I0078642

OFFICIAL REPORT

OF THE

FOURTEENTH INTERNATIONAL

CHRISTIAN ENDEAVOR CONVENTION

HELD IN

MECHANICS' BUILDING AND IN TWO TENTS PITCHED ON

BOSTON COMMON,

BOSTON, MASS., U.S.A., JULY 10 – 15, 1895.

First Fruits Press
Wilmore, Kentucky
c2015

First Fruits Press
The Academic Open Press of Asbury Theological Seminary
204 N. Lexington Ave., Wilmore, KY 40390
859-858-2236
first.fruits@asburyseminary.edu
asbury.to/firstfruits

COMMITTEE OF THIRTEEN.

H. G. DIXON.   E. A. GILMAN.   F. W. WALSH, JR.   CHAS. E. ALLEN.   A. J. CROCKETT.   GEO. K. SOMERBY.
ROBT. H. MAGWOOD.   GEO. W. COLEMAN.   C. H. KILBORN.   WM. SHAW.   W. F. BARTHOLOMEW.   F. F. DAVIDSON.
SAMUEL B. CAPEN.

OFFICIAL REPORT

OF THE

FOURTEENTH INTERNATIONAL

CHRISTIAN ENDEAVOR CONVENTION,

HELD IN

MECHANICS' BUILDING AND IN TWO TENTS
PITCHED ON BOSTON COMMON,

BOSTON, MASS., U. S. A., JULY 10-15, 1895.

COPYRIGHTED, 1895, BY U. S. C. E.

PUBLISHING DEPARTMENT
UNITED SOCIETY OF CHRISTIAN ENDEAVOR,
646 WASHINGTON ST., BOSTON, MASS., U. S. A.
1895.

FOURTEENTH INTERNATIONAL CONVENTION

OF THE

YOUNG PEOPLE'S SOCIETIES

OF

CHRISTIAN ENDEAVOR.

BOSTON, MASS., U. S. A., JULY 10—15, 1895.

CROWDS! crowds! crowds! An old gentleman of eighty years came all the way from Ohio to see the Fourteenth Christian Endeavor Convention. He had never in his life been out of his country town, and he came to Boston, as he said, to see the people. His humble wish was abundantly gratified. The Christian Endeavorers had *higher* ends in view, but doubtless the vast throngs were an inspiration.

How they poured in! The reception committee had sent its scouts far out along the railway lines. The expectant white caps waited in eager companies at every station and steamboat wharf. Early in the week the long trains began to arrive. All through trains were broken up into sections. Scores of trains were necessarily late, but the young men and women of the reception committee were patient; every delegation was welcomed by a group of Boston Endeavorers of the reception committee.

Boston frigidity? Forever henceforth let that phrase hide its head in shame! To say nothing of the crowded, enthusiastic rallies that have preceded this Convention, where audiences of seven and eight thousand went wild with Christian Endeavor zeal; to say nothing of those bands of beautiful-faced maidens and energetic lads that were striking warm hands with each incoming delegate, holding aloft " Wel-

3

come " placards, and beaming a welcome most unmistakable in their happy faces ; to say nothing of homes thrown wide open and churches with doors taken from their hinges ; to say nothing of newspapers bubbling over with hundreds of columns of vivid narrative and bright pictures, and of the universal interest shown in shop and street ; — to say nothing of these and a thousand things more, there were the decorations !

" When *did* Park Street Church ever do such a thing before ? " asked an astonished lady as she saw the dignified front of that grand old church festooned with the gayest of bunting in honor of Park Street's Illinois guests. Far out in Boston's galaxy of lovely suburbs the railway stations and the homes had blossomed out in white for purity and scarlet for love — pure love ! As for the city streets, they were all in a flutter of bright color.

The great mercantile establishments vied with one another in ingenious arrangement and lavish use of the red and white. The wholesale dealers in cloth of the popular hues told pitiful stories of the immense quantities of bunting they might have sold if they had only made sufficient provision for Boston's — frigidity ! THE GOLDEN RULE offices, within and without, were ablaze with bunting, banners, and electric lights ; and the constant throngs pressing in and out testified that the big " Welcome " on the front of the building was taken to mean what it said.

The Convention banner proper appeared everywhere, — tied to the trolley arms of the electric cars, adorning the headlights of locomotives, flying from windows innumerable. Red and white flowers in the Public Garden had grouped themselves into the same pretty banner, and into " C. E. " monograms as well, open Bibles, Christian Endeavor mottoes, badges, and the like. Never before have the charming Public Gardens put on such festive attire, rustic archways adorning the entrances and the bridges, and an admirable array of flowers and shrubs delighting the eyes of the ever-present throngs.

But we started to tell how the throngs arrived, — and now, we cannot ; for each of the hundreds of delegations had its special characteristics. Many were very winsome, with their cars bravely bearing noble mottoes, with bright banners waving from the windows, and sweet songs rising from the crowds that poured out into the stations.

There were State badges and banners, of all colors of the rainbow. There were State songs, lustily shouted forth. Everywhere through the stations and wharves the story was of excellently managed excursions, fine weather, and glorious times on the way.

And our friends were here from England, Scotland, Ireland, from Africa, India, Japan, and other distant lands, the breezy folk from the great West, the singing hosts from the South, Canada's enthusiastic cohorts, and the thousands on thousands from the States near at hand, — all were here to the number of 56,425, making a great Convention, by far the greatest of all the magnificent series of Christian Endeavor Conventions.

Now that it has passed into history, and we can look quietly over the events of the last crowded days recorded in the following pages, certain features of the greatness of the vast gathering appear conspicuously.

The most prominent, of course, though not the most important, is the majesty of overpowering numbers. The young Christians of the world have held the largest religious assembly ever convened in the world's history. Christian Endeavor is no Jumbo. Its meaning is far more than its mass. And yet it is significant of a blessed new power and hope for this old earth when more than fifty thousand young men and women spend time and money, and travel, many of them, enormous distances, to attend a purely religious convention.

Looked at a little more deeply than the surface, however, the main feature of the Convention was undoubtedly its splendid exhibition of patriotism. It is right to say that no gathering since war times — if any single gathering then — has done so much as this to fire young America with loyalty to its country ; nay, — for we must not forget our many friends from over the border, — to inspire a true love everywhere for all that is noble and worthy in one's native land, at the same time arousing a burning indignation against all that would pollute her or fetter her progress.

The historical surroundings of the Convention did much to suggest this trend of its thought. Many thousands for the first time saw Faneuil Hall and stood on Plymouth Rock. Many thousands, indeed, for the first time were brought into vital, visible contact with their country's past. What wonder " the little red schoolhouse " became in many sessions the centre of eulogium and almost frantic applause ? What wonder that every reference to the temperance reform, and to the reforms of our national and city governments urged by such men as Parkhurst, Clarke, and MacLaurin, should raise a tempest of enthusiasm ? The requirements of citizenship — Christian citizenship — will be felt far more deeply by thousands as the result of this Convention, and a demonstration so striking and so emphatic cannot but have its effect on politicians also.

Another element in its greatness akin to this was the fact that never before was there in a Christian Endeavor Convention so full a " parliament of nations." Not only were Endeavorers present from India and China and Japan, from Armenia and Spain and Germany, from Persia and Africa, from Bermuda and Mexico and Alaska, from the Indian tribes of North America, from Canada, Australia, England, Scotland, Ireland, and Wales — not only were all these present, but those representing the largest bodies of Endeavorers came as accredited delegates, — Rev. W. J. L. Closs for the 1,509 societies of Australia, Rev. W. Knight Chaplin and Rev. James Mursel for the 2,500 societies of England, Rev. John Pollock for the 200 societies of Scotland, Rev. J. L. Lamont and Rev. H. Montgomery for the societies of Ireland, and Rev. R. Burges for those of Wales.

This, moreover, meant something, and what it meant was made evident when it was announced that at a certain time in the Convention there would be held a meeting of all interested in the formation of a World's Christian Endeavor Union. This World's Union has now become a reality.

Until formal election can be made by the various national, state, provincial, and colonial unions, an informal organization has been effected, — a world's committee, in which Dr. Clark and Secretary Baer represent the United States ; Rev. William Patterson, Canada ; Rev. W. J. L. Closs, Australia ; Rev. W. Knight Chaplin, the United Kingdom. Dr. Clark was chosen president, Mr. Closs, secretary, and Mr. Shaw, treasurer. Triennial World's Conventions are to be held, the first at Washington next year.

No student of the Christian Endeavor movement will fail to see the immense significance of this step. Hitherto the United Society of Christian Endeavor of the United States has directed the movement, first appointing superintendents of Christian Endeavor societies in foreign lands, and then, as the societies multiplied, allowing them to form their own United Societies of Christian Endeavor virtually inde- pendent of the mother organization. Thus were formed the United Societies of Christian Endeavor of China, Japan, England, and Aus- tralia. This loose system is now to be changed for a compact body, which will have all the enthusiasm and power that come from a welding of forces, the close touch of shoulder to shoulder. May God bless the World's Union of Christian Endeavor !

The Convention was great, in the fourth place, because, more than all previous conventions, it was evangelistic. When in heaven we come to read heart histories as now we read our newspapers, we shall doubtless see that in this lay the supreme greatness of this mighty gathering.

These evangelistic services lay quietly beneath the entire Conven- tion, like a vast stratum of pure gold. They were planned and carried out by men of the widest experience in such undertakings, and of the most thorough consecration. They were led by the greatest evangelists of the world. The meetings exceeded in number those of the Conven- tion itself. During those five days was poured out upon the sin, the wretchedness, the need of Boston, a flood of righteousness, of eloquent pleading, that bore many a soul into the pure haven.

Much of the results can be counted. We know of the hundreds of requests for prayer, of promises of amended lives, of blessed conver- sions to all that is happy and noble. But there is one side of the results that cannot even be estimated, and that is the effect on the delegates themselves that aided in these services. To many of them it was their first experience in this sort of work. As morning after morning in the early prayer meetings these delegates gave their reports, it was clearly to be seen that each had gained from the work an impetus to the blessed service of soul-winning that would last him all his life.

Other points crowd for space, and can only be mentioned.

It was a most satisfactory Convention. Cleveland set the standard last year for completeness of arrangements and systematic, efficient working, and Boston has equalled Cleveland. All honor to the noble Committee of Thirteen and their thousands of faithful, self-sacrificing assistants! Boston's many stations and congested streets, together with the wide range of her suburbs and the vast numbers of her guests, gave the reception committee a task of no ordinary magnitude; but these splendid young men and young women were equal to it. The work of the choruses this year, for thorough training and ready obedience to leadership, has never been surpassed. The ushers were a fine band of young men, and accomplished their difficult work with a firmness and tact that were greatly appreciated. The decoration committee produced results most gorgeous and charming, and did much to open the eyes of Boston to the Convention. The accommodation committee, the hall committee, the press committee, the excursion committee, the committees on printing, music, and finance, — all deserve high honor. It is perfectly safe to say that a better-managed Convention was never held.

The Juniors should by no means be omitted from this catalogue of the great features of this Convention. Every Junior rally has been an improvement over that of the preceding year, and this was no exception. In plan and execution it was magnificent, and the more than ten thousand present, mostly Juniors, received an impression of the joy and beauty of Christianity such as they will never forget.

No previous convention has exhibited so fine an interdenominational fellowship as this. At Boston an unprecedented number of religious bodies were represented, but all met as brothers in Christ. Misunderstandings with regard to the spirit and purposes of the Christian Endeavor movement have almost altogether passed away. There was at Boston no word regarding the organic union of Christendom, but many words regarding its spiritual union, and every such word was applauded with a vehemence that showed how dear was the thought to the thousands of pastors and young people present.

It ought to be said, before we close, that this has been by far the most interesting of all Christian Endeavor Conventions. Boston is the most interesting city of the country (beg pardon, but this article is written by a Bostonian, you know), and the programme of this Convention was more varied, and offered more attractive and novel features, than any preceding programmes. These two things — the interesting city and the interesting programme — reacted the one on the other, and unplanned-for meetings, scenes, and incidents sprang up on every hand with bewildering frequency.

It was a Convention of high aims, an inspiring Convention, a far-seeing Convention, a fearless Convention, — and many more adjectives could fittingly be applied to it. In short, it was a Convention of *Christian Endeavor.* That includes everything. Because the spirit of true, eager Christian Endeavor was at the heart of the Convention, and because that spirit is growing among the churches, for that reason this monster gathering was country-loving, soul-seeking, fearless, and inspiring.

For that reason, also, we can be sure that every bit of good seed sown in this Convention is going to spring up and bear fruit a thousand-fold. The delegates to Boston carry home with them a great responsibility. They will be true to it. The inspiration they have gained they will pass on. The plans for better work suggested at the Convention they will put into practice. The songs of the Convention are to ring out in constantly widening circles of music. The Convention prayers are to be prayed over and over again as coming weeks go by. And as we gather in Washington next year, there will certainly be shown such splendid results from this Fourteenth Convention of Christian Endeavor Societies as will make joy in earth and heaven. God grant it!

OPENING SESSIONS — WEDNESDAY EVENING.

Boston was bombarded by a broadside of eloquence on the opening night. Nineteen churches of Boston and vicinity were thrown open, and crowds came, and in many instances overflow meetings were held.

Among the features of the evening was the editorial programme, filled out by Dr. Horr of *The Watchman,* Dr. Dunning of *The Congregationalist,* and Dr. Ward of *The Independent;* Dr. J. Wilbur Chapman's words of wisdom and power; Dr. John Henry Barrows's eloquent patriotic address; H. L. Hastings's scriptural talk; Dr. Rondthaler's bright and glowing summary of Christian Endeavor principles; and the forcible and witty remarks of the two Drs. Tyler.

Equally noteworthy were the stories by Grace Livingston Hill and Dr. J. F. Cowan; "Tom" Murphy's heart-born plea for temperance; Rev. William Patterson's magnificent tribute to men of faith; the exaltation of work for sailors and surfmen, made by Antoinette P. Jones, Rev. J. Lester Wells, and Rev. S. Edward Young, with the enthusiastic welcome given to that brave, life-saving man, Captain Tunnell. Then there was Dr. F. N. Peloubet's problem in spiritual arithmetic, — "The Sunday school, multiplied by Christian Endeavor, equals what?" Dr. Selah Merrill's scholarly talk, with its memories of the Holy Land; the consecrated and hearty greetings of those delegates from far away, — Rev. H. S. Jenanyan, of Tarsus, Turkey; Rev. K. Tsunashima, of Japan; Rev. Richard Burges, of Wales; Mr. Prabala Ramachaudrayya Garu, of India; Miss Ben-Oliel, of Jerusalem; Rev. Jesse Malex Yonan, of Persia; and Dr. Berry, of Japan.

And Dr. H. C. Mabie spoke, and Dr. Wayland Hoyt spoke, and Dr. H. C. Farrar, Dr. M. Burnham, Dr. Elijah Horr, Bishop Samuel Fallows, Dr. Roland D. Grant, Dr. W. H. McMillan, Dr. Arthur Little, Dr. John H. Boyd, Dr. Robert McDonald, Dr. Gilby C. Kelly, Dr. Teunis S. Hamlin, Canon J. B. Richardson, Dr. J. T. Beckley, Dr. James B. Brady, Dr. A. P. Foster, General Morgan, Dr. W. J. Darby, Dr. H. C. Wood, Rev. Messrs. H. B. Grose, W. H. Allbright, James M. Gray, S. B. Meeser, W. E. Barton, H. L. Shupe, M. M. Binford; and those eloquent ladies, Miss Charlotte T. Sibley, Mrs. Emily McLaughlin, Mrs. George W. Coleman, and Mrs. Elizabeth Campbell; and, besides these, many more. When before was such a feast spread before a city?

Brookline Baptist Church.

The First Baptist Church was prettily decorated for the occasion. At the entrance to the church was a massive arch of evergreen sprinkled with incandescent electric lamps, and on top was a sign in red and white — "Maryland Headquarters." The interior of the edifice was one mass of national colors, with banners bearing the State seals of Maryland and Massachusetts everywhere in evidence. On the platform was a neat display of ferns and tropical plants.

Rev. Henry C. Mabie, D.D., of Boston, presided, and the order of exercises proved to be a genuine treat, not only for the visitors, but also to the residents of Brookline. The church was crowded to the door, and standing room was at a premium.

The musical portion of the programme was given under the direction of Mr. C. J. Buffum, and the organist was Mr. George Caine.

The opening devotional exercises were conducted by Rev. S. W. Duncan, D.D., Boston, and Rev. O. P. Gifford, D.D., Buffalo, N. Y. Dr. Mabie, the presiding officer, before introducing Rev. H. S. Jenanyan, of Tarsus, Asia Minor, said, among other things, that the day for which the Christian Endeavorers had been waiting, and for which Boston had been waiting, had arrived. He was sure that the expression of feeling manifested in Boston, with bright skies and gala decorations hung out by all sorts of secular and business people, only represented a slight portion of the good will extended to us, not only by Boston, but by all New England. "The movement stands for much. It means the future devotion of the people to the Church of Christ. It means that young people are interested in the study of Christian religion. It stands for education, patriotism, and religion."

Dr. Mabie then introduced Mr. Jenanyan and spoke of the fact that the man who would address the audience was an Armenian, in whose race the Christian people of the whole world were now taking such an interest, because of the recent ravages of the Turks in their land.

Address of Rev. H. S. Jenanyan.

I consider it a great privilege and pleasure to be permitted to address this gathering of young people from all parts of the world, and to tell them something of the progress of their Society in my oppressed country. My mission to this country is not a social nor a political one; it is made solely for religious and missionary purposes.

I bring you to-night salutations from the countries of the Orient. St. Paul was the originator of the idea of salutations, and he taught it to the Eastern nations, with whom it is still the custom. So again I say to you that Armenia and Iconia and the Orient give you Christian salutations.

Who are they who thus greet you? They are the oldest of Christian nations. They are people from that part of the Turkish Empire who have not yet yielded to the threats of their oppressors. The Turkish Empire is divided into three parts: Armenia in the northeast, Palestine, the home of the Saviour, in the south, provinces of Cilicia and Iconium in the west.

The people of Armenia have no relations with the Turks, but keep as entirely separate from them as they are allowed to do. They are the original Christians of the world, receiving their teachings from Jesus direct. Tradition says that one time the king of Armenia fell sick and sent for Jesus to come and heal him. The Saviour was unable to go, but sent one of his disciples; and after he had healed the king he remained in the country and taught the people lessons that they have never been able to forget, and cannot if they would.

How much truth there is in the tradition I do not know, but I do know, and am sure, that in Armenia Christianity had its birth. In fact, the human race had its second birth in Armenia, for it was on a mountain in that country that the ark with Noah rested after the flood had passed from the earth.

At the end of the first century the Gospel was just starting in the country, but in the second century it was preached by some powerful teachers, and the king and all the people were converted.

With this history in mind, it amuses the Armenians to be looked upon as barbarians by the countries of the world. It was from Armenia that Europe, and through Europe the world, heard the Gospel; and while the ancestors of the present inhabitants of England and America were savages, the Armenians were the ones who sent missionaries to them.

The questions you, of course, ask are, Have these institutions stood? Are the Armenians to-day as strong in the Christian faith as they were of yore? To these questions I must answer no, but at the same time must ask you Americans a question. How long could you remain Christians if you were deprived of the right to study, deprived of your Bibles, persecuted from morn till night because of your religion?

Could you stand two hundred years? Could you stand one hundred years, or even fifty? I think you would hesitate to say yes, and yet the Armenians have stood for over ten centuries.

They have stood in spite of a constant series of wars waged against them because of their faith; they have stood against the most horrible oppression; and yet, although, as I said, their faith is not what it once was, they are yet Christians and eager to be taught more of their faith.

Do you know how the people live in that country to-day? In journeying through the country you will see scarcely a dwelling. Whenever you see a little hill, however, examine it closely and the chances are that you will find therein a hole. Descend into this hole and there you will find, fifteen feet under the ground, a room; beneath this room there are others, down as far as fifty feet. In these rooms are the dwellings, the schools, the churches, and the cemeteries of the people of Armenia.

In these rooms will be found carvings of the saints, hundreds of years old, and surrounding their base the bones and ashes of hundreds and thousands of Armenians who have died as martyrs or victims of the persecution that the country has constantly endured.

Because of these things, the nation that was once the world's teacher is now in need of being taught. To-night I bring you good tidings. The nations of the world have awakened to the needs of their Christian fatherland, and have sent over a great number of missionaries. These teachers are eagerly welcomed, and once more the light is dawning on the darkened and stricken shores of Armenia.

Mr. Jenanyan then gave a number of personal experiences, and touched briefly on the recent outrages in his country, ending with an impassioned plea for help for his people, both in a temporal and religious way.

The next speaker was Rev. K. Tsunashima, of Tokyo, Japan. Mr. Tsunashima came to Boston as the official representative of the United Society of Christian Endeavor of Japan, and came bearing greetings from its president, Rev. T. Harada.

Mr. Tsunashima gave a very entertaining address, and we regret to announce that a copy of it cannot be had for this report. His dialect was pleasing, and he had sufficient command of the English language to make himself understood. In opening, he apologized for his defect, and told a little story of an American lady who went to Japan and tried to learn the Japanese language. The lady learned one word the first night. It was "Ohio," which means "good morning." When the lady awoke on the following day she tried to say "good morning" in Japanese, but the nearest she came to it was "New York."

The Japanese Endeavorer said, " You Americans have done much for us. Japan is a small country, about twice the size of New England, but we have a large population, over 42,000,000."

The next address, of which we give an abstract, was made by Rev. Roland D. Grant, D.D., of Portland, Ore., pastor of the White Temple Baptist Church.

Address of Rev. Roland D. Grant, D.D.

The more difficult the task before us, the more liable we are to do it, and do it well. Life consists of doing large things, but in every undertaking there is a series of opposition; in other words, a conflict. In our activities of life we constantly come in contact with that which is directly opposed to us. Force is not power. It is a combination of forces that gives power.

From the very beginning man was informed that there were certain things which he must not do. There was a tree, and God ordered that it should be let alone. That tree was just as valuable as any other. It was planted for one purpose, and that was to be let alone. But you know the old story, poison is always the sweetest and medicines ever bitter. Steam escaping produces nothing but whistle and noise, but this same steam properly controlled makes the locomotive speed over the iron rails. Human character is developed much in the same manner. Don't allow yourselves to waste your energies, but use good sound judgment in all your transactions in life. God never wants to take the will away from any man. He has placed his own will where our will is brought in contact with it. All he wants you to do is to recognize that there is another will, and that is the Divine will.

The child becomes aware that it has a will, and then realizes that there is another will. The child can resist the Divine will, but afterward submits and enjoys sweet peace.

You are a combination of forces, and any one left alone to itself will surely come to ruin. Even in religion, a man may go so far as to be a crank.

Now what has all this to do with Christian Endeavor? It is easy to see. We hear a great deal to-day about a possible union of churches and of religions. The Christian Endeavor Society is pointed out as a step that way. It is no such step. Christian Endeavorers are strong because they oppose each other in the right way. They are powerful because the denominations in the union strike against each other and sparks of truth have to come.

The watchword of the Society might well be " Solidity by Individuality." No weak giving-up of personal ideas, but a constant rubbing of those ideas into a friendly opponent, which, if it does n't change his views, surely strengthens your own.

At present I hear a great deal of talk about solidarity, that we must all think alike, and that we are going to have one great union of thought. I, for one, do not want that ideal. The kind of solidarity I would like is best attained by individuality. You can't mix oil and water. I want something to live for and die for, if necessary. Endeavor means conflict—something to fight for. I don't care for the kind of religion where you have only got to sing. Stand ever with the consciousness that you are facing a severe problem, and so move on like an army conquering vice and wickedness. The Christian Endeavor movement in Boston is not weak-kneed, but is a vigorous movement with a mission to perform. These are great moments, crucial and critical, throughout the world.

Everywhere people are awakening to the great missionary spirit, and God permit you and me to have a hand in it.

Second Church, Dorchester.

Seldom, if ever, has the historic Second Church of Dorchester held such a large and enthusiastic audience.

The meeting was announced for 7.30, but fully an hour before that time the seating room was taken.

Rev. Arthur Little, D.D., pastor of the church, presided, and in a few words extended a cordial welcome to the visiting delegates. In the pews were a large number of delegates from Missouri and South Dakota.

After prayer by Rev. Mr. Bolster, Dr. Little introduced the first speaker of the evening, Miss Charlotte Thorndike Sibley, of Belfast, Me.

Address of Miss Charlotte Thorndike Sibley.

"Summer" and "sunshine" are kindred words. Both summer and sunshine are America's heritage and belong to you and to me. In the western States are long stretches of flat prairie so level that, as they say, when one stands on his threshold he can see day after to-morrow's sun coming up over the horizon. The old adage that to-morrow never comes is quite obsolete. We American Endeavorers have the right to both these words, "summer" and "sunshine."

Sometimes it seems otherwise. There are so many valleys which the sunrise does not touch until it is almost noon on the hilltops! I have just returned after several months spent in three of these dark valleys of the earth, from Egypt and Palestine and Turkey, from regions where life seems one long riddle and the question of the Sphinx has never been solved. Millions of human beings are herded together there in places and under conditions which a respectable American dog would disdain. I have felt that it is still night in the world, a night without a star.

All about us we saw poverty and ignorance, sin and suffering untold. One generation succeeds another and inherits only bestial appetites and awful wretchedness. As I looked and listened, all the efforts of Christian workers seemed to me only to play upon the surface and around the borders of this great area of woe. The heaviest burdens of man are not yet lifted. Thorns are upon his head, his shoulders ache beneath the cross, his brain reels, his weary limbs fail. Aye, there are so many dark corners and murky shadows in the way that we cry, "Day is dead. Night is the only reality. The people that dwell in darkness—we cannot tell when they shall see a great light."

Day has dawned in America. The Sun of Righteousness is already high in the heavens. But what are we to do with our sunrise? Every day I am more thankful that I live in America. I can but turn again to Egypt and Syria and Turkey, the darkest countries of this wide world. There is no home life, no intellectual life, a hard struggle for physical life even. "Is there any reason under heaven," exclaimed one of my travelling companions, "why God should have made such a miserable country as Palestine?"

It takes something more than a precious history to make a prosperous country. A rich past alone cannot hallow a country. A rich present must combine with a rich past before a land is blessed. Shunem and Nain are two of the most wretched places I ever saw, with low, mud houses and unimagined filth. The places where the Prophet Elisha was a guest, where the widow received her son from death to life, are localities in which no decent American would care to linger. Compare conditions here and there: freedom here for tyranny there; schools here for squalor there; here the Bible, there the Koran; churches here for mosques there; here practical Christianity, there poverty and superstition; prayers here, and there meaningless whirlings and howlings of the dervishes, hypocrites. Here are homes, while harems are there. Here is a happy childhood, there no childhood at all. As soon as a child can toddle it must carry a younger baby in its arms. I sometimes wondered if they did not toss up a penny to decide which baby should carry the other. Here in America is law, there in the East the caprice of tyrants. It is full day here, there are only faint streaks of light along the horizon. All the little light they have comes from Christian lands.

England has brought to Egypt all the sun that shines there. Now let English influence be felt in Armenia. It would bring the light of day even into that oppressed and well-nigh hopeless territory. Let us be thankful that we live in a land over which the sun has already risen. The sunrise lands do not lie in the East, but in the West. We are part of the sunrise. We can make our splendid morning lighten the world. It is the duty of England and America to shine brightly in the East.

Our Christian missionaries are stars in the East. What they are doing may give us fresh courage for work. As we travelled, wherever we saw them we learned to admire them. We are sometimes inclined to think of missionaries as they go out from us as young men and women, poor and pious, rather fanatical withal, and not very wise, going hand in hand, expecting when they reach their fields of labor to open their mouths and let the Lord fill them with words suitable for converting souls. But our missionaries, both English and American, as we have seen them, have been gifted, brilliant, with good stores of intellectual treasure and a wide knowledge of human nature. Why, it takes some ability to learn to talk intelligibly in one of those strange Eastern languages, where the consonants play leap-frog over each other in the speaker's throat, and the rumble of the gutturals and the sharp sizzle of the ss make each sentence seem one long, scolding, sibilant monologue. And the way the missionaries begin their labors is not by preaching to the people, and saying, "You are all miserable sinners." They win the children. They coax them into the schoolroom, teach them the rudiments of learning and good behavior, diffusing in that schoolroom the conquering atmosphere of a Christian spirit. They implant in the boys and girls the fundamental principles of American morality, truthfulness, courage, and independence, and make them the motive principles of their lives.

Our sun shines brighter as the knowledge of our consecrated young men and women grows. Sunshine does not spread into darkness without reflection. Most of the good men who have been powers in the world have been men of thoroughly trained minds. Moses was learned in all the wisdom of the Egyptians ere he tried to transform a race of slaves into a strong nation. Paul was a scholar and a diplomat before he became a missionary. Cromwell's speech was rude, but his thoughts were deep and his judgment keen and sure ere he hurled his Ironsides against weak royalty, and bade Charles yield place to Puritan virtues. In the words of Christ Jesus we find the garnered wisdom of time and of eternity. He spake as never man spake. Older than Christian Endeavor is the saying, "Knowledge is power." We Endeavorers should always advocate Christian education.

In learning there is always light. In Christlike wisdom there is full day. It is not enough for us as Endeavorers to be patient, to be cheerful, to rise each week in our meetings and say, "I love God and man." Love for God and man can do much, but love and wisdom together are the powers that move mountains. An untrained enthusiasm for the salvation of souls cannot work out the world's problems. We need full hands, tender hearts, and cultured brains to do God's service. Not every man, not every woman, must have a college education or a high school or academy course to do acceptable work in God's kingdom; but over and over again would I say that it is the duty of every Christian to make the most possible of himself, physically and mentally and spiritually.

We must remember that it is Christian education whereby we hope to spread Christ's light in the dark lands of the East. A scholar without Christ is like a well-planned machine. But mechanism can never supply the place of manhood. Christ said, "I am the way, and the truth, and the life." It is the knowledge of his truth which we need, and Christ's way is endless. His truth is limitless, and the life he offers is eternal. The mind and the soul are closely bound together. Neither can lie fallow without loss to the other. We dare not rest on the path of progress. We must not rest on the path of progress. We must not merely keep step and beat time — we must march. We must go steadily onward, upward. The progressive spirit of America has brought us near the

East and the sunrise. In the United States we are not clogged by the conservatism of older countries. Our stones roll too rapidly to gather any moss. The readiness of youth to learn new methods of work, to prove that which is good, is bringing us into consciousness of to-morrow.

And now, nerved by hope and trained by education, nourishing in our hearts an enthusiastic purpose to spread the light of hope and of Christian learning from our sunrise land into the distant East, we must go on to be God's heroes and heroines. At the opening of each new era in the world's history stands the man who dares. Abraham dared go from the land he knew into the great unknown. Savonarola dared the stake for freedom's sake. Abraham Lincoln dared to proclaim the brotherhood of man. Christ with sublime courage inaugurated the days of the years of our Lord. The sun at its rising shines always upon some hero's uncovered head. The belt of heroism has moved from East to West, from Chaldea to the United States, from Abraham to Abraham Lincoln.

The first duty of every church and every Christian is to be a light set where it can enlighten the whole earth. It is day here, but it is night over yonder in heathen lands. Every light we can set there will be seen and will help dispel the shadows of sin and of suffering. Trained by education to teach others Christian knowledge, with enthusiastic hope and heroism in our hearts, we can do a noble work as missionaries, at home or abroad, as God may call us. Once a traveller in the East met a little boy who was carrying on his back a plump brown baby only a size or two smaller than himself. "Is n't he too heavy for you?" queried the foreigner. With an air of surprise the little lad rejoined, "Why, no, of course he is n't heavy. He 's my brother!" Labor is wonderfully lightened by love. The burdens we bear for a brother are not so heavy as those we carry for a stranger. Every man is our brother. Love compels labor.

Let us be great in small places, and never be small anywhere. Let us hope great things, learn great lessons, do great deeds. Hope, wisdom, heroism — these three embody the elixir of life, of youth, of the morning.

The next speaker was Bishop Samuel Fallows, D.D., LL.D., of Chicago, Ill., a trustee of the United Society of Christian Endeavor, representing the Reformed Episcopal denomination.

Address of Bishop Samuel Fallows, D.D., LL.D.

The great trend of the age is toward unity. Races are seeking affinities. Nations are consolidating. Churches of the same faith are coming together. Many Presbyterians are praying that the thirteen distinct churches of their order may be united in one. Many Lutherans are looking toward the bringing into closer relationship of the twenty distinct Synods of their common creed. Many Methodists are hoping not only for the consolidation of the two great divisions of the church North and South, but of the fifteen minor bodies that bear their name. Many Baptists are believing that there must be a sheltering in one fold of the thirteen branches of their church. Many Episcopalians are working not only for union between the two divisions that claim to be Protestant, but for union between all evangelical churches through the Historic Episcopate; while the pope of Rome is striving through kindly words and fervent appeals to bring all the churches of Christendom into organic union with the Roman Catholic Church. We must make a fundamental distinction between Christian unity and church unity. Christian unity is the oneness of believers in Christ. Church unity is the oneness of membership in a visible church. Many advocates of Christian unity confound the two. There may be Christian unity where there is no church unity. And there may be church unity where no true Christian unity prevails. Christian unity is not, therefore, uniformity either in the human statement of doctrine or in modes of worship. It does not imply an outward organization to which all Christians must belong. The prayer of our Divine Lord, "that they all may be one; as thou, Father, art in me, and I in thee, that they also may be one in us, that the world may believe that thou hast sent me," was not a prayer for church unity, but for spiritual oneness of the believer with the Father and the Son. Amid all the divisions of church forms and governments this oneness may prevail. The history of the Church has revealed too often a struggle to make church uniformity prevail.

The mother church of England, in which my parents and my remoter ancestors were born, baptized, confirmed, and married, has changed in her spirit and methods since the days of Queen Elizabeth, when non-conformists were subject to banishment and death, "when the English inquisition was instituted, and the star chamber positively revelled in religious persecution;" since the days of King James, when hundreds of conscientious clergymen were silenced, and excommunicated, some of whom our then savage continent roughly received,— noble, God-fearing men, both Pilgrims and Puritans, who helped lay the foundations of the Republic and create the Christian civilization which makes it possible for a general convention of an Episcopal church to be held alongside of a national council of the Congregational churches. It has changed since the days of Charles the Second, when the Corporation Act was in full force, and the infamous Act of Uniformity was created, followed by the English Black Bartholomew Day, when two thousand of the ablest and most devoted clergymen of the Church of England were turned out of her communion — an act followed by the still more infamous Conventicle Act, by which any person over sixteen years of age present at any meeting for religious services other than those connected with the Church of England was subject to fine, banishment, and even death without the benefit of clergy. It has changed since 1632 in our own country, when the commonwealth of Virginia declared it a misdemeanor to attend any service except that of the Episcopal Church, the third offence involving banishment; when no one could be a school-teacher unless a member of the Church of England, and a shipmaster was liable to fine if he imported into harbor a non-conformist passenger. It has changed, also, since the days when the non-conformist fleeing from persecution thought it his Christian duty not only to have fellowship with the secretaries springing up around him, but to suppress them by laying unsparingly the lash on the bare backs of Quaker and Quakeress and banishing the intruding Baptist. It has changed since the days of the Revolution and our own early history days, and since the younger days of some of us who are not now very old, when the Methodist was fighting his way against the all-but-established Congregational Church.

In those days to have talked of an exchange of pulpits between Methodist and Congregationalist, or between the Baptist and Presbyterian, would have been as great an anomaly as to propose that Cardinal Gibbons, of Baltimore, should preside over the Evangelical Lutheran Council now being held in our own city.

The question was solemnly discussed years ago, by churchmen across the ocean, whether, for instance, "a pious Congregationalist" was in a better condition than "a pious heathen like Socrates or Antonine," since both were beyond the Apostolic polity. The learning, didactical skill, eloquence, and Christian catholicity of the renowned Prof. Wm. Archer Butler were enlisted to prove in a most elaborate manner that "the pious Congregationalist" was in a better condition than "the pious heathen;" that he was saved, not by the extraordinary mercies of God, "nor by his uncovenanted mercies" but by the great fundamental law of redemption, which was deeper and broader than any church or polity. By this law faith in Christ to come, exercised through obedience to God's commands, through imperfect signs and symbols and ceremonies (these all being also imperfectly understood), brought salvation to the Patriarchical Church and to the Mosaic Church. And so the grace of God, unlimited and free, would bring salvation to all who used the means and light they possessed, however deficient their privileges and opportunities might be.

I find in the report of the sermon of my Right Reverend brother Bishop Tuttle, of Missouri, delivered on the consecration of Bishop Gilbert, the following words: "Were not Christians of other names that were around about them staunch adherents of the faith? Were not all who were baptized in the name of the Father, Son, and Holy Ghost members of the same church?

" If holiness of life, untiring devotion to other souls, trust in the Scriptures, undying love for the Lord, are marks of true devotion, were not Methodists and Presbyterians, Congregationalists, Baptists, and other multitudes walking within the way, appointed true disciples of their beloved Lord and in their way doing the work of their mother, the Holy Catholic Church, though they may not carry the truth in all its fulness?

" To the Christians of other communions, we say we do not wish to be pharisaical, we do not say or think we are holier than others, we know how much nearer to God many of these are than we, and how much brighter crowns some of them will wear than we shall. Let them know we esteem their goodness and know of the multitudes of souls they have saved. God bless them all.

" But let us say also to them that they would be helped by the ministrations of our holy communion, by our everlastingly iterated creed, and our Apostolic ministry. These we hold in trust for them and would be glad to deliver to them. Meantime, we will thank them that they have done so much as they have in making the land as Christian as it is to-day, and in bringing so many souls into the Church. The Jerusalem which is above is free and the mother of us all. Limits were not the mother's. She with a mother's love and the graciousness of a queen asked not for limits. Might not we take some limiting fences down, that are tightly drawn and barbed? "

I like the ring of the words of my esteemed brother bishop. He has clearly indicated the way in which church unity is to be brought about. It is by removing the tightly drawn barbed fences between our Episcopal Church and other communions of saints. We must all tear down that barrier which was erected some years ago forbidding an interchange of pulpits between Episcopal and other non-Episcopally ordained ministers. We must cordially co-operate with them in the great religious and philanthropic movements of the age. We must thus get out of the narrow inclusiveness of our exclusiveness. We must be in the forefront in every united effort to reach the unsaved and the degraded masses of our fellowmen.

We bishops, and elder clergy, must teach the rising ministry that it is at once both a sign of callowness to speak of these great denominations about us, towering up in the magnitude of their numbers, in the magnificence of their contributions for the cause of Christ, and in the grandeur of the results they have achieved, as " secretaries," and to inform our laymen and our devoted church-women that it is neither Scriptural nor American nor becoming in them to speak of these earnest Christians as " dissenters." Let us away with such barbed fences as these, which hurt us on the inside infinitely more than those on the outside.

I have said " we " in speaking of the relation of the Episcopal Church to the other churches in the land, for the Reformed Episcopal Church is but the Protestant Episcopal Church Evangelical. Its creeds are our creeds, containing the primitive Catholic and Apostolic faith.

Its sacraments are our sacraments, its historic ministry is our historic ministry. Separated in name, but not in spirit, from that portion of the Church which still glories in the name of Protestant, she has in the good providence of God led the way (as the child has often to lead the parent) for the mother church to enter into the deeper and richer experience of the words of the beloved apostle, " Jerusalem which is above is free and the mother of us all." She has torn down and thrown away the barbed wire fences. She has stricken out " secretary " and " dissenter " and " uncovenanted mercies " and " priest," as a sacrificing sacerdotalist, from her vocabulary. She has thoroughly revised and enriched her prayer-book on the Protestant and Scriptural basis. She has gone out with a passionate hunger for the souls of men into the highways and by-ways of society and into the abandoned districts of our great cities. She has proclaimed herself a church of the poor as well as the rich. To her the Holy Catholic Church is the communion of saints.

The providential movement of the centuries toward Christian unity is the young People's Society of Christian Endeavor.

With its watchwords, loyalty to the individual church, loyalty to interdenominational fellowship, and, above all, supreme loyalty to Jesus Christ, the great Head of the Church, it is bringing together and binding together as nothing else has yet done the diverse branches into which that Church has been divided.

Its true work is not seen in these grand gatherings full of stir and ardent enthusiasm. It is seen in the devotional meetings and services of the sanctuary of the home church, in visitations of the sick and poor and needy, in concert of action in civic and philanthropic work, in the banding of societies of the different churches in the same town or city for prayer and praise and militant, spiritual action.

Thanks be to the God and Father of our Lord Jesus Christ for a Christian unity which is beneath all intellectual and ecclesiastical distinctions; which underlies every confession of the true faith of the divine love of God; which binds by ties never to be broken, church with church, congregation with congregation, soul with soul; which gathers the vast worshipping host within the protecting walls of the one Fold of the one Great Shepherd, where "there is one Lord and one faith and one baptism," where there is the same sublime accent of praise, the same soaring flight of love, and where to the upturned rapturous sight comes the same vision of heaven and God.

Rev. W. H. McMillan, D.D., of Allegheny, Penn., was the last speaker of the meeting. Dr. McMillan is also a trustee of the United Society of Christian Endeavor, representing the United Presbyterians.

Address of Rev. W. H. McMillan, D.D.

Nations are not the creatures of man's device. The civil powers that be, are ordained of God. In this nation every citizen is a part of the governing power. Every voter is a law-maker, an executive, and a judge; he is responsible for every law made, for the way it is executed, and for its correct interpretation. All the rights and all the interests of all the people are in his hands to preserve or to betray them. Citizenship, therefore, in this land, means a vast deal, where the government of all the people is *by* all, and should be *for* all. The people elect the law-makers; therefore, every law made is the work of the people acting through their chosen agents. The people choose the executives; therefore, whatever is done or not done in the matter of enforcing the laws, the people in the persons of their chosen officers are responsible for. The people elect the judges, or those who appoint them, and therefore they are responsible for the way the laws are interpreted by the men who are acting for them.

If the rights of the people are preserved, if truth and righteousness are fostered and crime punished, it is the people who have the honor of doing it; if wrong is licensed, or its commission winked at, if right is trampled down, the people are guilty of the crime.

In the old world, those who are born to reign come into the world with a vast responsibility hanging over their heads. It is said that when the young and beautiful Victoria was told that the crown of England was hers, she trembled at the thought of what she was to assume, and said to the bishop who brought the tidings, " My Lord, I will be good." In this land every man child is born to the responsibilities of sovereignty. All the rights and all the interests of all the people are to be protected or injured by the decisions he will give at the ballot-box.

The word "politician" ought to have a great and sacred meaning among us. It should mean one who gives special attention to the great questions of good citizenship, with all the duties and interests connected therewith. But its use in our day suggests only shrewd scheming for selfish ends. The word is like the man in the parable, — it has fallen among the worst characters, and has been trampled under foot, and left half dead. The misnamed politicians of our country have been having things pretty much their own way of late, and the consequences are apparent. The rights and interests of the people are being bartered for political advantages, and the whole country is suffering for wiser legislation, while the shameful pulling and hauling of the "ins" and the "outs" goes on. As for statesmanship, our political leaders have got no further than the Mint and the Custom House, and they are all at sea among themselves even about those questions. And all this time there is the trembling of a social earthquake beneath our feet, and every thoughtful person must look forward with anxiety to the future, when our children shall have succeeded us on the stage of action.

When our honored President, three years ago, suggested that the subject of good citizenship was one that should occupy the special attention of Christian Endeavorers in this country, I believe that the Spirit of the Lord moved him to the thought. I believe that He who has so wonderfully guided and preserved this nation in the past intends to save it now from the evils that so greatly threaten it, and it is to be saved by means of the Christian Endeavor Society. There must be about a million voters now in these societies, or those who will vote very soon, who are being trained to weigh carefully the duties of citizenship, and to vote according to God's will rather than the behest of a political party. The number of such voters is going to increase mightily as this work goes on, and our country will soon hear from them at the polls. Here is a power that is going to wrest the control of affairs from the hands of political demagogues and place it in the hand of Him who sits king over all, and rules the world in righteousness. Our political leaders have been carefully counting the saloon vote, the illiterate vote, and the stay-at-home vote, and all the other elements that have hitherto entered into their canvassings of probabilities, but they have not yet learned to count the Christian Endeavor vote. I want to serve notice on them now, that the time is drawing near when they will discover that a political revolution has occurred, and they will be found coming home from Washington and our State capitols out of a job. Let it not be supposed that this religious organization of young people is going to be turned into any sort of a political organization. It is simply going to train men to stand above all political organizations, and vote for God and his eternal right instead of party, and that will produce the revolution I have suggested.

In the first place, the Christian Endeavor training is going to give to the nation, in the coming century, voters who will recognize their personal responsibilities as voters, and *they will vote.*

I have been told, by those who know, that usually not more than seventy-five per cent of the actual voting population ever appears at the polls, and these stay-at-homes are generally the better class of citizens. Your foreign-born citizen who has received a hurried naturalization, and knows and cares little about our institutions, is seen going to the polls to vote under the leadership of demagogues; while your elegant, easy-going citizen, who is too busy with his own affairs, or too æsthetic to mix with the vulgar throng at the polls, stays away and allows the sacred interests of the country to go by default into the hands of the baser sort. Any citizen who indolently allows the sacred interests of his country to fall into such hands deserves the severest condemnation. The ballot in the hands of an American citizen is a great power for good, and one who has such a power in his possession and does not use it is betraying a great trust. The Christian portion of our people has undoubtedly the power to control the politics of the country, if they only would, but they do not. The Christian Endeavor is going to give us a class of voters who will vote. They will have too keen a sense of their responsibilities as Christian citizens to be stay-at-homes. The rights and interests which they can defend by their ballots will be seen to be too sacred for them not to cast it. The School Laws of Pennsylvania provide that any director who neglects to discharge the duties of his office for a certain length of time forfeits his position. I think it would be a good regulation to disfranchise all voters who persistently neglect their duties at the ballot-box.

But I am certain that no such regulation will be necessary for the voters which Christian Endeavor is going to give the country. They will be voters who will vote.

Another result of the training of citizens in this Society will be the existence of a class of the best quality, who will be willing to accept office whenever the interests of the country demand it. It has come to that in most places, that good men shun official positions from fear of contamination. They fight shy of politics on the theory that " He who lies down with dogs will get up with fleas." But when our citizens have grasped the true thought of their citizenship, for which their training in this Society will prepare them, they will come to the great duties of making, or executing, or interpreting law with a conviction of obligation to God and men which will not allow them to refuse the solemn trust.

And then the Christian citizens which Christian Endeavor is going to train for the future state will be men, and women, too, I hope, who will vote as Christians, and not as partisans. There stands before the voters of our country to-day a moral question of tremendous importance, one that involves the lives of hundreds of thousands of the people, and money interests to a degree that overtops every other, and the domestic happiness of the people to a degree known only to Him who puts the tears of breaking hearts into His bottle, and interests, too, that stretch on into the endless life beyond the shores of time. That question is this: *What shall we do with the saloon?* There are two great political parties to-day seeking to control the nation, and the saloon stands between them offering to throw the mighty weight of its influence in favor of the party that will give it most aid ; and it distinctly intimates that being let alone is the very least it will take from either party, and to meddle in the least degree with its interests in favor of the life and purity of society will be to forfeit its favor and receive its united and bitter opposition. I have a profound sympathy for political leaders, they have such a difficult task on their hands; they have to try to keep the saloon and the church people going along together in political action. The saloon is quick to resent any interference with its devilish traffic, and the church people have some conscience on the subject, and wish to see the evils of the drink traffic diminished ; so the politicians must look for a course that will offend neither, and keep them together within party lines. It is a humiliating fact that they have far more trouble keeping at peace with the saloon than they have with the Christians. The saloon will stand nothing, it is ready to bolt the party at a moment's notice if it is interfered with, but the Christians will allow the saloon to have its way while their convictions are persistently trampled upon. Christians are meek enough, as has often been proved, to allow their party to slap them in the face and still go on voting for it. It is high time for Christian people to consider the fact already stated, that every voter is a law-maker, an executive, and a judge, because his vote elects the men who make and interpret and execute the laws as his chosen agents. What a person does through his agent he does himself. If, therefore, the saloon is legalized and allowed to go on with its killing work, the voters are responsible for it. There it stands, the nameless curse of modern life, blighting the bodies and souls and estates of men, sweeping the land everywhere with black desolation ; to cast a vote in any way in its favor is to incur a degree of guilt in the sight of God which cannot be described or fully stated in words.

I am sure that Christian Endeavor is going to raise up for the future years a class of voters who cannot stain their hands with the crime of voting in favor of the saloon.

It is one of the distinctive purposes of this Society to lay upon the consciences of its members, and to diffuse everywhere as far as possible, the principle of good citizenship, and the obligations resting on the sovereign voters of America. The habit hitherto has too generally been for Christians to leave their religion at home when they went to the polls. Christian Endeavor is going to develop a class of voters that will soon number into the millions, who will take their religion along with them and put it to important uses.

It is well that our Lord is very patient, else he would have smitten many who bear his name with his bitter curse, for their inconsistencies in this matter. In all our religious assemblies where it is the proper thing to utter strong protests against all forms of evil, resolutions have been regularly passed expressing the strongest opposition to all unrighteousness, and then the members went home and voted to perpetuate the evils which they had in resolution condemned — in word, loyal to Christ and his kingdom of righteousness; by vote, against him.

The reason of this has been an idea somehow wrought into the minds of Christians that there is one code of morals for religion and another quite different for business and politics. English bishops, you know, are members of the House of Lords, as well as officers in the church. Once, when that church was not as good as it is now, a bishop was heard uttering very profane language, and when taken to task for it, he said, " I am swearing as a member of the House of Lords and not as a bishop." His reprover replied, " When the Lord goes to hell for his swearing, where will the bishop be? " Our modern Christian voters have not seemed to understand that there is a difficulty right there in preserving separate personalities that is hard to overcome. They have not clearly understood that, when the voter goes to perdition for aiding and abetting wickedness, there will not be a good estate in store for the church-members who, while voting up wickedness at the polls, have been resolving and praying on the side of righteousness in religious meetings. Our people have been playing off their patriotism against their religion when it came to voting. They have said to their twinging consciences that their party had policies so important to the interests of the country, and the party's success was so essential to the interests of the country, that it was right to wink at some sins supporting it. They have concluded that it would be better to be implicated in a large amount of wickedness than allow the other party to win. Do we not see that there has been an unlawful divorce between religion and politics, and that the holy banns should be celebrated anew? It is righteousness that always and only exalteth a nation; and sin is a reproach to any people, and an element of weakness and decay in the national life.

In our solar system, the comets amount to nothing except on dress parade. They come riding across the sky once in a while behind their fiery steeds, with robes of light trailing behind, and then are gone nobody knows where. The reason is that their orbit is not a circle, but a parabola or an ellipse. They have not one centre, but two, and that gives them their strange movements. The planets, on the other hand, move in a circle around one centre, and this one of the number at least is fit to be the footstool of God and the home of man. The voter who has been trying to revolve around two centres, a political and a religious one, is no better in society than that comet is in the solar system. You will never know where to find him, his orbit is such a strangely shaped thing. You may see him to-day moving splendidly through a prayer meeting, uttering holy protest against all evil; but when it comes to attacking any popular evil at the ballot-box, it is found that he has sailed off into the mysterious realms of nowhere, and is not to be found. The course of the true follower of Christ, such as Christian Endeavor is training up for citizens of this country, is a circle; his life moves around Christ as his only centre, and his conduct is just as near his centre at one point as at another—just as near when he is standing at the ballot-box to vote as it is when he is sitting at the holy communion; and the distance of such a soul from Christ at all points is just that mysterious negative expressed by the words, " Christ in him and he in Christ." When Christian Endeavor has trained a few more millions of young men to act as citizens along the circumference of that Christocentric circle, then Longfellow's prayer for this nation which he and we love so much will be fulfilled : —

> " In spite of rock and tempest roar,
> In spite of false lights on the shore,
>   Sail on, nor fear to breast the sea.
> Our hearts, our hopes, our prayers, our tears,
> Our faith triumphant o 'er our fears,
>   Are all with thee — are all with thee."

Pilgrim Congregational Church, Dorchester.

The auditorium of the Pilgrim Congregational Church, Dorchester, the headquarters for Minnesota, was filled with Endeavorers, who showed their appreciation of the excellent addresses by their undivided attention and hearty applause.

The church was elaborately decorated. The pulpit was draped with the national and Christian Endeavor colors, and the balconies were festooned with red, white, and blue bunting. Behind the president's desk hung the coat of arms of Minnesota, which could be seen from every seat in the hall.

The organ niche, also, was tastefully adorned. The two sides of the choir chancel were draped with a large American flag, and at the corner of the chancel was hung the Christian Endeavor monogram.

After prayer and singing by choir, chorus, and congregation, Rev. W. H. Allbright, D.D., pastor of the Pilgrim Church, spoke a few words appropriate for the opening of such a significant meeting.

In a few words he welcomed the delegates present, and then introduced Mr. Ernest Miller, president of the Pilgrim Congregational Y. P. S. C. E.

Mr. Miller welcomed the western delegation, and expressed regret that so many of the party were delayed in reaching the city. He then spoke of Dr. Allbright as an advance delegate from Minnesota, who five years ago came to the Pilgrim Church from the State whose delegates he was then entertaining. He referred to the society and to the new church as evidences of Dr. Allbright's efforts and ability.

The first speaker of the evening was Rev. H. B. Grose, of Chicago, Ill., a Baptist trustee of the United Society of Christian Endeavor.

Address of Rev. H. B. Grose.

One hundred and nineteen years now this has been a free and independent nation. What a miracle in this period has been wrought on this continent! The tale of Aladdin and his lamp is not to be compared to the story of the growth of this Republic. The truth of our history is stranger than any fiction.

Ninety-five years ago Washington died. What would be his sensations could he return to the land which he so nobly served! We call him "the father of his country;" but I fancy he would find himself a total stranger in it, save in that one spot, Mt. Vernon, which has been sacredly preserved. With what bewilderment he would survey a population increased from three to sixty-five millions, and a civilization advanced from the tallow dip and smoky oil lamp to gas jet and electric blaze; from log fire to coal, furnace, and steam; from sloop and stage coach to steamer and lightning express; from courier despatch to mail and telegraph and telephone! With what awe would he behold the bicycle bloomer! With what emotion would he gaze upon that proud pile in Washington city, the capitol! But with what diverse feelings would he witness the kind of legislation — or the imitation and mockery of it — that often goes on within those many-columned walls! And as he passed from city to city with railway speed, swiftly crossing by bridge the river which once he crossed so slowly and hazardously by boat; and as he was borne from East to far West, across the prairies, coming ever upon populous towns and cities, climbing up and gliding down mountain sides till halt was made on the Pacific slope, how would his wonder grow until the wearied mind could grasp no more of this marvellous reality! Well might he say that it was one country of which he was President in 1796, another country quite to-day.

Scarcely less difficult is it for us, looking back, to realize from what conditions we have grown. Read McMaster's graphic picture of the national development. Go back a hundred years, and the area of the Republic shrinks to less than half its present extent. There were then but thirteen States. Vast stretches of upland, now an endless succession of wheat and corn-fields and orchards, were then overgrown with dense forests abandoned to savage beasts and yet more savage men. The hamlets of a few fishermen marked the sites of now wealthy havens bristling with innumerable masts, while the great cities of to-day then had dimensions scarce exceeding those of our frontier towns. Of the inventions and discoveries which abridge distance, annihilate time, extend commerce and agriculture, save labor, and transmit speech, which turn the darkness of the night into the brilliancy of the day, which alleviate pain and destroy disease, not one existed.

Can you realize it? A hundred years ago only, and what do we behold? The States were but little better than a great wilderness. A narrow line of towns and hamlets extended along the coast from Maine to Georgia, but fifty miles back from the Atlantic the country was an unbroken jungle. Portland, Me., was founded, and here and there along the shore now dotted with summer cottages and hotels were a few fisher's cots. In New Hampshire a few hardy settlers had marked out the sites of settlements in the mountains. In New York, Albany and Schenectady were settled, but the rich valleys through which the Mohawk and the Genesee flow down to join the Hudson were still the hunting-grounds of the native red man. In Pennsylvania, dense forests and impassable morasses hid the rich iron and coal mines. In Virginia were to be found a few straggling villages. Beyond the Blue Ridge, Daniel Boone was fighting the Cherokees in the cane-brakes of Kentucky. Pittsburgh was a military post. St. Louis was a mission station. Chicago was not dreamed of. Of the country beyond the Mississippi almost nothing was known. The entire population of the country was not greater than that of New York, Brooklyn, and Philadelphia to-day. That gigantic system of manufactures which has made the streams and rivers of New England an endless succession of mills, and covered it with factory towns, had not begun to exist. The housewife spun her own flax and made her own linen. Not one existed of those implements of agriculture with which American ingenuity has revolutionized a great branch of human labor, cheapened food, and brought millions of acres into a high state of cultivation. The farmer of the Revolution plowed his land with the wooden bull plow, sowed his grain broadcast, and when it was ripe cut it with a scythe and threshed it with a flail. His house was without paint, his floors without carpets. The place of stoves and furnaces was supplied by huge fireplaces that sent half the smoke into the room and half the heat up the chimney. His food was of the simplest kind, served in the coarsest of dishes. The minister alone had white bread, as a special distinction. School meant two months a year in the little red schoolhouses, for boys in the winter and for girls in the summer. It was co-labor rather than co-education in those days. The minister was held in high esteem. To speak disrespectfully of him or his sermons was to incur a heavy fine. How have the times changed, indeed! In New England, to be absent from church on Sunday was to be hunted up by the tithing-man, admonished, and, if obstinate, fined, or exposed in the stocks, or imprisoned in the cage. The people had their revenge for the two-hour sermons, however, for the preacher often had to take his pay in turnips, corn, beans, and bacon, and as he could get it. Of newspapers in the sense of the modern daily there was none. The interviewer and telegraphic despatch were alike unborn. The mails were few and irregular. More letters are now delivered every day in New York than were distributed in the entire thirteen States in a year only a century ago. No bridge of any length had been built. It often took an hour to be rowed across on a flatboat from Brooklyn to New York, and a journey from Boston to Washington was a far more important under-taking than a trip to Europe is to-day.

From such a condition we have in a century developed into our present greatness. From a simple stretch of colonial territory on the world's map, the United States have spread over a continent and come to be recognized as one of the first nations of the globe, foremost in all that pertains to the liberties, the highest hopes and interests of man. No free government like ours exists in stable form elsewhere. No prosperity like ours tempts the poor. No liberty like ours invites the oppressed of foreign lands, and no mistaken generosity like ours lets in freely the thieves and trash of the earth. Since the War for Independence we have passed through two further eventful struggles, one of which established our ability to shake off foreign interference, the other to preserve forever inviolate the Union. And after a century marked by such vast conquests over opposing nature and opposing man, we can still fling out the stars and stripes as the world-honored emblem of "the land of the free and the home of the brave."

But free what? We know what the poet means, — that this is the land of free men as no other land can equally claim to be; the land of men who will brook no kingly tyranny, recognize no rank save that of manhood, suffer no oppression, permit no unnecessary restraints on personal liberty, hold no human being in the shackles of the slave, submit to no dictation in matters of religious faith; the land of men who would lay down their lives, if need be, to guard the principles of liberty, the leaving of every man free to worship God according to the dictates of his own conscience, the legal status of every man as free and equal. "The land of the free" — this has been our pride and boast.

The question is not wholly useless. Must we abandon the poet's and patriot's idea and substitute something else for it? Along with our astonishing growth in wealth and power, and the development of material resources, have there also been developments of a political and social and moral kind that demand serious consideration, and that threaten to change radically our national character and civilization?

"The land of the free!" Our fathers fought for it. See that gallant company sail away from oppression in England in the good ship *Mayflower*, crossing trackless seas into voluntary hardship and exile — why? That when they set foot upon the soil of the new world they might make it a land of the free. Again they fought for it. Under colonial oppression see them throw off the tax as they throw out the tea. Follow Freedom's flag all through that long and exhaustive struggle of the Revolution, in which right lent resistless might. When at last on Saratoga's field the British Burgoyne surrendered, and Freedom's victory was won, I can imagine that the celestial choir caught up with joy the mighty chorus, and sent the message ringing out, "The land of the free!" But once more our fathers fought; yes, and our brothers, too. This time it was a war at home, sad fratricidal strife in Freedom's cause. And when, after countless cost of life and treasure, the flag of union once more floated aloft and unrivalled, I can imagine that a white-robed angel, coming down as a messenger from heaven, dipping his pen in the life-blood of Freedom's martyrs, wrote across the white lines of our flag the motto, "Free men, free government, free ballot, free speech, free schools, free labor, and free conscience forever!"

For this our fathers fought and toiled and died. For this our stars and stripes still stand. Shall this ever be changed? Shall the letters written in with the best life-blood of the nation ever foully be erased?

No, no! And yet it is threatened. Out of the abyss of atheism and anarchy and the foul passions of base men, out of the saloons and the slums, see creeping forth a demon of the night, fired with the most malign purpose of hell. Blotting out from the flag the inscription just described, he would put in its place the black words, "Free rum, free riot, free love, free Sunday, free interference with the rights of labor, free assault on capital, free gambling, free bribery, free bigotry, free trusts, free bullets, and free irreligion."

This is not altogether fanciful. It rests with the Christian men and women of America to say whether such changes as these shall be made. It is a question of vital concern. Already the demon has begun to plot and blight. It is high time that the young people of the nation awoke to the perils which threaten the heritage bequeathed to us. Is the systematic organization of labor into compact opposition to capital merely a play? Then it is playing with danger, as those who were present at the Cleveland Convention, and still more, those who were kept away by the railroad tie-up, will vividly remember. To make this the land of the free, African slavery was abolished. The slavery resultant from present labor organizations is equally inconsistent with free institutions, and destroys the right of a considerable portion of the population to the title of free men. Again, are the socialism and anarchism so rapidly developed of late years only spasms of braggadocio and revolt? Let us hope so — under the stern restraints of law. And yet let us not forget that the rapid and unrestricted immigration has brought in upon us not only the densest ignorance of the European masses, but also the most dangerous leaders of the worst classes. And as a result, thousands of our working men who would otherwise have remained peaceful and contented have been stirred up by demagogues until the foment and disturbance are too great to be disregarded by any thoughtful student of the country's welfare. The labor problem will never be settled until it is settled right; and it will never be settled right until this is the land of free labor.

And then free liquor! It is almost that. The temperance uprising has had one good result beyond what was directly aimed at. It has revealed a peril that was partly concealed, — a cancer eating its deadly way into the nation's vitals. The truth is that in far the larger part of this country rum rules. It does not merely madden and murder men and damn their souls and ruin their homes; it rules. In the legislative halls of many States, in common councils and in civil courts, in police headquarters as in vile resorts, rum rules. If not, how is it that the liquor laws are openly and defiantly violated? How is it that the great political parties are tied hand and foot by this tanglefoot power? The facts are indisputable, and one of two things must come to pass: either the rum power must be overthrown, or this will cease to be the land of the free. No citizen is free whose platform or vote is dictated by the liquor power. Free rum and free government cannot permanently exist together. Here is a field in which our young people have a mighty work to do. The saloon as a factor in American politics must be abolished. This will only be when the saloon itself shall cease to be. Suppress the saloon and you smite to death the liquor traffic.

The land of the free — assaults on the people's rights in the shape of illegal and pitiless trusts. The octopus Combination is swallowing the Independent Individual. Along with this go free lying, gambling, cheating — not in the hiding-places of crime in the slums, but on the stateliest avenues of business, in magnificent speculative exchanges. Everywhere are to be seen the effects of lowered standards of morality in commercial competition, through the absorbing craze for wealth that is consuming honor and life itself. Then there is the free, which means the desecrated, Sunday, and many other things that might be named. But these are enough. And while we thank God with patriotic pride for our national greatness and his goodness, it is wise also to pray for wisdom to detect and Divine strength to face and conquer such foes of freedom as must accompany such swift development. Over against the dark picture we can put the free Church and the conquering Christ. Every enemy can be overcome if only the Christian citizens will heed the injunction, " Stand fast therefore in the liberty wherewith Christ hath made us free." This nation owes its liberty to Christ. The principles of his Gospel are the principles of human liberty, fraternity, equality. Man's obligation to his brother man was never taught by any other as by the Lord Christ; and this mutual obligation is the basis of our free government. Hence it is true that in the Christian freedom this nation was founded. The more you study our history the more will you discern the hand of Almighty God in it. As in our past we recognize his presence, so in our future we recognize his purpose. How shall we help work out this purpose and show to the world the enduring worth and glory of a Christian nation? By standing fast on Christian liberty. By resisting every assault of evil. By learning the meaning of patriotism, and by applying the truths of religion to actual citizenship. By being Christian citizens. That means to do what in us lies, by the grace of God, to preserve this as "the land of the free."

This shall be. I believe in God. I believe in the Divine destiny of this nation. I believe that we shall yet give to Europe and Asia, to all the world, such a sublime view of true Republicanism, of American independence, of the royalty of untitled citizenship, as shall lead them up with rapid step to civilization higher, better, purer, than any of which their statesmen, reformers, or poets have dreamed. God help us to do our part. To lead others we must be ever in advance. Keeping the Bible and our Constitution before us, let us march onward and upward in the great highway of political, social, and religious progress, raising to heaven the glad refrain, as both hymn and prayer : —

> " The Star-Spangled Banner,
> Long may it wave
> O'er the land of the free
> And the home of the brave."

The next speaker was Rev. Gilby C. Kelly, D.D., of Owensboro, Ky., also a trustee of the United Society of Christian Endeavor, a representative of the Methodist Episcopal Church South.

We regret a report of Dr. Kelly's admirable address cannot be given. His theme was, " Variation of Protestantism," saying that not variation but opposition to Protestantism is the evil which America has to contend against. He then stated that the practical advantage of the Christian Endeavor Society was that it had the power to destroy this evil, — first, by fostering good fellowship among all Protestant denominations. Secondly, it is the body through which the moral questions which imperil our nation are certain to be conceived.

He then spoke of the growth of the Society, and the influence it has on the American public to-day. He cited the fact that the closing of the World's Fair on Sunday was due to the protestations of this Society.

In closing, Dr. Kelly reminded the Endeavorers that the future of the Society lay in its ability to remain united, and in doing so the Christian Endeavor was destined to become the basal religious society of the country. "We may all be singing different parts," remarked Dr. Kelly, in referring to the various Protestant denominations, " but we are all singing the same tune."

The last speaker of the evening was Rev. John H. Boyd, D.D., pastor of the Southern Presbyterian Church of Charlotte, N. C.

Address of Rev. John H. Boyd, D.D.

When John Robinson, pastor of those brave spirits whom we know and revere as the "Pilgrim Fathers," delivered his farewell address to them, then setting sail in the *Mayflower* for the New World, he used these words : " I charge you, before God and his blessed angels, that you follow me no further than you have seen me follow the Lord Jesus Christ. I am very confident that the Lord has more light and truth to break forth out of his Holy Word. Luther and Calvin were great and shining lights in their times, yet they penetrated not into the whole council of God. I beseech you, remember it, — 't is an article of your church covenant, — that you be ready to receive whatever truth shall be made known to you from the written Word of God."

These are prophetic words, honoring to Divine truth because recognizing its infinite depth and perennial freshness; they are words of hope, because in this ability of the Sacred Writings to speak forth new truth, at new exigencies and in new times, lies their power to bless the world and aid man in his effort to realize the kingdom of God on earth.

I am before you to speak of a new light which I believe is breaking forth from God's Holy Word, and I am here to plead with you to be ready to receive it.

We read that our Saviour, in that hushed hour of midnight when the shadows of Gethsemane and Calvary were gathering about him, prayed, prayed thus: "That they all may be one; as thou, Father, art in me, and I in thee, that they also may be one in us; that the world may believe that thou hast sent me."

At another time he said, "A new commandment I give unto you, that ye love one another. . . . . By this shall all men know that ye are my disciples, if ye have love one to another."

The very spirit of the Master breathes through the words of the apostles: "And above all things, have fervent charity among yourselves." "Walk in love." "My little children, let us not love in word, neither in tongue, but in deed and in truth."

Let these few passages out of a multitude suffice. They are holy words, and must be richly significant. What do they teach? Three things: —

1. The vital unity of God's believing children, — a unity so real that it is comparable to that which subsists between the life of the Father and the life of the Divine Son.

2. The basis and bond of this union is *love*, — a love as spontaneous, as full and sincere as that wherewith the Father loves the only begotten Son.

3. This unity and love should find practical expression, and manifest itself in the attitude of believer toward believer.

The unity of God's true people is one of those unmistakable truths of Revelation which have never been denied or overlooked. It is one of those sublimely comprehensive conceptions which the mind eagerly grasps. It is pleasing to the fancy. It delights the affections. It is easy to believe, and the Church has always held to it as an article of its faith. Whatever external differences there may be, the whole body of Christians announce, in one language, their belief in "the Holy Catholic Church" and in "the communion of saints." The psalmody of worship rings with the glad thought that

> " We are not divided,
> All one body we,"

or in humble thanksgiving declares,

> " Blest be the tie that binds
> Our hearts in Christian love."

The Church has thus fixed this great fact in her creed, in her theology, and in her worship; but the conception of the nature of this unity has been such that men have been content to let it remain an idea, an abstraction. It is a reality, — no doubt of that, — but one purely spiritual, a bodiless reality, needing not to be seen or felt or in any way to reveal itself to the outer senses. The condition prayed for by Christ was thought to be a transcendental something so far removed from actual states and duties that it might be gloriously true and yet the earthly Church be marked by division, strife, separateness; might continue so as in no way inconsistent with it. The name of Christ might be lost under a hundred party names; hostile pulpits and factions might hurl anathemas one against the other; diverse schools might teach antagonistic doctrines; truth might be expressed through numberless creeds, and the hosts of religion stand isolated, and such confusion and separation was called a necessity, evidence of loyalty to truth, a bulwark of faith, a precaution against decay, a purifier of corruption, an incentive to activity, and the Church was still Catholic, and believers, "members one of another."

Would that I might say that such had been the idea of what Christian unity and love meant in the past that is now dead, but we know that such is the dominant idea — very much alive — in the world to-day.

But a new conception is winning its way into the mind, a new light dawns, a new truth is breaking forth from God's Word, and is endeavoring to get itself heard. Many wise, deep-hearted disciples, lying on the bosom of the Master, and hearing the throbbing desire of his own heart, are beginning to see that this vital relationship of God's children is not a mere ideal, a fancy, a vision; not a fact for the inner life alone, but one so great and real that it must be expressed, it must find a means of manifesting its vitality and reality; and this passion of love, binding all saints together, is not a mere sentiment, a passing feeling playing over the chords of the heart, but a holy affection and abiding principle, overmastering all other emotions and finding its right expression in action. It must be so. Such a truth as this must find its end and last issue in a concrete fact, such a relation must have its life of outward duty, and such an emotion must manifest itself by word or look or touch or work. It refuses to remain silent, hidden; it will not be repressed; it irresistibly embodies itself in some outward shape of practical sympathy, brotherhood, fellowship, union.

This is the necessity which is seeking recognition in these times, the truth that is trying to get itself believed — unbelieved, unrecognized, and unfelt through ages past. The treasure hidden in the field is being brought to light, the spirit of love is seeking a body, the voice drowned in the din of noisy, contentious years is winning attention.

It seems to me that across the lost centuries I can hear the plaintive cry of God's Holy Son going up through the midnight air, pleading for the fellowship of his followers: " I pray that they may be one — that the world may know that thou hast sent me. Without this unity and the love that prompts it, the world will not — cannot know me ! "

Oh, what large, terrible meaning lies in such language ! The absence of that intimate, visible relation between his disciples which attests their brotherhood and warm-heartedness is an opaque something, a curtain, a fog, a funereal mantling, which conceals his true divinity. His love and loving work for man, the significance and efficiency of all he did and experienced from manger to tomb, depend upon the maintenance of peace and fellowship among his followers.

You have sat, perhaps, in the hush of the evening hour, beside a lake whose bosom was all unruffled by even the gentlest breeze, and saw beneath the perfect image of the o'erarching heaven, — the scimiter moon lying softly almost within reach, each star blazing its message of Divine immensity and mystery into the inner deeps of your being, while across the waters came music, faint, distant, yet bearing a message to your soul, the very echo and reminder of celestial melody; then, while thus lapped in the delight of such a moment, a crowd of merrymakers, with splashing oar and ribald laughter, passes, breaking the soul's sweet restfulness, hiding the reflected glory, and driving moon and star back to their places in the far off heavens, and drowning the tones of music.

I think that this picture may represent the meaning of Christ's words. By the discords of his disciples the image of his divinity is marred and obscured, and his words of grace are drowned. And yet our ingenuity has invented so many apologies that we are not far from deeming the present state of the Church ideal; and he who questions this or would alter it is set down as a vain disturber, or a dreamer of hurtful dreams.

The actual condition of suspicion and isolation is justified by many plausibilities; division is defended with acute reasoning; obstacles are thrown across pathways leading to a common meeting-place; the elements of religion which make for disintegration are fostered and emphasized on the plea that this is essential to proper loyalty to truth. It is loudly announced that *principle* is involved. Yes, my beloved friends, this whole subject of interdenominational fellowship does involve principle. We must be unflinchingly loyal to truth. What principle is this which is so involved? With what principle is loyalty to begin? Is not the sum of all Divine commandments, "Thou shalt love"? Do not the law and the prophets hang on this? Are we not "members one of another"? Are we not to love, not in word and tongue only, but "in deed and in truth"? What principle more radical, higher, holier, than this? Let us learn to be loyal to this truth and to this principle for a while.

It is urged that any attempt to draw God's people together on a platform of mutual recognition and friendliness will endanger the best welfare of the Church, leading to corruption and indolence. Do you believe it? Is party spirit and the green eye of jealousy the guardian of ecclesiastical purity? If so, the devil's policeman is on watch in God's city. The true Keeper of the blood-bought Church is the Spirit whose very name is "Holy." The promised, abiding presence of the Head himself insures the continuance of that Light from which darkness and corruption flee away. The true motive for service in the Kingdom is not sectarian rivalry or aggrandizement, but love — love to God, love to brother man. This greatest, brightest, best, divinest, thing in the world is the appointed source of zeal and devotion. Heat begotten of denominational friction is hell-fire, and the hotter it is, the more hellish it is.

Would that I could thrust this fact of the real unity of all Christians into the inner deeps of your soul, there to be fixed forever, causing your hearts to thrill with brotherly love, and creating a noble thirst and resolution for the exercise of whatever sincerest fellowship implies. We are gathered from almost every land; many races and nations are represented; we are named by diverse party names; yet we are unified by the masterful fact that we are all "hid with Christ in God." Whether touched by the hand of confirmation or not, baptized *with* or *into* water, to each there was an hour, sacred above every hour, when the Spirit of God came and touched the soul as the breeze touches the cheek in that shadowy hour between the lights. We felt him. He was strangely near and real to us then; we lived, we loved, we vowed — loved Jesus and vowed loyalty to his divine name and service to his Church. That experience has made us one — not one externally, one in that which the senses announce, but really one: one in that inner life, one in the supreme fact respecting ourselves, that we are the sons of God. This glorious fact must not remain invisible, mute. It must reveal and substantiate itself in some material form — in fellowship, heart touches, hand touches, lip touches, in co-worshippings, prayings, workings.

God's great idea of unity and the duty of love has wandered through the centuries, a ghost, a dream. The creeds said that men believed it, but it was unseen, untouched by good mortals, and scoffed at by evil mortals. God has commanded brotherly love from the beginning, and Jesus pleads for it, but the dulled ears of earth heard only a sound, and tongues fell to disputing whether it were angel voice or thunder. Thanks be to God who speaks, there are ears which hear this command to-day. Hearts growing sensitive to the evils of strife and division are feeling the glow of a passion so full and sweet and kindly that it must be the very inspiration of God himself. Endeavorer, are you not such? Do you not hear the call to fellowship? Do you not feel a love embracing the whole brotherhood of Christian faith? This great Convention testifies that you do. This whole movement, running around the globe with swift passage, touching every shore, entering all denominations, quieting all differences, loudly acclaiming all correspondences, announces to the world that some of the Father's sons have grasped the truth that Christianity stands for practical love, outwardly expressed in substantial, helpful sympathy, in a fellowship which draws us heart to heart, uniting our voices in praising Christ and in pledging fidelity to his Church, and sending us down to our several places and relations with pulse bounding in generous enthusiasm for the success of his kingdom.

We are not yet able to measure the arc in which this Christian Endeavor Society is moving; nor may we know the full purpose for which the idea was at this time divinely projected into the life of the Church. The marvels of

God's approval are known to us. The quickening of the religious life of youth, the large fruitage of consecrated devotion, the inestimable impulses for righteousness flowing from innumerable organizations throughout the world, are become commonplace, well known, and yet fondly told over and over. I believe firmly that there is something in the movement beyond all this, larger and higher than aught else which has yet been effected. I have said that God was trying to find a voice, a vehicle, through which he might announce to the universal Church the fact of its unity, and to all his people the necessity of love. May we not expect him to utter himself through this movement? We believe that Christian Endeavorism is a plant of Divine setting. Then remember that one of its root principles is interdenominational fellowship. It does not antagonize the present order. It has no aim to permanently obliterate dividing lines. It seeks no fusing nor confusing of parties or sects. Historic landmarks are undisturbed. It widely recognizes that enough doctrinal ground has not yet emerged from the sea of controversy for all Christians to stand upon, but it has discovered that while separated by intellectual conceptions of truth, within the heart the same love throbs, the same loyalty to the Master is felt. Forgetting the differences of the head, it seeks to place heart to heart; and on a basis of love and fellowship we stand together, and the will, controlled not by logic, but affection, is harmonized in one sacred vow of devotion to Christ and his Church. This movement affords a trysting-place where the separated family of God may meet and exhibit to the world the hidden, mystical cords which bind them even amid apparent isolation, and is the hint and prophecy of that more glorious unity, to be one day consummated, when the dissevered multitudinous constituents of the Holy Catholic Church shall be regathered and blended into unjarring harmony.

This mighty annual gathering, attracting representatives from every division of the sacramental host, is already the highest expression which the fundamental principle of the unity of the sons of God has ever had in the world. It is the most splendid exhibition of the fellowship of Christians since the days of the apostles. For this reason I glory in it. For this reason I hail it as the messenger of hope. It points to a glowing light on the horizon; and that light is the dawning of a day which shall reveal the method by which the infinite number and variety of elements now forming the divided Church may be combined, and the very comprehensiveness of the scheme marvelously enrich and strengthen the Kingdom, and we, devoted to Christ, enthusiastic for his glory, shall have one banner above us, and stand united as comrades, brothers, lovers. This day shall come. No prophet or seer can tell when or how it will come. The issuance of a new creed with a minimum of articles is not going to bring it; nor invitation to gather upon a platform of essentials; nor endless resolvings and discussings. It will not come by any scheme of man's devising. God will bring it in his own way. He will usher in this day as every day comes, with all the phases from gray dawn to the glare of meridian splendor. He will grow it as he grows the plant, blade, stalk, full ear. He is no artificer, mere earthly working with noise and dust, with hammer and saw. No tool is ever heard on his temples. He will work this work of peace by breathing more love into our hearts, by drawing us together in such meetings as this, revealing more and more to us our identity and kinship. Our part is to open the heart to all that makes for peace, and to conserve the right to meet and greet those who love and serve our common Lord. There are those who would destroy our communings, and confine our association to party limit, unclasping our hands and trying to make us believe that sympathy and fellowship beyond the bounds of sect are dangerous. Brethren, if this movement be of God, the right to love and embrace a brother Christian, whoever he may be, is a sacred right and duty which is as inalienable and unquestionable as the right to ask for Divine pardon or to hope for glory land. We should hold to this, and rising above the narrowing influence of a confined horizon, stand on the mountain-top, where breezes from other lands shall waft messages of hearts warm and lives true though unknown and distant.

Thus prepared by residence on the heights of liberality and fellowship, God shall speak unto us the benediction sung by the angels, and send the fullest answer to his Holy Son as he pleads that his disciples may be one.

Dudley Street Baptist Church.

The announcement that Mrs. Emily McLaughlin, of Boston, and Rev. Teunis S. Hamlin, D.D., of Washington, D. C., were to speak drew an immense congregation of Christian Endeavorers. Not only were all the seats in the body of the house and in the galleries and choir loft occupied, but the aisles were crowded with people who were content to stand, and the vestibule was packed clear out to the sidewalk.

But still the Endeavorers kept coming, and it was necessary to hold an overflow meeting in the Dudley Street Opera House, and even there the seating capacity was taxed to the utmost.

Prior to the opening of the meeting in the church, there was a service of song, lasting fifteen minutes and conducted by Mr. George K. Somerby.

At 7.30 o'clock, Rev. A. S. Gumbart, D.D., the pastor, opened the regular meeting by announcing that, although he had been expected to preside, he thought it more fitting that Rev. H. T. McEwen, D.D., should assume that responsibility, Dr. McEwen being president of the New York State Union, and Dudley Street Baptist Church being headquarters for New York. Dr. McEwen accepted the suggestion, and, after a brief address of welcome, introduced Rev. Mr. Dunn, who read the Scripture lesson.

After a prayer by Rev. Mr. McCready, the colored quartette of Atlanta University sang.

They were obliged to respond to a rousing encore, after which Dr. McEwen introduced the first speaker of the evening, Mrs. Emily McLaughlin, whose subject was, " Temperance."

She expressed the difficulty which she felt in giving full expression to the feelings of her heart as she looked into so many faces and realized the blessed meaning of the assemblage and the Divine work of which the crimson and white decorations were the symbol.

The speaker then spoke eloquently upon temperance and the power of the blood of Jesus to wash away all sins. She was glad to see so many young faces among the older ones, but said that Christians, those who are one with Christ, never grow old at heart. Mrs. McLaughlin referred to the enthusiasm which she noticed everywhere.

After the singing by the Atlanta University Quartette, Dr. McEwen gracefully introduced Rev. Teunis S. Hamlin, D.D., one of the trustees of the United Society of Christian Endeavor.

Dr. Hamlin's subject was, " The Personal Element in Christian Work," and received the closest attention from his auditors.

At the overflow meeting in the Opera House, Rev. B. F. Hamilton, of Roseberry, N. Y., read the Scripture lesson, and Rev. C. A. Barbour, of Rochester, and Rev. H. C. Lamden, of North Berwick, made interesting addresses. The musical conductor was Mr. Lawrence Greenwood.

Phillips Congregational Church.

The meeting held in the Phillips Congregational Church was a decided success, and the audience was so large that it was found necessary to hold an overflow meeting in the Fourth Presbyterian Church, on Dorchester Street. The main auditorium of the Phillips Church was a perfect mass of color and buntings. Over the speakers' platform were two large English and American flags, and surrounding these were numerous small Christian Endeavor flags.

The meeting was opened with a ten-minute praise service, conducted by Mr. J. S. Robertson, the musical director of the Fourth Presbyterian Church.

Scripture reading by Rev. A. E. George, pastor of St. Matthews Episcopal Church, followed, and a brief prayer by Rev. W. T. Perrin, pastor of St. John's M. E. Church.

Rev. Minot S. Hartwell, the pastor of the Fourth Presbyterian Church, who presided, then delivered a brief address of welcome to the delegates present and introduced as the first speaker, Rev. Richard Burges, of Cardiff, Wales.

Address of Rev. Richard Burges.

There is great binding power in the International Bible Reading Association. In the first place, it binds thoughts. It does this because every week each member takes the same topic from the Bible, and thus each day every member has the same lesson, and his thoughts are on that lesson and that alone. We do not consider it the best plan to read the Bible here, there, and everywhere, skipping from one place to another, but the members of our association have a separate and distinct topic each day. These topics are six months in the year from the Old Testament, and the other six months from the New Testament.

Monday morning one topic is read, Tuesday and Wednesday other sections are taken up for consideration, and so on through the week.

The Bible is the living book; if we continue to read it we love it more and more. If we read one portion of the Bible and do not thoroughly understand it, we always find another section which, by reading, makes the first part better understood. As members of this association we are supposed to memorize a verse every day. In the morning we are expected to read a portion and select a particular verse to our liking, think and ponder on it all day, thus becoming thoroughly acquainted with it.

The International Bible Reading Association not only binds our thoughts, but also our Christian activity, by the agencies of the Church. It binds together families, and members of the same family think of the same subject during the day. This is a splendid method of binding friends together. It binds nations and it binds worlds, because it brings heaven and earth together. It binds together different denominations. We bind nations together by sending missionaries to the heathen. Five hundred thousand members of the British section voluntarily contribute one cent each year, and this supports a missionary in India. Our missionary in India at the present time is an American, and we thank you for sending so noble a man as Dr. Phillips.

In Great Britain, among the students of our colleges, there are one thousand young men who have volunteered to be missionaries in the foreign field — one thousand young men who are ready and willing to lay down their lives in the work of the Lord.

OFFICES OF
THE UNITED SOCIETY OF CHRISTIAN ENDEAVOR
AND
THE GOLDEN RULE.

Information Booth, Union Railway Station.

The next speaker was Rev. Spenser B. Meeser, of Wilmington, Del., president of the Delaware Christian Endeavor Union. Mr. Meeser's topic was, " Christian Endeavor Fellowship."

Address of Rev. Spenser B. Meeser.

If we examine simply our religious life we shall see that it may be broadly analyzed into (*a*) the influences of God upon us, (*b*) the beliefs we hold, (*c*) the affections that are aroused, and (*d*) the deeds we endeavor to do.

All religion arises in the act of God upon the soul; and Christianity lays its chief claim upon this fact. It insists, not only that it originated with God and not with man, but, equally, that each true Christian is first influenced by God before the Christian life is his. This life involves beliefs, affections, and holy conduct.

By which of these elements in the Christian life are the denominations differentiated? Not upon the ethical nor the emotional nor the spiritual, but always upon the creedal, the matters of belief.

There must be some reason for this, because it always has been true that the divisions of Christianity have rested upon creedal differences; while all our thought about Christian unity rests in the explicit or implicit claim that the only basis of union or constitution of a church is a common belief.

I wish to raise the query, and partly answer it, why a common affection for Christ, or a common spiritual nature, or a common service, should not be a sufficient basis for the existence of a church? These, as we have seen, are integral and fundamental parts of the Christian life; why should the whole emphasis be laid upon a common creed? We must recognize the place of belief in Christian experience. Beliefs lie at the root of perennial emotions, and emotions when true lead to true conduct. Much of our Christian life is imperfect because of imperfect ideals and beliefs. It is rational and plain, then, why this matter of a creed should so deeply affect the unity of Christendom. But two things must be remembered. The mind is affected by the moral sympathies, the sympathies by the conduct, conduct by the sympathies, and the belief by the conduct; they are all retroactive. It is to all a familiar fact that *love* will aid one to believe, and Christ has said that *doing God's will* enables one to know what is true doctrine. The Church is partly in error, therefore, in isolating the creed and in unduly emphasizing it to the dividing of Christians. For even if we admitted that, after the influence of God upon the soul in regeneration, the *true belief* is the most important thing, because of its emotional and ethical influence, a question would still be pertinent, — whether the beliefs which divide the churches into separate bodies are of that fundamental character; that is, whether these beliefs result in emotional and ethical types of especial value and of utmost importance.

For example, does the belief which makes one a Presbyterian or a Baptist or a Methodist, does that especial belief awaken the love for Christ and compel the conduct without which one cannot be a Christian? Unless it does, the claim of the fundamental relation of belief to affection and duty cannot be used to justify the Church divisions.

But interdenominational fellowship regards all the claim made for creeds and only insists that the common spiritual experience with God, the common love for Christ, and the obligations of service commonly recognized are a sufficient ground for a fellowship which is Christian, and which is higher and greater than the denominational brotherhood. Because God has regenerated us; because we love Christ, and because we all wish to serve him, we believe ought to prove sufficient reasons for our being together, even if we do not all think alike. This is more true when we realize that we even think alike when the great truths of Christianity are at stake.

But our fellowship does not mean the destruction of the denominations nor even that we are seeking such an end. It means only that we are exalting Christianity above denominationalism and putting the most important thing in a first place and a secondary thing in the inferior place.

International comity and law do not aim at the extinction of nations. They propose a method of association among nations upon the ground that the brotherhood of man is a higher ideal than the perfection of any nation. Humanity is more than any nation. So our fellowship proposes a method of association and work, without calling for the extinction of any sect, simply upon the basis that Christianity is greater than any church or body of churches, and because, as Lowell says,

> " Man is more than constitutions. Better rot beneath the sod,
> Than be true to church and party while we 're doubly false to God."

We do not aim at the sects, but above them, — at the Christian idea, large enough to include them all.

Our fellowship does not mean that we shall ignore the truths which differentiate us. The duty to know the whole truth compels one to study and know the sincere views of others. He is not loyal to Christ, nor is he true to his own denomination, who does not seek to know the truths which other honest Christians believe they have found. We need not fear to do this, for the diversity of opinion need not affect the unity of spirit, of love, and of service. First to know that we differ and why we differ, and then to find the principle of fellowship in something higher, is better then to ignore the differences, which, if not considered, may afterwards separate us.

So, then, our fellowship rises above mere tolerance; it must be based upon mutual respect and consideration. There is no lasting communion possible among Christians, if we cannot command each other's respect and love. A high and true spirited man can endure contradiction of belief because he knows equally strong and able persons differ. He may endure the dislike of those he differs from and not lose his self-respect. He can even endure that men should ignore his belief or hold him in contempt for it, but he cannot endure tolerance which carries contemptuous pity and condescension. Then he feels like fighting; and the nobler his spirit, the more he feels like it and the more he is justified in it.

This fellowship, then, will not ask the surrender of personal convictions; as Dr. Boardman says: "If there is in all this world a sacred right, it is the right of every human being to have his own personal moral convictions. If there is in all this world a sacred responsibility, it is the responsibility which every human being has before his God and before his fellows for those personal convictions. If there is in all this world a sacred obligation, it is the obligation which rests on every human being to be true, at whatever cost, to his own convictions." The fellowship we enjoy does not demand a surrender, a tolerance for, nor an ignoring of convictions; neither does it seek their destruction. It claims attention to the other integral parts of Christian life; namely, the common spiritual nature, the common love of Christ, the common service of Christ, and the wide range of common beliefs.

In the meanwhile we will not forget Browning:—

> " Ask thy lone soul what laws are plain to thee,
> Thee and no other, — stand or fall by them,
> That is the part for thee; regard all else
> For what it may be, — Time's illusions."

The possibility of such a fellowship is amply demonstrated in the fifty thousand or more delegates gathered in this Convention of the Endeavor Societies. That it is possible indicates some interesting things.

The denominations have learned from each other much of that for which each once contended. They may not have adopted all they have learned, but no student of Church history in the last twenty-five years can fail to see that the life and conduct of each denomination has been very largely affected by the thoughts and practices of the others. The standards may remain formally the same, but they are so differently interpreted, if not departed from, that the churches have grown together and believe more things in common. A member of any church may find this true by a test of simple comparison. The interdenominational idea is the fruit of this growth.

As a result of this, it may be seen that the lines of division in the churches do not entirely correspond to the lines of difference in the living thought of the people of to-day. If all the denominations could be abolished, it is improbable that they would be re-organized exactly as they are to-day. One can readily find in his Christian life affinities stronger than those of his denomination. Men are thus grouping themselves even while they remain in their churches. Numerous illustrations could be given of practices, resting on real convictions, which are finding their way into churches whose standards are strongly opposed to the innovations, and yet they are permitted without question, because they represent the present living thought of the people in the churches.

The sense of the problem of Christianizing the world grows upon us and dwarfs the sectarian question. We are being inspired with the Christian idea; and the common cause, against the enemy of us all, makes us nearer to one another. We crave the chances for expressing the love and obligation we have to Christ. The sense of unity grows. We need the touch of elbows.

In our fellowship there should be dominant, then, one idea, *comprehension;* one spirit, *the Holy Spirit;* one person, *Jesus Christ.* In these we have the unifying idea, the unifying Spirit, and the unifying Person. Of the unifying idea we have now learned. The Christian ideal should be comprehensive, not exclusive nor differentiating. It should recognize the originating influence of God, the common love, and the common idea of duty. It should also emphasize the truths we hold in common. It should point out, also, the fact that the beliefs on which we differ do not awaken the fundamental emotions nor inspire the essential ethical service.

The spirit of our fellowship should be the Holy Spirit. He has been given without question to all of the churches. If we stood in doubt of our loyalty to Christ because of our association with those of varied beliefs, this credential ought to be sufficient, that they have received the like gift of the Holy Spirit. Upon this we may rest assured. Indeed, we may even be guilty of "withstanding" God when we demand a national or creedal credential.

We have been a long time learning what the Apostle Peter was taught when he went to the house of Cornelius to baptize him and to eat with him. The council at Jerusalem called him to account for his conduct, so unbecoming a circumcized Jew. The answer he gave is full of import. He told of his vision, of his visit, of his preaching of Jesus Christ, and the descent of the Holy Ghost, and continued: "Forasmuch then as God gave them the like gift as he did unto us, who believed on the Lord Jesus Christ; what was I, that I could withstand God."

This credential Peter considered a sufficient reason for violating even the written word of God concerning circumcision. He sees in it a new word of God, in which, by the indifference of the Holy Spirit to circumcision, the old essential is no longer necessary. He accepts the facts as the bases of a new fellowship. The gift of the Holy Spirit is to him a sufficient reason for a common fellowship with the Gentiles. So it ought to be with us, that they who, with us, have had the similar Divine approval are worthy of our respect, our love, and our communion. So should it happen that we be accused of being indifferent to conviction, to our churches' polity, to our sacraments and ordinances, we may rest on the fact that God, to-day, as in the apostle's day, makes known to us his comparative indifference to these things. This he does by the common blessing of the Holy Spirit; and we need not hesitate to follow the lead of the Spirit.

Brethren, though I hold hard by the faith for which I stand, because ye are Christ's, attested by the Holy Spirit, I salute you sons of God, and count it a high joy to fellowship with you.

The unifying Person is Jesus Christ. He is the all-inclusive reason for our fellowship. He is the sun and centre of our communion. In him all differences are swallowed up. It is he who has made us a common people. He is the bond of unity. We are one in him. It is the redemption he has made, the inspiration he has given, and the love he has which have likened us to one another, because they have made us more like himself. And it is Jesus Christ who ought to be in our minds all through the fellowship of this Convention, and who should go with us to perpetuate the bonds of a holy unity.

I am impressed every day with the power the leaders among men have over their followers. I recall that return from Elbe, when the vanquished but ambitious Napoleon landed in the country from which in humiliation he had retired. I see the soldiers, sent to arrest him, fling themselves in a strange devotion upon his neck and at his feet, and then, for his sake, follow him, once more go to defeat, humiliation, and death. For the love they bore him, they sank every other consideration of belief and hope to be a united army. And the question rises, Can a Napoleon do this and Christ be impotent? Will the followers of Jesus be less loyal? Will never the call of the conquering Christ join his people for one great common warfare? Do they think less of him than of their creeds? *Christ is more than any creed.*

In a civil war men of every political faith, of every religious creed, of every social standing, under the impulses and convictions of patriotism and for the love they bore their country were made into one army, and in the one fellowship of that patriotism waged an awful conflict.

Is the Christ love less inspiring? Under his leadership and for his sake can we not do nobler yet than they? While every one stands true to his convictions of belief and duty, can we not become one army of Christ, one people of God, for the sake of our Divine Leader? Under his guidance can we not push more vigorously still the service and love for our fellowmen until they all shall have no more consuming thought than that of honoring God and doing all they can for Christ and the Church? *Let us exalt Christ above every conqueror, and Christianity above every creed.*

The last speaker was Rev. Michael Burnham, D.D., of the Pilgrim Congregational Church of St. Louis. The speaker gave a very interesting account of the work performed by the society attached to his church, which was enthusiastically received, and then made a very helpful address. A report was not secured.

The overflow meeting in the Fourth Presbyterian Church was largely attended. Mr. James Kemp presided, and the speakers were Rev. Walter Cally, of the Bowdoin Square Church, Boston, Rev. Richard Burges, Rev. A. E. George, and Rev. Mr. Canning, of Toronto.

Jamaica Plain Baptist Church.

The Jamaica Plain Baptist Church should have been double its present size to comfortably accommodate the crowd of enthusiastic Christian Endeavorers who filled every pew and even the aisles at the welcoming rally the opening night.

Crimson and white bunting was hung from end to end of the church, and the pulpit was draped with the stars and stripes.

A praise service preceded the regular exercises, consisting of a violin solo, by Mr. Fletcher, and a number of well-known Christian Endeavor hymns, sung by the two thousand people present, with Mr. O. E. Mills, of the New England Conservatory of Music, as leader.

The pastor, Rev. Ralph M. Hunt, then introduced Rev. Mr. Shatro, of the Jamaica Plain Methodist Church, and after a short reading from the Scriptures, he made the opening prayer.

Rev. Mr. Morgan, of the Central Congregational Church, then

made a short speech of welcome, after which Rev. Mr. Hunt introduced Rev. Elijah Horr, D.D., of Worcester, Mass. whose topic was, "A Reason of the Hope that Is In You."

Address of Rev. Elijah Horr, D.D.

"A reason of the hope that is in you."

The Prophet Daniel, looking down the long vista of the coming ages, spake of a time when "many should run to and fro, and knowledge should be increased."

Our era seems to fill out this outline. Our wonderful facilities of travel have brought the "ends of the earth" together, while general information upon all subjects of inquiry was never so wide-spread as now. In Christian lands all are expected to be well informed, — to have opinions and to be able to defend them.

Protestant Christianity has always enunciated the Biblical theorem of the "priesthood of the people," — the right of individual interpretation of the Scriptures, accepted as the rule of life, and the duty of all to be able "to give a reason of the hope that is in them with meekness and fear." Christianity has never appealed to the credulity of the people. Her impregnable system is founded upon accredited facts in revelation and experience. Historical Christianity is unimpeachable; it rests securely upon the demonstrated genuineness and authenticity of its records. The early apostles and teachers of Christianity always appeal to the facts in the life and concerning the death of Christ, alleging that "these things were not done in a corner."

An eminent historic critic has affirmed that there is better evidence, and more of it, to support the alleged facts in the life, death, and resurrection of Jesus, than there is of the life, deeds, and death of Julius Cæsar; and that the genuineness and authenticity of the Gospel records are tenfold better established than those of "Cæsar's Commentaries." We are not credulous or superstitious when we accept the well-proven facts of early Christian history; that they are not "cunningly devised fables" the general consensus of the scholarship of the centuries abundantly proves.

Historic criticism with almost one voice declares that the apt phrase coined by "the grand old man" of England — Gladstone, celebrated as deservedly for his rare and ripe scholarship as for his peerless statesmanship — is well-chosen: "the impregnable rock of the Holy Scriptures."

The scholars of the world have been buttressing this old rock through the centuries, but there has never been an era of such wondrous activity and such pronounced results in this direction as in this generation in which we are permitted to live.

Biblical archæology has exhumed its treasures from cities so ancient that their very names have been lost or antedated historic records; and the cuneiform inscriptions upon the providentially preserved tablets have established from these collateral sources the historic correctness of the Old Testament records. These investigations, conducted not by theologians, nor always even by Christians, but often by enthusiastic scientists and antiquarians, have thrown a flood of light upon the early history of the race, and established the substantial genuineness of the Old Testament accounts of events of which we have had heretofore no other records.

The same appeals to facts and results — to what it is, has done, and is doing— can most appropriately be made to-day in defence of the divinity of Christianity.

Neander, the celebrated church historian, said that "the introduction of Christianity turned the history of the world into new channels." History itself furnishes an unanswerable argument for Christianity. Its opponents must in some way account for the new force in spiritual dynamics, that appeared and marked an epoch so important that all history, ancient and modern, dates from it.

The value of this argument becomes more apparent as we note that all substantial progress in the world's history has been made during this era.

Christian civilization, that has changed or is modifying the face of the who... earth, is the mightiest argument for the Divine in our holy religion. It is fast bringing out the lost lineaments of God in human nature throughout the world. This recognized force that has steadily and persistently been working out the intellectual, moral, and physical regeneration of the race for nineteen centuries must be accounted for by those who question the divinity of Christianity.

How does it happen that a little company of proscribed men, whose leader has been apprehended by his own nation and crucified by the Romans, should become so inspirited as to boldly announce the audacious purpose of the conquest of the world, and in spite of persecution and martyrdom press steadily onward through the generations and centuries to its consummation? In less than three centuries from the ascension of Christ, Christianity, in the person of Constantine the Great, had ascended the throne of the Cæsars, wrapped itself in the royal purple, and ruled the Roman Empire. How may we account for this miracle of history, except by recognition of the Divine Christ, who, reincarnating himself constantly in his followers, has through them moulded and shaped the world's destinies.

The evidences of Christianity as taught in our theological systems are not the only or perhaps the strongest arguments for its divinity. They are many and cumulative from historic sources; they are embodied in the constantly multiplying institutions of our civilization; they are emphasized in her missionary conquests that girdle the globe with light; they are voiced in the triumphant songs that inspire her militant hosts as they march to new victories.

Every redeemed soul, every ennobled and glorified life, is a vitalized argument and evidence of Christianity, a "living epistle," that may be read by all men, the daily acts in every-day life forming an alphabet in conduct, habits, and character that spells Christianity.

Man is the God-appointed exponent of truth. The vitality of truth is demonstrated by human conditions, just as the vitality of the seed is proven by contact with the soil. The best evidence of Christianity, the most satisfactory proof of its power, is afforded by human experience. The questions that men ask to-day are not so much concerning its past as concerning its present efficiency as a regenerative agency in human life and affairs. What can it do for us here and now amid the distractions and competitions of business and professional life? Will it take out of my heart the lust for unholy pleasures? Will it free me from the dominance of low and base motives? Will it emancipate me from the love and power and guilt of sin? These questions are vital. They are answered in the experience of ten thousand times ten thousand Christians in our own time. The mighty army of Christian Endeavorers, the youthful contingent of the great militant host of God, answer it by their presence in our metropolitan New England city in these gracious days.

The Bible, our Christian text-book, makes it the duty of Christians to be teachers and defenders of the faith; but this ability to serve the cause of the Master comes not by accident, nor can it be attained without careful study and diligent training of our mental and spiritual powers and faculties. Mere religious enthusiasm and the exhilaration of meetings and conventions cannot alone, however excellent they may be as aids, fit us for this work. It can only be attained by diligent study of the Word, the judicious reading of carefully selected books, meditation, prayer, and the constant guidance of our religious teachers and pastors.

Whatever we accept as religious truth we ought to be able to defend. Knowledge is the foot-rest of faith — the fulcrum, without which her heavenly flights are impossible. These flights are often beyond the realms of reason; but true faith is never unreasonable.

The mysteries of faith may not all be fathomed by reason, in the sense that all her processes can always be formulated and demonstrated; but this is no more true of faith than of science. In both science and revelation there are revealed mysteries and mysteries revealed.

Some great facts and theorems of Divine procedure in both realms are revealed as stupendous mysteries. There is no attempt in revelation of explanation. In them are the "hidings of God's power." They are the mountain peaks of God, unscaled and unattainable by human reason. There are thus many secrets of God's operations both in the natural and spiritual world that we recognize but cannot reveal — processes that we may note, but cannot explain.

The doctrine of the New Birth or Divine Regeneration is so revealed to us by Christ. Its philosophy, its mode of operation, no one may explain; its effects every one may both observe and experience. The scientist admits these things in his realm. Why should any one be surprised, or object, if we find them in God's other realm of the spirit. Some of these great mysteries must be received by simple faith, but such faith is not necessarily unintelligent or superstitious. It rests securely and confidently upon the promises of an unchanging God, whose work for us and in us has been tested in our own experiences and that of others. What we can understand and explain, what we have proven and tested, is our basis of belief and trust in those great mysteries that our finite conceptions cannot reach or solve. " Secret things belong unto the Lord our God: but those things which are revealed belong unto us and to our children forever." Science and revelation stand upon a like basis in some of these particulars. Some of the great truths of science never have been, and probably never can be, demonstrated; but no one doubts them or has reason to, and they are properly made the basis of much other and clearly demonstrable teaching.

Christianity has ever been the fostering mother of education and science. She has built the observatories and the laboratories that have made the discoveries of science possible. There is hardly a college or university of sound learning upon either continent which has not been built or endowed by Christian munificence. There have been some scientists who have been so inflated by the real or supposed importance of some of their discoveries that they have hastily turned about and abused their mother.

The times both demand and provide for intelligent Christians in these days. While Christianity was never more thrown upon the defensive, there were never better facilities afforded for her defence than now. No Christian need, nor ought to be, either ignorant of the evidences of his faith or unintelligent in the practical marshalling of them in its defence.

The Christian Endeavor movement, one of the most remarkable in the history of the Church, may be made everywhere, through the co-operation of pastors, a school of theoretical and practical instruction for the Church of to-morrow.

It is a providential opportunity for the education of our young people in the evidences and doctrines of our faith, which no pastor can neglect and do his full duty. This instruction can be made at once so popular and interesting, in a series of monthly conversational lectures, that the young people of the congregation will enjoy them as much as any other portion of the services of the society. They should take the place of the regular meeting once a month, that they may not interfere with other church work, or crowd the young people too much in these days of constant pressure in church and social life. The need of this kind of instruction in these days is too obvious for argument.

Catechetical instruction in the evidences of religion and doctrines of the Church, once a function of the Sunday school, and almost everywhere a part of its regular curriculum, has very generally fallen into practical desuetude. Formal and regular instruction of this kind in Christian families has in these hurrying times been mostly discontinued. It must be admitted that a very general neglect of one of the most important functions of the Church, the religious education of her young people, is at present a characteristic of nearly all the denominations. It is culpable, and in time might become almost fatal to the development of strong religious character in the Church of the future.

A providential opportunity for resuming, under most favorable conditions, this work is afforded us in our Christian Endeavor Society. International in its scope, interdenominational in its reach and practical efficiency, it furnishes to every church alike a constantly recurring occasion that may be utilized for this purpose, leaving to each the adoption of such measures and methods of teaching as is adapted to its genius and polity. These teachings will have, and must have, new forms of expression; for the new thought of our times cannot be put into the old moulds of former generations. There will be also new methods of application, varied according to age and environment; but if it is judiciously commenced and persistently carried forward, it will insure stronger Christians in the next generation, and many times duplicate their influence and power. " A reason of the hope that is in us " should be the motto of all our societies. The new age of general and Christian intelligence asks for it. All should prepare themselves to give it. Our great army of Christian Endeavor must not only be strong in numbers and enthusiastic in zeal, but if its power and influence are to be abiding, they must be the result of intelligent convictions so inwrought into religious character and life as never to be eradicated.

The next speaker was a Methodist Episcopal trustee of the United Society of Christian Endeavor, Rev. H. C. Farrar, D.D., of Albany, N. Y. His topic was, " The Christian Endeavor Society as a Training School for Church Workers."

Address of Rev. H. C. Farrar, D.D.

This subject has been assigned to me; I accept it because it is a most fitting subject for discussion before this great Christian Endeavor Convention.

The subject has three distinct lines of thought; viz., (1) The Christian Endeavor Idea; (2) A Training School; (3) The Church Worker.

In speaking of these three thoughts I shall present them in reverse order.

1. *The Church Worker.* — It is an age of work. Evidences of it abound on every hand — in the great factories and great corporations and great enterprises.

The mightiest thought that comes to us in this world from all sides and sources is that of work. The greatest of workers is God. He is not an infinite quiescence, but rather an infinite activity. He has filled the ages past, and still he works on. Jesus said, " My Father worketh hitherto, and I work ; " and man, true to his origin and to himself, is a worker, for he is made in the image and likeness of God.

By work the body is redeemed from the curse of laziness, the earth from the curse of thorns and briers, the mind from the thraldom of ignorance, and the spirit from the habits and power of sin.

What has been achieved in this world without work? Absolutely nothing. Man has had no windfalls; the horn of plenty has been filled only as he has loyally coupled in and worked with God.

The " Micawbers " of the race, those who are everlastingly waiting for something to turn up, have been the world's biggest nuisances. By our very constitution work furnishes the missing link between Divine influence and human good. Neither coats, nor hats, nor houses, nor culture, nor character, grow. They are created, made through co-operation.

The material and the proferred help are at hand, and the Divine decree is, " Go coatless and hatless and houseless and knowledgeless and characterless, or else help yourself." That is God's order, and so he has locked up the treasures of this world and the next on a combination of four letters, W-O-R-K ; and no man can get anything of value without a knowledge of this combination and working it. The treasures of all works are before him and may be his if he work for them.

" Redemption by work " is the very heart of the Gospel. The Master said, " *I must work ;* " the servant must be as his lord. Hence this work law is *universal.* There are no exceptions, no favorites; no passes are issued over this royal road of life.

This work law is *individual.* "To every man his work." "He gave to every man according to his ability." "He gave five talents to one, to another two, to another one." So teaches the Christ. He says to everyone, "Go work in my vineyard." No one can fail to meet the employer. No one can evade the obligation, for no one can get out of the vineyard. The greatest vineyard I shall ever toil in is myself — my threefold being, body, brain, and spirit!

One says, "I am not educated." It makes no difference; work on without it. "I make no profession." That makes no difference. "I am not settled in my religious opinions." So much the worse for you, but the Divine order is not abated one jot, "Go work in my vineyard"!

Hear me: Your salvation, your peace, your success, your eternity, depend on your obedience to this order of Jesus Christ.

Young people, our religion should be not a creed, but an experience; not a restraint, but an inspiration; not an insurance for the next world, but a programme for this world! Church work is our royal heritage; to it let us pledge our best fidelity and loyalty.

2. *The Training School Is a Necessity.* — Trained thinkers and workers are ever in demand. The trained thinker is the secretary of his age, while the trained worker is its treasurer. The plea from all kinds of business and schools and shops and banks and offices and churches is, "Give us the best prepared men and women for our work." And so it is that the best trained teachers, clerks, book-keepers, servants, nurses, drivers, engineers, doctors, preachers, find quickly the best places and receive the best pay.

Magazines are pleading for articles from the trained thinkers. Heads of departments in great organizations and corporations put highest premium on best trained men and women. Preparation is more than half; in many things it is nearly all. Long apprenticeships are necessary for important work. Inadequate preparation foredooms to failure. So ever is there a demand for better schools, better books, better tools, better conditions, better brains, and better discipline.

Shall the day schools get the best teachers, and the Sunday schools take up with anything? Shall the lucrative professions command the best, and the ministry get but the dullest? All worldly departments best filled, and the Lord's work shoved off on the uncultured and the untrained?

Does God deal so with us? Does he not give us the best — the best world and atmosphere and light and body and mind? Has he not wrought out for us the best redemption? Does he not afford the best remedial agencies? Does he not furnish the best incentives?

Your best or none; that is New Testament Christianity! The best rendered, then he adds his blessing!

Work is the only universal currency which God accepts. "The purposes of God" nowadays march with quick steps along the highways of the world's history. Trained brains and hearts will discern these purposes and turn them quickly to the world's profit. Joshua became the easy successor of Moses because God and Moses had him in training forty years.

Training schools were never so needed as to-day, because better work is required and better work is being done.

Knowledge is power. Increased knowledge is increased power. There lies the alphabet, twenty-six letters, fine in form but forceless and useless. Let slumbering genius awake and seize those letters, and it will, by the power of its thought, write up all law and medicine and art and science and literature. Knowledge is power.

Henry Bessemer is working yonder in a sooty foundry, working on a knotty problem, "How turn iron into steel?" After years of experimentation he discovers and masters the art, and by its mastery revolutionizes every human industry in the world!

Knowledge is power. Power is the great need of life. By it we turn on our shortest axis and multiply the products. God waits to turn power on to human hearts and into human lives. But God is an economist, and will not waste his power and grace. He gives for use. Power to its last particle is duty! Oh that we may covet power for greater enterprise in the Church of God!

3. *The Christian Endeavor Society as a Training School for Church Workers.* — The Christian Endeavor Society was born of a providential necessity. How quickly recognized by the Church and utilized! What a growth! Unparalleled and phenomenal. What a history it has created for itself! What a power for good it has exerted! This is so because Christian Endeavor stands for "Christianity in earnest." It is literally packed with Gospel principles. It is not an institution foisted upon the Church, but has grown up from within, from its very heart. Hence it is a felt force. It has done and is doing most royal work. It has quickened many a church, comforted and inspired many a pastor, inaugurated many a revival, given fresh impulse to missionary interests, and created a new era in thousands of churches.

Christian Endeavor stands for orthodoxy, an inspired Bible, a Divine Christ, and an ever-present Holy Spirit perpetuating the work of Jesus Christ in the world's salvation. It stands for interdenominational fellowship and fraternity, for Christian citizenship, brotherhood of man, socialism in its purest and highest sense, aggressive missionary zeal, personal consecration and concentration. It is in full accord with the best means and methods of preaching Christ and saving men. Look at the factors at work in the Christian Endeavor Society making it effective as a training school for church workers. They are all concentred in one *pledge*. That is a wonderful pledge, and there is great power in it. It takes hold of the conscience like the marriage vow or the oath of loyalty to government. What opened doors of privilege and blessing has this pledge been to thousands! I need not quote the pledge in this presence — we know it and love it and keep it. It has helped us to do regularly what we used to do spasmodically. It has made the Bible as a new book to us through daily study. It has solved for us the matter of church attendance by making it a duty and not a mere matter of convenience or personal enjoyment. It has helped us to forego certain worldly pleasures that were disintegrating faith and blurring hope. It has opened up new paths of duty, and made the way delightful. Our Christian Endeavor pledge, if studied and kept, has in it the power of making first-class church workers! Daily face to face with Jesus Christ in prayer, daily studying his Word, meditating with care on the weekly theme, attending church regularly and taking active part while there, doing only what would please the Lord Jesus, working to help our fellowmen — these are the vital conditions of a healthful and aggressive Christian life.

But the pledge in all its bearings *must be worked*. I hold in my hand a pound of coal; it represents, when applied through steam to machinery, a man's day's work. We have in our country over 200,000 square miles of coal beds; but those mines must be worked in order to be made available.

Niagara has been running to waste for centuries; now they are harnessing its vast possibility of power to machinery, and going to make it do service all over the State as message bearer and illuminator and motive power.

Oh, the wasted power in all our churches! How can it be utilized?

The Holy Spirit is here to do it. He only can turn power into the human heart and make it fruitful and productive.

Oh, for a new Pentecost in all our churches! Pray for it and work for it, and the promise of the Father shall be again fulfilled!

Shawmut Congregational Church.

The Shawmut Congregational Church was crowded with Christian Endeavorers.

Rev. W. E. Barton, pastor of the church, was the presiding officer, and first announced the hymn, "Awake, My Soul." After singing this,

a chapter of the Bible was read and a prayer followed.   All then joined
in singing, "Arise, My Soul, and Spread Thy Wings."

Mr. Barton then gave a hearty greeting to those present, saying in
part: "I greet you on behalf of the Church and on behalf of the State
of Massachusetts.   I mean this greeting to extend from frigid Alaska
to torrid New Mexico, and to cover the plains of Ohio.

"I have been asked what the word 'Shawmut' means.   It's an
Indian word, and the translation is 'Living Waters.'   This was the
Indian meaning, and we hope to greet you at the living waters."

Mr. Barton then went on to show what a power Massachusetts had
been in the building up of Ohio especially, and the Western States
generally.   He described how John Adams "would not allow the trend
of empire westward to stop at the Ohio River, but claimed the Pacific
Coast as its nearest confines."

Then Mr. Barton turned to the decorations, and aroused no end of
enthusiasm by referring to Grant, Lincoln, and Garfield as memories
that belong to us all in common.

"We welcome you to our historic fields," said Mr. Barton, in conclusion.   "Concord and Lexington are yours to revel in.   We invite
you to where the old sexton climbed the stairs and hung out the lantern
that told the story of liberty and Paul Revere's ride."

The events of the evening were the reading of two Christian
Endeavor stories written for the occasion by two writers favorably
known to Christian Endeavorers.   The first was by Mrs. Grace Livingston Hill, of Germantown, Penn.; the other, by one of the trustees
of the United Society of Christian Endeavor, Rev. J. F. Cowan, D.D.
of Pittsburgh, Penn.   Later in the evening brief addresses were made,
by Gen. H. B. Carrington, Charles C. Coffin, Esq., and others.

Warren Avenue Baptist Church.

Notwithstanding the delegates from Wisconsin and Montana did
not arrive in Boston until late in the afternoon, they came in large
numbers to the big rally held in the Warren Avenue Baptist Church,
their headquarters, and apparently as fresh as when they started on
their long journey.

The church was handsomely decorated with red and white bunting
and Christian Endeavor flags, while the chancel was draped with the
national colors and flags bearing the emblems of Wisconsin and
Montana.

Above, on the organ, a large banner was displayed, with the greeting
written in red letters on a white ground: "Boston, '95.   For Christ
and the Church.   Welcome, Wisconsin — Montana."

The exercises opened at 7.30 o'clock with an organ prelude, after
which the pastor, Rev. Robert MacDonald, D.D., who presided,
requested the congregation to rise and sing the favorite Christian
Endeavor hymn, "In the Cross of Christ I Glory."

There was Scripture reading by Rev. Francis Perry, of Hyde Park,
and then Rev. Mr. Bluet offered prayer.

After another congregational hymn, Dr. MacDonald extended a very cordial greeting to the visiting delegates. He said he believed he voiced the sentiments of every one of his large congregation when he expressed the great interest which is universally felt in the Young People's Society of Christian Endeavor. "I speak truly and conservatively," said Dr. MacDonald, "when I say that it has been a great blessing to this church. I believe the young people's societies could never accomplish such excellent results without the aid of the Christian Endeavor."

Before introducing the first speaker, Rev. H. F. Shupe, of Dayton, O., one of the trustees of the United Society of Christian Endeavor, Dr. MacDonald said that while talking with the latter before service he asked him to what denomination he belonged, and the answer was, "To the United Brethren." "And can we," said Dr. MacDonald, "call ourselves Christian Endeavorers without being united brethren?"

Address of Rev. H. F. Shupe.

My theme is, "Every-day Heroism." Mary and John are my heroes. Their childhood days were passed before the days of the Junior Society, or both of them would perhaps have enjoyed the advantages of that institution. Mary was reared in a Christian home. Her father was a respected Christian; her mother, faithful and considerate. The Bible was honored, the Sabbath was a sacred day, and there was love in the home. In John's home there was no Bible and no Sabbath. If Mary had had the Junior Society she would have had the advantage of its help in developing courage in the discharge of public religious duty. If John had had the privilege of the Junior Society he would have enjoyed the benefits of early religious instruction. He was in the Sabbath school, which will account in part for his subsequent history. Mary and John are both married now.

Heroism does not consist alone in facing physical dangers or in doing brave deeds which win the applause of the multitude. God has provided that our first lessons in life shall be in moral rather than in physical courage, and there often is as much heroism displayed in developing dignity, integrity, honor, and self-respect in character as in facing an army. Heroism is not exhibited only in great emergencies, as when the engineer, seeing danger and death before him, holds on to the throttle, refusing to save his life that he may, if possible, save his train. It is not always necessary that there be some great epidemic to call forth heroic service, as when Miss Elizabeth Jones, a bright young woman of thirty years of age, in training as a nurse in Bayonne Hospital, on completing her course learned that the smallpox had broken out in the institution. Within a fortnight the physician and orderly were sent to the pest-house, but Miss Jones bravely begged to be allowed to care for them. Her request was at first refused, but finally was granted; and there in a few days she, too, sickened and died. It was a heroic deed; and a memorial, not in useless marble, but in an additional hospital building, is to be erected to commemorate her bravery. A great conflagration will sometimes develop heroism. A fire was licking up the homes in a residence district of a city. Bravely the firemen were fighting. Suddenly the owner of a beautiful home dashed forward and rushed into the burning building. Immediately there was a cry that some one was in the burning house. Soon he appeared at a window and an old trunk was dashed to the ground, and a moment later he appeared at the door bearing tenderly in his arms a feather pillow!

I have stood recently on two of the great battlefields of our country,—at Chickamauga, where the great conflict developed many a hero, and at Gettysburg, where the high tide of the Rebellion was beaten back with a heroism that will ever command the applause of mankind. But it is not in war alone that heroes are seen. We may say with Whittier: —

> " Dream not helm and harness
> The sign of valor true;
> Peace hath higher tests of mankind
> Than battle ever knew."

And with Carlisle we may say, " If 'hero' means *sincere man,* why may not every one of us be a hero?" There were no great emergencies in the lives of Mary and John, and yet they were heroes.

" Brother Baker will lead us in prayer." These words would have been altogether appropriate in a prayer meeting, but they were spoken on the street corner. They came from a group of boys standing on the street just as John walked by on his way home from the prayer meeting. John had just been converted, and the words were spoken with a sneer by a boy who had been an intimate friend of John's. The taunt stung him to the heart, and he felt a quick flush of anger and was about to make a hasty reply, but as nothing came to his mind for a quick retort, a better thought came. He remembered that he was a Christian and must expect some sneers from the world, as Mary Hilton had told him. Mary had been instrumental in leading him to Christ, and had told him that if any of the boys should taunt him he should send up a swift prayer to God for help, and not get angry or ever be ashamed of Jesus. John walked on, and as he passed from the group, who were still laughing at him, his heart ejaculated a prayer, and a sense of strength filled his soul, and he was ashamed of the angry thought that had darted into his mind. It was a sudden emergency and was neve. known to the world at large, and yet in the victory of that hour John had shown himself a hero.

This was not the only occasion for the development of the heroic in the life of our young hero. His home influence had not developed his moral sense so that one might expect the best type of religious life. On the every-day questions of Christian morals, such as the sacredness of the Sabbath day, and the character of the amusements proper for the Christian, and the duties of religious worship, his standards were low. He had never hesitated to join a Sunday excursion or to take a Sunday run with his bicycle club. Before his conversion he had often laughed at the Church's narrowness and prejudice in its opposition to the theatre, and he had not been trained to attend the services of God's house with any regularity. Now that he was a Christian and a member of the Church these questions had to be considered, but he had a faithful pastor who wisely placed upon the individual the responsibility of deciding upon a course of action with reference to those things concerning which the popular sentiment allowed great license. John was impressed with one thing. It was the rule Stonewall Jackson applied to all these questions. Jackson's rule with regard to the questions of right and wrong often raised concerning indulgences which many consider innocent was, " I know it is not wrong not to do it, so I am going to be on the safe side." To come to a decision on such questions when his habit had been to indulge his wishes, and when the sentiment of Christians was divided and uncertain, presented no easy course for John. He thought of it long, and looked at the question candidly, and at last bravely and courageously decided on the course of self-restraint and adherence to the safe side in every case of doubt. He was a hero. His pastor loved him, and his associates respected him.

Another act of bravery deserves mention. These acts of heroism — meeting quick provocation, facing ridicule harder to be borne than the assault of armies, conquering inclination, and facing popular opinion — prepared John for further acts of heroism. He was elected president of his Christian Endeavor Society. Unfortunately, many of its members had misapprehended the force of the pledge and were carelessly neglecting its requirements. The committee from which he had a right to expect faithful service required his constant attention lest they neglect entirely their duties. The withering, scorching drought of utter indifference settled down upon the society. He seemed to be alone, and every circumstance was disheartening. The heroism of the soldier is often more severely tested while standing faithfully holding his post, than in the heat of the battle's charge. So the heroism of John was tested, but through it all he stood firm, and in the end brought his society to a faithful discharge of their duty. It was a heroic act, and marked him as a hero. John is married now, and is still active in all church work, and is to be depended upon by his pastor, and we may safely conclude that he will continue to be a hero.

Mary was reared in a beautiful home. Her educational privileges and the sheltering influences of her home developed many beautiful graces, and she was a young lady of much talent. As was natural, she had high aspirations; and it was the fond dream of her young girlhood to shine as a useful member of society. This dream caused her to look above common things, and rendered doubly distasteful the duties that were thrust upon her by the circumstances in the home. Lofty as were her ambitions, she found herself occupied day after day with disagreeable household tasks. The future seemed to shut down hopelessly around these homely duties, and she was in danger of becoming embittered with her lot in life. Just then a useful lesson was taught her by her friend and faithful teacher, the family doctor. He pointed to some vials and said, "These are cheap and worthless things in themselves. In one I put a deadly poison, in another a sweet perfume, and in another a healing medicine. Nobody cares for the bottles themselves, but for what is put in them. So it is with our lives. Their usefulness and beauty depend upon what we put in them." It was a new conception of privilege to Mary, and she set herself to performing patiently and cheerfully the homely duties that were thrust upon her. Her self-sacrifice seemed hardly to be appreciated in her own home, but she continued her lowly work, every day growing more beautiful in character. She was a hero, although no huzzaing public cheered her.

One fair evening in June Frank Preston told his love to Mary. The home she entered as her own was not the elegantly furnished one her fancy had painted for herself, but to Frank there was no more beautiful spot on earth than the cosey room where Mary awaited him, clad in dainty gown, inviting him to rest and quiet. There was but one sorrow in the heart of this young wife. Frank was not a Christian. There were no morning and evening prayers and no grace at table. To all these she had been accustomed in her father's home. She knew that Frank would not object to these things in their new home, for he was not wholly averse to religion and would not for a moment oppose his wife's wishes in the matter. She had been accustomed to taking part in public religious services, and she was impressed that she ought to establish the family altar in her own lovely home. It required courage—more courage, she thought, than to do anything she had ever been called upon to do. Between herself and Frank there was the completest confidence, and why should she hesitate to speak of this particular thing? At length she spoke, and one quiet Sunday evening they knelt together and Mary prayed a simple prayer, while her husband in silent reverence assented. It required courage. It was a battle fought out away from the sight of men, but God saw it, and Mary was a hero.

While God does not give to many the opportunity to obtain the applause of the world through the display of physical daring or by meeting some great emergency, he does give to all the opportunity for moral courage. The Young People's Society of Christian Endeavor in its requirements of faithful service, proceeding from devotion to principle, is developing this kind of heroism, and the world is full of heroes. With Sarah K. Bolton, I may thus describe my hero:

> " I like the man who faces what he must
> With step triumphant, and a heart of cheer;
> Who fights the daily battle without fear;
> Sees his hopes fall, yet keeps unfaltering trust
> That God is God; that somehow, true and just
> His plans work out for mortals. Not a tear
> Is shed·when fortune, which the world holds dear,
> Falls from his grasp; better, with love a crust
> Than living in dishonor; envies not,
> Nor loses faith in man; but does his best,
> Nor ever murmurs at his humbler lot,
> But with a smile and words of hope gives zest
> To every toiler. He alone is great
> Who by a life heroic conquers fate."

The next speaker was the well-known evangelist, Rev. J. Wilbur Chapman, D.D., of Albany, N. Y. We have no report of Dr. Chapman's address, which was well received by the delegates. Dr. Chapman prefaced his address by a few congratulatory words. Said he : —

" I bring my congratulations to you, young people, and have good reasons for so doing. Coming over from New York a gentleman remarked to me that the Christian Endeavor Society deserved to be congratulated on account of its large numbers — its great size. But to me the size, if alone considered, might mean a loss. Not quantity, but quality, counts with the Creator.

" I congratulate the Christian Endeavor Society on account of its possibilities."

Dr. Chapman chose for his text, " The hour is come ; " and referring briefly to the crisis in the life of our Lord, suggested some hours of crisis in the life of the Christian Endeavorer.

In the first place, Dr. Chapman believed in the efficacy of prayer. " I believe," he said, " that if we enter into the right avenues, and with the right spirit, the evangelistic force of the Christian Endeavor will be felt all over this country.

" The spirit of the Church is changing. I believe we are on the eve of a great crisis in the life of the Church."

Continuing, the speaker emphasized very strongly the fact that the Church is not an end, but a means.

Dr. Chapman closed with an explanation of prayer. By prayer many souls are brought to Christ.

The meeting closed with the benediction pronounced by Dr. MacDonald.

First Baptist Church.

" The oldest evangelical church in Boston," the First Baptist Church the headquarters for the largest State Christian Endeavor Union, was naturally occupied by a large proportion of Pennsylvania delegates at the thronged and enthusiastic meeting, drawn by the announcement of such noteworthy speakers as Rev. J. T. Beckley, D.D., one of the trustees of the United Society, and the widely known temperance orator, Thomas E. Murphy.

The pastor of the church, Rev. N. E. Wood, D.D., presided, and, after a brief introductory service, introduced as the first speaker Rev. J. T. Beckley, D.D., of the Epiphany Baptist Church, New York, who was very cordially received, particularly by the Bostonian element that knew of his old-time association with this church. We regret that we were unable to secure a copy of the address.

The next speaker was Mr. Thomas E. Murphy, the temperance evangelist.

Address of Mr. T. E. Murphy.

I am not here to-night for the purpose of dealing in platitudes, nor of discussing theories, but to say a few words on the subject of " Gospel Temperance," which is, as you know, the highest type of self-control, — the self-control that was enjoined by our Saviour Jesus Christ; the placing upon not one in particular, but all our appetites and passions, a strong moral check; in fact, an abstinence from all and everything that prevents the development of the highest and noblest idea of Christianity. This is what I take "Gospel temperance" to mean in the general sense; but I want to be more specific to-night, and apply it specially to total abstinence from all intoxicating liquors as a beverage.

I am aware that many methods and plans have been suggested for the destruction and abolition of the drink traffic, and to every one of them I give my prayers and hearty "Godspeed." But the fact remains that the saloon, with all its concomitants of evil, is still with us, drawing its support, as it does, from the masses of the people; and before it can be wiped out, or any radical change for the better can come, public opinion must be revolutionized, and the individual drinker must be won to total abstinence. This can only be accomplished by education. The great Grecian orator, when applied to for information as to the most important requisite in elocution, said, "Pronunciation," meaning thereby not merely the correct utterance of a single word, but also attention to emphasis, tone, inflection, pauses, etc.; and when asked what was the next essential, replied, "Pronunciation," and gave still the same answer to the query as to the third essential in the art. So I would say to you, as Endeavorers, that to bring about that most-coveted time when the saloon shall be outlawed, and the drink evil dethroned, the first, second, and the last essential is education, Christian education. As education has led us out of that state of semi-barbarism wherein a standard of man's gentility was judged by the number of bottles of wine he could dispose of at a sitting, so by the aid of education shall we progress until the virtue and justice and patriotism of a perfect civilization shall abolish this great wrong. "Lead us not into temptation, but deliver us from evil" is our daily prayer; and it is obvious, then, as Christian Endeavorers, that it is our duty to teach and instil into the minds of all who may come under our influence the evil of intoxicating liquor, to so educate those whose salvation is in our care, and to so act before them that by our example and precept we may do something to help fulfil our prayers.

I am thankful and rejoice to say that the importance of education in this respect is coming to be more and more generally recognized. To-day there are but four States in the Union in which there are not statutory enactments making it obligatory that the evil of drink and narcotics shall be taught in the public schools. It is said of the Duke of Wellington that, as he stood on the playground of Eton and watched the boys at play, he remarked, "Here is where Waterloo was won." If we want total abstinence in this nation of ours, it is high time to realize that we must lay the foundation for it in the instruction of youth; and if we, as temperance workers, ever win the victory, it will be because we so laid the foundation.

> " The riches of the Commonwealth
> Are free, strong minds and hearts of health;
> And more to her than gold or grain,
> The cunning hand, the cultured brain.
> For well she keeps her ancient stock,
> The stubborn strength of Plymouth Rock;
> And still maintains, with milder laws
> And stronger light, the good old cause;
> Nor fears the sceptic's puny hand
> While near her school the church spire stands;
> Nor fears the blinded bigot's rule
> While near her church spire stands the school."

In the great movement of Christian Endeavor there are many teachers, and it is in their power to mould and fashion the manhood of the future. When boys and girls understand that alcohol shatters the nerve centres, clogs the brain cells, distorts the reason, vitiates the mind, and destroys that physical, intellectual, and religious liberty which God intended all should enjoy, they will, from conviction and love of the truth, avoid the snare of this "fowler." And it is imperative that they should be so instructed. Indeed, if we put the question on the most selfish ground, we cannot fail to succeed.

Another thing in connection with this subject which I think very necessary for us as Endeavorers not only to possess, but to inculcate in the minds of others, is self-knowledge. Self-knowledge directs to the proper discharge of one's duties. A man that rightly knows himself is acquainted with his peculiar temptations, and knows when and in what circumstances he is in the greatest danger of transgression. He knows what he is and what he ought to be, in order that he may live usefully and uprightly in this world; but how few of us possess this knowledge, or seek to acquire it! We spend a deal of time in studying useless things, but give little time to the study of ourselves. There is nothing in which men are more deficient than in a knowledge of their own character. We may be versed in Greek and Latin, we may be able to read Hebrew and Sanskrit, philosophy and science may be at our fingers' ends, but if we are ignorant of ourselves, if we do not comprehend the lights and shades, the weaknesses and frailties, of our natures, the great lesson of life has not yet been learned.

Pope, in his "Essay on Man," says : —

> "'T is only virtue gives us bliss below,
> And all our knowledge is ourselves to know."

A thoughtless remark, the slightest nod of approval on our part of some questionable act, may determine the destiny of some of our companions or friends.

Drinking customs and the evils which accrue from them could be greatly minimized if the young women of our land regarded them in the light which Christian duty teaches. For example, it is a common occurrence for a party of young men, young bloods, if you will, to go out upon what they are pleased to term "a night's spree," in the course of which they make the "wee sma' hours of the morning" hideous by their bacchanalian revelry; and when the mind has lost its balance, and the reason is dethroned, they stagger to their respective homes and sleep off the effect of their debauch. Surely the reputation of these young men must have reached the ears of most of their female friends, even if in a most modified form. Yet what do we see? These same young gentlemen, having succeeded in sleeping themselves sober, are again on the street, feeling, I am glad to believe, somewhat ashamed of themselves. They meet some young women of their acquaintance, girls from Christian homes, who probably move in the best society, and maybe regulate the atmosphere of the fashionable world. Greetings are exchanged, and perhaps a promenade together is taken. Are these young women altogether ignorant of the habits of these young men? I wish it might be so, but I am compelled to say I doubt it. The fact of the matter is, a little "rakishness," as society is considerate enough to term it, on the part of young men apparently adds an additional charm in the eyes of the young woman of to-day — simply because she has not a proper conception of life and its responsibilities. She trusts that when married her love and tender care will keep her husband from all such sin. Let me tell you that a woman who marries for the purpose of starting a reformatory institution is entering on very serious business.

Now let us look at the other side. Suppose a party of these same young women should determine upon an escapade of a similar character as that indulged in by the young men, and should carry it out as openly and unblushingly. Suppose they were seen on the street the next day; show me the young man, with any self-respect, who would speak to or promenade with them. My point is that a young woman has the same right to demand as lofty a standard of virtue and sobriety in a young man as he looks for and expects in her.

And as Endeavorers we should lay down this principle; and when it is accepted as a rule of life by the young ladies, the young man who drinks will be an exception, and the cause of reform will have achieved a triumph, the value of which cannot be overestimated.

"Honor thy father and thy mother: that thy days may be long upon the land which the Lord thy God giveth thee." This is the first great command which our Lord gave, and in our efforts for Christian Endeavor too much stress cannot be laid upon it. If the young men of to-day were ambitious to honor their parents, and if they fully realized their obligations in this direction, they would not cultivate convivial tendencies.

I appreciate that no young man who tipples ever expects to fall and be a source of sorrow and shame to his loved ones, but the devil of drink is so insidious and subtle that before its victim realizes it his will is weakened, his moral senses stunted, and his manhood is subjugated.

Doctor Johnson declares that "the diminutive chains of habit are seldom felt until they are too strong to be broken." How true this is of the drink habit!

"O thou invisible spirit of wine, if thou hast no name to be known by, why not call thee devil."

I am the uncompromising foe of this iniquity, and no ballot of mine has ever been given, except in condemnation of it. Gospel temperance recognizes the power and effectiveness of law, and its mission will not be complete until constitutional prohibition has been established in this land. But before we can hope to realize this much-desired state, our manners, habits, customs, and social amenities as a nation must be changed. Those who drink must be educated to abstain. The home must be permeated with the principle of total abstinence, for it is largely in the home that the principles are formulated which are to rule the destiny of this Republic; and if the home life be desecrated by the influence of drink, the welfare of the Republic is bound to suffer. It is necessary that parents shall be right on this question. Who were the inebriates of to-day thirty years ago? They were the young boys of those times. Who were the wives of the inebriates of to-day thirty years ago? The young girls of those times. And the inebriates and their wives of thirty years hence, if there are any, must come from the youth of to-day. Hence we see how important it is that every home shall be a schoolhouse for the promulgation of Gospel temperance truth. But, alas! many of the homes of to-day are furnished with the sideboard and wine cellar, and the children are brought face to face with this temptation. It is not sufficient for parents to admonish their children; it is not enough for them to stand as sign-boards pointing the way. They must themselves lead. It is stated that a father once said to his son, "My boy, I want you to go to Sunday school; there is beautiful music there, splendid singing, and charming books; you'll have a delightful time; you must go." He repeated this injunction several times, and then one day asked the boy if he had obeyed it. "No," was the reply. "'No'? Why not?" the father asked. "Well, father," replied the dutiful son, "if they have such good times there, why don't you go?" The father gave up preaching and commenced to practise. The boy went to Sunday school.

As Christian Endeavorers, we must labor to raise the standard of Christian self-denial as it applies to the drinking customs of to-day. We deplore the existence of the saloon, and condemn it; but let me tell you that the habit which too often culminates in a life of drunken debauchery is often formed under influences and surroundings which are looked upon as types of our highest civilization. I refer to the social party, the wedding feast, and the aristocratic club, where wealth and refinement, culture and dignity, lend their approval to the steaming bowl of punch, and to the case of "Mumm's Extra Dry." The guest is asked to take a glass of wine; he accepts, and in many cases is ultimately lost. We must be careful of our acts, for "Evil is wrought by want of thought as well as by want of heart."

I do not say, as some do, that one cannot be a Christian and drink. In no sense would I become the judge or censor of those who indulge in an occasional glass. But in view that it is everywhere acknowledged that the drink traffic is the greatest foe to Christ's kingdom, we ought to bring, as far as possible, every professor of religion who has a spark of conscience face to face with the declaration of God's words: "It is good neither to drink wine, nor anything whereby thy brother stumbleth."

"For if any man see thee which hast knowledge sit at meat in the idol's temple, shall not the conscience of him which is weak be emboldened to eat those things which are offered to idols; and through thy knowledge shall the weak brother perish, for whom Christ died?" If the Church universal were a total abstinence church, and all her great power and influence for education were directed against this monster, the victory would be assured.

We need to lay down the fact that drunkenness is a sin, and the sovereign remedy for all sin is the saving love of Christ in the heart and life. This is the force that has cast out the evil spirit of drunkenness, and lifted the inebriate from the depths of despair into the radiant splendor of a regenerated manhood. In proof of this, let me relate an incident known to you all. It concerns a young man who came to this country when a boy; and after spending a little time on a farm in the State of New York, he landed in the metropolis, and fell in with associations which led to the formation of an appetite which made a drunkard of him. He neglected business, and when his mother came from the Old World to visit him, the only shelter he could offer her was a room in a tenement, where she contracted a fever and died. In this trying hour, poverty reigned supreme, the young man had no credit, and the city had to bury his mother. She was placed in a coffin, without a shroud, and carried to the Potter's Field, where she sleeps to-night in an unknown grave. The young man went from bad to worse until, one rainy night, he was found standing on a street corner in the city of Worcester. A good Samaritan tapped him on the shoulder, and asked him to attend a service where there was an opportunity given to sign the pledge. He walked forward, and wrote his name to the declaration that by God's help he never again would drink a drop of intoxicating liquor, and God helped him. He kept his word, and evoluted on the line of righteousness until he became the most imperious orator in behalf of Gospel temperance that ever trod the platform; and the Love Divine which made a manly Christian of him holds out the same good tidings to every unfortunate.

Then as Endeavorers I would say, in closing, Let us carry on the work in the spirit and according to the teachings of our Master. Then shall we be made strong, stalwart, hopeful, and brave, bearing about in our daily life the poise and carriage of true Christian men and women. Always in the thick of the fight! Taking and giving blows in the war against all unrighteousness! In the home circle let us ever be loyal, tender, and true, so that the world may find us upright before God and downright honest before men. Let our hearts and our hands ever go out in sympathy and helpfulness to those who are weaker than ourselves.

Clarendon Street Baptist Church.

The rally held in the Clarendon Street Baptist Church was large enough to pack both floor and galleries. Rev. George Scholl, D.D., of Baltimore, Md., was expected to preside, but was prevented from being present. Mrs. George W. Coleman, the president of the Clarendon Street Y. P. S. C. E., took his place.

A feature of the meeting was the singing, which was both congregational, by a special choir, and by a quartette of negro students from Hampton Institute.

Rev. J. A. McElwain, of the Clarendon Street Church, read from the Scriptures, and Rev. J. W. A. Stewart, D.D., of Rochester, N. Y., invoked a blessing upon the work of the coming Convention. The speakers of the evening were Mr. Prabala Ramachaudrayya Garu, of Guntur, India, and Miss Florence Ben-Oliel, of Jerusalem, and Prof. James Lewis Howe, of Lexington, Va., one of the trustees of the United Society of Christian Endeavor.

"Necessarily and most delightfully," said Mrs. Coleman, "the presence of these speakers gives this meeting the character of a missionary meeting," and with this thought in mind the church had been appropriately decorated. Over the pulpit hung a large map, giving the areas (in colors) occupied by the chief religions of the world.

We do not have a report of Professor Howe's remarks, nor a full report of Mr. Garu's.

Address of Mr. Prabala Ramachaudrayya Garu.

My country, India, was a home of civilization as much as forty centuries ago. The one thing left of the glories of her ancient civilization is the system of caste, that pernicious barrier to progress. The caste system is not like any class system. Class systems allow a man to earn a position in a higher class than that into which he was born; but the caste system allows no moving upward whatever.

Under British rule, and with Christianity influencing the whole country, great changes are taking place. The chief change is the gradual unification of the people. It is the chief glory of Christianity in India that it is doing this.

The policy of missionary work in India is fourfold, — evangelical, educational, medical, and industrial.

The evangelical is, of course, the most important. The Gospel is now being carried among the people of all the villages and towns. The work is done chiefly among the lower classes. It is said that if the rate of progress which has been attained during the last century is continued, in another hundred years India will be a Christian country.

The educational work done by the missionaries varies according to the denominations which carry it on. Some denominations believe that it is of no use to give the children more than a primary education, or just sufficient to teach them to read, write, and cipher. Other denominations believe in maintaining colleges for the higher education. The advantage of these latter is that the missionaries have in the students who attend them a permanent audience which they may daily instruct in the truths of Christianity. And it is only through some such system of education that the missionaries are able to reach out to the higher orders of the people and carry Christianity to them.

I will say, in regard to the medical work which I have referred to, that the influence of the medical missionary is enormous. It is, indeed, incalculable. He reaches thousands of people, by first gaining their confidence through his use of his medical knowledge, who could never be reached in any other way.

The industrial work of the missionaries is also very important. Most of the million native Christians in India are of the lower classes. When they become Christians they are liable to be persecuted, for their religion, and lose their chance to earn bread for their families. It is, therefore, necessary to supply them with industrial work, by means of which alone can the Christians in India become a power

Address of Miss Florence Ben-Oliel.

It is my privilege and joy to come before you to-night with a message red-hot from Jerusalem, which we love to call "the city of the Great King," not only because there the King of Glory humbled himself for our salvation, even unto the death of the Cross, but because we know that the very city where he accomplished the work of redemption is also to be the throne of David's greater Son when he comes once more in power and glory to establish his Kingdom of Peace.

The last time that it was my privilege to address an American audience in behalf of my people, it was in this city, but with such a difference! Israel's greatest friend in Boston, the sainted pastor of this church, brought me to the meeting and closed it himself with such thrilling words of confidence in the final restoration of my nation and of their ultimate salvation that sent me back to my share of the work in my father's mission with heart aglow and determination to look steadfastly beyond the difficulties of to-day to God's great purpose. The following night his people bade me farewell as his "watchword" missionary to Jerusalem; but we had only reached Genoa when we heard that he had been called up higher. Shall we not believe to higher service? We miss that noble, sweet presence; but may we not be certain that he who worked and prayed so tenderly here below, now being with Christ, which is far better, still intercedes for the Lord's work committed to our care? The warm, noble, loving heart that had ever a welcome and a prayer for a Hebrew Christian is at rest; but Boston, while she mourns one of her greatest men, will not forget his teaching; and looking to the future, one sees her becoming a centre of spiritual blessing to Israel, and being blest herself. "They shall prosper that love Thee."

To-night, for a short time, we are to study the people and the land of the Book. God had one great mission — shall we not say the greatest of all missions? — for his chosen people. "Ye are my witnesses," was his repeated word, "called from amongst an idolatrous people to know the true God in his unity, and to receive and to give to the world the revelation of his character and the hope of Messiah's coming." The people and the land are inseparably united in God's word and purpose, whether for blessing or curse. One finds an epitomized history of the Jewish nation in the twenty-sixth chapter of Leviticus. The first verses call up to our imagination a beautiful picture of prosperity, a brave nation of successful warriors dwelling in peace, God-blessed families cultivating the land of promise, and proving it to be a land "flowing with milk and honey;" above all, God dwelling and walking with them. Then comes a warning of the curses that would fall upon land and people if they obeyed not his commandments, and we see a sad picture of what has in fact been the state of both for the long centuries of their separation, — the nation a prey to their enemies and their fears until their pride be broken, their beloved land desolate and fruitless, their proud cities waste, and their holy sanctuary desolate. The subjugation of the people was completed in the reign of Zedekiah, 688 B.C., but it was only after their rejection of the Messiah that the final separation and dispersion came.

After a long Sabbath of rest, the latter rains, almost entirely withheld for centuries, are on the steady increase, and are a strong factor in returning the land to some measure of its past fertility. Of the plain it has been said with truth that one has only "to tickle it with the hoe and it will laugh a harvest." Even the bare mountain slopes, which look so desolate and waste, respond smilingly to the farmer's efforts, in oil and wine.

Palestine is being prepared to support the nation to whom it belongs by promise. All have heard of the railroads that are being built across Palestine. But have you realized that they are the fulfilment of the prophecy of the Prophet Isaiah? "And an highway shall be there, and a way, and it shall be called The way of holiness; the unclean shall not pass over it; but it shall be for those: the wayfaring men, though fools, shall not err therein." The Hebrew of "highway" describes, as closely as the prophet could, the railroad, so strange to him. The words translated "way of holiness" in the original are, "the way to the holy," the present Arabic name for this very road. The poor lepers of Palestine are not allowed in our train, and the prophet noted with surprise that not even a fool could lose his way on this new road.

Jeremiah xxxi. speaks of the building and extension of Jerusalem, and describes minutely the ground at present being rapidly covered by buildings which can compare with the suburbs of a European town. Ten years ago there were scarcely any houses outside the city walls. Now Jerusalem without the gates covers an area more than twice as extensive as the old city within. As regards the people, the changes which the last fifty years have brought have been greater. 1844 saw a firman from the Sultan of Turkey promising the Jews protection. In 1867 the Sultan issued a firman permitting Jewish citizens of other countries to own land in Palestine, and revoked the law which forbade more than 300 Jews living in Jerusalem. 1881 heard the outbreak of the persecution in Russia, and anti-Semitic demonstrations in Germany, Austria, and elsewhere. 1882 saw the great Mansion-House Meeting in aid of persecuted Jews, and the formation of Palestine colonization societies, which are bringing "bone to bone," and cementing the national feeling in all countries. Of these the Society of Lovers of Zion, which has now enlisted the sympathies of prominent Jews in every country, is doing the greatest work for the temporal benefit of the Jews who of recent years have flocked back to Palestine. While ten years ago there were scarcely 40,000 Jews in the whole land, there are now over 100,000, and some 43,000 living in or around Jerusalem.

In Jerusalem you would see little boys taken to school even in their mothers' arms; and seated around some old master the little fellows will learn to read Moses in the original — all this with their first lispings. Is it much wonder that boys who, instead of reading, "The mouse ate the cake. The cat ate the mouse," etc., commence their study of the revelation of God's power and grandeur in the creation of the world, of his guiding providence and his commandments, are able at the early age of thirteen to take upon themselves the responsibility of their own actions? When he is twelve years old the Jewish boy takes his place at the regular services at the synagogue with the grown men. These services are so frequent that a pious Eastern Jew spends a third of his year in religious services and observances. They consist very largely of the reading of the Old Testament, and, as is only natural, the Jews become very familiar with the Word. It is a rare thing for my father to begin to quote any verse in the Old Testament to the Jews who gather around him, without their taking it up and going right on with the passage. In their own synagogues, let the reader at the desk make the slightest mistake in the reading of the Law and the congregation will cry out *en masse* to correct him, so jealous are they of the Inspired Word.

Now, if we believe, as we must believe, in the light of prophecy, that the Jews are to return as a nation to Palestine, our wisest plan is to seek to bring them to a knowledge of Christ ere they wander further from the old paths. It was this thought which led the British Society to ask my father whether he would leave his work in Rome for a new field of labor in Palestine, and we have not regretted the step.

All over the world an eager spirit of inquiry is being raised among the Jews, and thousands are ready to listen to the Gospel. They must always be met on their own ground. It is only what Moses and the prophets said concerning Christ that will convince them. One challenge which my father often gives them is this: "The prophets foretold that Messiah should come to the second temple before the destruction of the city. Then either Christ has come and you have not recognized him, or the prophets were false." And to that they exclaimed, "God forbid, God forbid!"

To-day the Jews occupy a place in the world which cannot be overlooked. In intellectual pursuits they have been leaders in many lines. In philosophy, we have Maimonides, Spinoza, and Mendelssohn; in astronomy, the Aragos; in music, Mendelssohn, Meyerbeer, and Halevy, and many others. To-day the press of Europe is largely under their control. Only recently the Chancellor of Exchequer in France was Fould, and in England, Disraeli. In philanthropy you have such leaders as Cremeaux and Montefiore.

To-day it is stated on good authority that some 600 Protestant pulpits in Europe are occupied by Hebrew Christians. Amongst these we have such shining lights as Neander, the church historian; Cassel; the Herschels; Ginsburg; Edersheim, who has written the most wonderful "Life of Christ" ever given to the world; Hetzenburgh, the prolific commentator; and many others. And in the mission field, Dr. Stearns, the Abyssinian captive; Rabinowitz, in Russia; Rabbi Lichenstein, in Germany; and others well known to you, — men who have been an inspiration to the whole Church of God. What, therefore, is to be our attitude toward this people to whom we owe so much that we hold dearest and most sacred? Here is an immense conference of 50,000 delegates gathered to study the messages of God given to them through the Jews. Shall we not, in gratitude, seek to open their eyes to the Gospel and Saviour which belongs to them? Shall we not extend to the nation, especially to those of them in our midst, the right hand of fellowship and sympathy, and ask them to accept the unspeakable riches found in Christ Jesus?

Many who are jealous of the growing power and influence of the Jews in all countries complain that they are getting control of so much of the wealth of the world; but we Bible lovers and believers can see in that, also, God's wonderful purpose, and reading Micah iv. 13, " Arise and thresh, O daughter of Zion, and thou shalt beat in pieces many people: and I will consecrate their gain unto the Lord, and their substance unto the Lord of the whole earth," rejoice that a day is coming when the Lord of Hosts will consecrate the rich coffers of the Jewish financiers, and we see missionary enterprises, now so sadly hampered for the lack of silver and gold, flourishing as never before.

People's Temple.

The only standing room at the People's Temple, the largest church in Boston, was on the rafters, and they were inaccessible. The crowd overflowed into the vestry, chapel, and hallways.

The decorations were worthy of notice as being tasty and appropriate, consisting almost exclusively of red and white bunting. A gorgeous " Welcome " greeted all, while a legend in large letters urged, " Let All the People Sing."

Rev. James Boyd Brady, D.D., pastor of the church, acted as presiding officer, and made brief introductory remarks.

Rev. Dr. Archibald led the meeting in prayer, after which selections were read from the Scriptures.

Dr. Brady introduced Rev. J. Lester Wells, secretary of the work of the Christian Endeavor Society in life-saving stations, lighthouses, and light-ships in all lands.

Dr. Wells said that he would like to introduce Rev. S. Edward Young, of Newark, N. J., who had something to say; and Mr. Young said that the organization had done a noble work among the surfmen, and a work that was appreciated and bore results. He spoke of the thousands of lives and the millions of dollars' worth of property saved by the lighthouse, life service, and kindred work. He said he wanted to present to them a life-saving man, a man who had saved many lives, who was a member of the Christian Endeavor and a Presbyterian, Captain Tunnell, of the Delaware Breakwater Life-saving Station.

Captain Tunnell, who was dressed in the regulation uniform of his rank, arose, and was given a hearty cheer, the great audience rising at the suggestion of Mr. Young.

Then followed the address of Mr. Wells.

Address of Rev. J. Lester Wells.

Christian Endeavor, being an aggressive organization, and quick to seize upon every opportunity to bless mankind, has traversed world wide, on land and sea, in desolate places, isolated and lonely spots, and is bringing sunshine to the bravest of men; viz., life-savers, lighthouse keepers, and light-ship crews in all lands.

All along the dangerous coasts where the angry waters roll, life-saving stations are located, manned with the strongest, bravest, and best-disciplined men the world ever had. Why do they patrol the shores, even in the darkest nights, and in the midst of fearful hurricanes, but to rescue upon the high seas the vessels in peril, and to save precious lives and property from loss in shipwreck? Thousands of persons have been snatched, as it were, from watery graves, and millions of dollars' worth of property saved to the nations by the heroism of these men. Equally with them may be classed lighthouse keepers, who always keep the lights burning, and they may be numbered by the thousands. As civilization advances and commerce extends, their number increases. The lighthouse is located, like the life-saving station, along the seaboards, the coasts of lakes, bays, and rivers, as a beacon to the mariner, and is becoming more and more a necessity to travellers and a safety to the commerce of the world. Neglect on the part of these public servants in letting the lights go out or burn dim would be announced in every country, and raise a cry of alarm in the vast marine world. Far out from the harbor are the light-ships, anchored in deep water and with never a moment of rest. They are continually tossed by old ocean, and in storms the experience is something awful. The heroic men of the light-ships are called upon to endure many hardships, as others of the service. In the time of danger, whether in fog or tempest, the alarm bells and whistles must be kept active, and lights bright and clear. The light-ship crews have also proven praiseworthy life-savers, as they are frequently summoned by vessels in danger in their vicinity to come to their rescue. Why, now, are these thousands of heroes glad for the sympathy, religious influence, and cheer of the Christian Endeavor Society? In answer we would say, The most of them are practically shut out of society, and live lives of loneliness. They are located on isolated spots, some far-off island, a barren sand-bar or rugged promontory far out at sea, away from home and dear ones, cut off from religious privileges, and in thousands of cases deprived of literary and intellectual benefits.

The International Committee would urge all Christian Endeavor Societies in every land, located near life-saving stations, lighthouses, or light-ships, to use their utmost endeavor to comply with the united request of the keepers and crews to visit the stations and hold such services as they in their good judgment think the surfmen would appreciate. Make the meetings cheerful and of an uplifting character, and leave out all sectarianism. Visit the stations for the good you can impart to the men, and let these visits be sometimes of a musical and of an entertaining character.

Another way in which Christian Endeavor can help these noble servants of world renown is by sending comfort bags; and every society, even the Juniors, can do something along this line of work.

From the time Rev. S. Edward Young, chairman of our International Committee, held the first service in a life-saving station on the New Jersey Coast, in 1891, until now, the interest in keepers and crews has not abated, but has gone sweeping around the world. During the year, thirty representatives have been appointed in foreign countries on work in life-saving stations, for lighthouse keepers and light-ship crews, and the total number of miles of coast reached by our present representatives amounts to ninety-two thousand, one hundred and forty miles (92,140).

We are now in communication with thousands of stations, and so are coming into touch with these heroic men everywhere. We are learning day by day, more and more, about the lives they are living and the toils they endure for the safety of the travellers upon the high seas, and for the commerce of the world.

We are also getting a better insight into their environment, their social life, habits, etc., while, on the other hand, they are becoming educated in the noble work Christian Endeavor desires to accomplish for them. Since the keepers, crews, and surfmen have found out the spirit of our international movement, a new world of hope and blessing has loomed up before them. The keepers, surfmen, and crews have been the recipients of thousands of comfort bags, and on opening them, beholding the wonderfully convenient and useful articles therein, have expressed their thanks in words of delight. The hundreds of letters which have been received from them, not only by the secretary, but by societies themselves, overflow, as it were, with heartfelt gratitude to the friends who have thus remembered them. The thousands of copies of *The Golden Rule*, and other papers sent them, are eagerly read; and one result is that their minds have been set to thinking new thoughts, and we have reason to believe their hearts moved to action. We can never recount the value of the visits made to the stations, and the meetings held there. During the past year religious interest has been manifested in many places, and the most remarkable has been along the New Jersey banks. Where the first work was done the first great fruit is gathered. The interest extended from one station to another, and scores of surfmen have resolved to live Christian lives.

The last speaker was Rev. John Henry Barrows, D.D., of Chicago, Ill., one of the Presbyterian trustees of the United Society of Christian Endeavor. Dr. Barrows's topic was, " Samuel Adams as a Type of Christian Citizenship."

Address of Rev. John Henry Barrows, D.D.

There are several great chords to be struck at this International Convention. Among them are foreign missions and Christian citizenship. I shall confine my address to-night to the duties which belong to the Christian citizen, and I count myself most happy that I can take for my text the life and character of Samuel Adams, the greatest of Boston's heroes, who offers a most unequalled model of high devotion to the public good. I hope that what I say to-night will inspire within us a new thankfulness that we can hold such a convention as this in the Puritan metropolis, in the cradle of American history. You will find memorials of Samuel Adams scattered all over this historic town, and I am most happy in being able to help you to a better acquaintance with one whom, since my young manhood, I have cherished in my heart of hearts. I shall attempt to revive the fame of a half-forgotten hero, who, as John Fiske declares, "was second, in the history of the American Revolution, to Washington himself," a judgment which the Hon. Robert C. Winthrop has also expressed. " The noblest valor," it has been said, "may sleep unrecorded, like the heroes before Homer." Such, for a long time, was in some measure the fate of Samuel Adams.

He was born in Boston, the city which divides with Chicago the right to be styled "the emporium of modesty." According to New England conceit, those who are thus highly favored do not need to be born elsewhere or again. He was a son of Captain Samuel Adams, a deacon in the Old South Church and a member of the Massachusetts Assembly. This wise and good man, as his son calls him, organized, with twenty others, an association of ship-builders' mechanics, called the " Caulkers' Club," whence, we are told, our word "caucus." I believe that my hero's skill in the management of men — and he never had a superior on this continent —was in part a native inheritance from his father, the founder of that much-abused, much-neglected, but truly American institution, the caucus. His mother was a profoundly religious woman, and from her Samuel Adams inherited a moral earnestness that would have driven him to the pulpit had not family misfortune interfered and prevented. In this respect he was not like the Boston man of to-day, who, it is said, falls back for his living on the immortal soul.

During his boyhood the Colony was in dispute with the royal Governors, and young Adams was eagerly interested in these preliminary contests between the people and the crown. The chartered rights of Massachusetts were violated, and the boy's blood was stirred as he listened in his father's house to discussions with the leading men of the day as to what measures ought to be pursued. A deep interest in public affairs tinged his studies under Master Lovell, at the Boston Latin School, and his four years at Harvard College, where he became a proficient classical student, a citizen of Greece and Rome. His speeches abound with classic reference and quotation, like the English

orations of to-day. What Trevellyan says of Lord Macaulay is true of Samuel
Adams: that he was as much at home with Cicero and Atticus as with the
statesmen of his own day. While in college he read the English writers on
Government, especially John Locke. To the illustrious author of the essay on
"Human Understanding," and the "Principles of Free Government," he was
largely indebted, and he fortified his later arguments against British oppression
with the logic of British philosophers.

In 1743 Samuel Adams took his master's degree at Harvard College. His
mind was aroused by the arbitrary interference with American trade and the
continued violations of the Massachusetts Charter. He chose for his thesis the
question "Whether it be right to resist the Supreme Magistrate if the Commonwealth cannot otherwise be saved," and boldly answered in the affirmative.
Thus thirty-three years before the Declaration of Independence, while the boy
Washington was strolling through the streets of Fredericksburg, and Patrick
Henry was wasting in idle sports his earlier school-days, — the very year when
Jefferson and his wife Jane first rejoiced amid the tobacco fields of central
Virginia over a boy whom they called Thomas, — the young orator of Boston
began his long war against the encroaching injustice of England.

There is little difference of opinion to-day as to the merits of the Revolution.
As John Bright and John Stuart Mill championed the cause of our nationality
during the late Civil War, so the greatest English statesman fought for us a
hundred years ago. The Whigs in Parliament were true to the cause of political liberalism in always speaking of Washington's army as "our army." Now
that the Old South Church has become a memorial building of the Revolution,
it ought to contain the statues not only of Benjamin Franklin and Samuel
Adams, but also those of Edmund Burke and William Pitt, who strove to save
England from injustice, and rejoiced when America resisted it.

The chief arena of Sam Adams's influence, as Governor Hutchinson wrote
to Lord Dartmouth, was the Town Meeting, that Olympian race-course of the
Yankee athlete. The throne of his power was the platform of Faneuil Hall
or the Moderator's Chair in the Old South Meeting-house. He knew his
townsmen well, better than any of his contemporaries, as John Adams
testifies. Unlike the great Roman censor, Cato, with whom he was frequently
compared, he neither spoke to the rabble of Romulus, nor dreamed himself in
Plato's Republic. Like Lincoln, he had great confidence in the strong, good
sense of plain people. A famous illustration of this occurred in 1788, in his
later life, when the vote was pending on the ratification of the National Constitution in Massachusetts. Samuel Adams had not yet committed himself to
the stronger government which the chaotic times demanded. A company of
ship-builders' mechanics determined to gain his consent. A meeting was held
in the Green Dragon Tavern, and resolutions favoring the Constitution were
passed, and then a committee waited on Samuel Adams, headed by Paul
Revere, who, on that April night of 1775, had ridden through the towns of
Middlesex with the fate of the nation in his hand. Adams took the resolutions and inquired, "How many were at the Green Dragon?" "More than
it could hold," was the answer. "And where were the others?" "In the
street," was the reply. "And how many were in the street?" "More than
the stars in the sky." Sam Adams felt that what these men of the "worsted
cap and leathern apron" wanted they ought to have. He addressed an
audience politically better educated than that Parliament of country squires
that grossly insulted Franklin, hated Pitt, sneered at Edmund Burke, one of
the greatest of the sons of men. The Boston of pre-Revolutionary days was
probably the most perfect democracy that ever existed. She was the culmi-
nation of American life. When the brave city was in danger, the Colonies
trembled with sympathetic fear. When the Port Bill blocked her harbor,
relief was sent by the backwoodsmen beyond the Alleghanies, while fifty
pounds were forwarded by a celebrated Virginia planter then living at Mount
Vernon. When George Rogers Clark was fighting the British and the
Indians in the West, he found that the Indian allies of Great Britain expressed
their idea of the situation by saying that they had gone out "to fight Boston."

Even to-day, among the Chinook Indians on the Pacific Coast, the word for "American" in their jargon is "Boston-man." Among his sturdy townsmen Samuel Adams moved about like Agamemnon among the Greeks, as both an equal and a prince; and when he rose to speak "his earnest look drew audience still as night or summer's noon-tide air."

In revolutions, the essential element of great statesmanship is a wise boldness. In Samuel Adams this was joined to an inflexible virtue. "A man of steadfast integrity," John Adams calls him. He was a poor man and died poor. When preparing for the first Congress, it was needful that his friends and neighbors should provide him with clothes suitable for his proper appearance among the dignitaries at Philadelphia. In his last years, when Governor of Massachusetts, it was only the economic arrangement of his capable wife that made his small salary available for his decent support. He was in political life as long as Palmerston or Disraeli, and yet escaped the chief bane of politics,— self-seeking. He never learned the trick of developing a small salary into a princely fortune. Like St. Francis, his bride was poverty. I fear that in this generation she has no suitors, and may die an old maid. He lived in the age of Walpole, when every man was thought to have his price. Parton says that "Lord North fought the American Revolution from the Stamp Act to Cornwallis, with a bought majority in the House of Commons." He acted on the theory of King Philip of Macedon: that a mule laden with gold was the surest key to the strongest fortress. He knew that Samuel Adams could not be frightened. When Governor Gage had recommended to him to make his peace with the King, he replied: "Tell your master that I trust I have long since made my peace with the King of kings, and no personal considerations shall induce me to abandon the righteous cause of my country." Not being able to scare him, Lord North resolved to buy him. Immense bribes were offered to tempt his integrity, just as the Roman Pontiff sought to silence the voice of Savonarola, the great Dominican monk, who in the Duomo of Florence had thundered against the corruptions of Rome. Poor though Adams was, he scorned the proffered peerage, a place amid the august ranks of British aristocracy, with a salary of two thousand guineas for life, and preferred a name on "the brief immortal list of exemptions from pardon."

For nine years Samuel Adams represented Boston in the General Court, and was annually elected clerk of that body, thus wielding the pen of Massachusetts in its controversies with the royal Governor. No man that ever lived was a more diligent writer, and few so direct and convincing. His private correspondence, like that of Calvin, was a miracle of industry. Every leading man of America, and every leading friend of America in England was made to think his thoughts, and if he deemed it wise, to know his plans. Then, too, he knew the power of the newspaper and the pamphlet. From the dusty files of the Colonial journals you may exhume the philosophy of the American Revolution written out in the forceful English of Samuel Adams. But what shall I say of his public political writing? John Adams declared that they would illuminate the history of fifty years. He was New England's and the nation's pen. In 1764 he drafts the Boston instructions, the first bold protest against British taxation, "one of the grandest of State papers," as Winthrop called it. In 1765 he writes the Massachusetts Resolves, which rang throughout the continent. He is the oracle of the Town Meetings, whose written declarations are the guiding hands of the Colonies. His pen never allows a persuasive and misleading speech of the Governor's to go unanswered, and Governor Bernard said, "Every dip of his pen stings like a horned snake." He writes the Assembly's addresses to the British Ministry, and they are read, and not, as formerly, thrown in the waste-paper basket. An English wit said that as soon as a British minister began to read American despatches he lost the Colonies. According to Hutchinson, Samuel Adams was the chief obstacle to the success of the royal schemes in America, and from him Dr. Franklin, in London, took his directions when the General Court was not in session. Samuel Adams corresponds continually with the towns, keeping them informed of every movement, and making sure of their support. The Honorable Joseph White, for many years secretary of the Massachusetts Board of Education, a thorough student of the history of the State, once said to me, "Sam Adams finished the American Revolution before he began it. He made sure of his men in every town of the State."

Have you seen in Samuel Adams the elements of a great statesman? He had thorough knowledge of the problem in hand. He knew the facts in the case, both in Parliament and in the Town Meeting. He was vigilant and industrious. He was bold when boldness was wisdom. He never flinched in the storm. Serving his country with a halter about his neck, he saw no future, in the chance of defeat, excepting the scaffold, and I am confident that he would have mounted its narrow step with the firm tread of John Brown or Algernon Sidney. Benjamin Franklin's famous joke, that we must all hang together or hang separately, was no joke to him. He was a practical statesman, seeing with Lord Bacon the necessity of committing the beginnings of great actions to Argus, with his hundred eyes, as well as the ends to Briareus, with his hundred arms. It was always his policy to keep the enemy in the wrong. He grounded himself and his cause, as he believed, on righteousness. The pen that wrote the Declaration of Independence and the sword that led our Colonial armies were both in the hands of slave-holders. In 1764 a negro slave woman came into the possession of Samuel Adams. "A slave cannot live in my house," he said; "if she comes she must be free." Above all, he was a religious man, as Motley said of William the Silent, whom Samuel Adams remarkably resembled in face and figure, as John Adams discovered from portraits at the Hague. His constant prayer was that Boston might become a Christian Sparta. For this reason he opposed the introduction of theatres, fearing the demoralization of the people, and for this reason he favored the abolition of public whipping as being degrading to free men. His last letter was one of rebuke to Thomas Paine: "Do you think that your pen or the pen of any other man can un-Christianize the mass of our citizens?" But he was no bigot, as he told the General Congress when with great shrewdness and boldness he moved that an Episcopal clergyman lead that body in prayer. Mrs. Beecher Stowe tells us that Benjamin Franklin represents the earthly and material side of the New England character, and that Jonathan Edwards represents its spiritual half. In Samuel Adams the two were united, the earthward grasping sense and the heavenward reaching faith. Lacking either, he would have failed; possessing both, he was a master. Warm in his friendships, free from jealousy, inspiring a passionate attachment in others, knowing nothing of despondency, as Bancroft has said, sublimely hopeful "as if his confidence sprang from an insight into Divine decrees," possessed of boldness, wisdom, prudence, incorruptibility, and piety, with a fascination of manner which enhanced the power of his great qualities, with an eloquence of tongue and pen to which America responded, with an iron industry that never wearied, undiscouraged by difficulties, and cool and firm amid the gravest perils, devoted with all his heart to a great cause, Samuel Adams had a shining list of qualities to which it would seem that little could be added; and yet this also must be said, that, more than any other of his contemporaries, he saw the end from the beginning. He was the pioneer of independence and the founder of the American Union. The elder Pitt thought the Continental Congress in 1774 the most sagacious body of men known to history. Only one of them had dreamed of separation from Great Britain. Six months before Lexington, Washington wrote, "No thinking American desires independence." Six months before Lexington, Samuel Adams exclaimed, "Independent we are; independent we will be!" and long before this he had foreseen the possibility of severance from Great Britain. As Governor Hutchinson told George the Third, Samuel Adams was the first to assert the independency of the Colonies. All his measures for uniting the people had reference to this foreseen contingency. Through storm and sunshine he pursued his way to this one shining goal. From 1764, when he first proposed union, to 1768, when he began to labor directly for independence, down to 1772, when the Committees of Correspondence were appointed, down to 1773, when he first called for a

Continental Congress, down to 1774, when the first Congress met, he stead. fastly moved on to this greatest achievement in the politics of mankind- Nothing deflected him from his purpose. While others slept, he toiled; while others doubted, he flinched and failed not. While others looked every-whither, his eye turned to the North Star of Independence. And when at last the storm-cloud burst in the lightnings of war, he rejoiced. The British troops marched to Lexington to capture "the great incendiary." The dawn of the 19th of April, 1775, shone over the quiet vales of Middlesex, soon to resound with the clash of arms; and looking up into the sky, Samuel Adams, the hunted fugitive, exclaimed, "What a glorious morning this is!" He foresaw the end. The seeds that he planted were seeds of fire.

The natal hour of American life, which embittered and maddened the ministry of George the Third, was a glorious hour for England as well as for us. Says the last of her great historians : "From the moment of the Declaration of Independence it mattered little whether England counted for less or more with the peoples around her. She was no longer a mere rival of Germany or Russia or France. She was from that hour the mother of nations. She had begotten in America a great people, and her emigrant ships were still to carry on the movement of the Teutonic race from which she herself had sprung. It is this thought which flings its grandeur around our story. The struggles of her patriots, the wisdom of her statesmen, the steady love of liberty and law in her people, were shaping in the past of our little island the future of mankind."

It is an inspiration to revive once more this legend of old Roman virtue transplanted to our Puritan shores. We may wander amid the broken marbles of the Parthenon and the moon-pierced shadows of the Coliseum, questioning the venerable wisdom of the classic ages, and find nothing worthier the emulation of the citizen than the story of Samuel Adams. He was willing, like John Milton, to undertake the lowliest duties; and his example teaches that vigilance and virtue are the only safeguards of liberty. With more men willing like him to work unselfishly for good government, faithful to the primary meetings which are the head-sources of our politics, and devoted to something higher than the loaves and fishes of party-success, we might witness a deliverance of our American cities from the rule of corruption, the next great act of emancipation for which a patient Providence waits. We might expect more brains and less "boodle" in the United States Senate, more conscience and less corruption in municipal and State affairs, more patriotism and less partizanship in the Civil Service, more Scriptural politics everywhere, and, ultimately, no saloon politics anywhere. Who that has read Professor Bryce's great book on "The American Commonwealth" does not long for such an uplifting? The American Commonwealth! That majestic name for the nation was first used by the man who organized it—Samuel Adams. He deserves a place not only among the great apostles of liberty, but also that glory which Cicero and Bacon ascribed to the founders of States, the glory of Charlemagne and Alfred and the first William of Orange. It was not given to him, as to some other men, to die at the supreme moment of his life, and thus to take his place at once among the immortals, like Wolfe expiring before Quebec, like the Earl of Chatham and John Quincy Adams, stricken down spear in hand on the field of debate, and like Abraham Lincoln, with the martyr's crown pressing with sudden splendor the victor's laurel. But in these great days of memory, the time has come when every American and every lover of civic virtue and political freedom should erect in his heart a statue to the memory of him who launched a new nation on the stormy, inspiring sea of democratic liberty.

I have sometimes thought that no worthy monument would ever be erected in his honor, but I was mistaken. There still abides in Boston the old State House, for more than forty years associated with his life so intimately; and as one has said, "In the whole history of Anglo-Saxon freedom, since the times when the Teutons clashed their shields in token of approval in the forests of the Elbe and Weser, what scenes are there more memorable than these old walls have witnessed?" And there still stands on Washington Street that building which has not been destroyed by the foe, the storm, the fire. The body of the great Puritan lies at rest in the Granary Hill Burying-Ground, but his spirit abides in the Old South Church. Thither let pilgrims throng and learn that American freedom was not born in the club-rooms of French and German unbelief, but in the hearts and homes and churches of men who knew their rights and duties as the children of God. Thither let our statesmen go and hear the voice of Liberty, speaking from their holiest shrine, saying : —

> "I, Freedom, dwell with knowledge ; I abide
> With men whom dust of faction cannot blind
> To the slow tracings of the Eternal Mind."

And thither let us send the youth of the coming generations, not to listen to

> " The stringed lute of Old Romance,
> That cheered the trellised arbor's privacy,
> And soothed war-wearied knights in raftered hall,"

not to catch the spirit of military glory which breathes through the galleries of Versailles, or the sentiment of an antique chivalry which still lingers in the Kaiser Saal, the throne-room of German Emperors, in Frankfort-on-the-Main, but, better far, to listen to the trumpet-voice of the civic hero who bore the burden of a mighty conflict and achieved the renown of an endless triumph ; for within those walls, which God and good men and women have spared,

> " The herald's blast was blown
> Which shook St. Stephen's pillared roof
> And rocked King George's throne ! "

First Presbyterian Church.

The meeting of Christian Endeavorers in the First Presbyterian Church, Columbus Avenue, was one typical of the great Society. It was not a meeting of curiosity-seekers, but workers.

The seating capacity of the church is large, and it was considerably overtaxed.

The active body of Christian Endeavorers connected with this church had decorated the interior in good taste. Crimson and white bunting, United States flags, official Convention flags, and various inscriptions were given prominent positions.

From the opening hymn to the closing address the evening's programme was a strong one, and held the closest attention of the large audience.

Rev. Scott F. Hershey, Ph.D., pastor of the church, presided. Mr. W. H. H. Smith, of Washington, D. C., chairman of the Committee of '96, read the Scripture lesson, and prayer was offered by Rev. Robert Hunter, D.D., of Philadelphia.

Dr. Hershey was brief in his address of welcome, having made an engagement to speak at another meeting during the evening. He said his people had looked forward to this gathering for months. He announced that Rev. Pleasant Hunter, D.D., of Minneapolis, who was one of the advertised speakers, could not be present on account of the serious illness of his wife.

Rev. J. O. Paisley, of the First United Presbyterian Church, Cambridge, presided during his absence.

The first speaker was Miss Antoinette P. Jones, of Falmouth, superintendent of the Floating Societies, who delivered the following address.

Address of Miss Antoinette P. Jones.

Christian Endeavor voices from the sea greet you to-night because " God so loved ! "

God said, " Let there be *light,*" and there was light. " I am the *Light of the world,*" Christ said. Fourteen years ago the white light of *Christian Endeavor* shone out, generated by the finger of God.

The four million seamen sailing into the world's ports often saw beacon lights held by brave disciples of our Master, sometimes lighted from them little torches to bear away, but soon sailed out into the darkness and forgot the light, and their own went out.

Brighter and higher " for Christ and the Church " glowed the great light, radiating the *land* afar. Why might it not shine out upon the " great and wide sea " ? So five years ago the " light " was made possible for *all* who " do business in great waters," the " power " from God, a line of love attached to the land, that we all may be one. " Is it well with thy soul ? " we can now signal far out to sea !

The Floating Society of Christian Endeavor, a branch of our Young People's Society of Christian Endeavor, instituted in April, 1890, is arranged for now on shipboard in every grade or service.

It is not limited to one section of the world's great highway, nor to one class of men, for "*all ye* are brethren " in Christ, whether in uniform or without, on a ship that steams or one that sails ; always Christian Endeavor in principles ; interdenominational, international, intermarine, — " afloat " the world around.

Each branch of Christian Endeavor has its distinctive pledge and Constitution. Floating Christian Endeavor retains our original Young People's Active Membership Pledge intact, simply inserting a clause, heartily endorsed by men and officers, relating to pure living, total abstinence, and non-profanity.

Amid trying daily experiences, in forced companionship with men often mature in sinful living, a declaration of principles is of great service. In the great lantern of a lighthouse near my home was placed a red sector invisible on the true course, but miles away on the verge of a dangerous shoal the red light shows. So we have placed in our Floating Christian Endeavor pledge "light " the red sector, invisible on the safe course, but flashing out a warning ray when nearing the shoals of temptation.

No provision is made for associate membership, experience emphasizing the decision, as men of fixed habits, *not yet* Christians, often disown the name, or disgrace it, proving a hindrance to faithful members. Evangelists' " Christian life " cards are frequently used effectively.

The pledge, gummed in signer's Bible ; the coupon, detached and kept on file ; the introduction card, for presentation in other ports ; and our widely recognized regulation C. E. badge pin, worn by members, are each a reminder and a testimony to the valued world-wide brotherhood in Christ.

The Constitution is arranged from the Christian Endeavor Model Constitution, and includes a Covenant for small bands.

The Floating Society of Christian Endeavor, first planned for enlisted men where crews remain comparatively unchanged for some time, was soon claimed by crews of merchant ships whose members must sooner scatter, but upholding Christ among other crews.

Much work on the Pacific Coast of the *United States* is with British deep-sea ships making long voyages, doing good work during months at sea, a society necessarily disbanding on discharge of the crew, but the members continuing to report where they signed.

A full record of *prayer meetings* held on *naval* and *merchant* ships by Floating Societies cannot be given — sometimes they are held semi-weekly, one for members, one public.

Who can estimate the power and influence, on officers and men, of prayer meetings held by loyal Christian Endeavor men and boys whose daily life must bear, for long months, the scrutiny of a whole crew, or the practical jokes of the godless.

Frequent letters, full of touching incidents, from Floating Societies of Christian Endeavor in all parts of the world, are received by the superintendent from these heroic bands of from three to thirty-five members. "It makes my men more contented and willing," testifies many an officer. "Oh that men would seek God! Then they could bear these hardships," exclaims a Christian Endeavorer on a "hard" ship.

An ordinary seaman's record emphasizes the fact that he frequently changes from coasting to naval, from naval to merchant ships — the same man with different environment. Prejudice exists strongly between *classes* of seamen, even between men of different rating on the same ship, but *Christian Endeavor* unites men of various service or rating to work for one Master.

Arranged first for shipboard, a society on shore, in church, mission, or reading-room, composed of members from the sea, officered by Christian Endeavor workers, is called a Floating Society, the membership, but not the organization, "afloat." Representatives from local Christian Endeavor Unions in seaports form Floating Christian Endeavor Committees from consecrated young men and women workers, who receive cordial and practical endorsement of churches and societies in the union. Sub-divisions of this committee are frequently necessary to cover different lines of work in a port, including ship visitation with paper distribution, on steam and sailing vessels; gospel services on shipboard, dock, and shore; navy yards, receiving ships, training ships, marine barracks, and naval hospitals; reading-rooms, boarding-houses, and marine hospitals; and organizing Floating Societies of Christian Endeavor on ship or shore whenever advisable.

A new reading-room, steam-launch, or portable organ is often discovered to be a necessity.

Our shore members and inland societies serve by holding many Floating Christian Endeavor missionary services, collecting barrels of good reading, making comfort bags, and furnishing libraries. Experience has proven the advisibility of local unions inaugurating their work *first;* and as the number of such committees increase in a State or Province, a State superintendent may then helpfully encourage them, and enlarge the work by arousing local interest, or suggesting new openings. Uniformity is strongly advised in printed forms and methods which are broad enough to meet local peculiarities. Our member from the sea should find no confusing changes as he studies Christian Endeavor principles, and familiarizes himself with the work of societies in many ports. The essentials of Christian Endeavor, a pledged membership and participation in services, are always upheld, while soul-winning and training for service is our highest aim.

The one who at the beginning arranged the society and printed forms, under the sanction and cordial interest of the officers of the United Society of Christian Endeavor, was then appointed, and has been continued, superintendent of Floating Societies. Helpful interchange of plans, and general extension, printed matter, supplies, and information can at all times be obtained of the superintendent.

Five years since the first pledges were signed, the first society organized on shipboard! Who can estimate results? Surely this is God's plan for his children on the sea.

Over 3,000 have become members, all *active* members except in one or two societies. Seventy-one Floating Societies, 52 on shipboard, 19 on shore, and 15 Floating Christian Endeavor Committees.

Organized work is now in the United States enrolled in about the following order: On Vineyard Sound, Mass.; New York, now four Floating Societies, and a Floating Christian Endeavor Committee; Navy Yard, Brooklyn; Cleveland, O., two societies; San Diego, San Francisco, and Oakland, Cal.; Philadelphia, two societies and a Floating Christian Endeavor Committee; Valloy's, Cal.; Tacoma and Seattle, Wash.; Chicago, Ill.; Portland, Me.; U. S. Training Station, Newport, R. I.; Key West, Fla.; Boston, Mass.; Galveston, Tex.; Santa Barbara, Cal.; and Norfolk, Va.

The past year records the inauguration of organized work in other lands.

MAIN ENTRANCE, MECHANICS' BUILDING.

PLATFORM, MECHANICS' BUILDING — THURSDAY MORNING.

In St. John, New Brunswick; Wellington, New Zealand, Sydney, and New-castle, New South Wales, Australia; in Liverpool, England; and news comes from the society among the marines of the Imperial Japanese Navy, whose members, in the recent war, went to the front, two of whom were killed.

And the 52 Floating Societies of Christian Endeavor on the ships! A brave and commendable record! Souls won from sin to service, holy ambition aroused, lives definitely consecrated, co-operation in gospel services, with missionaries, on ship or shore! Many have united with the church of their choice. Some societies ashore in ports report all the members — 75 at Key West — church-members.

Sailors are quick observers and generous to "lend a hand." While no appeals are made, some generous gifts have been made to Christian work. Many tithe their pay. The Floating Society of Christian Endeavor on *U. S. S. Charleston*, of fifteen members, realizing the great need in Nagasaki, Japan, have donated $450 and enthused others to give like sums, whereby a *Christian House for Seamen* will be established under care of the Christian missionaries. The Floating Society of Christian Endeavor on *U. S. S. Thetis*, together with their officers, gave $200 toward establishing a Bethel in San Diego, Cal. One "blue jacket" out of his "tithe" supports a boy in an academy in Turkey, besides a recent gift to his favorite Turkish missions. Two members pay toward the support of a church at either end of their trips.

Floating Christian Endeavor Committees and Societies in ports have held hundreds of services during the year on shipboard, with blessed results, San Diego Committee holding 304. Reported and unrecorded services held ashore, socials, individual soul-winning; hundreds of letters written to aid and encourage the members; voluntary gifts of time, and strength, and money to defray necessary expenses! Remember, our work is *in addition* to established seamen's work, which it in no way intends to supercede.

Christian ministers and missionaries have written testifying to the encouragement given them in their work by the presence and assistance of Floating Christian Endeavor brethren.

A foreign missionary wrote one Floating Society, " You will wield a mighty power to assist us to conquer heathendom." Another, "I had felt almost hopeless concerning a navy that had as few chaplains as ours, but the Floating Societies of Christian Endeavor will do more than chaplains, I am sure."

A member on a ship writes, "I never knew what this brotherhood in Christ *was* until I came in touch with those large-souled people."

Thousands of comfort bags, each filled with thoughtful gifts, the letter reminding our sailor boy that some one cares for his soul, causing him to tenderly turn the marked pages of the little Testament, have been supplied.

Philadelphia Floating Christian Endeavor Committee heads the list with 2,400 bags solicited and judiciously distributed.

Seamen compass the globe! Shall "the people that sit in darkness" see a "great light" as the ships sail in?

The rule of missions — "If you cannot go, send "— is literally true when you send the Gospel by our sailor brother.

Does no call come to you? Does no responsibility *to do*, responsibility if you do not do rest upon you?

> " Let the lower lights be burning,
> Send a gleam across the wave,
> Some poor, fainting, struggling seaman
> You may rescue, you may save."

Some mother's boy! Some sister's wandering brother! Some praying wife's dear one! Worth saving? "God so loved that he gave *his Son*." Christ so loved that he said, "*Go ye*." "Lovest thou Me?" "Inasmuch!" Remember, "One is our Master, even Christ; all ye — seamen — are brethren!"

The next speaker was not on the programme, but he is always welcome upon every Christian Endeavor platform, the Rev. B. B.

Tyler, D.D., of New York City. He made a happy speech and said many good things that were enthusiastically applauded.

The last, and, in some respects, the best-known speaker of the evening was Rev. J. Z. Tyler, D.D., of Cleveland, chairman of the Convention Committee of '94, that arranged for the Cleveland Convention. Dr. Tyler was particularly impressed at the warm welcome which was extended the delegates, hospitality which the oldest saints could not have imagined. Dr. Tyler's address was not reported, we regret to say.

The meeting was brought to a close by the singing of a hymn.

Berkeley Temple.

Berkeley Temple was aglow with spiritual enthusiasm and the bright colors of the Endeavorers. A large audience was present, and it frequently applauded the fervid utterances of the speakers, making the old church fairly echo. The Temple never looked brighter than it did that night. The organ front gleamed with the Stars and Stripes, the Christian Endeavor red and white, the Berkeley Temple white banner, showing an open Bible on its silken face; and the seal of the Commonwealth was prominently displayed.

The front of the platform was festooned with red and white streamers, and about it, on the floor, were the handsome silk and velvet banners of the Middlesex, Meriden, Bridgeport, Hartford, Rockville, and Danbury Unions, all from Connecticut, in the midst of which stood the Nutmeg State Union banner. Rev. W. S. Kelsey, associate pastor of the Temple, lead a service of song, while the people were gathering and finding seats. For a choir a call was made for Endeavorers from the audience. The response was generous, so that a good chorus was obtained, and it sang with stirring effect.

The occasion, in a notable sense, was a newspaper one. All the speakers were eminent editors. Rev. George E. Horr, D.D., of Boston, who presided and welcomed the Endeavorers, is editor of *The Watchman;* Rev. William Hayes Ward, D.D., of New York, is editor of *The Independent;* and Rev. A. E. Dunning, D.D., of Boston, is editor of *The Congregationalist.* Each was cordially greeted when announced, and applauded most heartily for what he said.

The services opened with a song, followed by the reading of the Scriptures by Rev. Edgar J. Penney, chaplain and head of the Bible School of Tuskegee University, Ala.

The Divine blessing was invoked by Rev. Asher Anderson, of the Meriden (Conn.) Congregational Church.

"Scatter the Sunshine" was sung, and then Rev. Dr. Horr spoke the words of welcome to this city,— as he termed it, "the capital of the Puritans." They were most hearty and cordial.

The first speaker was Rev. Wm. Hayes Ward, D.D., of New York City.

Address of Rev. Wm. Hayes Ward, D.D.

It is no part of my purpose now, to give the statistics of the religious press, nor to utter its praises. I do not care to tell how many religious papers there are, nor how great is their circulation or influence. I will not enumerate the different leading denominational or undenominational journals, nor will I classify nor describe nor criticise them. I remember that I am talking to a multitude of Christian young men and women, every one of whom reads from one to a dozen religious papers, and I may assume that some hundred or more of you are, or will be, editors or correspondents of religious papers. As one who has had nearly thirty years of experience in religious journalism, I may venture to tell not what kind of a religious paper you want, but what kind I think you ought to want and demand.

What you want and need is what any intelligent young Christian wants and needs. I do not suppose that because you are Christian Endeavorers, you have therein become any different from what any other intelligent, young, and active Christians ought to be. You take an additional pledge, or, rather, you take a second time, and in a different form, the pledge you took when you joined the Church. Your Christian Endeavor Society simply tries to make you an intelligent and active and faithful young Christian. You band together to help each other be what every young Christian ought to be. So I do not need to talk about the religious paper which Christian Endeavorers need, but about the religious paper which intelligent, active, faithful young Christians ought to want. For I want to make it clear that you are a certain band among young Christians, a big band, — I wish a great deal bigger, — but among them, a part of them, and not at all a band possessing any different or superior graces, or any different needs from those of other young Christians of your class.

It is a very simple thing to tell you what sort of a religious paper you ought to want. It is merely the paper that will help you to be the intelligent, active, and faithful young Christians you ought to be. That is all there is to it.

Notice the adjectives, *intelligent, active, faithful,* and *young.* You are *young.* That you cannot help, and the paper cannot affect. Time will change that, and give you the experience and perhaps the wisdom — perhaps the folly — of age. We need say nothing more about that adjective.

Then come the adjectives *active* and *faithful.* They mean very nearly the same thing, for faithfulness will show itself very largely in activity. Not wholly, for patience, truthfulness, honesty, purity, are a part of the faithfulness; but common morals I assume. Of course you are pure, and honest, and truthful, and patient. Of course you are good sons and daughters, brothers and sisters, scholars and teachers, housekeepers and workmen. These are the first principles of the Gospel of Christ, like conversion, and repentance, and faith. Your righteousness you are taught by your religion; but you are also taught by the whole civilization into which you are born.

If your ideal, as young Christians, is, on one side, faithful activity, and on the other side, *intelligence,* you have the right to demand of your religious paper that it shall help you on these two lines. By these two tests, in large measure, you must judge it: does it, in the first place, spur you and urge you and encourage you in the way of active service for the Lord, as faithful soldiers in his army; and does it, also, instruct you in those principles and methods and facts which you ought to know and which will control your judgment and conduct?

Faithful activity is taught by both precept and example. We are generally told that example is the best teacher. You should then demand of your religious paper that it should afford you good exhortation and especially good illustrations and examples and reports of the Christian activity of others. I believe in some preaching in a religious paper. I do not mean necessarily reports of sermons, though these are good — if they are good — but I mean brief, pointed exhortations to a Christian life, addressed, as the case may be, to believers or to the impenitent. They may be in the form of editorials, or articles by contributors, or of expositions of Scripture lessons. In any form, not overdone, they are good. But a paper should not have too much exhortation. It makes it soft and flabby.

Very much more important, in my view, is the incitement to Christian activity that comes from learning what is the success that attends the activity of other people in their Christian labor. These words, "the success that attends the activity of other people," sound very tame and commonplace, but they mean nothing less than the progress of the kingdom of God. That is all we are at work for. Our prayer is "Thy kingdom come;" it is toward that that all our activity is directed. It is the one constant, absorbing thing that interests us. In pursuing it we should have all the encouragement that can come not only from knowing, by faith, that God will somehow and sometime give us the victory, but from watching the progress of that victory as the campaign advances. I suppose that when in battle one wing of the army makes a successful advance, and pushes back the enemy, the knowledge of that success gives courage and enthusiasm to the other wing, and they press on with a fresh assurance of victory. Faith is good; it ought to be enough; but sight adds enthusiasm to the dogged determination of faith. Many a revival has been started because the news came of a revival near-by; and we sing, " Lord, I hear of showers of blessing," and we expect and get the same.

Now your religious newspaper must, *must,* whatever else it fails of doing, *must* tell you of what others have been accomplishing; it must tell you of the progress of the kingdom of God. If it merely exhorts, then it is a weekly tract, nothing more; it is not a newspaper, and a *newspaper* you want it to be. The editor of a certain religious paper once told me that during a six months' sickness, when he could do nothing for his paper, he told his assistant to go back ten years in the file and reprint the old editorials, one after another. He said nobody knew it. They were nothing more than sermons, with no reports and comments on current Gospel history, and so they were after ten years just as timely, and just as worthless, as at first.

The Book of Acts was Gospel history, the Gospel history of the times of Paul and Peter. It is most instructive and inspiring Gospel history. It has the report of Peter's sermon on the Day of Pentecost, and the wonderful revival of religion that followed it. This is just as truly a day of Gospel history as that was; and we shall be inspired, if not instructed, just as much by current Gospel history as by ancient Gospel history. Our current Church history concerns us ten times more than does the Church history of the times of Athanasius or Augustine. I despise the intelligence of a theological seminary which teaches its pupils all about Origin and Arius, and leaves them ignorant of the Church history of this current century, which is really more important than that of any other century since the apostles. Rather than neglect the Church history of this century, I would have you skip the whole of it from the death of the Apostle John to the day when the Missionary Carey started, a hundred years ago, for India. You ought to require your religious paper to give you this history as fast as it is created.

Consider what is the greatness, the majesty, of this current Church history. See the mighty currents of religious progress flowing with enlarging volume down the century. Observe the great divisions of Christendom, Greek, Roman, Protestant, all spreading and developing; and the smaller ancient divisions, Jacobite, Nestorian, Coptic, Abyssinian, encroached upon and crowded back by the three stronger and more enlightened ones. See how religion is affecting politics, the highest politics of nations sometimes identified with their religion, sometimes controlled by it. See how Russian internal politics appear to be mostly religious, the Jews persecuted, confined in territorial limits, restricted in trade, and forbidden higher education or the posts of office. See the same thing done to the Stundists, banished, for no crime but their religion, to the Caucasus. See the Lutherans in Russia in a scarcely less evil plight, and their German University taken from them. See the Turkish Empire divided, not into territorial, but into religious, nationalities, and the Armenians butchered by the unspeakable Turk, and Armenians, Greeks, Jacobites, and Protestants too jealous of each other to unite for their common advantage. See to-day a purely religious uprising in Macedonia, which is likely to tear another province from Turkey; and Bulgaria and Greece and Austria, three religions, quarreling to see how they can divide the prey between them, while Russia, a fourth religion, attempts to grasp the whole. See the Sultan of Turkey claiming to be not only a temporal ruler, but the spiritual head of the whole Moslem world, and the Czar equally the chief of the Greek Church, and the Queen of England also the Defender of the Faith and ruler of the Church of England. See the English Parliament taken up with the religious question, How the Church shall be conducted in Wales or Scotland, how schools shall be managed religiously, and who shall be buried in the churchyard ? See the concordats and agreements between the Church of Rome and France and other governments, by which all over the Roman Catholic world the Church is supported by the State, and the State, in return, is allowed to put its veto on the consecration of bishops, and its bit and bridle on the Church.

These, and much more of the same sort, are examples ot the interaction of Church and State in the current political and ecclesiastical history of the day, which an intelligent young man or woman ought to require his religious newspaper to record. But this is far from all. We are happy to possess that rare sort of government that does not allow this meddling of the State with the Church, nor this evil dependence of the Church on the State. Scarce any vestige do we yet retain of Church establishment, although the little mischievous shadow of it which yet unfortunately lingers, such as the exemption of churches from taxation, and the compulsory reading of the Bible in public schools attended by Jews, Catholics, Protestants, and unbelievers alike, is still valued by many as if it were a substantial advantage. But if we have little occasion in our own country to study the interference of the Church and the State with each other, we have the more interesting study of the Church itself and by itself. The State has nothing directly to do with this magnificent gathering of the young Christians of the country — nothing except to protect you on your way and after you reach this ancient city; but this meeting is an event in current Church history, and the work of your Society, and the kindred societies that have unfortunately separated for sectarian purposes from you, has a very important part in the current history of the Church. You cannot but demand of your religious newspaper that it shall inform you of what are all the important drifts and movements and forces in the Church to-day, here about you and in foreign lands. Here comes in the great importance of special and denominational papers. You need a special paper which shall with great fulness inform you and stimulate you as to this Christian Endeavor Society; and you need your denominational papers, which shall not neglect the wider view of the religious world, but which shall most fully represent the work and progress of your own denomination. This is of prime necessity to you; not the largest, perhaps, but the nearest necessity, the same sort of necessity that makes you take a closer and more engrossing interest in your own household than you do in the affairs of your town or State. Yet you do not neglect your town or your country ; you are patriotic as well as filial, and you must be interested in their welfare as well as in that of your own family. Through your religious newspaper, if it deserves the name, you must get your information of the doings of the great Commonwealth of God to which you belong, as well as of your sectarian household.

Consider, once more, how large this subject is. Do you see with what generous rivalry Methodists and Baptists, and Presbyterians and Congregationalists, and a hundred other denominations, are trying to conquer the land and the world to Christ? Do not confine your view to one denomination's work. Your Christian Endeavor Society is interdenominational. That fact helps you to a larger view. But do not fail to see what other societies are doing, which have gone out from you. Watch the steady progress of a feeling of Christian unity among these denominations, and rejoice whenever two of them arrange that their rivalries in the service of Christ shall be purely friendly, and that they will yield to each other for the common good. You must also be interested to study what are the great movements of theological faith in all these churches, what is the gain in liberty of thought, or what the defence against unbelief. You will watch to learn what is found to be essential, what important, what indifferent, and what erroneous and therefore hurtful in the larger or shorter creeds which we have been in the habit of hearing taught. There is no other study so fascinating as theology, and no science more important, or more studied, or showing greater advance. We must ask our religious paper to tell us plainly what the discussions in our several denominations are teaching us about the Bible and other topics in debate.

We must observe the movements in these denominations. What is there more interesting than to watch the current history of the Roman Catholic Church in this century? We live in a land by far the larger part of whose territory used to belong to that Church. Protestant England settled a narrow strip on the Atlantic Coast, and not all of that, for Catholicism held the Penobscot Valley in Maine, and all America north of it, also Maryland; Catholic France held the interior with its trading settlements from Canada, along the Lakes and the Ohio Valley, and also all the Mississippi Valley, which we had to buy from her. Then Catholic Spain held Florida and all the region west of the Mississippi Valley to the Pacific. The Catholic Church has held Mexico and South America, but there is not now a Catholic State in this nation. This is an amazing fact. The country is possessed by Protestanism, and the same thing is true of nearly all British America. But it is not to this fact that I wish to call attention, but to the amazing and beneficent change that has taken place and is still taking place in the Roman Catholic Church, owing to the influence of the Protestantism in which it is. The best, the most spiritual, the most beneficent Roman Catholicism in the world is in the United States. Compare it with that of any wholly Catholic country, or especially with that of Mexico or Brazil or Peru or Cuba; observe its noble system of Sunday schools, its temperance societies, its missions, its preaching, the faithful attendance of its adherents, the growing spirituality, the rapid decay of superstition, the ardent patriotism of its people, the zeal with which they, even mistakenly, maintain their parochial schools, and the increasing regard for the public schools, and we cannot but rejoice at all this current Church history right before us, which it is the duty of your religious newspaper to observe and record. Let me take a single example of what I mean, coming under my own knowledge. The priest in charge of a large Catholic church in Brooklyn observed that his people were getting negligent in their religious duties. So he invited, this spring, one of the two or three religious orders which are devoted to this work, to hold a mission in his church. The first week they asked the attendance only of married women; the second, of married men; the third, of unmarried women; the fourth, of unmarried men. Services were held twice a day, at five in the morning and at eight in the evening. Through those four weeks the great church was crowded at both services, from 1,500 to 2,000 present, often the aisles filled with people standing and listening to the most pungent, drastic preaching which could be delivered. Such revival meetings are held now all over the country, and such progressive Catholicism as this is one of the wonderful movements of the day; and these revival meetings and these Sunday schools and temperance societies, and their fellowship in good work, are drawing all our people closer together—and how are you to know what is all this religious movement except as you require it from your religious paper? These are just the distinguishing marks of the Christianity of the present day: one is its evangelistic activity, and the other is its eagerness for Christian unity. The importance of the first is now everywhere acknowledged, and it only needs to be developed. The value of Christian unity is not wholly understood, but the tide is rapidly rising. Your religious paper should understand and promote these two objects more earnestly than any other if it is to be the spokesman of the best spirit of the age.

Doctrine is important, theological correctness is to be valued, but far more important is it that a man should live right than that he should reason right. They that do the Lord's will have the promise that they shall know of the doctrine; and they may be sure that they will know all that is essential, and they will probably think they know a great deal more. It is well that your paper should teach the oldest or the newest theological doctrine; and what we think truest depends much on our faith in the Holy Spirit ever dwelling in and teaching the Church. But your paper may err here, and yet be a grand paper if it is earnestly devoted to the growth of the kingdom of God.

The kingdom of God! It has begun; it is extending; it *will* become universal. God's purpose, the very purpose of the death of our Lord, is the pledge of it. But it is for us to say it *shall* become universal. We must put our wills with God's will. Your religious paper must express that will, must labor for it, must encourage its accomplishment more earnestly than anything else. Why, that is the one great purpose of the Church, the conquest of the world to Christ. Everything else is subordinate. Your own personal sanctification is part of it, and therefore important and your personal duty. But it is only the beginning of your duty. The bigger part of it is not taken up with your own spiritual state. You probably will not have time to bother much with them. The day for introspective religion will never quite be over, but the millennium must come before it is anything more than a subordinate spiritual occupation. We have too much to do for others to waste much time on ourselves. When the era of missions came in, the era of religious diaries went out, with their daily or hourly records of one's spiritual thermometer. Now we want to draw this drunkard out of the gutter, to comfort that old woman in the poorhouse, to tell this young friend that Jesus died for him, to close that saloon, to expose that shop of political corruption, to send a teacher to those ignorant negroes or Indians here in our own country, or to the pagans abroad. Your religious paper must hold up this religious activity as of the first importance, and, not satisfied with preaching the duty, must direct you how to do it and report to you how it is done. We want to know what is the news of the Holy War. Where shall we go to fight Apollyon? Give us religious papers, and many of them, of every denomination, and of no denomination, that shall be eager, enthusiastic, on this greatest of all subjects.

Give us religious papers that will do this first, prime work, and I can forgive almost any other fault. They will do good even if they fail of doing all the good they might. They will do some good even although they fail of being in sympathy with all the intellectual movements of the age. They will not be bad religious papers even if they do some things that are wrong and injurious.

But there are bad religious papers, and chief of all is the paper that is too anxious to make a living for its owner to be interested in the kingdom of God. The chief fault, the one damning fault, in a religious paper is that it does not care much for the kingdom of God. Thank heaven we are passing out of the age of sectarianism. Christians now forget their sects in their love for the Church of the living God. They will do this more and more. For the present we must have denominations, and our denominations must have their religious paper. And you and I are born and converted and work in denominations, but our papers, whether denominational or not, must not make the kingdom of God bend about their denomination. For this reason I thank the good Providence that has led you to cling to this interdenominational Society. Your wise religious paper will understand the signs of the times, and will make your denomination the servant, not the master, of the Church. You are learning here a lesson which sectarians would not want you to learn: that your denomination does not have all the truth, and that others are just as faithful to the Master as yours is.

I have said that the bad religious paper is the one that is lukewarm, heedless about the extension of the kingdom of God. There are other minor faults. One of these, and perhaps the most dangerous of them, is what I may call religious Toryism, old fogyism, invincible conservatism. Many papers are too conservative to welcome the Christian Endeavor Society, because they think it will supplant the old Church. As if every religious meeting in a church were not a church meeting! Your young people's meeting is just as much a church meeting as a mothers' meeting, as a mid-week prayer meeting, as the Sunday school, as the Sunday preaching service. The Sunday preaching service has no claims to being the one only real church meeting, and some ministers who think so are really only jealous for their dignity and prerogatives. Such is the conservatism that is frightened if women take part in a religious meeting, and for that reason is afraid of your Society. A similar and perhaps worse conservatism is that which is so enamored of its old interpretations of Scripture that it refuses to welcome any study or investigation that calls them in question. It is a fearful error in your religious paper if it seems to be suspicious generally of science or Biblical criticism, or afraid that something will be discovered that will discredit old views about the age of the world, or the Flood, or the authorship of the Pentateuch. Remember that the paper which flouts at learning is flouting at the pursuit of truth. Remember that you care for your religion only because you believe it true; and if anybody can show you that any one of your religious beliefs which you may have put in your creed is not true, you owe him many thanks; for he has made your religious belief truer and purer, and the result will be good and not bad. Your religious paper should welcome research and not fling at it. The religious teacher, in the pulpit or in the sanctum, who is all the time flinging at science or criticism is making infidels; for it is the scientific men who are nobly devoted to finding out the truth, and they are sure to prevail; and Satan will be glad if the people can be taught that if they accept the teaching of science they must give up the Bible and their religion and become infidels or atheists. God is truth, and the search after truth will prove a search after God.

One thing more about your religious paper. Don't read it when you ought to be studying your Bible. In these days we are in danger of reading our newspapers when we ought to be studying our Bibles. You must read the Bible as you would read other literature,— to get its story, to get its drift of teaching, to get its spirit. You must read First Samuel or Hebrews through at a sitting, as you would read a newspaper or a novel. Did you ever sit down and read your New Testament through, or run it over, just to see what it teaches on inspiration, or the human nature of our Lord, or why Christ came into the world? Don't imagine that when you read a verse or a chapter out of its connection you are studying the Bible. You are probably getting a false view of it. That way of reading the Bible would teach you that women must not speak in your meetings. It is the spirit, not the letter, of the Bible that allows and commands it. I wish there were not so many of our religious papers that are crazy literalists in their teachings about the Bible. This literalism, applied to healing and especially to prophecy, is one of those things that make bad papers, and it is allied to the fear of scientific and critical study.

But it is not the faults but the merits of religious newspapers of which I have desired to speak. I have not sought to urge on you the duty of reading religious newspapers. I have little fear that you will neglect that duty. I much more fear that you will neglect real intelligent study of the Bible. It has been my desire to impress on your minds what are the great religious duties of evangelism, of Christian unity, of fearless search for all truth, and to show you that you must demand of your religious papers that they shall be intelligent, truth-loving, charitable, hospitable, and, above all, devoted to the unity and the extension of the kingdom of God.

The next speaker was Rev. A. E. Dunning, D.D., editor of *The Congregationalist*. Not having a report of Dr. Dunning's address, we can give only a thought or two as reported by one of the daily papers:—

Rev. Dr. Dunning, speaking of the relation of the religious press to the Christian Endeavor movement, began by remarking that it might be a little difficult just at present to draw the line between the secular and religious press of the city, as the great dailies had suddenly become a religious press, giving column upon column of space to news pertaining to the Convention.

He maintained that the growth of the Christian Endeavor movement to the proportions in numbers, power, and influence exercised by the organization to-day had been in no small measure due to the religious press, which had given circulation to the idea, and had helped to steer it over some critical periods. He frankly admitted that he had looked to see it go under long before this, but now believed that it was on the broad sea where no sectarian controversies could overturn it.

Referring to the work of missions and the Turkish atrocities in Armenia, he said: "God loves the Turks, but he does not like them," and then saw hope for the future in that the domain of the Turks had been reduced one-half in the past thirty years.

Touching upon good citizenship as essentially Christian, he brought forth a storm of applause by declaring that "a man who doesn't vote when he can cannot go to heaven, for if he does not think enough of his country to put his voice in where he can, what would God do with him up there?"

He styled the English secular press as more decorous than the American, but less religious, for while the English press only recognized religion as it entered into affairs of state, the American papers had come to realize that in matters of Church news and religious questions there opened a field which was ripe with matter of deep and abiding interest to the people, and had been prompt to give generously of its space to religious news.

Park Street Church.

Christian Endeavorers took the Park Street Church by storm in the opening rally held there — the headquarters of the States of Illinois and Nevada.

The church was beautifully decorated with patriotic bunting in profusion, and flags in bewildering numbers. Over the pulpit platform was placed a long red strip upon which was the phrase, in large gold block letters: "Our Home, Your Home." The banners of Illinois and Nevada were scattered here and there throughout the church.

Considerable disappointment was experienced at the non-appearance of Hon. Neal Dow.

The other speakers spoke as scheduled. They were Rev. C. H. Daniels, D.D., of Boston, who also presided; Rev. Jesse Malex Yonan, of Persia, and Rev. Thomas J. Morgan, LL.D., of New York.

Mr. C. W. Meacham led the singing, which was interspersed at intervals throughout the speaking.

The opening devotional exercises were conducted by Rev. E. K. Alden, D.D., of Boston.

Address of Rev. C. H. Daniels, D.D.

It is a most impressive sight which greets one in Boston these opening days of the Christian Endeavor Annual Convention. The hosts of Christian young people from the churches of our land have come to no mean city upon a religious errand. The coming of these youth has nothing to do with social patronage, or prestige of wealth, or advancement in philosophy, or political preferment, but simply the things of the kingdom of God.

There are certain specific forces transforming, controlling, and elevating such a company as gathers in our city this week. These forces are the peculiar marvels of our Christian religion, and the incontestable evidence of its Divine origin. This company of Christians in our city answers in actual experience, though unbelief denies it, that no truth has ever been so potent as the Gospel truth. It has won its way against kingdoms, empires, and Cæsars.

We may name the inherent forces of the Christian religion which will be carried into the future and which will conquer all that opposes God: —

1. *The Truth of God.* It is the doctrine which makes men free. It is a deeper force, and is internally stronger than error. The strength of its truth is in its teaching. Its greater power is when that which we speak is exampled. Then before truth's majestic power and penetrating radiance our unbeliefs and doubts fade away and die.

2. *The Living Mystery of a Personal Christ.* His pretensions were ridiculed and his mission rejected, yet there was a something in that life, — it was a ministry that strangely won men. He was incomparably above all other men. He was worshipped and deified. He was truly God and truly man. There are thousands of societies, and as many endeavoring societies, but the distinctive character bears his name. His power is his personality.

3. *The Living Presence of the Holy Spirit.* This Divine, supernatural power, transforming life, at the same time enlightening the mind and subduing hostile influences, is the mighty force engaged in the pre-eminent work of the kingdom of God among men. None too soon will this great Convention hasten to the source of its success, "not by power, nor by might," nor by numbers, "but by my Spirit." None too soon will individuals yield to his gracious leadings.

4. *The Over-ruling Providence of God.* The Father, God, intensely interested in the scheme of redemption, threw about it the almighty protection of his providential care and support. The great movements of these days in temperance, in missions, in Christian Endeavor, are all magnificent proofs of an all-wise Providence directing in the affairs of men. Timely, efficient, pervasive, we are attracted and won by his presence and guidance.

5. *The Holy Living of Believers.* Nothing carries such consternation to the enemies of the truth as a loving, pure, square, elevated, Christian life. This commands respect and reverence when all other appeals fail. Lives must count for truth, temperance, virtue, and godliness.

These are the battling forces; nothing more, nothing less. Christ has been more loved than father, mother, or friend. To be like him is to be recognized as having the highest type of character.

Rev. Jesse Malex Yonan, of Persia, was then introduced. He is a young man, with great vigor, warmth, and energy of expression. He captured his auditors immediately by exclaiming with great energy, " It makes me feel good to be here." This feeling was caused, he said, for three reasons : —

The first missionary from the American Board to Persia was sent from Boston, Rev. Justin Perkins; Miss Fidelia Fiske, that most noble missionary woman of the world, also started from Boston to preach in Persia, and she had done more than any other person for the elevation of the women of Persia; and last and the best reason, "because my wife is one of the most excellent Christian Endeavorers alive."

Mr. Yonan then kept his auditors deeply interested in his résumé of the religious history of Persia, and the account of the condition of its people, especially the inferior status held by the women there. The condition of women there even now was deplorable, and the speaker begged the help of their sisters in America in uplifting and giving to women their proper rights and protection.

The last speaker was Rev. T. J. Morgan, LL.D, of New York City. Dr. Morgan said in part : —

This movement has in it the promise and potency of great things for the Church and young people and communities.

There is one thought that lies without the religious motives of this Society, and that is that it is not only "for Christ and the Church," but also for the country.

This is the greatest movement toward good citizenship ever started, and we should develop talents on this specific line.

I would call your attention to three great processes now unfolding, toward the consummation of which we are surely drifting.

The first is the process of nationalizing the herds of people who come to us from abroad bringing an exaggerated love of liberty. This expresses the typical idea of independence carried to the extreme.

The second process is that of Americanizing these people. Distinctions of nationality and language exist among us which are barriers to national loyalty and feeling. The English should be the only language spoken on this soil, not because it is the superior language, but because it unfolds our national traditions and is our native tongue.

The third process is that of Christianizing this great mass. A republic must rest ultimately on the religious convictions of its people, and a country like this, which recognizes no earthly sovereign, must call God its king.

I do not believe that we shall have a republic which will endure, in spite of our boasted institutions, until we incorporate the golden rule into our civic and social life.

The national conscience must be aroused and quickened, and the peoples coming here become subjects of these three great processes before we shall be truly mighty.

What can the Christian Endeavorers do? In this work of Christianizing the world, be first Americans and put behind you all sectional differences, feeling only that you belong to the Republic; and as you reach out the hand of welcome to the foreigners, seek your own good as well as theirs.

Central Square Baptist Church.

The opening meeting at East Boston in connection with the Convention was in the Central Square Baptist Church, the largest Protestant edifice on the island. It was filled to the doors.

The body of the house was reserved for the Vermont delegates, who arrived last evening and have their headquarters in East Boston. A delegation of Lynn Endeavorers was in the balconies.

The auditorium was tastefully decorated in the Convention colors, and with flags, banners, and inscriptions of welcome. In front of the pulpit was a silver maltese cross.

The programme opened with an organ selection by Mr. A. C. Mc-Mann, which was followed by the hymn, "For Christ and the Church," by the church choir, directed by Mr. Sanford Kimball. Next came devotional exercises led by Rev. Dr. Smith Baker, pastor of the Maverick Congregational Church, East Boston. After singing "Scatter Sunshine," the address of welcome to Vermont delegates was made by the pastor of the church, Rev. F. M. Gardner, who presided over the meeting, and it was responded to by Pres. E. G. Osgood, of the Vermont Union.

Mr. S. E. Kimball sang a solo, after which the first speaker, Rev. M. M. Binford, of Richmond, Ind., one of the trustees of the United Society of Christian Endeavor, was introduced. Mr. Binford's topic was, "A Call for Men."

Address of Rev. M. M. Binford.

When the ancient Spartans were taunted for having no walls to their city, they pointed to their young men, and said: "These are our walls, and every man is a brick." Jerusalem, in Ezekiel and Jeremiah's time, was not so highly favored. "I sought for a man," said the Lord, "that should stand in the gap and make up the breaches before me, but I found none." "Run ye to and fro through the streets of Jerusalem and see if ye can find a man that executeth righteousness and seeketh the truth." Alas, the demand far exceeded the supply.

When ruin threatened the Holy City, the Lord was "among them as a mighty man that could not save," for there were no men to stand with him. There were not lacking optimists whose hopes were built upon their desires; prophets who preached, "peace, peace," for selfish gain; politicians who were busy contracting alliances with Egypt or Syria; but God said there were no *men* in all the city.

What is manhood? The sarcastic cynic, Diogenes, once stood in the streets and cried, "O ye men of Athens." When the crowd gathered round him, he said, "I called for men — not pygmies." Carlyle once described the population of England as so many millions, mostly fools, and probably he would have pronounced no kindlier judgment on us; but there is an unequalled pathos in Ezekiel's description of the magnificent City of God left defenceless for lack of righteous, truth-loving, incorruptible, God-fearing men.

Our word "character" comes from "*charasse,*" to carve, and it is charactered men — not carved stone — that are the walls of defence for both Church and State. The realization of what constitutes true manhood has been the lesson set for all ages. Tennyson says: —

> " Ah, God, for a man with heart, head, and hand,
> Like some of the simple ones gone
> Forever and ever by I
> One still strong man in a blatant land,
> Whatever they call him — what care I?
> Aristocrat, democrat, autocrat — one
> Who can rule, and dare not lie.
> And ah, for man to arise in me,
> That the man I am may cease to be!"

King Solomon, in the premature senility of a wasted life, exclaims, "All is vanity, vanity of vanities." "There is nothing new under the sun." Beware of the early fading out of high moral ideals, the unnatural disgust and weariness of all life. It has grown fashionable in many circles. We hear again the old Epicurean cry, "Let us eat and drink, for to-morrow we die;" or else, the Stoic dictum, "Be not astonished at, nor admire anything." "Discount all altruism, regard as visionary all high moral ideas, yield yourself to the materialism of the present; as for the future — ah, nobody knows." The answer, the only hopeful answer to all this, must come from him who said, "Behold, I make *all* things new." There *is* a perpetual newness and freshness of life; all is *not* old and worn out and involved in hopeless mystery. The prevalent unbelief has a thousand enigmas where faith has one. It robs men of courage, blights hope, and covers all with pitchy darkness. There is a perpetual new creation in the faith of Jesus Christ. It is the rejuvenescence of manhood, the antidote for soul weariness, the perpetual mainspring of action.

A second element of true manhood is a profound sense of moral responsibility. The materialism and atheism of our time have violently assailed the idea of duty. It has been treated as a mere figment of traditionalism, an obstacle in the world's progress toward simplicity and purity of life.

A recent defender of suicide contends there is no such thing as duty or purpose in life, hence no sin or wrong in self-destruction. Also, realistic literature seeks to obscure distinctions between right and wrong, plays fast and loose with virtue, and divorces art from morals. Politicians relegate to the rear all moral convictions in politics, and exalt party fealty and political expediency as God upon the throne; fattening, meanwhile, like the idolatrous priests of old, upon the sacrifices of their victims and the spoils of office. "Men have no backbone," says Sam Jones, "they have only a cotton string with a few ribs tied to it." Kingsley once classified the race as, "First, men who mean to do right and do it; second, men who mean to do wrong and do it; third, men who mean to do whichever is most convenient." "We no longer meet individuals," says a French writer, "but only samples." The sense of responsibility to God makes men able to stand *alone.* "God made men upright." They do not need to be propped, and patronized, and pampered, and patted. "Here I am, I cannot do otherwise, may God help me," said Martin Luther at the Diet of

Worms. Caleb was such a man when he faced the angry, unbelieving, clamorous 600,000 men of war at Kadesh Barnea and declared they could go up and take the land; and he was all the more such a man when, in all the trying scenes of the forty years' wandering, he patiently bore with his brethren, and retained, undimmed, the freshness of his faith in God. Joseph was such a man when he cried, "How can I do this great wickedness and sin against God?" Moses was such a man, preserving unsullied his childhood faith amid the idolatries of the Egyptian palace and the long waiting in the desert. Daniel was another, standing alone for God again and again in Babylon. Every-day life is still full of such opportunities. You meet them when you enter school, or business, or society, and the unexpected test that reveals character and determines destiny is suddenly upon you.

A third element of true manliness is religious belief. There is a false idea that unbelief is a sign of manliness. There may be a period in the life of young men when the great problems of all time come crowding thick and fast, and they are in doubt, not willingly, but because the answer is not yet clear to them. Give them sympathy and light, not repression and reproach, and they will come out all right. There was a time in our childhood when we could not believe the world was round nor turning round, else why should we not fall off? But it does not trouble us now. The larger knowledge has swallowed up the smaller doubt. Hume once boasted that the dawn of the nineteenth century would mark the overthrow of the Bible and Christianity, the breaking of the shackles of superstition, and the liberation of human thought; but we stand to-night upon the threshold of the twentieth century, after a hundred years of the world's most marvellous progress, and declare that if faith in Christ be superstition, and belief in the Bible a shackle upon human freedom, then the chains are hopelessly riveted upon the most prosperous nations of earth, and the links are fast forging to bring the world captive to the Word of the lowly Nazarene. Still, there are multitudes who have abandoned all faith in Christ, and his Word and Church—who, as Henry Ward Beecher once said, "have cut down the venerable trees around their paternal homes, and spend their lives in delusive hopes under a few stunted saplings." How graphic is Carlyle's description of the soul struggles in the realm of the "Everlasting No,"—the negation of all things, until all slips from beneath its feet, the sky overhead is the blackness of darkness, and no voices are heard save those of the harpies of despair. Out of this comes the soul into the land of the "Everlasting Yea," and where is that land save where "all the promises of God in Jesus Christ are Yea and Amen forever"? "Faith is the one thing needful for the world's well-being; with it martyrs otherwise weak can endure the shame of the Cross, and without it worldlings puke up their existence by suicide, in the lap of luxury." "Religion" means "*religare*," to bind again to God. It is the acceptance of the cords of love and truth wherewith he draws us, until, so bound, we cry, "Nothing shall be able to separate us from the love of God, which is in Christ Jesus, our Lord."

A one-sided theory of the world's development has been founded on the selfish "struggle for life," and a cold, heartless theory it seemed, subversive of all that was holiest and best in human life; but now we hear of the "struggle for the lives of others," the dawnings and developments of the life of sacrifice, — the life of love. This, then, has been the true progress of the race; and Christianity, which *is* love, and manliness, which is the climax of evolution, find their realization in the new life of faith in Christ Jesus, our Lord. But we may safely assume to-night that the battle between Christian faith and the atheistic materialism of philosophy and science, which has raged so fiercely for several decades, is practically fought to a finish. Faith and reason are no longer antagonistic, but the complements of each other. Is the work of the world then nearly accomplished? Are the great questions all settled? When Charles Sumner entered upon his duties as a member of the United States Senate he was commiserated by a statesman of the old school because all the great questions in American politics were already settled, the provisions of the Constitution having been clearly determined; but we know that the really great questions of United States history since the adoption of the Constitution have been settled *since* 1850. The relations of the States to each other, and the translations of Constitutional theories into practical realities have been work enough for nearly half a century. In like manner the interdenominational relations of churches, and the application of religious truth to all departments of life afford to us a most glorious field of Christian effort. While every age is in some sense transitional, we are confronted with the gravest problems since the breaking up of the feudalism of the Middle Ages. This is far from being a finished world. The kingship of Jesus Christ is far from being recognized. Though Christianity has been driven from the cloister, it is still too often sheltered in an ecclesiastical system. There have been many men who have stood upon mountains of spiritual vision and discerned the "signs of the times"—men who, like the children of Issachar, have had understanding of the times to know what Israel ought to do; but the visions of the prophets slowly become the convictions of the masses of Christians even, and they are slow to become the heroes and martyrs of their own convictions. The rapid advancement of science, the increase of the material benefits of civilization, the closer fellowship and affiliation of communities and nations, the increased possibilities of organization and combination, fill the entire horizon with perplexing problems. Government is declared by many to be wholly a secular matter, the opposite extreme from the unholy papal alliance of Church and State. "Sociology," says Benjamin Kidd, "is yet wholly without a science," or rational method of procedure. Notwithstanding the wonderful progress of the "Century of Missions," Alexander Duff could truly say, "We are only playing at missions." So ignorant of practical Christianity are even multitudes of professing Christians that real personal piety is compatible with most unrighteous corporate or political iniquity. Whichever way we turn, the world is full of work. There is a call for men. There are uncompleted tasks for more men than can be found to do them. We do not want more men who can *rise*, but more men who can stay down alongside of their personal duty, however small the sphere, and faithfully discharge it day by day. It is an inspiration to be connected with the movement which calls us together here, and which, under such wise leadership, addresses itself so heroically to the work of our time. It seeks no new channels of doctrinal and experimental Christianity, but follows the trend of the Christian ages. Supreme faith in the Word of God, and deep spiritual life are the taproot of its existence. But it believes most profoundly in the right of Jesus Christ to rule in this world; to rule supreme in all nations and over all faiths and non-faiths of men; to rule supremely in our own land in politics, in municipal reform, in all social and industrial movements. Unrighteous men can never rightly administer a righteous system. Unrighteous men will never rightly reform a wrong system. The application of the principles of Christianity to all these problems is the duty of our lives. We believe in the establishment of the authority of righteousness in all secular affairs. Men must be made too righteous to become the tools of unscrupulous politicians. The State belongs to God as much as the Church, and the duties of the Christian and of the citizen do not conflict with each other. The piety of the vestryman or member of the "official board," and the piety of the director of a bank or corporation, are alike obedience to the will of God. The dawn of the perfect day may yet be far away. Only God's watchmen on the mountain may be able to cry, "The morning cometh." There may yet be nights of seeming victory of evil, chaotic upheavals of the solid crust and inrushing of the floods of evil, but God is making a world. The deliberateness of his mills, that grind so slowly, may be equalled by the deliberateness of the advance of a Christian civilization. Scepticism still cries, "What is truth?" and pessimism says, "Who will show us any good?" But we have caught a vision of the dawn that all the prophets from the beginning of the world have seen:—

> "God to the human soul,
> And all the spheres that roll,
> Wrapped by the Spirit in their robes of light,
> Hath said, 'The primal plan
> Of all the world and man
> Is Forward. Progress is your law, your right.'"

The long weary struggle of ages for life — that fearful law that, viewed alone, makes the heart sick — must yield to the higher law. The self-sacrifice and co-operation which began with the family, and has slowly grown to the tribe and clan and state and nation, must yet be perfected in its details and widened in its application. It is no less the affirmation of the new science than the declaration of Divine revelation that war must cease on earth. Sooner or later pacific principles must prevail; conflicting interests between nations must yield at last to the law of human brotherhood. No prophetic voice crying out in the darkness of past ages shall be unheeded. There shall yet be a "restitution of all things spoken by the mouth of all God's holy prophets since the world began."

In the long waiting ere it comes, every deed of every true man counts in the fashioning of the stones of the temple which is building for the revelation of the glory of the Lord.

The next speaker was the representative of the Cumberland Presbyterians upon the Board of Trustees of the United Society of Christian Endeavor, the Rev. W. J. Darby, D.D., of Evansville, Ind. Dr. Darby's topic was, "What These Things Mean."

Address of Rev. W. J. Darby, D.D.

With the youth of the land in full possession of the city, a speaker may readily assume that his audience is composed wholly of this class, or of those in close sympathy with them. I come to you, young people, with suggestions as to the meaning of what you behold and the import of the times through which you pass.

You are getting a largeness of view which promises breadth of character and wide usefulness in life. The whole range of Bible truth is opened before you, and weekly topics introduce you to a variety of themes whose bearing will touch and quicken every side of your being. He who grows into a one-sided manhood is without excuse, and a narrow Christian developed from Endeavor ranks ought to be a rare product in these days.

What means the phrase, "World-wide Endeavor," that is upon the lips of all our youth, and has crystallized into the title of a book in which the founder of this movement tells its remarkable history? It means not simply that the Christian Endeavor banner is planted among well-nigh every people on the globe, but it is suggestive of heart-beats that yearn for the salvation of a whole race and for the bowing of every knee to Jesus, our Lord. World-wide Endeavor stands for thoughts and plans that take in all nations, for affections that circle the globe, and for work that is to win the world for Christ.

Another product of the times is definiteness of aim. That is necessary to successful execution of the plans and work of life. Without exercise the undeveloped powers of the young Christian will never find their natural outlet.

This great religious movement is characterized by a growth of Christian intelligence that augurs well for the future of the Church.

This wonderful stir among our Christian Endeavor millions means a great increase of the readers of good literature; it means a growing appetite for knowledge that will swell the attendance at our colleges and universities; it means a familiarity with the Bible and books growing out of it such as was never known before.

One step beyond is that other feature of our Endeavor fellowship, the helpfulness of sympathy. Young people are readily attracted toward each other, and their association in these relations is natural. They are a source of strength, and deserve to be maintained with scrupulous care — each a stepping-stone to help others to heaven, not a stumbling-block in the way.

The last speaker was another trustee of the United Society, the

Rev. William Patterson, of Toronto, Ont. "The Need of the Age" was the title of Mr. Patterson's address.

Address of Rev. Wm. Patterson.

The age in which we live is one of the most advanced and wonderful that the world has ever seen. It has been called "The Electric Age,"—an age of invention, of discovery, of learning, and of culture surpassing all the ages which have gone before, and the question might be asked, "What lack we yet?" To this question we emphatically reply, "More 'men of faith.'" We have many men of faith in our land, but the supply is nothing compared to the demand.

I am well aware that selfishness and covetousness are the great sins of the age. These lie at the foundation of the liquor traffic, the opium traffic, and other forms of iniquity which are blighting the nations of the earth; but faith will kill these sins. Just as soon as faith got into the heart of Zacchæus selfishness and covetousness fled, and half his goods went to feed the poor, while fourfold was restored to those he had wronged. If a man comes to believe with all his heart that the things of earth are temporal, while the unseen is eternal; if he believes that God is, that his promises are true and his power unlimited, he will no longer be "of the earth, earthy," but he will have his affections set on things which are high and holy. Abraham was a man of faith, whose eye caught sight of the City of God; he was lifted above self, so that he could say to Lot, "Choose to the right hand or choose to the left; the land is before thee." What a marvellous contrast we see between the man of faith and the man of sight—when we look at Abraham and Lot!

It was faith which led Moses to turn his back on the glory and wealth of Egypt and identify himself with despised Israel; it was by faith that he led forth the enslaved nation, bringing them across the sea and through the desert.

Now, if we look back over the history of the world and the history of the Church, we will see that the men who have been instrumental in accomplishing anything for God or humanity have been men of faith. When the Israelites were at the border of the land of promise they sent twelve men to spy out the country. Ten of these men were men of fear, who saw the walled cities of Canaan and the giants who dwelt in them; then they looked at unarmed and untrained Israel and said, "We cannot take the land, we are only as grasshoppers in their sight." Two were men of faith; they saw the walled cities and the giants; they saw unarmed and untrained Israel; but behind that they saw Jehovah, who subdued Pharaoh and divided the sea for his people, and they said, "If he delight in us, we can take the land." What Israel wanted was more men like Joshua and Caleb, men of faith, for God did not intend to keep Israel forty years in the wilderness, but through unbelief they could not enter the land of promise. Israel in the wilderness, when she should have been in the land of promise! What a picture of the Church of God in our age! Has God not promised that he will pull down the strongholds of evil, and exalt the land by righteousness? This has to be done through his people. But what do we see? The liquor traffic, and the opium traffic, and all forms of iniquity lifting up their heads in proud defiance of the Church of God, just as the walled cities of Canaan lifted themselves up in proud defiance of the hosts of Israel. I know that we have in the Church men of faith who believe that all iniquity could be overthrown, just as they had in Israel men of faith who believed that the walled cities could be taken. But it is now as it was then—the men of fear far outnumber the men of faith. Consequently, little is attempted and little is accomplished, for unless we have faith in God we will not attempt great things, and if we don't attempt great things we will never accomplish great things.

Look at New York City. Many of the people of God saw iniquity in the high places, and sin, like a plague, destroying the city. They shook their pious heads and said, "It is really too bad; what can we do?" Dr. Parkhurst saw the same things, but he said, "What ought to be done can be done." His faith in God led him to attempt great things, and great things have been accomplished. Just as the hosts of Midian trembled before the faith of Gideon and his three hundred, so the host of iniquity workers in New York trembled before the faith of Dr. Parkhurst and his followers. If the Christian people of America had the faith of Joshua and Caleb, if they had the faith of Washington and Lincoln and Garfield, before the close of this century there would not be a tavern, an opium den, a house of ill-fame, or a gambling hell in the great Republic. What applies to the States will also apply to other countries. What we need is men who believe and, therefore, speak; men who believe and, therefore, act, — men whose faith can be seen in their works.

This subject can also be applied to foreign missions. Why is it that after nearly 1,900 years there are still ten hundred million of the human race without the Gospel? Are not these heathen nations the promised land? As God promised to give Canaan to Israel, has he not promised to give the heathen to his Son for an inheritance, and the uttermost parts of the earth for his possession? And as God commanded Israel to take possession of Canaan, has he not commanded the Church to take possession of those heathen lands? What is the command? "Go ye into all the world and preach the Gospel to every creature." "Make disciples of all nations." And the Church has been doing what Israel did. We have not taken possession — because we have more men of fear than men of faith. The great heathen nations are waiting to receive the messengers of the Cross. Hundreds of young men and young women from the different colleges and schools are prepared to go, but the Church is afraid to send them, lest she should not be able to meet the expenses. Of course, times are hard and money is not easily gotten, but has the Lord become poor? There was a time when he owned the cattle on a thousand hills and he could say, "The gold and silver are mine." When Jesus Christ gave the command to take possession of the nations in his name he said that all power in heaven and earth was given unto him, and he promised to be with his people in the carrying-out of his commission, even till the end of the age. Do we act as if we believed that "the earth and the fulness thereof" is the Lord's; that his power is unlimited; and that he has given us the command to evangelize all nations? Surely what we most need is men of faith, men who will say to the Lord, as Isaiah said, "Lord, here am I, send me;" men who will bring of their gold and silver to the treasury of the Lord, because they believe the words of the Lord Jesus: "It is more blessed to give than to receive."

Faith is the channel through which God sends his blessings to humanity. We have many statements in Scripture proving this, such as, "According to your faith be it unto you," "Thy faith hath made thee whole," "All things are possible to him that believeth." Without faith it is impossible to please God, and without faith it is impossible to accomplish anything in this world for God or our fellowmen. It is said of our Lord Jesus, himself, that in a certain place he could not do many mighty works because of the unbelief of the people; and the same thing might be said of many churches and communities in the present age. Too many people are putting their trust and confidence in the things of time and not in the Lord. Look at the Church of Laodicea. That church was trusting in her riches and culture and power, but the Lord was outside knocking at the door, seeking admission. There are many churches at the present time like this one — churches trusting in the eloquence of the preachers, trusting in the singing of the choirs, trusting in the respectability of the people, trusting in the gold that fills their treasuries, and saying, like Laodicea, that they have need of nothing, while the conversions are few and far between, and iniquity continues to abound under the very shadow of the buildings where those meet to worship themselves. "It is not by might, nor by power, but by my Spirit," saith the Lord, that the world is to be saved. It is only through men of faith that the Spirit will work. Read the eleventh chapter of Hebrews, and you will find a list of the worthies of whom the world was not worthy; men of faith through whom God subdued kingdoms and wrought righteousness; men by whom he delivered nations and saved peoples; but they were men who believed his word and obeyed his command.   Read the Acts of the Apostles and the story of the Reformation; read the history of missions and the accounts of the great revivals, and you will find that God always honors the men who honor him, and trusts the men who trust him, making them the channels through which he sends his blessings to humanity.

The question may now be asked, How shall we get this faith, so that we may become a blessing to our age and a power in the earth?   We are not left to speculate as to what answer should be given to this question, for the Apostle Paul distinctly tells us that faith cometh by hearing and hearing by the Word of God.   I think it is impossible for a Christian to be full of the Scriptures without being full of faith in the God of the Scriptures; and I think a Christian will have very little faith if he is ignorant of the Word of God.   If you read the history of the Church in any age you will find that men who were mighty in the Scriptures were always men of faith.   Look at Stephen, the first martyr, — a man full of faith and the Holy Ghost.   When you read his address to his murderers, you cannot help noticing his wonderful familiarity with the writings of the Old Testament.   Did not the great faith of Luther come from his knowledge of the Bible?   He heard the voice crying in his ear, " The just shall live by faith," and it made him strong as a lion and fearless of the foe.

Now, if any one should ask me what I considered to be the strongest feature in connection with the Christian Endeavor I should answer, " The place which the Society gives to the Bible."   So long as a society makes the Word of God its text-book and continues to train young men and young women in the Scriptures, so long will the society prosper and go forth conquering and to conquer in the power of the Holy Ghost who caused all Scripture to be written.   This is an age of literature, and we cannot be too thankful for all that has been accomplished through the printing-press, for the millions of books and periodicals and papers that have come from the printing-press to bless the world; but we must see to it that these do not take the place of the Bible.   We are thankful for the oil and gas and electric light, which have been such a boon to our age, but these, no matter how useful they are, cannot take the place of the sun, the giver of warmth and light and life.   So this Christian literature, no matter how good and useful it is, cannot take the place of the Bible, — God's revelation to man; inspired by the Holy Ghost it becomes the power of God to the salvation of all who believe.   Those who question its authenticity and doubt its inspiration are those who know least about it.   On the other hand, those who meditate upon its truths find them sweeter to their taste than the honey that droppeth from the comb, and through its precepts they become wiser than their teachers.   To their feet it becomes a lamp, throwing light on their pathway and guiding them through the changing scenes of life; and as they grow in the knowledge of the Sacred Volume, their faith becomes stronger, so that they can mount up with wings as eagles, and looking at the last enemy, can shout out in triumph, " O Death, where is thy sting? O Grave, where is thy victory?" and beyond the shores of time they can see the city with foundations whose builder and maker is God, and hear the songs of the ransomed as they praise him who is the alpha and omega, the fulfiller of all prophecy, and the end of the law for righteousness to every one that believeth.

> " Trust in the Lord, forever trust,
>   And banish all your fears;
> Strength in the Lord Jehovah dwells,
>   Eternal as his years."

First Baptist Church, Charlestown.

It was a very enthusiastic meeting which took place in the First Baptist Church, corner of Austin and Lawrence Streets, Charlestown. This was the central point of interest to the Christian Endeavorers in Charlestown.   It was the place of reception for the Hampshire County delegates, many of whom registered in the gayly decorated Sabbath-school room.

This meeting was fortunate in being attended by Rev. Wayland Hoyt, D.D., of Minneapolis. Dr. Hoyt delivered a most excellent and stirring address, sustaining the interest of the Endeavorers to the very last word of his utterance. His remarks were devoted to enjoining the Endeavorers to cleave steadfastly to their pledge; and he made an impression which is sure to have a lasting influence toward the good of the great Christian Endeavor movement.

The church was decorated with streamers, flags, and banners, in which the colors red and white were represented in profusion.

There were about one thousand people in the church when the pastor, Rev. Arthur S. Burrows, D.D., opened the meeting.

The chairman's preliminary remarks were directed toward welcoming the delegates in the most hearty fashion. After singing another hymn, the congregation joined in prayer, with Rev. S. L. B. Spear, of West Newton; Rev. William J. Spear, of Littleton, Mass., read a chapter of Scripture.

Then John C. Berry, M.D., of Japan, delivered the following address, his topic being " Medical Missions."

Address of John C. Berry, M. D.

The name "Christian Endeavor" carries with it the thought of *practical work*, of applied Christianity; and the programme of this great Convention shows that the subjects to be brought before it for consideration are along those practical lines which characterize the daily work of Christian Endeavorers the world over. It is for this reason, I suppose, that I am requested to speak on that special branch of service with which it is my privilege to be identified in the foreign field, — the medical arm of missionary work, — a branch whose especial aim it is to give to those to whom we go practical illustrations of Christian charity, and of that noble civilization which in our age Christendom represents.

Our Saviour was the first Christian Endeavorer, and it is interesting to note that the line of practical work he especially emphasized was the *service of healing*. The glimpse we are afforded of his actively consecrated life at Capernaum, when " all they that had any sick with divers diseases brought them unto him; and he laid his hands on every one of them, and healed them," gives us an idea of the first Christian dispensary service; and so, also, in this same Gospel of Luke (it is natural that Luke should make reference to the medical side of our Saviour's work), where we are told that " Jesus went about all Galilee teaching in their synagogues, and preaching the Gospel of the kingdom, and healing all manner of disease among the people," we have a record of the first medical missionary tour. Indeed, during all his life of active work of which we have a record, he made prominent this same service of healing; and in his commands to his disciples he said, " Into whatsoever city ye enter and they receive you, heal the sick that are therein, and say unto them The kingdom of God is come nigh unto you." The apostles and early disciples to whom was thus committed this miraculous power over disease were faithful in carrying into effect our Saviour's command; the early Church gave prominence to the same work; and when it became evident that this Divine gift had been withheld from the Church, the founding of Christian hospitals at once assumed prominence, several such institutions being in existence at the time of the Council of Nice — one of the articles of that council enumerating the necessary qualifications of a Christian hospital steward.

History, therefore, shows that the charity hospital is an outgrowth of our Saviour's own work and teaching; that medical missions, too, were founded and encouraged by Christ; that the apostles gave great prominence to this line of work; and that the Church, in its purest and most aggressive age — an age when, within three hundred years after the crucifixion of our Lord, and in spite of the fiercest opposition, it planted its colonies throughout the vast Roman Empire, with its population of one hundred million souls — during this time, I say, the hospital was a prominent factor in the practical work of the Church.

In time the monastery, rather than the hospital, came to represent the spirit of Christianity as prevailing in the Church, but to-day the Church and Christian communities generally have returned to primitive and better practices, and applied Christianity has come to take the place of penance and monasticism.

And it was doubtless due to the growth of this spirit in the Church that medical missions were again adopted as auxiliary to the work of the Church; and in an experience of sixty-nine years (for it was not until 1826 that Dr. Dalton, our first medical missionary, was sent to the Jews) we have abundant proof that the work of medical missions is the divinely appointed substitute for miracles. According to the testimony of a prominent English merchant in Canton, Dr. Peter Parker, our first missionary physician to China, did more by his hospital to open China to the influences of modern civilization than all the embassies of Lord Amherst together. So highly were his services appreciated by the people that ladies of rank have been known to wait all night in their palanquins before the gate of the hospital that they might be in season to secure tickets for admission to the hospital service next morning. Of him it was graphically said, " He opened China with the point of his lancet."

And as in the early history of Christian missions, applied Christianity did more to touch the heart of that nation than diplomacy, so recently, in the great struggle in the far East, Western civilization has been recommended to China more by the humane operation of the Red Cross Society from Japan than by every other influence of the war; and to-day no missionary agency in China has a higher value attached to it, both by Church and people, than the well-conducted mission hospital. We therefore find these numerously employed throughout that vast empire, with its population of nearly four hundred million souls, quietly and unostentatiously doing their double work of healing and of love, and representing what is highest and best in our precious faith and noble civilization.

And as in China to-day, so in Japan during the last quarter of a century. Indeed, it is probably true that in no mission field has applied Christianity, as witnessed in the Christian hospital and dispensary, had a more salutary effect, in allaying prejudice, winning confidence, and preparing the people for the truth, than there. As a result of two hundred and fifty years of legislation to keep Christianity from the nation — a legislation following, and perhaps rendered necessary by, a conspiracy to seize the throne and place upon it a prince more in sympathy with the Roman Catholic faith; a legislation preceded by the remarkable edict, " So long as the sun shall warm the earth, let no Christian be so bold as to come to Japan; and let all know that the King of Spain himself, or the Christian's God, or the great God of all, if he violate this command, shall pay for it with his head;" a legislation requiring an edict board against Christianity in every village, and a yearly official visit to every family in the realm — as a result of all this, I say, there was the most bitter prejudice against Christianity, so that when the preacher reached Japan with his message he found few who would come to hear him. At this juncture the influence of Dr. Hepburn's work at Kanagawa was far reaching and potent for good, and later the medical work of Dr. Adams, Dr. Palm, Dr. Taylor, Dr. Lanning, Dr. Whitney and others became, not infrequently, the source or centre of a religious influence rapidly ripening into a church. This was my own experience at Sanda and Takahashi; while at these places and at other centres, among the first deacons in our early churches, six were physicians who had been associated with me in dispensary or hospital work. Dispensaries thus directed become at once centres for physical relief to thousands by day, and places for Christian meetings at night, while Christian assistants hold personal conversation with inquirers, and distribute to them tracts and Scripture portions.   I well remember with what telling effect an evangelist made use of a hospital incident at one of these evening services.   It was at Himeji, and Mr. Suzuki's address for the evening was on " The True God." He had attended the surgical clinic in the afternoon, and in his discourse said, " To-day, as I saw the foreign teacher preparing to open an eye and remove a cataract from a 'grandmother,' I wondered to myself: Supposing now we Christians *are* mistaken, and that instead of one God there are many gods, and that the one who made the Americans did n't consult with the one who made the Japanese, and as a result there is a difference in the minute anatomy of the eye, as a result of which this operation proves a failure. What a calamity for this 'grandmother'! But no such thoughts seemed to disturb the doctor. He made his preparations and cut into the eye in confidence, took out the cataract, and, to the joy of all, the patient could see.   Truly there is but one God, the Creator and Father of us all, and we are brethren."

Time would fail me to tell of these hospital and dispensary experiences, of touching expressions of gratitude, of awakened interest in truth.   I recall with tender memory a touching scene at the earthquake dispensary service at Ogaki.   Sad scenes had been witnessed there; our hearts were subdued in the presence of an awful power and its terrible results; and as the large yard and street in front of the clinic room would fill up at an early hour day after day, our work for the relief of the suffering seemed almost endless.   It was on the third day of the service, when a woman of eighty years came for relief.   She had suffered a dislocation of the shoulder which physicians had failed to affect other than to increase her suffering.   The dislocation, however, was easily reduced, and when, three days later, she came to have the bandages renewed, so profound was her gratitude that, standing where she could see me at work, she lifted her clasped hands and bowed her head to me in profound worship. One of the nurses directed my attention to her, and my feelings may well be imagined as I hastened to her side, took her little wrinkled hands between my own, told her I was but a man sent by our common Father to do her and her people good, a Father who had preserved her life all these eighty years, and even amid the perils of the great earthquake. Let her and her people worship God.   To-day there is a church in that locality.

I have spoken of the influence and work of the trained nurse, that newest arm of missionary service.   It was in 1887 that this was established.   I had witnessed the rapid development of medical science in Japan, and the salutary change in the treatment of the sick, from the basis of Chinese superstition and religious fanaticism to that of a humane and intelligent appreciation of scientific principles, and concluded that, both as a practical missionary agency and as an important step in the humane and scientific treatment of disease, the time had come for the trained nurse.   As Fleidner has so well said : " If one enters a house of suffering to carry a helpful Gospel message it is well; but if, in addition, one is able to extend a helpful hand to a weary and discouraged wife and mother, to show her how to make a new and acceptable article of diet for a sick husband or child, to ventilate the sick-room, to bathe the patient, and do many other practical features of nursing, she carries to the burdened heart and weary body an uplifting ray of sunshine and of joy." And this has been the work of our trained nurses sent out from our school. Many have entered who were not Christians, but every one of the fifty-four graduates have been Christians when they have received their diplomas and have consecrated themselves to the service of humanity and of Christ. Are they devoted to their work? Since the time when the school was first opened, and Miss Linda Richards, my first superintendent, devoted herself to a little child during an entire night, and by the frequent application of necessary remedies saved its eyes from destruction, to the present, when Miss Helen Fraser, with a self-sacrifice beyond her strength, teaches her nurses both in hospital ward and lecture-room to consecrate themselves to the sick under their care, the nurses have been true to their instruction, and have won for themselves and their school the respect and confidence of the nation. Are they brave? I have never seen but one faint away at the sight of blood,— a new nurse,— and the following incident will answer the question. It was at this same earthquake service. A surgical operation had just been performed when, as I was finishing a delicate part of the work, a seismic shock occurred so strong as to threaten to bring down the already shattered building upon our heads. A general rush for the door of the clinic room at once took place among such patients as could walk, and their friends; but not an assistant or a nurse moved from their posts. Bracing themselves to meet the shock, they stood bravely at their work, each performing her duty, and the operation was completed and the patient saved.

In accomplished results, therefore, and in prospective usefulness, the Christian Nurses' School is now recognized as a missionary agency of great value. In furnishing women suitable for this work, no less than in supporting needy native students, a vast field of labor is opened up to Christian Endeavorers in all lands. A trained nurse, consecrated to the service of Christ, in the foreign field is a double missionary.

Great, however, as has been the power of science and of truth, as combined in medical missions, in advancing the interests of rational medicine and of hygiene; in caring for the sick and emphasizing the claim of Christianity that the strong shall bear the burdens of the weak, and a community care for its suffering and unfortunate; in contributing to national greatness and to the purity of social life; yet the chief glory of medical missions has been that they have brought comfort and satisfaction to longing souls, and given a victorious tranquillity in the supreme hour of human need. I remember as yesterday the return of my wife from a visit to the mother of a physician who had been much associated with me in Christian medical work, and who had, therefore, come much under the influence of the power it represents; and from this old lady my wife had received and brought home with her this garment. [Garment shown.] It is not unusual for faithful Buddhists in Japan to make their burial-robes and take them to the temples and have the priests write upon them passages from the Buddhist scriptures, prayers, etc., and these you see written all over this garment. They number about twelve hundred, and the probable cost was about twenty-four dollars. On the occasion mentioned she gave it to my wife with these words: "I once felt a certain sense of satisfaction in the possession of this robe, but I don't want it now. When I fall asleep I shall rest in my Saviour's love, and I shall awake clothed in his righteousness. Take it to your people, if you will, and thank them for their kindness in sending the messengers of the Gospel to us." The dear old lady has passed on to the sublime realities of her faith; her Buddhist burial-robe is with us to-day, an evidence of the victories of the Cross in the island empire of the far East.

And as with the grandmothers, so with the strong men. I recall with delight an experience with a Samurai, those useful men in old-time Japan who were the soldiers and the scholars of the land, who did the fighting and the thinking of the nation. Self-satisfied in his strength of arm and in his Confucian philosophy, he came to the hospital for treatment, disdainful of that faith of whose life he soon saw evidences. Christian love and kindness, however, soon touched his heart, and not long after he began to study the Bible, gave his heart to God, and became an earnest and humble follower of Christ. And later, when asked what most influenced him in this step, he replied, "Why, the reasonableness of Christ's teachings and the perfection of his life." And this, dear friends, is the strength of the Christian missionary to-day. Wherever and whenever he speaks the word of life and of love he realizes that God's Spirit is with it; and this, backed by the perfect system of ethics embraced in the teaching of our Lord, and by his perfect life, produces immediate results.— the Gospel of Christ thus proving itself "the power of God unto salvation to every one who believeth."

And, fellow Endeavorers and Christian friends, it is *such* a Gospel that we are privileged to present to the non-Christian world, and at a time, too, when God, in his infinite wisdom, has fitted his Church for grander and more aggressive work, and has opened wide the nations to receive his truth. The ideals and requirements of the noble civilization of Christendom command the respect and awaken the ambition of aspiring nations. Steam and electricity stand harnessed at our very doors to convey our messengers and our messages to the uttermost parts of the earth; the broad highways of the oceans and the gateways of the nations are thrown wide open to our passage, while the Holy Spirit of God is working mightily upon the hearts of all. It is a day for which the nations have waited; a day for whose preparation the providences of God have long been active; a day when, in order to the rapid consummation of the great work of establishing the kingdom of righteousness and truth in the world, we have but to move forward along lines God has prepared, and to make use of the means he has so plentifully placed in our hands.

Of members of the Christian Endeavor Societies, and of the Christian Church generally, it may be said to-day: —

> " There is a tide in the affairs of men
> Which, taken at its flood, leads on to fortune;
> Omitted, all the journey of their lives
> Is lost in shallows and in miseries.
> On such a full tide are we now afloat,
> And we must take the current as it serves,
> Or lose our ventures."

Shepard Memorial Church.

The historic old Shepard Memorial Church, " the first church in Cambridge," opened its doors to welcome the Christian Endeavorers who were sojourning in the university city.

The pastor of the church, Rev. Alexander McKenzie, D.D., was unable to be present to welcome the delegates, as he was in Europe.

The services were begun by the singing of several familiar pieces by a special Christian Endeavor choir from the North Avenue Congregational Church, under the leadership of Mr. A. F. Roberts. Mr. B. B. Gillett, the organist of the Shepard Church, presided at the organ.

The presiding officer was Rev. A. P. Foster, D.D., of Boston. All the speakers were men prominently identified with the work of the Sunday school; consequently, as planned by the programme committee, this meeting bound the Sunday school and the Christian Endeavor Society closer together.

The first speaker was Rev. Rufus W. Miller, of Reading, Penn., one of the trustees of the United Society of Christian Endeavor, and president of the Brotherhood of Andrew and Philip.

Address of Rev. Rufus W. Miller.

The Apostle Paul sets forth forcibly an important truth of Christian Endeavor when he says: " As we have opportunity, let us do good unto all men, especially unto them who are of the household of faith." He suggests that our good-doing is limited by our surroundings. How true! One hundred years ago as an individual Christian you could have done much less for Christ than now; not because the need was not as great, but the opportunity was lacking. Three hundred years ago you could have done still less. Modern church work affords us, as Christians, opportunities for good-doing such as has never before been witnessed in the history of Christianity. It has emphasized individual religious effort, and opened the way for a brighter re-setting of the ancient God-given agencies for the right rearing of the race, — the Church home and the Church school. And justly may it be said no modern agency has greater potency in these directions than the Young People's Society of Christian Endeavor. Christian Endeavor means opportunity for good-doing. Opportunity! Did you ever examine the word closely? Evidently it is formed of the two words: "ob," meaning "near," and "portus," a "port" or harbor. So that the entire word "opportunity" used to mean "harbor-nearness." We can well understand how the old Roman sailors, tossed about on the Mediterranean Sea by many a storm, at last with beating hearts and straining eyes sighted the familiar head-lands of the harbor, and joyfully entered its quiet waters, finding in the harbor the end of anxiety and the supply for all their need.

We see that the word is full of joy. Every syllable pulsates with gladness. It is obligation that has forgotten its own name, and calls itself happiness. And so Christian Endeavor has come to mean opportunity, glad harbor-nearness, a haven of rest, a treasure store of blessing to the Church and her divinely given agencies.

Disturbing disintegrate forces are at work in these modern days to nullify and overthrow the usefulness of the Sunday school and the home. But with every new danger the all-wise Head of the Church gives to his people fresh spiritual means to meet the evil. Christian Endeavor in its development seems to be such a Divine solvent. To-night, amid the uplifting, enlarging influences of this world-gathering of Christian Endeavorers, let us consider how Christian Endeavor acts as a solvent in the sphere of the Sunday school and home; or, in other words, how helpful certain fundamental features of Christian Endeavor are and may be to emphasize and cultivate indispensable factors in the work of the Sunday school and the home.

It is well to recognize clearly that God has for all time assigned work in the right rearing and training of the race to certain agencies, and no subsequent manifestation of his will has in the least abrogated the responsibility or lessened the sphere and purpose of these first agencies. In the beginning God committed to the family the religious training of the race, and for the first fifteen centuries or more no agency of God shared with the family the responsibility and the privileges of that exalted mission. The Divine injunction to parents was and is, "These words which I command thee, shall be upon thine heart: and thou shalt teach them diligently unto thy children, and shall talk of them when thou sittest in thine house." (Deut. vi. 6, 7). "Command your children to observe to do, all the words of this law. For it is not a vain thing for you; because it is your life." (Deut. xxxii. 46, 47.)

The family did not prove faithful to the trust committed to it. And after the flood we find that God established the church school as a co-working agency with the family for the right rearing of the race. Rev. Dr. H. Clay Trumbull ably shows that Abraham was a teacher before he was a parent. He had at least three hundred and eighteen instructed retainers before he had a child of his own. Of the days of Moses it is declared, in Deuteronomy, that the Lord's command for all Israel at certain stated periods was: "Assemble the people, the men and the women and the little ones, and thy stranger that is within thy gates, that they may hear, and that they may learn, and fear the Lord your God, and observe to do all the words of this law : and that their children, which have not known, may hear, and learn to fear the Lord your God, as long as ye live in the land whither ye go over Jordan to possess it." And so it was that the church school in its germinal form was brought into the world to make the family what it should be. It is intensely interesting to trace the development of the Jewish training, with its progress from the service of the tabernacle and of the temple to the social services of the synagogue and accompanying exercises of Bible study and teaching. It attained its crowning glory in the earthly training of the Holy Child Jesus.

The Christian Church, from her inception, progressed along the line of the family idea and of the church school. This modern age has witnessed a renewal and rejuvenescence of the Bible schools of the early Church.

The Sunday school of to-day is, too, a wise and necessary adaptation of the church school to the needs of our times. And with the growth of the Sunday-school system the standard and character of family life has advanced and improved. Now the fundamental means of instruction in the family and the Sunday school is the Word of God. The Protestant idea emphasizes the truth as the first and greatest means of grace; hence the supreme importance of Bible instruction. But just here appear dangerous tendencies.

The hurry and rush of our modern time find no time for religion and instruction in the family. The crowding together of vast multitudes in our large cities, the isolation of numerous families in country hamlets, alike tend to the neglect of the use of the Bible.

The Sunday newspaper and the turning of Sunday into a day of recreation contribute largely to the want of the family life. The Sunday school, with its added exercises and its multiplied "lesson helps," is in danger of falling away from its emphasis of the Bible as the one text-book. And the demands of the day school, with its wide range of studies, oftentimes draining mental activity and filling every moment of time, make it easy to neglect the study of the Book of books at home.

In the emergency of the Church there is always provided a remedy; so, in the providence of God, the Young People's Society of Christian Endeavor is coming to be seen as a solvent, the new application of an old idea, church vows reduced to particulars. Two principles, with accompanying particulars, underlie Christian Endeavor, and in these respects it is a solvent.

First, it insists upon the appropriation and use of the Word. Our pledge, taken by millions, requires a daily reading of the Bible at home. In the prayer meeting the most common mode of participation is by the recitation of Scripture passages. Who can estimate the value of the fulfilment of these simple, definite obligations? The habit formed cannot fail to permanently influence character. The opportunities presented are boundless in their outreach. The strategic position of Junior Christian Endeavor needs emphasis. The Junior superintendent touches at once the Sunday school and the home. There is the mighty force of fellowship. The personal spiritual intimacy between the Junior superintendent and the child means something more than fellowship at almost any other period in life.

Another matter of detail is worthy of note. It is this: childhood seems of all others the time for committing things to memory, and in religious training this holds true especially. And herein Christian Endeavor is powerfully aiding the Sunday school and the home. The use of the Bible and the memorizing of Scriptures is a felt need in our Sunday schools, and how to secure home-study of the lesson is another pressing problem. Let us thank God and take courage, Christian Endeavor can justly claim a Divine authorization, as it proves its efficiency in the line of unqualified co-operation with the family and the Sunday school. God is not a God of confusion, but of peace.

The second solvent principle underlying Christian Endeavor is a principle of education, which has been greatly emphasized by educators in these days. It is the principle that we learn by doing. It has found its application in almost all departments of modern educational work.

The work of primary education has been almost entirely reorganized on this basis. It is a principle which admits of application to Christianity possibly with greater force than anywhere else. Christian Endeavor is strong and sound, because it stands squarely upon this principle of self-activity. Its assumption is that Christian character is formed, not when the intellect is properly instructed in sound doctrine, not when the instruction has entered the heart and moved the feeling, but when the truth has so informed the intellect and penetrated the heart that it again comes forth through the will in the form of loving activity. Christian Endeavor insists that the only religious training worthy of the name is that which through its instruction produces consecrated activity. The various committees in Christian Endeavor and the active participation in the weekly prayer meeting afford an unbounded field for the exercise of this principle, — that we learn by doing. Here, too, Christian Endeavor becomes a resolving and recharging force in the Sunday school and the home. The Sunday school is a school for study; the Young People's Society of Christian Endeavor, for training. One is for nourishment and food; the other, for nurture and exercise. The reflex blessing of working for others penetrates the atmosphere of the home and the school. The associated Endeavor "for Christ and the Church" permits a larger, more frequent, more free, more simple fellowship in prayer, praise, conversation, work, and study, where the duties of Christians are learned, and help in living the Christian life is imparted; especially needful is this help to the growing and developing boy and girl. There comes a time when the best of home influences need to be complemented in the training activities of the Church. To each life, whether thoughtful and prepared for it or not, there comes a period marked by a great change. One has called it the "ephebic stage of youth," where we find that adolescence is a physiological second birth; new trials and diseases, organs and cells, are developed; boys and girls become independent; must devote themselves to others and to causes. The religious sense is deepened. "Happy is the child when in such time he can find in the Endeavor Society a training school and a harbor of refuge for his developing, but as yet weak, powers." Frœbel said that the kindergarten had its place and work in the promotion of family life; and very beautifully is this idea carried out in all his writings, also the games and plays, where even the fingers are represented as members of a family. So with truth we may say Christian Endeavor has its place and work in the promotion of family life; and by its principle of self-activity, its social fellowship, and its appeals to the religious life, it becomes a well-spring of blessing and an invaluable coadjutor of the parent in the spiritual culture of the son or daughter.

Great dangers and perils there are to the work of the Christian home. We ought not to be blind to them, nor underrate them. Neither should we ignore the teaching of Scripture in respect to the high place of the home in the plan of God. Think, for a moment, how deep the foundations of the kingdom were laid in parental instruction and family religion. With Israel at the Passover, in the laws of Moses, in the Psalms, how much more mention is made of the teaching of the parents than of the priests! To elevate the standard of thought and faith and duty among the parents is one of the noblest and highest purposes a church can have. And can we not believe that God has raised up the Christian Endeavor as a means to this end? The Christian Endeavor movement, in its surprising results, reminds us, we think not inaptly, of the well-known old Scandinavian tradition, — which savors at once of parable as well as legend, — how once the daughter of a great giantess, walking in the field, saw a husbandman ploughing there; she ran and picked him up with finger and thumb, ploughshare, oxen, and all, and putting them in her apron, ran home to her mother, saying, "Mother, mother, what sort of beetle is this I have found wiggling in the sand?" But the mother said, "Ah, put it down, child, put it down. We must be gone out of this land now that this kind of people have come to live in it." Almost did we seem to hear the voices of the giant spirits of Ignorance, Superstition, Greed, Lust, and Irreligion say, as Christian Endeavor and kindred young people's organizations began to move across the unfurrowed fields, "Now we must be gone; these people have come to live here." And out of the home spectres of parental neglect, worldliness and passion vanish. For the teachings of the Sunday school, as for the home, the Christian Endeavor Society acts as a solvent in affording a field of exercise and practice. Information and instruction concerning the pleasures and profits of Bible reading and of prayer, and concerning the benefits and methods of self-denying beneficence, are here complemented by actual practice. The soul of the child in his play should be trained to that sort of excellence in which, when he grows up to manhood, he will have to be perfected. "Now Christian Endeavor incarnates this idea of practice of Bible instruction and Christian truth as an essential factor in the training process. Young People's Societies are, as some one has well called them, the Church's 'gymnasia.'" Here provision is made for promoting the growth of the individual disciple of Jesus unto "a full-grown man unto the measure of the stature of the fulness of Christ." And underneath it all is the simple yet profoundly philosophical solvent principle, — we learn by doing. Self-activity is the law of the spiritual realm as well as of the natural. Now, in view of these facts, the closest alliance should be made between Christian Endeavor and the Sunday school, and Christian Endeavor and the home. Their co-working and their complementary relations should be clearly recognized and emphasized. On the one hand, Christian Endeavor should centre its efforts and should develop its work in and through these two great institutions of the Church, ever acting as a supplementary agency in supplying incentives and helps and a field of exercise ; and on the other hand, the Sunday school and the home should recognize and utilize Christian Endeavor as its best friend and ally, a spiritual solvent of its training and instruction. May this Convention enable us to apprehend more profoundly in our own personal experience the abounding opportunity of this signal miracle of God's providential grace. Let us see our commission and our strength in the threefold cord of Christian training. Let us see how the triune oneness of the home, the Sunday school, and Christian Endeavor Society in the Church of Christ is made manifest by this trinity of effort. Historians of art tell us that when Michael Angelo was living in Rome, the Pope, his patron, was so much interested in his work that he had a secret passage created from his own apartment to the studio of the artist,—which was in the same chain of buildings, — so that he could go unseen, whenever he pleased, and watch the work that the artist was carrying on. At this time the artist was preparing to decorate a building with certain heroic figures. It is said that he wrought with wonderful power upon the marble ; that he would fly at it with inconceivable ardor ; and that the chisel would strike fragments off from the statue faster than three men could carry them away.

God commissions us to decorate the earthly and heavenly future with conquering heroes. Those that " overcome shall be pillars in the temple of God." Realizing this, let us feel the enthusiasm of a grand work as the mind and heart are touched with the chisel of noble influences.

Remember, also, that we work not unobserved. Between the throne of heaven and the home circle or the school or the Christian Endeavor Society, where we do our work, there is an unseen passage, and through it comes the King of heaven to watch and cheer us in our glorious task, and " a book of remembrance is written."

The next speaker was Rev. F. N. Peloubet, D.D., of Auburndale, Mass., well known to all as the author of one of the very best " Helps " for Sunday-school teachers and scholars.

Address of Rev. F. N. Peloubet, D.D.

Twice two, in spiritual arithmetic, are more than two plus two. According to the promise, if " one can chase a thousand, two can put, not two thousand, but ten thousand to flight." Twice two are ten. The Sunday school multiplied by Christian Endeavor is a great deal more than the Sunday school plus Christian Endeavor. Added, they are four colors ; multiplied, they are a cathedral window. Added, they are four sounds ; multiplied, they are an anthem. The hope of the world's progress of the millennium lies in this: that the results of spiritual arithmetic are not by addition, but by multiplication. It is not ten and one, but ten times one ; not ten plus ten, but ten times ten. Christianity is doing a great deal more than add ; it is putting in seed, each grain of which is a multiplier. New methods and societies and institutions are being developed almost every day, and each one is a multiplier. And this is the secret of the marvellous growth of Christianity. The first thousand years ended with 50,000,000 under its influence. This was doubled in the next 500 years, and there were 100,000,000 ; doubled again in the next 300 years, and there were 200,000,000 in A. D. 1800. But it took only 80 years to double this again, and now there are more than 400,000,000 under its influence, because there never were so many multipliers as in these times of education and commerce and invention and evolution.

One of the speakers in the parliament of religions relates a legend: that " when Adam and Eve were turned out of Eden, the earthly paradise, an angel smashed the gates, and the fragments flying over the earth are the precious stones." He carries the legend further; he says that "the precious stones were picked up by the various religions and philosophies, each claiming that his own fragment alone reflects the light of heaven, and is the true material of which the paradise gates are made." Patience, my brother; in God's own time we shall all of us fit our fragments together and reconstruct the gates of paradise. In our country there are five chief forces making for Christian union, — the Young Men's Christian Association, the Women's Christian Temperance Union, the International Sunday-school Lessons, our hymn-books, with hymns from every denomination of Christians, and last, but not least, the Young People's Society of Christian Endeavor, all gathering up the scattered jewels, and uniting them again in the gates of paradise. No Lambeth articles, no papal encyclical, can begin to do as much as these five are doing to bring the Church into Christian union, into one great league of every land and every race, under our one Master, Jesus Christ.

1. In the first place, to accomplish this end, the multipliers must come together. The Christian Endeavorers must be in the Sunday school. Mr. Spurgeon once asked if we spelled "we" with an "I" in it. Do we spell "Sunday school" with a "C. E." in it?

2. In the next place, permit me to give a hint from personal experience as to the method of working with others. Early in my ministry I learned that one secret of working with others was to put all desire for recognition or honor of leadership out of sight, and to seek with the whole soul only the progress of the cause, let whosoever will have the glory.

3. The Christian Endeavor is to be multiplied by the Sunday school, as well as the Sunday school by the Christian Endeavor. To be good workers we must be full of God's Word, as an engine that would draw a train must be full of fuel, and fuel on fire; and there is no one thing that will so help us to this as the Sunday school.

There is an old familiar comparison of a Christian worker full of knowledge to a cannon made of the strongest steel, loaded with the best powder, and the latest form of shot, but as useless as a heap of sand, unless touched with the fire of the Holy Ghost. But the comparison is equally true if we turn it around. All the lightnings of heaven cannot fire off an unloaded cannon. God does not use an unloaded soul for his work. We need most of all the Holy Spirit, for every man has something in him to be used. But if the Holy Spirit wishes to use a man where intelligence is required, he leads the man to gain the knowledge necessary for his work. If you imagine the Holy Spirit is leading you to teach the Bible, while he does not lead you to study the Bible, then you may be sure it is some other spirit that is leading you. This is where the Sunday school multiplies the Christian Endeavor and its power to do the work God has given it to do; or rather, where the two are multiplied together.

4. Now let us turn to the other side and see how the Christian Endeavor can multiply the Sunday school. There are many directions in which this can be done. Your spiritual power multiplies the spiritual power of the Sunday school. Your gain in Bible knowledge multiplies its Bible knowledge, whether you be a scholar or teacher.

I do not know so much about the model Christian Endeavor meeting; but I know that we sometimes mistake what a model school or Sunday-school class is, and we are discouraged because we are so far from our wrong ideal. It is not a selected number, who are perfect in deportment, who are always present, and always know the lessons, a kind of show-case in which are placed the best specimens of what a Sunday school produces. It is a factory, not a show-case; a studio, not an art gallery. Of all persons those should not be left out who do not know how to behave, who have no home training, who are ignorant of the Bible, and will not study their lessons, but, like Gallio, care for none of these things. Shut out your deacons if you must; send away your perfect ones if you will; but by all means in your power keep these in your meetings and in your Sunday school. "These are our treasures."

It is a blessed privilege to live now; to be young now. No times since

Pentecost have been so good to live in as these times of ours. Heaven is blessed. I love to think of it; but I would rather stay here longer, and work for the Lord, than have the sweetest harp ever sounded by cherubim or seraphim. It is better to help make the millennium than to live in it. It is better to help bring " the good time coming " than to enjoy it when it comes.

The Federal Convention had been sitting for months, in Philadelphia, forming that wonderful document, the Constitution of the United States, and had come to a definite conclusion amid the greatest differences of opinion. On the back of the President's quaint black arm-chair there was emblazoned a half sun, brilliant with gilded rays. As the meeting was breaking up and Washington arose, Franklin pointed to the chair and made it a text for a prophecy: " As I have been sitting here all these weeks," said he, " I have often wondered whether yonder sun was rising or setting; but now I know that it is a rising sun." I have been watching the Christian Endeavor movement from the beginning. I have rejoiced in its phenomenal development under God's providence, and the wise guidance of Dr. Clark, both in numbers and usefulness. I see your faces still toward the vision of what may be, and I know that the Christian Endeavor is not a setting, but a rising sun.

Pilgrim Congregational Church, Cambridge.

The inaugural meeting in the Pilgrim Congregational Church, Cambridgeport, was a most successful and thoroughly interesting one. The auditorium of the church is spacious, with ample accommodations for the seating of a good-sized audience ; and, although some of the delegates who were expected to attend were unable to do so on account of delayed trains, the church was filled. Everywhere was to be seen the Convention colors. The church itself was prettily decorated, the young people of the society connected with it using the colors and emblems tastefully about the walls. Rev. Charles Olmstead, the pastor of the church, presided.

Mr. Olmstead, before introducing the first speaker of the evening, bade all the visiting delegates a warm welcome to Cambridge, the church, and the Y. P. S. C. E. connected with the church. He then introduced Rev. Canon J. B. Richardson, of London, Ont., an Episcopalian trustee of the United Society of Christian Endeavor. Canon Richardson's topic was, " Christian Endeavor ; Its Record and Its Sphere." We regret a report of his splendid address was not taken.

The next speaker was Mr. H. L. Hastings, of Boston. Many were anxious to see and hear this noted man, who for years has stood for the right. Extracts from Mr. Hastings's address follow.

Address of Mr. H. L. Hastings.

On the high road passing eastward from Babylonia to Ecbatana, near the western border of old Media, in the province of Irak. Persia, a long, narrow, limestone ridge, the eastern boundary of the plain Kermanshah, terminates abruptly in the Rock of Behistun, a vast perpendicular cliff, rising thousands of feet above the adjacent plain.

Four or five hundred feet up this cliff a space upon the face of the rock has been cleared and smoothed, its hollows and crevices filled with lead, and on this broad tablet, "graven with an iron pen," are chiselled a series of inscriptions, surrounding a centrepiece of colossal human figures. Here, upon the face of this mighty cliff, inaccessible and unintelligible, have stood for thousands of years those strange inscriptions in the unknown characters of a long-forgotten tongue; and for ages and centuries that mysterious record baffled the wisdom and the curiosity of mankind. But in the autumn of 1835 Maj. Henry Rawlinson contrived to copy a considerable portion of the record, which he deciphered and translated. In 1844, and at a final visit in 1848, he finished his copies and carried away a complete set of paper casts of most of the inscriptions, which were subsequently translated. The inscriptions were the words of Darius, son of Hystaspes, the Persian monarch (B. C. 550–485), and contained a record of his exploits and victories. And thus, at a distance of more than twenty-three centuries, we read the undying record of the prowess, the glory, and the cruelty of an ancient Persian king. Such pains do men take to perpetuate their fame or their infamy! Man hates to be forgotten; but in what way may we, the common people who have heard the Saviour gladly, have reason to expect that our names shall endure, while the names of such multitudes are lost in utter oblivion? Let a single significant example furnish an answer to this question.

Nearly 2,000 years ago there lived in a little Lycaonian city, just west of the boundary of ancient Cappadocia, a young man who, we may suppose, did not differ greatly in character or native ability from thousands of other young men around him. Yet, while they are forgotten, he is remembered.

His name to-day is a household word in millions of homes; it is read in hundreds of languages; it is borne by multitudes of living men; and it will be remembered to the latest hour of time, and be known along the ages of eternity.

It was this young man, thus trained and equipped, whom Paul, on his third visit to Derbe, selected from all the young men of his age and his country to go forth with him as " a good soldier of Jesus Christ." So to-day the name of Timothy shines through the ages like an unsetting sun, and shall shine in the ages to come like "the stars forever and ever." And the secret and cause and foundation of his fame was that "from a child" he had "known the Holy Scriptures," which are able to make us "wise unto salvation." If we would be sharers in such fame and honor as Timothy has won, we must also know the Holy Scriptures, and be permeated by their vitalizing power.

Men thus trained and taught from childhood in the Holy Scriptures become mighty through God to the pulling down of the strongholds of Satan. They make their mark in the world, while others, wasting their time on other things, vainly seek to know the secret of their power.

Waiting one night in the darkness on the railway platform at Framingham camp-ground, I heard two ministers discussing the secret of a certain noted evangelist's power. After listening awhile, I ventured to intrude the suggestion that if they could get a look at that evangelist's old Bible they might learn the secret of his power; for it contained more marks of use than fifty ordinary ministers' well-kept Bibles. It reminded me of the old Scotch warrior's claymore. He had been in twenty-four battles; there were twenty-four hacks in the edge of his well-tempered blade. He had struck fire every time. A well-studied Bible, believed and preached and practised, is a source of power which will ever remain a mystery to those who neglect the Word of the living God.

Franklin Street Congregational Church, Somerville.

The first gathering which gave Somerville people an opportunity to indicate its Christian Endeavor temperature was held at the Franklin Street Congregational Church. That it had reached a high point was shown by the fact that the great auditorium was packed, the platform being occupied by a large choir which led in the rousing singing of the Endeavor songs.

Rev. James Gray, pastor of the church, presided, and, after a brief, but hearty welcome, introduced the speakers of the evening. One of these was Mrs. Elizabeth Campbell, of Allegheny, Penn., who was presented with warm indorsement by Mr. Gray, and was received with hearty applause. The subject assigned her was, " Intemperance,"—" An old, hackneyed theme," she said ; " but still a terrible evil, which must be grappled with by the Endeavor army." We do not have a report of her address, nor of the breezy and characteristic address of Rev. J. A. Rondthaler, D.D., of Indianapolis, Ind. We can, however, give the address of Hon. Selah Merrill, LL.D., of Andover, Mass.

Address of Hon. Selah Merrill, LL.D.

Seven thousand miles from Boston, far up among the hills of Judea, is Jerusalem, a city venerable with age and cherished as no other city on earth is cherished by many millions of our race. That city and every section of the Holy Land is as familiar to me, after ten years' residence there, as is the town or region to yourselves where you individually reside. Let me ask you to go eastward and visit with me that wonderful city and a few of the holy places of that wonderful country.

There is Bethlehem, the place where Christ was born; there is Nazareth, the place where he grew up to manhood; Capernaum, the city which was his home during a large part of his active ministry; there is the " green hill " near the walls of Jerusalem, where Christ was crucified and buried; there are the fair slopes of Olivet near Bethany, whence our risen Lord ascended to glory. Even if I were dumb, the mention of these names ought to unseal my lips and clothe my tongue with power to move your hearts.

As I regard the Society of Christian Endeavor, it is not wholly a product of this inventive age and of our own time. For the reasons of its existence we must go back to Judea and Galilee. Its warrant is the great event which was enacted there eighteen centuries ago. Its life, its power, its hopes, are intimately connected with the Cross and open grave at Golgotha, with Olivet and its mysterious cloud of light. Its name, its spirit, its works, are centred in the life of Christ. Its triumphs are the triumphs of the Man of Nazareth.

As it was in the beginning so is it now, — the motive is always the same. The cause — *your* cause — is redemption, and years and centuries do not change its character. Once it was a single voice speaking to an eager group by the wayside or upon the shore of Galilee's beautiful lake; it was a single messenger telling to men the good tidings of the Father's love. By and by other voices were heard, other lips prayed, other heralds went forth; through the ages the numbers increased, till to-day " great is the company of those " that are preaching Christ. Once it was a single heart bearing the burden alone; to-day the Christian Endeavorers number nearly two-and-a-half million souls. At Waterloo the allied armies had 70,000 soldiers against 80,000 French. At Gettysburg there were 93,000 loyal troops against 70,000 rebels. Unite these vast masses of men into one body, and you outnumber them by eight to one. We cannot possibly estimate the moral and spiritual force represented by this youthful band. There is an inspiration in numbers when men are disciplined, armed, equipped, and fired by the noblest motive that can stir the soul. Such a band as yours was organized for conquest, — it means victory when you realize the fact, which I trust you never lose sight of, that your work is the work of Christ. As such it had an origin. There was a moment when human eyes first greeted the dayspring from on high. There is, therefore, sufficient reason why you should look eastward to that ancient land.

It is not my intention in this address to give you descriptions of Palestine as I have seen it for many years, — its mountains, plains, valleys, sea and shore, its atmosphere and marvellous sky, its ancient cities with their buried treasures, its checkered history, its people, its poverty, its hopeless degradation,— or to dwell upon any other of its special features of interest. It seemed to me, however, that it would be useful to look back to the place where all Christian work began, to the first laborers called into the vineyard by the Master himself, to some of the characteristics of the new religion, and to some of the methods of work which were successful then and which are just as appropriate now.

The example of Christ shows that Christianity was designed to be an active religion. The Master went about doing good. He travelled with the companies that were journeying on the highways; he frequented the villages; he went to the places on the lake-shore where fishermen resorted; he mingled with the curious groups that gathered by the fountains or wells; he joined the multitudes that thronged the temple at Jerusalem. Not everywhere was he cordially received or fully believed, still everywhere he found some receptive souls, and it was for these that he was on the alert. Occasionally his divine vision was fixed upon some thoughtful person even before that person was aware of his presence. Did not he say to Nathanael, "Before that Philip called thee, when thou wast under the fig tree, I saw thee." (John i: 48.) My friend, if your heart is ever touched, if your soul ever looks up with longing to heavenly things, you may be sure that the Master has seen you before you thought of him.

How Jesus labored till he was weary! How he visited! How he comforted! How he healed! How he cheered! How he blessed in body and mind all them that labored and were heavy laden! The disciples caught his spirit. Early Christianity was an active religion. Its object was redemption. It carried the Gospel over the world as fast as its heralds could go. In this particular I believe the Christian Endeavor Society strives to follow the example and the spirit of Christ.

I said that our fellowmen in Palestine had forgotten Christ. They claim to be Christians, but how is their Christianity shown? Many of them neglect their persons, wear filthy clothing, eat coarse food, shut themselves up in stone cells, and imagine that thus they are serving Christ. A higher grade of the same class wear low shoes with silver buckles, knee-breeches, long black robes, low felt hats, and read perpetually from some service book, and persuade themselves that thus they are honoring Christ and living a Christian life. I am sure they are making an awful mistake. Why not go out among men and labor for their welfare? Christ went to Capernaum, one of the most active centres in Palestine, where he could meet and mingle with men of every class and country.

Christianity was a religion of thought. The early Christians were intelligent and studious. Following the example of Christ, they discussed, they persuaded, they reasoned with men. No one was ever forced to accept the Gospel. An awakened conscience and an enlightened understanding were always preliminary to becoming followers of Christ. This feature of our religion at the very commencement of its history was always to me a most interesting fact.

The new religion was remarkable in that it could not be deterred by obstacles. Even taking into account its Divine character, its spirit, considering the moment in the world's history when it appeared, was heroic. It appeared in the Roman Empire characterized by intellectual strength, pride, and an intense martial spirit. Moreover, it appeared in Judea, the strangest place on earth to be chosen as the cradle of the New Life. The elements about it were elements of opposition,— sneer and scorn, contempt and ridicule, and at last actual violence. It was not many years before the early Church could name its first martyr. Still, with composure and serenity it went on doing its Master's work. The persecuted remembered their enemies and prayed that they might be forgiven. Considering the spirit and circumstances of that age, I think we do not now realize the significance of the fact that men prayed for their enemies. The narrow-minded Jew, the martial-spirited Roman, could not understand it. It was to them a phenomenon without explanation.

Steadily the Tree of Life waxed tall and strong, and steadily the forces antagonistic to it increased in hostility. The world began to learn what Christians could endure for the sake of Christ. The trials of the early years of Christianity we can read about, but can never measure the agonies through which it passed. If we follow Paul in his journeyings from city to city, we get some idea of Jewish enmity and spite. Those who labor among the Jews in Jerusalem now meet with the same spirit of intense hatred to Christianity. It

MECHANICS' BUILDING — SATURDAY MORNING.

View on Boston Common — Convention Tents.

requires the Divine power which overcame Saul to move the heart of a Jew. The opposition on the part of Mohammedans is just as great, although it is not so spiteful in its manifestations. Judaism and Mohammedanism — wherever these prevail, Christianity has to face appalling obstacles. Still, it is not deterred by obstacles nor by opposition, hatred, spite, bigotry, threats of violence; but everywhere it lifts up a cheerful voice in song, it prays for its enemies, it heals the sick, it helps the helpless, it redeems and saves.

It is not the sword, it is not death in terrible forms, that Christian Endeavorers have to fear; there are, however, obstacles which must be encountered and enemies which must be faced.

Early Christianity was a religion of hope. Its earliest motto was " Let not your heart be troubled." This should be your motto now and through life. You are young, and all the fascination of life is yours. You are many in number; you are strong, and with Christ you can conquer the world. Your success in the past promises a wonderful future. Historic Boston, Faneuil Hall, and Bunker Hill, in welcoming you has not welcomed a shadow; it has welcomed a mighty army that is to win great victories for Christ. There is no room for discouragement; let us banish the word.

Early Christianity was a religion of helpfulness. I think if an entire stranger to it were to read candidly the Gospels, he would say, " These contain the life of one who strove to help men, — the sick, the outcast, the wretched, the dying."

One notable fact in Mohammedanism will illustrate this. The idea of a hospital is entirely foreign to the Mohammedan religion and Mohammedan life. The Mohammedan world is destitute of such an institution unless where it has been introduced by Christian nations. If one is an outcast, let him save himself if he can. No effort is made to reclaim the intemperate, no kind advice is given, no friendly hand or asylum offers to secure or relieve. To help the poor, the outcast, the afflicted, the drunkard, the vicious, is no part of the religion of Mohammed. That is altogether a cheerless religion. It has no Saviour. The Mohammedan world is a dismal world because of the absence of hospitals, charitable institutions, societies for the relief of suffering, and all those agencies for helping men with which we are so familiar. The disposition to create and support these agencies comes from the Gospel of Christ. Christianity is a religion of helpfulness. The more of this spirit that Christian Endeavorers possess, the more they will be like Christ.

(1.) Christ was active. Christian workers must act where men are. (2.) Christ established an intelligent, reasonable religion; his followers should be thoughtful and studious. (3.) Christ was not deterred by obstacles; Christian Endeavorers should be courageous Christians. (4.) Christ's religion was one of hope. (5.) Christ's religion was one of helpfulness. Hope and helpfulness, — they breathe upon men the breath of life.

The Christian Endeavor Society is after all but a section of the great body of Christian workers. The Salvation Army belongs to that body ; so does every Sunday-school worker, every teacher and missionary of Christ, in every land. In our Grand Army organization our motto is, " One Country, One Flag." As veterans we hear but one bugle-call, one loyal drum-beat.

The motto of the great army of Christian workers is, " One Lord, One Faith." There is no other name given under heaven among men whereby we can be saved. This is the old, old story. This, Christian workers, we have always preached. We preached it by our Brother Stephen, who laid down his life under the walls of Jerusalem. We preached it by our Brother Paul to Agrippa and his courtiers at Cesarea-by-the-sea. We preached it on Mars Hill. We preached it in the pulpits of Antioch, Constantinople, and Rome. We preached it by Brother John Knox, and fired Scotland for the truth. We preached it by Brother Hannington, who was slaughtered by the savages in Africa. We preached it by the devoted Vicars amid the horrors of the Crimea; by the saintly and heroic General Gordon, who fell at Khartoum. We are preaching it to-day by every disciple of Christ. As a Christian Endeavor Society we are preaching it by more than two million voices ; and I trust that day unto day will declare new and splendid victories which you shall achieve in the name of Christ.

THURSDAY MORNING.

Mechanics' Hall.

Conventions have witnessed many phenomenal openings whose scenes have thrilled the world; but Boston has made history. Never before has such a great and enthusiastic throng got together at such an early hour as did the delegates in Mechanics' Hall on Thursday morning. They did not saunter into the building by ones and twos. No; they seemed to really roll in, as a mighty, ceaseless stream.

A full hour before the time of opening, six thousand people were in the building. When Dr. Clark struck the platform railing with his Oregon gavel, nine thousand people looked upon him.

Rev. Smith Baker, D.D., of East Boston, conducted the opening devotional exercises. Mr. Percy S. Foster, of Washington, D. C., led the chorus in the song of welcome, written for the occasion by Rev. S. F. Smith, D.D., author of "America:"—

> " We welcome the hosts of our glorious King,
> The King whom we worship, whose praises we sing.
> His triumph we seek; His dear cause cannot fail.
> ‖Christ's servants, Christ's soldiers, for His sake, All Hail!‖
>
> " Our hearts are as one, and one Name we adore;
> We lean on one Arm of Omnipotent Power.
> Come, Prince of Salvation, come, reign, Thou alone,
> ‖All worlds be Thy kingdom, and all hearts Thy Throne.‖
>
> " As o'er the wide earth bends the blue arch above,
> Brood o'er us, O Spirit of wisdom and love;
> Our Life, our Redeemer, our Saviour, our God,
> ‖We yearn for Thy coming, we wait for Thy nod ‖
>
> " We march forth, unshrinking, to battle for Thee;
> The armies of sin shall not tempt us to flee.
> We bow to Thy will, and we honor Thy word,
> ‖And follow Thy banner, our Captain and Lord.‖
>
> " Ride on to new conquests, new glory attain,—
> How grand is Thy kingdom, how blessed Thy reign!—
> And wear — for no being is worthy, but Thou —
> ‖The crown of the earth on Thy glorified brow.‖ "

Sing? Christian Endeavorers can no more help singing than can the angels themselves. They entered with song; they assembled with song; they sang in accompaniment to the incoming delegations. They greeted arriving companies with song; they sang one to another; they sang in sections; they sang in choruses.

As the approach of a summer shower over a forest, so would a song begin at a remote corner of the hall, sweeping onward steadily and increasingly, until a mighty storm of music swept over the Convention. The music was from the popular new hymn-book, " Christian Endeavor Hymns," published by the United Society. Among the many soloists, none aroused greater enthusiasm than Rev. John W. Becket, of Baltimore, Md., who sang at this opening service.

It was a magnificent, indescribable, inspiring scene. Cameras in every corner, artists in every alcove, bright eyes everywhere, tried to catch and keep the wonderful gathering. But all these, focused and coupled with the words of throbbing hearts, cannot mirror that scene. It has no parallel this side of the great white throne, with the surrounding innumerable companies of singing ones. Dr. Dille described the meeting in a sentence. "What are you going to do at your Convention?" some one asked him on the way. "Do? Do? Why, we will do what they do in heaven. We'll sing and pray, and pray and sing, and tell the glories of the Lamb."

Chairman S. B. Capen, of the Committee of Thirteen, spoke like the royal good citizen and great-hearted Christian Endeavorer that he is, when he gave a pulsating right hand of welcome to the Convention. Hearty, indeed, was the welcome he received when introduced by President Clark.

Address of Hon. S. B. Capen.

As chairman of the Committee of Thirteen, it is my privilege and pleasure to speak this first word of welcome. But I speak not only for the committee of an unfortunate number, but also for the whole chorus of 3,000 voices, for the committees on entertainment and accommodation and all the rest, yes, for the more than 5,000 Christian Endeavorers who have in some way been joyously helping to prepare for your coming.

We welcome you, first, because you have come in the name of Christ. Christian Endeavor stands for Christ enthroned. It must never be forgotten that this is first, last, and always a religious gathering. There is no other name but that of Christ that would draw this more than 50,000 people together.

Massachusetts and Boston, its capital, have many attractions. It is the old Pilgrim Commonwealth to which the children and the grandchildren love to come from all over the land. Here is Plymouth Rock and the Cradle of Liberty; but it is not for these that you are here to-day, but because of your loyalty to a personal Christ.

Some of you have come a long journey across the ocean and the continent, at a sacrifice of time and strength, to gather with us at the feast. We are from different nations, and live under different flags; we belong to various religious sects, but as Christian Endeavorers all such distinctions are forgotten.

In the English army, when on dress parade, the various divisions have a badge upon the lapel of the coat so they may be readily distinguished. But when the battle is on, the lapel of the coat is turned over and all distinctions are forgotten. We have obliterated all our distinctions, and we stand as absolutely one under the banner of the Cross. The Union Jack of England, the Tricolor of France, the Stars and Stripes of America — we put the Cross of Christ above them all.

> " In this sign we conquer; 't is the symbol of our faith,
> Made holy by the might of love triumphant over death.
> He finds his life who loseth it, forevermore it saith;
> The right is marching on!"

This Christian Endeavor army is the grandest the world has ever seen. It speaks of the greatest movement of this generation, and is rounding out magnificently this great missionary century. With its nearly three millions of members, it is belting the world with its light and with the enthusiasm of its service for Christ. And yet we are only two years in our teens, and we have only just begun to live and to grow. We have no less a purpose than to conquer this whole world for God and truth.

We welcome you, therefore, as a part of this great, all-conquering army of the King. We have enjoyed the hospitality of other cities and States, and we are glad indeed that it is our turn to be the host. "Giving is better than getting," and we know that "the more we give the more we live." We have been getting from you in royal entertainment in the past; we want to "give" now; and we do give you all our warmest greeting, not to our city only, but to our homes and our hearts.

We welcome you because we want our citizens to see what splendid people you are. We have been boasting about you for months, and we know you will more than fulfil our proud boasting, for you are fulfilling one of the last injunctions of Bishop Brooks: "Be godly for man's sake; be manly for God's sake."

We welcome you to this city, which is so proud of its intellectual and material things, because it needs above all things a "religious stirring-up." We want to get upon a higher level if we may, and breathe oftener and deeper of spiritual things. Many of our people think religion is a good thing for old men and women; we want to show them it is a better thing for the boys and girls. They think religion a good thing to die with; we want to show them it is a better thing to live with. They think it is gloomy and sad; we want to show them that it is the most joyous and glad thing in all the world.

We welcome you because you have, during the past few months, been witnessing, as never before, how to do practical things for God and humanity; and it is just because of this that the Christian Endeavor movement is having more and more the confidence of all. It does not spend all its strength in singing and praying; for it believes in a gospel of service, and it adapts its methods of work to the conditions in which it is placed.

It was a Christian Endeavorer that led the splendid work in Montreal for better government.

It was a Christian Endeavor Society in the State of New York which recently found that deception was being practised upon young girls from the country, and that they were being enticed into boarding-places which were not worthy. They found them better places and stood guard till their sisters found the way thither.

It was the Christian Endeavor Societies in Kansas that helped put legislation upon the statute books which struck gambling and lottery a deadly blow in that State, a Christian Endeavorer drafting the bill in the exact form in which it was passed.

It was the Christian Endeavorers that in Indiana helped to pass the recent Local Option Law in that State, bringing terror and confusion to the liquor interests. Five hundred meetings of Christian Endeavorers in Chicago in one week, and similar work in New York, have helped materially to redeem those cities from corruption.

Yes, we can never forget that it was a Christian Endeavorer in Troy, in the person of Robert Ross, who gave his life to protect the ballot-box; and when that young martyr fell in this holy cause tens of thousands of young men had a new impulse given them to do their duty as patriots at any cost.

And this leads me to say that we welcome you to our city just at this time in our history because you all stand for good citizenship. We believe in "God in politics," and that allegiance to God and patriotism are synonymous. I say all without reservation, for our young women, as well as our young men, are thoroughly in sympathy with and using their influence for this revival of patriotism.

Was it not a young lady who was a Christian Endeavorer who said, "If we cannot have a vote, we can have a voter?"

The women are recognizing their responsibilities for good government, and much of the success of reform movements in Brooklyn and New York is due to their efficient service. Women are often braver than men, and can inspire all. It was Barbara Freitchie who "took up the flag the men hauled down."

We welcome you because you believe not only in the prayers and preaching of God's house, but also in the caucus and the ballot, and that the ballot-box should be sacred as the Ark of the Covenant. There can be no separation of piety from patriotism, and the man who neglects his civic duties is not a Christian citizen.

We welcome you because you are the foe of the political " boss," and you will not have this man to reign over you. We welcome you because you are opposed to the saloon and the evils which go with it, and to all who are trying to undermine in any way the Christian Sabbath and the sanctity of the home. We have some very clearly defined moral issues at least, and we have enlisted, not for three months or nine months, but for the war. We propose to lay aside all that hinders and go in all over and for all we are worth, to win.

At one time the English war department was considering a change of uniform. The Duke of Wellington, thinking he would get the opinion of an old soldier, said, " If you were to fight the battle of Waterloo over again, what kind of uniform would you like to wear? " Quick as a flash the reply came from the scarred veteran: " General, if I were going to fight it over again I should want to go in my shirt sleeves."

The Christian Endeavorers metaphorically have put on this garb for service, and the devil's kingdom is doomed. And if the politicians think this Christian Endeavor movement for good citizenship is only a passing wave of excitement and will soon be over, we will give the same answer that was given by John Paul Jones when asked, " Have you lowered your flag? " " No; we have not yet begun to fight."

Your coming this year has been especially propitious. Massachusetts is proud of its splendid list of governors, and we honor to-day in that position a fearless and incorruptible man, of spotless character, whose voice is ever ready to speak in the cause of righteousness,— His Excellency Governor Greenhalge.

And then we have in His Honor Mayor Curtis one who is also in full sympathy with the moral purposes of our organization. In his position as chief magistrate of our city, he has from the beginning done everything in his power to assist the committee in their preparation for your coming. Nothing has been done by him in a half-hearted, perfunctory way, but ungrudgingly and generously. As a part of the welcome to our city, we want you all to see our Public Garden, which our superintendent of public grounds, Mr. Doogue, has, with lavish hand, decorated for us, making a floral exhibition which has never been equalled. He has made the very flowers in all their beauty speak the welcome in crimson and white of Boston, '95. Yes, welcome, thrice welcome, to the home of Hancock and Winthrop, of Sam Adams and Paul Revere, of Governor Andrew and Colonel Shaw, of Phillips Brooks and A. J. Gordon, the capital of the old Pilgrim and Puritan Commonwealth.

Loyalty is first, and the delegates were ready and glad to listen to the strong words of Rev. A. H. Plumb, D.D., pastor of the Walnut Avenue Congregational Church, speaking the welcome of the Boston churches.

Address of Rev. A. H. Plumb, D.D.

If the generic Christian Endeavorer stood in this presence now, representing after the manner of a composite photograph, in one person the average qualities of all our many thousand guests, and if, too, I could be looked upon as embodying the traits of all the pastors and church-members for whom I speak, then this scene would seem to reproduce one of the most memorable conventions of all the past, when two representative characters came together at an important crisis in the history of the Church; for, about 1,850 years ago, in a city more renowned than Boston, a young Christian Endeavorer, Paul's sister's son, moved by his affectionate enthusiasm for the right, and guided by the wonderful providence of God, went forth to carry a message, and to perform a service, which secured large blessings for all ages to the end of time. And in the office he then fulfilled, he resembled, in important respects, the typical Endeavorer on his visit here to-day.

And when Paul's sister's son met in convention there with Claudius Lysias, the chief captain of the Roman army at Jerusalem, he brought his message to the source of highest power in the ancient world. And in the larger sense there is no higher power in Boston to-day, or in the land, or on earth, than the power of the Christian churches, such as I have the honor here and now unworthily to represent, — power to give light and guidance, power of wholesome, salutary control; for our Lord, who said, "All power is given unto me in heaven and on earth," says to the members of his churches, "Ye are the light of the world; ye are the salt of the earth." The greatest triumphs gained on this planet, the mightiest deeds, the worthiest works, are those spiritual conquests by which the churches recover souls from sin, and build up character in exalted and imperishable worth. This government of ours, of state or nation, could not last an hour but for the presence and power here of the Christian Church. All right progress depends on that power; all true advance is chiefly valuable as it contributes to the aims of the Church.

And it was because Claudius Lysias was the chief captain that great interests depended on the sort of welcome he should give to the young Christian Endeavorer as he came into that convention. It was worth a great deal to Paul's sister's son, and to the coming ages, that the chief captain took him by the hand. And it makes a vast difference to the young Christian Endeavorer who comes up here to-day, it makes a great difference to the world at large, how the Christian churches receive this youth.

And so I magnify my office now, as in behalf of the greatest power on earth, the churches of Christ, I meet this typical Christian Endeavorer as he comes up to this Convention, the Paul's sister's son of our time; and like the Roman captain of old, I take him by the hand and give him cordial greeting as a welcome messenger sent of God.

Great as the chief captain was, he was not too great to learn from the youth he held by the hand, nor too proud to ask for the information that youth had come to impart. Even such is the attitude of the Christian churches toward Christian Endeavorers now. "Your young men shall see visions" is the old-time prophecy which has a springing and germinant fulfilment from age to age. It greatly concerns the churches of our time to learn the purport of the visions God is giving to the young. And so behold me now, one and all, as I stand here, the representative of the churches, and in imitation of Claudius Lysias of old, I take by the hand this nephew of an apostle whom God has sent to us to-day, and with attentive ear and open heart, I inquiringly say, "What is that thou hast to tell me?"

For it is no true welcome of the messenger unless his message is received. And so when I say to this Christian Endeavorer to-day, "What is that thou hast to tell me?" I hear him answer thus: "*The desperate malignity of evil now demands from Christians an alert activity hitherto unknown.*" That, in effect, was what Claudius Lysias heard, as the young man told of the conspiracy against Paul's life. The exigency required action at once. It would not do to wait till to-morrow. There was rallying in hot haste, and all night endeavor with the utmost energy and despatch. Well, now, that is the spirit young Endeavorers show. So imminent now is the peril to all the interests we love, the times are so prolific in dangers for the souls of men, that Christians must be more prompt and aggressive than ever before. The universality of the obligation to testify for Christ and to work for his kingdom must be pressed upon all. Enlist the young early in the work. Organize and train them. Emerson says, "Great is drill." Let them fling out their banners, "The World for Christ," and resolutely, persistently, in all varieties of ways, seek to bring every individual soul here and everywhere into vital union with Christ. The prayer of one of old, "Would God that all the Lord's people were prophets," is being answered now. And it is by the highest authority that any and every true Christian may take up this holy office, for the risen Saviour himself says, " Let him that heareth say Come."

Again I take the young man by the hand and say, "What is that thou hast to tell me?" And this further word he speaks: "*Christians must rise up in the interest of righteousness and take control of civil affairs.*"

Oh, what a sublime spectacle was that when that young Christian Endeavorer, strong in the righteousness of his cause, appealed to that representative of the Cæsars, and, unveiling the plots of the enemies of law, boldly cried, "Do not thou yield unto them." His weak hand, as it lay in the chief captain's palm, held all the power of the legions of Rome at command; for the stern justice of the old Roman made instant response, and by nine o'clock that night an army of soldiers, spearmen and horsemen, 500 strong, were escorting the apostle beyond the reach of fanatical priests and murderous mobs.

So now let good men assert themselves and lay their hands to the helm of affairs. It is not so much the violence of the bad that hinders progress, as the ignorance, apathy, and cowardice of the good. It is a time of fearful agitation and social unrest. And the example of Paul's sister's son, and of the Christian Endeavorer now, plainly says to us that good citizenship comes by improving and strengthening our social institutions, and not by overturning and destroying them, as the anarchist is trying to do, and as some Christian socialists, in their blind ignorance and criminal recklessness, urge us to do.

That early Christian Endeavorer induced the chief captain to act in the interest of law and order; not to take Paul out of the hands of the courts, but to maintain the regular procedures of the law. And the courts and legislatures now, which some of our fanatical teachers malign and deride, the social institutions they traduce and undermine, are the precious fruits of ages of heroic struggle and glorious achievement. The fabric of our Christian civilization is our rich inheritance from a noble past, and it is to preserve and increase its blessings that the young Christian Endeavorers are taking hold of politics now.

Moreover, the young man is telling us, too, that Christians should take control of civil affairs; not to unite Church and State, but to keep each in its place, friendly and helpful to each other, and never either hostile or joined. Paul's nephew invoked the civil power simply to protect the apostle in his right of free speech, equally with the Jews. No special favors were asked. To use the sword to prevent argument and to compel assent is Mahomet's way of promoting religion, though some who have borne the Christian name, unhappily, have often tried it. And like the endeavor of Paul's nephew, that of the good-citizenship Endeavorer now is not to control the government for the benefit of any particular church or form of religion, but simply in the interest of general righteousness, of fair and honest dealing among men, equal protection of all religions, a fair field for each, no special favors for any, leaving every church free to make its own way as it shall be able, by the only legitimate means—the force of the better reason and of a more constraining love.

Once more when I take by the hand this young Christian Endeavorer and say, "What is that thou hast to tell me?" you will observe that he tells me a great deal by what he does not say. He does not speak of himself, but of the great interests he serves. Why, we do not even know the name of that early Christian Endeavorer. He is simply Paul's sister's son, known only by his worthy relationship and his helpful service to an important and imperilled cause. And so this is what he has to tell us more; that *all agencies are to be valued in view of their helpful relationship to Christ and his Church.* The Christian Endeavor Society is called the Church porch. It is nothing in itself, only as it is helpful to the Church of God. What was the name of the lad who had five barley loaves and two small fishes at Galilee? Nobody knows; but this we know, he gave all he had to Jesus, and when the Saviour blessed it the whole multitude were fed, and so the little nameless one is forever dear to our hearts.

We read that the Saviour once spake to his disciples that a small ship should wait on him because of the multitude. And in these recent years an almost innumerable fleet of Endeavor societies has been launched. And

not one of them is christened *Valkyrie* or *Defender*, or is sailing up and
down to make its name great. Oh, no! They are all just small ships that wait
on Christ and help his work. They are not yachts at all, but just "tenders"
attending continually on this very thing, the need of Christ's Church, which is
his body. What wonder, then, that both Church and State hasten here and now
to give hearty welcome to the whole flotilla of the helpful little craft, and their
unselfish captains and crews. Now the spirit of wise co-operation shown by
Claudius Lysias and Paul's sister's son made that early Christian Endeavor
convention a great success. Why, just those two working together added ten
years to Paul's life, ten years of abounding labors, years in which seven of his
mighty epistles were written, to go on blessing the ages while time endures.
Oh, it was worth while to hold that Christian Endeavor convention, in Jerusalem
so long ago, although only two persons came. All the world is glad it was held,
and all the world will be glad of this Convention if the same spirit prevails here.
If we take this visiting Endeavorer lovingly by the hand, and if with a candid
mind we ask him, "What is that thou hast to tell me?." and if we act on the information received, as Claudius Lysias did, no tongue can tell the imperishable good
that will result. For God has not exhausted his gifts to his Church. "Greater
things than these" he is continually saying as he leads us along. And may we
not say that unnumbered souls will bless God through all eternity, because
chief captains not a few, and many young kinsmen of apostles, meet here in Convention to-day?

Then Gov. Frederick T. Greenhalge welcomed the Convention in
behalf of the State, being introduced by President Clark as follows : —

Particularly for the last few years, Christian Endeavor has stood for good
citizenship, not for partizanship, and I believe it never will. We are in all
parties, and we shall probably stay in all parties, but we shall work for the
best citizenship and for the purest political atmosphere. Is it not, then, particularly appropriate that to these royal welcomes should be added the welcome
of the Governor of Massachusetts — especially when we can welcome him not
only for his official position as Governor of the State, but when we can welcome
him for his personal character, for his interest in all good things, for his devotion to civic purity, for his interest in this Convention which he has attended,
and to which he has given not a little thought? It is a great pleasure to me
that I have the privilege of introducing to you Gov. Frederick T. Greenhalge
of Massachusetts.

Governor Greenhalge was received with the most intense enthusiasm ; handkerchiefs were frantically waved, and the chorus gave their
salute. It was several minutes before he was allowed to speak. When
the applause subsided sufficiently to allow him to be heard, he welcomed the Endeavorers to Boston, in behalf of the State, as follows : —

Address of Gov. Frederick T. Greenhalge.

Mr. Chairman, ladies and gentlemen, and if I may be permitted to say so,
brethren and sisters, it is given to me to perform the pleasant task of welcoming
you officially to the Commonwealth of Massachusetts. It has been said that
sometimes it is given even to ordinary mortals to entertain angels unawares.
I cannot say it on the present occasion, because you gave us due notice of your
coming. But I think I do not speak extravagantly when I say that Massachusetts, with all her heart and soul and mind and strength, welcomes this noble
Society to its borders. I think I may say, too, that it is fitting that the representatives of a Christian Commonwealth should extend its greeting. I care not
who plants; I care not who waters; it is always and forever God who giveth
the increase.

I am not disposed to challenge the honors won by any member of this Society I will not say that Dr. Clark was not the first founder of this great Society. I simply desire to point out that from the beginning Massachusetts, kneeling upon the desolate seashore and committing her fortunes and her future to Almighty God, was a Christian Endeavorer in the highest degree, and I will say to Brother Clark, if he will permit me, that this is only a rediscovery of a very ancient society. Why, John Winthrop may be supposed to step down from his pedestal in the public square to join in this hearty greeting which I try to give you. Was he not in the old days a member of this Society? We hear about the man of saintly life who was a priest forever after the order of Melchisedek, and so it is that every true working Christian was, whether he knew it or not, a member of your distinguished order; and so, my friends, I say first, in order to convince you that you are welcome, all Massachusetts, from her Atlantic islands on the east to her mountain barrier on the west, shall be turned into a shrine where your white and saintly Society may kneel, and gather and give back new inspiration and new consecration to the work which you are performing for God and for humanity; and what fitter place could you hold your assembly in than this where you are gathered to-day? I admit there are cities of larger population than Boston, with wider streets, cities that make more noise than Boston, but after all it is the quiet work that tells, and Massachusetts is a quiet worker. You have seen the captain of some great steamship standing on the bridge guiding the great vessel along in the storm in safety. He is not given to loquacity; he is not voluble; he is not shouting out boasts every five minutes; and so Massachusetts, standing on the bridge of the ship of state, does her work and leaves the world to judge of it afterwards. Yes, we welcome you to Boston, to Massachusetts, to Concord, to Lexington, to Bunker Hill. It seems to me as if you may readily fancy that the old hill in Charlestown blazes again to teach you the doctrines of civil liberty; that you can hear again the shot heard around the world more than a century ago. You can hear in Faneuil Hall echoes which teach you the grandest stories of human liberty and human law, of order, progress, justice, equality, and education,—the grandest story ever told to mortal beings! And so, my friends, as you walk about these streets, as you think of the Old South-Meeting-house, you will seem to hear Otis and Adams and Warren again. All these grand traditions and recollections will come back upon you, and you will remember that it is not in natural wealth that the greatness of a State or a municipality consists. It is in the richness of the spirit. It is in the cultivation of the mind. We put our citadel forward as the citadel of ideas which can never be taken except by the superior force of superior ideas, and then we are ready to capitulate, but never before. So as you go about and look at libraries and art galleries and museums, everything that learning and science and art and wit can furnish, always remember that after all and under all and above all is the spirit that has moved 50,000 human beings to gather in Boston to-day, to profess, in the name of the Master, their willingness to go into his service whose service is perfect freedom. My friends, in the name of the Commonwealth of Massachusetts, I welcome you all here to her soil. From whatever State you may come, from whatever territory, from whatever country, whether it be from Palestine or the British Isles, whether it be from California or Canada, you are all welcome here with all the welcome that the great heart and soul of Massachusetts can give; and let me assure you that long after you have departed the sunshine of your presence will live and abide with us. In the name of the Commonwealth, then, I bid you a cordial and hearty welcome.

Then Dr. Clark introduced Rev. E. R. Dille, D.D., of San Francisco, Cal., a Methodist Episcopal trustee of the United Society of Christian Endeavor. Dr. Dille responded to the words of welcome in behalf of the Board of Trustees of the United Society and of the delegates present.

Address of Rev. E. R. Dille, D.D.

The task assigned me, — that of voicing, in behalf of the trustees of the United Society and these delegates, our grateful appreciation of the right royal welcome we have received, — is one that might occupy me delightfully for an hour or two, but that I am limited as to time, and in this respect am less fortunate than was a young minister in our country once upon a time.

A young lady organist in a neighboring church was captivated by this young minister, and was delighted one Sunday morning to see him in the pulpit, where he was to preach that morning in exchange with her pastor. The organ was pumped by an obstreperous old sexton, who had a habit of stopping when he thought the voluntary was long enough.

This morning the organist was anxious to make a good impression on the young visiting minister, and as the service was about to begin she wrote a note intended solely for the sexton's eye.

He took it, and in spite of her agonized beckonings, handed it right to the preacher, unopened. Imagine that gentleman's feelings when he read, in the fair organist's handwriting and over her signature, this message: " Oblige me by blowing away until I give you the signal to stop ! "

I have unfortunately no such *carte blanche* as that this morning !

Gentlemen who have spoken, I thank you for the words of welcome you have uttered, for the greeting we have received, and for the princely provision you have made for our comfort and entertainment; and to be straightforward about it, we accept the splendid hospitality of your great city and Commonwealth in the spirit in which it is tendered.

We already feel that it is a delightful thing to come under your roofs and into your sanctuaries, and to dwell with you during these blessed days of fellowship and council and peace and prayer; that clasping each other's hands and looking into each other's faces, we may feel anew the pressure of the Hand that was pierced and of the Heart that broke on Calvary for us and for all men.

As we stand to-day in this historic city, where cluster the most thrilling memories that can stir the heart of any American, we feel that we are on holy ground; for Faneuil Hall and Bunker Hill Monument and the Old South Church and the Washington Elm make this forever the Mecca of American patriotism.

And yonder in your classic Cambridge is Harvard College. And our hearts, beneath our Christian Endeavor badges, shall beat with a quicker bound as within those storied walls we remember that General Gage called Harvard College a nest of sedition — and in that nest was hatched James Otis, who proposed calling the Continental Congress without the king's leave, and Joseph Warren, who went gaily to his death yonder on Bunker Hill, quoting with scholarly grace " *Dulce et decorum est pro patria mori.*"

When Sam Adams was a college stripling and took his master's degree at Harvard he argued in his master's thesis that it was lawful to resist the crown itself if the State could not otherwise be preserved; and that college student's thesis, declaring the higher law, was the morning gun of the Revolution; and that morning gun soon found its echo yonder at Lexington and Concord,

> " Where the embattled farmers stood
> And fired the shot heard round the world,"

and in the glorious thunder of Bunker Hill.

And then it were worth the long pilgrimage we have made to drop a tear over the sacred dust that is within your keeping; for sacred shrines to every American are the graves of Channing and Willis and Sumner and Agassiz and Longfellow and Wendell Phillips and Webster and Emerson and Oliver Wendell Holmes and Lowell and Whittier and Phillips Brooks.

And then we are glad to find ourselves in Old Massachusetts, one of the most regal in all the queenly sisterhood of States.

We shall continue our pilgrimage, some of us, to Plymouth Rock, which your Rufus Choate declared to be not a boulder, but the outcropping of a ledge which undergirds the continent. Faneuil Hall, and Independence Hall, Philadelphia, are built upon that granite ledge, and the apple-tree at Appomattox struck its roots into a cleft of the same. Certain it is, the germ of the Republic was in the cabin of the *Mayflower.* Columbus brought the crucifix, but the Pilgrims brought Christ himself.

The hosts of Christian Endeavor gather to-day from every part of our land —from the far North to the Gulf, and from sea to sea; nay, from all continents and from almost all islands of the sea, for our fellowship is world-wide. The United Society says to the North, "Give up," and to the South, "Keep not back;" "Bring my sons from far and my daughters from the ends of the earth," and they have listened and obeyed.

We are here from every land where the language of Shakespeare and Milton is spoken, for our imperial, unconquerable race is one, on both sides of the St. Lawrence, both sides of the Atlantic, and in Australia, that Greater Britain beneath the Southern Cross.

See yonder host hailing from the Dominion,—an empire that has an area forty times that of the British Isles, seventeen times that of the Empire of Prussia, and twelve times that of the Republic of France; a land that has rivers and lakes still unknown to song, and valleys untrodden by the foot of civilization, which will yet resound to the tread of a population as vast as that of Europe.

And if we ever needed a high and pure type of patriotism, it is to-day, when we are confronted with problems more serious and complex than any that ever before appeared in the history of the world,—problems that, like the Sphinx, will have an answer or they will have the life of the nation.

A force mighty and irresistible is at work day and night thrusting upon us graver and graver social questions. These vexed and vital questions cannot be settled by policeman's club or soldier's bayonet; only righteousness can solve them.

There are ominous clouds rising above the horizon; they come seething out of the black depths of ignorance, want, and intemperance, and the unbridled sins and shame of our great cities, and they hold within their depths the sullen thunders and vivid lightnings of anarchism and lawlessness. The Huns and Vandals of the twentieth century are likely to come from our great cities.

If Christianity fails in America, America fails, and if America fails, humanity fails, while if we can make the United States truly Christian we can give to Christ the sovereignty of the world; with America for a fulcrum and the Cross for a lever, we can lift the whole round world up to God.

And here is an army of whole-hearted, true-hearted youth, consecrated to their finger-tips, standing at the golden gateway of the dawn, rich in the high enthusiasms, the unwasted powers, the unspent energies of youth, who shall march into the twentieth century with the swing of conquest, and crown Christ king of nations as he is already king of saints!

The twentieth century! "Before its noon," said Victor Hugo, "war will be dead, the scaffold will be dead, oppression will be dead, bigotry will be dead."

What is the America of the twentieth century to be?

Is it to be the America of the boss and the boodler, of the predatory rich and the wretched poor, of Dives and Lazarus side by side, of labor and capital in senseless and godless strife—the America of the Continental Sabbath and the saloon and the vices, whose name is legion, which are born of the saloon and fostered by it?

And in response to the glowing words of the minister of God who has welcomed us to the churches, the homes, and the hearts of the people of this fair city, let me say that this young people's movement is the re-enforcement to the Church of God that Blucher was to the allies at Waterloo, when the Iron Duke prayed, "Oh that night or Blucher would come!" Blucher has come, and the tide of battle is turning as it turned in that pivotal hour when the eagles of

Prussia, on Blucher's banners, soared above the field, and shone like meteors in the dun smoke of battle in which the sun of Napoleon set to rise no more.

Said a gentleman to me on the way hither: " It seems to me that your conventions are like McClellan's grand reviews—they are magnificent, but they are not war. Does it pay to bring all these people together to do nothing ? "

Pay? As if you could measure this meeting—called not for legislation, not for creed-making, not for the dispensing of ecclesiastical loaves and fishes, but for inspiration and fellowship — by any material computation !

I tell you, the fellowships, the blessed friendships, the contagious enthusiasms, the high ideals, the spiritual uplifts, the equipments for service, that come from such a meeting as this are worth more to America than all the products of all the Minneapolis flour mills and Chicago stock-yards and Boston factories and shipyards and California mines.

And, then, the presence of these International Conventions in our great centres of population, of commerce, and of thought — the presence of these mighty hosts dominated by conscience and consecrated to Christ — is a tremendous rebuke to the pessimism and scepticism and materialism of the age, and a timely testimony to the fact that holy enthusiasm, sincere faith, and a sterling Christian manhood and womanhood are not obsolete in this old world of ours, but are more real and vital to-day than ever before.

To me these great conventions are like visions of heaven to the soul, of the multitude whom no man can number, who have washed their robes and made them white in the redeeming blood of the Lamb, and who sing the new song of redeeming love.

I thank God that we are to have the Convention of '97 in California, the land of sunshine, fruit, and flowers, and in San Francisco, the queen city of the Pacific, throned yonder by the West.

But that Californians are all as modest as violets, outblushing the strawberries that grow there all the year round, — blushing like their world-famed fruits at praise of their own loveliness, — I would tell you something of California; though had I the tongues of men, and even of real estate agents, you would still say, when you come to us in '97, " The half has not been told! "

We have a wonderful empire out there; we have arable land enough to support a population of thirty millions, and then our population would be less dense than that of Europe; an empire of our own, as large as Spain, — larger than the nine States of Delaware, Maine, Maryland, Massachusetts, New York, New Hampshire, New Jersey, Ohio, and Rhode Island combined. Then the salubrity of our climate makes California the sanitarium, the fairer Italy, of the world; its scenery is grander than any beneath European skies, and its variety of productions and climate is so wonderful as to defy even the California genius for exaggeration.

Come, ye wise men and maidens from the East, and help us to make that Ultima Thule, that stopping-place in the westward march of humanity, as happy by man's obedience to the Divine law, as peaceful and holy under the benign sway of King Jesus, as it is marvellous in its beauty, rich in its opulent resources, and splendid in its promise of future development.

Do you know that while Boston is the hub of creation, San Francisco is the hub of America? It is precisely half-way between the easternmost part of Maine and the westernmost point of Alaska ! We invite you to the hub; you are but fellows ("fellys") out here, — the right good "fellows," as this reception demonstrates.

At the conclusion of Dr. Dille's address, General Secretary John Willis Baer read his annual report.

The Christian Endeavor Wheel.

Annual Report of General Secretary, John Willis Baer.

Every useful wheel must have its hub. Every hub, to be useful, should have its wheel. Figuratively speaking, Christian Endeavor is a useful wheel; certainly Boston is the Hub. As we are in the Hub, let us turn the wheel upon its axis, and from the Hub view its revolutions. Its circumference equals that of the globe, and its spokes number thousands upon thousands. Each year the circumference of the Christian Endeavor wheel widens; each year thousands of spokes are added. Last year our wheel was strengthened by 7,750 new societies (or "spokes," if you please). This is the largest increase for any one year since the wheel commenced revolving, fourteen years ago.

Spoke after spoke passes our vision rapidly in this whirl of inspection, in all 41,229. Of these 4,712 are from other lands, the United Kingdom heading the list with 2,645, which figure includes 180 from Wales, 112 from Scotland, and 53 from Ireland. Australia now has no less than 1,509; Africa, 30; China, 32; France, 64; India, 117; Japan, 59; Madagascar, 93; Mexico, 25; Turkey, 39; West India Islands, 63; and so on until every country is represented save five, Italy, Russia, Iceland, Sweden, and Greece.

And now the spokes from· the Dominion of Canada come into view. Ontario, with her remarkable growth of the last year, leads, with 1,995; Nova Scotia, 388; Quebec, 264; New Brunswick, 152; Manitoba, 156; Prince Edwards Island, 62; Assiniboia, 53; British Columbia, 40; Alberta, 15; Saskatchewan, 5. In all, counting 5 in Newfoundland, 3,105, an increase of 1,223 during the past year.

And now our view from the Hub discloses the balance of the wheel, all bearing the familiar colors of the Stars and Stripes. Pennsylvania still leads, with 4,139; New York next, with 3,822; Ohio, 2,787; Illinois, 2,446; Indiana, 1,762; Iowa, 1,563; Massachusetts, 1,309; Kansas, 1,247; Missouri, 1,133; Michigan, 1,082; New Jersey, 1,045, etc. In all, from the United States, 33,412, as against 28,696 last year.

These figures from the United States include 18 Senior Societies, 33 Mothers' Societies (a splendid movement, first started in Kansas), 62 Intermediate companies; and it includes the societies in our schools, in our colleges, in·public institutions of various kinds, in prisons and schools of reform, to the number of 169. It includes that noble regiment of 250, known as the North American Union of German Christian Endeavor. It includes the 7 among the " boys in blue " in the regular army and in the navy of the United States. It includes the societies among the policemen and patrolmen. It includes the companies among the Indians of the North and West. It includes our comrades enlisted in work among the life-saving crews, lighthouses, and light-ships. It includes the Travellers′ Union of Christian Endeavor, an enterprising company. It includes 158 Floating Societies. It includes a regiment of 8,859 Junior companies.

And now for the Juniors. In addition to the 8,859 Junior spokes from ·the United States, there are 339 from Canada and 224 from other lands, making in all 9,122 Junior Societies, with a membership of 340,000. While the numbers of Juniors were included in the enumeration by States, it will be of interest to know that Pennsylvania still leads the Juniors, with 1,023; New York, not very far behind, with 920; Illinois next, with 746; Ohio, 623; Indiana, 470; California, 414, etc.

And now we have counted the spokes as they have swept by our vision,— a total of 41,229 societies, with an individual membership from every clime and every nation, with skins of varying color, of which 480 are red, 20,300 are yellow, 109,400 are black, and 2,343,560 are white; in all, a great interracial brotherhood of 2,473,740.

Our eyes are now directed toward familiar ribbon badge banners, which have been displayed at our conventions of late, and will be presented here during the sessions of the Convention. The banner for the greatest *proportionate* increase in total number of societies during the year, that was first given to Oklahoma, then to Manitoba, then to New Mexico, and which has been in the custody of West Virginia during the last year, will now pass across the imaginary line for the coming year into the hands of our comrades in Assiniboia.

Pennsylvania first captured the badge banner, which is awarded each year for the greatest *absolute* gain. Ontario took it the next year, then returned it to the Keystone State. Pennsylvania last year was obliged to give it up to England, where it has been displayed this year. It is in Boston to-day, and our honored guest who brought it from England's shores can proudly return with the banner, for none of the States have been able to equal the excellent record of the Mother Country. Ontario and Pennsylvania, in order named, were not so very far behind, however. For the second time this banner crosses the " briny deep." Guard it well; we intend to capture it for this side, another year.

There are other banners, however, to be awarded, — the Junior badge banners. Pennsylvania carried two Junior banners from our last convention,—one for the largest total number of Junior Societies, the other for the *largest gain* in one year. Pennsylvania is again entitled to both of those banners.

The Junior banner for the largest *proportionate* gain in number of societies was delivered last year by the District of Columbia to Delaware. Delaware this year must pass her banner to Assiniboia, for that province has surpassed the record of all others. Shall Assiniboia hold two banners another year? When we gather next year we shall know.

England, Pennsylvania, Assiniboia, yours has been a successful year, and the banners you carry from this Convention show that Christian Endeavor is not decadent within your borders. Your efforts, put forth in a spirit of friendly rivalry, were not for the banners, — we know there is no real value in them, — but for the blessings that come to those that valiantly fight " on the Lord's side."

Last year, at the Cleveland Convention, New York State received from China a richly embroidered " umbrella of state," for having reported the largest number of societies that had adopted the Fulton plan of giving "two cents a week " per member for missions. The "umbrella of state " is a peculiarly Oriental object, and is usually presented by the Chinese to high officials that have faithfully performed their duty. New York brings the umbrella to Boston, and this year it will be New York's pleasure to place it in the hands of our lively friends from the District of Columbia, it having been decided that this year the umbrella should be awarded to the union having the largest *proportionate* number of societies using the Fulton plan for giving systematically to missions.

And that leads me to make mention at this time of the missionary roll of honor which will be unrolled in our meetings on Monday. Upon it are the names of over 5,000 societies from 35 States, 7 Territories, 7 Provinces, 4 foreign lands. Each society has given not less than ten dollars to its own denominational home or foreign missionary board for the cause of missions. The total amount as reported on this roll of honor is $149,719.09. In addition to this amount of money which has been given by these 5,551 societies that we have enrolled upon the roll of honor, we find that $190,884.45 has been given by these same societies " for Christ and the Church " in other ways, making a total of $340,603.54, the largest amount given by any *one* society being the $1,900.00 of the Clarendon Street Baptist Church of Boston. So much for the roll of honor, which measures nearly five hundred feet if we use a yardstick; but who can measure its real length and breadth but He who guides us all in our endeavor?

Let me make it plain that the $149,719.09 given direct to mission boards by the five thousand societies, and their gifts of $190,884.45 for other benevolences, represent only the record of the societies that have *asked* to be enrolled upon the missionary roll of honor.

After careful gathering of other statistics and information, and from advice received from the representatives of missionary boards, home and foreign, we find that the societies in the United States and Canada have contributed not less than $425,000 for *missions at home and abroad.*

The largest amount reported to me by any one board is from the Presbyterian Foreign Missionary Board. The treasurer of that board states that during the last year $33,160.53 have been received, and that in the last five years the total is $106,704.77. When you take into consideration that that represents but *one* board in but *one* denomination, and that the Presbyterian Home Missionary Board received $21,330.90 last year, we can praise God for the missionary uprising among the young. But we can do better. We ought. We will.

Each year, too, an increasing number of our members make the following or similar covenant : " We covenant with the Lord, and with those who enter with us into the fellowship of this consecration, that we will devote a proportionate part of our income, not less than one-tenth, to benevolent and religious purposes."

At our convention last year, the Cleveland Local Union was presented with a banner for its excellent record in this revival of practical Christian stewardship. The Cleveland friends have reported another excellent year's work, and Cleveland is entitled to the banner again this year.

Let me mention now, and briefly, too, that the battle for Christian citizenship, which was begun three years ago at President Clark's suggestion, has been fearlessly waged, and has been blessed in promoting a more intelligent spirit of patriotism. *Christian Endeavor is against the gambling-dens, the lotteries, the violation of the Sabbath, and condemns intemperance in every form, stands for total abstinence, for the suppression of the saloon, and for the annihilation of the power of the saloon in politics and in all "parties." Aye, we believe the liquor traffic is the implacable enemy of righteousness and purity, and of Christ and his Church. The saloon must go ! The saloon must go !*

The Chicago Union has had it in its possession for a year the banner awarded at Cleveland for the most aggressive Christian citizenship warfare. Chicago's record this year is even more worthy than her last. It has been decided, however, after careful deliberation, that the report made by the Syracuse Union entitles them to the custody of the Christian citizenship banner for the coming year. How I wish I could share with you the excellent reports of this union and a dozen or more others ! Not one has been accused of partizanship, but each has, through its individual members, stood for the enactment of good laws and election of good men, and has sturdily opposed the enactment of bad laws and the election of bad men. Yes, there *is* a new moral force in the world, and Tammany in New York and Tammany everywhere must meet it, and be overcome by it, for God reigns.

There is one more city union banner to be mentioned at this time, — the one known as "our fellowship banner." It was carried away last year by the largest city union in our world-wide fellowship, — the Philadelphia Union, — and Philadelphia's report for this year secures a firmer grasp upon the banner, for that union has increased "our fellowship" by organizing the largest number of new societies during the last year, the present membership being 452 societies.

The Christian Endeavor "local-union" idea is assuming larger and better proportions every month. It contains so much of the blessed idea of interdenominational fellowship, and its possibilities in the way of inspiration and fraternity are so large, that it is evidently an institution that has come to stay. Many of these unions are doing practical work through their missionary, executive, citizenship, correspondence, lookout, evangelistic, press, and visiting committees.

If one thing has been made clear by the history of these fourteen years, it is God's design to bring the young people of all evangelical denominations together, not for the sake of denouncing denominations or decrying creeds, but in a common fellowship that respects differences and believes in diversity. The fears of those who thought that the Society would destroy all distinctive beliefs, and demolish the principles for which the fathers suffered persecution, have been largely allayed, for it has come to be acknowledged that the Society makes every young person more loyal to his own denomination, at the same time that it makes him more generous toward others.

From our position in the Hub we were counting the spokes in the Christian Endeavor wheel. To carry out our figure, it is time to remark that we have reached the rim of our wheel, the felly. Our "felly" is made up of the fellowship of over thirty evangelical denominations.

Stop the wheel, and the different divisions of our felly are easily marked, bearing different colors as they do; but turn the wheel again, and the felly shows no divisions, though they are actually there. The various colors, as they revolve, have blended into one, so that our felly shows but one color,— the blood of the Lamb that was slain for the sins of the world.

In the United States the denominational representation is as follows: the Presbyterians still lead, with 5,283 Young People's Societies and 2,269 Junior Societies; the Congregationalists have 3,990 Young People's Societies and 1,908 Junior Societies; the Disciples of Christ and Christians, 2,687 Young People's Societies and 862 Junior Societies; the Baptists, 2,686 Young People's Societies and 801 Junior Societies; Methodist Episcopal, 931 Young People's Societies and 391 Junior Societies; Methodist Protestants, 853 Young People's Societies and 247 Junior Societies; Lutherans, 798 Young People's Societies and 245 Junior Societies; Cumberland Presbyterians, 699 Young People's Societies and 231 Junior Societies, and so on through a long list.

In the Dominion of Canada the Methodists of Canada lead, with 1,057 Young People's Societies and 122 Junior Societies (most of the societies known as Epworth Leagues of Christian Endeavor); Canadian Presbyterians are next, with 979 Young People's Societies and 108 Junior Societies; Baptists next, with 160 Young People's Societies and 26 Junior Societies; Congregationalists next, with 122 Young People's Societies and 36 Junior Societies, etc.

In the United Kingdom the Baptists lead, with 791; Congregationalists next, with 733; Presbyterians, 182; Methodist Free Church, 175; Methodist New Connection, 132, etc.

In Australia the Wesleyan Methodists lead, and Congregationalists, Baptists, Presbyterians, follow in the order named.

And while this is a long list of denominations, first and last, I believe you will agree with me that, whether in the United States or Australia, in Canada or the Mother Country, Christian Endeavor makes a Presbyterian a better Presbyterian; makes a Methodist a better Methodist; makes a Congregationalist, a Baptist, a Lutheran, an Episcopalian, a better Congregationalist, a better Baptist, a better Lutheran, a better Episcopalian. And, while that is true, it at the same time demonstrates *that the crown of the movement is our blessed inter-inter-*INTER*denominational fellowship.* As a Presbyterian, I say, for one, let us have more rather than less of this fellowship. The Christian Endeavor Society is as loyal a *denominational* society as any in existence, as well as a broad and fraternal, interdenominational, interstate, international, interracial society. "One is your Master, even Christ; and all ye are brethren."

This report is already too long. Time will not permit me to touch in detail upon many practical results of our societies and individuals, such as increased attendance upon the part of the young people upon all regular church services and the midweek prayer meeting; the definite and practical work of the various committees in the local societies; the systematic study of the Bible and an ever-increasing knowledge of its use in hand-to-hand work for the saving of souls; a clearer understanding that the Society is only a means to an end; a determination to get good and to do good. No!—no one man, however privileged, can give you a complete report of what has been accomplished by thousands of societies when the members of those societies declare first, and foremost, personal devotion to our Divine Lord and Master, Jesus Christ; when they adhere to the covenant obligation embodied in the prayer-meeting pledge, without which there can be no true society of Christian Endeavor. Let me drop everything and close by mentioning the best of it all, the very best. I have been speaking a good deal about the growth of local societies, local, State, Territorial, Provincial, and national unions, etc., and have not referred to the additions to churches that have been made from our societies. You will agree with me, of course, that the growth of the local societies " is marvellous in our eyes," but what of the large number that have taken the "next step " and have joined the various churches east, north, south, and west? *In all, 202, 185 have joined the churches since the last convention.* In 1890, 70,000 new church-members were reported; in 1891, 82,500; in 1892, 120,000; in 1893, 158,000; in 1894, 183,650; and now, in 1895, 202,185. In the last six years, 816,335. What a ransomed host!· "Praise God from whom all blessings flow."

How much or how little our individual work or that of the Society has gained this blessed victory, we know not; sufficiently happy and thankful are we to know that these recruits to the number of 816,335 have come from our ranks in six years. Again I say, " Praise God from whom all blessings flow."

Now turn from this retrospect of magnificent achievement, pleasing, cheering, and comforting as it may have been, and with the spirit for the exultation of Christ in our hearts and lives, let us think, plan, and act for the future, believing that if each one of us stands strenuously for the preservation and faithful observance of the Active Members' Pledge, *which is the golden tire that binds the Christian Endeavor wheel together, felly, spokes, and hub,* we shall have before us, when we gather next summer in Washington, a report which shall be a vision as splendid as ever fell on John's anointed eyes on Patmos. God grant it !

The closing prayer was made by the venerable father of President Clark, Rev. Edward W. Clark, Westboro, Mass.

On Boston Common.

Tent Williston.

It is rarely that a more picturesque scene is witnessed on Boston Common than that which was presented in the shadow of the Soldiers' Monument.

The two tents, Endeavor and Williston, with their immense spread of canvas, the moving throng of delegates, decked with badges varied in color and striking in design, the flags and streamers waving in the gentle morning breeze, all presented a picture of enthusiasm not often seen.

The first comers of the great crowd who attended the services in Williston arrived about 8.45. The interior of the tent was richly decorated with flags and streamers. The motto, " For Christ and the Church," was suspended on a banner over the speakers' platform, with the word " Welcome " directly underneath the motto.

The platform for the speakers and chorus was trimmed with laurel, flags, and bunting.

The audience enjoyed itself in singing before the meeting was opened, and it was ably assisted by the chorus many of whom were in their seats a half-hour before the time for opening the meeting.

At this meeting the chairman of the music committee, Mr. George K. Somerby, of Boston, was the leader of the chorus.

At 9.30 Rev. Wayland Hoyt, D.D., of Minneapolis, one of the trustees, who presided, called the meeting to order, and led in prayer; but, before this, he called on the audience to sing one or two hymns.

The devotional exercises were led by Rev. Asher Anderson, of Meriden, Conn., and the Convention really opened with "All Hail the Power of Jesus' Name."

Then followed the Scripture reading, which included Psalms XXIII., XXIV., and C. A prayer followed, by Rev. E. K. Alden, D.D., of Boston.

After another song Mr. Charles E. Allen, president of the Massachusetts Christian Endeavor Union, stepped to the front, and presented a gavel to Dr. Hoyt.

He said that the gavel was made from two ancient buildings. The head was turned from the railings of one of the old pews of the Old South Church. The handle was made from a piece of the gallery of Faneuil Hall. The block was manufactured from a piece of wood from the tower of the old State House.

The gavel was a gift from the excursion committee of '95, while the block was given by the Massachusetts Christian Endeavor Union.

Dr. Hoyt received the gavel with a few appropriate remarks, and then introduced Mr. George W. Coleman, vice-chairman of the Committee of Thirteen, who gave the committee's welcome.

Address of Mr. George W. Coleman.

It is indeed fitting that you should have a cordial "How-do-you-do" from one of the boys on behalf of the Committee of Thirteen. Not only the city and the churches, but the hearts of the young people as well, are open to you, and wide open at that. We have been looking forward to your coming for nine months. And now that you have come, we are going to hold on to you just as long as we can; and if some of you meet your fate and settle here for life, so much the better.

My word of welcome to you on behalf of the Committee of Thirteen is, like all other words, only the shell of the thing it represents. The real kernel, the meat, the soul, of this welcome, is found not in my words, but in the long months of prayer and preparation, the many days of service and sacrifice, and the long hours of anxiety and anticipation that have gone before. But with all its cares and perplexities this has been a sweet and precious season of joy to us, for we have looked forward with radiant hope and exuberant joy to the time when you should come from all quarters of the earth, and bring to this city and to our young people the sweet blessings of your life with Christ.

Perhaps you have heard that Boston is a cold place, that Boston people are cold. Don't you believe it! Our hearts burn within us, and we are consumed with a desire to give you a warm welcome. It is in our hearts to give you such a greeting and welcome as would be fitting if the Angel Gabriel himself should pay the city a visit.

Perhaps you have heard that Boston is very cultured and exquisite. Well, that is so, but we are not. We "don't know beans," but you will, in all probability, before you leave the New England country.

The Committee of Thirteen represent 10,000 Christian Endeavorers who have been especially active in these plans of preparation; and indeed, in some respects the Endeavorers of the whole State are represented by the committee in receiving, as the hosts, this great company of young people, and it is in behalf of the multitude of earnest, wide-awake, consecrated young Christian Endeavorers of this State that I extend to you, one and all, the hand of interdenominational fellowship, the hand of international fellowship, the hand of interracial fellowship.

Make yourselves thoroughly at home among us. Our committees number over 5,000 strong. We desire to leave nothing undone that would administer in any way to your comfort and pleasure. The white caps number over 900, and they stand ready, every one of them, to answer all questions, give advice, and furnish escort. There are over 400 red caps who will be at your service in all matters of registration and entertainment. On all sides you have seen evidence of the greeting prepared for you through the efforts of the decoration committee. And after the sessions of the Convention have closed, the excursion committee will take you in hand and lead you to many places famous in the annals of religious and civil liberty, where all may unite in praises and thanksgiving to Freedom's God.

As it occurs to me now, I know of but one thing that we have neglected in all our plans for giving you a hearty welcome, and that is this : in addition to the beautiful map of the city that has been prepared for the delegates ; in addition to our walking city directories with the white caps, we ought, as a committee, in all fairness, to have provided each delegate with a mariner's compass, so that you might navigate our crooked streets with some hope of arriving at your destination. A Westerner says our streets are nothing but cow-paths, and that you can see where the dog headed the cow off. While we "deny the allegation and would eat the alligator," we have provided every possible help to assist you in your journeying through our highways and byways.

But let us remember that all our plans for a welcome to you, and all your enjoyment and comfort and pleasure are but a means to the end we all seek in this great Convention,— to exalt Christ, to receive the power of the Holy Spirit, to impress and convince the world of the love of Christ.

A little story illustrates my thought. A minister, hearing that a returned missionary was to preach at a certain church Sunday evening, made up his mind that he would find out what church people thought of missionary preachers. He went to the meeting early, and stepping up to an usher asked, "Who preaches this evening ? " "A returned missionary," was the reply. " Do you think it worth my while to stay ? " "Well, you would enjoy it more when our pastor is here; he is a very eloquent man." The minister then passed on to another usher, and then to a third, receiving much the same response in each case. Finally he approached an old lady down near the front of the church. And when he asked her if she thought the service would be interesting, she looked him straight in the eyes and replied, " My dear sir, that depends upon the state of thy heart."

And so I believe the success of our welcome to our guests, and your enjoyment of our hospitality, and the entire success of this whole Convention depends not so much upon the programme or the speakers, not so much upon the officers of the United Society nor upon the Committee of Thirteen, as upon the state of your hearts and the state of our hearts. We welcome you, therefore, above all, in the name and for the sake of Jesus Christ.

The pastor of the Dudley Street Baptist Church, Rev. A. S. Gumbart, D.D., was then introduced to give the welcome of the city pastors and churches.

Address of Rev. A. S. Gumbart, D.D.

It gives me more than ordinary pleasure to extend to you a welcome on behalf of the ministers and churches of Boston. We are glad to welcome you because we believe that your visit will teach us many needed lessons. Any religious movement which has been so signally blessed of God as the Christian Endeavor must contain many important lessons. One of the great lessons which Christian Endeavor teaches us is the value and blessing of interdenominational fellowship.

I am not one of those who senselessly decry denominationalism. Denominationalism, as so many appear to assume, is not the expression of unbrotherliness, or jealousy, or enmity, but of conviction, of differences of interpretation, and arises largely from the fact that men cannot see alike or think alike. A man who thinks, a man who has convictions, naturally gravitates to one or the other of the denominations, even if he does not accept every doctrine held by the majority of the particular denomination with which he is identified. It is only the man who does not think who escapes denominational classification. But denominationalism is dangerous in the proportion in which it prevents or interferes with the harmonious co-operation of God's people in the spread of the Gospel. Christian Endeavor shows us that a man may be true to his own denomination, and at the same time emphasizes the usefulness and blessedness of interdenominational co-operation in Christian work. I regard the Christian Endeavor Society as the grandest illustration of interdenominationalism this world has ever witnessed.

I am free to admit that, at first, it seemed as if the tendency of this interdenominational fellowship was toward a dangerous disregard for formulated doctrine. There was, perhaps, a tendency to lead a few light-headed young people to suppose that it was almost a foolishness to believe anything specific; but that this is no longer so, to any considerable extent, can hardly be disputed.

Another reason why we are glad to welcome you is because Christian Endeavor, as represented at this Convention, will lead many to see that there must be other unused elements of power in the Church.

Before the advent of the Christian Endeavor no one dreamed that we had in our churches the material for the constitution of such a mighty army of enthusiastic workers. Never before were the laity so actively engaged in Christian work as now; and a very large share of the reason for this is due to Christian Endeavor methods. There are about 30,000 Christian Endeavor societies in the United States. This means 30,000 prayer meetings more every week than before the Christian Endeavor was organized. It means, at least, one and a half million meetings every year added to the regular church meetings. It means even more, for there are thousands upon thousands of young people's meetings, every week, held under the auspices of societies not enrolled as Christian Endeavor societies, but which owe their existence, primarily, to the Christian Endeavor movement.

When I first entered the ministry, in certain quarters it was enough to cause a man to be regarded with grave suspicion if it was said of him that he was in favor of "new methods." Methods are not to be despised because they are old, or accepted because they are new, but the reverse of this is likewise true. For this reason, if for no other, we thank God for the Christian Endeavor, — because on account of its existence the Church is growing less shy of new methods, and is developing hitherto unused forces by which her usefulness and power are being multiplied many times over.

Again, I am glad to welcome you to our city because this Convention will emphasize the fact that Evangelical Protestantism is not a failure.

Every now and then some loose-tongued orator volunteers the statement that Protestantism is a failure, or that Orthodoxy has lost its vitality, and is dying of heart-failure. But we have no fear of any such thing coming to pass when we think of the great army of Christian Endeavorers,— noble sons and daughters of Evangelical Protestantism, every one set for the promulgation and defence of the truth. And if Evangelical Christianity in Boston does not receive a tremendous impetus on account of the Christian Endeavor Convention, we may almost expect God to rain down fire and brimstone upon us as he did upon Sodom and Gomorrah of old.

As we look back over the history of Evangelical Christianity, we find many occasions for thankfulness to God. Bohemia, with her plea for the free preaching of the Word of God; England, with her mighty reformatory movements; France, with her memorable struggles; Germany, with her stubborn fight against intolerance; Hungary and the Netherland; Savoy and Piedmont; Scotland, Sweden, Denmark, and Switzerland, with their altars bloody with sacrifices paid to intolerance and fanaticism and misguided zeal for the emancipation of truth, and the victories for religious freedom in our own beloved land, — all these struggles, so painful, so needless, so much to be regretted, God has made to work together for the strengthening of the cause of New Testament Christianity. But I firmly believe that the future will show that the Christian Endeavor, with its spirit of love to all and malice toward none, without sword or torch, without strife or imposition, without fanaticism or intolerance, but with its motto, " For Christ and the Church," as truly expressive of its principles, has done more under God for the advance of pure gospel truth than any reformatory movement the world has ever known.

Mayor Curtis was unavoidably detained by official duties, and Mr. Alpheus Sanford, the chairman of the Board of Aldermen, was deputed to welcome the Endeavorers in behalf of the city.

Address of Mr. Alpheus Sanford.

His Honor the Mayor of this city, being unable to come here, asked me to come as his messenger and extend to you the welcome of the city of Boston. Excuse me if I say this hardly seems necessary. On all our streets, our stores, and our buildings you see the gay decoration of flags and bunting; at our railroad stations and elsewhere you have met the hearty handshake of our citizens ; our homes are open to you, and your banner—" C. E., '95 "— has become familiar to us, as it is seen on every hand. And so I say that these things speak more distinctly and more eloquently of Boston's welcome to you than any words of mine can. The papers of this city have been telling us that you were coming. We have been looking for you and, honestly, we are glad you are here.

Now, Boston is an interesting city. By the way, Mr. Chairman, your committeeman, your efficient committeeman, who spoke to you a few moments ago, told you so much about this city that he has not left much for me to say. Boston is an interesting city in many ways, and we hope you may be able to visit some of our public buildings and many places of interest. I think at this moment of the Public Garden. It is very near to you now, only across Charles Street, and I want you all, before you go, to be sure to visit the Public Garden. As a Bostonian I take pride in it, and Boston herself is proud of the Public Garden. We think here that no place of a similar character can be found in any other city. We hope you will visit as many of the places of interest as you possibly can.

Boston is proud that you are here holding your Convention, and feels honored by your presence. We know something of your Society. We know something of the principles upon which it rests. We believe they are good, and we know you are making an honest and a noble effort. Personally, Mr. Chairman, I feel proud, in Tent Williston, — that tent named after the church in which your Society was formed, — in behalf of this city, this city of Boston, to extend to you a royal and heartfelt welcome. Our city is yours. Our citizens are ready, willing, and generous. Your time here will be limited, but the generosity of our people is without limit. We hope that your deliberations will be successful; that the Society will continue to prosper. And we hope that when the time comes, and it is necessary for you to go, you will not forget this city or the many friends you have met; and, Mr. Chairman, if you permit me one more word,— I have been thinking of this since I began to speak, — should you have a spirited contest as to the place where you will perhaps hold your next convention, and should you feel that the lines are drawn rather sharply, and that it will make some disappointment in deciding the question, let me just give you this word: I think you will make no mistake if you hold the Fifteenth Convention in the same city where you held the Fourteenth.

After the singing of "America," the following responses to the words of welcome were delivered on behalf of the visiting Christian Endeavorers : —

Response by Rev. W. N. Page, D.D., of Leavenworth, Kan.

It is certainly a great privilege and honor to respond to these welcome words on behalf of the great West; but somehow we Western people feel very much at home here in Boston, for either ourselves or our fathers and mothers were the younger brothers and sisters who, years ago, asked for their portion, and went away into a far country. Many of us did not get it, but we went all the same; and we have been there all this time; and during the last year, when Boston sent us the invitation, we came to ourselves, and we said, We will arise, and go to Boston, for she has beans and brown bread and veal enough to spare. And so we have come from the great West — not in rags, and neither are we hungry for husks; we have been, and are, well fed; but the dear old mother, Boston, Massachusetts, like the parable of the Bible, met us afar off, and gave us the kiss. And I am sure she has the best robe, if we can believe the advertisements of all the clothing merchants. And I am sure the fatted calf has been killed; for we, many of us, had roast veal last night. We are here to-day to get a cup of tea out of Boston Harbor; we want to get the old taste in our mouths.

This welcome has touched our hearts. Let me say more seriously that we in the West have gone forth from the North and the East oftentimes with precious seed, but with tears; and, thank God, by the power of Christian Endeavor, we come to-day rejoicing, bringing our sheaves with us.

The great question to-day is a financial question before the country. Many of the politicians and some statesmen say that the next division will not be of latitude, but of longitude; not a Mason and Dixon's line, but a line dividing the West and the East. The leader of the Colorado delegation told me that all along they had their car with the legends on it saying that they were from Colorado and going to Boston; and, at the various places where they stopped, men asked them, "See here, are you silver men going to Boston to teach them what the right currency is? Is that your mission?" I am glad to say that that is our mission. One of your colors is white, and we come to you with the white silver of the West in kind, loving words, thoughts, and deeds. God grant that there may be no division, but that we may be one in Christ. And yet, I am a Western man, although born in New England, in a valley so deep that it took us till nine o'clock before we could see the sun rise. I am a Western man, as some one has said, "from the sole of my head to the crown of my foot." I am reminded of the Babylonian king's dream, which Daniel interpreted, concerning the image whose head was of gold and whose trunk was of silver. We are here to-day in the golden head of this Union. Of course, the head contains the brains. Well, to be honest with you, to tell you the truth, I believe that is true very largely. Our men of science, our poets, our literary men, our wide-awake, best thinkers, have either been New Engand men or from New England descendants. We acknowledge the thought, the power, the culture, the force, of New England, and that Boston is her Hub. And yet, when you take this great Union, and remember that the larger share of New England sons and daughters to-day are not in New England, — they are throughout the great South and the West everywhere,— instead of the Hub, Boston is but a fly-speck on one of the spokes. Another thing you will remember is, that if the brains are in the head, the vital powers are in the trunk; and we, in the great central West, represent a great central figure. The forces of this great Union have been poured into it. All along through the valley of the Mississippi and the Missouri to-day there is smiling in the face of the Lord one of the most wonderful harvests the world has ever seen. The heart is not in the head; it is in the trunk, thank God. The heart is in the West. As for the spinal cord, — the great sympathetic nerve, the great nervous system between the head and the heart, — you see it here to-day in Boston; it is here in the power of the Church of Jesus Christ. The whole body under God is bound together.

Some few weeks ago I was in the city of Pittsburgh, which is the centre of a great iron mining district. I never saw such magnificent horses as they have in that city. One day I saw a magnificent team of four mighty horses with a load of iron get stalled. They could not move it. The driver was a wise man. He got down and went to one of the magnificent horses and talked to him, and then to another, and then to another, and then to the fourth. Then he quietly got up on his load, and said just one thing : " Now, boys, pull." And every horse settled down into his collar, and you could see the muscles work; together, they drew that mighty load, and went on. It seems to me to-day that we are gathered here one mighty team in the service of God, and the Christianity of the Holy Ghost was given to our own people, and we settled down into that yoke which is easy and which is light, but oh, how strong! We are gathered together, the people of the North, South, East, and West, to glorify and honor Christ and God.

Response by Miss Cora B. Bickford, Biddeford, Me.

Mr. Chairman, Endeavorers, and Citizens of Boston and of the Old Commonwealth of Massachusetts, — What could be more affecting to a band of halting pilgrims than your stirring words of welcome, words that cause the hearts of Endeavorers to glow with enthusiasm? We are indeed moved by the expression that greets us on every hand, and yet we were not wholly unprepared for this wealth of welcome. We had premonition of it when we received the official invitation to make your city our gathering-place for '95. There was an earnestness that sent it speeding on its way. We heard, and our hearts were made glad as we listened. From the moment the echo of that true-hearted welcome reached us, Boston became the Mecca of every Endeavorer. And with faces turned westward, we have looked on your thoughtful preparation for our every want and comfort, and, as we have watched, we have prayed that the richest blessings might attend you, that this gathering might be a Pentecostal season in spirit and fact; and when our hearts have been too full for other utterance, we have found expression in song. We have sung with the spirit that would help the cause along; we have sung with the spirit of the 50,000 strong. And your summons has not been unheeded; we have come up to keep with you the annual Feast of the Passover, to celebrate anew our liberation. The journey has led many of us into new pastures and by untried paths. Our message to you to-day has already been recorded. The Lord Jehovah is our God, and in him do we trust. We have little need to ask of you, " How fares it, fellow pilgrims ? " The light of peace shines in your countenance ; the joy of hope is in your hand-grasp, and no good thing has been left out. The reality exceeds all expectation. It is worth all these miles of pilgrimage to look into your faces. You have opened to us your city gates, your homes, your hearts, and may we merit the confidence. During these days of conference, prayer, and song, may our hearts be united with yours in one common purpose, loyalty to the King of kings. And when this gathering-time is over may we go forth with songs of courage for the victories to be won; may it be with faith, may it be with love and the blessed memory of true-hearted service, to go on, till within the gates of the Eternal City we again meet and hear the perfect greeting — not " Welcome," but " Well done."

Response by Rev. Walter H. Brooks, D. D., Washington, D. C.

When, a few weeks ago, I was invited by one of the trustees of the United Society of Christian Endeavor to be present on this occasion, I knew not what to say, but finally I decided, after receiving an invitation from the secretary, to be present, and to make some remarks at this meeting. I am glad to be present, glad to look into your faces, glad to hear these words of welcome which have come to us in this stirring song that has been sung; words of welcome which have come to us from those who spoke for the city of Boston, and for those who spoke for the pastors and churches of the city; words of welcome that came from every side. And as I think of these words of welcome, inviting me and the millions whom I represent in my blood and lineage to a prouder and a nobler fellowship, I thank God and take courage. I walked only yesterday through the garden just beyond this, and I saw written over an archway these words: " Fidelity — Fellowship," and I thought on them. We must be faithful to God, faithful to all that gives truth to us; and we must enjoy, as far as possible, the highest and the sweetest Christian fellowship. I confess, brethren, I long for the fellowship of the saints of God, and this is an occasion that inspires me with hope. Think of those who are confined simply to themselves; they become despondent at times. There may be at this very day a question whether a man like myself shall speak in an audience like this. I thank God for this privilege, and I thank God that it has come unasked, unsought, and that you have shown that out of the one blood God has created all men for to dwell upon the face of the earth, and One is our Redeemer, even Christ.

And, Mr. President, I want to say that we are Americans, though our fathers came not here in the *Mayflower*. We speak the language of this country — not German, not French, not any other tongue, but the prevailing tongue of this land. We think after your modes of thought; your God is our God; and this land is ours, here to toil, here to live, here to die, and I welcome this work.

We have a society in our church. I will say that in my own denomination there are a million and a half colored people. We have one colored Baptist in every five black men in the land. We have a society of two or three hundred in my church. I see the power of this organization, these thousands of young people under a higher, deeper, and broader Christian culture. And this is the method, this is the thing under God that shall lift the masses so that we shall be sober, upright, straightforward, conscientious Christians. And the songs that stir your hearts shall stir our hearts and make us greater.

Dr. Hoyt then announced that Rev. H. G. Scudday, of Tyler, Tex., was prevented from being present by a delayed train, and Rev. Gilby C. Kelly, D.D., of Owensboro, Ky., a member of the Board of Trustees of the United Society, was announced to speak in his place. Dr. Kelly's speech was as follows : —

Response by Rev. Gilby C. Kelly, D.D., Owensboro, Ky.

A first visit to Boston, the seat of " ancient founts of inspiration," would be an unforgetable event to any impressionable person. The circumstances of this, to many of us, first visit; the presence here on the historic Common of tens of thousands of Christian young people from all the States and Territories and the Provinces; the threefold welcome that has been so cordially and eloquently spoken by the Committee of Thirteen, his Honor the Mayor, and the churches and pastors through their respective representatives, make the occasion epochal in its suggestions and experiences.

This astonishing Convention is a witness to the unifying force of Christian Endeavor.

The chief minister of religion in ancient pagan Rome, as subsequently in Christian Rome, was called, " Pontiff," which, being interpreted, is " *a maker of bridges.*" It is surmised that the name was applied because the first bridge over the Tiber was consecrated by the High Priest. The Christian Endeavor Societies have raised up more than two million pontiffs who are joining the opposite banks of the rivers of Zion and converting the dwellers thereon from rivals into allies.

They are not only uniting in brotherly accord the parted, and alas ! sometimes warring tribes of Protestant Israel, but also former alienated divisions of the American Commonwealth. We are here from the South, from every State of the South. Yesterday forenoon, as the special train that bore the delegates

from Kentucky and Alabama was speeding hither across the State of Massachusetts, it stayed for a brief while at Pittsfield. In a moment a group of our
young people were on the platform waving Christian Endeavor banners and
singing Christian Endeavor songs. Presently, as I sat in the coach, I heard
"Old Kentucky Home" swelling on the air, then "Dixie." I wondered for a
moment, "How will Massachusetts receive the singing of our Southern songs on
her soil?" Before I had quite satisfied myself that she would be pleased, "My
Country, 'T is of Thee" burst on my ears. Misgiving gave place to assurance.
Christian Endeavor beautifully exemplifies the principles: Many denominations, one Christ; many States, one America.

You will pardon me for adverting to the fact that you are indebted to the
South for some of your best gifts. There is Patrick Henry, who, with your own
James Otis, fired the souls of the colonists to the highest pitch of resistance of
oppression; there is George Washington, "the father of his country;" there is
John Marshall, thirty-four years Chief Justice of the United States, of whom
your own Judge Story says: "The Constitution, since its adoption, owes more
to him than to any other single mind for its true interpretation and vindication;"
and lastly, there is the Gulf Stream.

I was pleased to hear the words of the colored brother who preceded me.
I am no exception among public men of the South when I say it is with feelings
of utmost good-will that I stand with him upon this platform, doubly hallowed to
patriotism and Christianity.

Observing men in the South see the course of empire turning our way. I
would give you generous warning to-day. The South is reaching for the iron
crown of Pennsylvania and the distaff, the sceptre of Massachusetts. The time
is coming and now is, as we verily believe, when she will carry iron to Pittsburgh and cotton cloth to Lowell. Year by year the attendance from the South
at this annual feast of tabernacles increases. When Christian Endeavor comes
to be better understood among us we confidently predict that the representation
from the Southern States will equal that from other parts in which Christian
Endeavor has had free course almost from the beginning.

Response by Mr. G. Tower Fergusson, Toronto, Ont.

It gives me pleasure to be here and speak on behalf of Canada. If I might
be permitted to follow the brothers who have preceded me, I would say we
have good things up there, too, — plenty of iron, plenty of coal, and the influence
of the Gulf Stream. We have a noble history, and we have a solid financial
structure built on a gold basis. No trouble about it.

Now, in coming here to speak, it has occurred to me that while these
addresses of welcome have been delivered in eloquent words and in kind sentiments, they come too late. Most of us have had twenty-four hours of welcome
before we heard these addresses at all. We found the committee's arms open
to receive us. We have seen Boston beans. We have known that this city
was indeed welcoming us. There is just one thing in connection with the
words that fell from the lips of the first speaker, when he said that if any delegates here were to meet their fates he would be inclined to wish that such
should make their stay in Boston, to which I would make reply. I may tell him
frankly that if any of our delegates meet their fate while here, that fate has
got to come to Canada, whether male or female.

While we are separated politically, while we are separated because of our
different denominations, there is the one grand and broad platform on which
we stand, — love for a common Saviour and a desire to be of service to him.
In our Christian Endeavor fellowship we ever must keep this before us, because
if the Christian Endeavor principles and the Christian Endeavor movement are
to spread, we must have this mighty, this grand, this common, standard. We
cannot give up our denominational differences, we are not likely to give up our
international differences. There is that grand common ground on which we
stand and must stand ever, — love to the Divine Saviour and a desire to be of
service to him. Yet in that is there not the thought that with all our differ-

ences we come together, and with a united effort against the enemy, standing shoulder to shoulder, we shall speak for Christ with a voice and with a tone that could not otherwise have been uttered or heard?

We from Canada thank you heartily for your welcome. We are going to stay the five days. I am perfectly sure that we will go back again better satisfied with Boston, better satisfied with Christian Endeavor, and more firm in the conviction that "One is our Master, even Christ; and all we are brethren."

The morning's programme was completed by the reading of Secretary Baer's annual report, by Rev. John Barstow, Medford, Mass.

Tent Endeavor.

Ten thousand people listened to the Christian Endeavor speakers in Tent Endeavor.

Every seat under the tremendous spread of canvas was occupied, and the ushers had to roll up the sides of the tent, in order that the crowd outside might catch the voices of those who spoke.

Lieutenant-Governor Wolcott received a tremendously enthusiastic greeting.

Trustee Rev. John T. Beckley, D.D., of New York City, presided. Before introducing the Lieutenant-Governor, Dr. Beckley said that for three years he had held office in the city of Boston; had been a member of the School Board, and he was much prouder of that connection than he would have been if he had been a member of the last congress.

The interior of the tent did not look bare, although it was so large. The platform was decorated with evergreen wreathed over wide stripes of red, white, and blue bunting. Just back of the sounding-board, under which the speakers were to stand, hung a great banner, marked "C. E. For Christ and the Church," and below this the single word, "Welcome." On each side of the sounding-board the English flag fluttered, and just outside the American Stars and Stripes were stretched. Here and there throughout the tent the flags of different nations were seen blended with long streamers of the Endeavor colors.

At 9.30 Rev. W. H. Allbright, D.D., of Boston, stepped forward under the sounding-board to begin the regular morning service, although it had really commenced some time before, while the singing was growing stronger. He asked the chorus and congregation to sing, "Onward, Christian Soldiers;" and Mr. George C. Stebbins, of Brooklyn, N. Y., the musical director, whose name is known by every one, led the singing.

At 10 o'clock, when Mr. Stebbins stepped forward again, after Dr. Allbright had declared the devotional service ended, to lead the singing of Dr. Smith's "Hymn of Welcome," which is given elsewhere, there were at least 10,000 worshippers under the immense canvas covering; and the volume of sound, when Winslow Simond's cornet rang out, was tremendous.

And still the crowd poured in and filled the space back of the benches. At 10.20 Mr. A. J. Crockett, president of the Boston Local Union, made an address of welcome for that body. He also presented to Chairman Beckley a gavel, the head of which is made from wood taken from the old John Hancock House, built in 1737, on Beacon Street, and the handle from wood cut near the famous prison pen of Burma.

Address of Mr. A. J. Crockett.

If anything more can be said to assure you that you are welcome to this beloved city of ours, tell me what it is and I shall be only too glad to say it.

Before you had touched foot upon this historic soil, many of you, if not all, were welcomed by representatives of the reception and accommodation committees; but the rank and file of our young people have not yet had the opportunity of greeting you as they would like. On their behalf, on behalf of the six thousand members of the Boston Christian Endeavor Union, who have nobly supported the Committee of Thirteen in their work, and who have done all in their power to make everything ready for this great Convention, I bid you a most hearty, and cordial welcome. We have found great pleasure in preparing for your coming, and now we are glad to receive you.

The Endeavorers of Boston are a loyal body of young people,—loyal first of all to their Master, Jesus Christ, loyal to their church, loyal to their pastor. Their motto is "Boston for Christ." To that end they are laboring; and we rejoice that the people of our city must now see and must now come in contact with fifty thousand of the most devoted, most enthusiastic, representatives of the vast army of nearly three million Christian Endeavorers who are consecrated to the work of bringing the whole world to Christ.

We welcome you because this Convention will impress upon our citizens as never before the fact that Christian Endeavor stands for good citizenship, for missions, for evangelistic work, and for the observance of the Lord's Day after the good old New England fashion.

We realize that one of the greatest enemies of the Church and of all that pertains to Christian citizenship is the licensed, the legalized, saloon. During the past two years we have been working to break down this giant evil. The presence of such a vast army of fellow Endeavorers who are working along these same lines will give us fresh courage for future battles.

We welcome you because your very presence in this city will be instrumental, in the providence of God, in doing more to advance the cause of Christ here in our midst than all the Christian people of Boston could do in many years. There is power in numbers, when every individual of the mighty host is filled with the spirit and the power of God.

We have been praying that you might come to this Convention full of the Holy Spirit; that we might have a Pentecostal season the like of which we have never seen here before. I know that our prayers have been answered, for the spirit is already manifesting itself in power, and will more and more until the close of the Convention.

We welcome you, fellow Christian Endeavorers, because conservative Boston needs the stimulation of your enthusiasm. You have brought consecrated enthusiasm with you; you will leave unbounded enthusiasm behind you. We are glad of that, and we are also glad that you will take back with you more enthusiasm than you brought.

We welcome you because we want you to see Boston and all its places of historic interest. We want you to visit Faneuil Hall and the Old South and Old North Churches, and Bunker Hill and the grave of John Eliot, and let them speak to you of the past. May they send a thrill of patriotism through your veins, and may they inspire you to rally again and again around the standard of good citizenship, until politics shall have been purified and our cities set free from the bondage of the godless, unprincipled, political boss, wherever he may be found.

The Endeavorers of Boston who have attended previous conventions and who have enjoyed the unlimited hospitality of other convention cities are glad that it is our turn, our privilege, to act the part of the host; and if it be possible, our welcome to you is doubly warm and cordial because of the many kindnesses we have received at your hands.

To none of our guests do we extend a more hearty welcome than to our brothers and sisters from the other side of the imaginary line, from beyond the broad Atlantic, from the British Isles, from the countries of Continental Europe, from India, from China and Japan, and from the Islands of the Sea.

May we not forget that this is an International Convention; that while we may speak different tongues, and our homes, our fields of labor, may be in widely separated parts of the world, we have met here in this city, with its cosmopolitan population, as brothers and sisters, one in Christ Jesus, fellow laborers with God and for humanity, — one in heart, one in aim and purpose, serving one and the same Master, marching under one banner, and that the banner of the Cross.

We as young people welcome you to our homes — your homes, for what is ours is yours for the time being; and I am sure the pastors of Boston will not object if I also, in the name of the Endeavorers, welcome you to our church homes.

Next Sunday we shall have you with us in our churches. What delightful meetings of prayer and conference we shall have together! We are looking forward to those meetings with great joy and hope. It is a privilege and blessing which no other convention city has enjoyed, — one of the many advantages of having no general session on Sunday.

Almost immediately upon the return of our delegation from Cleveland, fired with the enthusiasm of that convention, the Boston Union appointed a committee to secure the Convention of '98. The latter part of August that committee was thoroughly organized and had its work well under way.

The life of that committee was short. You know how San Francisco was obliged to give up this Convention. We sympathize with her in that great disappointment, and we trust that in the near future her patience may be rewarded with the grandest convention ever yet held.

The Endeavorers of this city stepped in to fill the gap, and before the close of September we were wondering how we could take care of the great Convention of '95; how we could do in less than ten months what most convention cities have had two years in which to plan for. But we have done it after a fashion; we have done our level best in the short time we have had. You are welcome to what we have to offer you; we wish we could have done far more for you.

In the midst of these decorations of crimson and white, the colors of the Boston Union, we welcome you, and we beg that you take the lessons they are meant to teach. The crimson is the symbol of the shed blood of Christ; the white is the symbol of purity. May these colors impress upon us the thought that our lives have been made white and pure through faith in the shed blood of Jesus, our Lord. May we never cease to labor to bring lost men to Christ, that their sins may be washed away in his blood, that their lives may be made as white as wool. That is our mission as Christian Endeavorers.

May the blessing of heaven rest upon you while you are in our midst! May you leave blessings for our churches, for our Christian Endeavor Societies, and take rich blessings to your churches and to your societies!

Then Rev. M. D. Kneeland, D.D., pastor of the Roxbury Presbyterian Church, Boston, extended the welcome of the city pastors and churches.

Address of Rev. M. D. Kneeland, D.D.

We surrender. The Goths took Rome. Coxey took *in* Washington. Christian Endeavor has taken Boston. Our English cousins thought it wise, nine months after Bunker Hill, 120 years ago, to make a trip into the country, and no foreign army, from that day, has held Boston; but now, we surrender,— surrender unconditionally, surrender enthusiastically, bag and baggage, streets and markets, homes and buildings, lads and lasses, and bow our best welcome to this victorious army of the nineteenth century knights and maidens. The upper half of the white flag of surrender is the crimson of hospitality.

At last, the world has come to the Hub. You are all spokes of the Hub to-day, — fifty or sixty thousand spokes. Quite a wheel that! Its buzzing, whizzing, singing, are heard around the globe.

Christian Endeavor is God's high-gear bicycle, by means of which he is girdling the world with righteousness. Boston is certainly the hub of this wheel, because this is the centre, and in the Portland suburb of "greater Boston " the first Christian Endeavor cradle was rocked. That baby has proved to be, in fourteen years, a very Medusa, since every hair of its head is to-day a Christian Endeavor Society. All honor to that man of a magnificent idea, which God inbreathed, and has so signally blessed, — Francis E Clark.

The churches of Boston welcome you, one and all, of whatever order and faith, to this largest *religious* gathering in the history of the world. We welcome you to the religious life of our city, which you will find to be eminently practical and large hearted, — as its numerous hospitals, asylums, and charitable organizations witness. You will not find our hand-grip as stiff and icy as you have imagined it to be, nor our faith weak and flabby, nor our piety formal and worldly. A few years' residence in the home of my Puritan ancestry has convinced me that the reputed icebergs of Boston culture are largely melted in the Gulf Stream of honest, hearty appreciation of true worth; that a genuine faith in God and righteousness is flowing strong and pure underneath ceaseless surface questionings and agitations, and that conscience controls public opinion in this very city as in few cities of the land, and when once awakened, it is simply invincible.

We welcome you to our throbbing *literary* life, with its genuine as well as its fictitious culture, and its superior educational and musical advantages. The common school, the direct offspring of " the little red schoolhouse," is the heart of that system which begins with the kindergarten and graduates at Old Harvard. Palsied be the hand that would apply the torch to the destruction of that bulwark of liberty — *the public school.*

We welcome you to our homes, and promise you our best, — not forgetting brown bread and baked beans, and that sacred emblem of our Commonwealth, "Cape Cod turkey." We cannot, however, promise to give you tea dipped from the harbor, which, it is slanderously reported, we have never ceased to drink since that famous tea-party, and called it Old Hyson. We will give you the best beds we have been able to improvise, but assure you that whether they be cots in the hall or eider-down in the spare room, we will keep you so busy all day that you will not wake in the night-time to find out how much solid sleep there is in them.

We welcome you to our magnificent history. Every street is eloquent with the voices of Pilgrim and Puritan. The oxone of patriotism fills the air. The old Common is no common spot. Faneuil Hall, Bunker Hill, and scores of historic centres are holy places. Boston is nothing if not loyal to the old flag, and proud of " America " and its author. Still, our loyalty is not petty and narrow, but so broad that we rejoice to see before us to-day the emblems of all nations and representatives of different climes, especially subjects of that noble mother to us all, Queen Victoria.

But why do we give you glad welcome? Why? Simply because you are what you are, — members of the Young People's Society of Christian Endeavor. You are all "young people," whatever your age, — and Boston is too polite to question these ladies on that point, — young with everlasting youth, young at heart. Youth means strength, courage, enthusiasm. Youth wins the world's victories. Youth shall usher in the millennium. We welcome you because of the promise and potency of youth.

We welcome you because you are a "society," an organization. Organization to-day, more than ever before, is point, purpose, and power. The world bows before power, especially moral and spiritual power. We would not be mortal were we not stirred, thrilled, and captured by what we see here, which

I do not hesitate to call the grandest exhibition of spiritual possibilities since the time of the Reformation.

We welcome you because you are " Christian " men and women. The close of the nineteenth century has little need of anything that is not Christian. The more fully Christian it is, the larger shall be its place in the future. This Christian Convention means more than a lark, a picnic, a dress-parade, more than talk, crowds, hip-hip hurrahs, more than statistics and theories; it means light, life, " Christ for the world and the world for Christ." Henry Thoreau was once asked how much wood he burned. The philosopher answered, " It is not how much wood I burn, but what I do when I am warm." Christian Endeavorers, it is not the amount of show and noise that we make, but what we do with our light and heat for God and humanity. " Christian " means that Christ, crucified and risen, is our central Sun. Reading the Bible, uniting with the Church, yes, keeping the cast-iron pledge, however important, are but steps in the Divine life. Underneath must be a saved soul, a Christly character, a Christlike enthusiasm for humanity. God pity that small type of Christian who in this age of our Lord is not longing and struggling to help save somebody, somewhere, somehow.

There are other things which the " C " in our five letters denotes, and to which we need but allude. It means always *temperance over against the saloon; purity over vice; the Sabbath Day over against seven days' work, the Sunday theatre, the Sunday baseball, the Sunday newspaper.* It means, every time and everywhere, *good citizenship over against municipal rottenness* and political demagogism.

We welcome you once more because you are " Endeavorers," i.e., Christians on duty. It is one thing to be merely a professing Christian, all properly enlisted and uniformed, and an infinitely greater thing to be a Christian on duty. Such a one says, with the prophet whose lips had been touched with a live coal, " Here am I, Lord; send me." The Apostle Paul is our Sir Galahad, the knight errant of Christian Endeavor, as he rises from the Divine vision with, " What wilt thou have me to do? "

Endeavor; do. We cannot all go with Paul on missions to the heathen; but we can and will be missionaries of Christ at home, on the street, in the shop, the store, the study ; and we will, with God's help, enable our mission boards to send forth, the coming year, a still larger number of missionaries than ever before in the history of the United Society.

We welcome you, not only because of what you *are*, but also because of what, after fourteen years of testifying, we believe that you *do, and will, stand for* in the eyes of God and man.

First, *Christian unity.* In our judgment the *United Society of Christian Endeavor* has done more in its short life to break down sectarian barriers, and to draw different denominations together, than all other forces combined during the same period.

Second, you stand for the *salvation and training of the young.* In your Junior and Senior work you follow not only the experience of the most successful experts of the ages, but also the example of the Divine Teacher, who said, " Suffer little children to come unto me; of such is the kingdom of heaven." If Christian Endeavor methods shall aid in making such an impression on the twentieth century that it shall spend less time on hopeless old sinners and far more time in saving the coming generation for Christ, it has done a magnificent work, and, though it do nothing else, shall leave a royal heritage to the generations that follow.

Third, Christian Endeavor stands for fidelity to Jesus Christ. It bears in its heart the world's Redeemer. It clings to him as its living, personal friend. It shows its love to him by loving those for whom he died. " Christian Endeavor " may mean " Christ exalted." It says, not only " Back to Christ," but " Forward with Christ." As long as it halos his brow — and may God grant that it may never bow to any " other name " — its mission shall be as broad as Christendom itself.

We might give one other reason, a selfish one, for welcoming you to Boston.

We need you, — your spiritual enthusiasm and uplift; the Christ whom you know. We have a right to expect great things from these vast gatherings. Boston needs more than anything else *a genuine revival of true religion.* Our prayer and expectation is that the Holy Spirit may brood over these assemblies, revive the hearts of all listeners, and baptize our beloved city and Commonwealth with saving power.

It was once my privilege to see the sun rise over the Jungfrau in the Swiss Alps. The glowering morning was clad in mists and clouds. Every bush and shrub was bedewed with the tears of midnight. Our early morning excursion seemed in vain. Even the guide said, "We'll have to try again." He had no sooner spoken than a strange sight occurred. Far yonder, one corner of the curtain which hides the face of the sun lifts gently at first, then rapidly, as though moved by an eager hand. All along the line, a battling of mighty forces. Now the mists are masters. Now struggling sunbeams shine shimmeringly. Ten thousand times ten thousand slender darts pierce the black dragon, and his quivering form rolls backward. The soft footsteps of the glad morning angels are followed at last by the mighty rushing battalions of victorious day. Splendor on pinnacled peaks; glory on snow-capped and ice-crowned mountains; inexpressible and never-to-be-forgotten beauty and grandeur. The sun had risen on Jungfrau, the beautiful maiden of the Alps, and banished mists and darkness.

Fellow Endeavorers, our mission is the mission of God's sunlight. "Let there be light" is the first command. "More light" cries the dying Goethe. "Ye are the light of the world" witnesses the Christ. Our work is to reflect the sunbeams of our adorable Enlightener "until the day dawn and the day-star arises." Our united prayer shall be, "Come quickly, Lord Jesus."

Chairman Beckley then introduced Lieutenant-Governor Walcott by saying, "No Commonwealth has had nobler men at its head than the old Bay State; and I am proud this morning to present the distinguished representative of the State, Lieut.-Gov. Roger Walcott." His Honor received a tremendously enthusiastic greeting, and the applause was warmly and frequently given throughout his address.

Address of Lieutenant-Governor Roger Wolcott.

I esteem it a high privilege that I am able to bring the word of greeting on behalf of the old Commonwealth of Massachusetts to this vast host of earnest men and women. I have not the right to speak to you as one of your own number; but short-sighted must be that man, as he walks our streets or as he faces this great host, who does not feel the deep significance of this great movement; sluggish must be the pulse of him who does not feel in his blood the inspiration of these great numbers, the uplift of these scenes, the feeling that here is a host gathered from every part of our own broad land,—from the generous and broad West, from the warm-hearted and sunny South, from the lands beyond the sea,— brought together here by a high religious and moral purpose, to feel the high inspiration of numbers and the splendid impulse of a lofty common purpose.

My friends, it seems to me that in the very inception of this movement the thought that inspired it, the thought that gave it name, was happy and blest. I know of no two words in the English language that are more freighted with deep significance. I know of no title that you could have chosen that would be more heavily weighted with blessing and Divine inspiration than these two words. I know not what to you may be the special inspiration and significance of your colors; to me the white speaks of moral purity that is as clear and as pure as the snow upon the sunlit mountain-tops. The crimson speaks not alone of the blood shed for mankind by our Redeemer, but it speaks also of that strong current of human blood cours-

ing through the veins of man to-day which has shown in all ages that it
flows with the pulse of high appeal, that it is ready to pour itself out for noble
causes, that it responds to-day, as it has done through all the centuries, to the
blood of martyrs, to the blood of heroes, in the long past. And so, my friends,
we open our hearts to you to-day. I know not whether the hospitality of New
England springs quite as freely to expression as that of the great, boundless
West, that magnificent empire of the Mississippi Valley, or the cordial and
friendly hospitality of the States of the great and new South; but I know, my
friends, that when the hand of New England is held out in friendly grasp
the heart of New England follows it. I know that when Massachusetts greets
a man or an assembly with the right hand of fellowship the cordial heart-
beat goes with it, though it may come through halting lips. And so our buildings blossom out with decorations in your honor; the neighboring Public Garden
shows you floral designs the only drawback to which is that I have sometimes
feared that Nature herself might retire from the business of floral display and
confine herself to an all-consuming green of envy.

My friends, Massachusetts, for which I am privileged to speak to you to-day,
Massachusetts greets you with sympathy and respect. We rejoice to know
that you are pledged not alone to carry out a life of devotion, so far as in you
lies, to the pure and lofty example of Jesus Christ. It is not an individual
virtue that you cherish and foster; it is that virtue that goes out into the world
and holds out a helping hand to suffering humanity,—to the poor, to the ignorant, to those less favored than yourself. I rejoice that all through your movement, as I understand it, runs the thread of good citizenship. There is place
in our Commonwealth, there is place in the nation, there is place in every
country on the face of the earth, for devoted, loyal, fearless, incorruptible
citizenship that shall make also the type of effective Christianity. I rejoice
that while, as is your right, you abate not one jot of devotion to your own
denominational creed or belief or organization, whatever that may be, you
see, even above that, the great interdenominational fellowship of Christianity.
It is even, my friends, even as behind and above the devotion that we all
feel to the banner of our own State, we recognize, flying above that, nearer
the empyrean, glowing in colors of splendid brilliancy, the flag of our
own broad nation, "Old Glory," the Stars and Stripes of our country. That is
the larger conception, the greater idea, to which, as I understand it, you are
pledged. And so to-day we rejoice, we are proud, that our city of Boston and
our Commonwealth is honored by this great outpouring of men and women
who are prompted by a high, a noble, a Christian, a patriotic, purpose. My
friends, Massachusetts welcomes you. She asks you to listen as you stand, as
I hope many of you will, upon Plymouth Rock; she asks you to listen to the
lesson of devotion to principle, of sturdy courage, of heroic and splendid enterprise, that Plymouth Rock teaches. As you stand by Concord Bridge, or as
you stand on Bunker Hill, we ask you to learn there the lesson of patriotism,
willing to pour out its blood for a great cause. We ask you to study our school
system; we ask you to visit our schools and learn what public education means
in the Commonwealth of Massachusetts. We ask you to go to our Public
Library; we ask you there to see what splendid opportunities for general education the city of Boston holds out with lavish hand to all its people. We ask
you to visit our Art Museum, not the finest in the world, not the greatest in this
country, but open to all the people, teaching its refining lesson that shall elevate
and purify their lives. We ask you to see, in our public grounds and in our
great park system, the provisions that Boston makes for the enjoyment and
pleasure of her people. We ask you to go to Faneuil Hall and listen to the
words that Webster spoke. We ask you to stand in historic places in all this
eastern part of the State, and we ask you, from whatever country you come, to
carry away with you the inspiration of patriotic devotion, loyal citizenship, yes,
and of high moral purpose. And so, my friends, we welcome you. We thank
you for your presence here this week. We know that we shall owe much to
your presence and to the inspiration you have brought. You will leave the
city of Boston not quite the same as you found it; you will leave the city of

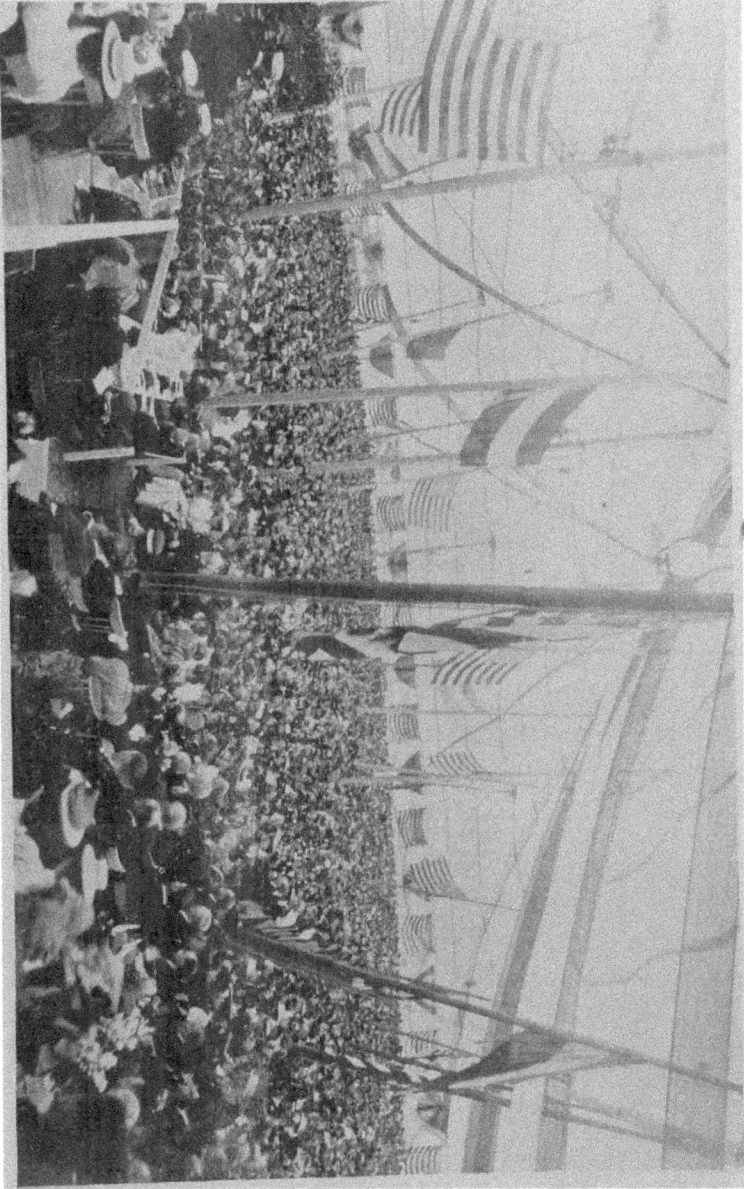

TENT ENDEAVOR — FRIDAY MORNING.

A SECTION IN STATE HEADQUARTERS, MECHANICS' BUILDING.

Boston thrilled through and through by the splendid vigor, the splendid inspiration of your presence; and you will carry away, as you will leave behind, that sense of Christian unity, that sense of national unity, on which our people must build, on which the future of this Republic depends, if it shall continue to be, as it has been in the past, a nation whose God is the Lord.

Then came the response to the addresses of welcome. This was made by Trustee Rev. John Henry Barrows, D.D., of Chicago, Ill.

Address of Rev. John Henry Barrows, D.D.

Our hearts beat with joyful and grateful enthusiasm as we find ourselves in this historic city on this memorably historic occasion. We have been thrilled by these cordial speeches of welcome from the representatives of the Christian Endeavor Societies, of the Boston churches, and the representative of the old Commonwealth of Massachusetts. And now, as representing the United Society of Christian Endeavor, a noble body of men with whom I am proud to be associated, I am asked to reply to these words of eloquent welcome, and to say what is in my heart, and what I believe is in your hearts, at this glad hour. I thank these speakers, and I thank the city of Boston, its churches, its newspapers, its homes, its Endeavor Societies, its Committee of '95, for the princely preparations for our coming and for the royal greetings of to-day.

A few years ago the International Convention was held in the great city of the West which I have the honor to represent, and, with our usual Chicago pride, we called the meeting enormous and amazing and unparalleled. But the Christian Endeavor army sweeps on to grander conquests, and compared with the Boston Convention that Chicago assembly was almost nothing, and as I recall it I have some of the modest feelings of the colored man who joined a secret society with high-sounding titles, and when another colored brother asked him what position he held in the secret organization, he answered, " I am the Most High and Exalted Mighty Supreme King, but I ain't anywhere near the top!" And that is just the way that the truth-speaking Chicago man must feel when he thinks of this Convention.

We have come, in response to your invitation, from every part of America and from all quarters of the globe. We who belong to the great American Commonwealth are especially glad to walk once more, or for the first time, the streets of Boston. We feel that we have come back to the cradle of the nation, to the birthplace of its noblest institutions and ideas. We expect to return with a loftier conception of the meaning and mission of America. We expect to return with a grander faith in our future, springing from a truer knowledge of the greatness of our past. Some people, reading American history, appear to have missed its higher, more Christian, and more distinctive elements. They look upon this land as an Eldorado rather than a possible kingdom of God.

There is a nobler side to our history which only the God-fearing and Christ-honoring student appears to discern and applaud. There is also, I am well aware, an America, both of the past and present, that is despised at home and abroad, — the America of the hoodlum, of the debased politician, of the boodler, the rum tyrant, and the unscrupulous corporation, — which is as much below the America of Winthrop and Washington and Samuel Adams, the America of Whittier and Lowell and Lincoln, as the pavements of Pandemonium are beneath the battlements of heaven. Our nationality is sometimes flaunted before the world as chiefly the arena of machine politics and domestic scandals, the paradise of railroad slaughters and vulgar money-getting; but here in Boston we should learn anew that this is not the true America. In the name of Him in the light of whose Gospel our history has been illumined, I claim that the real, the vital, the nobler, the conquering, America is represented by our Christian patriots, our great statesmen, our martyrs and sages and poets, our law-abiding and Bible-reverencing common people, our Sabbath-observing Christian Endeavor Societies, and that this America is to be guarded and applauded and held up by public teachers, even though she is sometimes so modest that she is not always recognized as the rightful ruler of this New World, — the world which the Spaniard and Englishman pried out of the stormy Atlantic to be a golden continent of hope and freedom for the sorrowing hearts and aching eyes of the older nations of mankind.

Colonel Higginson once said, "To have loved America is a liberal education," and we shall applaud this sentiment when we begin to understand what God has lodged in our past, and what is to be our imperial future; when we begin to comprehend the genius of humanity, of freedom, of independence, which has shaped all that is best in our life; when we realize that the hand of the Puritan whose brain received the training of Oxford and Cambridge laid the foundations of our nationality, and that the spirit of generous fraternity and of faith in God has characterized everything worthily American. The America which we reverence floated across the Atlantic in the *Mayflower*, the fairest seaweed that ever drifted to these shores; it was found in the common schools of New England; it wrote the Declaration of Independence as the charter of universal liberty; it was regarded by Washington when he insisted upon the observance of Sunday by the Continental Army, and declared that every officer and man should endeavor to live as became a Christian soldier.

The true America found expression in the order of President Lincoln requiring the observance of Sunday by the Union forces; and the nobler America rang out in the words of General Hawley at the time of our Centennial celebration, when he said, "Before God, I am afraid to open the Exposition gates on the Sabbath." The true America lives in the hearts of those who are attacking the infamous spoils system, of those who are building up our far Western civilization on the foundations of the Christian church and school. The true America has spoken in these last few years to the forces of municipal corruption through the voice of the great New York reformer, who attributed the downfall of wicked Tammany to the people's faith in the Ten Commandments.

I cannot forget that this is the city of that Christian statesmen, one of the chief founders of America, whom I have reverenced for thirty years, who was once a Lieutenant-Governor and also a Governor of Massachusetts, and whose constant prayer was that Boston might be a Christian Sparta, and who believed that the New World, dedicated to freedom and justice, would ultimately give laws to the Old. I am glad that the delegates to this Convention may see on every side of them memorials of that "last of the Puritans," as he was called, Samuel Adams. They may stand by the old Granary Hill Burying-Ground, on Tremont Street, and see where, near the tombs of Hancock and the parents of Franklin, repose the ashes of him whom Wendell Phillips regarded as the greatest man, excepting Sir Harry Vane, that ever walked the streets of the Puritan metropolis. They may enter the New Old South Meeting-house, and there read the memorial tablet which honors the most illustrious member of that historic church.

They may go to the Massachusetts State House, whose corner-stone Gov. Samuel Adams laid in 1796, dedicating it to freedom and the rights of man, and there see his marble face in the Doric Hall, where the eye rests on the statues of Andrew and Sumner, of Lincoln and Washington. They may walk down Winter Street, now brilliant with shops, and remember that there Samuel Adams once dwelt in humble poverty; and may recall how Gov. Caleb Strong halted his inaugural procession at the old man's door, and, alighting from his carriage, grasped reverently the palsied hand of Samuel Adams, while the soldiers presented arms before him who had marshalled the towns of Massachusetts against the mightiest monarchy on earth. They may stand by the Old South Meeting-house, on Washington Street, and think of those stormy times when his voice thrilled the men of two continents.

They may walk down School Street, and see the site of that famous Latin School where he and so many illustrious men were trained, and remember how in his last years the aged Governor was often seen in the streets, surrounded by troops of school-children, — a scene which yet waits the historic painter. In

Dock Square—now called Adams Square, in his honor—they may look at the bronze copy of Miss Whitney's statue of "the incorruptible patriot who organized the Revolution and signed the Declaration of Independence," representing him as he stood before the royal Governor defiantly waiting an answer to his demand for the removal of the troops from Boston. They may see the site of the old Green Dragon Tavern, where he so often counselled with patriots; and the old State House, where, for so many years, he led the Commonwealth; and Faneuil Hall, where his voice roused, and his wisdom guided, not Boston only, but thirteen Colonies. And when we remember what other great and sacred names and events are associated with this town, and with its neighbor, Cambridge,—what interests of learning and religion, what splendid and enduring gifts to letters and art,—we shall ourselves, for the day at least, be Bostonians. We shall murmur sympathetically the lines of Emerson:—

> " The rocky nook, with hill-tops three,
>   Looks eastward from the farms,
> And twice each day the flowing sea
>   Takes Boston in its arms.
> What care though rival cities soar
>   Along the stormy coast,—
> Penn's town, New York, and Baltimore,—
>   If Boston knows the most?"

and we shall go back to our homes by the Potomac and the Mississippi, by the St. Lawrence and the Sacramento, by the Penobscot and the Merrimac, by the Susquehanna and the Tennessee, the Ohio and the Rio Grande, by the James and the Oregon, by the Lakes and the Gulf, praying, not only that God's richest blessing may abide with this Puritan mother, but that we ourselves may be girded with new zeal and wisdom for those battles of righteousness which are to test the young Christian citizenship of America.

But we are the representatives not only of one people, but of many nations, and far greater than America is that kingdom of Christ, which overleaps mountains and streams, and border lands, "by bloody sword-points traced;" which stretches beyond political boundaries, and clasps ages and nations within its celestial confines. And this majestic Christian Endeavor movement has vast significance in the missionary conquests of the globe. Looking out in the Madison Square Garden upon more than 10,000 Christian faces at the New York Convention of three years ago, the venerated Dr. Schaff said to me, " Christianity is not dead." No, Christ, our King, whose royalty was written in the three great languages of antiquity on his dear Cross, never looked out before on such a broad and fast-widening dominion. Within seventy years from the day when Jesus gave their marching orders to his little band of followers the messengers of salvation had penetrated every civilized land from Babylon to Spain; and within seventy years after the first American missionaries sailed from Boston and Salem harbors conquests equally memorable had been achieved.

Christendom was never so great a fact in the world as it is to-day. We are brought face to face, as never before, with the forces and claims of other systems; and, as the most famous of all the students of comparative theology has said, " However highly we prize our Christianity, we never prize it highly enough until we have compared it with the religions of the rest of the world." Furthermore, such comparison discloses the fact that Christianity alone presents to-day the aspects of a world-wide religion. We see Judaism, the historical root of Christianity, shrinking into a national cult and numbering less than ten millions of our race. We look at the religion of the noble Parsees, the heirs of the venerable faith of Persia, and they have dwindled, as we know, to a few score thousands, dwelling mostly in Bombay; and from the Malabar Hill they send out no missionaries to convert the world. We see Confucianism, which is older than historic Christianity, but it has never reached after a world-wide supremacy; it is simply Mongolian ethics, and its strongest ambition has apparently been restricted to national boundaries. It has influenced with its philosophy the military literati of Japan, but it has gone little further, and, instead of furnishing the aspects of a world-wide system of belief, it presents, to-day, the sorry spectacle of the most populous of empires corrupted, humiliated, broken and barely escaping the shame of seeing the horses of the Mikado stabled in, the pagodas of Peking.

We see Hinduism, — the most seclusive of all the faiths, forbidden to cross the black water,— pre-eminently an ethnic religion, and conspicuously lacking in that missionary spirit which takes men out of themselves, and sends them across oceans and deserts to tell the life-giving truth to other hearts. There is no other religion than our own that could have gathered a convention like this, filled with such hopes, animated by such purposes, and representing such varied nationalities. When President Clark made his voyage around the world he found only one faith in all lands, and supreme in the civilized and progressive nations. He met only two other religions at all missionary in character and seeking to become universal. One of these is Buddhism,— an ethical philosophy, humane, but pessimistic, rather than a religion,— which appears to have flourished only among peoples who were out of the track of the world's chief development. It has been driven from its native home in India; and in the countries where it now prevails, according to Mr. Dharmapala, it is in a comatose state, for he sends me word that " In all Buddhistic countries the monks, with a few exceptions, have failed to influence the people, and they are sadly wanting in the desire to spread abroad the teachings of their great Master."

The late Dr. Happer once wrote to me that, according to his calculations, which agree with Prof. Max Muller's, " There are less than one hundred millions of genuine Buddhists; " for he eliminates from the enormous figures which are usually proclaimed the four hundred millions of the Chinese who are really to be reckoned as Taoists and Confucianists. Mr. Gladstone has recently written that " No other religion approaches the numerical strength of Christianity; " and he adds that " The art, literature, systematized industry, invention, and commerce of the world are almost wholly Christian."

The other missionary faith is Mohammedanism, the only non-Christian power left in Europe and Africa,— a system which is aggressive, intolerant, and out of sympathy with our humanitarian and progressive century. With but one powerful Moslem monarch left in the world, and that ruler permitted to remain in Europe only through the jealousies of Russia and England, Islam is not in the least likely to conquer mankind. It belongs to races which, at the best, are linked with forms of despotism and types of narrowness which modern civilization is sweeping away.

These two non-Christian missionary faiths, that of Buddha and that of Mohammed, are being penetrated, and in some respects modified, by the radiance of the Christian Gospel, while all their attempts to carry on missionary work among Christians have scarcely yet reached the dignity of a farce. The nominal disciples of Christ in the world are more than 400,000,000, while under Christian governments, dwelling beneath a reign of law and the radiance of Gospel light, are more than 600,000,000 of the world's inhabitants. And when the Turk is driven out of Europe, and when the colossal Empire of China is broken into fragments and brought into line with the world's progress, and under the sway of Christian governments,— all of which may happen within a generation and possibly within a decade,— four-fifths of the world's population will have come under the direct and powerful influence of the Christian faith. Christianity holds the field to-day. It has been truly said that " The non-Christian nations could not exclude Christianity if they would, and the most enlightened of them would not if they could."

Thus more and more Christianity presents the appearance of a world-wide religion. On every shore,—Australasian, Chinese, and Siberian, Japanese, Javanese, and Indian, Singalese, Persian, and Arabian, Malagasy, Zanzibar, and Egyptian, Barbary, Syrian, and Turkish, Grecian, Italian, and Spanish, Portuguese, French, and English, German, Dutch, and Scandinavian, Russian, Icelandic, and Hawaiian, Brazilian, Mexican, and American,—from the North Cape of Europe to where the sailor beholds " the long wave rolling from the Southern Pole to break upon Japan," are the manifold evidences that Christianity is a vital, progressive, and conquering force. A large work of preparation has already been accomplished. The world is being made ready— through governments, through steamships and railroads, through international communication, through a better and a friendlier feeling toward Christians, through a new knowledge which discriminates between a true and a false Christianity, through a better understanding of the loving spirit of the true — is being made ready, I say, for the universal faith. All nations and religions find in the Christian system a common meeting-ground; and some of the ethic and some of the so-called universal faiths are acknowledging and adopting the noble truths of the Christian Gospel. The missionary uprising of the Christian Endeavor Societies is an event big with prophecies of Christian triumph.

But all the Christian progress which the nineteenth century has achieved appears but a faint prediction of the Christian victories that await the twentieth. On June 23, 1861, Sir Samuel Baker and his party were sleeping in the dry bed of the Atbara, one of the tributaries of the Nile. In that dry river-bed they had been travelling for days. On this night Sir Samuel Baker was awakened by a noise like distant thunder. Soon his native attendants rushed in upon him, shouting in their terror, " The river! " and with all speed they hastened to the parched and sandy shore, and soon the torrent which had gathered its volume of waters among the snows of the mountains of Abyssinia, rushed by ; and on the morning of June 24, when the sun arose, the English traveller looked out over a river 1,500 feet broad, and from 15 to 20 feet in depth, rolling on in freshness and fertilizing power, moistening the roots of 10,000 palm-trees, at last to be spread over the immortal fields of Egypt. So the waters of our Christian civilization and of noble missionary zeal have been long accumulating on the high lands of Europe and America, and a mighty, rushing river will suddenly descend on the thirsty African plains, and over the tropic fields of India and the freshly opened provinces of the Celestial Empire ; and the roar of the oncoming torrent will be a new fulfilment of Ezekiel's vision of a sacred stream which shall go out into the east country and down into the desert, healing the waters of the bitter sea.

Old Cotton Mather, speaking of John Eliot, the apostle to the Indians, said, " We had a tradition among us that the country could never perish so long as Eliot was alive." The fire of Eliot's missionary zeal has not been quenched, but rather made more luminous and beneficent in the ampler and milder air of the present age. It will not die out with expanding knowledge, or if it does sink down or flicker in our own land it will be reilluminated here by a Christianized Africa and a regenerated Asia. The promise of our Divine Leader standeth sure. He who has all power is behind his church, and he wearies not. Therefore, we lift again the prayer of John Milton, " Come, O thou that hast the seven stars in thy right hand. Come forth out of thy royal chambers, O Prince of all the kings of the earth! Put on the visible robes of thy imperial majesty ; take up that unlimited sceptre which thy Almighty Father hath bequeathed thee, for now the voice of thy bride calls thee, and all things sigh to be removed."

At this point Rev. Henry T. McCook, D.D., of Philadelphia, Penn., was introduced, and made a brief but vigorous address. Mr. J. E. Cheesman, of Cleveland, O., then read Secretary Baer's annual report, and the meeting adjourned.

THURSDAY AFTERNOON.

The Denominational Rallies.

" The best we ever held," was the verdict of almost every denomination in regard to its rally. So large were three of these gatherings that they were assigned to the chief auditoriums, and the result showed that the space provided was none too ample. The Presbyterians filled Mechanics' Hall, where they listened to appeals from the representatives of their missionary boards. By a rising vote, the meeting authorized the appointment of a committee to present to the General Assembly's Committee on Young People's Societies the facts that call for recognition of Christian Endeavor. Tent Endeavor was crammed with the Baptists, who heard from their missionary boards, and then had an open parliament on "Advance, Endeavor." The Congregationalist thousands in Tent Williston discussed the relation of their principles to freedom, spiritual, mental, political; considered the resulting obligations to the churches and to missions ; and then heard brief addresses from several State presidents.

The gathering of the Disciples was marked by its missionary purpose, foreign, home, and city evangelization being considered. Resolutions were presented, to the effect that the young people should work through the established agencies of the Church. Sixteen States were represented at the Lutheran rally. Marked features here were the emphasis on the value of an interdenominational society, a powerful address by a converted Brahman, and an open parliament on Christian Endeavor work.

The Methodist Episcopalians, the Methodist Episcopal Church, South, and the Methodists of Canada held an enthusiastic joint rally, whose spirit found expression in the resolutions affirming the strongest loyalty to the denomination, and urgently appealing to the General Conference to arrange for the affiliation of Epworth Leagues with Christian Endeavor Societies. At the union rally of the African Methodist Episcopal and African Methodist Episcopal Zion Churches, the heartiest approval of Christian Endeavor was expressed, because of its enthusiasm, fellowship, and educational power. About two hundred Methodist Protestants assembled to take part in a programme that included reports from Conference Unions, and from the recent denominational conventions, and to give their reasons for being Methodist Protestants.

The Cumberland Presbyterians discussed Christian Endeavor possibilities in their church, and the method of attaining them, emphasizing the importance of increased gifts and the promotion of a higher standard of intelligence. The conviction was strong that the nine hundred Endeavor Societies must be made fifteen hundred. The mission of the United Presbyterian Church, and the means of fulfilling it, occupied the attention of the delegates of that denomination ; and the duty and responsibility of the Church in regard to civil government were strongly urged. "Christ, our King" was the motto of the Reformed Presbyterian gathering. Christian citizenship was discussed, and the Church's work in Syria was described by a missionary from that field. At the Southern Presbyterian rally all but three Southern States were represented, and every delegate had come at least five hundred miles. Numerous testimonies were given as to what the societies are doing, and answers were given to the question as to what more they may do, missions receiving a prominent place in the discussion. Of the two hundred Canadian Presbyterians, nearly eighty were from Nova Scotia. They devoted their time largely to a consideration of the dangers confronting Christian Endeavor, and the best means of avoiding these.

The Protestant Episcopalians, in the largest rally that they have ever held, took a survey of the progress of Christian Endeavor among them, and passed a solemn resolution pledging themselves to do all in their power to further this progress. The Reformed Episcopalians emphasized the thought of fellowship and the need of a baptism of the Spirit to carry on the work. Suggestions were made looking to a closer union between the societies of the denomination.

The representatives of the Reformed Church in America were stirred by remarks dealing with the record of that church, reports of what it is doing along missionary lines, and statements as to the outlook for Christian Endeavor. Nearly two hundred were present at the rally of the Reformed Church in the United States, and not one had come less than three hundred miles. The meeting was marked by the address of a missionary from Japan, by the emphasis on Junior work, and by the consideration of systematic giving and a denominational course of reading.

The Christians had the largest and most rousing rally that they have ever held, the large attendance of ministers being especially marked. The possibilities of Christian Endeavor was the general theme, and missions and Christian citizenship came in for a large share of attention.

Every State was represented at the Free Baptist rally, where the attendance surpassed expectation. Greetings came from all parts of the home field, and from India, the denomination's mission field. Resolutions affirming loyalty to Christian Endeavor and to the denomination were unanimously adopted.

The United Brethren considered the topics of literature, Junior work, and missions, and listened to brief addresses by Endeavorers.

The Friends received from their secretary an encouraging report, showing, among other points, that fifteen missionaries are supported, in part at least, by the Endeavorers. A strong plea was made for interdenominational fellowship in the interest of denominational loyalty. The Moravians have formed a national Moravian Christian Endeavor Union, and the annual meetings are to be at the same time and place as those of the Christian Endeavor Conventions. Measures have been taken, also, to circulate more definite information about missions.

The success of the Mennonite rally greatly surpassed expectations, and was especially notable because the place of meeting was so far from the nearest church of the denomination.

The delegates belonging to the Church of God felt the need of a Christian Endeavor denominational organization to promote the cause of Christian Endeavor, and the Pennsylvania members effected a permanent organization for the purpose.

The two hundred Advent Christians received reports from nineteen societies, one of which is in Asia Minor ; and the outlook was found to be very encouraging.

At the gathering of the United Evangelicals it appeared that one-fourth of the entire membership of that church belongs to the Keystone League of Christian Endeavor.   The Junior work and missions received special attention ; and it was determined to raise for missions, during the coming year, one dollar for each member of the K. L. C. E.

The representation from the two hundred and fifty German societies was quite small ; but this was largely because the convention of the North American Union of these societies was to meet at Sandusky, O., within three weeks.   Encouraging reports of progress in this country and in Germany were given.

THURSDAY EVENING.

Mechanics' Hall.

Three giants, Moody, Conwell, and Woolley ; how were the Endeavorers to choose ?   Evidently they chose *each ;* for, quite an hour before the time for beginning, far more than enough Endeavorers to fill it were waiting in front of the Mechanics' Building ; and when several thousand found that there were too few seats for them in the great hall, news came that there was no room for them in the tents either, so that overflow meetings had to be hastily extemporized ; and during the evening Rev. Henry Montgomery, of Ireland, and Rev. John Pollock, of Scotland, Rev. Anderson Rogers, of Nova Scotia, President Clark, and Secretary Baer spoke from the steps outside the building to the crowds outside.

The packed throng in the hall was in a very happy temper.   They applauded the music ; they applauded the electric light when it came ; they applauded every point made by the eloquent speakers.   A fine keynote for next year's convention was struck by Mr. W. H. H. Smith, chairman of Washington's committee of arrangements, who described in glowing terms the admirable prospect before us for enjoyment and spiritual profit next July.

Very striking was his reminder that, though Washington Endeavorers had already contributed from their own funds $10,000 for the great gathering to come, yet this year they carried off Mr. Fulton's Chinese umbrella for the greatest proportionate number of systematic givers to missions.   Then the audience sung with gusto Washington's rally song, which was printed on fans distributed throughout the hall and tents by the enthusiastic Endeavorers of the capital city.

Address of Mr. W. H. H. Smith.

Knowing, as one in best position to know, all that which is in preparation and promise, added to what is already in possession, in the District of Columbia for our great gathering next year, I count it a royal privilege to stand here as the representative of the Christian young people of the capital of this grand Christian nation, and to invite the Endeavor hosts of the world to our homes and hearts, and to the feast of fat things which will there be spread for our convention in 1896.

We are to meet in one of the most beautiful cities in the world, with its more than 300 miles of well-paved broad streets and broader avenues, shaded with 70,000 trees, thickly emeralded with its more than 400 acres of public gardens, and bordered with above 2,000 acres of great parks, and filled with buildings, both public and private, illustrating every variety and combination of architecture and decoration.

Our meeting is to be in one of the most interesting cities in the world. It is our nation's capital, crowded with historic places, relics and memories of valuable and thrilling interest alike to foreign and native born. Here, also, in the sessions of Congress in our great-domed Capitol, and in the various departmental buildings, the wheels of government may be seen and studied, while the navy yard, arsenal, and forts may be visited to see our "peace compelling" appliances and plans; and, not least of all, the wealth of exhibits in the Smithsonian, the National Museum, and the Fish Commission buildings affords opportunities to the student well worth a trip across a continent to see.

We are to gather from all lands in one of the most cosmopolitan cities of the world; where those who shall come from every considerable hamlet, township, state, or country, from all over the earth, will be almost sure to be met by some former friends or neighbors with their warm welcomes and hospitalities, from the chief executive officers of our government, and the ambassadors and representatives of foreign powers, who have their official homes here, down to the humblest clerk or laborer in the departments or marts of the city.

We are to assemble in our ideal convention city, where the compactness and regularity of arrangement, close proximity of its hotels, churches, and places of interest, excellent means of city transit, and absence of noise and dirt incident to large manufacturing-places, with its splendid railroad and water approaches, and the faultless manner of receiving and entertaining visitors, to which it is accustomed, make it the most desirable place in which to hold such a great Christian Endeavor gathering.

Time will not permit of my speaking concerning the amplitude of the preparations to house and care for the expected 80,000 to 100,000 who shall come, nor to describe our plans for the four amphitheatre-seated and well-ventilated auditoriums for the 40,000 and more persons at one time, proposed for location almost within the shadows of the Washington Monument and the much-coveted White House; we will press this into a sentence. Remembering the pithy proverb that "Money talks," the mere mention that our Endeavorers contribute $10,000, and our merchants promise $15,000 more for this convention, at once places the perfection of our preparations for the comfort of all who may come beyond question.

But, dear young soldiers of the cross, this is not all. Great and desirable as are these things, which we are so glad to offer you, and which we are sure will most amply repay every one who comes, from whatever distance, for every dollar and hour expended in the trip, we yet hold them less than the least of all that for which we are most earnestly desirous, and for which we are so carefully preparing. I think we may confidently look to our United Society officers to provide us with the very best programme of topics, speakers, and exercises that we have ever had, and so we are sacrificing, laboring, and most earnestly praying for your coming, as God's chosen ones, to the most Christian capital of the nations of the earth, where Christian people, young and old, will vie with each other in giving you full measure of true Christian hospitality, and with the intense longing that the Holy Spirit may fill the place in every service, song, and sentence as never before; so that not only shall every Christian enterprise and effort in our city receive a mighty impulse for wonderful work and success for the glory of God, and that every one who comes to this convention shall return to their homes better and braver to help win this redeemed world back to its Redeemer, but that also the impress of this host of glad young lives consecrated to Christ and the Church shall mightily stir serious thoughts and plant a greater leaven of righteousness in the minds and hearts of congressmen, diplomatists, and representatives, so that its fruitage shall go out to the world in such manner and in such measure as shall be beyond our powers to plan or to conceive. For this we are consecrated in our motto, chosen at the beginning: "Not by might, nor by power, but by my spirit, saith the Lord of hosts," and for this we ask the daily prayers of you all.

Therefore, I count it a royal privilege to stand before you to-night, and in His name, and in the name of the Committee of 1896, and in the name of the Christian Endeavor Union, and of the Christians of the District of Columbia, to invite you, and through you the Christian Endeavorers of the world, to come to Washington, D. C., in July, 1896, for the Fifteenth International Christian Endeavor Convention.

How describe the welcome given to Dr. Clark as he came forward to give his annual address! The Endeavorers had in mind his absence from last year's convention, and his happy recovery of health. The great room blossomed into a flood of fluttering white, led by the red and white handkerchiefs of the choir. Then a round of applause, and another, till our beloved leader had to appeal for silence.

"The Responsibilities of Success" was his appropriate topic. He had in view the unparalleled Christian Endeavor growth of the past year and the assured success of the movement, not only in regard to numbers, but in all helpful ways.

Annual Address of President Francis E. Clark, D.D.

Judged by all standards it is no immodest statement that the Endeavor movement is a success. An organization which in fourteen years has grown from one society to forty thousand, from fifty-six members to nearly two millions and a half; an organization that has belted the globe; that finds itself as much at home in Old England as in New England, under the Southern Cross as under the North Star, under the Dragon flag of China as under the Stars and Stripes of America, can claim surely to be no provincial and temporary expedient, but a world-wide, providential movement.

Especially is this true when it is remembered that this success has been achieved without any ecclesiastical patronage, such as has brought into existence and assiduously fostered other societies of the Endeavor type. That this success is no evanescent, temporary affair is shown by the fact that this year has been the year of greatest and most substantial growth, as well as of highest spiritual attainment, of any of the fourteen.

Our secretary's report told us of nearly 8,000 societies added to the ranks, with their half-million members, 500 full regiments of the young soldiers of the Lord, marching on to victory. This Convention will tell you of the battles fought and won for Christian citizenship; of the war waged against the saloon and the brothel, the Sunday ball game and the Sunday theatre; for good government and righteousness in municipal affairs. It will tell you how Christian Endeavorers have relieved the poor and sick, lightened the squalid misery of the despairing, strengthened the prayer meeting and every church service, while from its ranks scores of thousands have come into the churches of Christ. It will tell you of the advance of missionary spirit and systematic giving, and of thousands of eager Endeavorers who are only waiting the word of command from their respective churches, like the new settlers on the edge of a reservation, with one foot over the line, waiting for the government pistol-shot, to go in and possess the land. It is not within my province to rehearse these matters, though our hearts leap with joy as we consider them.

There are no considerations which so belittle man's agency in the movement or make one feel so humble as those which tell of the undreamed-of success of this God-sent, God-guided movement. Had its success been less, self-congratulation on the part of some might find room. Its very scope and reach preclude vanity and boastfulness, as a vastly bounteous crop can be attributed by the farmer only to God's fruitful soil, and sun and rain.

But success brings its own responsibilities. If the crop is large, the duties of stewardship are also large. The greater the fortune, the greater the obligation to use it aright. The responsibility for the future of Christian Endeavor rests not with any leaders or officers or United Society or union, but with the Endeavorers themselves, in every one of the 40,000 societies the world around. What *you* make it, Endeavorers, the future of the Society will be. Upon your modesty, teachableness, wisdom, devotion, aggressive zeal, depends the still larger success for which we pray to-night. What, then, are the providential responsibilities thrust upon Endeavorers by the very success of this movement? What is demanded of us by the very triumphs of this good year?

First. I would mention humble, unselfish devotion to the cause we represent, which is the cause of Christ,— a devotion which is not measured by loaves and fishes; a devotion which is entirely independent of offices and emoluments and honors. This Society, thank God, has never yet been at the mercy of designing, mercenary schemers. Its very genius, its spiritual aims, its lofty purpose, its loyal dependence on the church which it serves, will, I believe, preserve it in the future as in the past. Everybody, from the pill-man to the railroad ticket-scalper, wants to sell you his wares, just because you are numerous. Everybody, from the political hack, who is in the business for revenue only, to the prophet of a new dispensation, who is sure that his spiritual panacea is the only one to usher in the millennium, wants your patronage because there are so many of you. Don't be beguiled. The Endeavor Society is "for Christ and the Church;" for home and native land; not to boost or bolster any political party or to sell any nostrums, be they for the body or soul.

Above all, let us beware of ecclesiastical politics. Suffer no boss, not even an "easy boss," in Christian Endeavor. If any one in your State or local union attempts to lord it over God's heritage, elect him to stay at home at the next opportunity. The Society has prospered in the past in every State and Province because of the *unselfish* devotion of a myriad of unheralded workers. I know of no organization that is so indebted to recruits who ask for no pay, no uniform, no epaulets, no decorations, no reward except the reward of a meek and quiet spirit and a consciousness of duty done.

If I may be allowed to refer for a moment to the United Society of Christian Endeavor. Its great missionary work is done; the Constitution is translated into and circulated in two scores of languages; it serves as a bureau of information for societies in forty-four states, five territories, eight provinces, and half a hundred countries outside of America, on a total yearly expenditure of about $12,000, all of which it earns. This it is enabled to do largely because there is so much gratuitous service given by those who love the cause. So it is in our State and local unions. They employ no paid officers; they have no large expenditures; they afford no opportunity to the selfish adventurer. We have no votes, no patronage, no influence, which, as an organization, we can or would deliver to him who seeks them. The limitations and functions of our National and State Endeavor Unions are clearly defined. Their functions are, as they always have been, those of inspiration and stimulus, never of legislation. The conventions are mass-meetings for spiritual uplift and fellowship, where almost no business is transacted, and to which no wire-pulling schemer need apply. Our success in the past has been won along these lines. The guide-board to our success for the future points in no other direction.

Second. Past successes have all been won along the lines of fidelity and intensest loyalty,— loyalty to God and his Word, loyalty to our individual churches and their interests. These very successes thrust upon us the same course for the future. In order that we may be more intelligently faithful, may I suggest that greater attention be paid to the study of God's Word, systematically and consecutively? To be sure, it may be said with much force that the Sunday school is the place for this study, for the Sunday school is the Church instructing the young, the Endeavor Society the Church training the young. This is all very true, but it is also true that there is much special Bible study which may well be taken up by Endeavorers. There is also study for each one of his own church, her institutions, her creed, her polity, her missionary work. This, under the direction of the pastor, if possible, is most appropriate to any Endeavor Society.

It is the proud boast of this Society, and it is no empty boast, that it is as loyal to its own church as any purely denominational society possibly can be. Statistics recently obtained relating to the Sunday services, the mid-week prayer meeting, the missionary treasury, and other departments of church work, abundantly prove this. Let this loyalty be as intelligent as it is intense. Let us know why we are Baptists and Methodists and Presbyterians and Lutherans and Disciples of Christ and Congregationalists and Episcopalians. Let us base our service on intelligent devotion as well as on traditional veneration.

Third. The successes of the past have been due to certain distinctive principles, which have come to be known as CHRISTIAN ENDEAVOR PRINCIPLES. This Convention is not an agglomeration of all kinds of young people's societies. It is not a gathering of musical and literary and social and amusement societies. It is a convention of CHRISTIAN ENDEAVOR SOCIETIES. The growth of these fourteen years is not a happy combination of odd elements which have come together by chance. As every plant has a root, so every Endeavor Society has a root. Rather, it has three roots: the pledge, the consecration meeting, and a system of committees by which its practical service for Christ is performed. You might as well expect a plant to grow strong and vigorous if you hack away at its roots as an Endeavor Society to grow strong without these cardinal principles; and yet some people have not only pulled up the Society to look at its roots, but have deliberately cut off one or more of them. They could not accept the experience of ten thousand others, but must lop off one or more of the roots for the sake of having an *original* society, and then they have wondered that it has so soon withered and died. Originality in organization is sometimes a good thing, but it often costs too much, as many an Endeavor Society can testify.

To speak with all seriousness, so far as my experience has gone, in every part of the world, in every climate, under all circumstances, in all denominations, among young people of every color and condition, I have never known a Christian Endeavor Society to long flourish which ignored the pledge, the consecration meeting, or the essential committees. All of the untimely deaths of which I have heard, — except those due to ecclesiastical strangling or freezing, — can be traced directly to a neglect of these fundamental ideas, which make a young people's society a Christian Endeavor Society.

While there is the utmost flexibility and adaptability to circumstances, doctrines, church polity, and ecclesiastical conditions in all lands, there are also in all lands these common and essential elements which the Endeavor Society has introduced into the organized Christian life of young people, and which differentiate this Society from every other. The vast significance of this truth is found in the fact that these three features (the pledge, the consecration meeting, the leading committees) embody the distinctive *religious idea* of the Society. No form of words is contended for; no exact uniformity of method is my plea; but for the predominance of the *supreme religious thought* embodied in the pledge, the consecration meeting, and the essential committees, I do plead.

The God-ordained purpose of the Endeavor movement is to raise the standard of practical devotion and consecrated religious enthusiasm of young people. It is constantly saying by means of the pledge, the consecration meeting, and the leading committees: " Make of your religion *the first thing* in all your lives. Place it before your business, before your social pleasures, before your school, before your amusements." "There is one supreme thing in the world, and that is the service of the Master." "Allow no paltry excuse, no mood, no inclination, no whim, no worldly pleasure, to come between you and your religious duties." O friends, this is the burden of my message to-night! Raise and keep aloft the spiritual standard of service and devotion as you ever have done in the past. Raise it higher and higher if you would win new victories. Our Christian citizenship, our missionary zeal, our fellowship, depend first of all and draw their power from this lofty devotion. *This gives Christian Endeavor a right to live. This accounts for its success in the past. This guarantees its success in the future. Not only the success of the movement as a whole, but of every individual society, teaches us this lesson; loads us with this responsibility; forces upon us this inevitable conclusion; faces us with this necessity: that the spiritual standard must be maintained, that the means to this end must be observed;* in other words, that an Endeavor Society must be an Endeavor Society, and have the distinguishing marks of a pledge and a consecration meeting and a lookout committee, which God has crowned with his seal of success.

Fourth. But while the absolute necessity of keeping the movement " true to type," as the gardeners would say, is laid upon us, a necessity no less strenuous is ours *to wisely follow the later providential paths which God has marked out.* When, two years ago, at Montreal, the suggestion was made to you, Endeavorers, that as individuals you had unfulfilled duties along the lines of Christian citizenship and missionary enlargement, who would have believed that your response would have been so prompt and generous? How you have leaped forward to your duty and your privilege! How the rapid contagion of these ideas has spread from society to society, from local union to local union, from city to country, from state to state, and province and nation! Not a death-dealing contagion is this, but a blessed inoculation which, please God, will make forever impossible the smallpox of such municipal misrule and corruption as we have known in the past. May this be a lymph, too, which shall render forever innocuous the wasting consumption of indifference to the spread of the Kingdom in all the world!

To speak first of our efforts for a better citizenship. It behooves us to be very modest. I make no extravagant claims for the Christian Endeavor Society, but it is fair to say that the Society has had no insignificant part in the general uprising of Christian people which has buried Tammany under fifty thousand white ballots in New York City and is now fighting an equally corrupt foe of another breed in the same State; which has voted for reform, fifty thousand strong, in Chicago; which is now engaged in cleansing the dirty streets and the dirtier politics of that and other cities; and which, in a hundred places, has awakened the civic conscience and purified a fetid political atmosphere.

Nor is it too much to say that the aroused interest in world-wide missions among Endeavorers has done something toward furnishing the army of volunteers, six full regiments, each a thousand strong, who are eager to march forward into the enemies' country, to do battle for the Captain of their salvation, whenever the churches shall furnish the " sinews of war."

Ten years ago the cry was for men and women. That will never again be the unanswered cry, I believe. Now the imperative call is for money to send the thousands of ready volunteers whom, in part, Christian Endeavor has equipped, and called, and sent forth with the ringing cry of aggressive consecration upon their lips: " Here am I, send me." The fact, too, that the societies of Christian Endeavor, for the most part, over and above what would otherwise have been given, have put hundreds of thousands of dollars into the misssionary treasuries of their respective boards shows that there are consecrated pocket-books as well as hearts among us.

But the very success of these movements for a better citizenship and a larger missionary zeal, unprecedented and unexpected as it has been, brings with it responsibility for further effort along the same lines. Grant's laconic commentary on success in arms was, " Push things." Napoleon's tactics were to follow up a victory; to crowd the enemy; to pursue the flying foe. I believe our Captain issues no other orders to us, fellow Christian Endeavorers. I can find no other interpretation of the success he has already given us. Not as a political party, but *in all political parties* stand for righteousness, for honesty, for purity, for good men and good laws. The Endeavor Society is a quick and tender conscience in these matters among the young people of a community. It is an indignation meeting against misrule and corruption which never adjourns. Its true mission, as of every similar organization, is to awaken and keep awake righteous public sentiment, until organized wicked-ness slinks away abashed and ashamed of itself. Not as an organized society, but as well-organized individuals, simply because we are followers of Christ, the Righteous, let us stand everywhere for the right. Do not be content with overthrowing one Tammany in New York and another in Chicago. Do not be content until a Tammany in America is forever an impossibility. Do not be content until a corrupt political deal is as impossible and intolerable as an open cesspool would be in your own parlor. Follow the flying foe. Push things. The sword of the Lord and of Christian Endeavor!

So for the other great twin movement of the day. Push things, and keep on pushing. Do not be content with holding meetings and arousing enthusiasm or even volunteering for the mission field, but *pay the debts.* Enthusiasm is well; arousing meetings are important; but consecrated, systematic, propor-tionate *giving* alone justifies the enthusiasm and saves it from ridicule. Neither let us be content, Endeavorers, with helping to pay for this once the debt which hangs like a dark pall over many of our missionary boards; let us make a debt forevermore impossible. By so stimulating the generosity of our members; by so appreciating our stewardship; by making proportionate giving to God as much a part of our religion as praying and believing, let us make a debt in any mission board in America an unheard-of thing.

A Tammany in America forevermore impossible! A missionary board debt forevermore impossible! Those are two of the responsibilities of the future from the successes of the past in Christian Endeavor.

May I suggest as a practical way of realizing this last impossibility (if you will excuse a seeming Hibernicism) that we all band ourselves together, after the manner of some societies, in the support of some particular missionary both in the home and foreign field? If your missionary board is willing, have your own field, your own missionary, your own native helper, for whom you are definitely responsible. Definite responsibility of this sort, I believe, will go far to make possible the blessed impossibility of another missionary debt.

Fifth. Once more, our success in the past has been the success of a united host. It could never have been won as a sect, as a segment of the hosts of God's people. *So far as we have been allowed by our superiors we represent the undivided evangelical young people of America.* For this spiritual unity Christian Endeavor stands, as well as for the pledge and the consecration meet-ing. Thank God that in every denomination, but one, the world around during the last twelvemonth this fellowship has been growing broader and more com-plete. " *E. Pluribus Unum* " is our motto around all the world as truly as it is the motto of the United States of America. State and provincial pride and loyalty are no less intense because of the union of States in the United States, of the Provinces in the Dominion of Canada, against common foes. Denomi-national loyalty and love are only more marked when we are bound together in this alliance, offensive and defensive, against the hosts of evil. It is true in Christian Endeavor ranks as never before in the history of Christendom : —

> " We are not divided,
> All one body we."

This spiritual fellowship is necessary to future successes, as is proved by past victories. There is only one country in the world where Christian Endeavor is forbidden, and that is the land of the Sultan, where our Arme-nian fellow Christians have endured such awful indignities and sufferings. The unspeakable Turk is afraid of the unity of spirit brought about by our fellowship and brotherhood! May he have no allies and co-partners in destroying our fellowship in this country! God puts upon us by reason of his former blessings a mighty responsibility to preserve flawless and perfect this blessed spirit of unity in the bond of perfectness. In such a fellowship only can we go forward to the largest victories. But this fellowship, I believe, is assured. Never again will the hosts of God be divided into warring factions as in the past. Never again will churches be multiplied, as often in the past, only to struggle and die, or, worse still, to live to perpetuate sectarian rivalry. Never again will united wickedness triumph because Christians are divided. Never again will the devil laugh because Christians are busier fighting each other than they are fighting him. The proposed World's Christian Endeavor Union, which perhaps wiL be consummated this week, will still further cement our unity. For such a fellowship as this has Christian Endeavor come to the Kingdom.

Then let us enlarge our boundaries, Christian Endeavorers, not for the sake of the organization, but for the sake of the Kingdom; because enlargement means a larger federation, a sweeter fellowship, a wider unity, a stronger army to fight against hoary and venerable wrongs. Let us enlarge our fellowship for no selfish motive, but because the God-given successes of the past show that enlargement means the spread of the intense devotional idea for which Christian Endeavor stands, because it means civic purity, missionary extension — the world for Christ. Let us enlarge our fellowship because thereby we are answering our Lord's prayer "that they all may be one."

I have thought you might grow tired of our old annual motto, and I have tried to find another one as appropriate, but I cannot do it. The successes of the past year only emphasize it, for they are all of Christ and of Christian fraternity; so I must give it to you again for the coming year,—the motto which tells of one Captain and of one fellowship; the motto which points backward to past successes; the motto which shows the only road to future victories; the motto which tells alike of our leadership and our brotherhood. Here it is. Take it, O Christian Endeavorers, take it, and live by it for another twelvemonth. "One is your Master, even Christ; and all ye are brethren."

After the address of Dr. Clark the chorus and congregation, under the leadership of Mr. George K. Somerby, joined in singing "The Banner of the Cross," after which Mr. Baer introduced Mr. Dwight L. Moody.

Address of Mr. Dwight L. Moody.

An occasion like this does not occur many times in a man's life, when he can speak to so many churches at one time, and before I speak I am going to ask the congregation if you will be kind enough to bow your heads in silent prayer and ask unitedly that God will help me speak so that it will be a help to every one. Let us all bow our heads in prayer. [Then Rev. Dr. J. Wilbur Chapman led in the following prayer, at Mr. Moody's request:]

"Almighty God, our Heavenly Father, we pray thee that at this moment every one of us may be sensible of the presence and the power of the Holy Ghost. We thank thee that we are not strangers unto him. We thank thee that many of us have opened our hearts to the Saviour, and we pray thee, O God, that as never before in all our experience, so to-night we may be sensible that he is filling us with his Spirit; and if there should be one in this great throng still a stranger to the Spirit of God, we pray that that one's heart may be touched with the Word of Jesus, with the message of the Spirit. Oh that there might come to us to-night a Pentecostal experience! Come, Holy Ghost, and fill us, every one. We thank thee that from the first until this moment there has never gone forth from the lips of thy servant an uncertain word for the Son of God. We pray that thou wilt so honor his message to-night. We thank thee for the privilege, but we ask thee that in all things in this service Jesus Christ, and he alone, may be glorified. Bless us, we pray thee, and we shall praise thee throughout the unending eternity through Jesus Christ our Lord. Amen."

Mr. Moody then continued : —

The President, in his report, sounded out a note of warning. He said that what he wanted in all these Endeavor Societies is to cling close to the line. Now there is a class of people who are afraid that this movement may drift away and become a power for evil instead of good. I have no fear of this movement if we can only keep close to the Word of God. I believe it will become a greater power as the years go by, if we can get all these young Christians in all these different societies to honor the Word of God, to cling to it.

Let me come back again to this question of the Word. I believe that every movement that is built on Scriptural lines is going to last because the Word of God is going to endure. That is never going to pass away; but any movement that is living on experience, or on excitement, or on mere numbers, is soon going to run ashore. The people will soon lose their interest. I have seen it over and over again; but I have never in my life seen a movement where they have been led to study the Word of God but that it has increased in power and influence. What is a doctor good for if he has n't any medicine? He may tell you that you are diseased, but if he has n't any medicine he cannot help you. What is an organist good for if he has n't any organ? What is an army good for without weapons, or if they have weapons and do not know how to use them? That is what has been the trouble with China in the last year. Japan, that little country, has been marching right through the nation. Why? Because China does n't know how to use her weapons and can only fire off a few fire-crackers. There is the trouble, and many a Christian enterprise and many Christian workers have come to naught because they did not know how to use the Word of God, which is the sword of the Spirit.

Now, in Psalm CIXX., David prayed nine times that God would quicken him according to his word, according to his law, according to his judgment, according to his precept. Now that is a quickening that is going to last, and I do not believe there is any other quickening that will last.

These meetings are very inspiring and very good, but we have got to have something besides these meetings to keep up the interest. When I pray, I am talking to God, but when I read this Book, it is God talking to me, and it is more important that God should talk to me than that I should talk to him. And let me say here to-night that I do hope that the Christian Endeavor will cling to the whole Bible and not a part of it. A man is not going to do much with a broken sword. If I believe that only half of that is a sword, I am not going to be much of a fighter. I have yet to find a man who is picking the Bible to pieces who is successful in any work.

I heard a good thing a few years ago. A certain man went to see his minister and took his Bible, and he called it the minister's Bible. The minister said, "Why do you call it my Bible? I have never owned it." "Well," he said, "I have sat under your ministry about five years, and when you say a thing is not authentic, I have cut it out." And he had all of Job cut out, and all of Revelation, and he had got about a third of it cut out. The minister did n't want him round town showing it as his Bible, and he got him to give it to him. "Now," says the man, "I have got the covers, and I will hold on to them;" and off he went holding on to the covers. If some men had their way, I think you would have just about a third or half the Bible in the course of a few years. If one minister can say, "This is not authentic," and another can say, "That is not authentic," I would like to know where you will soon be. We will be without a Bible.

Now what we want is to remember that Christ says, "The Scriptures cannot be broken," and he had reference to the Old Testament then, the New had not been written. And when Paul wrote to Timothy, "All Scripture is given by inspiration of God and is profitable for doctrine, for reproof, for correction, for instruction in righteousness," that man of God had reference to the Old Testament; the New was not written then. "What!" you say, "All of the Scripture given by inspiration?" Yes, all given by inspiration, but, mark you, it does n't say all is inspired. Would you like to have me make a distinction? When the devil told a lie in Eden he was not inspired to tell a lie, but some one was inspired to write it for us. If he had n't, we would n't have known about the devil's lying. When Ahab spoke he was not inspired, but some one was inspired to write what Ahab said. When I take up this Book I bear in mind that all is not inspired, and the Bible has never claimed that it is inspired, but it is all given by inspiration.

Did you ever notice that the things men question most in the Old Testament are the very things that the Son of God set his seal to when he was down here on the earth?

Men say, "You don't believe the story of Noah and the flood!" Why, I believe it just as much as the Sermon on the Mount. "Shall the servant be above his master?" The Son of God believed it; he connected it with his return to this earth. "As it was in the days of Noah, so shall it be also in the days of the Son of Man." They were eating till the flood came and took them all away.

Men say, "You don't believe in the story of Sodom and Gomorrah and Lot's wife, do you?" Why, Christ believed it. He said, "Remember Lot's wife." "So shall it be in the coming of the Son of Man." He connected that with his return to this earth.

Men say, "You don't believe people were healed by looking unto a brass serpent on a pole, do you?" Look and see. As Christ said, "As Moses lifted up the serpent in the wilderness, even so must the Son of Man be lifted up, that whosoever believeth in him should not perish but have everlasting life." He connected that with his own Cross.

Men say, "You don't believe, do you, that the children of Israel were fed for forty years with manna?" Christ believed it: "Your fathers did eat manna in the desert." He connected that with his own broken body.

"Well, you certainly don't believe, do you, in the story of Jonah and the whale?" Yes, I believe that. Christ connected that with his own resurrection. In Matthew twice they came and said, "Show us a sign," and he said, "The only sign this generation shall have is the sign of Jonah in the whale's belly. As Jonah was three days in the whale's belly, so the Son of Man shall be three days in the bowels of the earth."

I was going to say that scientific men tell us that it is a physical impossibility for a whale to swallow a man; that a whale's mouth is not large enough. But you turn to the book of Jonah and you see that "God prepared a great fish to swallow Jonah." Bring God in on the sea and there is no trouble. Could n't God create a fish large enough to swallow this whole world at one swallow? It is an absurd thing for people to say that God could not do it. I believe it is a master-stroke of Satan to get us to doubt these portions of the Scripture; because, if you throw over the story of Jonah, you throw over the doctrine of the Resurrection, and when you get as far along in life as some of us have got you will get as much comfort out of that doctrine as any doctrine in the Bible.

My friends, let us hold on to every scrap of that Book; not a part of it, but from Genesis to Revelation, the whole of it.

I pity any Christian worker who thinks he is going to succeed by picking the Bible to pieces.

But people say, "What are you going to do when you come to something you can't understand?" A man comes to me and says, "Moody, what do you do with that? How do you understand it? How do you interpret it? How do you explain it? What do you do with it?" "Why," I said, "I don't do anything with it." "How do you understand it?" "Don't understand it." "What do you do with it?" "Don't do anything." "You don't believe it, do you?" "Yes, I believe it. There are lots of things in that Book I don't understand. There is a height that I know nothing about; a depth that I know nothing about; a length that I know nothing about; a breadth that I know nothing about. If I could take that Book up, read it and understand it, I could write a Bible, and so could you. I thank God it is beyond me. It is a proof that it came from God and not from man."

But this man says, " I would n't believe anything I can't reason out, or that I can't see." " Why," I said, " do you know anything about higher mathematics? " " No." " Do you believe in it? " " I suppose I do." " Do you know anything about astronomy? " " Why, yes, I know a little about it." " Can you tell us all about it? " " No." " But you believe in it? " " Why, yes, I believe in it." " But I thought you would n't believe anything you could not explain. If you can't understand earthly things, how do you expect to understand heavenly things, and understand them all at once? " I asked him if he ever saw his own brain.

There are a good many things about this body I don't understand, yet I believe I have a body. I have n't any doubt about it. There are things I come across every day I don't understand, but I don't say that they 're not true; and so, my friends, when we come to this Book, let us not be wise above Scripture.

The materialist says, " We have got to have a new Bible." That is the trouble; the old Book is good for the Dark Ages, but we have come into an enlightened age now, and we have got to have a new Bible. My friend said, " Well, before we give up the old one, let us find out a little about it. Can you tell me what is the first book in the Bible? Is it Genesis or Revelation? " He could n't just answer that, but we had got to have a new Bible. It is easy enough to talk about something we know nothing about, and of all the sceptics I ever met, I never met but one that ever claimed he had read it through. He could n't quote but one verse, " Jesus wept," and yet he was talking against the Bible.

It is an absurd position for a man to say that he believes in the New Testament and does not believe in the Old. There are only eighty-nine chapters in the New Testament, and one hundred and forty quotations in that from the Old Testament. Take that short Epistle to the Galatians, — only six chapters and sixteen quotations. In Hebrews there are only thirteen chapters and eighty-five quotations. In these two short Epistles to the Corinthians there are fifty-three quotations from the Old Testament; in Revelations, twenty-two chapters and two hundred and forty quotations. And yet men say they will believe the New Testament but not the Old! How can you believe the New without believing the Old? How can you believe one without the other? It is all interwoven. Take the New without the Old, and it would not be worth reading. In Matthew, alone, there are sixty-five quotations, not just isolated passages, but great blocks taken out of the Old Testament and pasted into the New.

People say they will believe the natural part, but they won't believe the spiritual; the things that are supernatural they throw out. There is no part of that book that does n't teach supernatural things. " Abraham fell on his knees, and God talked with him." If that did n't take place, the man that wrote Genesis knew that he was writing a wilful, deliberate lie. The children of Israel going through the Red Sea, and Moses striking the rock with that rod; if that did n't take place, the man who wrote Exodus wrote a deliberate lie. Break down his testimony; throw it out. Go into Numbers, and there is the story of the brazen serpent. If that did not take place, the man that wrote Numbers knew he was writing a lie. In Leviticus, the strange fire going out and consuming the two sons of Aaron; if that did not take place, the man that wrote Leviticus wrote a deliberate lie. And so you may go right on through the Old Testament, and you can hardly find a book that does not teach supernatural things. Go into the Four Gospels, and that is the last portion of the Bible people give up when they begin to pick the Bible to pieces; and there are more supernatural things in the Four Gospels than in any other part of the Bible.

Why, you cannot touch Christ anywhere that there is not something supernatural about him. Five hundred years before he was born the Angel Gabriel drops down into Babylon and tells Daniel; he drops into the Holy of Holies and tells Zachariah; that was supernatural. He dropped into Nazareth, and told the Virgin she was going to bring forth that Son; and then when he was born there came the heavenly choir and sang, " Glory to God in the highest, and on earth peace, good-will toward men." That was supernatural.

Our Gospel was born in the fires of supernaturalism. Look again when he was baptized, and the heavens opened, and the Spirit of God descended in a bodily form, and a voice coming from heaven said, " This is my beloved Son, in whom I am well pleased; " and after he was baptized hardly a day passed without something supernatural. One day he cleanses a leper; another day he curses a tree that withers away; another day he feeds five thousand miraculously; and so, day after day, miraculous things were taking place; and when he died the sun refused to look upon the scene, and veiled its face.

Thank God Christ is not dead yet. Do you think you would see these 60,000 people in Boston gathered here in the name of Jesus Christ if he was in Joseph's sepulchre? Thank God Christianity is not dead; it is alive, and I have never seen it more alive than it is to-day in this old city of Boston.

I want to say, very emphatically, I thank God I live to-day. I thank God for the outlook. I am no pessimist; I can tell you that. I thank God for what I see. I believe we are going to see greater things. I believe that we are coming back to the old Book. Why, some infidels, running up and down the country, tell us the old Book is going out of date. Thank God, it is just coming in. Do you know — now listen, mark — there have been more Bibles printed in the last twelve months than there were in the first eighteen hundred years. Don't forget it. At the first of this century it was estimated that there had been five thousand Bibles printed. In the last twelve months the National Bible Society, the Bible Society in London and New York, those three societies alone, have printed between six and seven millions of Bibles; and there are a good many private individuals — one house in New York City sold one hundred and ten thousand Bibles last year — that do not come from these three societies. There never was a time when the Word of the Lord Jesus Christ was so widely distributed. Why, it is printed in three hundred and fifty different languages! His words are going to the very corners of the earth.

Do you remember what he said? " Not one jot or tittle of the law shall pass until all is fulfilled." You turn over to the thirteenth chapter of Mark, who wrote, " Heaven and earth shall pass away: but my words shall not pass away." Have they passed away? Come, my friends, have they passed away?

Supposing that some sneering, jeering infidel had stood near Christ when he made these remarks. I see the scornful look as he says, " Hear that Jewish peasant talk; he says heaven and earth shall pass away, but his words shall not pass away." And mark you, he had no shorthand reporters taking down his words, no publishing-houses trying to publish a volume of his sermons. He was not liked by the Jews of that day; he was detested by what they called the Christians of the day. They looked upon him as a deceiver, an impostor, and yet he says, " Heaven and earth shall pass away: but my words shall not pass away."

Suppose some prophet had prophesied that in the sixteenth century this continent should be discovered and in the nineteenth century lightning should carry messages right across this continent; would it not have been considered a greater miracle than any Christ wrought? Thank God that has taken place. When they brought out the New Version it was arranged that it should be thrown on the market in New York and London together, and the two came out the same hour. It was thrown on the market in London at nine o'clock Friday morning. That would bring it out in New York at three o'clock Friday afternoon. An enterprising concern in Chicago had ninety men put to work, and they telegraphed every word of the New Testament from Matthew to Revelation, telegraphed it to Chicago, and it came out in each of the daily papers, and every class of people were buying that paper and reading the Word of the Lord Jesus Christ. Has his Word passed away? Thank God the sun shines on more Bibles to-day than it has ever shone on before in the history of the world;

and, my friends, what we want now — we have got the Bible and we have got the machinery to put it in motion — is to put the words of the Lord Jesus into the hearts of the people as well as into their minds. What we want now is men and women who are willing to go out and proclaim and teach it.

As I look over this audience to-night, I see a good many weak, struggling churches, some willing to carry on the work that can't afford to hire a minister. Let the Christian Endeavor carry on the work. We would have fires burning in all these churches that are perishing because they can't afford to hire a minister. Oh, I thank God for this volunteer movement, and I believe the Lord Jesus is calling for volunteers. And let every man and every woman who loves the Lord Jesus Christ go into training so that you may teach the Word of God. Just as quick as you can, my friends, learn to feed yourselves spiritually as well as physically. There are a lot of people that have to be fed with the ecclesiastical spoons. If the minister gives them the Word of God, they get a little bread. Go to the fountain-head; learn to read and study the Bible for yourselves. When my little boy could get his spoon from the plate to his mouth and not tip it over, the other children clapped their hands and cried, " See, papa, Paul can feed himself." They thought that was a great accomplishment. Some have to be fed every Sunday morning with an ecclesiastical spoon. Learn to feed yourselves; go right straight for the Word of God. There are a great many helps that we can get. O Christian Endeavorers, make up your minds to feed, to sustain, yourselves; train yourselves to be useful.

Why, you are not going to be carried away with every wind and doctrine if you know, actually know, the Word of God. Let me tell you how to do it. Get a Concordance; if you have not got one, get it before you leave Boston. Go to the bookstore, — they will give it to you, — and then just take up the Bible and study it properly; take up atonement, justification, sanctification; take up any one of those doctrines and spend a whole month. Study it for yourselves and by and by you will be armed and equipped, and if any man tells you that the doctrine is not true you can defend that doctrine and quote Scripture to that man; and I don't know anything that will down a man quicker than quoting Scripture. I would rather have " Thus saith the Lord" than tons of argument. It is not what this man thinks and that man thinks as much as what God says, and what we want is more men and women who can expound the Scriptures. A man says to me, " Well now, Moody, the Americans don't like it; they want eloquence in the pulpit; they want a man that can stand up with logic and with sound arguments and with beautiful elocution, and deliver His message." I think people have got awful sick of it. I believe there is a mighty famine in the land for just want of having the Word expounded.

A man said to a friend of his that he had made an artificial bee that was so natural he would challenge any man to tell the difference, and it would buzz like a live bee; and the man said, " Put the two bees down together and I will tell you which is the live bee and which is the artificial bee." He put down a drop of honey, and the live bee went to the honey. The artificial bee went buzzing round — he didn't know anything about honey. Well, I will admit these artificial Christians know nothing about the Word of God, but the real, true child of God knows honey every time; and I thank God we are willing to give them the honey.

I would like once more, before I close, just to urge upon all you young people to study the Word of God. Study it, make up your minds that you are going into active service, and therefore you must be armed and equipped. Let us pray that God may bless that Word that has been said anywhere throughout this city to-night and forever.

Prayer by Mr. Moody.

Our Heavenly Father, we pray that thy blessing may rest upon all that are gathered here to-night and in different parts of this city. We pray that the

Pentecostal fires may be kindled to-night; that the Pentecost may come upon this city as it did upon Jerusalem, and may there be fires kindled that shall be taken back into the country and the churches that shall set the churches on fire. May there be streams of salvation breaking out throughout the length and breadth of this land. We pray that thou wilt give us greater love for this Word; may it be a lamp to our feet and a light to our path, to guide us to those mansions thou hast gone and prepared for them that love thee. Oh that there may come a breath from Heaven upon us now! Holy Spirit, come with all thy convicting and converting power. May it be revealed to us to-night, and may every one here turn from sin and turn to God with all their hearts. We pray that heaven's blessing may rest upon the officers of this Society, and as they have been guided in the past, so may they be guided in the future. May every step be upward and onward, Godward, Christward, and heavenward. And may the blessing of God come not only upon them but upon all societies in this land and other lands; and Christ shall have the praise and glory forever. Amen.

Tent Williston.

From the throng that crowded Tent Williston, and made a wide fringe about it, came an urgent call for more after the colored quintette from Atlanta had sung " Do You Think I 'll Make a Soldier of the Cross ? " As usual, the limits of time made it necessary to veto the recall, and Trustee Teunis S. Hamlin, D.D., of Washington, painted in glowing colors the attractions of Washington, '96, to which the audience responded heartily with the Washington song. The prospect of San Francisco, '97, called out another burst of enthusiasm. The introduction of the Park Sisters was followed with the warm welcome that always awaits them. Rev. Henry T. McEwen, D.D., always remembered as the chairman of the famous Committee of '92, read Dr. Clark's address, the points of which were re-inforced by the vigorously expressed approval of the audience.

Rev. Russell H. Conwell, D.D., LL.D., a pastor with nine Endeavor Societies in his church, made the address of the evening. Treasurer Wm. Shaw presided, and Mr. Geo. C. Stebbins conducted the music. Rev. B. B. Tyler, D.D., of New York City, led the devotional exercises.

Address of Rev. Russell H. Conwell, D.D., LL.D.

A friend writes to me from a distant State that in his town there has for many years stood a church, the denomination of which I will not in this presence mention. But such a church has been seen in other parts of the world. He says that for many score of years the spiders have woven their webs in the corners and have partially hidden the desk itself, that the carpet remains only in rags, that the seats are many of them eaten by worms and whittled by roguish boys. One day not long since a Young People's Society desired to hold a meeting in that church. They petitioned the officers of that church for the privilege of having it one evening in the week to hold their religious services there ; but one of the good old officers of the church, too good to remain on this side of the bright gates, said that he was afraid that if the young people came into the church they would not behave reverently toward that sacred place. But the permission was at last granted to that society, and they went in with their brooms and their sponges for the purpose of rejuvenating the old ark of a building, when lo ! one of the officers who had consented to their presence came forward and said, " No, no ; lay not unholy hands on this sacred place." One of the number said, " But, grandfather, look at that cobweb in yonder corner; is it not a disgrace to have a cobweb here?" "O no, you young people are working a dangerous revolution. Remember that our prayers have been strained through that cobweb for twenty-five years."

Such a church as that has existed in more places than one, and many an old father in Israel has sat down in the dust, thanking his stars, not his Providence, that he had the opportunity to sit in the old place where brooms never come, where water is never seen, and where spiders are not interfered with in their share in the worship. But my friend writes to me that in the last cyclone that swept over that part of the country, only a few weeks ago, the lightnings descended and struck that old chimney and tore it apart, and the winds lifted the roof and carried it over into the next yard. The rains descended upon the old pews, and the grace of God came down upon the old pulpit, and the Christian Endeavor Society now hold open-air meetings; all of the denominations meet under the blue sky, perhaps under the stars, I know not. They have torn up the old carpet, and have cleared out the spiders; the old saints in Israel, — God bless them every one! — the old saints have departed from the ancient walls, and the new have come in under the light God let in by his own mighty cyclone. The storm will howl over those old churches, and if they do not permit the new life to come in and clear away the old webs and spiders and wasps, every roof will be lifted, letting the sunlight of God shine in. The Christian Endeavor movement was born for that purpose, if I may speak in the words of a prophet, for the churches of these later days have many of them needed new life, needed new blood.

I stood by the side of a patient in a Philadelphia hospital, and saw the blood transferred from the daughter to the father; and as the daughter's blood entered the veins of the father and saved his life, the new blood of the young life of Christianity is needed to preserve the very existence of Christianity in many churches in our land. And such a giving of God has now come, and in this Christian Endeavor movement I see its most vital purpose used for the purpose of renovating, making over into the image of God, those places called churches, but which should not bear that name unless the Spirit of God is in that place to keep them clean and welcome bright young faces. There are churches like that, and there are others that are like unto the great magnificent assembly of artists' genius to be found in the Louvre at Paris. I walked in Paris one day, and looked upon the wonderful productions of the sculptor's chisel. That night I had a dream, and in my dream I walked again in those halls, and some strange spirit of life had come into them, and the Venus de Milo and the Venus de Medici and the Apollo Belvidere arose and walked forth, and spoke with words of love and with an expression of kindness, and looked up to the stars. I felt in my dream what to-night I feel as I walk amid the rejuvenated churches, — a church life, which I find in all parts of the country, and which we see is coming into being in all parts of the world. Many of the churches are saintly and godly and happy, but they lack the very life of Christianity, the very heart's experience which cometh in with the new life of the young people, so greatly needed by the Church. I do not believe there are any church too holy to do good in. I do not believe there is any church people too pious to help their fellowmen. I do not believe there is any society bearing the name of Christ that has any right to that name, unless it is full of earnestness for the salvation of the souls of men.

The Christian Endeavor Society has this important safeguard and merit, that it is non-sectarian. It is one of the most liberal movements on the face of the earth; one of the most non-sectarian under the stars. Liberty is liberty regulated by law, and the highest type of Christian liberty is liberty regulated by the law of the living God. No people are so high-minded, generous, and hospitable as the rising people that are connected with this non-sectarian movement. The grandest thing to my mind is that it is non-sectarian. Christ was not sectarian. God is not sectarian. God is father over all. It is so grand in this that it brings necessarily forward this type of the future Christian. The Christian Endeavor movement is intended to make possible a pure, perfect, Christian man ; and when Dr. Clark, in his magnificent address, called for men, oh, how it touched the deepest vibrations of my soul! What the world needs is men, men, men! Not theology, but men!

I would not want to be moved by the theology of my denomination even a hundred years in the past. I would not desire to organize a church on the principles laid down by Calvin himself, or by the fathers of any of your denominations a hundred or five hundred years ago. Let that theology go. Who knows anything about the theology of St. Augustine? No one but musty old theologians, obliged to delve there to find something they do not need to find. Who cares? No one; but he was a good man, and the fact still lives and will live notwithstanding the mistakes in his theology. Some one has made a mistake in this tent to-night. Either you are wrong or I am wrong. Here are several different denominations that hear me speak, and we differ. Somebody's wrong. I hope it is not I. But if it is I, as sure as the sun rises, when I discover it I will change my theology. But the world does n't care much about your theology, anyhow, my brother, and it does n't care much about mine; and the Presbyterians don't know much about my theology; I don't know much about theirs. I don't care much about it.

I recognize the force of the Christian Endeavor Societies in their churches, upon the poor and the weak and the suffering and the needy. What I want is a man, not theology. O friends, I want that my church should be the last surviving church of all the churches in the world. I am very anxious that my denomination should be the denomination when all denominations unite, as they are going to do very soon. But I am comforted by this magnificent fact: if my denomination does survive all other denominations, it won't be because of its theology; it will be only because of the greater number of good men to be found in that denomination. If your denomination survives, and God grant that it may, then it will only survive because of the number and influence of good men, and it is for that purpose that the Christian Endeavor Societies are organized, — not to advance theology, but to make good men; to make righteous men and women. That is the purpose of these societies; hence it is non-sectarian. Of course it is. We are loyal to our own because we believe that in some things it is better than the others. We must meet that test whether we will or no. We must meet it. If your church is the church of the world, it must be judged by the Christian character of its membership and not by its theology. What the world wants is men, men, men. And this Christian Endeavor movement is building them up on every side. It is building them up first by creating a great standard of honor. Dr. Clark talked about the pledge, and said that it ought to be maintained in all our societies. It is an element of manhood to sign a pledge. We had a man in Philadelphia that said to a brother of mine, " I don't believe in taking pledges." So he went courting one of our sisters, and he said, " Will you marry me, Mary?" She said, " I don't believe in taking any pledges." Yet that same man signed his name to a pledge for $37.00, and owes it now, and probably always will owe it.

I believe that a pledge is a good thing. It makes society safer; it makes mankind purer; it lifts the standard of Christ higher to take a pledge. It makes men and women. Hence I believe in the Christian Endeavor pledge to speak every week in the meeting; it makes men. I believe in the advice of studying the Holy Bible for itself; it makes men. I believe in this mighty gathering from all quarters of the world because it makes men and women. Boston will be purer, her streets more peaceful, and the whole country will come nearer to the standard of liberty. The influence in every town and city and State and in this mighty gathering is for the uplifting of a Christian manhood, a type of Christ living and moving among men. Let me say just this: we want to save the world the other side of the earth. How will it be saved? Not by putting in two missionaries where there is a single convert and fighting over our sectarian differences. The heathen will only be saved when you can send to them better examples of Christianity than they find among the heathen. When you can send to them a perfect manhood, a manhood that they can see living, moving among them, as Christ moved among men, then and only then shall the whole world be saved.

Treasurer Shaw announced that it had originally been the plan for the convention to meet in San Francisco in '95, but that on account of being unable to obtain satisfactory rates on the railroads, the plan was abolished, and it was decided to come to Boston. Washington has claimed the Convention of '96, and we are already talking about where to go in '97. Los Angeles, the beautiful city of Southern California, has presented its plea with all power and sweetness and eloquence. Seattle, the beautiful city of Washington, has also come, and I hardly know which one presented the most urgent request. Portland, Ore., followed with, if anything, twofold earnestness — three of these great States asking for the Convention of '97. San Francisco also renewed her request, and desired that the convention should meet in San Francisco in '97. After careful and prayerful deliberation, the Trustees have decided that, if satisfactory rates are named by the railroads, the Convention of '97 will be held at the Golden Gate, in the city of San Francisco. After the benediction was pronounced the great meeting adjourned.

Tent Endeavor.

There were only 9,000 seats, but these were all filled an hour before the opening; and, by persistent pushing and crowding, the anxious horde of people outside, who had come to hear the speeches, — some of them from across the continent, — and who would not be disappointed, worked themselves gently but surely into the aisles and under the platform steps, until the "Endeavor" tent was holding 1,500 or more people than it was built for.

Inside, the scene was vastly more brilliant than at the morning meeting. Over 100 arc lights brought out with magnificent effect the colors of the decorations.

In the presiding officer s chair was Trustee Rev. J. Z. Tyler, D.D., of Cleveland, O.

The meeting was opened by a half-hour service of song, Mr. Percy S. Foster acting as musical director. The singing was grand; its beauty was not lost on any of the 10,000 inside, and thousands outside heard it.

Rev. Thomas Mulligan, D.D., of Allegheny City, Penn., read the lesson of the evening, selecting Matt. v. 1–12. Rev. Mr. Hardin made the opening prayer, and this was followed by a selection from the male quartette of Hampton Institute, Virginia; and the young colored men sang with such spirit that they were obliged to respond.

Mr. W. H. Pennell, of Washington, was introduced as the first speaker. His subject was, "Washington, 96." Mr. Pennell, the first signer of the first Christian Endeavor pledge in the first Christian Endeavor Society, was received with enthusiasm, and gave all a hearty invitation to the next convention, which is to be held in Washington.

After that, Trustee Prof. James Lewis Howe, of Lexington, Va., read Dr. Clark's annual address, and then Mr. John G. Woolley delivered an address which is herewith reproduced in full.

Address of Mr. John G. Woolley.

The bewildering paradox of the Christian reformer, in these days, is that he must speak of politics without mentioning politics, unless, indeed, he feel constrained to say something contemptuous of the only political party that stands for the only political thing that the Church, politically, stands for. You smile, but that is the indispensable condition of commanding the respectful attention — not to say cordial sympathy — of that touchy fugitive from Divine justice that goes by the alias of "Christian Public Sentiment." I refuse to try to do it. I hold myself at no great value in these Olympiads where the horse-leech's daughters, with Eutyches, Ananias, Balaam, and Judas, represent the Church in the dominant politics, but incalculable star-flights beyond any fear of the contemptible boycott that, under pain of ecclesiastical starvation and partizan rack and wheel and thumb-screw, would consign the greatest of reforms to worked-out mines of bathos and old tales, or the more recent and even more hopeless levels where sanctimonious expediency sorts junk from the garbage of its two hundred and fifty thousand social catch-basins and hooks rags from the ashes of its own accessory arson.

I should despise myself for such capacity of shrinkage in my manhood as would fit me to scull an argument along the devious larvæ-breeding lagoons that go by the name of "policy," — creeping on under bare poles, navigating lily-pads, with half a crew hoisting distress signals and the other half heaving the lead, — reaching up for the desperate help of wreckers and down for the oozy assurance of mud, when just outside a little bar of *sand* lay God's illimitable and unfathomable ocean of truth, with power blowing a gale off shore.

This is a fight, and I, by the grace of God, am in it, to win, or lose or suffer, as events dispose, and I will not, now or ever, charge the enemy with hortatory turf, when hard, hot, jagged facts are ready to my hand.

Away back at the sky line of history, limned in heroic outline on the flushing East of legendary time, whoever looks may see a glorious crank, or, in theological language, a minor prophet. And like a bugle blast of some blenched and horror-stricken but unflinching Titan, sounding a challenge to Perdition's envoy extraordinary and minister plenipotentiary, his voice splits the great deep of twenty-five centuries of cruelty, as rapiers of the lightning flash through summer clouds, and scandalizes the "good form" of decorous and perfunctory litanism, hallooing, "Woe unto them that supply drink to other men!"

Voices of his critics do not survive, but doubtless, prude, "per diem" orthodoxy shrunk aghast into its gabardine and said, "This Prohibitionist is a nuisance and a seditionary." "You cannot make men sober by law." "Statutes should never be in advance of public sentiment." That was the blunder of the Golden Rule, the weakness of the decalogue, the farce of Sinai. "I am as good a Prohibitionist as he is, but not third party." "He is throwing his influence away." "He is setting the cause back twenty years." "He wants an office." "He is a sorehead." "He is in it for money." "He is paid by Babylonish gold." "The best we can do now is to work popular vices on shares, confine them to the tenement districts, — and build more jails." "Why does he not content himself with scorching sin in general, or tweaking the nose of heterodoxy as the major prophets did?" "Noah made wine, and so did David." "Solomon said, 'Wine is a mocker,' a thing to use — and so, to sell — for medicine and pudding." "Let this upstart fanatic stick to *that,* or hold his peace!"

But he said, "There is no muzzle in Palestine that will stop my mouth. I will wear no armor that does not fit me. I will worship no book nor retrogress to any other man's ideal. I refuse to be careful for anything, but in everything, by prayer and thanksgiving, let my wants be made known unto God; I will stand upon my watch-tower and see what *he* will say unto *me.*"

So I, least of the prophets of the great reform, a fugitive from the black galleys of the pirate ship of drink's despair, with the purple welts of a thousand whippings on my heart, and whom it is as lawful for any priest, doctor, or drink-seller to entrap and damn as it is to kill a rat, have come again, dead spent with toiling up and down the land, to tell you, in the name of the transcendent citizen who threw his vote away on Calvary, what God has been saying to *me* in the swish of the cat-o'-nine-tails of two hundred and fifty thousand licensed bastinadoes in this Christian land.

Expect no soft, sheeny sentences from me to-night. Let no sleek, politic doctrinaire admonish me to be careful. The white faces of my dead father and mother came to me this morning before the dawn and said, "Get up and curse the saloon!" O friends, O father, O mother, O graves of my dead, O my country, O earth, O heaven, O Christ, hear me! If I held here in a crucible, white hot, the most scalding, corroding, and consummate curse of God I would pour it out upon the liquor traffic with a steady hand!

But stop! Who knows how far that curse would burn its way? Who is it, in the great white Dominion and in these States, that keeps the drink on sale?

I hold up before you here the greatest public document the world has ever seen; Magna Charter was a trifle to it. I am afraid you cannot see the beauty and suggestiveness of the design. Let me describe it in a word or two. The margin is a silver trellis set up against a background of gold, with vines of morning-glory wreathing to the top and doves mating in its verdurous meshes. The central picture represents a scene in a saloon. Back of the bar is the inevitable mirror, flanked by decanters and pyramids of cigar-boxes, over it a dumb clock face, and over that the laconic rhetorical gem, "No tick." To the right, a sign, "Hot Punch," and to the left another, "Tom and Jerry," and two bartenders, one in the act of drawing beer and the other putting a black bottle upon the bar. In front three men are leaning, with glasses in their hands and cigars in their mouths, and three others sit at a table gambling — one holding up three fingers, signing for more drinks.

Listen, while I read it: —

State of Indiana. Retailer's liquor license. To whom it may concern: This certifies that license has been granted by the Board of Commissioners of——— Indiana, to ———, for one year from ——— day of———, 189—, to sell spirit-uous, vinous, and malt liquors in less quantity than a quart at a time, with the privilege of allowing the same to be drunk upon ——— premises at ——— place of business only; viz., ——— in ——— in——— township, in the county aforesaid, subject to the restrictions and under the provisions of an act to regulate and license the sale of spirituous, vinous, malt, and other intoxicating liquors; to limit the license fee to be charged by cities and towns prescribing penalties for in-toxication, and providing for the recovery of damages for injuries growing out of unlawful sales of intoxicating liquors; to repeal all former laws regulating the sale of intoxicating liquors and *all laws and parts of laws coming in con-flict with the provisions of this act* (that abolishes mother-love, common sense, conscience, God), prescribing penalties for the violation thereof and *declaring an emergency*.

Approved March 17, 1875.

In testimony whereof I hereunto set my hand and affix the seal of the Board of Commissioners of said county, this ——— day of ———, 189—.

{ SEAL }

——— ———, *Auditor.*
——— *County.*

That, I say, is a legal document, the letters patent of a great State, the sov-ereign voice of a great people, the muniment of a great title, a royal bond and charter for the safety of the saloon. I got it in Indianapolis, but you may get the same thing in Boston, — less ornate, as befits the quieter New England taste, — or in Canada, or in any State but four; and the bargain is made, and in process of fulfilment, to put *them* back among the States of purchasable virtue.

That low, coarse, bestial instrument disgraces Indiana not only, but declares the law of the whole land to-day; for although the prohibitory States and towns issue no license in their own name, they all and singly consent to this.

On your peril, pray for the mildew of God's wrath upon the saloon. The petty, venial, criminal, infernal tyranny and treason of the party boss have made every saloon-keeper the *people's licensee, and every one of us his licenser.* And less than two per cent of us have even entered a protest at the general election!

Christendom is Saloondom, and ninety-five per cent of male church-members are on the pay roll of the drink — as gaugers, collectors, storekeepers, or *silence-keepers.*

The liquor traffic is an industrial and political trinity; it gears to the social system at the saloon, but gets its life in the "still-house" and its hopes of immortality in the still church.

I have no word to utter here against the distiller, the brewer, or the drink-seller. The public virtue was for sale; they bought it at its own price, and paid for it in hard cash, — bloody dimes wrung from the hands of folly, poverty, and toil, — and while they own it they have a right to enjoy and profit by the usufruct. My voice is to the voting church. "Awake, thou that sleepest, arise from the dead, and Christ shall give thee light. Awake, awake, put on thy strength, O arm of the Lord. Put on thy beautiful garments, O Jerusalem. Shake thyself from the dust. Arise, loose thyself, O captive daughter of Zion, for ye have sold yourselves for naught, and ye shall be redeemed without money!"

The case is between church resolutions and saloon RESOLUTION, plural versus singular, miscellany versus solidarity, a pious sprinkling-pot versus an ocean current of practical politics, local option versus universal empire, multiplication of fractions, that is to say, *division,* pursuing the saloon, which is an integer.

The difficulty, dimly seen for years, has crystallized into the maxim, "Temperance people ought to get together." Of course we ought; but *where?* It happens at every change of the moon that some flabby philosopher pushes his peripatetic bandbox into the public square, and challenges the saloon to mortal compromise upon some contemptible Scandinavian basis of profit-sharing, or the more brutally straightforward and American method of a fixed price for taking civic honor out of politics, and for the debasement of public virtue to the plane of stark revenue, — like a brothel, — and simpers to worn and anguished women and haggard, beggared men, as they crawl out of the wreckage of their broken lives, "Behold, how good and how pleasant it is for saints and saloon-keepers to vote together in unity."

And when some heart-wrung man cries out against the truculent infamy this same philanthropist sneers at him as a new-washed, impudent drunkard, "over-scrupulous," "a maligner of the Church," "an auxiliary of the saloon," while the belle Pharisee, with honesty at half-mast, struts into politics, and delivers over the Christian vote into "a league with death and a covenant with hell," and answers the wail of stricken homes, the voice of the Church, and the plain Word of God with the pusillanimous logic of the bargain counter: "It is not what we want, but it is cheap;" and then, upon election day, the voting Church eagerly ambles after a party leader to the polls, and ratifies his offer of a lease of God's world to Satan for a mess of spoils, and would mitigate the perfidy by saying that wrong is sometimes right in politics. And that is a lie, as black as ever flapped its bat wings at the glory of a sunset.

And I, for one, dare stand apart and be a fool for Christ's sake, and call wrong *wrong* in religion or politics or New York City or hell or Norway. For a man, a woman, a church, a city, a state, or a nation to "buy the truth and *sell it*" is treason against the God of Truth, label it what you may. "Tax" in Ohio, "license" in Massachusetts, "mulct" in Iowa, or "bribe" in New York, it is shame everywhere and forever.

We would better stay apart eternally than get together in the *nicest* wrong. These elastic Empirics, who would vivisect a living political truth out of the politics of the Republic, ought to know that they never can unite the faith of the Church upon a wicked thing. How can "two walk together unless they be agreed"? Sin is the essence of disagreement, fermentation, yeast, the one tremendous contradiction of the universe. God has endued the very atoms of human dust with inability to lie still with evil. This is his only visible guarantee of saving this world. "The wicked are like the troubled sea when it cannot rest, *casting up* mire and dirt, " domestic or Norwegian just the same. No man is wicked enough to agree with *himself* in sin. There is but one place under the bend of that sky, or over it, where one human mind can come to itself, or more than one can get together, and that is in the " green pastures " and " beside the still waters " of righteousness.

Take a vote upon the various propositions that have come up in this reform, and there is just one that can command the universal sympathy of Christians, and that is that " the saloon ought to die."

Then why not kill it? Why have we not voted it to death long ago? The answer is very simple, and brings me at once to the gist of this argument. We have not voted the saloon to death because the ruling politicians *would not let us*. How could they prevent? Are Christian men slaves? Yes; abject, motley slaves, contraband of machine statesmanship, and annually put up and sold upon the auction block of *party*.

Do money-jobbers loot the treasury, and do the people cry out against it? " Shut your mouth, you wild-cat ignoramus!" Who says that? *The party*.

Does monopoly grind the face of independent industry, and does some faithful preacher or college professor flame out against the villany? " Resign, you incendiary anarchist!" Who says that? *The party*.

Do railroad corporations use the people's franchises to their hurt, and do the people dare complain? " Silence, you idiot!" Who says that? *The party*.

Why has Iowa violated the express will of her people, and by a general statute compounded the felony of liquor-selling and consented to become the laughing-stock of courts? Because she supposes that she has a statesman so neutral tinted that he can make an invisible race for the presidency midway between whiskey and water, and between gold and silver, provided he can go before *the party* free from the fatal blemish of hailing from a State that is unfriendly to the saloon.

Why has Rhode Island gone back into the service of the saloon, and concentrated her intelligence and conscience upon a measure to establish free gold-cures for her home-made drunkards? Because the hand of Providence,— Rhode Island,—a private office broker, points out the *party* peril of being steadfast.

Why has Christianity been insulted in Ohio and denied the right of self-defence against the saloon? Because her favorite son was a candidate for President, and the leader of the house said that to estrange the saloon-keepers would swamp *the party*.

Why has the enforcement of the prohibitory law of Kansas been betrayed in difficult cities into the hands of its notorious enemies? In order to hold the saloon vote in *the party*.

Why did those senators of New Hampshire find it necessary to cringe and squirm and lie to prevent the prudent and necessary strengthening of the prohibitory law? Because that sacrifice of patriotic manhood was necessary for *the party*.

Why does Maine's Chief Justice habitually insult the law that he has sworn to enforce, and permit himself to be known and despised as the saloon-keeper's friend in a prohibition State? Because *the party* interest in that State requires that Christianity and crime should be politically harmonized by a flexible judiciary.

Why did Michigan disfranchise a large number of her noble citizens? Because they felt in honor bound to unite against the ruling *party*.

Why has New York disfranchised *everybody* except Platt and Croker, the " twins" in the zodiac of dirt? Because the recent wave of civic honesty in the city was a common menace to both *parties*, and so, in self-defence, they make the empire robber's roost *bipartizan*.

And so throughout the land the Christian vote cries craven, hangs its harp upon the party willow on election day, and sings the *party* version: —

> " All hail the power of Jesus' name,
> Let angels prostrate fall;
> Bring forth the royal diadem,
> And *sell it*, Lord and all."

This is plain talk, but not a word at random. Somebody *must* talk plain, and I have no parish to please, no trustees to satisfy, no session to consult, no subscription list to consider, no career to foster; no presiding elder has an eye on me, no bishop counts me in his diocese, and this is Boston, the home of independent thinking and free speech.

The defeat of the Church, the disgrace of the law, the despair of reform, is the all-but-universal substitution of partyism for patriotism. This country will go straight for prohibition whenever it shall suit the interest or convenience of the two great parties to let the people loose with the saloon. We await their pleasure.

Meanwhile, a young Christian man arriving at his majority and entering into *respectable* party affiliations must shed his greatest and clearest political convictions, as one would leave his mackintosh and rubbers, at the door. But in the face of that truth ninety-five per cent of Southern Christian men, and about forty-eight per cent in the whole country, pour out the blood of their civic virtue in defence of a *party* which is the open enemy of prohibition, and this they do for the utterly unpatriotic and unworthy motive of "beating another *party*."

And again, ninety-five per cent of Northern Christian men, and about forty-eight per cent in the country at large, annually bind the Son of God and lay him on the altar of unpatriotism as a sin-offering for a *party* organization which is as destitute of honor to the Church as the moon is of atmosphere, and they do this because they hate another *party*.

Quadrennially, the voting Church dissolves into a bipartizan mob and goes to the Gethsemane that we call a general election, where the son of man lies on his face and prays, and saloon-keepers, distillers, brewers, gamblers, and all the unclean brood of politicians, scoffers, and libertines seize him, put a scarlet robe upon him, arm him in derision with a reed in his right hand, plait a crown of thorns and put it upon his head, bow the knee before him and mock him, crying, "Hail, Saviour of men!" and then spit upon him and smite him in the face; and ninety-five per cent of the Christian voters stand with the mob *and do nothing* until they are challenged by a *party*, and then they say, "*We do not know the man to-day;*" and the politicians drag him to the polls and crucify him there, and as he staggers up the bipartizan Aceldama, they hoot and jeer and call him "mugwump," "Sunday-school statesman," "fanatic," "fool," and subservient priests wag their heads and say, "He undertook too much," and when he gasps and faints from pain they thrust the vinegar and gall of party ridicule and hate into his mouth, and party bosses gamble for his garments, and five millions of his disciples stand by until the polls close to have the poor privilege of seeing their despised, deserted, broken-hearted lord *buried* and his grave sealed with the stamp of the internal revenue.

Have I made you understand? I tell you that when the Democratic party looks into the face of a dead drunkard his wounds identify *a murderer*, and open and bleed afresh. And nearly half of you are Democrats! And upon the staring, wide, wild eyes of the broken-hearted woman who was murdered last night by the frenzied brute who called her "mother," the Republican party is photographed, a co-assassin with the saloon-keeper and the felon-maniac, her son. And nearly half of you are Republicans!

For us to be mixed up with that is at once infamous and imbecile, for we are not cowards, traitors, or murderers at heart, but victims of partizan education, slaves of partizan habit, tools of the vilest hypnotism of partizan suggestion.

If we believe it to comport with Christian profession to keep silent about the saloon at general elections, or that it is indifferent what we do about it there, we ought to expunge our toplofty resolutions like honest men, and stop the braggart lies that have been published in our name.

Be patient with me! I know you will scorn to take such action. Well, then, for the sake of the chivalry of your manhood, the luxury of self-respect, the strength of your youth, the truth of the Church, stand up like brave men, and make your resolutions good.

Do not ask me to instruct you how or when you may achieve the victory, or what party will win it. I don't know. No men can tell you that, for no man's mind is big enough to calculate the tension of ideas, the strength of organizations, the lines of least resistance, the resultant of infinite forces and antagonisms, the percentages of friction, or the quantum of inertia in the civic world. I have but one clear vision to-day about it, and that I have come a thousand miles to give you. It is this: we must overcome the sag of dirty politics. How? *Get out of it!* But where shall you go? Never mind. Get out of the slough, and *then* inquire the road.

Let me be very clear about this. For instance: you are a young man, a Presbyterian, a Christian Endeavorer, a Carolinian, and a Democrat, and the election is coming on. Your church says, " No political party has the right to expect, nor ought it to receive, the support of Christian men so long as it stands committed to the license policy, or refuses to put itself on record in an attitude of open hostility to the saloon."

The United Societies of Christian Endeavor are pledged to annihilate the saloon in politics. Your State is impoverished, betrayed, debauched, by it, and your party is pledged *not to interfere.*

What are you going to do about it? Your Populist neighbor says, " Come with us, and we will crush monopoly, throttle the banks, and establish the saloon upon a less obnoxious and more profitable basis." He may be right about monopoly, but that iniquity is not so clear to you as the saloon is, and the Church has not yet taken position as to it, and you do not feel ready to rip up the financial system about which great statesmen appear honestly to differ very widely, and you cannot consent to engage in *improving* saloons.

What are you going to do about it? The Prohibitionist says, " Come with us, and help us enfranchise every woman in the land, and we will *vote* the saloon out." But you are not ready to enfranchise women, nor hopeful of the effect of their influence in politics.

What are you going to do about it? Your Republican friend says, " Come with us, and we will do you good." Well, what good? Republican victory means many things problematically, but it surely means saloons. Where shall you go? I don't know, I tell you. But remember the call of Abraham: " Get thee out, . . . and I will show thee." Go out of dirty parties, and God will tell you where to go next. The rudder is at the stern of a boat, or an idea. *Move;* then steer.

Christian citizenship means at least two things, — Christianity and Citizenship. The voting church by trying to be true to parties has been untrue to both. The Christianity that stays in dirty parties loses its savor precisely as the fishes of Mammoth Cave have lost their eyes. Politics is *the average virtue.* The first duty of a Christian is to *raise the average* by as much as his character weighs. Because we have lost sight of that, the parties have been able to disfranchise civic Christianity and transmute the power of the Church into saloons.

There are men enough at this Convention to stop that *now*, and we have no business to ever pass another resolution against the saloon until we have made up our minds to march out of that fellowship. To compromise with wrong is a surrender of integrity. The supreme business of Christian Endeavor is to bring Christianity to *par.* If it were capitalized to-day upon a basis of five million shares at one dollar each, they would be selling in the political stock exchange at less than five cents apiece. That is appalling, but it is true. Last general election ninety-five per cent of Christian men consented to shut their eyes to the saloon to help one moderate drinker beat another to the White House, and yet that ninety-five per cent are continually asking us to propose something practical. *Wash your hands;* that is practical.

Somebody is sure to say that I have spoken here in the interest of the Prohibition party. I make you my witnesses that I do *not*. No party owns me; no party claims me. I speak in the interest of a *clean church;* and in my judgment the very day the Church *cuts loose* from dirty politics there will come a new cleavage of voters, new ideals of citizenship, new measures of candidates, new meanings of loyalty, new victories, and a new country, and the Prohibition party will have done its work and will disappear, except in its one clean, noble page of American history, and there will be a new party either for Christians or for saloon-keepers, for no honest party can hold both. I speak in the interest of a robust and vital Christianity, that will not be under obligation to saloons, nor mix with cowardice or lies.

O my friends, come up where the Church stands, an impregnable fortress upon the crown of the Rock of Ages. Come up where the air is better, the horizon wider, and where in the skyward silence you can hear God speaking. Let the unclean parties know of you what they know of J. Wilbur Chapman, Ballington Booth, Bishop Fitzgerald, Joseph Cook, and some two hundred and seventy thousand others in the States alone,— that though their citizenship go mute and inglorious forever for want of a party, their vote *cannot be had,* on any terms, for a man or a party that does not say, *on the platform,* "Down with the saloon." Join every one of you to-night in the pledge of Habakkuk: " I will stand upon *my* watch-tower and *see* what *God* will say unto *me.*"

General Grant said, "There is a moment in every battle when the first advance means victory." The battle royal of the centuries is on. The Church that never lost a *fight* with wrong, nor ever succeeded in a *stratagem* against it, faces the saloon upon the fairest field and fairest terms the universe could furnish,— the ballot-box of a republic where, by Divine right, the people rule. The voice of the trimmer is heard in the Church and the State, saying, " Let the saloon alone one more campaign, and let me lead you *round about* the good by stealth and the aid of enemies." Away with trimmers, great or small! Cowards, to the rear! Call in the pickets! Close ranks! Guide center! Forward, with this new battle cry: *The Church for Christ!*

If the delegates in Tent Endeavor on Thursday night entered the canvas doors without any definite convictions about the liquor question, they left bearing in their hearts a perfect hatred of that minister plenipotentiary of the Evil One. They left, likewise, with an overpowering realization of the truth that party is not principle, that truth is not entirely included in any platform, and that the starry firmament is all too narrow to cover the saloon and the Christian Church. "Down with the saloon!" will be re-echoed in thousands of deeds because of this mighty meeting in Tent Endeavor.

FRIDAY MORNING.

Mechanics' Building.

The very skies seemed to smile Friday morning, and that was, perhaps, why the crowds of Thursday evening were repeated at Mechanics' Hall.

The beginning was prompt, and the singing went better than ever before. It was indeed a scene of beauty and inspiration that Director Stebbins looked down upon as he arose to announce the first hymn.

After Scripture reading and a prayer by Rev. John Pickles, D.D., the pastor of Tremont Street M. E. Church, Boston, the programme of the morning was started. The chairman of the morning was Trustee Rev. M. Rhodes, D.D., of St. Louis, Mo., who introduced Mr. William T. Ellis to give a sample committee report.

Information Committee's Report.

By William T. Ellis.

The information committee is the field-glass with which Christian Endeavor sweeps the wide world. It keeps Christian Endeavorers up to date. It makes them one in fellowship and work. It takes but five minutes at each meeting of the society for the hearing of its report. Material for these is culled from denominational papers, from *The Golden Rule,* and from other sources. The aim of the present address is to give simply an ordinary example of an information committee report.

Around the world in five minutes! Begin at the antipodes, if you please, and pay a fraternal visit to that unique society in Australia, among the members of a private family. Here we find a complete and prosperous organization with no members that do not dwell under one roof.

With the speed of imagination we are now in Laos, among the dark-skinned Endeavorers who call themselves "the company of young people that endeavor to do, with sacrifice, the work that is proper in a Christian." They tell us that on January 10 they were but a feeble folk — only fifteen of them. Now they bless that heathen land with nine societies and two hundred and forty-five members.

Another jump, and we are in the British Isles. We spend a moment in the reading-room of the Portadown Society, in Ireland, which is maintained for the youth of the neighborhood. Another Irish Society held a social recently, a. which seventy of the poorest people in town were entertained and banqueted.

Look stern as we enter the land of the "unspeakable Turk," and glance at the smallest society in the world, with its two faithful members. It has been larger, but the lookout committee was faithful, and a violated pledge meant a purged society with these conscientious boys.

Back now to "the home of the brave," but not "the land of the free," for we are going to visit some brethren who are "ambassadors in bonds," the members of the society in the Kentucky State Prison. Their first greetings are praises of the Kentucky Endeavorers who sent a Christian letter to each of the convicts, thus leading many to the Lamb of God.

From effect to cause is not a geographical journey, so we may glance for an instant at the drink monster, and rejoice in the set-back the Endeavorers of Indiana have given it in the famous Nicholson Bill. Montreal, New York, Rochester, and Syracuse — all are jubilating over temperance victories. We joy with you.

Our journey is ended — ended at the Cross. Here we can stand and bid Godspeed to the sixty volunteers who offered themselves to the missionary cause at Tennessee State Convention, and to the fifteen members of a single Maryville (Tenn.) society that have their faces turned toward the foreign field. The host of missionary givers and goers increases before our vision, and we close our eyes, and cry "Thank the Father, thank Jesus, thank the Holy Ghost, for the missionary baptism of Christian Endeavor."

Dr. Rhodes then introduced the Rev. W. Knight Chaplin, of London, England, as follows : —

We are now to have a voice from the other side of the sea, and we all want to hear him. It is written in our annals that there was a time when America and England were not engaged in Christian Endeavor. It was about the time that Boston had stopped drinking tea for a season. I am happy to say that that day has passed. I wish we had a British flag here this morning as large as a small section of the Atlantic Ocean. I wish we had a choir of ten thousand voices, that we might sing "God Save the Queen;" but in the absence

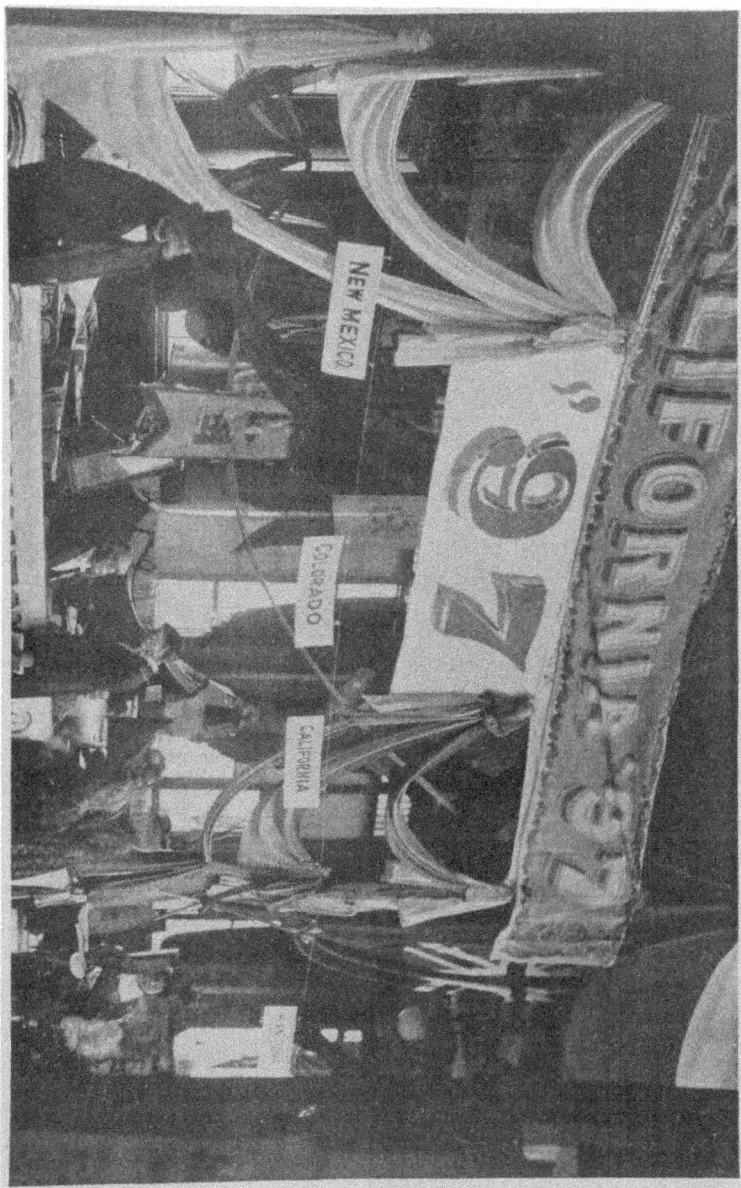

A Section in State Headquarters, Mechanics' Building.

of these, I am sure there is something of America here, and there is something of England here, and I am very glad indeed to clasp hands with this my brother in a fellowship which in some measure beautifully illustrates that for which Christian Endeavor stands, and that peace which was sung in the skies of Bethlehem. It pleases me to introduce to you the Rev. W. Knight Chaplin, of London, England, who will speak on, "The Cardinal Principles of Christian Endeavor."

Then followed a scene seldom witnessed in any convention. Dr. Rhodes clasped Mr. Chaplin by the hand, and as they stood together the audience stood and cheered to the echo.

Address of Rev. W. Knight Chaplin.

I bring you greeting from the great and growing army of Christian Endeavorers in the Old Country. There our population is increasing at the rate of half a million every year. This one fact is most eloquent and forceful in declaring that the church of the future will be that church which most earnestly and successfully gives itself in the present to winning the young for Jesus Christ. It is, perhaps, the recognition of this fact that has caused the churches of Great Britain and Ireland, and indeed the churches of the whole world, to give so warm and ready a welcome to the Young People's Society of Christian Endeavor. That that welcome has been both warm and ready those who best know the facts will be the readiest to admit. In Great Britain this has been most undoubtedly the case. Commencing at Crewe, in 1887, the movement at first took root slowly and advanced very gradually. At the end of the first five years there were but 425 societies registered in the British section. That brought us to the beginning of 1893. During that year the growth became more rapid. Commencing the year with 425 societies, we closed it with 1,004. In the early hours of 1894 I sent out a little article entitled "1894," in which I made the suggestion that we should set it before ourselves as an ambition to make the number of societies at the end of the year correspond with the number of the year, thus causing 1,004 to become 1,894. By very many this was regarded as a wild dream, but the year was not nine months old before we registered 1,894 societies, and we closed the year with a total registration of 2,112. Sometimes when we tell the story of this phenomenal advance we are reminded by our friends of Jonah's gourd—that sprang up in a night and withered away just as quickly. We thank them for the illustration and remind them that Jonah's gourd grew at the bidding of the Lord, and did not wither until it had accomplished the work which he had for it to do. In like manner we regard the growth of the Christian Endeavor movement as the work of the Lord, and are convinced that it will not pass away until it has accomplished his purpose.

I was in Ireland a little time ago and there heard of just such a man as you hear of nowhere else but in Ireland. This man, it was said, was one day busily engaged building a wall in an exposed part of the country. A passer-by addressing him said, "What's the use of your building a wall there?" "Why not here," asked the Irishman, "as well as anywhere else?" "Why, simply because the first gale of wind that comes sweeping across this part of the country will cause your wall to topple over." "Is that all?" said the Irishman. "Yes." "Well, if that's all, that is n't much." "How can you regard with such stoical calmness the probability of all your work being suddenly brought to naught in that manner?" asked the passer-by. "Well, yer see — yer see," he said, "it all depends on how yer build." "Are you building in any special sort of way?" "I should think I am." "Well, how are you building?" "Well," said he, "I am building this way — three feet high and four feet wide, so that if it blows down it will be better than it was before." There was a great deal of truth in what he said when he said, "Everything depends on how you build." When you are about to judge whether a building is likely to endure or not you ask, " What is it built on, and what is it built with ? " Now in this Christian Endeavor movement we are building upon the strongest and most enduring possible foundation. We are building into the movement material of sterling worth, material made up of the gifts and talents and powers with which God has endowed earnest, consecrated lives. This movement may have had a cradle; it will never have a coffin; but will go on in the achievement of victory and success "for Christ and the Church " until the Lord, the great Head of the Church, shall crown every member of the Endeavor host with a crown that fades not away.

But I must not forget that the immediate subject which I am to present this morning is. " The Cardinal Principles of Christian Endeavor." Let me say right away that I regard these as being: first, Service by all; second, Love to all; third, Separation from all; and fourth, Consecration in all. With regard to the first of these I may say that the abundant hope of the Church of Jesus Christ lies in leading the young people to offer the flower of their life to God while that flower is yet in the bud. The day has gone by for supposing that no good work could be done "for Christ and the Church " until the energy and enthusiasm of youth have been superseded by the wisdom and ripened experience of old age. We regard it as an honor, great and unspeakable, to be yoked together in service with God's veterans, but we recognize that there is a work and a place in the Christian Church for the youngest disciple. Looking around, we discover that many of the world's best-known men accomplished their best work in comparatively early years. The French Emperor who conquered Italy was only twenty-five when he did it. Newton had made many of his greatest discoveries before he was a day older than that. Wesley and Whitfield were still students when they inaugurated Methodism. And Melancthon had gained the Greek chair at Wittenberg and was keenly defending Martin Luther in the face of the whole world when he was but twenty-one years of age. The truth of the matter is, my young comrades, in Christian life and work, that it behooves us to make good use of the morning of our life, for when life's sun has once reached its meridian the night comes very quickly. Dr. Phillips, our British Sunday-school Union missionary in India, told me that he was sent for on one occasion to go to a little village in an out-of-the-way corner of his great diocese in India, to baptize and receive into church fellowship some sixty or seventy adult converts from Hinduism. He said: "I went very gladly, and that afternoon found these dear people all gathered together in the little mission church. I spoke with each one of them in turn (catechized them, as he called it), and at the end of the talk I came to the conclusion that I might safely and wisely receive all of them into fellowship with that church. At the commencement of the proceedings I had noticed a boy about fifteen years of age sitting away in a back corner, looking very anxiously and listening very wistfully the whole time. He now came forward. I said, ' What, my boy, do you want to join the church? ' He gave me to understand that he did. ' But,' I said, ' you are very young and if I were to baptize and receive you into fellowship with this church to-day and then you were to slip aside and turn back it would bring great discredit upon this church and do great injury to the cause of Christ. I shall be coming this way again in about six months. Now you be very loyal to the Lord Jesus Christ during that time and if, when I come again at the end of the half-year, I find you still steadfast and true I will baptize and receive you very gladly.' I had no sooner said this than all those people rose to their feet and, some speaking for the rest, said, ' Sir, what do you mean ? ' and I said, ' My dear people, why all this excitement? What 's the matter ? ' and then with a common consent they pointed toward that boy and said, ' Why, sir, it is him that 's taught us all that we know about Jesus Christ,' and so it turned out to be. This was the little minister of the little church, the honored instrument in the hand of God of saving all the rest for Jesus Christ."

I refer to this to-day in order that I may once more urge upon you that which is my profoundest conviction, that if the weakest and least talented among us will but unreservedly consecrate to God what power we have, he will accept the

offering and use it, and us, in a manner that shall surpass our wildest dreams.
I believe

> " This old world might be better
> If each hand would break a fetter,
> If each one would do his part
> To bind up one stricken heart."

SERVICE BY ALL. This, as you know, is one of the watchwords of this movement, — not sentiment, but service. The movement, indeed, exists in order to translate sentiment into practical life and work. That does not mean that either the founder or the leaders of the movement undervalue sentiment. We know that in the case of all Christly souls religion has its exalted visions, its moods of triumphant hope and transporting love; seasons when the cup of spiritual joy seems to run over and the whole nature is ravished with the beauties of the spirit world. But we also recognize that unpractised sentiments, be they ever so pure or noble or lofty, are of no more real use to either the man, the Church, or the world, than those raindrops which, falling in the summertime upon the leaves of the tree are dried up by the summer sun without ever falling to nourish the roots of the tree's life. Christian Endeavorers are taught to go from the quiet chambers of devotion, where they have been lifted for the hour into the very heaven of spiritual delights, and from thronged services and great conventions where the tide of spiritual joy has run high — to go from these scenes and privileges to the arena of manly service, and to the sphere of earnest activity "for Christ and the Church."

The second point I wish to emphasize is that the ever-present constraining motive of this service by all must be LOVE TO ALL. This, I am glad to know, is already remarkably characteristic of this great movement. Christian Endeavorers want to belong to that wing of the army of Jesus Christ that " picks men up out of the gutter." We want to be endowed with the promised power from on high that shall enable us to reach out to the one farthest away and out of reach, and to reach down to the one most sunken in sin, and to bring these lost and soiled souls into saving touch and contact with the Divine Christ, who died to save them.

This missionary fervor has hold of the very heart of this movement and is, I am convinced, one of the greatest secrets of its success and power. I have been told of two men who, some years ago, for the first time saw an engine. It was standing at the head of a train of coaches at the railway station platform, and, as they came near to it, one said to the other, " Jim, they say that there thing goes." " Don't yer believe it; that 'll never go." And by and by it was time for " the thing " to go. It went. The guard blew his whistle, and the train proceeded, slowly at first, and then increasing its speed until presently it dashed away out of their sight. For a time they stood looking after it with eyes and mouths wide open with astonishment. When they had somewhat recovered, the one who had said it would never go said, " Jim, she 'll never stop." But by and by another train came in and stopped, and they were more mystified than ever, and they said, " We must see into this thing ; " so they looked under it and over it and round about it, and examined it very carefully ; and at length the voice came again : " Jim, I have found it out." " Found out what, mon ? " " I have found out what it is that makes her go." " What is it ? " " Jim, come and see ; it 's the fire inside on her ; that 's what it is." And if you ask me to-day what it is that makes this Christian Endeavor movement go and grow, I say, " It 's the fire inside, that 's what it is ; " the fire of an intense missionary enthusiasm burning upon the altar of the heart of every Endeavorer, and burning, too, at the centre of the life of every society ; an earnest, burning, yearning, unspeakable desire to save men for Jesus Christ.

There used to be an old-fashioned theology called " The Little Remnant Theology " (of which I am very glad to say only a very little remnant remains). It was the darling belief of this theology that God delighted in saving as few as possible, and that it was to his glory to have a kingdom that could only be seen through a microscope. These dear people used to sing, " We Are a Garden Walled Around," and they were very comfortable in singing it, too, for they never looked "over the garden wall," and, therefore, they never saw the far-reaching landscapes that were ready at the laborer's touch to break into the brightness and beauty of golden and eternal harvests. But Christian Endeavorers better understand the world-wide empire of the Cross of Christ. They have raised the divinely ambitious cry, "India for Christ, Africa for Christ, China for Christ, the Islands of the Sea for Christ, the world for Christ." A grand battle-cry that! Never abate it by a single jot. It has the true Calvary ring about it. "And I, if I be lifted up, will draw all men unto me."

I am afraid that my fourth point this morning, CONSECRATION IN ALL, will have to go untouched; but I want in a word to enforce the importance of that which I have ventured to call the third of these cardinal principles of Christian Endeavor: SEPARATION FROM ALL. What do I mean by that? I mean very much what Dr. Clark has expressed in a booklet of his which has had wide circulation in our country. He there says, "This Society has its literary and its social and its other features, but it is firstly and paramountly a religious society." It is imperatively necessary that we preserve our weekly meeting as a weekly *prayer* meeting; it must never become less than this; it must never become other than this. The weekly meeting of the Christian Endeavor Society is not an entertainment, but a devotional service. Let us never forget that this is pre-eminently a spiritual movement. Its aims, its foundations, its centre, its circumference, are all spiritual. We are in the world, but let us see to it that we are not of it. It is right for the ship to be in the sea; peril and disaster come when the sea gets into the ship. It is right for this Society of Christian Endeavor to be in the world; there will come peril and disaster if ever the world is allowed to get into the Society.

Perhaps I can explain better what I mean by telling you what occurred to myself the other day. I was spending a little time with a doctor friend of mine in East London, and after dinner he said, "Come to my study, will you?" I thought of the spider and the fly, but I went. When he had closed the door he said, "I want to try an experiment on you." I immediately said, "Will it hurt?" "Oh no, it won't hurt you at all. Be quite comfortable about that." Then he brought out a sheet of glass and stood it on four glass feet; then placing a chair on the glass, he said, "I want you to get up on that glass and sit down on that chair." I did as I was told, and then said, "What are you going to do?" "Well, now," he said, "you understand that glass is a non-conductor of electricity, don't you?" "Yes." "Well, while I have you sitting as you do upon that glass, standing as it does on its four glass feet, you are completely cut off. separated, from everything that's around you; and while I have you in that isolated position and condition, I am going to fill you up full with electricity and fetch sparks out of you." And again I said, "Will it hurt?" "Oh no," he said, "you won't feel anything." I sat still; the battery was attached, and by and by he said, "Now you are full." "Oh, but," I said, "I don't feel anything." "Perhaps not, but you are full." And then, with a sort of little steel wand that he had, he touched me, here, there, yonder, and sparks came out. It was like striking half a box of matches all at once on one's coat. He said, "I can make your hair stand on end." And he did. "Well," I said, "that's very remarkable." "Yes; and now I want you to put your foot down to the ground." I did so. "Now," he said, "you are empty." "Empty?" "Yes, quite." "Well," I said, "that's queerer still." He went on to say, "Directly as much as a thread of you touched the earth, all that power that was in you ran out of you and left you just as you were before." I went away and thought about that. I remembered how many times the old Book had called upon me to be filled with the Spirit. I remembered that it is only just as long as I am filled with the Spirit that God can use me to the extreme limit of any powers which I may possess; and it is only while my life is entirely separated from everything out of harmony with the mind and the will of God that I can be in any real, full measure the temple of the Holy Ghost. And that which is true of the individual is true of the Society. It is only while our societies in all our activities and methods of work are in direct line and complete harmony with the mind and with the will of God, the Holy Ghost, that we can be used to the fullest extent in the achievement of success and victory "for Christ and the Church." I speak thus emphatically to-day because I am convinced that it is only along these lines that we can hope for permanent power and for multiplying victories.

Have you ever seen an engine on the line? Of course you have; and as you have watched it speeding along at the head of the express train you have said, "That is about the most powerful piece of machinery I ever saw." Have you ever seen an engine, perhaps the same engine, off the line? If so, you have seen it after it has plowed up the track for a few yards, lying wrecked and stranded and helpless, and you have said, "That's about the weakest looking thing I ever set eyes on." Ah, it makes all the difference whether the engine is on the line or off the line! To-day, I believe that this Christian Endeavor organization is on the line, and that on the line it passes the wit of man to tell where it will stop in strengthening the Church and building up the kingdom of God on the earth. But let us be sure that nothing short of the ever-watchful, guiding presence and power of God, the Holy Ghost, can keep us on the track. If we are true to these principles: Service by all, Love to all, Separation from all, Consecration in all, we shall attain to victories we cannot measure, and achieve unprecedented success which will astonish both the Church and the world. I adopt to the full the words of one of our own American poets, which reached me awhile ago, to this effect : —

> " A sage declared, in days of old,
> He 'd move the world if but a lever
> He might discover long enough,
> A fulcrum that was strong enough.
> He died, but found them never.

> " But we, though half as wise as he,
> Through God's own mercy found that lever;
> Its mighty arm is long enough,
> Young Christian hearts are strong enough;
> Its noble name—Endeavor."

The next thing on the programme was the presentation of the banner for the greatest proportionate increase in the number of local societies, by Dr. Hoyt.

Remarks of Rev. Wayland Hoyt, D.D.

This well-won banner goes into the hands of our comrades in Christian Endeavor in that outlying portion of our continent, the British territory of Assiniboia.

It has been quite far afield, this banner; it has flaunted its brave colors under many skies; it was captured first by the south-central territory of Oklahoma, where " Old Glory " waves; it was seized from there by our brethren in Manitoba, where the world-encircling banner of Great Britain flashes its crimson; it was captured from thence by our Christian Endeavor comrades in the far southwestern territory of New Mexico, and was brought again under the shadow of the great flag of our great nation. It was held still under that flag by West Virginia for the last year, and now it goes on its benignant mission, its longest journey yet, far to the northwestern corner of our great continent, and again under the shelter of the proud banner of Great Britain, to our brothers and sisters in Christian Endeavor in Assiniboia.

I think this far-travelled banner is significant of much. For one thing, it is significant of the universality of the heart of our Lord and Christ. Said Napoleon, at St. Helena, across a chasm of eighteen hundred years, " Jesus Christ makes a demand beyond all others difficult to satisfy. He asks for that which a philosopher may vainly ask of his friend, a father of his children, a bride of her spouse, a brother of his brother. He asks for the human heart." He will have it unconditionally, and forthwith the demand is granted. Wonderful in defiance of time and space, the soul of man, with all its powers and faculties, becomes an annexation of the Empire of Christ.

And so our Christ is a Christ for all the times and all the climes. This, to me, is the miracle of miracles: that this Christ, born in the most sectarian of nations, never passing beyond the boundaries of that little patch of Palestine, knowing only the culture of a Jewish village and a Jewish synagogue, should yet be not Greek, nor Jew, nor Roman, nor Celt, nor Teuton, nor Saxon, but the universal man, with heart so grand and great that all the men of all the times, of all the climes, for rest, refuge, rescue, may flock to that great heart as the birds flock to the summer.

And this travelled banner, representing, as it does, service for this Christ, passing from South to North, and from North to South, and now from South to North again, is emblematic of the universality of the heart of our Lord and Master. Also, I think this travelled banner is significant of the deep, spiritual unity of all believers in this one Christ. There is an imaginary line which must be crossed by this banner as it goes now into the glad grasp of our comrades in Christian Endeavor in Assiniboia. It may be other than an imaginary line in the mind of nations; they may sculpture such line deep by legislation, and make it emphatic by forts and guns, and put on the other side of it different ensigns, but hearts of believers flow easily across such lines and fuse together, for " One is our Master, even Christ; and all we are brethren." Christian Endeavor is international because on both sides such lines of nationality one Christ dwells and rules in believing hearts.

Also, this travelled banner is significant of the widening area of Christian Endeavor. They say that the Bay of Biscay is in the eye of all the storms, and that sometimes, for days together, the winds pile the waters on the lands, submerging them. There are benignant seas and there are benignant storms of the grace of God, and Christian Endeavor is such a sea and is such a benignant storm, and Christian Endeavor has flung its freshening waters far yonder, even unto the outlying corner of Assiniboia, and it shall go on with its storm of grace, and its submergence of spiritual benignant sea until the whole huge world is somehow under it.

And now, my brother, in the name of this Christ of the universal heart, and at the behest of the international feature of Christian Endeavor, and glad that Christian Endeavor is flinging itself so far, to you — not from Assiniboia, that is so far away that there is not even one representative of it in this great Convention, but to you who carry the banner of the Cross in Canada under the flag we just sang about when we sang "God Save the Queen"— to you I commit this banner, that you may see that it is borne to our brave brothers of Christian Endeavor, and sisters, too, in far Assiniboia. God bless it!

Rev. William Patterson, of Toronto, Ont., accepted the banner in behalf of Assiniboia, saying : —

Mr. Chairman and Christian Endeavorers, — I am not a Northwester, but I have been in the Northwest and I am very glad, on behalf of those who have received the banner, to accept it for them this morning.

It is the second time that this banner is to cross the line. The last time it was in Canadian soil it was taken by Manitoba; by that energetic and determined little province; by that little province that has declared by an overwhelming majority that they want to have nothing to do with the liquor traffic; by that little province that this year has put a law on its statute book that they will have no Sunday street cars; by that little province that has declared that they will have free schools. And now this little province of great territory to which the banner goes lies northwest of Manitoba; a territory that could swallow up, I suppose, several of the States; a territory that is new, but laying the foundations in righteousness. They have gained this banner honorably and well, and I have very much pleasure on their behalf in accepting it.

Dr. Rhodes then introduced Rev. A. F. Richardson to the audience as the president of the Christian Endeavor Union from West Virginia, from which the banner came. He addressed a few words thus : —

I acknowledge that we were very loath to give up that beautiful banner. I don't know whether I can say that it affords me a great deal of pleasure to see that banner go to the brother or not, but we certainly, as a State, congratulate them upon the acquisition of that banner. I hope that they will enjoy it to their hearts' content this year, for we have made up our minds that at Washington in '96 we are going to take that banner back to the State of West Virginia without a doubt. Now I hope that all of you who are here to-day will remember this and see it fulfilled in Washington in '96, because we mean it. I hope that this banner will be to these Endeavorers an inspiration, as it has been to the Endeavorers of the State of West Virginia, and that God's blessing may attend them in their effort to take the Gospel of Jesus Christ and to plant the banner of his Cross in that far-away land.

Then Mrs. Nellie Brown Mitchell sang a solo, "When Shall I See Jesus?" to the well-known air of "Annie Laurie," after which Dr. Rhodes introduced Rev. Otis A. Smith, D.D., of Evansville, Ind., with the following words : —

"The permanence of our government is symbolized by Plymouth Rock. So, my friends, the foundation of Christian Endeavor, the soil in which it is rooted and out of which it springs, and the diadem that crowns it, are our cardinal principles. We have heard from England; we will now hear from America on a like subject. It gives me great pleasure to introduce Rev. Otis A. Smith, D.D., of Evansville, Ind."

Address of Rev. Otis A. Smith, D.D.

The initial conception of Christian Endeavor was the enlistment and training of Christian youth for organized usefulness in the Church of Christ.

Fourteen years of history have justified the wisdom of that original design.

Providence answered the need of the times by bringing into existence this mighty brotherhood of Christian youth, united by one purpose, animated by one spirit, and dominated by the sovereignty of one Name.

And to have brought the youth of Christendom, with their irresistible energy and courage and enthusiasm, into an organization like this is a conception worthy of a master workman, and worthy of Him whose name is inscribed upon every banner which we unfurl to the breeze.

Where in all this world can you find a more inspiring sight than this great Convention of young people, representing nearly forty thousand societies and more than two and one-fourth millions of members, distributed in all the countries of the globe?

May the mystic chords of our spiritual brotherhood, which makes us one in Christ Jesus, stretching from Alaska to the Southern Sea, and from Boston to Africa and India and China and the Islands of the West, awaken in our hearts this morning the glad chorus of the Redeemed.

"Thou wast slain, and hast redeemed us to God by thy blood out of every kindred, and tongue, and people, and nation; and hast made us unto our God kings and priests." (Rev. v. 9, 10.)

"Blessing, and honor, and glory, and power, be unto him that sitteth upon the throne, and unto the Lamb forever and ever." (Rev. v. 13.)

As I witnessed the presentation of the banners this morning, I thought of an incident which happened in the life of our martyred Lincoln when he was on his way to his first inauguration as President of the United States. The train upon which he was travelling stopped at Dunkirk, N. Y., and a great crowd of people had gathered at the platform, expecting to hear a speech. A gray-haired man spoke out of the crowd and said, "Uncle Abe, what are you going to do when you get to Washington?" Lincoln replied, "My aged friend here has just asked me what I am going to do when I get to Washington." Then he reached up and took down one of the little flags used in the decoration of the train; and holding it before the assembled multitude, he continued, "By the help of Almighty God and the assistance of the loyal people of this country, I am going to try to defend the flag. Will you stand by me as I stand by the flag?" And the deafening cheers of the multitude attested the loyalty of their answer.

We, too, are here to stand by a flag, even the blood-stained banner of the Lion of the Tribe of Judah, beneath which we are marching on to the conquest of the world. And though we come from different States and different nations of the world, we profess allegiance to a King who is supreme over all. And beneath all the outward differences of race, nation, and ecclesiastical relationship, we hold sovereign, unifying principles, which bind us all together in one.

What are these principles?

The cardinal principles of Christian Endeavor are the primordial, constructive ideas by virtue of which, and for the sake of which, our Society came into existence. They are the Society's germ and the Society's norm. They have given the Society its character. They have regulated its movements. They control all its relationships.

They are the measure of the Society's usefulness and the prophecy of its permanence. They are larger than the Society itself. Societies die. Nations die. But principles and laws live on.

When I was in Colorado, three summers ago, I learned a lesson from the numerous mining-shafts which I saw upon the mountain-sides. In certain localities you will see, thickly scattered over the mountains, holes and tunnels and ugly scars, which mark the spots where the miners probed for ore. Many of those shafts had long been abandoned when I saw them, and were fast falling into decay. Were they failures, therefore? Oh no! For out of those ugly seams and scars and tunnels much of the precious ore which circulates in the money-markets of the world was drawn.

So, every organization which has blessed mankind in the progress of history has simply drawn out of the unfathomable depths of the Divine Mind some great truths, which they have liberated from their silent abodes, and caused to circulate through the commerce of thought in the common life of our race.

And this is one of the pleasing and reassuring characteristics of the Christian Endeavor Society: that in the espousal of its principles it dug deep into the Word of God, and has succeeded, beyond expectation and almost beyond precedent, in bringing the vitalizing principles of the Word to bear upon the ordinary relationships of every-day life.

What are these principles?

1. The first cardinal principle of Christian Endeavor is implicit trust *in* Christ, and unselfish, complete, and irrevocable devotion *to* Christ.

Trust in Christ is the source of devotion to Christ.

I know that there are very many who have thought intently upon this subject who would place loyalty to Christ as the first cardinal principle of Christian Endeavor. I am not surprised at this, for it is a part of it, but not the larger part, nor the most important part.

Loyalty, withal, is so soldier-like in aspect and bearing, so commanding and attractive, that I am not surprised that so many have been led to emphasize the outward concomitants above the inner secret and heart of patriotism which sustains it.

"Loyalty" is a term drawn from our civil life, which cannot be carried over into our religious life and applied without careful discrimination.

We are loyal to our country by the exercise of our wills, by those natural impulses which patriotism causes to swell within our souls. But we cannot be loyal to Christ in that way, "Because the carnal mind is enmity against God: for it is not subject to the law of God, neither indeed can be." (Rom. VIII. 7.)

Into that sphere of life where loyalty to Christ is exercised we enter by implicit trust, and day by day we are thus sustained in it.

This is the kernel and heart of the first cardinal principle of Christian Endeavor. It vitalizes and dignifies and glorifies our whole movement. It is expressed in our mottoes, written in our Constitution, and twisted into every fibre of our pledge. It disposes us to the use of the private means of grace. It prompts us to public confession of His name. It is the sustaining power of faithfulness in all personal and committee work.

Whenever we lead a meeting, read a verse of Scripture, testify, welcome a stranger, speak to the discouraged, seek out the straying, speak to an unconverted friend, visit in behalf of the Sunday school, carry flowers to the sick, scatter wholesome literature, contribute to missions, or take part in any of the established agencies of the Church, we do it all, humbly trusting in Jesus Christ for strength.

It is the vibrating chord in all of our conventions. It thrills in our hearts, burns within us in the emotion of prayer, and swells in all our glad choruses of song.

How simply and beautifully is this sense of dependence upon Christ recognized in the pledge, " Trusting in the Lord Jesus Christ . . . I promise him."

By the pledged avowal of this principle young Christians are brought out of the mass of indifferent and purposeless " professors " of religion, and organized into serried ranks of trained soldiers of the Cross.

This part of the principle cannot have too great emphasis. There is a tendency to emphasize the outward side of " endeavor " while we pass by the quiet, unobtrusive secret of " trusting."

But our outward activity cannot sustain itself. Our " endeavor " will cease without this inward life of trust and daily spiritual renewal just as inevitably as a river will cease to flow when the mountain springs which feed it are dried up. Where shall we find this principle, and how shall we get it?

We shall find it in the fifteenth chapter of the Gospel of John, in which Christ represents the union of himself and his disciples under the familiar figure of the vine and the branches. And we will get it by becoming a living embodiment of this chapter.

Let us leave for a while this morning the inspiring scenes of this Convention, and go to that " upper room," crowded with holy memories and filled with the glory of God, where Jesus gave his farewell discourse to his timid but beloved disciples. Hear him utter these words : —

" Abide in me, and I in you. As the branch cannot bear fruit of itself, except it abide in the vine ; no more can ye, except ye abide in me.

" I am the vine, ye are the branches. He that abideth in me, and I in him, the same bringeth forth much fruit : for without me ye can do nothing.

" If a man abide not in me, he is cast forth as a branch, and is withered ; and men gather them, and cast them into the fire, and they are burned." (John xv. 4-6.)

Here is the secret of apostolic devotion and heroism. By living this precious truth, the apostles came to be what they were, and to do what they accomplished for their Master.

And by this secret, too, we have in church history a long line of noble lives,— martyrs, confessors, and glorified saints,— which reach in unbroken succession away back to the Cross.

The principle has been handed down to us as a most precious spiritual heritage from Jesus Christ, our Lord, and we have taken it and embodied it as a cardinal principle in our Christian Endeavor Society. By it alone shall we be able to bring Apostolic Christianity down to date.

And looking away, for the time, from the magnitude and display and all outward features of our work, I affirm, humbly, reverently, but firmly, that the hidden source of power, the life and future promise of our Christian Endeavor movement, is found in these words which Jesus spake unto his disciples in the solemn stillness and tremulous air of that sacred upper room.

A father in Scotland was once walking out with his little boy, and came to a commanding prospect on the summit of one of the Cheviot Hills. And while there he used the opportunity to impress upon his little boy the greatness of the love of God. He pointed the boy to the East, and said, " My son, do you see that stretch of uplands and valleys all the way over to the place where the earth and the sky come together?" "Yes," said the little fellow, "I do." "Well, my son," said the father, "the love of God is as broad as that." And he successively pointed him to the North and South and West, and said, " My son, the love of God is as great as that." With a bright smile upon his face the little fellow looked up and said, " Then, papa, we are right in the middle of it, are n't we?"

And so when some one points away to Australia, and calls attention to the work which the Christian Endeavor is doing there, we are apt to feel and say in our pride, " The Christian Endeavor is as great as that."

And then some one will point to India and China and the Islands of the Sea, and say, " The Christian Endeavor is as great as that."

Others will speak of the work of missions at home and abroad, of good citizenship, and of the various lines of work in our own local churches, and say, " The Christian Endeavor work is as great as that."

Some one else will say, "Just see this mighty Convention. There has never been anything like it in the world before." And then we all feel constrained to say, " The Christian Endeavor is as great as that."

And all very true. But turning away from sights and sounds, from reports and statistics, from all outward display, and from every forward movement which represents the aggressive Christianity of the age in which we live, go back to Jesus Christ, and look deeply into the heart of the Gospel; look inward upon the fathomless meaning of Gethsemane and Calvary and Pentecost; recline as John did upon the bosom of his Lord, and feel his palpitating heart of sympathy and sacrifice and love, and hear him say, " Abide in me and I in you,"— then, and only then, can we say, as the little fellow unto his father, " We are in the very middle of it."

From this secret source of power alone will spring that devotion and loyalty which is complete and unselfish and irrevocable, which is the test of disciple- ship, and which is the prophecy of the conquest of the world.

To-day, upon the floor of this Convention, let us have it ; and if we feel that we do not have it, let us get it. But let us remember that no profession of loyalty can be sustained by the enthusiasm engendered here, but only by com- plete surrender, implicit trust, unquestioned obedience, and permanent abiding in Christ. With this prerequisite, there will be some meaning in our vows and pledges and professions of faith.

Then, like the brave followers of David who swam the Jordan at its flood, and cast themselves down in the presence of their king, and said, " Thine are we, David, and on thy side, thou son of Jesse," we can sincerely say, in a pledge which is complete, unselfish, and irrevocable, " Thine are we, O Christ, our Saviour and Lord, and on thy side, O thou blessed Son of God!"

2. A second cardinal principle of Christian Endeavor is devotion to the Scriptures. The Bible itself is our manual of devotion and confession of faith and rule of life.

We would deny our spiritual birthright and forfeit our privileges as sons of God if we should be disloyal to the Word, for by it we are begotten, "being born again, not of corruptible seed, but of incorruptible, by the word of God, which liveth and abideth forever." (1 Pet. I. 23.)

And through the Word come to us the most essential means of growth, the choicest privileges, and the sweetest prospects of our Christian life.

By the Word we are not only "begotten," but "nourished" (1 Tim. IV. 6), and "built up" (Acts xx. 32), and "perfected" in the love of God (1 John II. 5), and "thoroughly furnished unto all good works " (2 Tim. III. 17.)

What an example Christ has left us in the use of the sacred Scriptures ! How careful he was to conform his life and conduct to the prophecies con- cerning himself! Again and again during his life we hear him say, " This has been done that the Scriptures might be fulfilled." How confidently he appeals to its authority! How skilfully he uses it to repel the assaults of the Evil One, and how patiently he "opens the Scriptures" to the expanding apprehension and needs of his disciples!

Therefore it is a cardinal principle and a prime necessity of our Christian Endeavor movement to exalt the Word to that place of supreme authority in our hearts and lives which Christ enjoined upon us by special commands and by his own holy example.

Therefore the true Christian Endeavorer will allow no pre-conceived theological opinion, no personal inclination or desire, no selfish business interest, no tyranny of social custom, to take precedence of the plain and simple teaching of the Word.

How we ought to love the Word of God! How full of rebuke to our neglect of the Word is the devotion and affection of the psalmist: "O how love I thy law! it is my meditation all the day." (Ps. CXIX. 97.)

"More to be desired are they than gold, yea, than much fine gold: sweeter also than honey and the honeycomb. Moreover by them is thy servant warned: and in keeping of them there is great reward." (Ps. XIX. 10, 11.)

"When I read such passages as these," says Dr. Stalker, "and recollect that they came from the lips of men who possessed only the Old Testament, perhaps only a fragment of it, — men in whose Bible there were no Gospels, or Epistles of Paul, or Apocalypse, who never heard the Sermon on the Mount, or the Prodigal Son, the seventeenth of John or the eighth of Romans, the thirteenth of First Corinthians or the eleventh of Hebrews, — I ask what my feelings are toward the much larger Bible I possess; and I say to myself that surely in modern times the heart of man has become ossified, and the fountains of gratitude have dried up, and the fires of admiration and enthusiasm have been put out, so tame, in comparison, is our affection for the more perfect Book."

"Wherefore continue thou in the things which thou hast learned and hast been assured of." (2 Tim. III. 14.)

"Study to shew thyself approved unto God, a workman that needeth not to be ashamed, rightly dividing the word of truth." (2 Tim. II. 15.)

3. A third cardinal principle of Christian Endeavor is loyalty to the Church.

Human conditions have not so changed that we can get along without distinctive ecclesiastical organizations.

The best piety is still to-day that which is trained about some church altar. We cannot get along without the individual church any more than we can dispense with the home and the fireside. Any piety which has become so weak and diluted in its latitudinarianism that it cannot find room in one or another of the organic spiritual bodies of Christendom is certainly faulty and noxious.

Great and useful churches cannot be carried on after the plan of modern "apartment houses." The family table must not be supplanted by the restaurant and boarding-house.

Our large churches are already loaded down with a dead weight of members who join the Church simply from social considerations, without any doctrinal conviction, and with no idea whatever of being made useful, and of co-operating with the spiritual agencies of the Church in the great and stupendous scheme of world-wide evangelization and conquest. But the Christian Endeavor Society seeks to establish its young people in the principles of theology and church history, and to train them for practical and efficient usefulness in the Church.

We teach them that the Christian Endeavor is simply a part of the Church. It is a loyal subject in a great kingdom. It seeks to do, by division of labor, by co-operation and organization, what the whole Church ought to do, and what the Church will be compelled to do in order to win the world for Christ.

These are the cardinal principles of Christian Endeavor, which have won their way into almost every country on the globe, and which have organized the youth of Christendom into one stupendous Society whose acknowledged head is Jesus Christ, our Lord.

And wherever the Society has been established, and these principles have held sway, there has been increased spirituality, deeper knowledge of and devotion to the Word, and more efficient usefulness in the Church; and withal, more joy and sunshine in religion, and more gladness in the soul.

And now we confront the future. It is larger and richer than the most optimistic and idealistic Christian dares to dream. The Christian Endeavor movement has a place yet to fill.

These cardinal principles are forming the characters of the men and women who shall stand by the help of God for "Whatsoever things are true, whatsoever things are honest, whatsoever things are just, whatsoever things are pure, whatsoever things are lovely, whatsoever things are of good report." (Phil. iv. 8.)

> "For the cause that lacks assistance,
> For the wrongs that need resistance,
> For the future in the distance,
> For the good that we can do."

"Stand therefore, having your loins girt about with truth, and having on the breastplate of righteousness; And your feet shod with the preparation of the gospel of peace; Above all, taking the shield of faith, wherewith ye shall be able to quench all the fiery darts of the wicked. And take the helmet of salvation and the sword of the Spirit, which is the word of God." (Eph. vi. 14–17.)

Fight manfully onward. Live in His name; die in his name; and then, oh, joy and rapture, bliss beyond compare.! in his name we shall enter "within the gates."

When the troops of the great Frederick returned victorious from one of his wars they found the gates of the capital closed, and a sentinel from within cried out to them, "By what right do ye enter here?"

Then they waved their torn and weather-beaten flags, and shouted out the names of the battlefields on which their courageous leaders had pointed them to victory, and the gates of the city flew open, and they received the welcome of their monarch.

When, in the unknown future, we come to the gates of the Celestial City, in the exultation of that glad and glorious prospect we shall forget our distinctive theological creeds and denominational banners, and shall wave the blood-stained banner of the Lion of the Tribe of Judah, and mention the name of the battle where he won the victory over sin and the grave, and, humbly trusting in his name, enter within the gates. "And we shall serve him day and night in his temple." (Rev. vii. 15.)

"Thanks be to God, which giveth us the victory through our Lord Jesus Christ." (i Cor. xv. 57.)

Following Dr. Smith's address, Dr. Rhodes introduced Mr. O. W. Stewart, of Eureka, Ill., secretary of the Illinois Christian Endeavor Union, who conducted the open parliament on the topic, "The Pledge, the Backbone of the Society; Its Necessity and Its Paramount Value."

Remarks by Mr. O. W. Stewart.

I had intended making a speech of about an hour and three-quarters as an introduction to this parliament, but I thought possibly it would be better for me to cut down my speech to about a minute and three-quarters. It is enough to call attention to the topic, possibly in addition to that call attention particularly to some few things in connection with that topic, and then throw it open for short discussions from those in different parts of the house and representing the different parts not only of our country but the world.

You notice the topic is, "The Pledge, the Backbone of the Society." Now a backbone is a very necessary part of the human anatomy. Most men are unable to get along without it. Some seem to, but don't succeed very well. The backbone to a society is a very necessary thing, and its pledge is presented this morning as its backbone. Christian Endeavorers should know something of this pledge; they should know much of it; something of its necessity; something of its paramount value. Some make objection to the Christian Endeavor movement that it rests upon a pledge. I would call attention for an instant to the fact that the first word in the pledge taken by the Christian Endeavor is "trusting," — " Trusting in the Lord Jesus Christ for strength, I promise him." I should object, first, last, and all the time, to any pledge taken by Christian Endeavorers that was founded upon a trust in themselves, or in men, or in anything save the Lord Jesus Christ, who gave his life for them. " Trusting in the Lord Jesus Christ for strength," Endeavorers promise him something. They promise him that they will strive to do whatever he would like to have them do, and what wonders have been accomplished already by those who have gone out under that pledge! You and I have heard in our conventions, State and National, that " Here have I said and do I promise Christ that I will enlist under his banner. I will become a missionary of the Cross, ready to go into any land to preach his Gospel."

" Trusting in the Lord Jesus Christ for strength!" It is the very essence of the relationship that exists between the Son of God and the Lord Jesus Christ, that gave his life for us all. We trust in him; we promise him to do these things; we promise him to pray and read the Bible. Is there any possible objection to a Christian Endeavorer praying and reading his Bible? Why, most certainly not! There could be no objection to any one, howsoever far away he might be from Christ, reading his Bible and offering his prayers and petitions to him.

What have you to say with reference to the pledge? What have you to say with reference to its necessity? What have you to say with reference to its paramount value? Do you keep it? If you do, how do you keep it? How does it work among your people and societies? Can you get along without it? If you can't, why can't you? Tell us with reference to these things. If you do not take charge of it, I shall make that speech I prepared, of an hour and three-quarters, on the pledge. Now let us hear from you, — anything; what have you to say?

MINNESOTA reported 28,000 Christian Endeavorers during the last year; tried to keep the pledge by winning 1,600 to Jesus Christ.

JERSEY CITY: It makes the young people strong; if they don't keep the pledge they are weak.

CALIFORNIA reported that 12,000 Christian Endeavorers on the Pacific slope have organized and have to-day a pledge as the foundation, because they believe it expresses their loyalty to their Lord and Master.

WALES: The societies in our country which will not accept the pledge we call jellyfish.

ONTARIO: 1,995 Christian Endeavor Societies have been formed there, and all are working nobly under the pledge. They are endeavoring to push the order, and to push the cause, as far as the grace of God can enable them, and to win the world for Christ.

MASSACHUSETTS: The Christian Endeavor pledge is good for pastors. I am an active Christian Endeavorer.

MONTREAL: 2,500 Endeavorers. We find the pledge makes weak Christians strong, and strong Christians stronger still. It is of paramount value in our society, and makes our young people more active in the Christian work.

NEW JERSEY: Christian Endeavorers, trusting in the Lord Jesus Christ, are fighting for the Christian Sabbath and for the destruction of the drink traffic.

ALASKA: In the Christian Endeavor movement the pledge is at the head.

DELAWARE: It has brought to us great practical results.

JAPAN: Three years ago they had not a single Endeavor Society. Now they have some thirty-five or six Endeavor Societies, — something like three thousand members with their associate members; and, besides that, the pledge has been the means of bringing those young men from fanaticism and scepticism back into the Church of God to study the Word of God.

PENNSYLVANIA : Pennsylvania has sent the largest delegation to this Convention, and says that the pledge, the backbone of the Christian Endeavor Society, has become the backbone of the Church.

ILLINOIS: Not only the backbone but the whole skeleton. You see the Illinois delegates by the flag. The Illinois people are trusting in the Lord Jesus Christ. There are somewhere near 100,000 of us, and in that faith and trust we are trying to help clean out the city of Chicago.

At the close of the open parliament the chorus and congregation joined in singing the hymn, "True-hearted, Whole-hearted," accompanied by the organ and cornet.

Dr. Rhodes then introduced President A. E. Turner, of Lincoln, Ill., who addressed the audience on the subject, " I Ought, Therefore I Can," as follows : —

Address of Pres. A. E. Turner.

The appalling disaster which overtook a splendid German steamship last midwinter only added to the long list of heroic deeds, and served again to show that there is in man no common stuff. But though no new insight was given into human character, and though what happened was really expected, the world was spellbound with admiration as it beheld again devotion to duty which was not stayed though life itself was sacrificed. And the same nature which makes all the world akin was not less deeply stirred when, a half-year after the *Elbe* had sunk into its watery grave, a devoted husband dropped a handful of fragrant flowers into the bosom of old ocean, where his wife had met her death. Of the truly beautiful and heroic there can be no satiety. We cannot explain how, though oft repeated, these simple deeds of love strike a chord always responsive in human hearts.

There must be a spring of action, less hidden it may be, though not less strong, which furnishes the tremendous enthusiasm of the present unparalleled occasion. View it as we may, a chief glory of the Christian Endeavor movement is that it has not revolutionized but has simply directed energy. Marking out for itself no new path, blazing the way through no unexplored forest, but marching over much-travelled roads and amid familiar scenes it has achieved results marvellous in the eyes of all beholders. Is it not true that many of the movements inaugurated for the betterment of manhood and the vitalizing of dormant energies have come to naught because founded upon humanity as they would have it, and not upon humanity as it is?

Granted the existence of a lofty sense of duty, of obligation to a Divine Creator, Endeavor has wrought itself out through the *potentialities* of Christian youthfulness. The extent of these potentialities it has remained for our day to develop. Who cannot recall the dark ages of his own experience, when " Children are to be seen, not heard," was the vigilant mother's watchword? Who has not a sympathy of the sincerest kind for the earnest inquirer after truth who said, " Pa, will all the people in the world be resurrected at the judgment?" " Yes, my son," was the reply. " Well, if all the cannibals is resurrected, and then all the missionaries what 's been eat by cannibals is resurrected, things is going to be awfully mixed, aint they, pa?" Then, like hundreds of other inquisitive boys, he was consigned to a culprit's bed, his question still unanswered. Thank God for a Clark who has emancipated the young from a well-intended thraldom, and given to every one something to *do* and something to *say*.

Granted, I have said, a sense of duty toward our Creator, he lacks much of the stature of manhood who feels not within himself the ability which enables him to say, " I can *because* I ought." From such character no worthy action can issue, in it no uplifting ideal can be realized. Came this voice from New England's hills :—

> " So near is grandeur to our dust,
>   So near is God to man,
> When Duty whispers low, ' Thou must,'
>   The youth replies, ' I can.' "

The moralists tell us that no duties conflict; it is a law of Christianity that no duty too heavy to be borne is laid upon the weakest disciple. The very idea of duty carries with it the possibility of accomplishment, and a sad day it is for one of God's chosen when he knows his duty and does it not. It is a fact, lamentable as it is true, that many a will has made unconditional surrender to passion, to appetite, and to self. It is equally true that the largest returns come from the happy conjunction and co-ordination of an unimpaired will and a well-ordered sensorium. " A sound mind in a sound body " will never grow old, because it is true. The moral backbone of our youth needs not to be broken but, twig-like, to be inclined, and thus be enabled to make character, not driven by the wind and tossed, but that which may be trusted, as a pilot, amid the roughest seas and the most adverse winds.

Again, Christian Endeavor has recognized the principle, so long unrecognized in the Church, of division of labor. It is important that we be *at* the work and that we be at it *all* the time ; it is of vastly more consequence that *all* be *at* it *all* the time. We are not sounder preachers than the fathers, but we build better and larger than they because we say, " I ought." They said, " *You* ought." The burden *can* not, *must* not, be shifted. What a world of responsibility the age has thrust into your lives and mine ! And to us as a people this is great gain. Learning early the lesson of self-reliance and independent effort, when the time comes that tries men's souls, a line of well-disciplined regulars, and not raw recruits, faces the enemy. We fancy that we hear a voice — so late it has been stilled — saying : " Trust thyself ; every heart vibrates to that iron string. Accept the place the Divine Providence has found for you, the society of your contemporaries, the connection of events. Great men have always done so, and confided themselves, childlike, to the genius of their age, betraying their perception that the Eternal was stirring at their hearts, working through their hands, predominating in all their being. And we are now men, and must accept in the highest mind the same transcendent destiny."

How impressive our obligation to our Society becomes when we consider its quality and its comprehensiveness ! " I promise the Lord Jesus Christ that I will strive to do whatever he would like to have me do." " I promise the Lord Jesus Christ." Here is inspiration ; a pledge not to the world nor to the flesh nor to an earthly potentate, but to the King of kings and the Lord of lords. What weighty interests are committed to our charge,—interests to whose care we stand pledged with a faithfulness that clings not more to father and mother, to brothers and sisters, than to these. You will not break your word given to your friend ; surely it cannot be broken when pledged to our Master himself. " I will strive to do whatever he would like to have me do." His will, then, is the guide of my life. No other chart and compass are needed ; no rules of trigonometry ; no Greek roots ; no deduction ; no induction — simply his will. My law is his law. Whether life is worth living depends upon the one who lives it. With his Word as the man of counsel, the way becomes so plain that "the wayfaring man, though a fool, need not err therein." Our pledge becomes the *multum in parvo* of righteousness. With an eye single to it, no life can fail, no purpose fail of accomplishment.

And certainly none are worthier to take this obligation than the youth of the land. Rejoicing as strong men to run a race, full of the fiery energy of beginning life, how fit they are to carry as their standard the motto of the great Western metropolis, " I will," converting the synonym for the surpassing triumph of a World's Fair into a war-cry for Endeavor's valiant hosts. But might cannot make right, and back of the resistless energy, the deep-seated fervor, the redoubtable zeal which is thrilling this great centre of commerce and culture "for Christ and the Church" lies the spring of our power,—"Trusting in the Lord Jesus Christ for strength." In his service, right makes might.

> " Not to the strong is the battle,
> Not to the swift is the race;
> Yet to the true and the faithful
> Vict'ry is promised grace."

With Jesus Christ on our side what matters it if all the world be against us? The duty ethics as distinguished from the good ethics is receiving no little attention at the hands of the philosophers. Was it not Kant who said that no action is morally right that is not done from a sense of duty? We have no desire to go so far; to do so might be to undermine the foundations of natural affection, and to establish a Platonic reign as undesirable in its quality as it must be scant in the quantity. But much as duty has been abused, and often as it has been wounded, even in the house of its friends, there is a conviction born of live contact with Christian Endeavor heat, and fanned by its wonderful enthusiasm, that no sweeter experience comes to the soul than the consciousness of duty done, and well done. What unrest and discomfort harass him who follows not the line of duty! Having recognized, first of all, the obligation to loyal, active, and constant service to the great Jehovah, what noble mind, what virtuous soul, can restrain itself from a conflict as real as it is irrepressible ? So long as there is manhood of the Spurgeon type and the Phillips Brooks type, of the Moody type and the Clark type, so long will there be in Endeavor hearts a desire, which will be as a consuming fire, to do and to dare in his name. The thrill which we experience to-day, and which must reach the remotest lines of our organization, must strengthen the courage to *do* all that a Christian humanity *feels*. Endeavorers, we *can* take this land for Christ; we *can* conquer the world for the universal Church.

But our national regeneration will not be accomplished by such assemblies as this. We cannot hope for definite progress along definite lines of improvement as the results of our present convocation, and we must not for a moment conceive that political, social, and intellectual misery are to be relieved by the enthusiasm born of the hour and the day. In our homes conditions will confront us, problems will require our solution, and measures will demand our attention. We stand to-day in the engine-room. What the influence of the dynamo is, as it reaches out with its invisible arms of power, can be known only by a study of the sensible activities which it controls and energizes. Every shaft and piston is now receiving its polish; every valve and bearing, its oil. We are deeply impressed with the power and smoothness with which it works—the dynamo appears to be in perfect order, every bolt is secure, and every belt does its duty. What this splendid generator is to accomplish depends upon you and upon me. The connection must not be lost, the wires must not be grounded. Will these thousands of Endeavorers carry the current? Will every man and woman do his duty? If so, this Convention marks an epoch in the religious world.

May I suggest a few possible specific spheres of influence? We *ought*, therefore we *can*, better latter-day business methods. How sadly out of fashion is the old saw, "Honesty is the best policy"! All too few there are who believe that honesty *is* the best policy. The business philosophy of the "wild and woolly West" paraphrases the Golden Rule into "Do the other fellow, or he'll do you!" Fairy pictures are painted for the little tots, of the time when men were honest, when integrity was current, and when dishonesty discredited men even in the highest stations. It makes us shudder to be told that a business man cannot afford to be strictly honest if he wishes to succeed. The test of admission to the counting-house is ability to work the discomfiture of a competitor, regardless of scruples. An apprenticeship must be lengthened in order that the apprentice may learn the tricks of the trade. Endeavorers are to be the business men of to-morrow. They can call things by their right names; they can put conscience into ability to drive a sharp bargain. They *can* because they *ought*.

We *can* purify politics. The largeness of the field is attested by the long list of civic federations, investigating committees, and reform leagues. When the sentiment of a community becomes so outraged that its citizens gather in the city council-chamber and threaten mob violence against conscienceless law-makers, and when a stockholder in an immense manufacturing enterprise decides to withdraw his holdings because it is clear that the corporation has secured valuable franchises by foul means, it would seem that we are not ready to rest upon our oars. We would be fortunate, indeed, if the trouble were local only. That our highest legislative body should not escape the taint of corruption is alarming, not so much as an indication of individual depravity as that it shows the spread of the virus to every part of the body. What has been done by lawlessness and indecency will be done again, and what law and order have done they must continue to do. We must not be deceived by the sloughing-off of the old skin from the body politic; the disease is deeper seated, and the treatment must be thoroughgoing. Municipal purification needs to be something more than a fad. It calls for our best endeavors in the line of sound instruction and active participation in temporal affairs. Pharisaism in civics must go. Christian Endeavorers *can* put it away because they *ought*.

We *can* socialize society, — make it what in its very nature it ought to be: the means of uplifting and advancing our weaker brethren. We need, my friends, a social condition based upon our common brotherhood — one which will not shrink from giving the cup of cold water. Social aristocracy is strengthening its stakes, is deepening its trenches, and is establishing itself more solidly every day to resist the working of the law of love which the Saviour taught as indispensable to fruitful living. To quote another, the world has need of men in society, rather than society men. I have no quarrel with our social organization; indeed, I am convinced that much effort is wasted which looks to the obliteration of all lines of distinction; but it is plain that Christianity should be injected quickly and surely into what is fast becoming a veneered refinement and false culture. Christian people *can* inject it because they *ought*.

We *ought* to dominate the literature of our day, hence we *can*. Americans are truly omnivorous in their reading. Nothing escapes them. Discrimination is so little called into play that it seems to have lost its meaning. There are those who hold it great gain to have read much. It would be even greater gain, I take it, to read well a little that is good. There is significance, too, in the fact that our metropolitan newspapers are in the hands of men who are not pronouncedly and actively Christian. Experiments show that it is not wise for an editor to head his columns with texts of Scripture. It is not so much that these men are not moral men; if Christianity is to take the world they must be more. And shall we not confess with shame that the most popular story of the year — one which has produced a peculiar craze about itself — is essentially immoral? Christian principles can flavor our literature only as Christian men and women sit in our sanctums and handle our quills. Endeavorers *can* make it what they will because they *ought*.

But this is not a study in pessimism. The world is doing very well considering the chance it has had, but the Church is doing less. It needs the inspiration and zeal of fresh young blood, and the enthusiasm of youthful life. These it must have. The world can be made to go right. It will go wrong if left alone. We must take courage when we realize that such a host as is encamped about Boston to-day is shouting lustily and striking mightily in behalf of those principles which made this new world the asylum of distressed and oppressed conditions in every clime. Better than that, they are defending the faith, they are honoring Christ. They owe it to him to preach his Gospel at home and abroad, to make it the power of God unto salvation. They believe they *ought*, therefore I know they *can*.

Tent Williston.

Centred in Tent Williston was religious enthusiasm from every country. Long before the time announced for the meeting to begin the tent was two-thirds filled with delegates.

At 9.15 Mr. Foster, the musical director, came upon the platform. He was followed by President Francis E. Clark, the presiding officer for the morning.

Rev. Dr. Hazen, of Auburndale, opened the devotional exercises with Scripture reading, and then prayer was offered by President Mitchell, of Wilberforce University.

Dr. Clark introduced Mr. Amos R. Wells, the managing editor of *The Golden Rule*, who, Dr. Clark said, was better known to some of the delegates as " Caleb Cobweb." Mr. Wells was received with great hand-clapping, and gave the information committee's report as follows : —

Information Committee's Report.

By Amos R. Wells.

The information committee is the Society telescope. It discovers in the papers new Christian Endeavor movements and methods. It reports these during the first five minutes of every meeting. When you get home, organize an information committee. Without one you are like a hut built around the North Pole. With one you are like a central office of the Western Union Telegraph Company.

I want to give you a geographical information committee report. We are to take a five-minute journey through the Christian Endeavor world of the past year.

First MASSACHUSETTS, stopping at the Clarendon Street Baptist Church of Boston. These Endeavorers are supporting in China, as missionaries, two of their own number, and one is a Chinaman.

NEW YORK : More than 1,100 of its Juniors became Christ's Juniors last year.

PENNSYLVANIA : Held 50 evangelistic meetings at its great convention, and the angel's pen made a glorious record.

NEW JERSEY : We have heard of Christian Endeavor machinery. New Jersey has established the first factory Christian Endeavor Society.

MICHIGAN : A Christian Endeavor hospital built — not a hospital for Christian Endeavor Societies.

ILLINOIS : The first conference of 38 Mothers' Societies of Christian Endeavor. May there soon be a Mothers' Society for every Junior.

INDIANA : The Nicholson Temperance Law passed, and going to be surpassed.

OHIO : One pastor organized 19 new societies in one night in one town. Eight years ago there were 40 delegates at the first State Convention. At the convention just held 10,000 persons were present.

KENTUCKY : Christmas letters sent to all the State prisoners by the Endeavorers won many to the Babe of Bethlehem.

TENNESSEE : At their State Christian Endeavor Convention 60 foreign missionary volunteers. Now for the money to send them.

ALABAMA : At the State Christian Endeavor Convention 16 missionary volunteers.

DISTRICT OF COLUMBIA : At a missionary committee conference 12 missionary volunteers. They have been getting ready in the District of Columbia to hold, next July, the best Christian Endeavor Convention ever held.

NORTH CAROLINA : The State Union formed ; the first Christian Endeavor Convention held. All hail, North Carolina !

TEXAS : At the State Convention three decided for the ministry and 15 for the mission field.

KANSAS: The first kindergarten Christian Endeavor Society formed. Christian Endeavor is an early riser.

NEBRASKA: Seven societies of the Dakotah tribe formed the first Indian Christian Endeavor Union. Is " the only good Indian a dead one " ?

COLORADO: A nine weeks' Endeavor evangelistic campaign in Denver: 800 inquirers, and many join the churches.

WYOMING: Its State Union formed, and its first Christian Endeavor Convention held. Welcome to Wyoming!

MONTANA: A lady delegate to its last State Convention rode 117 miles by stage and 250 by rail. And it paid.

NEVADA: Endeavorers have converted a murderer under life sentence, who sends regular messages to their society.

CALIFORNIA: The Chinese Endeavor Society of Santa Cruz stands first in their country in the matter of giving to missions. "The Chinese must go!" California has five Floating Christian Endeavor stations, at which 605 sailors have found Christ.

BRITISH COLUMBIA: A Japanese Christian Endeavor Society of five in Vancouver has won to Christ in a year 80 Japanese, and sent to Japan several missionaries. What five American Endeavorers have done better?

MANITOBA held a Christian citizenship rally on the Queen's birthday, and sent greetings to Her Majesty. Long may she reign!

ONTARIO: The Endeavorers support nearly 100 missionaries.

QUEBEC: In Montreal a successful campaign against liquor-selling groceries. Down with them all!

PRINCE EDWARD ISLAND: Its first Christian Endeavor Convention. Greeting to Prince Edward Island!

SCOTLAND: Its first National Christian Endeavor Convention. Three years ago it had three societies; now it has 200. The Scots say well: " The movement has n't come to stay; it has come to go ! "

IRELAND: Its first convention, also.

WALES: Two years ago, 29 societies ; now, 120.

ENGLAND: Seven thousand delegates at its Fifth Annual Convention. The United Society for Great Britain and Ireland just established. Last year, 1,400 English societies; now, more than 2,500.

FRANCE: Three union Christian Endeavor meetings in one month in Paris. Forty-seven Christian Endeavor Societies in France.

SWITZERLAND: The Society introduced by an English society of three; taken up by a Swiss Methodist church, now going all through the cantons.

GERMANY: Five societies; one in the University of Berlin.

DENMARK: Start made this year; also in Sweden, Norway, Italy, and Austria.

TURKEY: The societies under the ban. That little society of two boys still holds out. So does the Syrian society of father, mother, and son. So do many more.

EGYPT: A society discovered in old Cairo.

SOUTH AFRICA: A strong Christian Endeavor Union formed, headed by Andrew Murray, the consecrated missionary and author.

INDIA: One society of natives has in the last five years preached nearly 4,000 times, in more than 2,000 places.

LAOS: No Christian Endeavor Societies before January; now, nine.

CHINA: First Provincial Union formed of the ten societies of Canton.

JAPAN: Floating Endeavorers on the *Charleston* are establishing, at Nagasaki, a home for sailors. At the Third National Christian Endeavor Convention of Japan, the United States and Japanese flags were entwined above the heads of the delegates, and we are proud of the honor.

AUSTRALIA: South Australia has 17 Endeavorers on foreign mission fields; Victoria has 32.

NEW SOUTH WALES has grown in three years from 13 to 237 societies; South Australia, in three years, from 38 to 324.

The first Christian Endeavor Convention for all Australia is to be held in September.
Now we have circumnavigated the globe in five minutes. God bless the Christian Endeavorers the wide world around!

President Clark then introduced Rev. W. J. L. Closs, the president of the New South Wales Union, who was received with great enthusiasm.

Mr. Closs made a fine presentation of Christian Endeavor principles. They differ in no point, it seems, under the Southern Cross and under the Northern one. " Our Christian Endeavor is yours, ' ditto, ditto, *one size larger,*' and we sum it up in four words, — ' Life, Liberty, Loyalty, and Love.' " Mr. Closs said that after it became known in Australia that he was to come to Boston as the delegate of the Island Continent, every mail brought him from ten to twenty letters confiding to him special greetings to the United Society.

Address of Rev. W. J. L. Closs.

I begin to feel as if I was right at home with the thermometer about 110 in the shade. It may be warm where you are, but if you want to know how warm Christian Endeavor can be, come right up here. And if you want to know how high it can go, so that the mercury jumps right out of the thermometer altogether, come right down to Australia. In that land beneath the Southern Cross, though out of 50,000 Christian Endeavorers we have only a handful, they are as seed sown in good ground, some of them to bring forth fruit thirty-fold, some of them sixty-fold, and, please God, some of them one hundred-fold. They are as the leaven which has been hidden in the three measures of meal, and by God's grace and Spirit in them, at last the whole of Australia shall be leavened for Christ from end to end. I give you greetings for them. The moment that it was known that I was coming to this Convention I received personal charges to give you greetings, and every mail that came to my study brought from ten to twenty letters sending their greetings to you. I knew I could not deliver all the messages, and realized that I must draw the line somewhere. So, at last, I had to come down to saying, "I will give Australia's greetings. What would you like me to say for those of you who live in this land of the Golden Fleece?" And at last they thought we could give no better greeting than our motto: " One is our Master, even Christ; and all we are brethren."

I have been asked to tell you to-day how Christian Endeavor is regarded in that land, and how the battalions that are marching on have dared, so small a handful, to fling out their banner to the Southern breeze and say, "We shall yet have Australia for Christ." It was very much like the case of a friend of mine who was to speak in a large meeting and had the experience of having his speech entirely taken from him. He got up and said, " I have nothing more to add to what Mr. So-and-So has said except ditto, ditto, a size larger." When you ask me what Christian Endeavor is in Australia I point to the manifestation of it in America, and I say, Australia says " Ditto, ditto, a size larger." But if you ask me to elaborate I will say, Australia holds four cardinal and essential points: life, loyalty, liberty, and love.

Without life there can be no Christian Endeavor Society, that is, the life which is found in Jesus Christ. We put him at the very heart of our movement, and we have his life surging along every fibre, along every nerve, every part of our being. Christ is the life of the Christian Endeavor movement; the life and the hope of the world. We enshrine him first of all. He vitalizes it from beginning to end. Away back in the beginning of the world God stood upon this world of ours, and he said, "Let man be; " and he breathed his own soul into man's nostrils, and man became a living soul. Christ has come to this world of ours, and he has called the Christian Endeavor Society into existence. He has breathed his life into it, and the Christian Endeavor is a living soul; it is that, or it is nothing. And if Christ so be in it and his life permeate it from beginning to end, then it must show itself. Life is not a dead thing. Life is an eager, active spirit, a great moving force. How did it manifest itself in Christ? He stood upon this earth of ours, and he said, " I am come to do the will of my Father." " I am among you as he that serves." " My Father worketh hitherto, and I work." " Not to be ministered unto, but to minister." If we be Christ's we must stand as Christ stood. Reverently we must say, " Our Father worketh hitherto, and we work." Did you ever hear of an inactive active Christian Endeavorer? The whole thing is an anomaly. And if we are to be Christian Endeavorers down in Australia, we hold to it that the life within, Christ's life, must show itself in our active service. Once again, there is a picture of that old world of ours when, by man's disobedience, he learned what it was to be alienated from God. In that hour He who was one with the Father stood in the Father's presence and said, " I pledge myself by our great holiness, by our infinite power and love of an almighty truth that is embodied in us, I pledge myself to go forth to the redemption of humanity. I will endure the Cross and despise the shame, if only I may bring these men back again to the heart of their Father."

You do not believe in pledges? Christian Endeavor does. Right down to the very heart of it, it believes in the Christian Endeavor pledge. In my own church there was a young lady who said she did not believe in pledges, not at all, not even in the temperance pledge; and as for the Christian Endeavor pledge, it was something outrageous altogether. But a young man came along and asked her to marry him, and at the altar she pledged herself, in my presence, to this man, that she would be true to him — this girl who did not believe in pledges. There is just about as much reason in the objections that are made to the Christian Endeavor pledge as there was in hers; for, as Christ pledged himself, we pledge ourselves to do the work to which Christ has called us, and to be true servers in that work. But Christ not only pledged himself, he was systematic in that work to which he was called and which he undertook. From the very first he kept his eyes fixed upon the Cross, forward through all the outrages heaped upon him, and at last his eyes closed as he uttered the words, " It is finished." Oh, we want to concentrate our powers, aim straight at one thing, and then, with all the forces of heart, with all the forces of intellect, and Almighty God behind us, to aim for that one point, — systematic service as well as pledged service. Because of the life within us, because of the Christ within us, we stand pledged Endeavorers in Australia, and we stand pledged to serve God, pledged to serve Christ, and pledged to do systematic work for the oncoming of his kingdom.

The second essential, so far as we in Australia regard it, is loyalty. You remember how, in the old Saxon lands, when a new monarch came to the throne, the nobles of the land came into his presence and put their clasped hands into his; and then, looking up into his face, they vowed that they would be his men, true to him in life and in death, to fight his battles and to do his bidding. We have put our puny hands between the nail-pierced hands of the King of kings, and we have vowed to be true to him, in life, in death, to be his men and to do his bidding. If that be so, we have no part with those who, like Peter, denied their Lord. It will be our utmost endeavor at all times, and in all places, to exalt our Christ and to be true to him, that men may see and know that we are following in the footsteps where he has trod. At all times be ye true to Christ, and aid us, down yonder in that southern land, by your example and force, to be true to him also.

Then we will be true to our own churches, to our own denominations, and to our own ministers, our own church officers. If we are true to Christ it follows, necessarily, that we must be true to our own individual churches and denominations. So, at least, we regard it in Australia. We believe in doing our service in that field where God has placed us, as Christ has given us opportunity to do his work. We may not have much power ; we may not have much ability ; the opportunities that come our way may be small; but still, what we can do, if it is only wiping the tear from the baby's cheek, we will do in Christ's name.

And then, the third essential is that of liberty. We believe in freedom, in our sunny Australian land, as much as you do here. We believe in our flag floating over a land of men and women who are emancipated, as you do in this land here. We believe in a government "for the people, by the people, and of the people," and so we live in a free land. I had almost said the freest land in God's great earth, but that flag floats over me, and I know the price with which you have purchased it, and I know I stand in the vicinity of Faneuil Hall and near to Plymouth Rock, and I thank God for liberty, and the lessons that this country has taught the world. As Christian Endeavorers we can exercise no authority over any single individual. We can exercise no authority over any society; no other union, no united society, not even a world-wide confederation, can for one single moment subject any, and say to a man, "Thou shalt," or "Thou shalt not." Christ, when he was here on earth, was so often asked to set up a standard! He utterly refused to do it. "How often shall I forgive my brother?" When he was asked to pay tribute to Cæsar, — "Render, therefore, unto Cæsar the things which are Cæsar's, and unto God the things which are God's." Christian Endeavor must re-echo Christ's voice. Live according to your conscience, do the best you know how in obeying the Divine Voice within you. And so we try to let men know that they can be free only as God makes them free.

But there is a wider liberty than that, the liberty for all men. In my fair country, and in my land, there stalk many giants, and these hold in their hands, as slaves, hundreds and millions of our fellow men and women. There is the giant of gambling, that has so blotted my own land; there is the giant of intemperance, against which you are waging such a noble warfare; there are the giants of lust and greed, and a thousand others. And I want to know what we are going to do about them. Are we going to be true to the truth God has given us, and seek to emancipate all men? O men whose boast it is that ye are brave and free,

> " Ye are neither free nor brave
> While on earth there lives a slave."

Ye have sown this land of yours with slaves. You may strike the fetters from the wrists of our colored brethren. What will you do to strike the fetters from your fellowmen whom God would make free?

Lastly, we believe in the great essential of love. You remember how Christ, ere his death, gathered his disciples together; you remember how he girded himself with a towel, and washed the feet of his disciples. What! washed Peter's feet, and in a few hours he was to deny him! What! washed Judas's feet, and in a few hours he was to betray him! What! washed the feet of those men who, in a brief time, were to forsake him and leave him alone in his sorrow and in his agony! Aye, every one of them. The great Christ, God incarnate, stooped down and washed their feet. What did it mean? "This have I done, that I might leave you an example that ye love one another as I have loved you." The old Jewish dispensation rose to the height of saying that a man must love his brother man as he loved himself. He could not go higher than that, and, oh, we would think we had come to our ideal if we loved our fellow as we love ourselves. But Christ said, "As I have loved you." Love that made him walk for thirty years this sin-cursed earth of ours. And have you ever thought what an agony it was, how every hour he met with sin, and evil, and wrong, and how it must have bruised his soul? Love that made him take up his Cross and hang on Calvary. That is the measure of my love and yours, that is our ideal, not less than that example which he has left us.

We believe with all our souls in interdenominational fellowship. In Australia, in our young people's movement, there is no division whatsoever. We are all Christian Endeavorers, and, by God's grace, we will keep it so.

I have heard how, in one of your great wars, two vessels of war met each other in the mists of the morning, and each mistook the other for a foe. Crash upon crash they sent the iron hail hurtling through the morning mists, and each one wondered how it was that his opponent was not slain. The morning sun rose and the mists grew thin and were dispelled, and it was all explained then, for at the peak of each there floated " Old Glory; " and they knew how it was that neither of them were slain. In the days gone by we have fired the hurtling hail of our harsh criticism into our opponents, but, thank God, the Sun of Right-eousness has risen; thank God that over all our interdenominational pennant floats out; over all there is the banner of our King, Christ Jesus.

We believe in these colors that you have flung out so widely to the breeze. We believe in the red, we believe in the white — in the blood of cleansing and in the white of purity. We thank God that you have hailed Australia with the colors red and white, for we believe in them with all our hearts.

> " Red, for the road we travel is blood-marked all the way;
> Red, for our consecration to the life, to the truth, and the way;
> Red, for the danger-signals for those who are going astray;
> Red, for the fount of healing open to all to-day.

> " White, for the shadows of ignorance must die in the dawning light;
> White, for the night of evil gives place to morning bright;
> White, for the wrong within us must bend the knee to right,
> And the midnight hour of battle shine out in the noonday light."

And so we live under these great powers. We live under the Southern Cross, the symbol of the world's hope as of the world's redemption. We, under the Southern Cross, say that life means to us service, systematic and pledged. We believe in the principles : life, liberty, loyalty, love — in this sign we conquer.

The fourteen two-minute reports from the denominational rallies were both enthusiastic and spicy. Rev. E. B. Bagby, the young chap-lain of our National House of Representatives, conducted the exercises as briskly as the speaker could.

Remarks by Rev. E. B. Bagby.

I remember one morning, upon a country road in old Virginia, I met an old colored man. He said to me, " Are you de young man dat preached down to church las' night ? " I replied, as modestly as I could, that I was. "Well," he said, " I was dere, and I certainly did enjoy your text." Now, I have a text to-day. It is a good one, and I hope that you will all enjoy it. This is the text: " Look not every man on his own things, but every man on the things of others." There was a time when we looked only upon the affairs of our own denomina-tion; when we did not know what the others were doing, and I am afraid we did not care, but that was the time before Christian Endeavor. Now, since we have learned the lesson that " One is our Master, and all we are brethren," we want to know what the others are doing, and we can, thank God, rejoice in each other's success.

Now the sermon this morning is to be a good one, as well as a good text. It is to be delivered by fourteen of my brethren here on the platform. The sermon is to be twenty-eight minutes long, and will be delivered in fourteen divisions of two minutes each. In two minutes' time these brethren are to tell us of what they did at denominational meetings yesterday afternoon. Now, firstly, Rev. R. Haywood Stitt, Philadelphia, Penn., is to tell us of the joint rally of the African Methodist Episcopal and African Methodist Episcopal Zion churches.

African M. E., and African M. E. Zion Churches.

Rev. R. H. Stitt, Philadelphia, Penn.: — I represent more than 200,000 black children of " Father " Clark. We followed you into this movement as we have followed you into other movements, 200,000 of us already organized, and 200,000 more to follow next year. But why not follow you? We followed you to this country when you came. You came to Plymouth Rock; we came to Jamestown. You intruded yourselves upon this soil; we came by special invitation. We tried to follow you a while longer. We followed you into the legislatures of the States; we followed you into the Congress of the nation; and we followed you into the jails and penitentiaries. Now we don't wish to follow any longer. We are with you in this grand movement.

Advent Christian Church.

Rev. A. C. Johnson, Lynn, Mass.: — Beloved friends, I come to you to report from one of the youngest and smallest denominations. We must remember the saying of the Prophet: "Who hath despised the day of small things?" We had a very successful rally yesterday. Some two hundred were present, and some nineteen societies reported, running all the way from the Pine Tree State to Asia Minor. I tried to speak about the benefits and blessings of the pledge as leading to definiteness of relation with Jesus Christ and definiteness and directness of service in his vineyard. Then we had an address from Rev. E. A. Stockman, earnestly advocating the Christian Endeavor name and pledge for all our societies. Some of them are loyal workers, and that grand, eloquent man advised them all to become loyal workers of Christian Endeavor; and so we trust they will all come into line, and we shall be with you in a body, undivided, when the year comes round again.

Baptist Church.

Rev. H. C. Vedder, Chester, Penn.: — In Tent Endeavor, yesterday afternoon, we had the largest gathering of Baptists ever held in Boston, in the United States, or in the world. Last year, at Cleveland, we had 2,000 Baptists in the Euclid Baptist Church, which was all that it would hold; and we thought that was a tremendous rally. A week later I was in Toronto, and between 5,000 and 6,000 young Baptists gathered there; we thought that was still more tremendous. But yesterday, at least 10,000 young Baptists gathered in this adjoining tent. Addresses were delivered by the Rev. L. A. Crandall, D.D., of Chicago, by the Rev. Clarence A. Barbour, of Rochester, N. Y.; and then we had two splendid missionary addresses by Rev. John T. Morgan, LL.D., the secretary of the American Home Missionary Society, and Dr. Henry C. Mabie, the secretary of the American Baptist Missionary Union. The meeting closed with an open parliament on the subject of "Advance, Endeavor," led by Dr. Wayland Hoyt.

Canadian Presbyterian Church.

Rev. W. R. Cruikshank, Montreal, Can.: — The young Presbyterians of Canada rallied yesterday 200 strong; 78 of them were Nova Scotians. We were reminded that the Christian Endeavor Society is fourteen years old — a dangerous age for a boy; he is apt to feel himself a man. We don't want him to be a man yet. He is sweeter as a boy, more gentle and loving. But, though he is not a man, he is a boy of giant strength. We warned him of his danger. We asked the audience to point out some of the weak points of Christian Endeavor, which they did. We endeavored to strengthen these weak points, and I think we did. We came away feeling that the boy was robust, and that if he would only eat a little more porridge, and take a little more of the shorter catechism, he would be all right.

Christian Church.

Rev. G. W. Morrow, West Randolph, Vt.: — The greatest rally of the Christian denomination yet held at the International Conventions was held yesterday, and was addressed by members on the subjects of missions and Christian citizenship, and very much enthusiasm prevailed throughout the meeting. The chief end of man is to glorify God, and that which adds to the glory of God and the salvation of man is what we are seeking to-day. The one sentiment that prevails, predominates, in the Christian Endeavor organization to-day is certainly that exaltation of Jesus Christ; and next to the exaltation of Christ is the honoring of Christ's Church, the bride of Christ.

Church of God.

MR. JOHN W. MACKEY, Harrisburg, Penn.: — We doubtless are in the minority as far as numbers are concerned, both as concerns our rally and our denomination; but we are with the majority on the great Christian Endeavor movement. We believe in life; we believe in loyalty; we believe in love. We were not satisfied with present attainments on the line of Christian Endeavor work, and the consequence was that our rally yesterday afternoon took the line of thought of how we could stimulate a greater activity among our churches in the direction of the Christian Endeavor movement. The result of that consideration, of that open parliament, was that we effected a Pennsylvania State organization to further advance Christian Endeavor; and we hope that, by thus systematically going at this thing, ere long we will be able to report to you a greater number of Christian Endeavor Societies in our churches, a greater work accomplished for the Lord Jesus Christ, than we have ever done before.

Congregational Church.

MR. W. H. STRONG, Detroit, Mich.: — The Congregational rally met in this tent, as many as could get in; the others met outside. The whole atmosphere of our rally told that the only value of our proud past lay in the courage that it gave for the present to meet the threatening and yet glorious opportunities that come to every one of us. We remembered how our fathers drew their inspiration from the Light of the world; how our fathers did their rugged duty with uplifted faces, casting a reflection and handing down the torch until the torch became a flame for our great world's light. In the inspiration of that thought, we are going out, as Congregationalists, more loyal than ever — more loyal to Christian Endeavor, to the local church, and more loyal to Christ

Cumberland Presbyterian Church.

REV. R. W. LEWIS, Meridian, Miss.: — I am here to represent a denomination in Boston on a visit — perhaps the only congregation that is here as such. I am glad, this morning, to represent a young denomination, born in 1810. I am glad to represent a revival denomination, born in a revival, and we are still living in a revival. I am glad to represent a progressive denomination and a church that knows no North and no South, and has never known North or South. I am glad this morning, also, to represent a denomination that took hold of Christian Endeavor at the start, and still holds on to Christian Endeavor. We have taken it unchanged; we have adopted it as our denominational society. We have 699 societies. Our motto for next year is: " One thousand societies as we go to Washington in '96."

Disciples of Christ.

REV. ALLEN B. PHILPUTT, D.D., Philadelphia, Penn.: — The Disciples of Christ have been loyal to Christian Endeavor from the very first. Numerically, they are the fourth of the Protestant denominations in size and third in the number of their Christian Endeavor Societies. It has been the custom from the first, in these rallies, to undertake some practical enterprise. We built, as a band of Christian Endeavorers, the church in Salt Lake City. Last year we agreed to assist in building a hospital in Japan. Yesterday we heard from the secretaries of our missionary boards and organizations, and voted unanimously to lift the debt from the only church we have in this great city, and to enable them to turn it into an institutional church. And also, that the western half of the United States, the people there, should do likewise for the city of Chicago, in a section of that city, on the north side, to assist in buying land, furnishing dollar for dollar, that they might build there an institutional church. We believe in practical work. We are in hearty sympathy with Christian Endeavor, and find there is no discrimination between denominational enthusiasm and this interdenominational fellowship.

Free Baptist Church.

Rev. O. H. Tracy, Somersworth, N. H.: — I have the honor to say a word for the denomination of Free Baptists. We are glad that we are free; we are glad that we are connected with the great Christian Endeavor movement, which is so much in harmony with the ideas of our own denomination, which has stood for freedom from the beginning, which believes that this great Christian Endeavor Convention is Free Baptist sentiment in full bloom. Yesterday we had one of the best denominational gatherings that I have ever witnessed. The Shawmut Avenue Church was crowded to its utmost capacity, and we had representative speakers from the East, South, West, and from far-off India, and Christian Endeavor sentiment ran high. We are glad to be connected with the Christian Endeavor movement. Christian Endeavor is better understood to-day among Free Baptists than it ever was before, and the tide is rising. Christian Endeavor is standing stronger and taking a more conspicuous part in the work of our denomination.

Friends' Church.

Mr. Winslow M. Bell, Milton, N. Y.: — Christian Endeavor in the Society of Friends has been thoroughly tested and proved. We saw it yesterday at our rally. In 1892 our church, as a body, merged all their young people's societies into the United Society of Christian Endeavor. It proved the beginning of a new era in our church, which has now advanced the young people so that they are recognized as they were not in the past. At our rally yesterday it appeared that out of over one thousand members, one has gone to foreign missions to advance the cause of Christ. Since the Cleveland Convention, Christian Endeavor has extended among the Friends. It has created a new bond of fellowship and united it with other denominations. We realize that Christian Endeavor was sent by God to further his almighty plans: advance his Church, extend the fellowship, and unite with other denominations. His hand can be plainly seen in the marvellous growth, unity, and strength of the Christian Endeavor movement.

German Societies.

Mr. Carl E. Wittwer, Buffalo, N. Y.: — The German rally at the Methodist Episcopal Church was a small gathering in point of numbers, but by no means small in importance of the benefits arising therefrom. The brotherly spirit manifested in this meeting was refreshing. Eight societies were represented, a small number out of the two hundred and fifty German societies in this country. But an explanation may easily be given. The Third National Conference of German-speaking societies will take place at Sandusky, O., within three weeks, and it is but natural that German Endeavorers should wish to attend that conference. It is not a question of preference but of loyalty on the part of German-speaking Endeavorers. They love their Heavenly Captain and Leader, and nowhere are more faithful followers or warmer admirers of Field-Marshal Clark to be found than in the German camp.

Lutheran Church.

Rev. Willis S. Hinman, Columbia, Penn.: — I am glad to represent the church that is the mother of you all, and the Mother Church of the Reformation is glad to be a child of Christian Endeavor. Though the church in which we met yesterday was not the largest in Boston, we filled it until standing room was at a premium. We had representatives from sixteen States, — Massachusetts the most eastern, and California the most western. We had one delegate from India, a convert of our mission there. The keynote that was struck at the

very beginning was young Lutherans at work for Christ, and it rung through
until the end. We came away happier that we were Lutheran Christians.

Mennonite Church.

REV. A. S. SHELLY, Bally, Penn.: — In Boston, hundreds of miles away from
our nearest church! And we feel at home in this City of the Pilgrims, the name
" Pilgrim " being suggestive of the experience of our forefathers of the past in
the Church, and the very name " Baptist " being sacred to our forefathers from
the time of the Reformation. Beyond all expectation, the gathering yesterday
in the Warren Avenue Baptist Church exceeded the rally of last year in numbers. The Lord is always willing to give more largely than we are willing to
expect of him. In the addresses special emphasis was laid on the need of
aggressive work, the need of carrying the warfare into the enemy's country.
Christian Endeavor stands for that part of the Church which is alive; which
has a full head of steam on.

Mr. Bagby then repeated his text in conclusion : " Look not every
man on his own things, but every man also on the things of others."

The next speaker received an ovation as he stepped forward to speak
upon " The Cardinal Principles of Christian Endeavor, as Presented
by a Scotch Endeavorer."

Address of Rev. John Pollock, Glasgow, Scotland.

My first duty is to convey the cordial greetings of the Scottish National
Christian Endeavor Union, constituted at our first Christian Endeavor Convention in April last, the greetings of Scottish Endeavorers generally.

Christian Endeavor, as you have already heard, is making rapid progress in
the Land of the Covenant. Scotland thinks twice before accepting any new
thing, especially if that new thing hails from America. Scotland, however,
when it gets a grip, holds. The Scottish terrier holds as tenaciously, when it
gets a grip of a thing by the right end, as ever the English bulldog did. We
have fallen in love with Christian Endeavor. We are now of opinion that of
all religious movements of the present day there is none so truly Scottish as
Christian Endeavor is. We believe in pledges in Scotland. Our fathers
pledged themselves in Grayfriars' Church. They opened their veins, many of
them, and signed their names in their own blood. Not only so, but many of
them sealed the old Christian Endeavor pledge of that day at the stake and at
the gallows in the Grass Market of Edinburgh. The mention of the Cove-
nanting times always makes the blood of a Scotchman tingle in his veins. I
believe I address an audience in which much Scottish blood is in circulation.
I have got it by the right hand.

We believe that Christian Endeavor means definite dedication of the individual to the Lord Jesus Christ. I am going to tell you some things I have
heard about you before I will tell you what I know to be a fact about Scotland.
There is not an active member of the Christian Endeavor Society in Scotland
who does not profess to have had a definite spiritual experience; who does not
profess to have passed out of darkness into God's marvellous light; who does
not profess to aim at holiness, without which no man shall see the Lord. I do
not say that all of them live in accordance with their profession, but I believe
this: that the profession, in every case with which I am familiar, is the profession
honestly made.

Now I have to speak to-day on the root principles of Christian Endeavor.
Do not look for these in the pledge. The pledge, to some extent, descends, as
it must do, to practical detail. I ask you to look at the motto. What is the
motto of Christian Endeavor? " For Christ and the Church." A loyal Christian
Endeavorer is loyal to Jesus Christ. He believes in his divinity; he believes

that he is sitting at the right hand of the Throne of God, and that he will one day come to judge the quick and the dead. He believes in the living Christ, working by his Holy Spirit in the hearts of all believers. He believes that he is on the winning side because he is under the banner of Him who shall one day lay unto himself his great power and reign. A loyal Christian Endeavorer is willing to do whatever Christ in any circumstances would have him do. If Christ commands him to stay at home, no amount of enthusiasm and interest in a heathen brother should ever close his eyes against that duty which is nearest, and which is always the clearest. If Christ commands him to go out to the uttermost parts of the earth, if Christ commands him to go to the torrid or the arctic regions, if Christ commands him to make his home in one of the mission fields of my own church, what has been called "the white man's grave," he has no right to spend the fraction of a second in thought; so soon as he is convinced that his duty stares him in the face, I say, he has no right to hesitate, but immediately should lay aside all that love of home which, at all events, would keep him at home. His duty, therefore, is to go forth with his life in his hands, proclaiming the message of Christ's command.

Loyal to Jesus Christ! My friends, did you ever notice how inopportune were the moments which Christ selected for the laying of his commands upon men? He went to the sons of Zebedee while they were mending their nets, almost as important an occupation to a fisherman as casting the net. His command was, "Follow me." Down went their needles, and immediately they followed the man of Nazareth. He did not wait until business hours were over, but there, with his laden scales at one elbow and his money-bags at the other, he went to Levi, and he said, "Follow me;" and immediately that business man, at the most business time of the day, left all and followed Christ. Now, my friends, I tell you this: the Christian Endeavor has come to teach Christians that they are bound to obey Christ, bound to lay aside likes and dislikes. So soon as they become convinced that the voice which comes to them is the voice of the Son of God, King of the conscience, Absolute Proprietor of the whole man, that moment they give themselves to the duty to which his finger points. Loyalty to Christ, the gospel of putting one's self about! We need it to-day. The gospel of putting one's self to inconvenience! We need it to-day.

But Christian Endeavor has another watchword, — "For the Church." And, my friends, we are doing what we can to emphasize that in Scotland. Christian Endeavor exists for the Church; it means loyalty to the Church. Now, my friends, do not tell me that that means loyalty to the Church invisible. No quibbling, my friends. It does not mean anything of the kind. I am glad to have an opportunity to say this in the presence of Dr. Clark. We mean the organized body of Christians which go together by the name of the Church. You cannot be loyal to that which is invisible. You cannot be loyal to that which is seen only of God. You cannot be loyal to that which is known only to the Searcher of hearts. How can you be loyal to a church, the communion rail of which lies in the presence of God? We do not know one another. A very good story is told of Dr. Chalmers' mother. Some one was praising up a certain individual very highly, and the canny Scotchwoman looked her informant in the face and said, "Weel, weel, that may be sae; but did ye ever live wi' her?" I remember a man of whom I thought a very great deal; I changed my opinion at college, when he and I were bedfellows. My friends, you cannot be loyal to the Church invisible. Christian Endeavor means loyalty to the Church; Christian Endeavor means loyalty to the denomination. By loyalty to the denomination I mean this: I believe that Presbyterianism is the grandest form of church government on the face of the earth, and that enables me to love very dearly the conscientious Congregationalist. I believe that my own church, the United Presbyterian Church of Scotland — I do not know about the rest of the planet — but I believe that it is the best church in Scotland; and the result is that I have a very warm side to the Free Church, to the Established Church, and to the other churches that are in Scotland. Christian Endeavor has come to stamp under foot the spirit of narrow sectarianism.

Christian Endeavor has come to possess the spirit of intelligent denominationalism. Be not enthusiastic for your church because you were born in it. I am not in the church in which I was born, and I believe I am in the best church of the lot. Don't be loyal because of that accident; be loyal because you approve of the principles upon which your particular denomination is founded. And then the Church — the Church means the congregation, your own congregation. I will tell you another thing that Christian Endeavor is putting an end to in Scotland. Stravaging (?). I am sorry I cannot translate. There is no word in the English language by which to translate the word. I will tell you what it means in a sort of a roundabout way. It means going and taking a very deep interest in some religious movement outside of your own congregation, while classes are remaining untaught in your own Sabbath school. It means going solo-singing at this meeting and the other meeting, while the conductor of congregational psalmody in your own church is at his wits' end. That is what it means. We are putting an end to that in Scotland by Christian Endeavor. Christian Endeavor means that it is a man's duty to rally round his minister, — to be one of those who rally round, yes, to make a multitude of himself, if he can, and rally round, in his multitudinous capacity, the minister of the congregation to which he belongs.

Christian Endeavor means interdenominational fellowship. I have a more accurate conception of what other denominations are than I had before Christian Endeavor arrived. Some of my dearest friends in Scotland now are men who do not believe a bit in Presbyterianism, who do not hold to the non-essential principles, if I may so speak, of the church to which I belong. We have got to know each other by being brought together under the banner of Christian Endeavor. Christian Endeavor means — I feel as if I must coin a word here — it is not undenominational; it is interdenominational. It is not only interdenominational, but I am reminded to-day, and as you listen to my broad Scotch accent you are reminded, that Christian Endeavor means *interpatriotism.* I remember being told when I was at school that *patria* was a noun for which there was no plural. *Patria* means one's country. My brothers, Christian Endeavor has discovered the plural for *patria.* I stand here to-day with the royal standard of Scotland on my breast, dominated, however, by Christian Endeavor, and, as a loyal subject of Queen Victoria, I congratulate you on the victory — for, essentially, a glorious victory it was — I congratulate you with all my heart upon the victory of Bunker Hill. My friends, that is what Christian Endeavor means: looking, each country, upon its own things, but every country also on the things of others. That is what Christian Endeavor means: one in Jesus Christ. I am amazed at the number of denominations that require to be represented on this and the contiguous platform. What in the name of common sense is the meaning of it? You have no State church here as we have in Scotland. If our State church were abolished — no, my friends, we do not want to abolish her, we love her too dearly — if she were set free, the result would be a flowing together of Scottish Presbyterianism. At all events, Christian Endeavor means, then, unity in Jesus Christ.

And now, in the precious five minutes that are left me, as I stand here to-day, will you allow me to say — I speak not now as the representative of Scottish Endeavor, but as representing my own church and representing myself. I belong to the American Church of Scotland. Did you ever hear of it? I belong to the only Presbyterian church of Scotland that will have nothing to do with State control, to the only church in Scotland which, from the very beginning has said, " Render unto Cæsar the things which are Cæsar's, and unto God the things which are God's ! " the church which the other churches are more or less rapidly sidling up to, finding their own positions somewhat unsatisfactory, and placing themselves beside us. But, my friends, I will tell you what I am far prouder of. I claim to belong to the Missionary Church of Scotland; not only the Missionary Church of Scotland, but to the church which occupies the next place to the Moravian Church on the list of the missionary churches of the world. A German writer some time ago said that next to the Moravian Church that church which had shown the most splendid missionary spirit was a small denomination (he was wrong there) in Scotland, called the United Presbyterian Church.

Christian Endeavor means the world for Christ. What does that mean when we break it down? It means, first of all, myself for Christ; next, my fireside for Christ, my ain fireside. It means, next, my companions for Christ, all the young men and young women in the particular warehouse department in which I am employed, for Christ. " For Christ and the Church ! " Oh, I fear that in many cases this must come before that, the Church for Christ. It means the extending of our influence at home, and sending abroad those who shall represent us in a foreign field.

> " Salvation, oh, salvation, the glorious sound proclaim
> Till each remotest nation has learned Messiah's name."

And, my friends, Christian Endeavor, with its glorious past, not of fourteen centuries, but of fourteen years, gives us reason to expect great things in the future. Why?

> " The Lord our God is good,
> His mercy is forever sure,
> His truth at all times firmly stood,
> And shall from age to age endure."

Mrs. Mary A. Livermore was then presented to the audience and given the Chautauqua salute.

A very interesting service followed the presentation of the banner for the greatest gain in number of societies in the year.

Presented by Rev. F. E. E. Hamilton, Newtonville, Mass.

The last words of Jesus to his disciples were the commission, " Go ye, therefore, and preach to all nations." Their first welcome when their work is done will be a plaudit : " Well done, good and faithful servant ; thou hast been faithful over a few things, I will make thee ruler over ten cities." We are here this morning to applaud faithful service. We will not forget, in the gratulations of this hour, that there are obscure and faithful workers who have wrought faithfully and well, but whose honors are as yet detained a little. The crown often belongs to him who fails. To England, however, — England, the mother of us all, — has been accorded the glorious privilege of seeing success. She has added over one thousand new societies to the united organization of the Christian Endeavor cause during the past year. England, therefore, through her representative, Rev. W. Knight Chaplin, of London, is called here this morning to be crowned *primus inter pares*, first among equals; and I have been asked in behalf of the organization to present to her, for the second time, this international banner.

Personally, I rejoice to see this emblem go back again across the ocean; I rejoice because it recognizes the adaptation and the adoption of some American ideas on English soil. England, my brother, can well afford to accept and to assimilate some things which are not peculiarly insular. I am glad, therefore, that every true Briton can say with every true American that he can hail the Christian Endeavor cause as coming to quicken and to strengthen the great non-conformist conscience. In these days of our American jingoism, when there has been so much criticism by zealous patriots of alleged and seeming violations of the Munroe doctrine, you may be surprised when I say that there is a warfare, however, which we, as Americans, are ready to take up with you, not only in the Colonies but in the very heart of England. I am therefore glad to say, in the spirit of Wesley, — you remember he said, " If thy heart is as my heart, give me thy hand," — with the spirit of Wesley, therefore, I am glad to say, and in the name of Him who said, "Go, teach," I am glad to say, Give to us your English hearts and your English hands, and together we will put our heel on devilism wherever found. Whether in London West or London East, we will put an iron heel on the dram-shop; we will teach anarchists and religious bigots that adherence to a red flag or a red robe shall never cloak violence or lawlessness. We will, by the help of Him whose Word is as a thousand swords, make trade and politics clean. We will shame, on both sides of the great Atlantic, religious shams. We will defy the organ of the tyranny of that public sentiment which builds on the love of money and the lust of spoils. We will lift up our hearts and our hands to welcome the purest patriotism that the world can know. We have here no continuing city; we are the patriots of a heavenly country; we are the sons of God, and God made woman to be God's equal. With our sisters of Christian Endeavor, therefore, we strike hands that all our Saxon peoples the world around may cast out their devils and, sitting at the feet of Jesus, be clothed in their right minds. We, as Christian Endeavorers, have a passion for the planet. Let us, therefore, we who are the heirs of all the ages in the foremost files of time, let us, here and now, consecrate ourselves anew to the one work of winning men to the standard of the Cross until all nations are come to the Christ.

My brother, I present to you this banner.

Rev. W. Knight Chaplin's Remarks.

We are glad to-day to bring you our heartiest greetings from the old country. We are a growing people, we are adding to our population half a million every year, and in the last two years we have added more than two thousand Christian Endeavor Societies to our ranks. We believe that Christian Endeavor has come to the United Kingdom to stay. I am afraid my voice will scarcely carry as far as I would like it to. Let me say, I am sorry that Ireland is not represented upon the platform, for Ireland, as well as Scotland and Wales, has had a part in the advancement of Christian Endeavor on our side of the water. We, in this Christian Endeavor movement, are building upon the strongest and most enduring possible foundation; and we are building into the movement materials of sterling worth, material made up of the gifts and talents and powers with which God has endowed young, consecrated, Christian lives; and because that is so, we say the movement may have had a cradle; it will never have a coffin, but will go on in the achievement of victory and success "for Christ and the Church" until the Lord, the great Head of the Church, shall crown every member of the Endeavor host with a crown that shall not fade away.

We thank you for our reception here to-day, and we invite you to come to London for the World's Christian Endeavor Convention in the year 1900.

Some one in the audience started "God Save the Queen," in which all joined, following with a verse of "America."

Then came a lively open parliament on the topic, "The Feet and Hands of the Society; How They Are Employed," conducted by Rev. J. A. Rondthaler, D.D., Indianapolis, Ind.

Remarks of Rev. J. A. Rondthaler, D.D.

We have had wonderful eloquence, wonderful patriotism, wonderful spirituality; now we are going to have wonderful common sense. Remember this: that these Websterian and Clay heads, from which has floated all this magnificence this morning, are finished, and now there is to come up from this audience all that which will make up the work for the year that is to come. I want to say to the men that are going to speak here now, "Roar like English bulls;" and to the women, "Scream like the American eagle, so that we can have the chance to hear you."

What is our subject? It is an anatomical subject; some fellow that has been studying medicine has been making up this programme. The backbone, that is the pledge; the beating heart, that is the consecration; the feet and hands, the committee reaching out. We want to make every fibre quiver; we want to make every nerve to be alive for Christian Endeavor.

(From numerous delegates the following testimony was derived, the questions being asked by Dr. Rondthaler.)

The Lookout Committee.

WHAT IS THE LOOKOUT COMMITTEE FOR? To bring in members.
WHAT OTHER WORK HAS IT? To keep in members.
HOW DO YOU KEEP IN MEMBERS? Make them work.
HOW? Give them something to do. Send them after other souls. Go where they are.
WHERE ARE THEY? Everywhere. Our lookout committee canvasses the saloons every Saturday night, and invites the men to our meetings Sunday morning?
DO THEY COME? They do. One lookout committeee has 900 souls at its Breakfast Association in Philadelphia. They feed the bodies first and then feed the souls.
HOW MANY STAY TO THE SOUL-FEEDING? The best part of them.

The Prayer-meeting Committee.

WHAT DOES THE PRAYER-MEETING COMMITTEE DO IN THE WAY OF THE HANDS AND THE FEET? Do not let anybody go away from the meeting until you have welcomed them. Our prayer-meeting committee tries to have each member lead a meeting during the year. Move around amongst the young people, and urge them to take their part. Get them to come early to the meeting.
HOW DO YOU GET MEMBERS TO COME EARLY TO THE MEETING? Wake them up; begin promptly; have a song service. In Chicago I have seen a sign. They hang it up in the front; on one side, in black letters, it reads, " I am early," and on the other, " I am late."
Encourage those who take part to take part again.
Call for them, bring them to the meeting yourself on time.
Bring before the Throne of Grace the needs of the Society.
Yes, earnest, intense, deep, constant prayer of the prayer-meeting committee for the highest, largest, sweetest blessing upon that Society will solve more problems than any other way.
Let the leader be short.
One society accepts the advice of *The Golden Rule.*
Meet the leaders regularly, and assist them with prayers and suggestions.

The Good=Citizenship Committee.

" We have a good-citizenship service on the first Sunday of every month, by the consent of the pastor," says one delegate. Vote as you pray. Another suggests the establishment of free drinking fountains of cold water, outside of the church, along the streets, wherever the great congregation meets the great world out-of-doors. When you are a good citizen yourself, go to work and make good citizens of the Juniors. Go to the caucus. One society kept beer from being sold on the picnic-ground on the Fourth of July. We of Colorado, in the interests of good citizenship, advise other States to give the women the right of the ballot. Keep the Golden Rule. One society shut up the race-tracks of New Jersey on Sunday.
Some one suggested, watch the caucus. How? Go there yourself, take the good man with you and be careful for whom you vote. Hold good-citizenship rallies, and teach the young men to be independent of their party.

BAND STAND, BOSTON COMMON — OPEN-AIR MEETING.

Entrance to Public Gardens.

Insist upon a proper observance of the Sabbath. How? By not taking Sunday newspapers. By not riding on Sunday cars. Shutting up the Sunday theatre. By not riding Sunday bicycles. By not staying at home on beds of sickness or sofas of wellness.

WHAT ARE YOU GOING TO DO FOR THE CITY? Insist upon having enacted and protected good Sunday laws. Stop the Sunday base ball, as they do in Canton, O.

WHAT DO YOU PUT IN THE PLACE OF IT? Put the Church in the place of it.

The Social Committee.

WHAT CAN THEY DO? Have socials to get members.

WHAT ARE SOCIALS? A place where you get better acquainted with the members.

Don't put all your time into sociables, but be social with strangers. Extend a hearty greeting to all to attend our meetings. Get a social committee consecrated to Christ. You have got to have as much spirituality in the social committee as in the prayer-meeting committee. Stand at the rear of the church and help the pastor shake hands. Be social everywhere.

The Missionary Committee.

WHAT ARE YOU DOING? WHAT CAN WE DO? Give wide-awake missionary concerts. Have our young people know what the boards of missions are doing. Make the main move obedience to the great commission. Study the life of Christ and the lives of missionaries. Teach systematic giving, beginning with the tenth for the Lord. Be vigilant; keep at it. Let the Christian Endeavor Society start a missionary library. Keep a table covered with small missionary tracts right at the church door. Have a missionary extension course. Encourage your missionaries by writing to them occasionally, bright, interesting letters. Have a specific aim. Take up a collection. Get the members to take missionary literature. Get a live missionary to talk to the young people. Pay all the expenses of your own missionaries, as the Clarendon Street Baptists are doing. Do something for the Chinese laundryman. A lady says, " Be a missionary yourself."

The meeting closed with music by the Park Sisters and a benediction pronounced by Rev. W. W. Sleeper, of Wisconsin.

Tent Endeavor.

During the half-hour previous to the opening of the meeting the crowd in Tent Endeavor whiled away the moments with impromptu choruses, singing " America " and a number of other familiar hymns.

Mr. George K. Somerby started his great human music-box at 9.30, prompt, with " Scatter Sunshine All Along the Way."

" Homeland Shore " came out strong and true from the chorus and congregation, followed by " Tell the Glad Story."

Trustee Rev. Howard B. Grose, of Chicago, presided. Mr. W. H. Pennell, of Washington, conducted the devotional services, reading Psalm CIII. and offering prayer.

Mr. Somerby selected " Still, Still with Thee " as a fitting song, and then Chairman Grose introduced Mr. George B. Graff, of *The Golden Rule.* Mr. Graff spoke on the information committee's report.

Information Committee's Report.

By Mr. Geo. B. Graff.

The information committee is supposed to take about five minutes at the beginning of every Christian Endeavor prayer meeting to inform the members of Endeavorers' and Endeavor doings, of methods that have been tried and proven, of successful meetings that have been held, and, in fact, of the progress of Christ's kingdom around the world.

This committee is the Society's telescope.

The wisdom of the world is not wrapped up in any one society. It may be that some society other than your own strikes a new and good idea. Then if your information committee has secured it the other society's experience is your gain.

The Christian Endeavor movement has made wonderful strides in foreign countries.

In India the Constitution has been translated into seven different dialects.

In Japan more than seventy different societies exist.

In South Africa the Endeavorers have the true missionary spirit, and are pushing out into the very heart of the Dark Continent, carrying the glad news of salvation.

In Laos, which lies in the northern part of Burma, the first society was formed less than six months ago. There are now nine societies, with 245 members. Meetings are held every week, and, although only three gospels and the Acts have as yet been translated into their language, the active members are faithful to their pledge, and find something to say for every meeting.

In benighted Egypt, too, the society is flourishing.

One significant fact in both Egypt and Laos is that the women, although heretofore considered far inferior to the men, now lead the meetings and are given an active part in the work of the Society.

The Christian Endeavor Society always has been and always will be a training school in the Church, and yet it is interesting to note how readily it adapts itself to other conditions, and how it is found in the most unlikely places. Societies have existed for some time in prisons, blind asylums, factories, in the army and navy, among sailors, travelling-men, and the police of New York City. Word has come lately to hand telling of the formation of a society in the Ohio State Hospital at Dayton; in the Masonic Home at Louisville, Ky.; in the Blind Asylum at Glasgow, Scotland; in the State Insane Asylum at Ossawatomie, Kan.; while a Junior Society has been organized in connection with the Y. M. C. A. at Kansas City, Mo.

The Junior State banners were presented by the Rev. J. F. Cowan, D.D., of Pittsburgh, Penn.

Remarks of Rev. J. F. Cowan, D.D.

Perhaps you have heard of a modest little State named Pennsylvania. It is full of modest people, and after I have proceeded further you will wonder that I did not say modest little people. Now to show you the delicate modesty, we have banners here which are handed to me by a Pennsylvanian to a Pennsylvanian, and I am to hand them over to another Pennsylvanian. Nevertheless they have been honestly earned. One of the delegates who came from our State, from the rock-ribbed portion of it, said he thought the Almighty must have made Pennsylvania by chipping up stones and then sprinkling a little dirt from some other State so as to make the fishing-worms contented to stay there. I assure you, however, whatever you may have heard of our mountains and our iron and our coal, we have broad, beautiful valleys and plains. Two years ago, at Montreal, Pennsylvania was over three hundred Junior Societies behind the foremost State, Illinois. We thought we would try to catch up; we were not just sure that we could; but there is a story of Abraham Lincoln which cheered us quite a little. It is said that he was the tallest young man in his neighborhood until one day some one came to this champion and said, " Abe, there is a fellow coming to town to-day who is half an inch taller than you." " Never mind," said Mr. Lincoln, " I have n't my highest-heeled boots on to-day." So he put them on, and he was half an inch taller than the other fellow. On the Fourth of July, or a Fair day, some great occasion, another tall man came to town, and they said, " Abe, here 's another man half an inch taller than you with your high-heeled boots on; what are you going to do now ? " The young man thought a moment, and then replied, " Well, if it 's necessary I can stretch half an inch." Pennsylvania has been wearing her high-heeled boots and stretching herself also in the matter of organizing Junior Societies.

Here are two banners. This one belongs to Pennsylvania forevermore, because it has been presented to the State having the largest number of Junior Societies. Of the 9,000 and more Junior Societies in the world, Pennsylvania to-day has over 1,000, or over one-ninth. We expect to keep this banner till we and it grow gray together. There is another banner here for the largest gain in Junior Societies during the last year. This banner, which we took last year at Cleveland, we brought up, willing to deliver it in case any one had a right to claim it; but no one has exceeded Pennsylvania, and so we modestly hand it back to the modest man who will now step up and receive it, Dr. McCrory, president of the Union.

DR. McCRORY: If this is not the most interesting performance in the world! For the State to present to the State its own banner produces something of the enthusiasm that went with it last year when we took it from the greatest people in the world, the people of Illinois. I say that because I was raised in Illinois, and I have not gotten over it yet. Over in Pennsylvania, however, we are laboring for Juniors, and we found a new meaning for " C. E."; it is " Castoria Endeavor," that is, a new way of getting the same old truths into the hearts and minds of the young. I was riding on the train through New York the other morning about daylight and looked out and saw, every once in a while, on the mountain-side that beautiful and significant sign-board, " Children cry for Pitcher's Castoria." And I said, We have it. That 's an idea. And I remembered how it used to be when I was a boy, and it has not been so long ago but what I can remember how we had to take our castor-oil. I remember how the boy did when he had to take the dose. Well, his mother said he must have a dose, and she went to the cupboard and she got out the black bottle and great big iron spoon. " What are you going to do ? " asked the boy. " You 'll have to take a little medicine." " I won't do it." " You 'll have to; you 'll die if you don't." " Won't do it." " If you do it I 'll give you a cookie." " Not for a bushel of cookies." " I 'll give you a shin-plaster." " Won't do it." And his father said, " If you don't, I 'll give you a licking." " I 'll take the licking." And so they got the boy, you know, and they laid him down on his back, and the father took hold of his nose, and they said, " You won't breathe until you swallow," and the spoonful of castor-oil was put into his mouth, and they held his nose until his father knew he would be on trial for murder, and when he let go it all went out. But the work had been done; the Russian bath that the boy had got in the struggle cured him ; it was not the castor-oil. Well, it used to be that way in learning the Bible. It is Castoria that we are getting into the children through the Junior Societies. It was the old castor-oil method I was raised on. Now my children take it and cry for it. So we say " Castoria Endeavor," and I hope every State in the Union, and Great Britain with her forty millions who struggled with Pennsylvania for the greatest number of societies, and beat us by a very few — forty millions over in Europe fighting with six millions in Pennsylvania beat us. We are not ashamed of it; but we are going to beat them next year. I hope every State and Province in the world will struggle for this banner, and I hope you will just get so near to it that we can keep it next year.

At the close of Dr. McCrory's speech Dr. Cowan said: —

We have another banner here. We were proud last year when little Delaware captured this Junior banner for proportionate increase. We are just as proud when the Province with the unpronounceable name captured it from Delaware. I have been looking into the etymology of that name. It is derived from the Chinese, "Ah Sin," meaning " I smile," with the suffix in Scandinavian, "Aboyia," which means " Christian Endeavor ; " thus the literal interpretation is " Smiling Christian Endeavor," and I think when the gentleman who is to receive this banner comes forward to take it, my interpretation will be justified. Prof. W. W. Andrews is to receive this Junior banner for proportionate increase.

Professor Andrews spoke as follows : —

Assiniboia! Assiniboia! Where on earth is that? Canada has this peculiarity: it is the only country in the world where flowers will bloom in May within the limits of the Arctic Circle. If one leg of a compass be set down on the Manitoban city of Winnipeg, and the other leg be made to touch your own Gulf of Mexico, and swung around to the northwest, it will just rest on the northwestern limits of Canada's great wheat-belt, where the finest wheat in the world, No. 1 hard, grows, — Manitoba No. 1 hard. Where is Assiniboia? Just almost in the centre of that great region ; a great territory in which we could toss a hundred Delawares ; in the centre of a great region in which, if those who have made the computation are correct, we could put the whole present population of the United States. It is something refreshing for a British-Canadian-American to come over to this region of Boston and to capture a banner. If you visit Toronto and Quebec, and some other places in old Canada, you will find that some banners will be shown you and some cannons which we happened to capture from you. At Quebec there are some cannons which were captured at Bunker Hill, — we got the cannons and you got the hill. Therefore it is with great pleasure that I receive from the brave little State of Delaware this banner, and will hand it over to my fellow countrymen in Assiniboia.

The presiding officer then introduced Rev. J. L. Lamont, of Belfast, Ireland, as follows : —

I am sure that those of us who represent the United States are only too glad to send a banner over into the Dominion ; and just as long as they continue to win these banners by their Christian Endeavor service we will say, " God bless you ! " And now we shall give our warm greeting to one of our Christian Endeavor brothers from across the ocean. We have in this Convention the evidence that Christian Endeavor belts the globe, and it is with great delight that I introduce to you the Rev. J. L. Lamont, of Belfast, Ireland, who will speak to us from his point of view upon " Cardinal Endeavor Principles." I should have supposed he would have wanted it green Endeavor principles, but no, it is " Cardinal Endeavor Principles."

Mr. Lamont was received with great enthusiasm.

Address of Rev. J. L. Lamont.

I ought to say in reply to that observation of the chairman that I had not the selection of my subject; however, he ought to know that we know something about cardinals in Ireland, and I hope we know something about principles as well. Now I have before me a very difficult task this morning ; I have to refer to a political matter, — I hope you are not alarmed, — it is a matter of political economy. I may say I am here to-day with this problem before me:

having to make a very little go a great length. It would seem to us on the other side of the water, if I had a task assigned me like the present one, as if I were requested to bring coals to Newcastle. It seems to me that my task might be explained to-day by saying that I have been asked to bring beans to Boston. It is somewhat presumptuous for a man from that Green Isle, who is himself somewhat verdant, to have to speak to you about "The Cardinal Principles of Christian Endeavor," seeing that we in this matter are of yesterday, and know nothing. It is to you we are indebted for this magnificent movement, which has accomplished such marvellous results, and which is destined in the near future to achieve still greater triumphs for Christ and his Church. You must remember that it is only about eight years since Christian Endeavor touched the shores of the British Isles. The first society was formed in 1887, and at the end of five years only four hundred and twenty-eight societies had been organized. All that time, however, men were beginning to look at this new thing, and prejudices were beginning to give way before the practical evidence of good which the societies already in existence afforded. One year later we had 1,004 societies; the next year we had 2,112, and to-day we have 2,700 registered societies, with a membership of 121,000. Now, Mr. Chairman, I don't mean to give you an address on statistics, because a great politician has said that there are three kinds of lies: "There are, first, lies; then, secondly, there are thundering lies; and third, there are statistics." Now those are not the kind of statistics that we furnish in connection with Christian Endeavor Societies.

"Cardinal Principles of Christian Endeavor"—that is my theme. I would like to emphasize the fact to-day that we have principle. There was a time when a multitude of people thought that Christian Endeavor knew more about pleasurable pastimes than about great moral and religious principles, but I am glad to say that that multitude is rapidly diminishing, and on our side of the Atlantic there are quite a number of persons who would be ashamed to acknowledge that they ever entertained such opinions. Now we do not claim to have made our principles, but we do claim that our principles have made us. We are quite ready to admit that the principles of the movement are old principles, and we are further ready to affirm as an article of our belief that old principles are the best for young people. We have no sympathy whatever with that Christian — I don't know to what denomination he belonged, it is sufficient for me to say that he was not connected with the Young People's Society of Christian Endeavor. I remember having heard that he applied for a certain position, and when he was asked what his doctrinal beliefs were, he said they were so and so; "But," said he, "if these don't suit I can change them."

In Christian Endeavor there are certain great fundamental truths, certain foundation stones without which no true edifice of Christian Endeavor can be safely constructed; notwithstanding this, I know that some have tried to raise a similar edifice, neglecting the character of the foundation, but I have never known such a structure to outlast the storms of ridicule, or of persecution. But a true Christian Endeavor Society stands four-squared against every wind that blows. The cardinal points in our country we regard as indicating the four points of the compass. We are assembled to-day in this monster Convention, from every point of the compass, to reaffirm our belief in the great principles and aims which have made Christian Endeavor such a mighty force throughout the wide world for Christ and his Church. Let me indicate in a few words what I consider these cardinal principles to be. First, covenant obligation to service. We are endeavoring in this grand Young People's Society to put the old principles of the Gospel of Jesus Christ into practice. I remember on one occasion attending a temperance demonstration in our country, and there was an English member of Parliament there. It is a great thing to get hold of a member of Parliament, and to get him on the temperance platform on our side. And he began by saying in a pre-eminently patronizing fashion, "Mr. Chairman, I am of your way of thinking, but I am not of your way of drinking." Well, it is not the theory but the practice of total abstinence that has troubled a great many people, and it seems to me that it is the same with Christianity. Speaking for myself to-day, I have found that more exception has been taken to the pledge than to any other feature of the movement. The annual conference of my own church closed just the day before I left home. I had the honor to be the convener of a committee on work amongst the young, which met during the past year. That committee brought in its report at our conference, and its strongest recommendation was the formation of societies of Christian Endeavor. I have to tell you that that report was adopted by a very large majority, and that it was supported by every pastor who had had any practical experience of the working of this grand Society. There was not one who was prepared to say, "I have tried it, and it has failed." And just before that debate closed there was one minister, than whom there is no man more beloved in our Irish conference, and he said he wanted to utter just one sentence. "At one time," he said, "I was opposed to this movement; after a while I was undecided; to-day I am thoroughly converted." I had the right of replying to all speeches that had been made against the report, but as I saw the battle was already won, I did not care to waste any ammunition. But there was one grand old man, a layman eighty years of age, and he came to me on the platform, and he said, "Mr. Lamont, tell them that I am eighty years of age, that I attend all the prayer meetings, and that I am heartily in favor of the Christian Endeavor movement." I gave them gladly this testimony, and there was no profounder argument used that day in favor of the Christian Endeavor Society.

In the course of that great debate there were objections made to the pledge. Now it seems to me that these objections might be classified under two heads. There were some men who seemed to say, "Obliterate it," and there was another class who seemed to say, "Dilute it." The one party wanted to wipe it out, and the other party wanted to water it down. Now there were others who in this convention said that they would not like to put such a solemn pledge in the hands of the young people. My reply was simple; I took up our covenant service, and I said that there were stronger pledges, stronger language, used in that covenant service than anything included in the pledge of the Christian Endeavor Society. The man who speaks of the bondage of the pledge does not understand the significance of the word "liberty" as we find it in the Gospel of Jesus Christ. No man can live a life of fellowship with Christ without entering into covenant with him. We do not say that the covenant must take the form that we have adopted, but we do say that our Heavenly Father disregards generalization. He would have us, as Christian men and women, particularize, enter into details. As Christian Endeavorers we enter into solemn covenant to strive to be and to do what Jesus Christ wills; it is a pledge to trust, and love, and serve our Master; and I think, my dear fellow Endeavorers, that in these days, when dogma is derided, when the cry is against the creeds, and when vague man seems to be the very man for the times, all true men will welcome a society that aims at the personal, and practical, and powerful presentation of the principles of the Gospel of Jesus Christ. There is one thing that Christian Endeavor grandly differentiates between, that is, between benedictions and benefactions. There are many men who will give us gladly their benediction, but will never give us benefactions. They will give you their "God bless you," but they will give you no hand of fellowship and service. "What God hath joined together let no man put asunder." Christianity and beneficence are married, and our grand hopes rest upon this practical character, this helpful character, of our movement. You remember, some of you, of reading that story of the two colored brethren who were engaged in some part of this country — we have to come to this country for all our illustrations — these two brethren were getting on a load of lumber. Both were Sunday-school teachers, and one was lifting all he could, and the other looking quietly on. And the working man said to the other, "Sam, do you mean to get to heaven? Well, if you mean to get to heaven, you will have to take hold and lift." This is what we Christian Endeavorers are trying to teach the young. If they mean to get to heaven they must take hold and lift; stoop and serve their brethren and sisters in the Gospel of Jesus Christ. Is there anything that the Church of Jesus Christ needs more to-day than a band of consecrated workers? Christian

Endeavor, therefore, proposes to train such a band; not by theological teaching, though we do not undervalue that, but by practical service. "Work for the young and by the young" is our glorious motto. Christian Endeavor finds something for every member to do. There are men in the Church at home in the Old Country to-day, — I cannot speak of yours, — and their bitterest regret is that they were not trained to serve Christ in the Church when they were young. And it is quite true to say that in all our churches there are many young people who owe their facility in speaking to-day to the training they received in connection with the Christian Endeavor movement.

The next principle that I shall present for a moment is denominational loyalty in Christian Endeavor. We have our preference without prejudice. We believe that young people can do more effective service for Christ when they are in fellowship with some particular denomination. We have very little belief, in the Old Country, in what we call "free lances." We teach our members to put their strength in somewhere, and that they must be intensive in their devotion if they would be extensive in their usefulness. The men who distribute their energy, the men and women who are here and there and everywhere, are nowhere in the real, practical work of the Church of Jesus Christ.

Another principle of the Christian Endeavor Society is to illustrate the teaching of the great Evangelical Alliance, whose motto is, "In essentials, unity; in non-essentials, liberty; in all things, charity." We ask Christian Endeavorers to believe in the communion of saints. We are in sympathy and heartiest co-operation in a very real sense with all Christians throughout the world. It has been said by some one who was an extreme sectarian, "I imagine that the denominations have been very useful as checks and chasteners." It is time surely that they were of some other use than that. In some places it would seem to me that ecclesiastical exclusiveness is the very master-stroke of the devil. "Come and see;" that is still the best remedy for suspicions and delusions existing between the churches. What a mighty impulse would come to our Christian beneficence if Christians would give to one another a larger measure of the spirit of love and brotherhood in the Spirit of Jesus Christ, and toward this great end we trust our young Endeavorers shall strive. Did you ever hear of those two men that lived in an English village — there is no member of the English deputation here; I believe he is in the other tent — and were very much opposed to one another on one thing? One man had a windmill, and he objected to the erection of the second because he said there was not wind enough to drive the two. That is just one of the grievances in living in a small island. You don't know anything about it here.

Now I will just mention, without expanding, as the preachers say, the "lastly," which is the consecration meeting. Christian Endeavor stands for Christian testimony. One thing the Christian Endeavorer knows: "Whereas I was blind, now I see." And knowing one thing he is ready to do one thing, and that is Christianity's greatest object. That is the unanswerable argument: "I know whom I have believed, and I am persuaded that he is able to keep that which I have committed unto him against that day." Dear brother and sister Endeavorers, we shall never look one another in the face probably on this side of eternity, but let us bear aloft the torch of truth and Christian testimony, and as a mighty army of witness-bearers we shall lead a great host into the light and love of our God.

When "Onward, Christian Soldiers" had been sung, Rev. J. W. Fifield, of Chicago, conducted an open parliament on the topic, "The Consecration Meeting."

Remarks of Rev. J. W. Fifield.

The great Convention is growing hot. We are coming down out of the air to walk the earth for a little while. We will now have together a parliament. If you have never been in a parliament you can remain and engage in this one for a little time. We have divided up the Christian Endeavor body into three portions. In one place they are going to study together the hands and the feet; over at another place they will look at the backbone; but here we have been asked to study about the heart of the Christian Endeavor movement, which is the consecration service. Now my part is simply to turn you loose and let you do the talking. I almost hesitate to give you the reins and let you go, but possibly if I try and guide you for a little time, we may get at some practical thoughts, and so we will have a number of things to take home with us. Yesterday we learned a good deal about Boston and her monuments and Plymouth Rock. You will not be permitted to take them home with you. Some one suggested yesterday that they proposed to take Faneuil Hall to Chicago; at once a resident of this city said he was going home to lock it up.

You may get some practical thoughts, then, for a little time, about how to conduct the meetings when you go home, receiving experience from all of the societies gathered here from our country and other countries. There is a verse in the Bible which says, "Let your speech be seasoned with salt." When asked to take this meeting I thought that I would have a few barrels rolled in, so that we might have the salt. S-A-L-T spells salt. Now you mind these four letters, and you will learn how you are to speak. You are to speak S, that stands for sharp, — something sharp and pointed; A stands for apt; I might stand for loud, — you are to lift up your voices like thunder, so that all may hear; S-A-L-T,— T will be true; sharp, apt, loud, and true. We will try and ask a few questions; you are to answer them. The consecration service, the heart of the Christian Endeavor Society! In the first place, possibly I might ask, Do your members keep the pledge and attend the consecration service? How is it with you in your societies, are they attending the consecration meeting?

PHILADELPHIA : Eighty per cent of our society.

MONTEREY Co., CAL.: Ninety per cent.

BERMUDA : One hundred per cent.

CHAMBERSBURG, PENN.: Eighty-five per cent.

SOMERVILLE, ILL.: About ninety-five per cent.

MR. FIFIELD: Those who do not attend — do they keep the pledge by sending in Scripture to be read or sending testimony if they cannot come? Is that true of your society? What per cent, when they cannot come, remember the society, and send in a verse of Scripture to be read at the consecration meeting?

PRINCE EDWARD ISLAND: Nearly every member of our society, when they cannot come, send in a verse to be read by some other person.

BERMUDA: We never knew one instance when the verse was not sent in when the person could not attend.

MR. FIFIELD: I wonder if that can be said of all the States and countries: that they are keeping the pledge, and when they cannot go are sending in the verse? If your members do not attend the consecration services, and do not send the verse, what do you do about it? When they are not there they have broken their pledge; what do you do? Does your lookout committee look them up? It is pledged to look them up.

SOMERVILLE, ILL.: We send out the lookout committee, five members, and attend to them right away.

LOUISIANA: Our society does not send out the lookout committee, but the committee look them up, anyhow.

MR. FIFIELD: What do you do? Some one else. Do you just let them go? One says they send out postal cards showing they notice they are away. If you let them go they think they are not missed. Another point: How do you conduct your consecration meeting? In the first place, do you call the roll of all active and associate members? I was spoken to before the services this morning and asked if some societies did not omit calling the roll. I would like to know if you call the roll, and ask, expect, and receive an answer to each name as it is called.

PENNSYLVANIA : We call the roll in full, active and associate members.

CONNECTICUT: We call the roll of the active and associate members. It draws the associate members in, it does not drive them away; it makes them offer their testimony, increases their interest in the society, and makes active members of them in a short time.

NEW YORK CITY: We call the roll in some societies; in others, the roll is not called. Those where the roll is called have the best societies.

MAINE: We call the roll of both active and associate members.

CLINTON, R. I.: We call the roll of the active members.

MR. FIFIELD: What would you do, supposing active members failed to respond to roll-call when present; what would you do with those members?

NEW YORK: We labor with them and bring them back.

RHODE ISLAND: We don't have such members.

EASTPORT, ME.: We don't have that kind.

HYDE PARK, MASS.: We send the lookout committee after them; if absent or unrepresented for three meetings, we drop their names. We call the roll, and they answer, "Here," and then in sections of twenty-five they unitedly read a verse of Scripture.

MR. FIFIELD: Suppose an active member is absent from three consecutive consecration meetings, notwithstanding all efforts in his behalf, what would you do with him? According to rules his name should be dropped. The person has been written to and does not respond; what would you do?

VERMONT: Go and see them about it.

MICHIGAN: Keep going till you get them.

MINNESOTA: We keep by the Constitution. When absent three times we drop their names.

MR. FIFIELD: A long list of names read, if not responded to, makes people feel as if they could play fast and loose with the pledge. Others catch the same spirit. Prompt measures should be used. These consecration services should be the rounds of the ladder, and we shall grow in Christian experience. How many at the consecration services ever had them respond all in prayer? Have any ever tried that?

BRIDGEPORT, CONN.: We have had responses all in prayer.

GRAND RAPIDS, MICH.: One hundred and twenty-four members all responded in prayer.

ROBESONIA, PENN.: Sixty members responded in prayer.

MR. FIFIELD: Now don't you find this true: that in the consecration service a great many will say a verse, and get through in a mechanical way? I believe you should have a definite outline. If you aim at nothing you will be sure and hit it; but you may aim at the sun, and though your arrow may not pierce the bright-orbed disk of day, you get in that direction. Now look out in your consecration work. If you find your young people are not studying the Bible, then arrange that every one shall respond by quoting a verse of Scripture. Announce it a week before; let the leader announce it; let every one learn a verse during the week. If you find that your young people are not praying, have prayer-meeting responses. We had one in the city of Chicago, and they were persisted in there until every one responded, and many voices that never prayed in public before were taught in that meeting how to pray. Are there any practical suggestions now? You remember the Saviour went out and gathered up the fragments, and he got many basketfuls. So we may get a few fragments of thought on how to conduct the consecration service. Did you ever have a real consecration meeting? Give us in just a word the thought that made it helpful, that we may fill up the baskets now.

WASHINGTON, D. C.: We have a new consecration every day; not once for all, not once a week only, not once a month only, but every day a new beginning.

MASSACHUSETTS: We have our consecration meeting Saturday, having the regular meeting and opening the consecration meeting afterward.

CHICAGO, ILL.: We found that the only way to keep our members consecrated was to give them responsibility.

PHILADELPHIA, PENN.: We have an alphabetical list prepared by the lookout committee, the members respond with testimony, then the president calls on those who have not spoken.

CHICAGO, ILL.: We have a consecration meeting with some definite point to work for each month.

MR. FIFIELD: Consecrate yourself for something particular, have something definite in mind. Near the Fourth of July consecrate your thought to Christian patriotism. If you are working alone, consecrate yourself to Bible study, to mission work. Carry it out through the month. Aim definitely at something in the consecration service and work up higher and higher in it.

EASTPORT, ME.: Have societies found that consecration meetings held in connection with business meetings are a success?

MR. FIFIELD: No. I hope we have gathered up a few of the fragments, which we may take home. Let us make this consecration service a great blessing. This is the heart; if the heart is sluggish, the whole society is sluggish. Make them spiritual, pray for them, make them Biblical, teach how to study the Bible, teach how to pray. Advance along Christ's lines, and your society will become fruitful more and more in the name of Jesus Christ.

Rev. D. O. Mears, D.D., of Cleveland, O., then conducted the reports from the denominational meetings.

Remarks of Rev. D. O. Mears, D.D.

God never meant that two stars in the firmament should look alike. "One star differeth from another star in glory." God never meant that two human faces should look alike. No two in the wide world are alike. God never meant that two churches in the great army for the conquest of the world should march alike, should be alike, should look alike. There is unity in diversity, difference in administration, difference in government. This is the law. God never meant that two flowers blooming in their beauty in the field should be alike. Go in the garden; suppose all the flowers were of one color, say blue. Suppose we begin where the surf of the Atlantic begins its music, and end where the clouds over the Golden Gate hang in their brilliancy and their beauty, and all through this nation every flower by the side of every railroad was blue. How would it look? Call the Presbyterians blue.

Suppose there were no blue, but that all were white, and that, in thus passing out, every valley, every mountain, every garden, should have flowers only white. Call these the Baptists. Not pond-lilies, but lilies of the valley. We should get sick and weary.

Suppose we should have all pink. That would represent a church that should stand in its beauty and in its purity. And from the Atlantic to the Pacific nothing but pink. We should grow weary, weary. Call that the Church of England.

Suppose they should be all red. No blue, no white, no pink, all red, — carnation in energy, in piety, in strength; great purity, great energy, great strength, all important. Call that Methodist. Suppose we should begin, and from one shore to the other nothing but red. We should grow weary, weary of the sight of red.

I 'll not pass through and call the list. If I were to send a bouquet to a friend, I would not take a bouquet of pink; it would look bad, when God has brocaded the full earth with beauty and that which is attractive. And I am here to-day to present the bouquet of the Convention, — flowers red, white, and blue, all the colors. I am only sorry that the Baptists are in the other tent, and I cannot introduce these white lilies I would like to include in this bouquet we present now. It is not for me to make any speech in introducing these brethren; I should have to be introduced to most of them myself.

Methodist Episcopal Church.

REV. WALLACE MCMULLEN, Philadelphia. : — We Methodists are very glad to have red assigned as our color, for red always stands first in the mention of the primary colors, and red always stands first in the mention of the trinity of colors that goes to make up these symbols of our patriotism about the tent. Therefore we are quite content with the assignment. We will stand by the red. We had a good meeting yesterday, a blessed meeting, and one which, in its spirit and in its probable results, we think surpasses any of its predecessors at any convention. We got a little enthusiastic over our Methodism, which was proper at such a time. We reaffirmed our loyalty to the church which has given and guided some measure of God's truth over the whole world. We reaffirmed our enthusiastic belief in her spirit and in her methods, declared once more that we would be forever loyal to that dear church in which our Christian life had its genesis, and from which, praise God, that same Christian life will have its exodus into the fellowship of the Church Triumphant some day. And then — this does not contradict the first — we got enthusiastic over Christian Endeavor. And we believed this was found to be true : that this great Society, in its pledged service, in its distinct religious consecration, in its enthusiastic spirit of toil, was in the closest affinity with historical Methodism; that the Christian Endeavor Society is a natural and effective ally to the Methodist Church and to the world. We resolved upon that, and we declared that we would be just as true to Christian Endeavor as we intended to be to Methodism.

Methodist Protestant Church.

Mr. PAUL M. STRAYER, Baltimore, Md. : — I represent one shade of red, — a Methodist red. I may look a little white, but I certainly don't feel blue. The Methodist Protestant Church is but a baby in years, but it disproves the text, " As thy days so shall thy strength be," for our faith is exceedingly great. It came into being in 1848, the same year gold was discovered, another precious article. But we are building strong for the future, because we are making the corner-stone of our structure of such material as consecrated young men and women. The only denominational young people's society given recognition in our church is called the Christian Endeavor Society; we recognize none other. It exactly meets our denominational needs; it fills the wants of our young laity, for our church is a church of laymen. Our rally yesterday was an echo of the convention of the Methodist Protestants. The Christian Endeavor meeting was the high-water mark of denominational loyalty and enthusiasm and our denominational fellowship. Our motto is the same as that of Maryland: " Increase and multiply."

Moravian Church.

REV. A. D. THAELER, Winston, N. C. : — The Moravian Church, though an old church, is one of the least among the princes of Judah. It seems strange that we happen to be sandwiched right in between the great denominations, but I suppose it is because we come in the M's. We had a glorious meeting yesterday. Boston has not many of our denomination ; however, we had representatives from eight different States of the Union. We formed something we never had before, a National Moravian Christian Endeavor Union. We are one all over the country, we Moravians are, and we gave definite instructions to the executive committee of the new union along two lines. One is that we are going to have an annual convention meeting at the same time and in the same city with the interdenominational convention at the time of the rally. The second instruction, however, it seems to me is still more important; that is, that the executive committee is to form a missionary bureau, that every Moravian in every part of the country may know more extensively about our own missions as well as the missions of others.

Protestant Episcopal Church in Canada and the United States.

REV. CANON J. B. RICHARDSON, London, Ont.: — Mr. Chairman, within our own communion we take very high ground, but when we come to the great Christian Endeavor Convention we don't take low ground, but very common ground with all our fellow Christians. There were a great many reasons which contributed to the success of our rally yesterday. We held it in Trinity Church, and we felt that the broad catholic spirit of Phillips Brooks was with us; and we re-echoed those glorious sentiments which have made him so popular and so universally beloved. You are very wise, sir, in giving to us the color of pink; pink protests against scarlet, and we from the very beginning have protested against the scarlet woman. We had the largest gathering of ministers yesterday that we have ever had before from all parts of the Dominion of Canada, from the North, South, East, and West of this great American republic. And we closed our convention by passing a solemn resolution that during this coming year we should accomplish more, if possible, in bringing our people into line with Christian Endeavor than ever we have accomplished before.

Reformed Church in America.

REV. ISAAC W. GOWEN, New Durham, N. J.: — We will undertake the contract to reform all of you if you join with us, because we carry the color of the national flower, the goldenrod. We of the Reformed Church in America had our schoolmaster at work while the Pilgrims in Massachusetts Colony were passing resolutions to build a schoolhouse. Our schoolmaster came over in the ship with the minister, and founded the first school in the New World; and we have kept it up ever since. Now if you want somebody to speak for the Presbyterians, I will take their two minutes and say that we are Reformed in name and Presbyterian in government, and the Presbyterians are Reformed in doctrine and Presbyterian in name. So I will speak for them. They are our big brother, and we always have our big brother stand by us, and we always stand by ourselves.

Reformed Church in the United States.

REV. HENRY T. SPANGLER, D.D., Collegeville, Penn.:— The first significant feature in the rally of the Reformed Church of the United States was the fact that there was not a single delegate there who had not travelled at least 300 miles to attend this Convention. The total mileage of the rally was between 75,000 and 80,000 miles. We are the oldest Reformed church of the whole Reformed family, dating our origin from Ulrich Zwingli, in the year 1516; and as is often the case with the more ambitious younger brothers and sisters, many of them live in a larger house and have more children than we have — though we represent a membership of over 200,000. Our church had a foreign missionary and a woman from Japan on the platform yesterday. The Christian Endeavor Societies of the church sustained the foreign missionary during the last year, — their first year's work in this line. The work of the Junior Societies was especially emphasized at our rally because ever since we have been a church our ministers have been taught to teach the children and the boys and the girls, and in this way bring them up into stalwart membership in the church.

Reformed Episcopal Church.

BISHOP SAMUEL FALLOWS, D.D., Chicago, Ill.: — The Reformed Episcopal Church, although the last, is, like the Moravian Church, not the least among the princes of Judah in her enthusiasm for and devotion to the principles of Christian Endeavor. Since our last interdenominational convention at Cleveland the Young People's Society has been made the official society of the western precinct of our church, and we confidently expect that when the next general council shall meet it will be the official society of the entire church. At the meeting yesterday the burden of the thought of the eight addresses was this: the need of a larger baptism of the Holy Ghost to carry on the work which God in his providence has given the Christian Endeavor Society to do. May that prayer be answered !

Reformed Presbyterian Church.

REV. SAMUEL MCNAUGHER, Boston, Mass.: — The Reformed Presbyterian Church rally was held in the First Church of Boston on yesterday afternoon; the subject which we had for consideration, as always in the Reformed Presbyterian Church, was Christ as King. We held that banner aloft as the Church has held it since the second Reformation; she has held that doctrine aloft since the time of the Covenanter Church in Scotland; she holds that doctrine to-day, and means to hold it as the solution of the great Christian Endeavor movement. We believe that Christian citizenship means Christ the King. We believe that this government and all nations throughout the wide world should recognize him as the King of kings and Lord of lords, and that that recognition should mean something in the fidelity and in the faithful service of God's people; and as a small church, if we are but few in number, we stand up with that great and that noble principle and ask the Christian Endeavor Societies of all sister denominations to take up the cry of Christian citizenship, " Christ, the King, " and under the leadership of our Saviour-King go forward conquering and to conquer. And we know that as this is done the Lord God Almighty will bring in the day of righteousness and of peace.

Southern Presbyterian Church.

PROF. JAMES LEWIS HOWE, Lexington, Va.: — At the rally of the Southern Presbyterian Church every Southern State but three was represented, and not one delegate but had travelled nearly five hundred miles, and some of them over fifteen hundred miles. We had an experience meeting and a conference. We were glad to hear there great encouragement as to what Christian Endeavor is doing throughout our church. It is not so strong in any one place; it is scattered all through the church, — scattered like a little leaven, — but it is leavening the whole lump. The Christian Endeavor movement is making itself felt in the church. So much so, that the Foreign Missionary Board had our secretary for foreign missions come on just to speak to our young people on foreign missions at this rally, in order that they might keep in touch with our young people, with our young Christian Endeavorers. As a church we are conservative, very conservative, we are afraid of a great many things that come from Boston ; but we are getting willing to accept good things, wherever they come from, even if they come from Boston. We are getting to recognize more and more that Christian Endeavor is the work of the Holy Spirit.

United Brethren Church.

REV. H. F. SHUPE, Dayton, O.: — The United Brethren are somewhat out of their latitude in New England, geographically speaking, the church having had its origin in the Middle States; and having developed westward from that centre, very few of our 250,000 people are in the New England States. While we are out of our latitude geographically, we are not out of our latitude in Christian Endeavor; and yesterday we had an excellent rally, representatives of our societies being present from Kansas and the States eastward. We have in our church a denominational union of young people's societies, and in that the Christian Endeavor Society has worked and been given right of way, and the societies are increasing in our church. We rejoice in the spirit of Christian Endeavor; and, while modest, we rejoice also that by our evangelistic methods from 25,000 to 30,000 people are being converted every year. Well, we have had an excellent rally here ; we shall have a better one next year in Washington.

United Evangelical Church.

PROF. OTIS L. JACOBS, York, Penn.: — Christian Endeavorers, I want to say that we had a splendid rally yesterday. We are not so large in numbers, but we made up in enthusiasm and earnestness. It has been charged that the Keystone Leagues of Christian Endeavor are becoming sectional and sectarian. I deny it. We love our church, but we love the great principles of Christian Endeavor, and we propose to stand by them. We are Christian Endeavorers, and we are going to stay Christian Endeavorers. We are taking care of our Juniors. We find that with great success we can organize mission bands in connection with our Junior work. We had interesting addresses on missions. I represent the youngest organization in existence, scarcely a year old; but we come here with fully one-fourth of the members of our church Christian Endeavorers. I want to say to you that we are going to keep at it. Somebody wanted to know what the initials K. L. C. E. meant. Christian Endeavor Keeping at it, and L., looking upward. And we are going to keep at it and look upward until we realize our motto: "Every member of the Church a Christian Endeavorer, every associate member a Christian, every child a Junior, and the Church and the world for Christ."

United Presbyterian Church.

Rev. R. M. Russell, D.D., Pittsburgh, Penn.: — Yesterday the United Presbyterians had a rally in the church at Cambridge, and it was agreed by all who were there that it was the best rally in the whole city of Boston, and we all came away filled with a deep commiseration for the 40,000 or 50,000 Christians that were kept from attending our rally by the unfortunate limitations of their denominations. We talked about a few things pertaining to the Holy Gospel. We had a man tell us what Christ's commission to the United Presbyterian Church means as defined by our opportunities, and when we got through we felt that this old world needs the theology of the United Presbyterians, and we felt that that wondrous field with its 5,000,000 away in the heart of Africa was a great enough work for us. Another brother spoke of our equipment for service, and when he got through we felt that it was a good thing to have our praisebook, — a book which although published in Pittsburgh was edited in heaven by the Holy Ghost, — and we thought a great deal about that old world-shaking power, and that he is just as powerful to-day to shake the world as in the days gone by. One of the speakers told us about what human government should mean as an echo from God, and he told us it ought to mean the kingdom of God against the modern political machine, the Ten Commandments should be absolute in politics, and it means the echo of the Divine Fatherhood in the natures of the men who hold the reins of government, and it ought to mean the thunder of heaven against unfaithful officials. The United Presbyterian Church means a good many things. It means look up and lift up until the clouds shall open for our Lord to come. We want the electric current to pass round the whole church until God's light shines on a new world.

The last speaker for the morning was Rev. S. P. Rose, D.D., a prominent Methodist pastor of Montreal, Canada, whose topic was, "Cardinal Principles of Christian Endeavor Presented by a Canadian Endeavorer."

Address of Rev. S. P. Rose, D.D.

The subject assigned me this morning has already been so amply and ably presented by our eloquent friend from Ireland that nothing remains for me to do beyond gathering up the fragments that are left, that nothing shall be lost. The cardinal principles of Christian Endeavor have been so frequently defined that it is not necessary to state them at length. What I should like to do is to suggest some benefits which arise from their application, from their translation into practice. And first of all I would venture to say that the cardinal principles of Christian Endeavor translated into conduct proffer to the churches a band of pledged Christian workers. It is universally admitted that the pledge is essential to the very thought of our Society. I am very fond of our pledge. I rejoice in it, first of all, because it presents the Lord Jesus Christ as the model of holy living. One of the most wholesome signs of the times in which we live is that increasing emphasis is laid upon the truth that Christianity is a life, and that salvation is salvation into Christ's likeness. We are saved just so far as we are made like him. This has always been the doctrine of the New Testament. It has not always been the truth emphasized by every part of the Christian Church. Too often we have thought of Christ as the Saviour from penalties rather than as the Saviour from sin, and too frequently we have looked upon religion as a moral bankrupt instead of that which would lead us up everywhere into "holiness unto the Lord."

The Christian Endeavorer who is true to his pledge makes the Lord Jesus Christ the model of his life. The pledge does mean this: it presents Jesus Christ as the inspiration of my conduct. I am to do what the Lord Jesus Christ would have me do, trusting in his strength. What is his strength? If you will study that life to see what made it the realized ideal, not of humanity alone, but of Deity as well, you will find that the strength of it is in the indwelling of the Holy Ghost. That same strength is proffered to us to-day. More than this, the Christian Endeavor pledge enables us to have the same abiding-places upon which the life of Jesus was lived. Seek how it was that his life was sustained, and you will find that the abiding-places of his power were mainly three. First is the habit of prayer. Pre-eminently Jesus was a man of prayer, and we ought to remember that Christ prayed not simply as an example, but he prayed because he had need to pray. He touched humanity at every point save that one place of conduct where Christians do sin and suffer. For that reason he stood on the same ground as Christians to-day stand in the need of prayer. Now a Christian Endeavorer pledges himself to make Christ his example in this regard, for prayer is to be a daily habit. A second abiding-place of Christ's strength is found in his knowledge of the Holy Scriptures. Possessing no Bible of his own, in all probability; becoming acquainted with its contents just in the very way that you and I become acquainted with them, by the exercise of memory; snatching his opportunities for study from the occupations of an exceptionally busy life, he became saturated with that Book, and walked the face of the earth a living Concordance. The Christian Endeavorer says that the study of that Book shall be the habit of his life. But there is a third abiding-place of Christ's power which must be kept in mind, his activity. He went about doing good. The Christian Endeavorer promises to do whatsoever Christ would have him do. Prayer and reading of the Holy Scriptures do not reach the highest possibilities; they cannot if they are not translated into conduct. And just at this point our society comes to our aid by these committees upon which it insists, which become to us an opportunity of the expression of the activity of our lives. Now because the Christian Endeavor Society by its cardinal principles offers to the Church a band of pledged workers, we may rejoice in these principles and accept them as sound. Moreover, these Christian Endeavor principles, their cardinal principles, translated into conduct offer to the churches not pledged workers only, but consecrated workers as well.

This morning's programme has placed great, but no undue, emphasis upon the heart of the Society, the consecration meeting. Where this is heartily conducted it reminds you of the need of a renewed dedication. This need is found in our forgetfulness. We mean well, but we forget so soon. There are very few of us so reformed, I take it, that we are reformed away from the need of the confession, "We have left undone many things we ought to have done." More than this, while we have as habits of life forgetfulness and neglectfulness we feel the need of renewed dedication. It is well said that our dedication should keep pace with our life. He who follows Christ works with light, and with that increase of light there comes to him the knowledge of new truth, and this new truth comes from the renewed consecration. Is it now not a good thing that from this Society, from the application of its principles to conduct, there is offered to the churches a band of workers whose consecration is up to date? More than this, the cardinal principles of Christian Endeavor translated into conduct give to our churches a band of consecrated, pledged workers, loyal to our denominational interests. Loyalty to our denomination is a fixed and unalterable principle, a cardinal principle, of our association. If it were not so, it would be a menace to Church life.

As a pastor I should be much afraid of an association of young people taking their orders from Boston or anywhere else as headquarters, if they were not loyal to their pastor and church officials, first of all. Such a thing could only come from one of two reasons. First, from misapprehensions of the cardinal principles of our association; and I presume it is that all such misapprehensions shall be cleared away that five times to-day there have been addresses made to this Convention upon the theme I am now speaking on. But where such disloyalty exists it is the outgrowth of a spirit of narrowness of the denominations. Thus, where it happens that Christian Endeavorers are treated by denominations or single churches as objects of suspicion, where they are spoken of as harmful to a denominational institution, where it is suggested that their loyalty is a matter of doubt, then what every one suggested would become true, unless these Christian Endeavorers were model Endeavorers, in which case — I wonder if I speak in the presence of any whose loyalty has thus been called in question by their denomination — I entreat them, for the sake of this great movement, to prove those mistaken by the uprightness, the loyalty, and the purity of their lives. I have thus far spoken of the benefit of the translation of these principles in conduct as to the individual churches. I would like for a moment to speak of one other feature of this movement: its interdenominationalism. Now for purely local and sectional reasons I should not care a fig whether my society was Epworth League or Christian Endeavor. If I had nothing to think of except sectional needs I could do with either of these societies, as I have done. But when our outlook is larger, then we see that there is in the interdenominational society that which possesses value over the denominational society. To-night, in another place, from the eloquent lips of Dr. Dixon, we shall hear more of denominational loyalty and interdenominational fellowship, and I must not trespass upon the ground that will then be most ably and aptly covered; but this I venture to say: that denominational loyalty and interdenominational fellowship are not only consistent one with the other, but that denomination gains nothing on the score of loyalty that holds its young people into denominational organizations. Our Epworth League is not one whit more loyal to the Church, it does not produce more loyal people, than our Christian Endeavor Society. Though our Epworth League may make intense sectarians, it does not make more loyal Methodists; it cannot, in the nature of things. I want to say further that that church which holds its young people to a purely denominational organization commits a denominational mistake, and I have upon me the spirit of predictive prophecy which leads me to say that it commits a mistake which, if not rectified, makes denominational suicide. I am persuaded that the trend of events is in one direction, and no denomination is wise — it is not brave; it is foolhardy — which puts itself in opposition to the acts of God as interpreted in the movements of these last years of this century. To go to the young people of a denomination and say, "You must not engage in interdenominational fellowship," is to forbid them to engage in forms of work that can only be carried forward by interdenominational societies. I do not see how a denominational organization could have done the work that has been done. Think of the work undertaken with the seamen, the railroads, the good-citizenship committees; a purely denominational society is debarred from that work. It is by the interdenominational society that this work can be undertaken for Christ through his Church — for Christ through his Church for the nation at large. Now it is because this Society stands for such principles that I believe in it. The form may change, but this Society will live in spirit and in some form, I am persuaded, in the days that are to come. These principles will be translated in some form or another into conduct until the morning of the great day when the prayer of Christ shall be answered, and we shall " all be one."

FRIDAY AFTERNOON.

A School of Practical Methods of Committee Work.

Nothing is better evidence of the solidity of the Christian Endeavor movement than the eagerness with which Endeavorers receive and carry out suggestions of new things to do or fresh methods of work. Always the series of committee conferences are among the best attended and the most enthusiastic meetings of our International Conventions.

There were sixteen of these schools of practical work, simultaneous sessions being held on Friday afternoon in many of the largest auditoriums in Boston, which were quite uniformly crowded to their utmost capacity.

Lookout Committee Conference.

Mr. H. A. Kinports, New York, N. Y., presiding.

"There was not a more animated, more intense, committee meeting of the series of practical methods of committee work than that of the lookout committee, held in People's Temple." The foregoing appeared in the *Boston Herald* as the opening paragraph in a brief report of the Lookout Committee Conference. The conference was opened by a brief service of song. Rev. Alexander Alison, D.D., of Seattle, Wash., was introduced to conduct the devotional exercises. Mr. Kinports followed in a few words, outlining the object of the meeting and the results to be accomplished. He announced as the first topic for discussion, "The Lookout Committee and the Associate Member." Mr. C. N. Hunt, of Minneapolis, Minn., was introduced and spoke as follows: —

"The associate member is one who has *not* yet trusted in Christ; for no follower of Jesus should ever be permitted to take the place of an associate. The lookout committee is to devise and carry out the wisest plan to win such to Christ, *first;* and to an active membership, *second*.

"It is not an easy task, but a noble one. 'He that winneth souls is wise.' The lookout committee is the soul-winner and soul-builder of the Society. The equipment needed is : love for Christ, love for humanity, tact, and patience. Think more of the *condition* of the associate members than of your own feelings! Be slow — painfully slow — to take offence. Never argue! Don't advise! Just let love and sympathy for the associate member plead more in your eye than in your word; more in your tone of voice than in the voice itself. Let him feel that you speak not because you are a member of the lookout committee, but because Christ constrains you. Look *first*, within your own heart. *Second*, look unto Jesus. *Third*, look out for those for whom Jesus died.

"Tact and patience go together. I might have called it plain *common sense*. We use less common sense in speaking to people about the welfare of their souls than about anything else. If we tried to win wealth as we do souls we should all be in the poorhouse within a fortnight. Study much the story of Christ and the Samaritan woman, in the fourth chapter of the Gospel of St. John. Reveal not yourself, but your Christ. She became an active member and chair-*woman* of the strongest lookout committee in Samaria. Her motto: 'Come see a man. Is not this the Christ?' Make that your cry."

A brisk and bright discussion followed; questions were asked and answered, and suggestions offered. The following are some of the more important points brought out: —

" Associate members won by active Endeavorers living the joyful life of a Christian."

" We had twelve associate members. Twelve active members each took one to pray for. In two weeks we had a revival, and now they are all active."

" Souls are to be hand-picked. We must seek them, plead with them, and love them into the Kingdom."

" We interest ourselves in them during the week, win their esteem in our social pleasures of ordinary and every-day life, and finally lead them to Christ."

" How To Secure New Members" was the subject of the parliament that followed. Suggestions from the floor came in quick succession : —

" Divide a list of the members of the Sunday school among the members of the lookout committee."

" We have an aisle committee, — two for each aisle, — who greet the strangers and invite them to the meetings of the society."

" A division of our lookout committee is called 'the strangers' committee,' who stand at the entrances on the gallery, welcome the strangers, invite them to the Christian Endeavor prayer meeting. They plan to present and welcome them; get them to register their names in 'The Strangers' Book,' kept for this purpose. After the meeting they are introduced to various members of the society."

" We secured a list of the young people of the church and made a house-to-house visitation among them."

A PASTOR : Our young men work through the Y. M. C. A., inviting strangers to the church and meetings of the society. We have found it a very profitable field.

" How would you influence young men to join who absolutely refuse to have anything to do with the society?" "Pray for them." "Pray." A young man arose and said he had been one of such a class. His name was brought before the lookout committee, and the members agreed to pray for him. He finally joined the society. "I thank God," said he, "for praying Endeavorers."

The monthly socials were also emphasized as a means of securing new members. There seems to be a strong sentiment in favor of a more earnest effort along the social line, at the close of each prayer meeting, as an excellent means toward this end.

Mr. Geo. L. Penney, of Philadelphia, Penn., was then introduced to read a paper on " The General Relations of the Lookout Committee."

He said that this committee should be in readiness to respond to pastor or church, and cited a church where there are ten societies, and where the church is so large that the pastor was forced to ask the young people to look after the spiritual welfare of many of its members. "Is not this a splendid field for the lookout committee?" "Again; this committee should do as much for the prayer meeting of the church as for its own meeting. The pledge says : 'I promise to support my own church in every way.' Do we do that when we let the mid-week meetings go unattended?" He dwelt upon the relations of the committee to the Society, saying that they were those of a mother to her child. It gives counsel, rears up the members, and by its love and ever watchful care keeps them in the straight and narrow way. It is responsible for all the members whom it recommends for membership, and sees that they keep their pledges. Each member of the committee is just as responsible as the chairman. This committee should also be a counsellor for all other committees, and through its acquaintance with all the other members can easily and quietly make inquiries, and so learn what they are doing. They should make the stranger a friend, and by their intercourse with the old members give them new inspiration for their work.

A general discussion followed the presentation of Mr. Penney's paper. Here are some of the gleanings : —

It was an almost unanimous opinion that no professing Christian should be permitted to join as an associate member.

The sense of the conference with respect to dropping members was decidedly in favor of an earnest effort, by prayer and personal visitation being put forth, to hold them " for Christ and the Church," even if months were required to bring about the desired result.

Two methods of calling the roll: (1) Print all names in bold type on a large card, and hang where all can see. Let the one whose name is first on the list begin, the others following in rapid succession. (2) Print the names of all members on a slip of paper, place in the hand of each member, and then respond in the order of their names.

Delinquents were to be reached by personal calls or personal letters, and not by a stereotyped printed letter. Prayer was also emphasized in this connection.

Plan the work of the committee as a whole, and not as individual members of it.

Divide members among lookout committee. Let each one become acquainted with all in their division. Look over each prayer meeting and see who are present, and notice in what manner they participate. Then fix your record-book accordingly; not *in* the meeting, but after you arrive home.

A large number of societies have a public reception of members, but on some other night than the consecration meeting.

Any person who professes to love and serve the Lord Jesus Christ should be taken in as an active member, even if he is not a member of the church at that time. The general opinion prevailed, however, that every effort should be put forth by the lookout committee to get him to unite with the Church.

A DELEGATE FROM TORONTO: We have a society of over 300 members. Each member is supplied with a badge containing his name and number. Active members, in addition, wear a white ribbon. These are all kept on a rack provided for the purpose. As each one enters they put on their badge and drop it in a box as they leave the room. We cannot help but know them, because their name is on the badge. After the meeting the lookout committee checks up their list, by the badges remaining on the rack, and sees that the absentees represented by the badges remaining are called upon during the week; the rack is then fixed for the meeting of the following week.

Use the " Monthly Report Blanks " for written reports. Published by the United Society. Price, 25 cents; postage, 4 cents extra.

Corresponding Secretaries' Conference.

Miss Lottie E. Wiggins, Toronto, Ont., presiding.

Almost every State and Territory in the United States and Canada was represented by local corresponding secretaries, fully 300 people being in attendance at the conference.

The session was opened with singing of Christian Endeavor songs by the Endeavor secretaries, which was followed by fervent prayer.

The conference then proceeded to open debate on the question of " Points To Be Considered by Christian Endeavorers in Selecting Corresponding Secretaries." In opening the debate, Miss Wiggins said: —

"The work of the corresponding secretary is perhaps the most important of any officer in the Christian Endeavor Societies, and if the secretaries of our unions are non-conductors of the electrical spirit of the great Christian Endeavor movement, they not only shut out themselves, but all those they represent, from the power of Christian Endeavor."

In the open debate that followed it was unanimously agreed that the office of corresponding secretary, particularly of the local Endeavor Unions, should be permanent; for unless the office is permanent, it was argued, it is an utter impossibility for the State secretary to keep track of the local society and of the local union.

Then the corresponding secretary must be full of the spirit of promptness.

He must not delay or neglect to answer correspondence, and important communications from State or international headquarters should be announced as quickly as possible, so that every member of the union may benefit by them.

It was voted by a large majority of the secretaries present that the best way to make announcements to the union is for the corresponding secretary to make the announcement himself at the first meeting of the society after the communication has been received. Another good plan is to post bulletins of the latest Christian Endeavor news where all may see them. Every corresponding secretary is overburdened with a vast amount of correspondence which is unimportant, and discretion should be used in such cases, and all unimportant matter should be thrown in the waste-basket.

Letters requiring him to secure information, or having to be laid before a business meeting, receipt should be acknowledged at once, and should state that the desired information will be forwarded in due time.

Secretaries should not be dead-letter boxes.

A prompt secretary makes the society *prompt.*

The secretary makes the reputation of the society.

Have a *system* for filing letters and keeping a correct record of business connected therewith.

The question of the duties of the corresponding secretary was next considered, and, on inquiry of the chairman, it was found that in twelve societies the office of corresponding and recording secretary is held by the same person, and in the great majority of cases the entire expense for postage and stationery is borne by the corresponding secretaries themselves. In such cases Miss Wiggins thought it proper for the secretary to send in a bill for expenses for postage and stationery to the treasurer of the local society. The welfare and reputation of his society depends more upon the character of the corresponding secretary than any other officer of the society; and it is the duty of that officer to pick up all the important Endeavor news, and to get all the new and helpful ideas possible by corresponding constantly with the different Christian Endeavor Societies.

Corresponding secretaries should be a live connecting link with every committee of the society, and with the pastor and the church. State secretaries should become acquainted with local secretaries throughout the State or Territory over which they have jurisdiction.

Very few corresponding secretaries keep a record of their work, but it was the unanimous opinion of the conference that it would be a good plan in the future for secretaries to keep a careful record of all their Christian Endeavor work, so they can answer correctly, when questions are asked by the international secretary or the State secretary, just what they have accomplished, and in just what state their work is.

The corresponding secretary has great opportunities to be of service to members of his society who leave and go to other towns, by informing the secretaries of those towns of the fact, and by requesting them to hunt the member up and look out for his welfare.

Many societies have committees specially appointed to do this sort of work, thus relieving the corresponding secretary of the burden.

Letters of transfer, it was decided, should be signed by both the president and corresponding secretary when a member of one union wishes to be transferred to another.

Conference of Floating Societies of Christian Endeavor.

Miss A. P. Jones, Falmouth, Mass., presiding.

A large and enthusiastic company of friends, workers and sailors, gathered in the First Presbyterian Church.

Floating Societies in seven ports and two ship societies were represented.

Work is in widely distant ports; members at sea are scattered around the world; twenty to twenty-five, expecting to come, were finally detained. Those present represented a constituency of 3,000 members.

Following devotional exercises and words of welcome, greetings were read from absent workers and societies in this and other lands.

Practical points were related regarding the fifty-two Floating Societies of Christian Endeavor on ships, the nineteen societies on shore, and work of Floating Christian Endeavor Committees, in their subdivisions for ship services, organizing Floating Societies, good literature, comfort bags, etc.

Mr. Madison Edwards, Vineyard Haven, who has experienced helpfulness in the use of the pledge, gave form of receiving new members and donning pin, with Scripture motto.

Mr. Harry Shaw, Brooklyn, told of three years' personal experience in navy-yard work. Appeal for Christian Endeavor for the sailor.

Mrs. Richardson, of Philadelphia, related campaign whereby 2,500 comfort bags were given, filled, and distributed.

Mrs. Seymour, of St. John, N. B., told of their new society and described a consecration service.

Arthur Chase gave greetings of Portland Floating Society of Christian Endeavor. Suggested " scrap " cards for hospitals. Miss Leavitt, same society, added valuable hints.

Pacific Coast work reported by a captain and a *U. S. S. Thetis* member.

Rev. D. H. Tribou, U. S. N., emphasized many points; advised practical Gospel messages without nautical illustration.

The conference could have continued with unabated enthusiasm, but was closed by sailor members from naval, merchant, and coastwise ships, testifying to great spiritual benefit derived from this world-wide brotherhood in Christ.

Mizpah benediction.

Conference of State Officers.

Mr. George MacDonald, Altoona, Penn., presiding.

The Conference of State Officers held in the rooms of the Y. M. C. A., Saturday afternoon, July 13, was very successful. About one hundred and twenty-five persons were in attendance, representing thirty-eight States, Territories, and Provinces. After prayer by Mr. H. H. Spooner, of Chicago, the various troublesome phases of State work were taken up and discussed in general with a great deal of benefit to all.

Previous to the meeting of State officers, a meeting of those interested in the work of the correspondence committee was held in the parlor of Hotel Huntington. The result of this conference was that Mr. R. B. Sinclair appeared before the State Officers' Conference to urge a more complete operation of this work by the State unions. Mr. Sinclair is connected with the New Jersey State Union.

Considerable stress was laid on the matter of evangelistic work at State conventions, etc., by the representatives of the States where work of this kind has been tried. All reports were very encouraging as to the results of this work in connection with State meetings.

The proper raising of money for State expenses was quite freely discussed, and with a single exception the plan of voluntary offerings is being used by the different unions, the general opinion being that this is the most satisfactory way.

The conference lasted from 2.00 P. M. until almost 5.00 P. M., adjourning to the reception at Cotillion Hall. All those present seemed satisfied that the time was well spent, and expressed themselves as glad of the opportunity of gathering together for the discussion of the troublesome things that confront the officers in State work.

Temperance and Christian Citizenship Conference.

Mr. Philip Y. Pendleton, Pittsburgh, Penn., presiding.

Park Street Church was filled to its utmost seating capacity, and there were several hundred persons gathered in the aisles and on the stairways when the meeting was called to order.

Mr. Pendleton's opening remarks were enthusiastically applauded. He said, in part: —

" In these reform movements we look to God for power. What we undertook but yesterday has been his chosen labor since the dial of time pointed to the first hour of human sin. And these powers of evil which exhaust the Infinite and well nigh weary God — how hardly shall unaided humanity withstand them. Heavens without a sun and ocean without water were each a minor paradox to a triumphant reform without God.

" Political reform is the sum of individual reforms, and individual reform is a Divine copyright. Only the Hand which fashioned us in the beginning can, out of our fragments, broken by the fall, reconstruct the forgotten image of the Invisible. To do this perfectly and universally, in man as an integer and man as a nation, has been the dream of promise in the life ot God.

" Since, then, all human reformation emanates from our Father, how momentous are these gatherings of his children!

" To purify the world is our Father's business, and wist ye not that we must be about it? Away with the false prophet who has collected all the grossest evils, most contagious sins, most diabolical iniquities, most damning leprosies, into one great family and called them all by one name, ' Politics,' and stands between them and the people of God, and says, ' Don't touch these; these are politics; go fight wickedness, and sin, and iniquity, but don't touch these, for these are politics, and Christians have no business to meddle with politics.'

" Yes, sir, we mean to lay hands on politics, we mean to wash politics clean and clothe her in white raiment, and make her an obedient handmaid to the Great King.

" And by what authority shall the Church undertake to reform politics? I answer, By a better right than any party, Republican or Democratic; by a higher authority than any other earthly power. When our opponents demonstrate that God has no right to reform the world and the politics thereof, then will we admit that the Church, his only authorized, his only accredited and sanctioned, agent upon earth has no right to attack political wickedness. But so long as God rules, so long shall I claim that the Church, acting in His Name, has the sole right to purify, and that all other reformatory agencies act by usurpation. True, God may have admitted the usurpation, and may hitherto have blessed the usurper, but the exception only proves the rule. God permits the thorn and thistle, the briar, the bramble, and the weed to grow far up the mountain, but when they reach the cloud-line they cease. The peaks that pierce the clouds toward heaven have from eternity known no other mantle than the spotless robe of driven snow which God has thrown around them.

" So it is with our nation. It is a world's model and a century's wonder, and our Father has permitted many worldly agencies and many political parties to garnish its rising glories hitherto. But to-day we are entering the cloud-line; we are marshalling for final victories, victories which only purified hearts and consecrated hands can win. The undertakings of to-day will bring us to the unapproachable curtains of Sinai; and all things worldly must pause, while the children of God ascend alone to receive new laws for God's highest achievement in earthly government."

Brief remarks were then made by other speakers, as in part follows: —

JUDGE A. S. TAYLOR, Washington, D. C.: — Our chief work in Washington is fighting the saloon. We have been fighting the last year with the Anti-saloon

League, and have succeeded in closing about seventy-five saloons, reducing the number to a few over four hundred in the city of Washington. The greatest national disgrace we are now under is the saloons in the basement of the Capitol Building, and they must go, too!

REV. WM. SHAW, Florida: — The Sunday newspaper is the foe of good order and Sabbath observance, the friend of the saloon and of corrupt politics. The evil of the Sunday newspaper is that Christians read it. The saloon must be banished by legislation, for it is beyond the reach of Christian boycott; but it is not so with the Sunday newspaper. Let Christians refuse to read it, and it will have to go out of business. It lies in our power. Let us stop it.

COLONEL HADLEY, New York: — One of the greatest difficulties is that all those wearing Christian emblems are not total abstainers. We should cease wearing Christian emblems when we fail to live as Christians. If total abstainers would only wear some badge by which the rescue workers might know them, they would know where to put a saved drunkard so that he would not be under the temptation of the "little black bottle" that aristocratic Christians sometimes take a "nip" at. "Take heed lest that liberty of yours be a stumbling-block to others."

REV. J. B. DAVISON, Wisconsin: — What is my work as a member of a good-citizenship committee? It is to enthrone Christ in every town and city in the State, to have every mayor and every councilman a Christian; then Christ will rule.

HON. A. M. HASWELL, Chicago, Ill.: — I want to file my protest here to begin with. Don't let us talk about good citizenship, but let us call it *Christian* citizenship. Let us honor the Name that is above all names. Every young man over twenty-one years of age has a weapon keener than the bayonet, — the ballot. You and I, Christian men, are responsible for the condition of things in this country to-day. I don't call myself a Prohibitionist any more; I call myself an Annihilationist. We must attend the caucuses, and capture them for the Lord. Christian Endeavorers, go home to work for clean politics; go home to attend primaries and caucuses; go home to whip any man who is a bad man in politics.

REV. MR. SCUDDER, Brooklyn, N. Y.: —Very few of our best citizens are familiar with the methods of politics and the law as to elections. Very few men know where their primaries are held or how to become a member of such associations. I would suggest that the good-citizenship committee of each society make itself an information committee, and secure and place before each voter of the church with which it is connected the information relating to the primaries and caucuses in time for the voter to take advantage of it. Let them be notified in due season to act.

HON. S. E. NICHOLSON, Indiana: — Indiana brings to this Convention to-day greetings of recent victory. We had a recent victory which we consider of very great importance,— the passage of the Sunday closing bill. The liquor men of Indiana are trembling as they have never trembled before. There are two hundred saloons less in Indiana to-day than two years ago.

REV. A. B. PHILPUTT, D.D., Philadelphia, Penn.: — The tide of independence is rising in Pennsylvania. I strongly advocate freedom in politics. The people have got to serve God in their business and in their politics the same as they do in their church. The trouble is, we have two different standards, one for our conduct as Christians, and one for our conduct as voters. We must learn to have only one standard; we must learn to be Christians everywhere and always.

MR. C. S. BULLOCK: — I advise each Christian Endeavor Society to appoint a caucus committee, whose duty it shall be not only to bring facts and information home to the people, but whose especial work shall be to get Christian voters to the caucus.

REV. W. G. CLARKE, D.D., Chicago, Ill.: — Five years ago there was something incongruous about a minister having any connection with politics. Now the situation is reversed. Dr. Parkhurst has been responsible largely for this change. The principles of Christ should never be compromised. In the interests of Christ's kingdom, we should spare no effort to destroy the evils which beset the world, and particularly the great evil, the saloon.

Speeches were also made by such men as Rev. J. M. Foster, Mr. B. S. Mabin, Mr. Wilson L. Gill, and many others whose very names are a warranty for the excellency of their words.

Christian citizenship and temperance committees will find the "Monthly Report Blanks and Outlines" very helpful. Published by the United Society. Price, 25 cents ; postage, 4 cents extra.

Conference of Sunday-school Committees.

Mr. Hugh Cork, Grand Forks, N. D., presiding.

A large and enthusiastic delegation, representing many States and some foreign countries, assembled in the First Presbyterian Church to discuss the relation of the Sunday-school committees to that most important auxiliary of the Church, — the Sunday school. An important fact was brought to light at the beginning of the meeting : not one of that large audience but had been a member of the Sunday school before joining the Endeavor Society. When it is realized that but seventeen and one-half per cent of our population are enrolled in the Sunday school, and from these only are coming the members of our societies, then the importance of such a committee's work must be felt. For the existence of the Society, if for nothing more, we owe it to the Sunday school to co-operate with it in every possible way in reaching the more than eighty per cent who are still out in the "highways and hedges."

No "set speeches" were prepared, but each brought of such things as they had, and it was literally a *conference.* An outline programme was followed, and under its five main divisions were brought out the following helpful suggestions : —

1. *The Committee's Make-up :* — Object, "To co-operate with Sunday-school workers." "Suggestions from a live committee will not be out of place." "Committee should be composed of persons of tact, common sense, and whose lives and beliefs are in harmony with both Sunday school and Endeavor." "The size of committee might vary, but should be as large as the supply will permit." "Meetings of the committee should be frequent, — at least once a month, and if possible, once a week." "Meet for a few moments at the close of Sunday school." "Keep a well-written report, and make it the record of the school as seen from a looker-on." "Note in the report the rise of interest." "Condense the report for reading at the *annual review day*."

2. *Work during School Sessions :* — "Committee should be at the door to welcome irregular attenders and strangers." "Should look after the material comfort of the little ones, assist in unwrapping and wrapping them warmly," etc. "By watching for singers a nice children's choir can be gotten together to assist with the music." "Young people can be persuaded to train for teachers, and thus take turns in supplying classes without teachers." "Each committee should so be understood by the superintendent of the Sunday school that they stood ready to support and carry out any measure he might direct."

3. *Work between Sessions :* — "Should watch carefully the attendance, and constantly try to increase it." "Get the names of all members of the church, and see that they and their children are there." "Find those who go to no school, and win them to Sunday school." "Get a list of the absentees, and visit those who are often absent." "Watch for the poor and sick and sorrowing, and carry them comfort and consolation." "Have a regular district for each member of the committee, and visit it systematically." "Assist in carrying the *Home Department of the Sunday school* into every home in the community." (If the Home Department is not understood, write Dr. Duncan, Syracuse,

N. Y., superintendent International Sunday-school Home Department, and explanations will be forthcoming.) " Co-operate with the teachers in following up spiritual impressions, and by personal visits and ' littles here and there,' land each scholar safely in the Kingdom."

4. *Work at Special Times :*—" See that the flower committee assist in having plenty of flowers for Easter." " Assist in getting the children together and drilled for any special time." " Clip pieces from papers suitable for these special times, and bring your collections to the programme committee." " At the rally day, which each committee can help work up, see that every class is instructed in the order of arrangements." " Stand ready to assist *any* teacher on a moment's notice." " Plan a town or county canvass, and enlist all the help possible to visit every home in the district, and besides gathering statistics, invite each to attend some Sunday school." (The plan of the St. Louis canvass was recommended for investigation.)

5. *Work in Special Ways :* — " See that the Sunday-school room is well ventilated, and not too hot or too cold." " Make the Sunday-school room as attractive as possible, by plenty of light, pictures, flowers, and even canary birds." " Visit the homes of the poor, and assist in making them brighter." " Get clothes for the poor so they can attend Sunday school." " Stay at home with baby while mamma visits the Sunday school." " Give class receptions." " Plan with the social committee for a *Sunday-school social.*" " Give the teachers and officers a reception, and bring in those whom you are trying to enlist as teachers." " See that the school is equipped with proper maps and blackboards." " Plan to keep a constant library fund." " Read and gather good things on modern methods of Sunday-school work, and give such articles to the superintendent and teachers to read." " Plan to have your teachers get to a good Sunday-school convention at least once a year." " Talk up such conventions with every Sunday-school worker, and if there is no regular county organization, start the movement to so organize." " Visit conventions and other schools to gain new methods to suggest to your own school." " Search out every needy neighborhood, and in such plant a mission Sunday school, and get the nearest pastor to preach to them sometimes."

Finally, " Whatsoever thy hand findeth to do, do it."

Use the " Committee Outlines and Monthly Report Blanks." Published by the United Society. Price, 25 cents ; postage, 4 cents extra.

Senior Mothers' Society Conference.

Mrs. F. T. Thompson, Chicago, Ill., presiding.

Among the conferences, perhaps that of the " Senior Mothers," or Parents' Society, held in the vestry of the Park Street Church, was as enthusiastic as any. There were young mothers, middle-aged mothers, and old mothers, many of whom were also grandmothers, and in the large gathering could be seen a slight sprinkling of fathers.

Rev. J. W. Fifield, of Chicago, made a brief but earnest address. The speaker said it was not information but inspiration that was needed to fan the flame of enthusiasm and give a perpetual impetus to the work of the movement. If we came for but a *thimbleful* we got it ; if we had deeper longings we received *wells* full of Divine inspiration ; if we hungered and thirsted we should be filled as *rivers* from the Water of Life. And only as we were filled from this great Fountain of Life could we hope to overflow and enrich other lives.

Rev. H. N. Kinney, of Syracuse, followed with a very interesting outline of the Senior work, and of the great rejuvenating power it has exerted in his own and other stupid mid-week prayer meetings. He said, " Every pastor should have a Christian Endeavor college with all its departments in his church. The Sunday school also needs their stimulus."

There are eighteen Senior Societies now organized, and this is only a beginning which must go on according to the true nature of Christian Endeavor principles. The Juniors must graduate into the Young People's, the Young People into the Senior's, and the Seniors into the Parents' or Mothers', and so complete the grand Endeavor circle, and thus foster and help to spread broadcast this inter-denominational spirit which is such a grand feature of the Christian Endeavor work. The ten minutes given for questions and suggestions were fully taken, and bright and apt were the replies by the speaker.

Greetings from Mrs. A. B. Fellows, of Chicago, were read by Mrs. W. H. Hogle, of Evanston, and were received with great applause.

The Mothers' Hymn, written by Mrs. Fellows and dedicated to the Mothers' Society of Christian Endeavor, was sung with much spirit.

Owing to illness, Mrs. F. E. Seagrave, of Toledo, a very enthusiastic Mother Endeavorer, was unable to be present, but sent her paper. We quote two or three paragraphs : —

" O mothers and lovers of youth, let us see to it that we hold that part which we have, lest others take our crown. Mothers, it is high time we were awake. Some one has aptly said that the spirit of the age is already calling for a higher standard of purity in individuals and in the nation. And where can we most surely look for this work to be inaugurated, and by whom ? Shall we not begin at the root, the home ? Let us rouse the mothers; for with more active and interested mothers will come, most surely, better homes, better mothers, better children, and a higher standard of morality throughout the nation.

" The Sunday school has long been regarded the garden of the Church. Here the seed is sown and principles implanted with which we hope to bring the child into the fold, but these efforts have often failed of the desired results; they need to be supplemented by other active and concerted work. The prayer meeting also required new life. There is need of young blood."

Rev. John Pollock, of Glasgow, Scotland, brought greetings from the Mothers' Society of Christian Endeavor of that city. He stated that it was the only one in the British Isles, and, he thought, the only one on the eastern continent; but it was doing good work, and other churches were upon the eve of forming these societies. He spoke very hopefully of the movement.

Mrs. F. E. Clark, wife of the President of the United Society of Christian Endeavor, was greeted with the Chautauqua salute.

It was due to her suggestion, at the International Convention held in New York, that a Mothers' Society of Christian Endeavor was ever formed.

She said, among other things, that she had long felt the need of mothers arousing themselves, banding together, and showing a live interest in the work for the children. Form some organization that shall be *tied* to the Juniors in some way, and so take an active part in the spiritual training of the little ones. This we feel that our pledge most effectually does by our promise to daily pray, and make daily effort in the home, for their spiritual development.

In the absence of Miss Belle P. Nason, of San Diego, Rev. H. N. Kinney gave a very clear statement of the Parents' Pledge, which has accomplished so much for the State of California the past year. Pledges were sent to every pastor in the State, claiming their interest, with a request that they incorporate it into their mid-week prayer meeting, by devoting one half-hour each month to this branch of the work. This was very heartily responded to by a large majority of churches, and they already feel greatly blessed by so doing, both in the church and in the work for the boys and girls.

Proportionate and Systematic Giving Conference.

Miss Frances B. Patterson, Chicago, Ill., presiding.

The conference opened with prayer by Mr. S. L. Mershon, of Evanston, Ill. The leader then briefly and pointedly defined systematic giving as " giving regularly and from principle, instead of spasmodically and from impulse," and proportionate giving as "involving still further the dedicating to God's use of a certain fixed proportion of one's income, not necessarily one-tenth, although it is generally held that *at least* that amount should thus be set aside." It is scriptural, a form of worship, business-like, an aid to more prayer and thought. It would bring Christ to the world in this generation. It quickens our spiritual life. It is as plainly taught in the Bible as the keeping of the Sabbath Day. We find Cain and Abel bringing offerings to the Lord; Abraham, the *friend* of God, giving tithes to Melchisedek, the Priest of the Most High God; Jacob vowing a tenth as a matter of course long before the Law was given to Israel. The Law itself says, "The tenth *is* the Lord's."

Then followed an open parliament on "How To Spread Proportionate and Systematic Giving."

1. *By literature :* — Send to Mr. Thomas Kane, 310 Ashland Bldg., Chicago, for a sample set of his leaflets, especially "Paying What You Owe," "Thanksgiving Ann," and the pledge of the Christian Stewards' League; to the A. B. C. F. M., 1 Somerset Street, Boston, for "Heathen Claims and Christian Duty," by Mrs. Bishop, for "A Sermon on Tithes," and for Dr. Vandyke's "A Brief Plea for Foreign Missions;" to the American Baptist Missionary Union, 2A Beacon Street, Boston, for "God's Tenth," by Dr. Gordon, and "A Question of Ownership," and "The Garden of the Great King," by Dr. Ashmore; to Mr. W. L. Amerman, 95 Broad Street, New York City, for "Learning to Give," a leaflet written especially for missionary committees; and to Mrs. Esther Tuttle Pritchard, Kokomo, Ind., for a catologue of publications on this subject.

2. *By wide-awake meetings :* — Prepare for them by wise and prayerful distribution of leaflets, so that every member will be prepared to take part in some way. Ask your pastor to preach a sermon on the subject. Make it your aim to have at least one meeting a year (two would be better) when you would ballot in some way to find out how the society stands. Always follow such a meeting by a careful personal canvass, noting progress from time to time. Vary your programmes. Let everything, song service, Bible reading, prayers, as well as papers and discussions, bear vitally on the subject. Have statistics given showing: (1) how the Church gives now; (2) how our converted heathen brethren give; (3) how we might give. Cite Dr. Gordon's church, and other self-sacrificing instances of giving. Have an objection-box, and let members answer the objections. Never fail to have testimonies as to blessings received in giving in this way. Always present the subject from a scriptural basis. If you want to convert some influential young business man among your members, get him to give a five minutes' talk on "Why I Should Give" from a business standpoint, supplying him with the above-named leaflets. Then claim God's promises, and you may be sure of the result. Use maps and charts. Get your young men to prepare the latter. You will find "A Missionary Pastor" — price 50 cents, published by the Student Volunteer Movement, 80 Institute Place, Chicago — very helpful in this work. Warn your young members never to borrow their tenth. Urge them to try it for six months, or to at least keep an account.

3. *By personal work :* — Always prepare for, and follow up, your meetings by personal work. Keep at it all the time. It is as important to convert men's pocket-books as their souls. In fact, the soul is never soundly converted unless the pocket-book is also. Expect results. Don't dishonor God's promises. We act as if they were a thin surface of ice over the pond in Boston Common, and are afraid to step out upon them; when, in reality, they are as firm and mighty as the everlasting hills. Step out upon them, and trust him for the result.

Then followed brief testimonies as to blessings received in giving proportionately and systematically, many prominent workers taking part, among them Miss Ben-Oliel, of Jerusalem, Miss Ella D. MacLaurin, Miss Kate Hamilton, Mr. W. L. Amerman, and many others. It was impossible to hear from all, and when the leader asked those who wished to add their testimony to rise, fully two-thirds of the audience rose at once.

Besides the large map giving the prevailing religions of the world, an immense chart hung in front of the audience, showing the great wealth, $13,076,300,000, possessed by church-members in the United States in 1890; the average annual increase of wealth of church-members from 1880 to 1890, or $434,790,000; the small amount in comparison given to home and foreign missions in 1890, $10,695,259; and the pitifully small amount, $5,000,000, given by all evangelical denominations last year to foreign missions. In contrast to the immense amounts in the hands of God's stewards was shown the debts of some of the leading boards of missions, amounting to about $1,300,000.

The leader closed with an appeal, among other things saying : —

" Is it not a shame, when the Lord has entrusted to his stewards for the furtherance of his harvest such immense wealth? If we gave but one-tenth (and remember that is the low-water mark of Christian giving), all these debts would be swept away in an instant, and there would be money enough in the treasuries of the Lord to bring Christ to the world in this generation. Think of it!

" One-half of the Protestant church-members in the United States give nothing. Over one thousand churches in each of the twelve leading denominations give nothing. We spend annually $1.50 to evangelize every soul in the United States, for every heathen soul one-half cent, or one three-hundredth part; yet they are equally precious in His sight. Last year the average church-member could only afford forty cents to spread the Gospel. But Christians yearly increase their wealth $500,000,000 above all expenses. While all the Christians in the United States could only give $5,000,000 to foreign missions, our bill for chewing-gum was $22,000,000, and $400,000,000 for amusements, $200,000,000 being spent for theatre-going alone. Our Lord has given us ' the heathen for our inheritance and the uttermost parts of the earth for our possession.' Are we taking possession? There is enough power in this church to-day to do it, if we will only step out on his promises. Is not our God, who made heaven and earth, able to open pocket-books? There is nothing too hard for him. Let us examine ourselves honestly and prayerfully to-day in the light of Calvary. Are we faithful stewards? Will we be faithful, remembering that God has placed in our hands power enough to bring Christ to the world, if we will but use it? God help us to realize our responsibility, and to do whatsoever *he* would have us do."

The conference closed with prayer by Rev. Thos. Marshall, D.D., field secretary of the Presbyterian Board of Foreign Missions.

Junior Superintendents' Conference.

Mr. Percy J. S. Ryan, New York, N.Y., presiding.

Every possible phase of Junior work was discussed at the conference of Junior superintendents held at the Warren Avenue Baptist Church.

The Junior is coming to be more and more an important factor in Christian Endeavor work. This was the largest and most enthusiastic gathering of workers ever held. Auditorium and balcony were crowded, every person present representing some Junior Society somewhere in the world. The Central and Southern States seemed most largely represented.

The first Junior Society was formed on March 18, 1884, at Tabor, Ia., by Rev. J. W. Cowan. Its purpose is to adapt the Christian Endeavor principles to the understanding of boys and girls.

Mr. Ryan's carefully-prepared programme was admirably arranged to make the afternoon truly a *conference,* for it consisted of questions that went straight to the hearts of the superintendents. "What Constitutes a Good Junior Meeting?" "Some of Our Difficulties, and How To Surmount Them," and, "Your Boys; How Do You Keep Them Interested?" were the general topics that brought out all kinds of suggestions, — from umpiring a baseball game, or making cookies for the boys, to the final emphasis placed on depending upon prayer and God's Spirit to bring success in all our work.

Following these discussions came the question-box, conducted by the well-known Junior workers, Miss Kate Haus, of Missouri, and Mrs. M. L. Hageman, of Indiana. After some practical thoughts on the Board of Mercy Junior work, by Miss Elizabeth W. Olney, of Rhode Island, this most earnest and helpful meeting closed with the appropriate words, "Blest be the tie that binds," and immediately after was followed by a wide-awake meeting of State Junior superintendents, under the leadership of Mr. Wainwright, of Chicago.

Gleanings.

" Do Juniors keep their pledge to the letter? "
Miss HAUS : Do Seniors? Do church-members?

The Missionary Committee Conference.

Miss Belle M. Brain, Springfield, Ohio, presiding.

The grand old church on Clarendon Street, whose walls for twenty-five years echoed the voice of Adoniram Judson Gordon as he pleaded for missions, was the scene of a meeting such as the greatest church in the world would be proud to place upon its records. It was a meeting which would have filled with gratitude the heart of the great man who was pastor of the church for so many years.

It was peculiarly fitting that this conference of the Convention be held in the Clarendon Street Baptist Church, and the audience that attended was a fitting tribute to the memory of Dr. Gordon, and the great sums the church has given to missions in all parts of the world.

Those who were there came from every State in the Union, from Alaska, India, Canada, England, and other countries.

The conference was led by Miss Belle M. Brain, of Springfield, O., herself one of the very bright missionary workers in the Christian Endeavor Society. On the platform was a picture of Dr. Gordon. Those seated on the platform with Miss Brain were Mrs. George W. Coleman, of Boston, Miss Frances B. Patterson, of Chicago, Dr. Pauline Root, of India, Mr. Robert E. Speer, of New York City, and Rev. S. C. Ohrum, of Boston.

Miss Brain opened the meeting in a very impressive way. She asked all to bow their heads in silent prayer for a blessing on the meeting, and announced that at the conclusion of a few moments Mrs. William H. Breed, of the church, would softly sing, " Nearer, My God, to Thee." She asked all to keep their heads bowed while the hymn was sung, and to make its words their prayer.

There was an opening prayer, then, by Rev. S. C. Ohrum, of the Clarendon Street Baptist Church, and, following, "Throw Out the Life-Line " was sung with a great deal of spirit by the whole audience. Miss Brain then read the Scripture lesson, which had for a central text, " Behold your God." Miss Brain introduced, as the first speaker, Mr. Edward Marsden, of Alaska, a delegate to the Convention, and a native of Alaska.

Mr. Marsden spoke briefly concerning the missionary work carried on in his country. He said, in part, that Alaska, a country about as large as the United States east of the Mississippi, was, and is now, a very hard country for missionaries to reach. At present there are some six thousand followers of Christ doing much good. He spoke also of the harm done by the importation of rum, and of the bad influence of unscrupulous traders from the States.

At this point of the meeting the missionaries present were invited upon the platform, and they were welcomed by the Chautauqua salute.

Then Miss Brain asked all the pastors in the audience to stand. There were quite a large number who did so. She then asked all the missionaries to stand. There were not a great many; but when she asked all who were members of missionary committees of Christian Endeavor Societies to stand, nearly the whole audience arose.

The next speaker was Mr. Robert E. Speer, of New York City. The subject assigned to Mr. Speer was, " How Shall We Lead the Young People to Pray for Missions ? "

He said, in part : " We are not going to lead young people to do anything we do not do ourselves. If we are going to lead young people to pray for missions, we must do it ourselves. Even Christ had to teach his disciples how to pray. The young people must be taught to pray. The first mission work started in prayer. Nearly all the miracles wrought were wrought in prayer. The whole story of missions is one long story of prayer. Almost all our missionary societies grew out of prayer.

" How is it to be done? It must be done by deepening spiritual life, by bringing one's life so close to that of Jesus Christ himself that one can't help praying. Use the prayer calendars of your churches. Use the Bible; the Bible is full of promises for yourself. As soon as you find a promise for yourself in the Bible plead it for yourself and others. Get your pastor to give missions a larger place in his prayers."

After this introductory address, Mr. Speer conducted a parliament for ten minutes, and during that time there were a great many who spoke a few sentences of suggestion. Some urged the reading of books, etc.; and it was interesting to see how eagerly the audience accepted the suggestions of whatever nature, and often asked a second time for the address of some publishing-house where certain literature could be had.

One delegate spoke of the Twilight Band, who prayed for those who at that hour were commencing their day's work for Christ in heathendom ; another, concerning the volunteer movement, who pray at noon each day. Prayer blanks and missionary calendars were recommended. The conclusion was that this is truly a matter of our own personal prayer-life. " Let us advance upon our knees," said Mr. Speer in closing, quoting the words of a famous Japanese missionary.

Mrs. George W. Coleman spoke concerning the cause and effect of systematic giving. " True missionary giving is spontaneous and joyful," said Mrs. Coleman. " It is personal loyalty to a personal God, our Master and our King." She referred most touchingly to the late pastor of the church, and spoke of his great work in the missionary world, and of his noble life, and what it all taught his people. As an illustration, she said that when the young people desired to show their love for him who had been taken from them, they thought of raising some two hundred dollars to aid in wiping out the missionary debt. When the pledges were recorded, it was found that over five hundred dollars were raised, and that this later reached nearly one thousand dollars. A noble tribute to the teachings of the eminent man of God !

The audience then sang Dr. Gordon's hymn, " My Jesus, I Love Thee."

The meeting closed with a general conference on missionary work, led by Dr. Pauline Root, of India. Over twenty-five arose, signifying their intention of going to a foreign field.

The Prayer-Meeting Committee Conference.

Dr. Jennette M. McLaren, St. Paul, Minn., presiding.

Berkeley Temple was the place of meeting of the Prayer-Meeting Conference. The conference was presided over by Dr. Jennette M. McLaren, of St. Paul, Minn. Dr. McLaren has a very quiet but insistent personality, and made a discriminating presiding officer. After singing a number of songs a brief devotional service was conducted by Rev. W. H. Allbright, D.D., pastor of the Pilgrim Church.

Dr. McLaren, in introducing the work of the hour, said the programme was to consist of no long speeches. It was to consider how the prayer-meeting committee could render more effective the weekly Christian Endeavor prayer meeting. She called for expressions of opinion and experience as to what had been tried in different societies.

For expedition Dr. McLaren asked them first to speak upon the theme, " The Prayer-Meeting Committee at Work before the Meeting." There were a number of responses.

The second division, to which Dr. McLaren directed the attention of the conference, was "The Prayer-Meeting Committee at Work in the Meeting." A delegate said he liked that division. It was the way Mr. Moody worked, who always had the audience sing for the first half-hour, and then was accustomed to say that most anybody could preach after that. " So," said the delegate, "if the prayer-meeting committee really does the work well before the meeting, all it need do is to metaphorically press the button and the society does the rest."

" What Constitutes an Ideal Prayer Meeting ? " was the first sub-topic. A number of responses poured in from all parts of the house, five and six delegates being on the floor at once. Here are a few of the suggestions as to what makes a good prayer meeting. " Be on time." " Take part yourself." " Every member prepare before coming." " No one to talk against time — merely to fill up time." " Every member stand on his feet." " Encourage ladies to lead in prayer." " Have chain prayers." " Scatter the faithful members among the back seats, where the whisperers sit." " Pray for the pastor every day." " Have good ventilation." " Secure a consecrated organist." " Have a judicious variety."

After considering the committee's responsibility and how best to conduct the consecration meeting, the conference closed with a question-box.

There must have been 500 questions, but the president was equal to them.

There were 1,400 delegates present. They filled the gallery, the choir seats, and the auditorium below, and many stood through the whole conference.

Local Union Officers' and District Secretaries' Conference.

Mr. Frederick A. Wallis, Hopkinsville, Ky., presiding.

The conference of local union officers and district secretaries was held in the main hall of the Y. M. C. A. building. The hall was well filled with interested Endeavorers, and Mr. Frederick A. Wallis, of Hopkinsville, Ky., the presiding officer, kept things going in a very lively manner.

The experiences of the different officers were told for the benefit of all, and that they were fully appreciated was shown by the questions and discussions which they provoked.

Mr. Wallis emphasized in beginning the conference that all speeches must be short. He wanted very short addresses from all rather than long speeches from the few. He himself set the example by making a very brief opening address upon " Personal Responsibility." " We do not feel this enough," he said, "but we cannot do good service without it. Out of his good pleasure, God has called us into his service. He chooses to call in human aid, so that if we do not work for the cause we rob God."

After several songs and sentence prayers Mr. Wallis announced the conference to be open, saying that the discussion would be divided under the sub-heads which he would announce, and to each of which five minutes would be given. In many of these subjects, however, the discussion was so spirited and the questions so numerous that additional time was asked for and granted.

The first subject to be discussed was that of district secretaries, and the case of delinquent corresponding secretaries was considered. One young lady suggested her scheme of making their life a burden to them until they would answer letters, and this was received with applause.

The general opinion seemed to be that district secretaries should become personally acquainted with as many as possible under them, and keep in touch with all the societies. It was especially urged that as far as possible the letters should not be typewritten, but should be personal letters.

As for the presidents and vice-presidents of local unions, it was a good thing for them to pay attention to the Sunday schools, and to write letters to the superintendents urging the building-up of membership. The vice-presidents were even more important than the presidents, for more work came in their way to do.

The secretaries of the unions were decided to be the most important officers. Their principal idea should be to keep in touch with the State secretary and with the United Society. If a secretary is good he ought to be kept for several years. As the president said, " He is the link which connects your union with the outside world."

The idea of a correspondence committee is a new one, and Mr. George M. Paul, of Philadelphia, explained the idea of it in a short speech. Briefly, the idea of such a committee is to give a Christian welcome and church home for every Christian Endeavor member in the country.

Every society ought to have a permanent correspondent who shall report all persons who move away. Notice of such removal is sent to their new location, and the persons are at once looked up and cared for by the society in that place.

In the discussion about a press committee, the president urged every society to have one, as most editors will give plenty of space to church news. By this means people are reached who could not be reached in any other way. A press committee is a necessity everywhere.

A general laugh was directed at the press table when one delegate suggested that a press committee was necessary to help the regular reporters, as they usually know nothing about Christian Endeavor work.

The last subject treated was that of missionary work. Under this was included the temperance movement, Sunday observance, good citizenship, care of the poor and destitute, and work in jails and hospitals.

Good-Literature Committee Conference.

Mr. J. H. Banton, Waco, Tex., presiding.

Quite a crowd of workers on the good-literature committee met at the First Reformed Presbyterian Church to confer with each other regarding their work. Every one seemed to be in a good humor, and all came loaded with fresh as well as time-tried ideas and methods. The discussion was divided into the following parts : —

" The Work of the Good-Literature Committee among the Converted, or in the Church." First under this head came the committee's work in creating and perpetuating missionary enthusiasm. Mr. Edward Marsden, a native Alaskan, spoke of the beneficial effects of good literature, well used at missionary points.

" Use a literature that has something about Christ alongside of some practical every-day article about something that some man is interested in, and he will read of Christ before he knows it," was one suggestion. He gave as an illustration how one man was saved by having something about Christ printed near a description of a steam-engine. The man was an engineer, and would read about nothing else but engines, but in reading about engines he read on into another paragraph about Christ. His interest was awakened, and his conversion resulted. " Write to missionaries and foreigners, and exchange papers of your country and theirs," was another suggestion.

Miss Lena Barnes, of Garner, Ia., on the same division, suggested carrying the church for missions as Neal Dow said Maine was carried for prohibition : "Sow it knee-deep in missionary literature." Let the good-literature committee act as an information committee, and by reading find out facts. Let the good-literature committee suggest books for members to read, and be familiar enough with the books to be able to tell some feature of them to arouse interest in their contents.

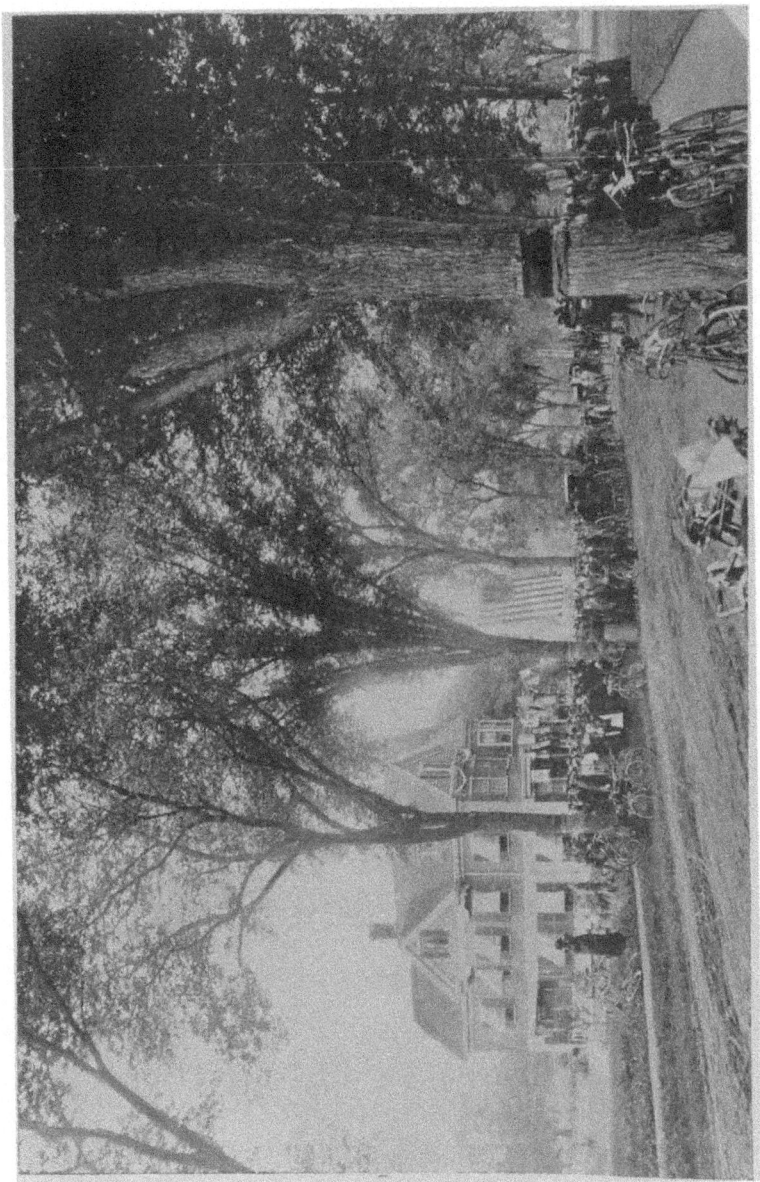

SECRETARY BAER'S HOME, MEDFORD, MASS.

RECEPTION TO WHEELMEN EN ROUTE FROM BOSTON TO LEXINGTON AND CONCORD, JULY 18, 1895.

SECTION OF PLATFORM DURING JUNIOR RALLY.

The next topic was, "How Can We as a Committee Assist Our Church Papers?" Bright and crisp ideas, prepared by Miss Martha Evans, of Indiana, and read by Miss Emma Donnell, of the same State, met with a responsive hearing. Canvass the congregation ; urge those who are able to subscribe; get funds and provide those who are unable to subscribe with papers. " Be useful in collecting arrearage on renewals," suggested another. One church paper gave ten per cent on all such collections, and the committee thus earned funds for other work. " An ignorant church is never a power for good. Let this committee fill the church with a consecrated intelligence by use of the church paper."

" The Work of the Good-Literature Committee among the Unconverted "came next. The responses showed that no committee there represented had been idle. "We combine the work of this committee with the flower committee, and send sweet flowers and good literature to cheer the hospitals," said one. "We do the same in the workhouse,' said another, "and though we can't hold meetings there, yet the authorities allow us to read the Bible to the inmates. This we do, and leave the Book with them. Our committee has succeeded in supplanting the degrading literature of the barber-shop with religious papers like *The Golden Rule* and *Ram's Horn*." "We put racks in the railway stations, and put good papers in them for persons to read while waiting for the trains." Another committee put marked copies of the Bible in similar racks. And still another use short pamphlets and card tracts in a like place. "The jail is regularly supplied by our committee with religious reading." " The penitentiary is our field for labor in this work, and six conversions have been the result of our placing good literature there."

" The Good-Literature Committee as a Press Committee "came in for a share in the discussion. Mr. C. C. McNeill, of Iowa, opened. His committee is divided into three parts, and each part has its work. One reports the sermons ; the second reports items of interest in the church, society, and Sunday school ; the third is always on the lookout for unusual events. The papers are anxious for news ; but be careful to give them news. One State had been informed on Christian Endeavor through the columns of a secular paper. " Get in line with the reporters, and they will run over you to get news items about your work." " Print and prosper." " One drop of ink can make a thousand people think." " Use the papers. The people are craving something about Jesus. Satisfy their appetites." " Sandwich the Gospel in between reports of baseball games, races, etc., and it will be the leaven that will soon raise such matter out of the columns of our papers."

But time would fail. The meeting grew red-hot. Only a few long talks. No one was allowed to advertise his book or paper; but all were urged to stick to this text : " What have you done? What are you doing? What will you do? " Some missed the mark and were lost in a fog of eloquence, but nearly all gave practical talks.

This glorious conference closed, for two reasons : time was up, and all the note-books were filled with good things. The chairman then announced that because the world was fast filling with a sickly, sentimental literature he thought it wise to give a practical illustration of what good literature was in short stories. He then introduced Miss Mattie M. Boteler, of Cincinnati, O., office editor of *The Lookout*, who read an original story written for the occasion. A general hand-shaking followed, and all was over on time.

Social Committee Conference.

Miss Mattie E. Race, Jacksonville, Fla., presiding.

A very important and interesting branch of the work of the Christian Endeavor Society is that conducted by the social committee.

More than a thousand of these earnest social-committee workers were present at the Union Congregational Church, on Columbus Avenue.

Promptly at 2 o'clock the session began, Miss Mattie E. Race, recording secretary of the Florida State Union, presiding. When a hymn had been sung, prayer was offered by Rev. E. W. Thompson, of Philadelphia.

Miss Race then said that she hoped that all were provided with good note-books and good sharp pencils, and introduced Miss Anna Peterson, of *The Youth's Companion* and also of the Bethany Baptist Church, who read a carefully prepared paper on the topic, " The Need of Every-Day and Every-Hour Social Committee."

She prefaced her paper by quoting from Dr. Clark, to the effect that no committee was more eager for suggestions, and none harder to furnish suggestions to, than the social committee, and continued substantially as follows : —

" What can we say when the need of an every-day and every-hour social committee is the question before us ?

" First, that the work in the past has seemed to be confined mainly to providing for an occasional entertainment; second, that we now look about to find a committee which will be always in a social mood, — a smiling, hand-shaking, a glad-to-see-you, a show-them-to-the-front-seat, and a linger-at-the-door committee; third, one which will make character a study, with the end of winning souls; fourth, one which will see the need of going deeper than the mere business surface in their dealing with men ; fifth, one which will carry the spirit of Christ in the lives of its members."

A verse of " True-Hearted, Whole-Hearted " was then sung, and Miss Race presented Rev. E. W. Thompson, of Philadelphia, who spoke upon " The Social Committee and the Pastor."

This relation, he said, should be very intimate, and could not fail to be of great value. All those who come into a church should labor with the pastor, and this should be especially true of the social committee. Politeness was an element of true Christian character; politeness often helped in the winning of souls.

The practice of the Golden Rule was necessary, and Christian love was essential for the best results in social-committee work. " Nothing so kingly as kindness, nothing so royal as truth."

Arthur Gale, of Jacksonville, Fla., spoke on " Social Work in the Church — Strangers within Thy Gates; How They Shall Be Reached." The power to convert belongs to those who can appreciate and take advantage of circumstances. Genial members are the best for social committees. There should be no cliques.

Rev. P. E. Zartman, of Sioux City, Ia., spoke on " How To Keep the Christian Endeavor Prominent in Our Socials." He said that the members must not wait till the socials are over. The Church is not doing its duty until it is open every day. Fight the saloons, not on Sunday only, but every day, and at night-time. If you have music, have good, inspiring music. Be cheerful, helpful, and charitable.

Miss Race next presented Mr. C. E. Smith, chairman of the press committee of the New Hampshire State Union. Mr. Smith's topic was, " Pleas for Printers' Ink," and he conducted a most interesting conference along this line.

He likened the conference to a railroad ride, he being the conductor and his audience the passengers. Tickets in the shape of suggestions were taken up all along the line, the three stations in the route being, " Use of Printers' Ink before the Social," " Use of Printers' Ink at the Social," and " Use of Printers' Ink after the Social."

The chairman, Miss Race, conducted the discussion of the three topics: " Refreshments at Socials," " Pay Socials ; Do They Pay ? " and " Don'ts for the Social Committee."

" Blest be the tie that binds " was sung, and the meeting adjourned, after the benediction had been pronounced.

The "Brotherhood" Committee Conference.

Rev. W. S. Kelsey, Boston, Mass., presiding.

A meeting of the "Brotherhood" Committee of Christian Endeavor was held in the vestry of Berkeley Temple, and was attended by about 150 men. Rev. W. S. Kelsey, of Boston, presided. The first speaker was Rev. Rufus W. Miller, of Reading, Penn., who explained the objects of the Brotherhood.

The Brotherhood, he said, was organized for definite lines of work. The committee pledges itself to do certain work, according to two principles, — prayer and service. By prayer the members pledge themselves to pray for the kingdom of Christ and the welfare of man; by service, they pledge themselves to make an earnest effort to bring one man each day into the Church. Hence the work has an endless outstretch.

This meeting was called to discuss what the Brotherhood can do and has done through the Christian Endeavor. A Brotherhood committee is a committee of three or more men, mostly voluntary, from the Christian Endeavor Society. The formation of these committees is not in opposition to the Christian Endeavor work, as is sometimes supposed, but is formed within that Society. The Brotherhood has as yet prepared no special literature, save its monthly paper and the report of the convention. The work has not yet been very strongly pushed, because it has been thought that such work could be done by the Christian Endeavor Society.

More than 260 branches of the Brotherhood have been established, mostly in places where the Christian Endeavor Society exists. Questions have been sent to each of these places, as to whether there is any conflict between the Brotherhood and the Christian Endeavor Society, and two-thirds of the places so questioned reply that the Brotherhood only intensifies the activity of the Christian Endeavorers.

The meeting was then thrown open to the discussion of the aims, problems, and the differences of the Brotherhood work in different places. Speeches and suggestions were made by Dr. Newman, of Washington, D. C., Rev. Mr. Haggardy, of Carlisle, Penn., Mr. Boynton, of Putnam, Conn., Mr. Hemingway, of Oak Park, Ill., Dr. Boyd, of Charlotte, N. C., Mr. Henry Franklin, of New Orleans, La., and many others.

Monthly Report Blanks for Committees.

The attention of all the committees is called to the "Committee Outlines and Monthly Report Blanks."

Every society of Christian Endeavor should insist upon monthly reports from each committee.

Many committees do not know what kind of a report is desired.

Some committees are doing so little they are ashamed to report.

All our committees would do more and better work if they had definite and practical suggestions.

Our new series of "Committee Outlines and Monthly Report Blanks" cover all the above points.

They secure systematic and accurate reports for the business meetings, and are so arranged that the committee retains a duplicate.

What a live worker says of them: "Upon a careful examination of the 'Outlines,' I do not hesitate to say that they are *the very best things for committee work that I have ever seen.* They not only solve the question of systematic reports, but they also outline the work for the committees, thus imparting more information as to the work of each than could possibly be obtained in any other way."

THE COMPLETE SET.

No. 1. Secretary's Book of Blanks. Contains outlines for reports to conventions, anniversaries, etc.; letters of introduction, special notice blank, and forms for treasurer's orders. Price, 35 cents; postage, 4 cents extra.
No. 2. Lookout Committee Report Blanks.
No. 3. Prayer-Meeting Committee Report Blanks.
No. 4. Missionary Committee Report Blanks.
No. 5. Social Committee Report Blanks.
No. 6. Calling Committee Report Blanks.
No. 7. Good-Literature Committee Report Blanks.
No. 8. Good-Citizenship and Temperance Committee Report Blanks.
No. 9. Junior Society Committee Report Blanks.
No. 10. Sunday-School Committee Report Blanks.
No. 11. Music Committee Report Blanks.
No. 12. Flower Committee Report Blanks.
Price of any of the above committee blanks, 25 cents each; postage, 4 cents extra. Price of complete set of twelve, $2.50; postage, 40 cents extra. (Cash with order.)

FRIDAY EVENING.

Mechanics' Building.

Although the exercises in Mechanics' Hall were not scheduled to begin until 7.30 o'clock, the great auditorium was completely filled as early as 6.45, and the multitude seated within the walls awaited patiently and with unbounded good-nature for the time to roll away.

One resource, unfailing with Endeavorers, and always answering sufficiently all drafts made upon it by them, was available, — they could sing; and sing they did with an unction, an appreciative heartiness, that gave their music a quality that a service of song does not always possess outside this organization.

The three-quarters of an hour thus passed was made memorable by the exercise, and another remarkable experience was added to the already long list of similar records of the Convention week.

The devotional exercises were led by Rev. Samuel McNaugher, of the Reformed Presbyterian Church, Boston. The reading of the twenty-fourth Psalm was followed by prayer by the leader. Hymn 10 of the Selection from Bible Songs, "I Will Joy," was then sung, and next came "For Jesus I Am Waiting." All the singing at this session was from the Psalms. This was arranged so that the young people from the denominations using only the Psalms of David for their songs of praise might have every opportunity to sing. The singing of these Psalms brought the following protest from some one in the audience : —

We emphatically protest against introducing denominational singing in this interdenominational gathering, with no ill-feeling toward the United Society or toward the brethren who sing the Psalms.

" I am surprised," said Dr. Clark, "to hear the Psalms called ' denominational songs.' Who is there in all this audience who thinks that we all have not a common heritage in the Psalms of David and the Bible songs? We rejoice and join in the common heritage which we all have in the Psalms and the Bible songs. I am confident when this is understood there will be no protest." This statement was greeted with applause.

At this point, Yong Kay, a Chinaman who, while in San Francisco, had been converted to Christianity, briefly addressed the audience.

After a selection by the Park Sisters, Dr. Clark introduced a pioneer Christian Endeavorer, Rev. Henry Nason Kinney, of Syracuse, N. Y. Mr. Kinney's topic was, " Senior and Mothers' Societies."

Address of Rev. Henry Nason Kinney.

" Old " people are Christian Endeavorers to-day. When in the year 1900 this International Convention is held in London, and the Christian Endeavor fleets, a steamship to a State, cross the Atlantic, Grandmother Lois, Mother Eunice, Simeon, and Anna, and Zacharias, " Uncle Martin," and " Aunt Ruth " will want a stateroom. They have taken the Christian Endeavor pledge! If the Christian Endeavor pledge is good for young people from seventeen to thirty-seven, for boys and girls in the Junior Society from seven to seventeen, why isn't it good for confirmed old bachelors, maiden aunts, and mothers and fathers in Israel from thirty-seven to one hundred and seven? " Father, why don't you know all about God?" said, twenty years ago, the toddling child of the philosopher, John Fisk, to him. " The girls in the kitchen do."

" Father, mother," we say to parents of Christian Endeavorers, "why don't you take part in the prayer meeting? Your own sons and daughters do."

1. From the first, patriarchal pastors, elderly elders, and white-haired deacons have been, ex-officio, honorary members of the Y. P. S. C. E. Older members of the congregation have been welcome and will always be welcome — if they behave well — in the young people's meetings.

2. Some members of the Y. P. S. C. E. were not so very young when they joined. The first signer of the Y. P. S. C. E. Constitution united, with his son.

3. Some of the members of the Y. P. S. C. E. are ten years older than they were ten years ago. Some of the delegates in this audience are older than they look; others are not so old as they look. At a recent prayer meeting of a city Y. P. S. C. E. the leader was over seventy; Miss Jane, the pianist, was fifty; the youngest young lady was twenty-five.

4. In some instances the whole church has become one Endeavor Society, its members from eight to eighty.

5. Those unable to attend prayer meeting at the church may now join the Home Department of the Y. P. S. C. E., i. e., the aged and disabled may keep the Christian Endeavor pledge at home.

6. The Senior or Adult Society of Christian Endeavor is simply the pledge to attend and speak in prayer meeting applied to the regular mid-week prayer meeting of the church. The Christian Endeavor pledge will do for the dear old prayer meeting of the church what it has done for the Young People's meeting. Graduates of the Y. P. S. C. E. and many before silent mothers and fathers, as well as young Christian Endeavorers, now take part in the church prayer meeting.

7. The Mothers' Society of Christian Endeavor was first suggested by Mrs. F. E. Clark, in 1893. It is an aid to the Junior Endeavor Society. The mothers of the Junior Endeavorers meet monthly for prayer and conference for their children. But Mrs. Clark might have known that Dr. Clark and other fathers have as much love for the children as the mothers; so in Chicago Mothers', in California chiefly Parents', Societies have been formed. Three

thousand fathers and mothers have taken the Christian Endeavor pledge for the sake of their children, and read the Bible and pray every day with them. As a result family altars have been set up, drunken fathers reclaimed, mothers led to Christ by their own little boys, non-churchgoers have been induced to attend a Sunday service. The Junior Endeavor Society is turning out little patriots, little pillars of the Church, pigmy Apostle Pauls; but sometimes parents are a hindrance to the work. The Sunday school and Home and Junior Endeavor Society and Fathers' and Mothers' Society have locked arms, and the child is safe!

The passage in John's gospel where Jesus says, "Feed my lambs, feed my sheep," by a better reading says this: "Feed my lambs, feed my sheeplings,"— *i. e.,* those neither lambs nor sheep, — "feed my sheep."

The Junior Endeavor Society feeds the lambs; the Y. P. S. C. E. feeds the sheeplings; the Senior, Mothers', or Parents' Society feeds the sheep.

The banner to be presented to the local union which had done the best work in promoting Christian Endeavor fellowship was presented by Rev. U. F. Swengel, of Baltimore, in the following words : —

Christian Endeavor means an aggressive Christianity. It is impossible to limit Christian Endeavor work within small circles. There is no city large enough to contain it, no State, no country, no continent. It is even now standing on the shores of many lands sighing for more worlds to conquer. Christian Endeavor means Christian conquest; its weapons are the sword of the Spirit and the arrows of truth. Its standard is the banner of love, on which is written the name of our one Master, whose we are and whom we serve. Christian Endeavor means to us a sweetness of fellowship and love. A Japanese convert said to a friend that the pleasures of the religion of Jesus Christ are enhanced by the freedom of fellowship and the fulness of confidence among the brethren. "We Japanese," said he, "are very careful as to how we express the fulness of our sentiments; but now when I see a man with a Bible under his arm, we are acquainted at once, and we talk over our most sacred secret experiences, because of the fellowship of the religion of Jesus Christ."

Our local societies feel the necessity of binding themselves together in Christian Endeavor unions. These unions are expanding; there is a reaching-out after other societies in order that the fellowship may be enlarged. Every one of these societies and every one of these unions rejoices in the enlargement and extension of every other one. One year ago the fellowship banner was presented to that wonderful union of the city of Philadelphia because it had gathered more societies into its union than any other union in the world. Of course no one believed a year ago, nor since, that the union of the City of Brotherly Love could be beaten in winning sister societies into her circle and into her fellowship, and because of this fact I am authorized to-night to present this beautiful banner again to the union of the city of Philadelphia. This represents to us the work, the great work, of that union. And now I have the pleasure and the honor, in the name of the United Society of Christian Endeavor, to present this banner to Mr. Louis S. Lee, president of the greatest Christian Endeavor City Union in the world.

Mr. Lee: It is an honor and a pleasure to receive on behalf of the union of the City of Brotherly Love the banner which has been given for Christian fellowship. There seems to be a peculiar propriety in that union whose motto is, "Let brotherly love continue" still holding that banner which is the highest type of brotherly love on earth, the Christian fellowship of the Society of Christian Endeavor. And while we take an honest pride in receiving once again from the hand of the United Society this beautiful and most precious symbol, we are filled with some degree of humiliation because this work, this great work which has given us the banner, has not been done by the Young People's Societies of Christian Endeavor. But what says the Scripture? "A little child shall lead them." Fifty-four societies have been added to the membership of our union during the year; fifteen Young People's, one Mothers', and thirty-eight Juniors. Can I as the representative of the Society at large hold this banner in my hands as the peculiar representative of the young people? Must I not in justice hand it over to the Juniors of Philadelphia? Endeavorers, on your behalf, in performance of the sacred trust which has been committed to you, I place this banner in the hand of the president of the Junior Union, Mr. J. B. Robinson.

MR. ROBINSON: I just merely want to add to Mr. Lee's remarks that those who are anticipating taking this banner from us had better look out. We have plenty of room for growth.

Rev. A. C. Dixon, D.D., of Brooklyn, N. Y., was enthusiastically received as he stepped forward to give his address, entitled, "Denominational Loyalty and Interdenominational Fellowship."

Address of Rev. A. C. Dixon, D.D.

In loyalty and honesty Jesus Christ was as narrow as a razor's edge ; in sympathy with struggling humanity he was as broad as the world. Narrowness is his mark of the way to heaven ; "Narrow is the way that leads to life." Breadth is his mark of the way to hell ; "Broad is the road that leads to destruction." And he builds Christian character along the lines of this narrowness and breadth. "Ye are built up a spiritual house," and a house is organized narrowness. The stone, once part of the great hills, has been narrowed into the block ; the wood, once part of the great forest, has been narrowed into rafters and boards; the clay, once part of the broad earth, has been narrowed into bricks. When a man becomes broad on the Ten Commandments, you had better watch your pocket-book. Virtue is always too narrow to include vice; honesty too narrow to include dishonesty; truth too narrow to include falsehood; righteousness too narrow to include sin.

"Ye are not come into blackness and darkness." Blackness is the absence of color, and Christianity is not colorless. But "ye are come into the general assembly and church of the firstborn, which are written in heaven." You are come into fellowship with all the saints of all the ages in both worlds, and the narrowness that is loyal to conviction does not prevent the broad fellowship that comes to us from Jesus Christ, the Lord. Listen to this word of God: "Ye are no longer strangers and foreigners, but the fellow-citizens with the saints, and of the household of God; and are built upon the foundation of the apostles and prophets, Jesus Christ himself being its chief corner-stone; in whom all the building fitly framed together groweth unto an holy temple in the Lord : in whom ye are builded together for the habitation of God's Spirit." No longer strangers, but fellow-citizens and in the family. I am not fond of the man who says, "I like one denomination just as well as another;" or will say, "I like one wife and one set of children just as well as another." But while I have a peculiar affection for my wife and my family, I can be in loving fellowship with all the families of earth.

Those of you who can walk back the path of apostolic succession, the Lord go with you; for my part I like an apostolic foundation founded upon the prophets and apostles, Jesus Christ having the prominent position. And you will notice, it is not the business of the Church to prop up the foundation, but the foundation holds up the Church. We need once for all to recognize that the apostles and prophets are well founded, and we need not spend our time in propping up but in building upon the truth that they have given us. "In whom the building fitly framed together;" and that phrase, "fitly framed" in another place refers to the joint of the body. The strongest part of my arm is not between the shoulder and elbow; you can break it easily there. The strong part is the joint at the elbow. The strong part of God's spiritual house is the joint, that unity of Christ's people. And if anything must give way, let the bone crack, while the joints sympathy and their ligaments of love hold. *Firm* as well as *blest* " be the tie that binds our hearts in Christian love." " In whom ye are builded together for the habitation of God's Spirit." On the Day of Pentecost the Spirit came as tongues of flame that sat upon each of them. And there is an individual enduement of power that we must have. But he came also as a rushing, mighty wind, and he filled all the house where they were sitting; we need above all things the rushing, mighty wind that fills the whole spiritual house. Such signs followed "them that believe," not him that believes; and when there is a union of faith and of purpose and of worth, then will come the Pentecostal power in the conversion of the lost.

In giving the portraiture of the heroes of faith, in the eleventh chapter of Hebrews, the author says time failed him to speak of Gideon and Barak and Samson and Jephthah, David also, and Samuel, and the prophets. Four of these men, Gideon, Barak, Samson, Jephthah, — five you may say, David, also, — represent phases of Christian fellowship and non-fellowship.

Gideon brought about a fellowship of common interest against a common foe. God called him before he called himself. God selected him to lead out the hosts of Israel against the invading, idolatrous Midianites. And there was a fellowship of danger and of loyalty to conviction. He turned at once upon the idols of his father's house and broke them down. Gideon was a narrow man, too narrow to take in his creed the altars of Baal and the prophets of the grove. Religion is mentioned five times in the Bible, only once with favor. " Pure religion and undefiled before God the Father " seems to be in contrast with the impure religion defiled before God to be displaced by the pure. Next to sin, the greatest enemy to Christianity is religion. It debases the heathen nations and throws up a Chinese wall about them, keeping them degraded century after century. The Pharisee that said, " I give tithes of all I possess," and then thanked God for the very thing that sent him to perdition, — that he was " not as this publican, " — was intensely religious. As Paul stood amid idol-cursed Athens, he said, " I perceive ye are rather religious," and he began to demolish their religions by preaching Jesus Christ and the Resurrection. I tell you, brother, the religion of Jesus Christ has no fellowship with idols, never did and never can. The mission of Christianity is to demolish all idolatry and bring about peace through victory, and not through surrender and compromise. When God had called Gideon he erected an altar and wrote upon it " Jehovah-shalom," — " The Lord send peace." The moment he came to war he said, " Peace." And there is a peace that comes only through war. " Not as the world giveth give I you peace." The world gives peace by sur-render, by compromise; Jesus Christ gives peace by victory and only victory. The Christian ought to love peace and pursue it; but next to peace he ought to love a fight, a fight with sin, with corruption in every form, a fight with every enemy of God until the last enemy shall be destroyed.

Gideon formed also a fellowship of enthusiasm. The Lord said, " You stand by the brook, and some whom you will see come down will be in no hurry to get at the enemy; they will kneel, and put their lips down in the water and drink to the fill, then put their hands in their pockets and, looking around, inquire what sort of weather we are going to have for the battle. Just set them aside; you don't want that kind. Others will be in such a hurry to get to the enemy over there on the hill that they will just scoop up the water as they run; they are the men you want, the men red-hot with enthusiasm, the men that have a fellowship of fire."

Westminster Abbey is a church in which they bury their dead, and there is perfect unanimity and uniformity. I know some churches in which the dead are not buried, but there is just as great uniformity. A delegate to a Baptist association said, " We are all united, frozen together." And there is such a union of ice that needs to be melted — unity without even unanimity or uni-formity that you get only in a graveyard.

You notice in Barak there was the fellowship of dependence. He could not go alone, and yet is a hero. God does not despise the fact that he wants some-thing to lean upon. He took Deborah along with him. I like that sort of fellowship. Now, thank God that the Christian Endeavorer won't go without

Deborah. Barak and Deborah began it together, and they are keeping up the march ever since.

Samson had fellowship with no one; he was a leader of nobody, not even himself. He had an alliance with the flesh. There was in him consecrated carnality. He was willing to use God, but not willing to let God use him. He could never fight until he got mad. He had to get up a personal quarrel, and then sail in and pile them up by the thousand. All his battles he had to fight alone. God honored the consecration and the prayers of his mother by giving him great physical strength, but he stands out as a sectarian of the flesh, as a sort of "peanut" politician over against statesmanship, as a narrow sectarian that has no fellowship and little following in contrast with a man that has a noble purpose for the glory of God. Samson spent his strength upon side issues. The Lord had called him as executioner, and he was a rough one, to be sure; but it does not take very polished men to put men in the electric chair or hang them up by the neck, and instead of having a noble motive he is prompted by personal consideration. When he came to die he said, "Avenge ME, Lord God, of my eyes." Killing lions, picking up gates and carrying them over thirty miles and flinging them down, as if to say, "Look what I have done!" and spending perhaps two weeks in catching three hundred foxes and tying them by the tails, and turning them out into the fields of the Philistines — that is poor business for a man that is commissioned of God to execute his sentence.

And you will find people that are sensual in their make-up; there is too much Egypt in them; there is not a fellowship of separation of those separated unto God. You remember what was the matter with the old Israelites as they crossed the desert, and they hungered for the flesh-pots of Egypt. They did not like the manna; it was not good, it was light stuff, they said. The trouble with them was their appetite had become used to onion and garlic, and when a man likes onion he never likes manna. When a member of my church refuses to come to prayer meeting I just take it for granted that he has been down to Egypt and had a square meal of onions. If some old Egyptian Yankee had caught the situation, and followed them with a cart of onions, he could have got all their spare change in no time. I tell you the devil is a sharp Yankee, and you can get onions in Boston and New York very cheap It is this alliance with the world, many a time, that keeps Christian men from being allied with the spiritual separated element for the conquest of this world for Jesus.

Jephthah was a man with a personal following. They were attached to him because they believed in his integrity. Whatever you may say about him, I, for one, don't believe that the context compels us to believe that he sacrificed his daughter as a burnt offering unto God; but whatever you may think, he was a man that kept his promise. He was conscientious; that little band believed in him because he was true, and cast their fortune with him.

And God has called men that were narrow to be great leaders. Luther was so narrow that he could not believe in anything but justification by faith. John Wesley was so narrow that he gathered a following about him on the basis of the witness of the Spirit. Calvin was narrow in believing in the sovereignty of God. And men that have believed in these men who have emphasized some great truth have gathered about them, and all have gathered about Jesus Christ for the same reason. My salvation depends upon his conscientiousness. He has promised and will perform, and every Christian that believes in the promise of Jesus may rally around him because he has faith in his integrity and power. And in however many other things we may differ, in this we may be together: "Ye are workers together with God." What is God working at? So far as I know he has gone out of the star-making business. He is now in the work of the new creation, seeking and saving the lost, forgetful of the ninety-and-nine saved, while he goes out after the one. It is ours to work together with him; yes, to work, and to work together, and to work together with God. Though we may not believe together in a thousand things, if we believe that Jesus Christ can save a lost sinner, and has saved us, we can work together with God for the salvation of others. Gideon divided the three hundred enthusiasts into three companies. They seemed to have been stronger for the division. They were separated, they thought differently about a great many things, they were from different tribes, of different shades of opinion, but there was one thing in which they agreed, and that was to do exactly what Gideon told them. It is ours to obey our Gideon. Let us break the pitchers, sound the trumpet, and let the light shine out together, and the conquest shall be ours. I believe that God called Gideon Clark to organize for the breaking of pitchers and the sounding of the trumpet and the routing of the Midianites all over the world. And as he follows Christ, we will follow him in this until all people shall have heard of the Name that saves.

David was all four of these men in one. A man to develop a fellowship of common interest, a leader of organized effort, he gathered a personal following about him; a man of conscientiousness that others believed in. And he could, when need be, fight his battles alone in the strength of God. David is the symbol of David's "greater son." He is a man that has individuality and yet fraternity, that's willing to be himself, bold in any great truth which God called on him to emphasize, and yet broad as the Spirit of Christ in linking hands and keeping step with the army of God as they march on. You have heard of the two Quakers, one of whom said to the other, "All men are queer but me and thee, and thee is sometimes a little queer." And the other man who said, "All men are dishonest but you and me, and sometimes I have my doubts about you." Be not like them.

There may be a narrowness of breadth which is truly pitiable. A man so broad in his liberal views that he has the utmost contempt for a man that refuses to be just as broad as he; so liberal that he fights the man that will not be as liberal — such narrowness of breadth should be as much condemned as the narrowness of sectarian bigotry. What we need is the narrowness of Jesus and the breadth of Jesus, that will make us as individual workers in harmony with all others. And there is a beauty in such harmonies. Beautiful songs mean many voices harmonizing; beautiful architecture, many minarets, or arches, or lines, harmonizing; beautiful pictures, many colors harmonizing. Just in proportion as we comprehend with all saints God's idea of dimensions, God's thought of breadth and length and depth and light, and comprehend it "with all saints," we shall be "filled with all the fulness of God!" That fulness of God will make us as individuals truly beautiful in character, and the great host of God's people in working together with him will present such a picture of beautiful service as no painting or music ever set forth.

> " Beautiful faces are those that wear —
> It matters not whether dark or fair —
> Whole-souled honesty printed there.

> " Beautiful eyes are those that show,
> Like crystal panes where hearth-fires glow,
> Beautiful thoughts that burn below.

> " Beautiful lips are those whose words
> Leap from the heart like the song of birds,
> Yet whose utterance wisdom girds.

> " Beautiful hands are those that do
> Deeds that are noble, brave, and true,
> Moment by moment, the long day through.

> " Beautiful feet are those that go
> On kindly ministry to and fro,
> Along lowliest ways, if God will it so.

> " Beautiful lives are those that bless
> Silent rivers of helpfulness,
> Whose hidden fountains few may guess.

> " Beautiful twilight at set of sun;
> Beautiful goal, with race well won;
> Beautiful rest, with work well done.

Beautiful graves where grasses creep,
Where brown leaves fall, where drifts lie deep
O'er wcrn-out hands; O beautiful sleep!

" Beautiful waking at dawn of day,
When the mists of earth have rolled away,
And Christ in His glory now holds full sway."

And as we gather about Christ and keep step with him and become like him,
the prayer to the Father has been answered: that we are one as he and the
Father are one.

The last speaker of the evening was Rev. J. T. McCrory, D.D., of
Pittsburgh, Penn.   Dr. McCrory is president of the Pennsylvania Chris-
tian Endeavor Union, and received a hearty welcome.   His topic was,
" Where We Come Together."

Address of Rev. J. T. McCrory, D.D.

What are we here for, Endeavorers?   I do not ask in elegant congressional
phrase, " Where are we at?"   We know.   In this respect we differ from present-
day politicians.   This is not the only respect in which we differ, I trust, but
this is one.   We know where we are.   We are at the " Hub of the Universe."
We are in the city which has been the social, intellectual, political, and moral
centre of this great nation, and which, for more than two hundred years, has
been sending out electric currents of mighty influence along all these lines.
Sometimes the true Boston has been but a small portion of the entire population of this city, but here the throbbing heart of the sublimest earthly endeavor
has always been beating full and strong, and its pulsations have been felt all
over this continent and clear around the world.   We are at Boston.   But again,
I ask, what are we here for?   No commonplace every-day answer will suffice.
This is no commonplace every-day event.   There are too many of us, and it has
cost too much to bring this concourse together, to answer with a commonplace.
Scores of thousands of busy men and women at a cost running into the millions
— you must have a good reason for that, a deep, broad, towering reason for
this expensive, this mighty, this magnificent, demonstration.   Well, let us see.
I am thinking to-night of another night, long ages ago ; and of a city which, like
this, had been the social, intellectual, political, and religious metropolis of the
country it adorned.   That was one of the darkest nights this sad world ever
saw.   That city, like this, was overrun with a mighty throng, a throng, too,
which had come from all quarters of the world and for religious purposes.   But
I am not thinking of the throngs.   I do not see the myriads, though they are
crowding all the streets.   I am not attracted by the joyous shout of a million
worshippers, though their temple is ablaze with light and their hosannas fill all
the heavens.   I am in a quiet suburban home, and in an upper room with a
select company.   There are twelve men here; there had been thirteen.   This
company is at prayer.   The sweetest, tenderest, mightiest, most wonderful, prayer
God Almighty ever listened to from human lips is now trembling up through
the night shadows of earth to the light and brightness of heaven's throne.
Jesus of Nazareth is giving voice to his deepest desires on behalf of his people.
He is praying for the Church; for the Church of to-day, of yesterday, and of
to-morrow.   The going-out of his heart in this prayer is all very wonderful, but
the petition, above all others, which just now impresses me is — listen, I think I
hear it as it falls from his own blessed lips — " That they all may be one; as
thou, Father, art in me, and I in thee, that they also may be one in us : that the
world may believe that thou hast sent me."

Who says Jesus takes no account of the unsaved in this great High Priestly
prayer?   Why here the whole, sin-doomed race is in his mind and on his heart!
And here, Endeavorers, I find the answer to the inquiry with which we began.
We are here for testimony.   We are here to bear witness before the world and

for the world to the oneness of the disciples of Jesus of Nazareth. We are here, praise the Lord, to help answer the petition he offered on the night before he died for us and for the world; a petition on whose fulfilment, to his mind, depends the triumph of his Cross. We are here, the tens of thousands of us, for this single and significant purpose. We may do some other things while here, but they will be secondary things—like the side trips compared to the main journey. For one thing, I suppose we will pass some resolutions which will become a part of the Convention record, and, like resolutions passed at our former international gatherings, they will help to shape and sway the future—but we did not come here to resolute. Then, for another thing, we will breathe in deep inspirations of patriotism in this birthplace of liberty and free institutions, as we see sights and hear words which will recall events and incidents that have made our history possible and glorious, and so return to our homes with new enthusiasm for the old flag, for "the little red schoolhouse," and for all that starry symbol stands for in the world—but we did not come here chiefly to be patriotically inspired. And then we will talk and commune and confer and conclude; we will be stirred by eloquent speech and great thoughts and wise suggestions and the story of splendid achievement in many fields and many lands, and thus influences will be started which shall tell mightily "for Christ and the Church" in the future operations of our growing, glorious, world-wide fellowship—still we are not here chiefly for talk and conference. Yes, and we will sing some, too. These tens of thousands of happy Endeavorers will sing their sweet songs and shout their glad hosannas until the very earth trembles and the high arches of heaven shall ring again and the great Atlantic yonder shall feel a new sensation creeping down to its fathomless depths and surging away across its three thousand miles of billowy surface, bearing the sensations of our gladness to foreign shores—but we are not here merely for songs. No, no. We are here as witnesses. We are here for testimony. This great host, representing the evangelical denominations of Christendom, gathered from the four quarters of the globe, is here in answer to the dying petition of our blessed Redeemer as it went up from the upper room in Jerusalem on the night he was betrayed. And this is the most practical answer that prayer has had for fifteen hundred years. We are here, moreover, to hasten the complete fulfilment of that prayer, and to bear the testimony that will persuade the world that Jesus Christ was and is, indeed, the sent of God for its salvation. And oh, how much such a testimony is needed! What pitiful sighs we hear from the hearts of the true disciples of the Lord everywhere over the strange, unaccountable indifference and unbelief of the dying world toward its most merciful and most mighty Redeemer! What is the matter with the world, anyway? Why will it not believe? we cry. Is sin a kind of insanity? Are unsaved men unamenable to reason? Are logic, fact, history, and demonstration of no force with the unsanctified intellect? Is the world clean gone mad? Then why does it not come to the open arms and loving heart of the blessed Saviour? For, you say,—and it is the joint testimony of millions,—Jesus is all the lost soul can need or desire. Why, you say, he has forgiven my sins, renewed my nature, cleansed my conscience, borne my burdens, comforted my griefs, refreshed my weary way with foretastes of heaven, and planted in my bosom a star of hope which sends forth a light that dissipates the shadows of earth and scatters the darkness of the grave and illuminates the eternities with a heavenly effulgence. "What a wonderful Saviour is Jesus, my Jesus." Why does not this sorrowful, dying world come to his open arms and loving heart? But it does not come. Why? Well, chiefly, because the testimony it needs has not been given. The invincible persuasive to belief, according to Jesus's teaching, has been wanting,—the testimony of oneness among the people of God. The world is waiting for that. It is waiting to see. It wants demonstration. Whenever evangelical Christendom shall give that testimony the Cross will be triumphant. Whenever it is made manifest to the eyes of the unbelieving world that there is a spirit of unity binding together the entire household of faith the last excuse for doubt will be taken away and the millennium will be ushered in with halleluiahs. Make manifest the supremacy of Jesus by his Holy Spirit in the entire body of believers, and the world will fall down and worship him.

Doing is the only thing that irresistibly persuades the prejudiced and unwilling. The Old World had been listening, for a whole generation before the Declaration of Independence, to the talk of the North American Colonists on behalf of liberty, and their protestations against tyranny — but Europe sneered at their protestations and discounted their spirit. It was only boasting, they said, which a slight experience of real war would silence forever. There was no spirit of unity pervading this conglomerate mass. The genius of liberty did not preside over the New-World destiny. This was all talk. A Patrick Henry, with his volcanic oratory, might set the hot blood of the Virginians boiling; an Adams or an Otis, with fiery eloquence, might even start the pulses of the cold-blooded New England rebels; but there was no supreme purpose pervading the land. The spirit of freedom was evanescent, and would vanish with the smoke of the first ten-pounder fired into the ranks of the rebels. And they could point, for justification, to the contentions between the various settlements, — Massachusetts against New York, Maryland against Virginia, the North against the South, New England against the other Colonies, — but when they beheld the whole population rise up after Lexington and Concord and Bunker Hill, yonder, and bear their bosoms to gleaming bayonets; when they saw the Colonists from the first enduring hardships which appalled the stoutest hearts, and contending for liberty with Spartan courage and Grecian patriotism and persistence, they changed their minds. They were compelled to concede that the boasting on behalf of freedom had not been a vain thing. They were persuaded then there was a real something inspiring this New-World movement which had in it the promise and potency of political revolution. And when that testimony, — the testimony of millions stepping forth intrepidly and gladly, to offer their sacred all, including life itself, for their country, — when that testimony, I say, got itself to the attention of the Old World, the contest was practically ended, and Freedom had won the day.

So, Endeavorers, it is in this world-wide, age-long contest between the powers of good and evil. Pentecost, with its baptism of fire, so melted down and fused together the hearts of believers that for many generations the unity of the body was unbroken, and the testimony on behalf of the mighty love of God was irresistible. The world was constrained to say, " Behold how these Christians love one another ! " Then, after the eclipse of faith for a dozen centuries, God sent a new Pentecost and baptized men with power to inaugurate the Reformation. Once more the Cross was lifted and a testimony borne for King Jesus. But alas! there were so many great questions closely related to the main issue — questions, too, which would hardly be put aside — that godly men found themselves contending with each other. And so the world said, " There is no harmony pervading their ranks." " They are not united in one purpose." " They do not seem to be under the dominion of one Spirit." " They have not one Lord." And so it has continued ; continued after every bottom reason for the earlier differences had passed away. And so the world is still unconvinced and unbelieving. And so it will continue until there is a manifest oneness among the disciples of the Lord Jesus. Now is there some one here saying in his heart, " Well, if the salvation of the world must wait on the unity of the Church, the prospect for the world is a dark one indeed"? Why so? " Because, " you say, " there is no fair and reasonable prospect for the union of evangelical denominations. " And you turn on me here in Boston, in true Yankee fashion, with a question which is to make evident the hopelessness of the case, and ask me, " Are you prepared here and now to give up your denominational preferences and join with others in new ecclesiastical relationships?" And I answer, promptly and positively, No. So vanishes, you think, the hope of the oneness of God's people, the answer to the Lord's prayer, and the conversion of the world. I do not agree with you. I understand there may be a deep, a Divine, unity even where there are differences in minor points of belief and of form and church order. When the liberties of the Colonists were assailed their united testimony and resistance against oppression did not involve the question of Massachusetts giving up her charter to Virginia or of Pennsylvania bceoming one with New York. It was not a question of the Quakers of Pennsylvania conceding everything to the Covenanters of the Carolinas, or the Puritans of New England adopting all the ideas of the Cavaliers of Virginia. It was not required that any of these should stultify themselves by repudiating their early history or disclaiming their ancestors or their honest convictions. It was only necessary that they appreciate the supreme demand of the hour, and, while respecting each other's honest differences, stand together against oppression, and cherish such a love for their common country and common heritage that the brand of traitor to these interests would be feared far more than ten thousand deaths. That was necessary, and that they did. Neither do we believe it essential, and, possibly, not even desirable, for all these evangelical denominations, in order that a united testimony may be offered to the world on behalf of Jesus Christ as the sent of God, to abandon their present grounds of belief, repudiate their ancestry, or fling to the winds their deep and settled convictions, though in some of these they differ from each other. When one recalls the history which lies behind these great bodies of believers, he does not wonder at the tenacity with which they cling to the names they bear or the reverence in which they hold their ancestors. Why, as I look back yonder to the early morning of the glorious Reformation and see Martin Luther erect and almost alone before an apostate Church and a reprobate age and world, looking fear itself out of countenance with his heavenly courage, and putting to shame the heroism of a dozen centuries with his sublime declaration, "Here I stand; I can do no other. So help me God!" and giving back to the world once more, at the peril of his own life, the doctrine of "justification by faith," I almost wish I had been born a German instead of a Scotch-Irishman. But then, when I see the brave Covenanters bedewing all the heather and enriching all the soil of Ireland and Scotland with the most precious blood that ever ran hot in patriot hearts or leaped living from patriot veins to consecrate a cause and maintain the "crown rights of King Jesus," I rejoice that I belong to the great Presbyterian family.

But here I open my Bible, the King James translation, and am reminded of the church which gave us, in our own tongue, this Book which, by the grace and blessing of heaven, has done more for the cause of humanity than all other earthly agencies combined; I recall the courage with which the English people threw off the papal yoke, and the wisdom and grace displayed in organizing a form of church order and promulgating a system of doctrine which, as Dr. Lord eloquently declares, "has survived two revolutions and all the changes of human thought, and is still a mighty power, decorous, beautiful, conservative, yet open to all the liberalizing influences of an age of science and philosophy,"—the church of Cranmer, Wilberforce, and Phillips Brooks; and I say, "From the people who see nothing to praise God for in the grand Episcopal organization, good Lord, deliver us." Again, I see the *Mayflower*, with its consecrated band, a race which had endured persecution unto the death for righteousness' sake in the Old World.

> " They could not live by king-made codes and creeds;
> They chose the path where every footstep bleeds.
> Protesting, not rebelling; scorned and banned;
> Through pains and prisons, hurried from the land."

I see this company landing yonder on Plymouth Rock, coming to these inhospitable shores inhabited by cruel savages, that they might find a place to worship God according to the dictates of their own consciences, and founding here "a church without a bishop and a State without a king;" and we say, "All honor to the Congregationalists." But there is Roger Williams, contending courageously for a church of spiritual persons and the non-interference of the magistrate in matters of conscience; and we say to our Baptist brethren, "You represent principles for which it is an honor to live and would have been immortal fame to have died." And then I reach out my hand across a hundred and fifty years, and feel a mighty sensation of power when I touch but the tip of the finger of one so surcharged with the Holy Ghost that, almost single-handed, he arouses an apathetic Church and startles the guilty world as with the trump of doom, and organizes, under compulsion, a religious organization which has proven a mighty inspiration to Christendom and has sent millions of redeemed ones home to glory, " sweeping through the gates of the New Jerusalem washed in the blood of the Lamb; " and then I say, " Who would not glory in the name and history of Methodism?" But, my friends, I look beyond all these and find that Luther, Calvin, Cranmer, Knox, Robinson, Williams, Wesley, and all the great men who have lived and wrought for God and the world, drew their inspiration from the Cross of Calvary and the Throne of Power — from the crucified but risen, exalted, and glorified Jesus. Then, I say, here is where we will get together — here at the Cross and the Throne. Not there with compromises which, if not meaningless, are stultifying, but here where are felt the mighty heart-throbs of a measureless love that will melt into oneness the disciples of Jesus of every name. I do not believe the difficulty in bearing this testimony for the Lord, as a united body, lies so much in the denominations as in the individuals of these denominations. You find less contention between different families of the Church than with the members of the same families. Let Jesus be enthroned in our hearts and lives, and all other matters will adjust themselves. That is what Christian Endeavor, as I understand it, proposes. That is its way of getting this witness of oneness before the world. It proposes to make every Christian like Christ, and then the whole Church will be like Christ; then the testimony for the unity of the Church will be irresistible and unimpeachable, and the world will believe. Whenever Jesus Christ becomes supreme in every Christian heart one purpose will pervade the entire body of believers and one sentiment find glad, swift response from every denomination; that purpose and that sentiment will be "the world for Christ and Christ for the world." You have heard the story of how, after one of the terrible battles of our great civil war, the bands from the Federal side gathered on the bank of the river that separated the contending forces, just as the sun was going down, and played " The Star-Spangled Banner," and the sentiment was cheered by the tens of thousands of the brave men who had come out to listen from the Northern camp. Then musicians from the Confederate army came down to the river on the other shore and responded with " Dixie," and were in turn cheered by their loyal comrades. The Federals responded with another national air, and the hills trembled with the shout of their fellows. This was answered with another Southern melody and a mighty yell from Confederate veterans. After a while one of the bands began softly to play a melody that silenced every voice and floated away over the river and was instantly taken up by the musicians of the other side, and all together they played the music of that sweetest earthly song, "Home, Sweet Home." Then, when the last soft note had floated off with the shadows of the dying day, there was a mighty shout that rent the very heavens, for two armies had joined in the response to the heavenly song. In that sentiment these great armies were one. So, Endeavorers, when the Spirit of the Lord pervades our hearts all differences vanish away and we are one to the glory of God and for the salvation of the world. This, Endeavorers, is a kind of oneness both practical and possible, and which, I trust, the dear Lord intends our blessed fellowship to further, and which is being mightily hastened by these conventions.

The benediction was pronounced by Rev. A. C. Crews, of Toronto, Ont.

Tent Williston.

The audience in Tent Williston was immense in numbers and magnificent in spirit and enthusiasm.

" All ye are brethren," we have said over and over again, but none of us ever more fully realized it than on Friday evening, the "fellowship night " of the Convention. Every corner of the earth gave up its best to these meetings. The speakers, many of them, bore unpronounceable names, and used picturesque dialects, but they all were intelligible in their Christian Endeavor badge and spirit.

Hearts beat quicker, eyes flashed brighter, souls rose higher, in this parliament of the world. England, Scotland, Armenia, United States, China, Spain, Mexico, Germany, Alaska, Wales, India, Australia, Bermuda, Japan, Persia, North America Indians — all had voices in this remarkable conference of Christians.

The presiding officer was Trustee Rev. H. C. Farrar, D.D., of Albany, N. Y. The music was in charge of Mr. George K. Somerby. The opening prayer was by Rev. W. H. Albright, D.D., of the Pilgrim Church, Dorchester.

Mrs. John M. Wood, of New York, sang a solo, and then Chaplain D. H. Tribou, U. S. N., delivered a very interesting address on "Christian Endeavor in the Navy."

Address of Chaplain D. H. Tribou, U. S. N.

I am to speak on, "Christian Endeavor in the Navy." The navy is almost all new; new vessels, new guns, new evolutions, and new methods. Nearly all the effective vessels are younger than the Christian Endeavor Society. It is an interesting fact that the Society and the new navy started about the same time. As to speed, the new ships have beaten everything except the Society.

The new ships have inaugurated a new era. The United States Navy has made several new eras in its history. The days of the sailing ship *Constitution* belong to the first era. The auxiliary steam frigates of the *Wabash* class mark another era. We revolutionized naval warfare with the first monitor. We put wooden ships out of date, and marked them " B. T." (Behind the Times), and the maritime nations of the world had to follow our lead. Now we put together a great mass of machinery that represents three years of labor and three million dollars in money, and that is the new defender of the nation's peace. Not a stitch of canvas except in the hammocks the men sleep in. No white-robed mast; no spreading wings; nothing of the old type, but in its stead fire and steam and machinery. It is a marvellous change. One can hardly realize it. But the sea has not changed. We have not penetrated its mystery nor conquered its power; and these immense fighting-machines must be driven and handled by men, men of the sea.

You all know what sailors are. You have been introduced to them in books and on the stage. Those sailors never change, and they never go to sea! I do not wish to speak of them, but of the actual sailors of to-day. They are not in any sense a strange species of the human race. They are just like folks. They are just like other men; no more generous, no more fickle, no more brave; only plain, honest men who have had experience, that is all. They are just as cranky as other men. They want to be coddled just as much as other men, and no more. All they ask is for an opportunity to range themselves alongside of other men, and be sized up by the common rules. No sailor wants any special pleading in his behalf, nor does he ask any special dispensation. You go on board one of the new ships, and two things impress you most of all: first, how handsome the men are; second, how young they are. If you pick out a hundred of them you will find a higher intelligence than among men of the same walk of life on shore. Talk with them, and you will learn that they are well informed and have an opinion on almost every subject, from prize-fighting to the latest society fad. There is a great difference in the effect of machinery on the man who lives on shore and the man who goes to sea. The man who runs a machine on shore is very likely to degenerate into a mechanical performance of his duties; at sea the man who runs a machine has to exercise his wits. When a piece of machinery breaks down he cannot send it to the shop or to an expert; he must learn to repair it himself. So at sea the tendency is to develop ingenuity.

The men who manned the sailing frigates in the older era did their work well. They had a responsible part in making this nation what it is, and they deserve the highest honors. The sailor of to-day is younger, more intelligent, much more temperate, less superstitious, and more religious. The religious atmosphere has improved very much during the last ten years.

What started the Christian Endeavor Society? The fulness of time. The hour struck, and in the little city of Portland a man was called to inaugurate it, just as truly as Mary was called to be the mother of the Saviour. The whole world was ripe and ready for it. That is what made it take. That is what comes of working with God, biding his time, but being on the alert to recognize its approach. Do you suppose your grandfather could have started it in his time? No, indeed! It is a society that can never have a grandfather! Why, some of the belated grandfathers did not want it started at all. A few of them thought to stop it by sitting down in front of it! They do not think so any more!

The first Christian Endeavor work on the sea began in 1890. It was started by that faithful, earnest, tireless woman, Antoinette P. Jones, of Falmouth, Mass.; and when it comes time to nominate candidates for Christian Endeavor sainthood I shall try to be on hand to nominate Saint Antoinette. On the first day of November, 1892, three Christian men and four seekers of religion, all seafaring men, met in the Chapel on the Cob Dock, at the Brooklyn Navy-Yard, and formed the first Christian Endeavor Society in the navy. They were led to this by that prince among chaplains, Donald McLaren, now the head of the corps of chaplains. Their president was that indefatigable worker, that brave and sincere friend, that devoted Christian man, John M. Wood, formerly of the navy, but now employed by the Seaman's Friend Society. He still holds the office, which he honors, and which I hope he will long continue to hold.

From that little society of seven members there have been enrolled at the Cob Dock no less than 550 members, representing thirty-five of the fifty ships of the navy now in commission. Besides this, there are societies on board the *New York*, the *Columbia*, the *Minneapolis*, the *Charleston*, and four other sea-going ships, with 140 enrolled members, a society on board the *Wabash*, and one at the training-station at Newport.

There are only about twelve thousand men in the navy, but there are more than three million men who follow the sea; and the world is yet to be evangelized — just as it was discovered — by the men who go to sea. Depend upon it, the sailor is the best ally in all missionary work. Get him first, and he will take the world for Christ.

> " There go the ships with precious freight,
> The souls of priceless worth,
> For whom the Prince of Glory died,
> With whom he lived on earth.
> There go the ships, and so, we pray,
> O Christ of Galilee,
> Rule o'er the stormy winds, and save
> Our sailors on the sea."

Rev. Rivington D. Lord, D. D., of Brooklyn, N. Y., then presented the banner to the local union which had done the best work in promoting fellowship, in the following words : —

Some one has said that a good speaker is like a good auger; he takes hold right away, goes all the time, and quits when he is through. And, permit me to add, such a speaker never bores his hearers. Dr. Clark in his courteous invitation to present this banner added that ten minutes only would be allowed for this service, and then I find that I must divide that ten minutes with my brother from Philadelphia. He is a very discreet man who never says either too much or too little. In a church business meeting—Baptist church, of course, for I belong to that church, Free Baptist—the chairman arose and said, "I hold in my hand the resignation of Brother Skinner. What is your pleasure in reference to it?" A deacon arose and said, "I move that the resignation be accepted, and a vote of thanks be tendered to Brother Skinner." That deacon said just a little too much.

But, seriously, I am delighted to-night to be present and to present this banner, for this banner means something and stands for something. That honored, world-honored, and world-beloved, that magnificent and peerless orator, than whom this nation or any other hath produced no greater, the lamented Henry Ward Beecher, once said, "When a thoughtful man sees the flag of a nation, he sees, not the flag, but the nation itself. Whatever may be its insignia, he reads in that flag the history, the principle, and the government of the nation that flings it to the breeze." So I say to-night, When you see a Christian Endeavor banner, you see, not the banner, but Christian Endeavor itself, and especially those vital and living principles for which Christian Endeavor stands. First of all, Christian Endeavor stands for Christ. It always has stood, it still stands, and it will stand for the Master. We know no other Lord nor Master. We know in whom we have believed. He is not only the Captain of our salvation, but the Commander-in-chief of all our forces; to him we owe—and, God helping us, we will pay—unflinching allegiance and undying devotion; such devotion as that wounded soldier expressed on the battle-field of Fredericksburg, who, when he was dying, said, "Boys, I am shot; don't wait for me, but unfurl the old flag and let me see its beauties once more." They unfurled the flag; he grasped it eagerly, kissed it, and then his spirit went heavenward.

Christian Endeavor stands, second, for the Church. I mean by that, the local church. You cannot be a loyal Christian Endeavorer without being loyal to some particular church. You cannot belong to the Church universal, for this would be like being a tramp. A tramp is a man who belongs everywhere in general and nowhere in particular; a tramp is a man who believes in eating everywhere and working nowhere. So a man who belongs to no particular church is a religious tramp. Let it be known now, henceforth, and forevermore that we have no room in the Christian Endeavor for tramps, even if they be Christian Endeavor tramps. You must work for your church.

But there is a third thing for which Christian Endeavor stands: Christian fellowship and interdenominational love. How much this means in these later days! Behold this wonderful sight,—that, as Christians, we have ceased to pick flaws with, but are beginning to court, one another's denominations.

Philadelphia has been noted as a city of Quakers, and if there is anything about a Quaker it is that he moves slowly, that he is quiet and reflective. But the Quakers that inhabit Philadelphia to-day have got a terrible hustle on. The banner which represents Christian fellowship and interdenominational love must go, as most properly, to the City of Brotherly Love. Philadelphia reminds me of those soft clams you have,—peaceable and quiet, but plenty of sand in them. To the brother representing Philadelphia I have this message to bring: "To the angel of the church in Philadelphia write; I know thy works: behold, I have set before thee an open door, and no man can shut it: for thou hast a little strength, and hast kept my word, and hast not denied my name. Because thou hast kept the word of my patience, I also will keep thee from the hour of temptation, which shall come upon all the world, to try them that dwell upon the earth. Behold, I come quickly: hold that fast which thou hast, that no man take thy crown."

Rev. Allan B. Philputt, D.D., of Philadelphia, received the banner with the following remarks :—

I am not the "angel from Philadelphia;" the angel could not be here, and about five or ten minutes before the meeting, asked me to represent him. The original angel can be seen later.

The eloquent address to which we have just listened did my heart good, for I am met everywhere I go with that stale joke that Philadelphia is slow. A little boy in New York asked his mother if the Schuylkill did n't run through Philadelphia. "No, my child," she said, "nothing runs in Philadelphia." For Philadelphia to capture a banner is a little like the Dutch capturing Holland, but, nevertheless, this banner has been honestly won; it is honestly come by, and the more so because this largest Christian Endeavor union in the world has already, as things go, worked its territory. This banner was won again this year by the Junior Societies. But for that field of her activity, she would have lost the banner, because there was hardly sufficient territory for churches within her borders to enable her to have captured it. The time is coming when the president of the Philadelphia Union, like Alexander the Great, will have to say, regarding that, "There are no more worlds to conquer."

Philadelphia is slow, you say; but, like the North Star, she is always there. She is true to Christian Endeavor and to the spirit of good fellowship. I reciprocate the eloquent sentiments of the brother in behalf of the Quaker City and of the Philadelphia Union to-night. We shall be only too glad another year for some other city to take the banner if you can, but, in the language of our plain Quaker talk, if thee takes it thee must get a hustle on.

The following speakers were in turn introduced by the Rev. H. C. Farrar, D.D.

For England, Rev. James Mursel: — I speak to-night for England. I am to give a message from young England to young America upon our fellowship. We find, in England, that our fellowship is helping to draw all English-speaking peoples nearer to one another. We find that though there was a time when things which came from America were looked at askance in England, that time has gone. Nationally, America is the child of England; and I hope that you will never, like some men when they grow rich, despise your parentage. But from the Christian Endeavor standpoint, England is the offspring of America. And we are proud of our parent. No name is held in higher and more affectionate honor than that of Francis E. Clark, and no movement is calling forth the chivalrous devotion of young England as Christian Endeavor is. We believe and we find that our fellowship, which is enshrined in our favorite monogram, has united the hearts of America and England by another endearing and most sacred bond. We also find that our fellowship draws us, as we believe it is drawing you, closer to Christ. To be near Christ is often to be near a fire; to be near him is to be near the sword; but Christian Endeavor is teaching us to bear the sword and to face the fire, if only in the furnace we may walk and in the battle we may fight beside our Lord and King. Still, as of old, the whole creation longs for the manifestation of the sons of God. We want those who are evidently the sons and daughters of God. We want those who can not only gather in the World's Convention of Christian Endeavor in their thousands, but who, when Hell summons a convention, dare stand all alone, unfearing and undaunted, and there believe that Christ stands still on their side. Those are the soldiers that Christian Endeavor fellowship is making the wide world over, and in our Old England.

Above the hum of your great city, I can hear the youth of England shouting their message. They bid me say we stand for truth, for Christ, for holiness, for God.

For Scotland, Rev. John Pollock: — I greet you in the name of Bonnie Scotland, land of the mountain and the flood, land very generally misunderstood. I greet you in the name especially of the Christian Endeavorers of Scotland. I was proud to stand beside my brethren from England to-day, representing my part of the United Kingdom. I am sorry that my brother, Mr. Montgomery, did not happen to be present to represent Ireland. I was glad to stand beside my English brethren, but I felt that I ought to have gotten a banner to take home to Scotland, because I am strongly inclined to think that had Scotland been considered separately, she would have run a good chance of securing the

banner for the largest proportional increase during the past year. I think one
hundred and twenty per cent is not bad; and we intend to do one better next
year.

There are a great many people asking questions about Christian Endeavor
in Scotland, and it is always after the questions and not till the questions have
been asked and satisfactorily answered that any one in Scotland will have any
thing to do with you.

FOR CANADA, REV. T. S. MCWILLIAMS:—I have the privilege to bear to
you the Christian greetings of Canada, and it gives me peculiar pleasure to
come back to the land of my birth and speak a word for the country of my
adoption. Perhaps I should begin by introducing Miss Canada to you, for I
fear that some of you are only slightly acquainted with her. Last year in
Lucerne a clergyman asked about a friend of his by the name of Smith, who
had emigrated some years before to Canada. We asked to which one of the
somewhat numerous clan of Smith his friend belonged and to what particular
part of Canada he had gone. In some surprise he asked, " Is there more than
one place in Canada?" A gentleman from Toronto went back to Ireland, the
place of his birth, and was asked similar questions about Irishmen that had
emigrated to Canada. In order to impress upon his inquirers the absurdity of
their inquiries and the greatness of his country, he said, "Why, in Canada we
have lakes that you could put the whole of Ireland in, and you would never
know it was there but for the smell of the whiskey." Uncle Sam sometimes
refers to Canada as his "little sister to the North," but if he realized the girth of
her waist and the measure of her stature, he would hardly refer to her in these
diminutive and patronizing terms — three and a half millions of square miles
of territory, the largest country on this continent, the United States not
excepted. It is true that our population is not quite as dense as this country's,
but then we have more elbow-room. And then give us time. The Dominion
is only twenty-eight years old; the Union is over a hundred years of age. Who
knows but in a hundred years from now Canada, too, will have 65,000,000
inhabitants, and be ready to annex the United States!

And Canada has something of quality as well as quantity of which to be proud.
Her banking-system, during this protracted period of financial depression, has
been pronounced the safest and best in the world. She keeps the Sabbath better
than any country of which I have any knowledge. There is scarcely a Sunday
paper published throughout the length and breadth of the land. The streets
of her cities are crowded on the Lord's Day with churchgoers; and in our
congregations are to be seen almost as many men as women. Canada embraces
the Province of Manitoba, which says, emphatically, notwithstanding the decisions of the Privy Council, " We will have no separate schools." Canada
embraces the Province of Assiniboia, which, this morning, bore off the banner
for the greatest proportional increase. But I have blown the horn of mighty
Canada quite enough.

This Christian Endeavor Society, under God, is one of the mightiest
agencies in promoting the fellowship of nations, the brotherhood of man, and
bringing about the beneficent reign of the Prince of Peace. It is one of the
greatest agencies for making wars to cease unto the ends of the world. Flags
of nations that have met upon the field of battle, and been shattered with one
another's shot and shell, here blend their harmonious colors, and float upon the
atmosphere freighted with peace and good-will. Nations that have met upon
the bloody field, nations whose sons have had their hands stained with blood
drawn by each other's bullets, have sent their sons and daughters to this great
gathering, where we clasp one another's hands in Christian affection and fellowship, and unite our voices in singing:—

"Let every kingdom, every tribe,
On this terrestrial ball,
To Him all majesty ascribe,
And crown Him Lord of all."

FOR ARMENIA, REV. A. M. BOULGOURJOO:—I bring you greetings from the
oldest nation — the oldest Christian nation — now existing. I bring to you the

greeting of the Christian Endeavor Societies of Armenia and its surrounding provinces, — from the Christian Endeavorers who are living and suffering for the name of Jesus Christ; from the Christian Endeavorers of a country where their Christian Endeavor banner could never be unfurled, and where to be a Christian is not tolerated, and where to be a Christian Endeavorer is regarded and punished as a crime. Under those circumstances, of course, we do not have very many Christian Endeavor Societies; and if you would like to know the reason more, you just read their book, " Our Journey around the World," by the honored President of this Society, and you will find the reason there. It is a country where they could not wear this badge; and this badge would cost me years of imprisonment, and perhaps death. The old Christian nation, the Armenians, are still working, endeavoring, and struggling for that dear name, Jesus Christ, the Saviour of the world.

While we have a very hard time, — and you all know about the great troubles we are having over there, — still the Armenians, the Christian people in Turkey, are not discouraged, but are still there to reclaim that country " for Christ and the Church." Dear friends, Providence has given us a great and important field. Just look at your maps; on the west of Asia there is Armenia, or Turkey in a larger sense, — " the Yankees of the East," as they are called. Then there are the Japanese, also Yankees of the East; and there is a great land between of heathenism; and a good Providence has called us to work for Christ, and Japan, on the other hand, to do her share.

I hope we shall have not only your sympathy, and your prayers, and your special interest in us, but a right hand of fellowship; and, God bless you, we are praying for you, and we are working with you.

FOR THE UNITED STATES, REV. S. W. ADRIANCE, WINCHESTER, MASS : — It is a long time since I looked into the faces of Christian Endeavorers. Since that last consecration meeting at Philadelphia, which it was my joyous privilege to lead, I have been laid aside from the busy world, and rejoice to-day that I can come again and look into your faces, and can speak to you. Sometimes the parents come to the homes of their children, and sometimes the children come to the homes of their parents.

It is hardly necessary that I should give you greeting in the name of America. You have certainly had a great many warm greetings in behalf of America by the city of Boston and by this beloved Commonwealth.

One of the most striking effects of Christian fellowship, as I see it, is the development of spiritual vision. However bright the eye may be, however strong the optic nerve, we need to be associated with one another to see well and to see strongly. I greet you all in the name of Christian fellowship, because it develops every part of you. It is true we need study and prayer, that we may have heart-growth; but it is quite as true that we need to be associated with one another, that our view may be broadened. Then we see both our landscape and their landscape; then we see both our views and their views, and we are so much the richer in attachment to one set of truths and to one line of duties. We have been disciples of meditation; let us now, through fellowship, learn to be disciples also of action. We have been consecrated in prayer. In fellowship we become consecrated in Christlike service. We are apt, all of us, to become too exclusive. We become not merely exclusive but also inclusive. I greet you all in the name of Christian fellowship because it develops distinctness of view. Fellowship does not merely show us new truths, new duties, new inspirations; it also makes us see our old familiar truths more distinctly than ever, and love them more dearly than ever. If we loved our work before, we love it with tenfold power because we have told it to others, and because we have heard the story of this work from others. I greet you in the name of Christian fellowship because it increases the range of our spiritual vision. By ourselves we do not see very far beyond the smoke of our own chimneys; in the love of Christian fellowship and Christlike fellowship, the ends of the earth are brought within our view. Fellowship gives to the near-sighted those magic glasses that sweep the whole world within our vision, and we are enabled to cry, " The whole world for Jesus."

For China, Yong Kay: — Thousands of miles we come from the end of this great continent to attend this great Convention, and we hope all of you will do the same in the year 1897, to attend the meeting of the Convention in California, and see about the work among our people.

Last May I was under the call of the Lord Jesus Christ to go from place to place in California, and make addresses. I will tell you about the work. At present we have fourteen active members and six associate members, making twenty in all. All the brethren of these societies we command to bring in others to attend all the meetings and the schools, and in this way our school has been enlarged. We thank God for the great blessing and the loving kindness which has been shown our society and school.

Can the Chinese be converted? This question has been asked many times by some of the American people. My answer is simply this: the Chinese can be converted as well as any other nationality. They not only can be, but have been, converted. If the Gospel of Christ has not the power to convert a Chinaman, why has it the power to convert an American? If the Gospel of Christ has the power to convert an American, what prevents the same power from converting a Chinaman? Let us see what the Bible says about it in the forty-ninth chapter of Isaiah: " Behold, these shall come from far: and, lo, these from the north and from the west; and these from the land of Sinim." According to the interpreters, "the land of Sinim" means China. But let us now go still further and see what Jesus himself says about it in the thirteenth chapter of Luke, twenty-ninth verse: " And they shall come from the east, and from the west, and from the north, and from the south, and shall sit down in the kingdom of God." And again in the twelfth chapter of St. John, thirty-second verse: " And I, if I be lifted up from the earth, will draw all men unto me. " " Men " means the Chinese as well as any other human being on the face of the globe. According to the Bible, there is no respect of persons with God. We may differ from you in color, in dress, in language, and in taste ; but we are one in faith and spirit, for the same God hath created us, the same Christ hath saved us, the same Spirit hath quickened us. We may have been separated from each other by land and by sea, but we are all drawn together by the cause of Christ's redeeming love. We thank God for that.

I hope you will improve every opportunity to teach our Chinese to accept the Gospel of Christ. God grant that our people shall be made known unto all the people as a God-fearing and God-loving nation. So your labor shall not be in vain, but bring you a fountain of blessing.

For Spain, Miss Catharine H. Barbour: — Perhaps it is due to the fact that our honored President, Dr. Clark, had for a playmate Louise Gordon, who, as Mrs. Gulick, was the founder and is the president of the International Institute for Girls in Spain, that in that land and in that school originated a society so similar to that known to-day as Christian Endeavor that it was found necessary only to translate the name " Christian Endeavor " into the Spanish for the same, while we retain the initial letters " C. E." and the initial principles. From the first, a large part of the income of this society has been devoted to benevolent objects, and this Christian Endeavor Society has in this way become a missionary society of such power, not only to take a share in Christian Endeavor in that land, but to take a scholarship and educate a pupil in the school. Our meetings are only fifteen minutes long, and we find that when every member is anxious to be true to her pledge and has so short a time in which to take part, a great deal more can be accomplished in fifteen minutes than is often done in an hour. We have special meetings on missionary subjects, which are held on Sunday afternoons.

The Endeavor Society now embraces all the members of our International Institute and others in the city, and it is spreading out all over Spain. I bring to you, therefore, the greetings of that land, and I cannot give them to you better than in the words of this girl who is a protégé of the Endeavor Society: " Pray for us over in Spain." I assure you that we have need of your prayers, that Christian Endeavor may have as free course there as it has in this land. When the International Convention of Christian Endeavor shall be held underneath the Castilian banner, sometime in the twentieth century, I invite you to meet us, and we will return your Boston welcome with a truly Spanish one.

For Mexico, Rev. A. C. Wright : — They of Mexico salute you. We have just come into the circle as an organized body. The Christian Endeavor Societies of Mexico met on the tenth day of last month and organized the United Society of Christian Endeavor of Mexico, and have sent me to represent them. I hold in my hand an organ of that society, a practical illustration of our fellowship. The light of the Gospel has begun to shine in Mexico, and that which we have seen and heard declared with enthusiasm you also heard ; you also may have fellowship with us, and our fellowship is with the Father and with his Son. The Mexican Endeavorers comprise 22 societies and 500 members, but we are surrounded by 12,000,000 people who offer us no fellowship, nor will accept any from us.

We want your fellowship ; and let me translate one line from a letter from one member of our Christian Endeavor Society who is all alone, four days' ride from the nearest church, and he says, " I beg you to remember me in your prayers, that God may help me in this enormous work, from which, when I contemplate it and then look at myself, I almost wish to run away, I am so small." May I tell him that he shall be sustained by the prayers of two and a half millions of Christian Endeavorers, bound together by that love which constraineth us ? We shall in time take Mexico and the world " for Christ and the Church."

For Germany, Mr. Carl E. Wittwer : — " Before God, there is no respect of persons." If that is true, then a German is capable of being a Christian Endeavorer. Germany has been set down last on the list ; certainly Germany is not the last in the array of nations politically, and will not long be last in the array of nations *Endeavorically*. For the past year or so clergymen and laymen of the German Empire have discussed the movement through the press, and have discussed it at the conferences. The Christian Endeavor banner has floated before the German eyes, and they could not help but see it. Many looked at it as if they had to guard themselves against it ; many tried to fight it ; but many others found that Christian Endeavorer, our beloved Christian Endeavor, brought them great joy, sweet peace, and many other blessed experiences. Christian Endeavor has become a new Reformation Hymn, a mighty battle-shout, the meaning of which cannot be understood. The Germans of America and the Germans of Germany have begun to take hold of Christian Endeavor. Christian Endeavor will be pushed and promoted with might and main. Germany will, next October, see its first Christian Endeavor Convention.

Germany is reputed to be slow. They are slow at times, but you arouse a German, secure his co-operation, and you have not only a faithful worker, but a fearless warrior. We are glad to-night to have a voice in this great gathering. I know that many of you pride yourselves on your Teutonic or Anglo-Saxon lineage. I bring you the greeting from the German societies.

Christian Endeavor has become with us the synonym for interdenominational fellowship. It stands for a mighty and blessed fact. My heart tells me to say, in the words of my own tongue, A greeting in God's name.

After singing, the audience listened to an address by Rev. Henry Montgomery, Belfast, Ireland, a man who made as strong an impression as any one on the programme ; who, although small in stature, has both intelligence and physical vigor in speaking, as well as the wit for which his race is proverbial.

Address of Rev. Henry Montgomery.

One of the speakers to-night made out that we made whiskey. But we make more than whiskey. We have sent to America the great Scotch-Irish race that you have that has risen to the top rank in many of the professions of this great land. We have helped to fill some of the finest pulpits of the country with the Scotch-Irish race, so I am glad to represent them, to bring you the glad greetings of the grandest isle on earth. You know we are fond of Ireland. There was a man who was about to visit Ireland, and he said to Bridget, "Bridget," says he, "what message will I take to Ireland for you?" She replied, "Kiss the sod for me." And so we love our native land. We make more than whiskey. We make fine ships; we make the best linen under the sun. Thank God that our industries are not confined to whiskey. Would to God we could banish every distillery off the face of the earth. Liquor is the devil's masterpiece; God wipe it out, that the regeneration of the world may come on.

I am glad to be here, dear friends, because this is the city of revivals. This is the land of Jonathan Edwards; the land where the Holy Ghost has been poured out in extended measure. This city has recently laid to rest the dust of one of the greatest men God ever gave to America,— Dr. Gordon. His name is loved across the sea because of the grace of God that burned in his heart and that shows on every page that ever God helped him to write. Would it not be a grand thing if we, as we went back to our various Endeavor Societies, should ask God to make this coming year the biggest soul-winning year that Christian Endeavorers have ever known? Would not that be right? And why not? We have God in it. Do you remember the difference between the two men who brought back the report from the land of Canaan? The ten men came back from the land of promise and said, "We are grasshoppers, and our enemies are giants. We cannot take the land." Joshua and Caleb, two young men,—thank God for the young men,—came and said, "Yes, we are grasshoppers, and our enemies are giants;" but they dropped a third G— God — in between the two, and said, "We will go and possess the land." Why shall we not "go and possess the land"? Let every young man and every young woman consecrate himself and herself afresh to Jesus Christ to-night, and I tell you the devil will know about it. I want that we shall be a downright nuisance to the devil. I want that we shall be that kind of Christians that the devil will be angry every time he thinks about us.

We have a great violinist in England called Paganini. He went before an audience one night to play. He worked with one string until he broke it, and the audience were much disappointed; then he worked with the second string, and they were more disappointed; but when he went on and broke the third string they fairly hissed. He walk forward and said, "Ladies and gentlemen, one string and Paganini," and he brought such wonderful music out of it that the audience gradually rose on their feet in the intensity of their excitement and applause. "One string and Paganini"—a surrendered soul and God Almighty. What can God not do by the young fellows and the young girls of America if they are surrendered to Jesus Christ? And so to-night I am here in this land of revivals and ask the Endeavorers of this great continent of America to get down on their knees and ask God the Holy Ghost to come and fill you, and if you ask him, America and the ends of the earth will be the better for this Convention. Do you remember how the Apostle Paul went to Ephesus? He did not go down and say, "Are there any Christians in Ephesus?" nor did he say, "There is no pith in them, no good about them." Paul's command to the Ephesians, when they said they had never heard of the religion of Christ, was, "Go down on your knees and you will get it." Then Ephesus was revived, and then the devil had to send a special despatch from hell and a great battalion to oppose him; and here to-night, if we are willing to go down before God and ask him to fill us with his blessed Spirit, there will be souls saved by the hundreds and by the thousands. There are better days before us. You know our friend spoke about the discovery of America. It was a Spaniard that did it. The people said there was no more beyond, but this bold explorer sailed away, and at last the keel of his bark struck upon this great continent. I want to tell you that in the Christian life there is more beyond; there are bigger blessings than we yet have known, if we will ask Jesus Christ for them. So to-night, fellow Endeavorers, one and all, God is willing to bless, God is willing to pour out his Holy Spirit. Before I came away the Endeavor Societies had half-nights of prayer for the outpouring of the Holy Ghost. Why not? We would have spent half a night at a party. And the young people arranged to go home in groups, and some of them arranged to keep one another in their homes. We prayed the Holy Spirit to come upon America and make the ends of the earth better for it.

Peter and John went up into the temple to pray. What do you remember they saw? A lame man. You remember how they said, "In the name of Jesus Christ of Nazareth, get up and walk." The power of the Holy Spirit on a man makes him see the needs of humanity. Turner once went out to see a very beautiful bit of country, and he forgot himself so entirely that finally a young apprentice who was with him said, "I don't see anything very particular in that." "No," said Mr. Turner, "but don't you wish you did?" And when the Spirit of God comes upon us, we begin to see as we never saw before. You know they kill seals with a club. A man whose business it is to kill seals said that one day he was killing seals, when one of them uttered a cry that was so human it reminded him of his child's cry, and he could not kill it. The feeling of kith and kin born in the big sealer's heart is the same spirit that is born in the heart of the Christian, that will lead him to speak to anybody that he can about the great salvation.

Oh, for a fresh anointing of the Holy Ghost for another Pentecostal awakening to breathe over this vast audience! May you go back glad in Jesus, willing to serve, and resolved that you are going to be the best Christian that it is possible for God to make you.

The benediction was pronounced by Rev. James Douglass, from the Island of Trinidad.

Tent Endeavor.

The services in Tent Endeavor were presided over by Trustee Rev. E. R. Dille, D.D., of San Francisco, with Mr. George C. Stebbins as musical director. The attendance was limited only by the capacity of the tent, and in addition to the singing by the chorus and congregation, the musical features of the evening included contributions by the male quartette from the Hampton Institute, and a solo by Mr. Knight.

The devotional exercises were conducted by Rev. Dr. Derrick, of New York City.

Dr. Dille then introduced Rev. H. W. Sherwood, of Rondout, N. Y., an old-time friend of Christian Endeavor, who presented the banner to the local union, for best work in promoting our fellowship, as follows : —

Remarks of Rev. Henry W. Sherwood.

This banner of gold and white is the United Society's banner of Christian fellowship, and is put in charge of that local union which adds the greatest number of new societies to its fellowship during the year. That union will hold it one year, unless it makes so good a record that it can keep its grip upon it for a second year. No word is more precious to Christian Endeavorers than "fellowship." We rejoice greatly in what this banner represents. We rejoice in the Christian fellowship that encircles the world; but we could not rejoice in such a fellowship unless the individual links that bind heart to heart, and society to society, and local union to local union, and State union to State union, and so on to the end — unless each one should perform its part.

This banner is to go to that local union which has done the best service in making Christian Endeavor fellowship a fact, in extending that which it so much enjoys to new churches and new societies which they have been instrumental in forming. It marks a step nearer to that blessed time when the Lord's prayer shall become an answered prayer, when they all shall be one, even as the Father and Son are one.

Christian Endeavor fellowship, in the Christian Endeavor language, does not mean that the individual shall trample under foot any honest conviction. It does not mean that he shall shut his eyes to any position which he holds intelligently before God. It means that hearts have become better acquainted; they more clearly understand the positions of those about them. It means that there is broader sympathy, and while convictions are held with the old tenacity, if not a greater one, hearts are still bound together in a method of work, and such objects as are furnished by the Christian Endeavor fellowship.

This banner was held last year by the local union of the city of Philadelphia, carried home from Cleveland a year ago; a proper place for it, it would seem, because the very name of that local union means " brotherly love." And so, as the Philadelphia Local Union has done the best work in the year past, in adding new societies to its fellowship, this banner returns to the City of Brotherly Love. We will send it back to them with that motto, " Let brotherly love continue," and I will place it in the hands of their representative.

Rev. Wellington E. Loucks, of the Beacon Presbyterian Church of Philadelphia, accepted the banner as follows : —

The locality which has already been named is a peaceful locality, containing a city which dwells in quietude and peace with all within its borders; a city that rises up to distinction on occasions of emergency, and having found out a good thing, knows how to keep it and to preserve it, adding strength and dignity as the days and the years go by.

On behalf of the city of homes we accept this tribute, this gift of the United Society,— a pledge that we are not faithless to the trust of those homes which we represent. Twelve thousand new houses went up in Philadelphia last year, which means the homes of the laborers multiplied, and the blessings of the home circle conserved. There is nothing better for the homes of the city than the life of energetic Christian Endeavor, emphasizing the principles of this Divine institution.

On behalf of her six hundred churches we accept this banner, in pledge that we will keep the committed trusts of " church enterprise," which is a new definition for Christian Endeavor ; and in the spirit of church enterprise we add to the ring the links upon links of societies, banding us in fellowship.

On behalf of the more than four hundred " little red schoolhouses " we accept this banner. We accept it under the enthusiasm of our beloved leader, who, three years ago, sounded the note of loyalty and patriotism united to Christian Endeavor, in the remarkable success which this year crowns in a convention so permeated with the principles of a patriotism that Boston shall never have seen, but possibly one day to eclipse the enthusiasm which she will witness to-morrow, and that the enthusiasm of the day when the blood of America was first shed in her defence, and for her final emancipation.

So we accept this banner, and we treasure it ; and we go back to our quiet city near Fairmount Water Works to engage in the business of Endeavor, in protection of our homes, and for the upbuilding of our churches, and in the defence of our institutions, knowing that the Christian people of any city have it in their power to maintain their institutions, to honor God, and to save souls.

Following the acceptance of the banner, Dr. Dille introduced Rev. G. F. Love, Jr., of Rochester, N. Y. Mr. Love's topic was, "The Christian Home Bureau."

Address of Rev. G. F. Love, Jr.

A novel work has recently been undertaken by the local union of Christian Endeavor of Rochester on behalf of the host of young people who annually come from the country to seek employment in the city. While it is important that these young people should secure good positions, it is not less desirable that they should be established in good homes; and in order to accomplish this our Rochester young people are attempting to assist the newcomers in finding boarding-places in Christian families.

The need of such a work is apparent when one considers how many young people our country churches are constantly losing from their congregations, and how few of them our city churches are receiving. These young people come to the city in large numbers, but few identify themselves with its religious organizations. This is largely due to the fact that all wholesome home restraints have been removed, and that the young people have been thrown among irreligious associates.

A committee, appointed by Congress, after extensive investigation in large American cities, declared the " boarding-house blocks " the source and seat of more vice than any other mode of human habitation. In such places all the religious influences of home life are lost, while bad companions are plentiful. These boarding-houses are frequently poorly furnished, dreary, and almost uninhabitable in winter; they foster homesickness, despondency, unrest, and poor health.

The chances of young people getting into bad boarding-places are more numerous than their chances of getting into good boarding-places, because the bad places are more easy of access, do more advertising, while the more desirable places are exclusive and quite difficult to discover. Those who have tried know that good boarding-places are hard to find.

The Christian Endeavor organization at large is especially adapted to assist young people in finding homes in Christian families. The method employed by the Rochester Union of securing Christian boarding-places requires each society in the city to appoint a committee of one, who secures a list of all members of his church who are willing to take young men or women into their homes. These lists of boarding-places are placed in the hands of a central committee, which is composed of one representative from each of the respective denominations included in the city union. This central committee is called the "Christian Home Bureau," and all applications for boarding-places addressed to it receive immediate attention. This bureau corresponds with the secretaries of societies in the surrounding country churches, and urges them to send on in advance the names of all young people who contemplate coming to the city to live.

It asks for their denominational relations or preferences, and if they desire homes, homes are sought out for them in Christian families of any denomination the young people themselves may designate. In all cases where young women's names are sent on in advance to the committee, a woman guide, who is employed for that purpose, meets the young woman at the railway station, and escorts her to the Young Woman's Christian Association, where she may board at moderate rates for a day or two until a permanent boarding-place may be secured. Guides from the association accompany young women to various homes offered by the bureau, and thus strangers are enabled to inspect the places before making definite arrangements.

This is practical Christianity, and no nobler undertaking could attract our societies of Christian Endeavor.

The earth was nearly encircled by the countries represented on the platform of Tent Endeavor. Not quite "every tribe and nation on this terrestrial ball" have been touched by the influence of Christian Endeavor, but many of them have, and this meeting brought their representatives together in a little "parliament of nations."

FOR ALASKA, MR. EDWARD MARSDEN: — I have the honor to convey to this great Convention the greetings of the Land of the Midnight Sun. Until recently, Alaska was known as nothing but a great refrigerator; but to-day we have learned better. It is not altogether a frozen region, but it is a country of timber for household furnitures, good stone for mansions, fish for dining-room tables, furs for winter clothing, gold and silver for wealth, fields of research for scholars, lofty mountains, grand and majestic sceneries for enjoyment, and peoples, patriotic peoples, for Christian churches, institutions of learning, and commercial and legislative houses.

Not long ago the Alaskans were without the Gospel. They ridiculed losing their old beliefs, their laws, and government. Russian, United States, and English powers could not help them to repent. Military display could not and would not civilize them. There is no earthly power that can change a heathen's dark heart. But there came a time when the Gospel was proclaimed. Some of the Alaskans stood still and listened. " Repent, believe, and confess " was the cry. Some of the Alaskans, as I have said, stood still and listened. It was really a voice in the wilderness. Somehow this voice was irresistibly powerful; it captured some strongholds, and levelled them to the ground. Heathenism is trembling. We have in my country to-day some 6,000 native Christians.

It is fitting that we sit and stand here together and talk about our fellowship, for it is only when we learn from the experiences of others that we can better do our work in our respective fields. In my country we ourselves become Christians first, before we attempt the conversions of others. Guided by the Spirit of God, we proclaim the Gospel in its purity and simplicity. We strongly encourage all kinds of industries, except the rum or other immoral habits. We educate the natives, and we teach them the good laws of the land. We are patriotic, and while we remember our sister nations, the "star-spangled banner" is to us the emblem of brotherhood, liberty, prosperity, victory, salvation. Alaska cries out, as she looks at this great army of Christian Americans, "All hail the power of Jesus' name." From the depths of heathenism and ignorance we have come, and are coming, and will come. Therefore, open your institutions of learning, and commercial and legislative houses, and kindly welcome us in.

For WALES, REV. R. BURGES: — The best proof that I know of that the Christian Endeavor Society is a good thing is that it has been received into our country. The Welsh people are a people who think twice before they speak once. The Welsh people are a people who think well before they accept any new thing, and for years they were thinking as to whether the Christian Endeavor Society was a good society; but, after thinking awhile, and after hearing of the grand work it was doing, Wales received into her midst this grand Society.

I feel it a very great honor to have been associated with the first society in Wales. It was in the year 1888. It was a very small society in the town of Swansea. We never thought when we worked with that society that it ever would assume such splendid proportions in our country, but I am glad to be able to tell you that we could fill this tent with Christian Endeavorers who are in Wales to-night. On our hills and in our valleys are thousands of young people who are singing the praises of Christian Endeavor.

Now, friends, I want to tell you it has revolutionized our people in Christian work; it has revolutionized individuals who were as cold as icicles in Christian work. It has revolutionized families, and made them very energetic in working for Jesus Christ. I know many churches, as dead as a cart-horse, who have been made alive by this splendid Society, and I am not saying too much when I declare that there are some denominations in our country who have been set on fire by this grand Society. I am commissioned by ten or eleven thousand Christian Endeavorers in Wales to bring you their greetings, and I feel that this is the proudest task that ever fell to my lot to perform. I voice all the Christian Endeavorers in Wales, and I bring you with all my heart the best wishes — the deep, heartfelt, best wishes — of the Welsh people. Not only so, but I am commissioned to bring you our thanks. We thank you as American people for sending us such a splendid Society.

For INDIA, MR. PRABALA RAMACHAUDRAYYA GARU: — I come to you from that old, historic country, India, with greetings of joy from the people of that country. They give you greetings because you have shown that in this world

Christianity can practically combine. I bring you tidings from all those who are working in the mission field, from all those whose business it is to fight with heathenism and darkness, and who look upon you with refreshment of heart and with strengthening of souls because they find in you more of the fellowship of Christian brothers and sisters. They look upon you for all help in the way of praying for them. As your name indicates, you are "Endeavorers," Endeavorers to uplift the people of all lands. You are Endeavorers because you have a new element in you, and that element is given one name, namely, "altruism." That is because you are placed under this civilization, just because you are what you are, on account of the practical statesmanship shown by your fathers; and so you are striving by this grand and mighty movement to help all the nations of the world.

In claiming your sympathy, in claiming your help, India is not behind other nations. If there is any country in the world which requires Christian influence, Christian help, Christian civilization, it is India. It is now thought that the whole of India — containing so many races, so many nationalities, no less than three hundred dialects, which the Christians have undertaken to unify — will be unified under one thought of Christian spirit.

Now, Christian Endeavorers, you see the statistics that have been sent to my country. A larger percentage of missionaries has been sent from this country to India than from any other Christian country in the Old World. Now on behalf of India I appeal to you, — in order that you may continue this good work, and in order that you may not be weary in well-doing, and in order that God may give you strength to do this work, — do the best you can. I plead in behalf of India, in order that your religious spirit may be sent to my country, and then, in the last day, before the Lord Jesus Christ, you may all be found there, and it will be known that you have done a great and good work for that country that has fallen and may some day rise through the help of the Christian Endeavorers.

FOR AUSTRALIA, REV. W. J. L. CLOSS: — I have already given a great many of you the greetings of Australia. It is but five years ago since the trade-winds of the South Pacific bore the germ of Christian Endeavor to our shores, and during those five years we have added each year to our Christian Endeavor host exactly the numbers that are in this tent to-night, — if this tent holds 10,000 people, — and we have added them from all denominations; into every evangelical denomination in Australia Christian Endeavor has come and been made welcome. We are the only young people's society in the whole of Australia. We know of no division; our fellowship is one, and by God's help we mean to keep it one. We believe in fellowship with all our hearts and all our souls; and for every thousand Christian Endeavorers in Australia to-day we have sent out a missionary to carry our Christian Endeavor idea of fellowship to the isles of the South Pacific, Japan, China, and India.

While from Australia came the idea of a world's band, a great confederation of all Christian Endeavorers of all colors, of all tongues, and of all lands beneath the sun into one great society of the World's Christian Endeavor Union, that idea found concrete form this afternoon in the Mechanics' Building, and there was formed the World's Christian Endeavor Union. You say, "Where is this thing going to stop?" I don't know. We have been told that if there is any hope of getting up to Mars and finding people there, we will annex that country; we will put a rope around it and bring it over here. At any rate, if we ever do come in contact with that distant planet, I believe we shall make it Christian Endeavor, "for Christ and the Church."

Those who are looking on, who are not imbued with the same spirit of fellowship as we, do not care for this great idea of welding into one.

What does it mean? It means this: all evil, all wrong, everything that disputes with Christ to-day, must cease. It means this: that an emancipated humanity shall claim the whole wide world for Christ. There are visions, not out of golden youth only; there are visions all over the world. What dreamers these Christian Endeavorers are! They have kept their eyes toward the sunrise, and we see the day dawning when the battle-flag shall be furled, when all men shall know Christ, the Nazarene, as their Leader. Shall we rest so long as there is one that does not call Christ master, or stretch out the hand of brotherhood in his name. We are his; he is ours; we live for him, we live in him, we are one in him.

FOR BERMUDA, REV. A. BURROWS : — I hardly know how to realize my own position sufficiently. Though I come from Bermuda and carry the greetings of that little island to this Convention, I wish you to bear in mind that I am not a Bermudan. Some of you know that; others may not.

I heard a good deal to-day about colors. Now I represent the blue. I represent the best of all blues,— a blue sky and blue waters, not to be found anywhere on God's earth the same; and further still, Christian Endeavorers, let me say to you that we need your sympathy. I hope you will give it. We have come a long distance. We have heard men say they came a long distance. I have come nearly one thousand miles to get some good at this Convention, to get my Christian weapons burnished and prepared for better service, to get spiritual strength renewed and spiritual enthusiasm awakened in my own soul. And now I will say to you in conclusion, Christian Endeavorers, go forward. Let that be your motto. Do not be satisfied with what you have at present accomplished, but go forward in the strength of the God of Hosts to do his work, to fight his battles, and to hasten that glorious day when, from the rising of the sun to the going down of the same, the name of our Immanuel shall be great in every land, and all shall acknowledge him as Lord of all.

FOR NORTH AMERICAN INDIANS, MR. DELOS K. LONEWOLF : — It is the very proudest moment of my life to bear the greetings of the former owners of this grand continent of ours. First, we claim your fellowship because you are Christian Endeavorers. We desire your fellowship because you, as an organization, have no committee on the foreign relations, or committee on the Indian affairs.

We love this organization, though few of us have any experiences in it; yet we love it because we are the natives of this country and the organization is a native of this country. We do not believe those have realized it, and know the power of Christianity, who think that education alone will civilize the Indians; but Christian education will civilize the Indians in much shorter time than education alone.

In my experience among white people I came across many so-called Christians who were no better than the Indians whom they desired to teach. Let us teach the Indians by our example, by our consecrated lives, and not so much by our preaching.

The old saying that "the only good Indian is a dead one" is true. But how? I may point, for example, to myself. I am a dead Indian, because the fire of the Gospel of our Lord Jesus Christ has killed the Indian that was in me. Therefore, I say, go to the Indians with the fire of the Gospel of our Lord Jesus Christ, and not with the powder of what you may call your guns. Let us treat the Indians as men, and not as Indians.

One thing I want to say to-night is this: do not call us Indians, but call us —what? [Cries of "Americans, Americans."] That is it; call us Americans, because we have no right to the name of Indians, but we have the right to be called Americans. So much has been said of love of country. We have more right to love this country than you have. Help us to know how to love this country,— not by your own teachings, but by the teachings of our Lord Jesus Christ,— that we may know how to love one another, and through this teaching we will know how to love our country; because if the right teaching will come to us, we will be better citizens, and we are willing and ready, whenever you will open to us the door of your civilization, and the door of citizenship, to enter and be one under one government, under one flag, and under one God.

FOR JAPAN, REV. K. TSUNASHIMA : — It is my honor and privilege to stand on this platform here this evening, and give you greeting in behalf of the United Society of Christian Endeavor of Japan. Here I hold in my hand a letter of congratulation from Rev. Mr. Harada, the president. By this record the Christian Endeavor Society of Japan send you greeting and congratulation here to-night. You call your president "Father Clark;" but we call our president "Young Harada." Yès, he is a young man; he is my friend and classmate. In Japan, not only the Christian Endeavor Society and its president are young, but everything is young. Japan itself is young. Although Japan is one of the old countries in the world, yet she is the newest country on the face of the globe. Her history runs back as far as the sixth century before Christ. The first Emperor of Japan reigned exactly twenty-seven hundred years ago.

Now Japan is new, just forty years old. The history of what we Japanese call "Sinipon," the new Japan, is very new. It dates from the time—I am glad to tell you fellow Endeavorers to-night—thank God, it dates from the time your Commodore Perry, under the Stars and Stripes, bombarded our shores, not with the cannon and quick-firing guns, but with the open Bible before him. You Americans always take so much interest in our country and have done so much we are grateful; we Japanese are grateful for what you have done for us. Here I stand to-night, holding this letter of congratulation, fellow Endeavorers. I congratulate you that you hold this great Convention of the Christian Endeavor Society in this historic city of Boston, in the city of Bunker Hill Monument, in the city of Phillips Brooks, in the city of Alpheus Hardy, who sheltered under his wings a fugitive Japanese boy and turned him, through God's blessing, into a perfect Christian gentleman—not only a Christian gentleman, but the founder of the first Christian University in the Land of the Rising Sun.

I give you greeting here to-night in behalf of my Japanese brethren in this country; in behalf of a hundred thousand Christians in my own native land; in behalf of forty-two millions of people of the sun-rising kingdom; in behalf of the beautiful island of the empire of the far East. May God's blessing rest upon this great land of freedom, upon that beautiful island of the Pacific. God grant a wider spread of his glory.

For Persia, Mr. Jesse Malek Yonan:—If we had a magnificent host of Christian Endeavorers like this in Persia we would have no trouble at all from Kurds. The noblest race in the world, the greatest nation on earth, is America, but America has never produced men so great as her missionaries abroad. From the fanaticism of fire-worship and Mohammedanism in Persia the American missionaries have given us a host of magnificent souls that are Christians. Fifty years ago Persia was the darkest country in the world; to-day we have more than fifteen big colleges for men and women. We have more than sixty missionary stations; but I may say, in spite of great missionary labors, thirty-five organized churches, and great institutions of learning, three hundred thousand square miles of my country has never been taught of Christ. Mohammedanism is going down. The Mohammedan religion is divided into numerous sects and is going to naught. But I may say the drift is not for Christ. This must be confronted with a great host of Christian Endeavorers.

A cry from women comes to you while you enjoy your magnificent meetings and while you sing. Persian women are groaning for freedom of religion. They ask for it. They steal to a mission tent; they sit and hear the words of life with tears, and get strength enough to endure the sufferings and beatings of profligate husbands. They ask for the Gospel; you have to give it to them. Men and women and children by thousands are killed, are buried alive, for the religion of Christ, and they ask your help. If there is a nation in the world that will bring freedom into Persia it is the Christian Endeavorers of America, and I shall live to see a great host of Christian Endeavorers joined with you in Persia.

For Africa, Miss Anna Cummings:—I hope none here to-night are disappointed that Afric's representative is not of dusky hue. The greetings I bring to you from the Christian Endeavorers of South Africa are none the less hearty. In no country in the world is history making faster to-day than in the so-called "Dark Continent." The nations of the earth are vying with one another in opening up the land through the extension of railway, telegraph, and other commercial enterprises. Even Thomas Cook & Son are organizing excursions to Bangweolo, the heart of Matabele Land, where we hope one day to welcome the Convention of Christian Endeavor. For what are these doors so widely opening? The Christian Endeavorers of South Africa are answering, "For Christ and his Church," and they are marching on from home and school, from college and training institute, to take possession of this promised land in the name of Christ, their King. The Christian Endeavor movement was born in South Africa, in the Huguenot Seminary, a school founded by Rev. Andrew Murray, that man of God whose life and words have brought blessing to many a soul the wide world around. Many here will be glad to know that he who represents also the head of the South African Christian Endeavor Union will visit these shores next month and bring to the Northfield Conference his words of help and inspiration.

The Christian Endeavor in South Africa is essentially a missionary movement. To its members have come with clarion call the command of Christ: "Go ye, preach the Gospel," and with ready response they are making answer: "Here am I; send me; send me." The diamond fields of Kimberly, the gold fields of Johannisberg, the mountain fastnesses and the upper waters of the Zambesi are echoing with the refrain: "One is our Master, all we are brethren," and to-night the message that this missionary of the Christian Endeavorers of Africa sent by me to you is that Christianity was wafted long ago over the waters. Come over and help us, that we may win Africa for Christ.

The concluding address of the evening was made by Rev. Edwin Heyl Delk, Hagerstown, Md., the subject being, "The Centrality of Christian Fellowship."

Address of Rev. Edwin Heyl Delk.

Our century has witnessed the rise and fall of three promised saviours of society. Democracy, science, and socialism have each, in turn, been declared the sure roads to civic order and social satisfaction. The attainment of our American autonomy and the French Revolution of 1789 made possible the experiment in Democracy. The Declaration of Independence, penned by Jefferson, and the Rights of Man, framed by the brilliant Frenchman, Dumont, came to downtrodden peoples like a new gospel of emancipation. In France, feudalism was overthrown, and the dogma of the equality of man proclaimed from the housetops. No student of history can regret or ignore the exhilaration and hope created by this bold Democratic manifesto. The promises made by the French National Assembly, and the glittering watchword of the Revolution,— "Liberty, Equality, Fraternity,"—came like the evangel of an opulent peace to the liberated Parisians. The ideal presented was entrancing. The promise of political equality and social satisfaction filled the imagination with visions of national glory and economic abundance. How did the promises of Democracy fulfil themselves? Let us give speedy honor to all the benefits that have come to us through the Democratic principle. Absolutism and class privilege have been broken. The sovereignty of the nation has been accepted. Every worthy citizen enjoys the privilege and duty of political self-expression. The people as a whole, and not a titled aristocracy, is the first class considered by modern legislation. Yes, Democracy has accomplished many reforms, and secured for us liberties for press and pulpit, school and forum. But the conviction deepens that, beyond the form of government, the real question is the question of individual character. Dumont himself asked, "Are all men equal? Where is the equality? Is it in virtue, talents, fortune, industry, situation? Are they free by nature? So far from it, they are born in a state of complete dependence on others, from which they are long of being emancipated." The value of Burke's attack on the exaggerations of revolutionary Democracy is receiving new evidence as we begin to realize that no one form of government assures social peace and perfection. You can't build a cathedral out of chunks of mud. However wise and just may be the plan of a government, the mere form will not save the individual or the citizenship as a whole. Democracy, as a social saviour, has failed us. The corruption and poverty of New York is

VIEW OF DECORATED BUSINESS HOUSES ON WASHINGTON STREET.

as pitiable and great as in Berlin or St. Petersburg. The very champions of Democracy cry out for a fresh ally in the work of civic and social betterment. The next aspirant for social regeneration was science. Disgusted with the scholastic restrictions and methods of Mediævalism, the seekers after nature's origins and actions discarded the formulas and speculative methods of the cloister and bookmen, and, by the path of immediate contact with rock and human organism, determined to ferret out the secret of the universe. "Give us time, and we will tell you the ultimate truths of all life — organic, inorganic, and spiritual." Science promised us the final revelation of truth and goodness. In the middle decades of our century she was boisterous, if not positively arrogant, in her claim to dominate all other teachers and leaders in thought. Who will deny that Bacon, Faraday, and Huxley, with their inductive method of approach to nature, have given us the true principle of discovery? Science has made splendid conquests in the realm of lower nature, and given us sure rules and sane ideas in the realm of hygiene and civic comfort. The reign of law is no small lesson to have taught the world. Her lesser gifts of electrical apparatus, chemical products, studies in primitive life forms, and her impressive tracings of the evolutionary advance toward man are joy and crown enough for any body of human investigators. But as a guide and motive power in individual and social life, science has failed us in our greatest hours of need. Geology, biology, sanitation, and vaccination do not touch the vitals of life. Proven science has no final word to offer on all the deepest and ultimate problems of life. Whence come all things? What is man, — his conscience, his prayer, — and whither is he going? Toward these ultimates science is agnostic or impatient. The first cause as well as the final cause of the universe are beyond her ken. In the presence of poverty, social injustice, moral depravity, and the spiritual outcries of the soul she sits like the impassive Sphinx amid the hot, throbbing desert of life. Her votaries, who once shouted themselves hoarse in the so-called "Warfare of Science and Religion," have finally discovered that, on the proper field of science, there is no battle with real religion at all; that science cannot even advance into territory of true religion without acknowledging a superior power to mere intellect. Pure science, as a social leader, has suffered defeat, and passes the ultimate problems of life over to the moralist and theologian. Man's social and spiritual questionings demand a more competent and effective leader.

Midway in the century, socialism arose to declare that the governmental ownership and direction of all the productive and distributive forces of the nation would usher in the reign of international peace and plenty. Poverty was declared the root of all evil. Labor was proclaimed the source of all values. Marx's book, "Capital," became the Bible of the discontented workmen of Germany, France, and England. "Once reorganize the industrial life of the nation," he advised, "on the basis of socialism, and then shall be ushered in the reign of social peace and plenty," How eagerly the cry was taken up! How true was much of the picture he presented! Poverty, hatred, a brutal fight for employment, disease, disgust, hopeless submergence of the lowest stratum, overcrowded poorhouses, useless charities, and aristocratic contempt for Democratic aspirations — all this was the groundwork and reason for industrial reformation. To transform the social order then seemed simple enough. His shallow philosophy and economic fallacy was hid in a mist of statistics and prejudice. Democracy had brought political equality; socialism would insure equal industrial opportunity. In time, this would lead to every social satisfaction. Industrial organization was declared the pivotal point in social well-being. Socialism had not yet accepted Hegel's words: "The social order, however omnipotent it may seem, is limited and finite, and man has in him a kindred with the eternal." In a word, man has other and higher needs than the merely economic and civil satisfactions. "Man cannot live by bread alone." No! nor by education, yachts, and brownstone fronts. The range of man's needs encompasses all loves, charities, and purities, both human and Divine. Slowly but surely even the leaders of socialism are beginning to realize the impotency of merely industrial and educational reform for the uplifting and completion of life.

One of the most notable books of the year was written by a brilliant and well-to-do Oxonian. The book is entitled, " The Melancholy of Stephen Allard." This modern Burton — after trying to satisfy his life, first, by scientific research, then in philosophic examination; by poetic form and insight; through artistic color and story; then by the moralities of Aurelius and Comte; later by the mysticism of modern religionism; afterward by the invigorations of travel and action; subsequently by the delights of love — came, at last, to realize the futility which follows every attempt at social and personal satisfaction. The *Journal of Amiel* and the pessimistic philosophy of Schopenhauer are not exceptional aspects of modern thought and literature. The " Decadents " are a respectable minority. Permit me to use the better words of " Ian Maclaren ": —

" We are living at the close of the century, and the last years of the century are suffering from the decrepitude and from the failings of old age. The blood of the century is running thin and cold, and the hopes of the century are few and dark. There is no great poet left us; there is no great novelist left us; there is no man now for the coming of whose books we hunger and thirst, or which would cause us to make preparations that we might sit up all night to read it to the breaking of the day. These men are gone, and smaller men are in their places. Science herself, which had a career of such singular success and glory, is not making great advances now, but is rather gathering up the fruit of earlier discoveries. No wonder there are men who are cynical; no wonder literature is pessimistic; no wonder an able writer, who published his book and died, declared that there are no more conquests for science and literature, no more achievements for the human race. There is only one institution on the face of the earth to-day that carries the dew of her youth, and that is Christianity. I do not mean the Christianity which is engaged simply in criticism, however useful these exercises may be; there is no heart for a man there. I do not mean, either, the Christianity which is peddling away with questions as to how long a man is to work and how much he is to get, for men of spirit want to work every moment, and ask only the reward of having done their duty; there is no inspiration there. I mean the old Christianity and first Christianity; the Christianity that centres around the person of the Son of God; the Christianity with the lifted head and the eternal sunshine upon her face. There are old men here to whom it is no matter how the century ends, for they have to do with the land where the centuries have passed away. There are some here who are past middle age; but I speak to you young men, before whom life is stretching far. If you despair of the life of the race, of yourselves, and the future that is stretching before you, you had better die at once. It is that which enfeebles a man, that which makes a man yield to fleshly sins. There is no future for him. Climb the mast, climb the mast till you are out of the mists and sea-fog that lie on the surface of the water; climb to the top, and you will see that marvellous spectacle of the spiritual world stretching far into the distant blue of the sea, and near at hand the sunshine on the vessel of sweet content. I do not say that any man can remain at the top of the mast; you will have to come down again. But how differently will you come down after a glimpse of Eternity! You will come down to work in the vessel that passes through many shoals, assured that the shadows may disappear, and you will see the kingdom of God in its glorious brightness where the sun is shining upon us evermore."

What are the factors in Christianity which give it the effective and central position among all the forces which go to the conserving and regeneration of society? In a sentence I reply. The Fatherhood of God, the brotherhood of man, and the regeneration of the individual life. These three factors find their expression and fulfilment in a person, — Jesus Christ and his continuous life throughout the centuries.

In these last days we have heard a great deal about brotherhood and fellowship. We have much so-called brotherhood which is only class organization for material benefit. Engineers, plasterers, Irish clans, privy orders, German turnvereins, Internationalists, and trades-unionism are but class or party clubs, not pretending to include employer, or women, or men of alien race, the poor, the rich, the strong, the weak, the saint, and sinner, but their basis and circle of brotherhood stop with a restricted membership and a section of society. Defiance of the public will and weal has characterized some of their actions.

At best, they are mutual benefit societies, not much higher in their spirit and operation than the insurance company and social club. A brotherhood with such an insecure and limited basis will not reach far nor mount high. Humanitarianism in all its phases, without religious re-enforcement, has proven a pathetic failure.

Christian brotherhood has a far richer origin, sweep of interest, and power of reconstruction. Christian fellowship has its birth in the belief in God, — in God the Father, who art in heaven, who has made of one blood all men who dwell beneath the skies. The one Father makes possible the many brothers. Eliminate his creatorship and will from the brotherhood and it goes to pieces upon the rocks of self-interest and racial antagonisms. God is the first cause, the author of the moral law, and the source of love's fellowship. He is the creative centre of all sympathies and all holy ideals of the State. His kingdom is the goal of history. He is the answer to humanity's perplexities and sufferings and aspirations. Society without God could be parelleled only by the chaos of hurtling planets without a central sun. Christian fellowship is unique because it has enthroned above it a creative power and intelligence guiding all cosmic and social law. Given this incentive and goal of God, the Father, and the whole of life is swept within the sphere of assured faith and abiding love.

Christian fellowship is no less unique in its conception of the solidarity of society. Long before the economic dogma of social solidarity became an accepted fact in practical statesmanship, St. Paul had declared: " Ye are all members one of another. If one member suffers, all the members suffer with it ; or one member be honored, all the members rejoice with it." It would be wrong to quote these words, however, as his belief in the modern theory of mutual social dependence. He believes that, and something more. His social solidarity was a spiritual oneness in Christ. It was an organism of dependence, but dependence upon a central spiritual Master. It was a brotherhood not for individual advantage through an organization, but an association of individuals for the uplift of the whole of society. The incarnate Son of God was to be its Supreme Head. His life and will were to be both law and life. As the Father had sent him into the world to be the friend of pauper and sinner, so Christ sent his work-fellows into the world to encompass with the gospel of peace all classes, all conditions, all nationalities. There is a brotherhood larger than trade, than Church, than black and white, than country ; that brotherhood is the kingdom of God. I call this brotherhood Christian because Jesus Christ is the only sufficient propulsive force for the realization of such a supernal ideal. No man cometh unto the Father but by him, and no man cometh unto his fellowman truly until he comes in the spirit of Jesus Christ. That modern Christian knight, the Earl of Shaftesbury, pushing a costermonger's cart along a London street, in order to express his sympathy and gain the experience of their hard life ; the modern university settlements amid the squalor and emptiness of the average day-laborer's section of the city; the self-consecration of many a city missionary to the rescue of criminal and outcast; the tender consideration of many a high-bred woman for the woes of orphaned childhood and more helpless old age; the resolute faith of the plain deaconess confronted by the hot passion and grief of a dissolute woman; the daring attack on slavery and intemperance and corporate greed by a disinterested minister; the outpoured wealth for pagan souls beyond the seas — all declare the supremacy and graciousness of that brotherhood which has Calvary for its controlling centre.

This recalls the third element in Christian fellowship, — the regeneration of the individual. The elemental defect in our social life is not organization, but character. The discord which breeds the bulk of our intemperance, crime, and pauperism has its source in a distorted moral nature. The root of all crime, pride, hate, lust, and murder is selfishness. Great as is the light and power given through education and legislation, not until these two splendid arms of the social body are directed in their work by a purified heart can they accomplish the highest civilization. Every member of an educational board or labor union knows that the most beneficent programme of social improvement is a mere paper constitution until invigorated and executed by strong moral impulse. It is because men are shiftless, arrogant, suspicious, and piggish that all our fine schemes of co-operation and universal culture go to pieces. At Exeter Hall, in London, at the close of a great labor demonstration, an old mechanic was called upon to make the closing speech. It was short, but it hit the nail on the head He said, "The speakers who have preceded me have spoken of the urgent need of legislation to redress our wrongs, and of education for the working men's children. This is all right. Legislate, legislate, legislate; educate, educate, educate; but let no man forget our greatest and most important work is to regenerate, regenerate, regenerate."

The great need of humanity is faith in God and man. Without the purity born of God, and self-sacrifice like unto the Son of Man, the social ideals painted by socialists and poets, however worthy, are but tantalizing and impossible fantasies.

To be more specific, permit me to indicate several spheres where this Christian fellowship should be made the central and controlling principle. First, in the industrial life of society. The labor question is not a question of mere justice. Whatever may be the form of industrial organization, whether it be the wages, system, co-operation, or State socialism, the ultimate question is the question of complete and satisfied manhood. Though the employer may pay every cent of a rightful wage; even if he is willing to share his profits with his employees; if in the co-operative establishment all the shareholders get their promised part of interest and benefit on the invested capital; granted, if you will, the establishment of nationalism or socialism in the industrial world, where "each according to his ability, and all according to their need" receive the benefits of production and consumption, still no true man would be satisfied with bare justice. *There must be a reciprocity of manhood as well as of dollars before we can look for social peace.* To give a man his wages and refuse him respect will not satisfy for long. To establish a public bath by the writing of a liberal check, and then to write with the same pen a supercilious article on "the lower classes" is a contradiction in form, if not in spirit, which will not be tolerated. To give a man his price of labor and not your praise of his workmanship is withholding the truest and most pleasing incentive to toil. Better than dividing your fortune is the distribution of manly sympathy. It is the invisible part of your estate, the part which the law, or the strike, cannot touch, which the working man really craves. I know they repudiate charity, and demand, in their platforms, "mere justice," but all the while they want something much richer and truer than simple justice. Justice does not cast out envy and jealousy. Among millionaires greed and hate are no strangers. Equal wealth is no defence against civil and moral distraction. The labor problem is pre-eminently a moral problem. It is a cry for the recognition of the essential manhood of every true worker in every sphere of life.

Now it is to this fundamental need that Christian fellowship directs its beneficent powers. "One Father, one blood, and one destiny." With these words emblazoned on its banner, it leads the world's teachers and philanthropists, its educators and artisans, its foremen and managers, its superintendents and boards of directors, into that larger justice which is sometimes mercy, but always love.

I wish, in the second place, to show the centrality of Christian fellowship in all movements toward a better civic order and morale. Municipal pride and economic taxation may arouse to spasmodic reform. Revelations of corrupt official life have shocked us into moral consciousness. Huge steals by bibulous aldermen and interested councilmen may cause us to rally around the public treasury, but neither civic pride nor a rifled corporation furnish a heroic or continuous motive in the fight for law and order. It is not institutions, but men, that most need saving. It is because such abuse of office breeds moral rot in every avenue of public and private life that we seek to reform an administration or an institution. I am sure our civil war took on nobler proportions when, added to the purpose of preserving the Union, it became a battle for the rights of man, — the liberation of four million slaves. It is because the city exists for man, not man for the city, that the arousement of the public conscience is such a splendid event in our national life. We Americans must never forget who has been our prophet in this new crusade. It is a man fired by Christian faith and determination. Parkhurst is first and foremost a lover of men; this makes him invincible in his fight for probity and decency in the administration of public trusts. It is not until we love men supremely that we can conquer our fear and sloth and march forth to retake the citadel of public justice. Christian fellowship answers the question, "Who is my neighbor?" by declaring, "Every tempted boy and tremulous girl, every unfortunate of the street and asylum, every lodger in our tenement-houses and majestic avenues, every bullied apple-woman and garment-worker, every boss-taxed clerk and harried millionaire." What are clean, smooth pavements worth, save as related to man's health and easy walk? What are wharves and piers, save as they make easy access for the cheapened food for the citizen? What significance has electric plant and water supply, save as they guide and refresh the homeward bound and thirsty? Why build the stately palaces of State, if not to impress the sense of reverence for law and order? Why paint our pictures and rear our art galleries, if not to call out man's latent power of observation and love of beauty? Why construct our noble cathedrals, unless to tell the story of man's unquenchable aspiration for the beauty of holiness? Man, it is man back of all sciences, arts, and institutions that gives vigor and value to all our toil and heroism. The truest patriotism is bred of Christian fellowship. Back of so much dirt and rock, streets and houses, charters and constitutions, stands a human history made by men of our own blood, and whose lives are our heritage, calling out our reverence and love and devotion to the arms and institutions they bequeathed. Well may Taylor sing: —

> " The bravest are the tenderest;
> The loving are the daring."

May I mention another realm of thought and action where fellowship holds the central place in the co-ordination of divided forces? I refer to the Christian Church. A union of the sects of Christendom or a synthesis of their various confessions is, in my own mind, a waning belief. I am still hoping against hope. There stands that prayer of Christ: " That they all may be one." So long as that prayer stands in Holy Scripture, so long I am compelled to realize the spiritual oneness of all believers. I am not sure just what he means. Good men tell us it means organic union, having one institution, and that organized on the Episcopal plan. Well, I am ready for that, provided the Episcopus is not an arrant autocrat. But would any form of church organization make us one in Christ Jesus? No; we need something more than polity. Some scholars would carry us back of all denominational history and creed-making, and put us down in the first century of the Church, and bid us be satisfied with the confession of the first disciples. But what was that confession? And, if we had it, would that insure Christian unity? No, not so long as men are born with their varied mental and emotional tendencies. There is something more precious than uniformity, and that is Christian liberty. What, then, must be the central power for the unifying of Christian activity? One thing is certain: we must have more Christian unity before we dare expect more church unity. Here our cherished power of love, which is considerate, humble, gentle, forgiving, generous, and full of faith, is the dominant factor in the co-ordinating of individual churchmen. It is to the men of this large Christian love in all the denominations, and not to the narrow ecclesiastics, that we look for that spiritual unity contemplated by Jesus. For " Christ " first, for " the Church " second, for " my denomination " last. This must be the historical and affectional order if we are really serious about the union of Christendom. One thing is certain: where there is constant rancor and self-assertion there can be no Christ. The faith once delivered to the saints was not an elaborated creed or a hierarchy of spiritual prerogatives, but an abounding trust in Jesus Christ as the Saviour and Lover of all mankind. I glory in my Lutheranism, because I believe it to be a pure Paulinism, and Paul the largest and truest interpreter of Christ. The nearer we get to Christ, the closer will we come to one another. This is the attractive feature in our Christian Endeavor Society. *We must have a confederacy of the churches before we can have a unification of the Church.*

The last sphere to be mentioned, in which I believe Christian love must be made the central and controlling motive of action, is in the individual life. Whether it be a system of theology or a single Christian life that is to tell for God, the love of God in Christ Jesus must be put at the core of the structure. The doctrine of the incarnation has taken on new significance in our age, because the recovered Christ has been seen to be the personalization of God's love. Among the Christian graces Paul makes charity, or love, supreme. Above the faith which clings to Christ for redemption, beyond the hope which strains its prophetic eye into the age of the completed Kingdom, reigns the constraining power of love, — love which suffereth long and is kind; love which envieth not, vaunteth not itself, is not puffed up; love which endureth all things and never faileth. Prophecies may fail, tongues may cease, knowledge shall vanish away; but love shall abide triumphant over every ill and sorrow of life. What force is more needed in our daily lives than just this Divine attribute? If men were ruled by this principle in the marts of trade, in the realm of science, in the home, in the church, in the university, on the playground, in the social circle, what a revolution would be accomplished, how like a new Eden this old brutal world would become! "A little child shall lead them." The day seems far off as yet. The vast standing armies of Europe, the struggle for existence among the masses of men, the ruthless licentiousness among all classes, the wasteful luxury among the unemployed rich and improvident poor, the blank materialism among so many, the reckless race for power among our political aspirants, seem to be all too resistless a combination to be halted and subdued by anything short of the Archangel Michael himself. But we hold by our central principle, — "Not by might, nor by power, but by my word, saith the Lord of hosts." Let us bring all our learning, all our discovery, all our art, all our science, all our legislation, all our poetry, to this central figure of love. Let her firm warm hand be laid in consecration on all your talents and opportunities and struggles. Let her lips rest upon your brow before you go forth to the battle of life. In her name Paul, John, Jesus, won their glorious triumphs over Pharisaism, Grecian thought, and Satan's power. By love's power the gory forum of Trojan and Nero was closed and Cæsar's palace captured. By love's might the German forests were pierced and made vocal by Christian song; by love's venture England's isles were redeemed from brutal butcheries and darksome faiths. By love's propulsion out into East, West, North, and South, the heralds of the Cross have gone to bring civilization and joy to haunts of vice and pestilence. By love's might Christ came down and bore in his uplifted hands a whole world's sin up to the pardoning Throne of God. And ever since, in nursery and on battle-field, the thrill of his redeeming love has given nerve and faith to mother love and manhood's noblest sacrifice.

I remember standing before the altar of Westminster Abbey. Behind that altar were the tombs of England's illustrious Kings and Queens, the shrine of Edward, and the chapel where the body of Henry of Agincourt sleeps its glorious sleep. To my left, in the north transept, were the marble statues of England's great statesmen and naval heroes. Turning toward the south transept, the tablets and busts of "Poet's Corner" recalled the pilgrims of Chaucer, the immortal dramas of Shakespeare, and the heroics of Milton. Standing in the north aisle of the Abbey, one looks upon the two floor-slabs which bear the names of Darwin and of Livingstone, the monuments to Harvey and to Pitt. Down the main aisle, as we approach once more the altar, bard, soldier, musician, actor, physicist, and philanthropist in silent effigy look down upon us. Around, above us, rear in sculptured symmetry, a forest of stone columns and over-arching traceries. The music of the great organ behind us commenced to move and swell into every bay and nook of the ancient minster. Slowly and unconsciously our eyes turned to the very centre and heart of this vast mausoleum of the world's great masters, — the reredos behind the altar. There, painted with his first disciples, stood the Man of Galilee, with hands outstretched to bless and to command the inmates of that vast cathedral. Yes, he was and is the true centre of the world's best thought and life. He is the commanding centre of all noble action and discovery. The uplifted Face, in the centre of the world's history, gives significance to every war and constitution, every grief and joy, every struggle for the emancipation of man, every poem and oratorio, every love and hate, every drama acted and king dethroned, every passion conquered, and every prayer wrung from the heart of stricken men. Here, at last, in his life, we have found the centre of all loves and Divine fellowships.

As I close, no one more than I realizes how imperfect and crude has been the presentation of this noble theme. I have wished that another voice than mine had plead for this principle and ideal of society. An inspired pen would be none too choice to arouse and declare the majesty of the fellowship which has Christ for its creative and controlling centre. But I am satisfied, if in any way, however rude, I have led you to the beginnings of that pathway which, broadening upward, opens at last into the City of God, where all great poetry and noble prophecy find their fulfilment in a fellowship made perfect in our joint-heirship with Jesus Christ.

Berkeley Temple — Overflow Meeting.

The overflow meeting at Berkeley Temple was characterized by brief and pointed addresses.

Rev. Smith Baker, D.D., of East Boston, presided, and introduced Trustee Rev. James L. Hill, D.D., of Salem, Mass.; Rev. D. M. Pratt, of Portland, Me., Pastor of Williston Church; Rev. H. M. Pope, of New Haven, Conn.; Rev. Edward S. Young, of Newark, N. J.; Col. H. H. Hadley, of St. Bartholomew's Mission, New York, N. Y., and others.

SATURDAY MORNING.

Mechanics' Building.

The vast auditorium was filled early, and the singing was of greater volume than on any similar occasion thus far.

The regular praise and prayer service was opened at 9 o'clock,— half an hour ahead of time,— under the direction of Mr. George C. Stebbins, of Brooklyn. Mr. Stebbins, in returning thanks for the greeting paid him, complimented the choir and audience very highly, saying they sang better than any body of similar magnitude he had ever conducted.

Trustee Rev. J. Z. Tyler, D.D., of Cleveland, O., and the audience read Psalm XXIV. in alternate verses, and the clergyman offered prayer, concluding with the Lord's Prayer, in the recital of which the assemblage joined. Then the choir and audience sang "Sweet Peace."

Trustee Rev. H. F. Shupe, of Dayton, O., the chairman of the session, in opening the regular proceedings referred to the fact that this was "International Citizenship Day," and introduced Rev. C. M. Southgate, of Worcester, Mass., who presented the banner to the city union having reported the best work accomplished for Christian citizenship.

Address of Rev. C. M. Southgate.

In promoting Christian citizenship, Endeavorers are saints, but not set up in niches, or to be put in glass cases.

There are several millions of them, and when those several millions get after anything, it had better surrender. I have noticed a sensational "scare head" at the beginning of a convention story in the newspaper,— "Satan is fleeing." Well, let him flee. Boston has been long enough "between the devil and the deep sea." Take him ten miles outside of Minot's Light and give him in charge of the Floating Endeavor Society. Young people have got longer to live in this world than old people, so that the evils of bad citizenship hurt them more than the old people. They own to-morrow. Whoever may be the up-to-date Christian century people of to-day, the young people are the to-morrow century people. They are going to see the next century well toward the twenty-first.

I do not hear anybody objecting to their taking hold. There is work enough for everybody. No school moderator has stood up and said, "Young man, you sit down; when God wants to convert these political heathen he will do it without your help or mine."

The young people own to-morrow, and they are bound to "get there," if you please. What is more, it is a society, a young people's society. The reason why bad citizenship is so bold in fight and so hard to conquer is because of its splendid organization. We are here as a society that has business on its hands. It is organization that is going to carry this thing through, and here is a Society that is organized already. This Society will be alive when special emergencies are past.

And then another thing: it has in its ranks womanhood, and there is nothing in this world so winning for a good cause, and there is nothing, let us say it frankly, so determined as womanhood. What she wants, she is bound to have. If she starts for anywhere she is going to get there, and anything that she takes along with her is going to get there, too.

The next word is Christian, Christian; and I dare affirm that no man can be a good Christian in these days without being a good citizen. He has got to be a citizen, and it behooves him to be a good citizen. The Lord Jesus Christ was not primarily a political reformer, but the spiritual force he embodied and the spiritual lives he inspired worked out into social and moral reform as surely as the heated, boiling water works out into steam-power. These evils of bad citizenship work through into souls and lives. You cannot keep them within the bounds of politics. They are wrongs upon God's children. They hinder the coming of God's kingdom. There was a man who went to New York because he wanted to get hold of the young men there. But he said, "I found the young men were walking all the week on the edge of a Tammany hell, when I had them only one day."

There is only one flag that ever floats above the Stars and Stripes. It is not the flag of any of these nations or of any organization; but on our great ships of war, when Divine service is being held, the Stars and Stripes float just below a white pennant with a blue cross upon it. We had a new holiday to celebrate here in Massachusetts,— Flag Day,— when the scholars sang in their schools, "Red, White, and Blue, Wave On." But there is one song that blends with that, and sweeps above it,— "In the Cross of Christ I Glory, Towering O'er the Wrecks of Time," and the conquests of time lift high the royal banner.

Then endeavor, endeavor. That means, "If at first you don't succeed, try, try again." There was a man who told me on the train this morning about an Irishman who was arrested for striking a man twice. "Did you strike him twice?" "Yes," he said; "I struck him once on the nose, and once where the nose was." During a military engagement a squad of men rushed up and cried, "We've captured a flag, general." Said he, "That's right, boys, take another." Lawrence tells a story about a camp of rebels in India, where a deputation from the fort came to meet the besiegers. They went out, and they saw a couple of huge elephants slowly and majestically dragging up eighteen-pound guns tandem fashion, with one pushing behind. They went back without a word to their fort, and in an hour the white flag was flying. Now, when Christian consecration is yoked with youthful enthusiasm, and pushed behind by a splendid organization, look out for the white flag of surrender.

Brother Kinney, of Syracuse, into worthy hands, with the congratulations of this great Convention, this magnificent Endeavor Society, and with the blessing of Almighty God, I give this banner because you have already fulfilled the prophecy: "When the enemy shall come in like a flood, then the Spirit of the Lord shall lift up a standard to them that fear him."

MR. KINNEY: We do not feel at Syracuse that we deserve this beautiful banner, but we will deserve it by the help of God.

Syracuse is an inland city of 127,000 inhabitants, beautifully located at the northern intersection of the New York Central Railway with salt water. Every Syracusan present wears a little badge, a bag of salt. It is labelled, "Christian Endeavor Salt." The bags are pendant from yonder Syracuse banner — of salt. Not that we are the "salt of the earth," however. But all you Christian Endeavorers and all good Christians are. In Syracuse we have but applied a little pinch of Christian Endeavor salt to the politics of the city. Salt is good for brine, and we have put a few politicians in a "pickle." Salt is good for freezing, and we have frozen some bad men out of office. From salt comes soda, and from soda comes baking-powder, and we are told that that is absolutely pure; and we have brought in a new purity into our politics. We are a little bit of leaven in the lump. Salt gives good taste to food, and things taste better in Syracuse because of our Christian Endeavor good-citizenship work. Salt is used in the making of glass, and we have let a little daylight in upon some dark political methods. From salt comes soap, and we have soaped Syracuse a little.

You remember that a little maid told the great Syrian captain how to get rid of the leprosy. The remedy was to go and bathe in the Jordan, and they put him in once, and it was said, "Put him in again; put him in again." Seven times he was bathed in the Jordan; and we have endeavored through our young women in Syracuse to see that the leprosy of our times in politics shall in some measure and manner be washed away.

We accept this banner in the name of Christ and our Christian Endeavor pledge and our Christian Endeavor purposes.

Mr. Shupe then introduced Hon. Elijah A. Morse, who spoke on the question of good citizenship. They applauded the well-known congressman, and it was several moments before the people quieted down to listen to his address.

Address of Hon. Elijah A. Morse.

This is "International Citizenship Day;" and one of the objects of this association and this monstrous Convention is to promote good citizenship. This great organization spans the continent and the world, and we have present here to-day representatives from other peoples and nationalities besides our own. A good Christian Endeavorer is loyal to the country and flag under which he lives. Under other forms of government than our own, the affections of the people naturally cluster around the monarch who sits upon the throne, — the King, Queen, Emperor, or Czar; and they are wont to cry out, "Long live the Queen," "Long live the King," or "Long live the Emperor." Having no such centre of attraction in our own free government, the affections of the people naturally cluster around the old flag, the flag whose azure blue set with stars symbolizes the starry firmament of God.

Good Christian Endeavorers love their country, their rulers, and their flag, and they are loyal to the same. And our foreign visitors will allow us, on this "International Citizenship Day," to do homage to our flag, and to cry out, "Long live the Republic." It is proper on this occasion, as we enumerate the qualifications of good citizenship, to recall the admonition of George Washington, which applies to every country and every land. In his farewell address he admonished his countrymen that education, virtue, and religion were the only enduring foundations of national greatness and glory. And the student of the Old Testament Scriptures, as he reads of God's dealings with his ancient people, gets this residuum out of the crucible: that when the children of Israel obeyed God's laws, and walked in his ways, honor, prosperity, and peace attended them as a nation. When they disobeyed God, and set at naught his council, and went after strange gods, and worked wickedness in his sight, then disaster and sorrow and misfortune overtook them as a nation. So it ever has been in the history of the world; so it ever will be, till time shall be no more.

Another element of good citizenship, and conducive thereto, is a sacred religious regard for the Sabbath Day as a day of rest and surcease from toil. The command given on Sinai, " Remember the Sabbath Day to keep it holy," was given for every nation and every people, for that century, for the nineteenth and twentieth centuries, and for the two hundredth century, if the world shall continue so long. And I firmly believe that the prosperity of any individual, family, state, or nation may be measured by their regard for the holy Sabbath Day. The command to observe it is side by side with " Thou shalt not steal," " Thou shalt not bear false witness," "Thou shalt not commit adultery." Christian Endeavorers love and defend the Sabbath Day.

Another enemy of good citizenship in every land is the awful saloon curse, an enemy of God and man,— that awful maelstrom that destroys the body and the soul. You are told there are millions in it, and you are asked " By what authority do you demand its surrender ? " I will answer for you: in the name of the great God and humanity. Of all the engines that the devil ever invented to destroy the bodies and souls of men, to destroy the peace of families, and to debauch and degrade the citizen, the saloon curse beats them all. Our cause is the cause of God ; we have a Captain that never lost a battle, and our final triumph over this enemy of God and man is assured. A hopeful sign of the time is the monstrous polyglot petition, praying the nations, monarchs, legislatures, and rulers of the earth to suppress the opium and drink curse. This monstrous petition was presented to our government last winter. It is now in England. It bears the signatures of one million, one hundred and fifty thousand persons, and the names of societies with an aggregate membership of over seven millions ; and is signed in fifty tongues, dialects, and languages. All honor to the Woman's Christian Temperance Union ; all honor to Lady Henry Somerset, who has championed this cause in England ; and all honor to Miss Frances E. Willard, Mrs. Mary Clement Leavitt, and Mrs. Mary A. Livermore, our American champions !

Still another important element in good international citizenship, for which this great Society stands, is the settlement of disputes among nations by arbitration, instead of by cruel bloodshed and war. A most wonderful event in the history of the world occurred a few months since, when W. Randall Cremer, a member of the British Parliament, crossed the ocean bearing a petition signed by no less than three hundred and fifty-four members of the British House of Commons, asking the government of the United States to join with Great Britain in framing a treaty to refer to arbitration disputes which diplomacy fails to adjust between these great English-speaking nations. I believe this to be the herald and forerunner of that glorious day, so long predicted in God's Word, "when nation shall not lift up sword against nation, nor learn war any more." Christian Endeavorers and good citizens will do all in their power to promote the settlement of international disputes by arbitration ; and I wish that this Convention might pass a ringing resolution in favor of it.

Mr. President, ladies and gentlemen of the Convention, I desire to say some practical word of counsel and advice to these thousands of young people who are before me to-day. I have often thought that if young persons in the morning of life would profit by the experience of those who have gone before, how wisely they might begin to live ! Most persons in my time of life have occasion to sing the hymn that says,

" The mistakes of my life have been many ; "

but I like the verse that says,

> " My mistakes his free grace will cover,
> My sins he will wash away."

In order to avoid these mistakes and make good citizens, it is of great consequence to these young persons in the morning of life that they start right and lay the foundations of their character well. Twenty years ago a reservoir dam above the city of Worcester gave way, and did great and irreparable damage. An investigation was held to learn the cause. It developed the fact that when the dam was constructed two plans were submitted. One architect said that the dam must be built in what is known in that kind of architecture as the reversed arch; another said that a cheaper and different foundation would do; his plan was adopted, and you have the result. The dam gave way, and hundreds of families in the path of the water were left houseless, homeless, friendless, and in tears. What was the matter with the dam? The matter was they did n't start right. Young man, young woman, it is of great consequence that you start right, and that you lay the foundations of your character well. Great opportunities and an open door stand before the young men and young women of to-day, just entering upon the twentieth century.

Representatives of other nationalities in this Convention will excuse me if I say to my countrymen that in this land above all other lands it is true that "There is no royal road to learning," and "Honor and shame from no condition rise ; " but, young man or young woman of every land, to the end that you may make the most of yourselves, and the world better for your having lived in it, let me exhort you to see to it that you start right, and that you lay the foundation of your character well. But you say, "What would you put into a young person's character, if you could have your say about it ? " I would put in first total abstinence from strong drink. Touch not, taste not, handle not, anything which intoxicates. Yes, and I would go further than that if I could have my say : I would put in total abstinence from tobacco. Tobacco is a dirty, vile, poisonous narcotic. It degrades any man who uses it. He may be a good man with it, but a better man without it. It creates an unnatural appetite that water will not satisfy, and leads to drink. With it you will not be so likely to succeed in life, and more liable to become a drunkard. Is that all? Oh, no ; if I had my say I would put you on the Lord Jesus Christ. If I had a voice that would drown Niagara I would say to every young man and young woman, in the language of the Book, " Remember now thy creator in the days of thy youth." I read a story of a party of young people who visited the White Mountains. Walking up the side of the mountain one beautiful morning, a young woman strayed away from the party and came to stand on the brink of a frightful yawning precipice. When warned of her danger she replied, "With my feet standing on this solid rock and my arm leaning on this one I feel secure." O young men and young women, on this "International Citizenship Day " put your feet on the Rock of Ages, and lean on the Lord Jesus Christ, and you are secure for time and eternity.

> " On Christ, the solid rock, I stand ;
> All other ground is sinking sand."

I have seen young people who were fearful that they would not be appreciated. I tell you, young man or young woman, you could n't make a greater mistake than that. The world will size you up about right, and you will pass for about what you are. In this favored land of ours, industry, ability, and virtue carry in their hands the sure prestige of victory and success. Am I addressing persons of obscure parentage and humble birth ? I am not here to say that it is not a good thing to be born well, because the commandment has a promise appended to it, " I will show mercy to thousands of them that love me and keep my commandments," or as the margin reads, "to a thousand generations." But I am here to say, young man or young woman, you can rise above the circumstances of your birth. Do you want illustrations? Abraham Lincoln was a rail-splitter ; Andrew Johnson was a Kentucky tailor ; James A. Garfield drove a horse on a tow-path; Henry Wilson said on the floor of the United States Senate that he was born in poverty, and Want sat by his cradle; Nathaniel P. Banks started life as a bobbin-boy in a factory.

But you say that these are political illustrations. Do you want illustrations in business and mechanical lines? John Roach came to this country a ragged, bare-footed, homeless Irish boy. He rose, as a ship-builder, master mechanic, and engineer, to stand on the highest pinnacle of worldly fame. Elias Howe, the inventor of the sewing-machine, was a poor mechanic, and worked in a machine-shop in Cambridge. With midnight oil, in a lonely attic, he worked out his machine, and died worth millions; and, what is of more consequence, he died acknowledged in every land and clime as a benefactor of his race. George W. Childs, a Philadelphia philanthropist and business man of affairs, began life as a newsboy, crying newspapers in the streets. George Peabody, the philanthropist, who being dead yet speaks, the man who endowed schools in this country to elevate the illiterate, the man who left millions for the benefit of the poor of London, began life a country store-boy.

Young men, young women, you are mistaken. I tell you that you will pass for about what you are. The world will size you up about right. If you drink and smoke and go with bad company, you won't amount to anything. Good character, industry, ability, and application are of more consequence to success then family, birth, or blood.

I leave this parting admonition with the young people, as I believe great things are to break upon your view in the twentieth century, now near at hand. On this " International Citizenship Day " resolve to set your mark high; enter upon its pursuit at once. Persevere, and adopt for your motto : " I live for the cause that lacks assistance, for the wrong that needs resistance, and for the good that I can do." Plato, the heathen philosopher, thanked God for three things : first, that he was born a rational soul; second, that he was born a Greek; third, that he lived in the days of Socrates. To-day, as I looked over the happy, joyous faces of this vast concourse of young people, I said to myself, " If this poor, benighted heathen, who knew nothing of the Gospel, who knew nothing of Jesus and heaven and eternal life, had that for which to thank God, surely what have we, who stand in this apex of the nineteenth century, enjoying all the blessings of the Gospel and modern civilization ! "

Mr. President, what a wonderful illustration this great Convention is of that good old hymn they used to sing in the churches when I was a boy, two lines of which are : —

> " Religion never was designed
> To make our pleasures less."

There is no rational, reasonable enjoyment that Christ denies to his disciples; and, more than that, Christ's promise is a verity when he says, " No man hath forsaken houses and land, father and mother and brethren, for my sake and the Gospel, but I will give him an hundred-fold in this life, and in that which is to come, eternal life." Christ denies to his disciples sinful pleasures. There is something to be borne, but " the yoke is easy, and the burden is light."

In the British Museum, in London, I saw the coat upon which General Wolfe died, at the Siege of Quebec, stained with his blood. Do you remember the circumstances of his death? It was a critical moment in the battle; he was waving his sword and cheering on his men, when he staggered, with a mortal wound in his breast. He did not want his men to know he was wounded; he said to the officers who stood around him, with his eyes growing glassy in death, " Hold me up, and don't let the men see me fall."

O you Christian Endeavorers, whatever else may betide you, resolve, on this " International Citizenship Day," that no man shall see you fall. And let all the aims thou aimest at be " thy Country, thy God, and Truth."

Mr. Shupe then introduced Bishop Alexander Walters, D.D., of Jersey City, N. J., who spoke on the subject, " The Responsibility of the Afro-American Race in America."

Address of Bishop Alexander Walters, D.D.

There exists such a variety of color among us that we have had considerable difficulty in selecting a suitable ethnological term which will take them all in. The terms " black " or " colored " people have been found inadequate to exactly meet the case. There are other people in this country who are so deeply colored that they might with equal propriety be called " colored Americans." Some who are forced into our ranks are so slightly colored that they can scarcely be distinguished from the pure white. The term " negro " has been so perverted (some calling us " negar," others " nigger," by way of derision) that it has become distasteful to us. We are Afro-Americans, not colored Americans, or negro Americans.

The subject which I am to discuss is an important one, especially so in the face of the efforts to disfranchise the Afro-American in South Carolina, Virginia, Florida, Georgia, Alabama, Mississippi, Louisiana, and other Southern States. The all-important question in the Southland is, " What is to be done with the negro? "

There is a base element of untutored whites in this country that say, " Kill him out! Trump up false charges against him, and lynch him without giving him an opportunity to prove his innocence, because he is becoming too strong, numerically, intellectually, and financially."

Others, a little better than the class mentioned above, say, " No, don't kill him, because that will bring down upon us the opprobrium of all good people here and elsewhere; and again, the wrath of God will surely overtake us. But disfranchise him by legal enactments."

They have done this in Mississippi, where the law is that no one is allowed to vote except he can read the Constitution, or understand it when read to him. The judges of election are the persons appointed to read the Constitution and to decide whether it is properly interpreted. Of course that means the disfranchisement of the Afro-American, for no matter how correctly he may interpret it, it will be considered incorrect.

They are about to adopt a little different method from this in South Carolina. The declaration has been made that the whole race of that State shall be disfranchised by constitutional enactment; how this is to be accomplished remains to be seen. The present registration and election laws, which favor all the people, regardless of color, have been waived.

There are others whose consciences are too sensitive to approve of this plan, and they say, " Transport him to Africa! " But after careful consideration of the ten millions to be transported, the expense, etc., together with their unwillingness to be transported, they have come to the conclusion that this plan is impracticable. Hence they are at sea as to what is best to be done. They would transport him if they could.

Thank God, there is a class of right-thinking white people in the North and in the South (some of whom compose this Convention), who believe in fair play; believe in treating the Afro-American right, regardless of consequences, and leaving the result with God.

General Wade Hampton, of South Carolina, in a recent speech said : " I have no fear of ' negro domination,' — a cry used only to arouse race prejudices and to put the coming convention under control of the ring which now dominates our State. The negroes have acted of late with rare moderation and liberality, and if we meet them in the same spirit they have shown, they will aid in selecting good representatives for the convention. I, for one, am willing to trust them, and they ask only the rights guaranteed to them by the Constitution of the United States and that of our own State, and that ought to be allowed to them."

I feel assured that every fair-minded person will agree with the ex-senator.

A proof that we have many friends in the South is the recognition which has been given us in the Cotton States and International Exhibition to be held at Atlanta, Ga., in the fall, by the appointment of I. Garland Penn as chief of the Afro-American department, and the large amount appropriated for the establishment and maintenance of that department.

I am sorry to say, however, that the predominant sentiment in the South is against us in many respects. We are discriminated against on nearly all public carriers; no matter how intelligent, fair, or well-dressed an Afro-American may be, he is forced into what is known as the "Jim Crow" car, which is little better than a common smoking-car. He is maligned and traduced upon the right and upon the left. No matter how hungry or how weary he may be, no matter what his station in life is, he is not allowed to stop at a white hotel or eat at a white restaurant. In many instances our wives and daughters are insulted without redress at law.

In the East, West, and North we are treated fairly well. We are given first-class railroad, hotel, and restaurant accommodations; indeed, we are allowed first-class accommodation in most public places and on public carriers. We have the advantage of mixed schools. This I consider a fundamental advantage; the co-education of the races is the most effectual method of eradicating race prejudice. Public sentiment in the North in our favor is far ahead of that in the South. It is true, in some instances we are shut out of the trades-unions, and kept off the public works; this, however, is more than overbalanced by the recognition of our manhood.

1. Upon the Afro-American rests the responsibility of preparing the coming generation for worthy citizenship.

The indispensable qualification for worthy citizenship is intelligence. We are laboring diligently to educate the young men of the race, in order that they may be able to use the ballot intelligently. The perpetuity of our nation depends upon the intelligence of its voters. We are teaching our boys and girls to love our institutions, thus inspiring in them true patriotism.

No one doubts the loyalty of the Afro-American to the Stars and Stripes. He has been often weighed, and never found wanting. The first blood which was shed in Boston in defence of American independence was that of an Afro-American, Crispus Attucks. Whenever the nation has called upon us to take up arms in its defence, we have gladly responded to the call, from Bunker Hill to Appomattox. The Afro-American has mingled his blood with the blood of the loyal citizens of the North and South on a hundred battle-fields in defence of the Union. Notwithstanding the discriminations and outrages which have been perpetrated against him, he has never been known to take up arms against the nation which gave him birth and freedom. It is a part of the Afro-American's make-up to be loyal. Who ever heard of him combining to destroy property and annul law?

2. Upon the Afro-American rests the responsibility of securing his civil and political rights.

Our enfranchisement must be maintained. The doors of hotels, restaurants, and other public places which are now closed against us must be opened. This can be achieved by intelligence, character, wealth, and wise agitation.

With character, intelligence, and wealth we will not have to go out of our way to demand respect, for we will command it — especially if we exercise good judgment.

No one need fear Afro-American domination. Numbers and everything are against that idea. Again, the Afro-American does not desire to dominate; all he wants is fair play. The cry of domination, as General Wade Hampton has well said, is only raised to prejudice our cause.

As to social equality. I have great faith in the American conscience. It is on the side of liberty and fair play; all it needs is to be awakened. It is our duty to rouse it; this can be done by agitation. Once aroused it will sweep injustice into oblivion. Remember the results of the anti-slavery agitation. In my opinion the conscience of the American people is being rapidly quickened.

3. Upon the Afro-American rests the responsibility of the industrial training of his race.

One of the means to be used in order to become wealthy and influential is industry. It is not enough to be industrious, but to be skilfully so. The demand of the hour is for skilled labor, — men and women prepared to execute their work in the most perfect manner. As a rule the Afro-American is shut out of the great manufactories and machine-shops of our land, hence he is deprived of the practical experience which a person receives who has an opportunity to serve an apprenticeship under skilled workmen.

This disadvantage was discovered some years ago, and in order to remedy it we established industrial schools, where we might at least obtain theoretical training. We must have more such schools. More assistance from our white friends is needed in this direction than in any other. We ought to be allowed to enter all the industrial schools in the land, and where there are no such schools supported by the State, they should be established at once.

Unskilled labor cannot compete with skilled labor, neither North nor South. In the past we were given certain positions by our white friends as the result of sympathy — not because we could perform the work as skilfully as others, but because of our poverty and oppression. The sentiment which actuated them to help us was a noble one, but that kind of sentiment is a thing of the past; now we are required to stand or fall, according to our merits.

When anything is to be manufactured, machines constructed, houses and bridges built, clothing fashioned, or any kind of work performed, the most skilled workmen are required.

There are a great many employers who care but little about the color of the workman; with them the question is, "Can he do the work?"

4. Upon the Afro-American rests the responsibility of the further elevation of his home.

We can accomplish this by defending our homes at the cost of our lives, by honoring our women and protecting their virtue, and by giving them more liberal education and broader culture. Again, we can elevate our homes by strengthening and respecting the marriage bond. This will be done by creating a strong sentiment against divorces and free-loveism.

5. Upon the Afro-American rests the responsibility of the religious training of his race.

This will be consummated by well-trained, religi.us parents and teachers, and educated and pious ministers; also by taking advantage of all the new organizations, such as Christian Endeavor Society, Young Men's Christian Association, etc.

Our future happiness, usefulness, and prosperity largely depend upon our loyalty to God and strict observance of religious duties. The stability of any people rests upon their adherence to religious principles. In Holy Writ we read: "Righteousness exalteth a nation, but sin is a reproach of any people."

The Afro-American has always had the reputation to being religious, and this is no mean reputation. Some of our non-religious leaders deride us because of our religious proclivities; they claim if we had less religion it would be better for us. This is a grave mistake; no one can have too much piety. A person can have too much superstition, too much emotion, but not too much common-sense piety.

Mighty agencies are at work in the interest of the religious development of the race; the most powerful factors in the solution of this problem are the following religious organizations: —

The African Methodist Episcopal Zion Church, which I have the honor to represent, has 3,880 preachers, 14,145 teachers (Sabbath-school and otherwise), and 425,768 members; the African Methodist Episcopal Church, 4,252 preachers and 497,350 members; Union American Methodist Episcopal, 115 ministers and 7,031 members; African Union Methodist Episcopal, 42 ministers, 3,500 members; Colored Methodist Episcopal, 124 ministers, 128,817 members; Colored members in the Methodist Episcopal Church, about 265,000. Total: Methodists, 1,350,024; Presbyterians, 1,000 ministers, 5,000 members; Baptists, 7,550 ministers, 1,292,394 members.

Besides these we have over one hundred and fifty denominational schools. There are also a great number of Afro-Americans in white churches outside of the Methodist Episcopal Church. What a tremendous force is being used for the religious development of the race! There is no doubt but that the Afro-

American will play an important part in the civilization and evangelization of Africa.

Tent Williston.

There was no diminution whatever in the attendance at Tent Williston; and when the devotional exercises, led by Rev. Henry T. McCook, D.D., of Philadelphia, were opened, every seat in the vast tent was occupied.   Trustee Rev. Wm. Patterson, of Toronto, Ont., presided, and Mr. George K. Somerby, of Boston, officiated as musical director.

The Park Sisters' Quartette rendered one of their popular cornet selections, and the Hampton Quartette was enthusiastically received as it stepped forward in response to an introduction by Mr. Somerby.

Then the regular programme was taken up, and the chairman introduced the various speakers from different sections of America, to speak on the general topic of "Christian Citizenship."   The Rev. C. D. McDonald, D.D., of Grafton, N. D., was too ill to be present, and the chairman then called upon Prof. W. P. Taylor, of Birmingham, Ala., to speak for the South.

Address of Prof. W. P. Taylor.

I suppose the main thing in our minds this morning might be, perhaps, the question, in the familiar Alabama phrase, about Endeavors, "Where are we at along good-citizenship lines?"   The South is behind in Endeavor work, but we are slow to adopt anything new.   The conditions of life in the South are different from the conditions of life in the North and elsewhere.   But the South is rapidly coming to the front.

All I have to say may be summed up, perhaps, along two lines: something of a defence for the South; something of a plea for the South.

Along the lines of good citizenship I know the idea is prevalent that the South is disloyal.   As an adopted son of the South, I want to give that statement the lie this morning.   The South is all right along the lines of good citizenship.   As we delegates sent up our songs on our journey, we sang, " I Wish I Were in Dixie," and always followed that — and singing with a warmer thrill at our hearts — with, " My Country, 'T is of Thee." Always it was significant of the new South.   The South is all right.   I firmly believe, after six years' residence in the South, that if any hand should ever dare to take one star from yonder " Old Glory," no section of the land would rise sooner to repair the outrage than Old Dixie.

My plea is prayer for the South; prayer for the Christian Endeavorers in the South.   No section of people — no people — have ever been called upon to solve such questions.   There is the evil of gambling in all its stages.   Then we have the Sunday violation to fight; we have the Sunday ball-games to overcome.   And I am so glad in so many parts of the South the young people have risen in defence of the Puritan Sabbath !

Once more, we expect sometime to welcome you in Dixie.   Next year you will go closer than you ever have before to the South line.   We expect that we shall see you in Dixie's land, and you will receive the heartiest welcome you have ever had in any convention.

Address of Rev. Alexander Allison, D.D.

I have come a long distance to talk to you, and I only have a few moments to do it.   Seattle, Wash., has been trying to get the Convention for 1897, you know; but we are going to take right hold and make the convention at San Francisco the grandest convention we have ever had.

We are doing our very best to increase our membership as fast as we can. We like the Christian Endeavor movement because it is from the East. A large portion of our population is from the East, largely from New England, New York, and Pennsylvania; eight-tenths are American born. We find that these young people who come to us from the old homes of the East come with everything in favor of Christian work, and we rejoice that we have so much of this kind of work to do, and we could tell you a great deal of what it is doing for us.

I believe in this movement because it is giving us the old-fashioned idea of young men and young women marrying in Christ. Some people have objected to this movement because they say it is only a sparking-school. I am glad there is some place where young men and young women can be brought together beside the ball-room and the card-party. I rejoice that in all our local unions and State conventions we have an opportunity of bringing Christian young men in contact with Christian young women. We are going to see a grand and godly population arising in the West, and if Boston does not look out we will have the Hub at Seattle. We rejoice to think that we are raising such an army out there to send into India and China and Japan and all the Islands of the Pacific Ocean. God bless this work ! We will start this morning the grand shout, "Seattle, 1900!"

Address of Miss Charlotte Thorndike Sibley.

Christianity implies good citizenship. No man can be a good citizen of the kingdom of heaven unless he is a good citizen of the kingdom of earth. No man can be ready for citizenship in the heavenly kingdom when he is a faithless or indifferent citizen on earth. We owe it to our fellow countrymen to make them good citizens. "Patriotism" and "brotherhood" are kindred terms. Christian Endeavorers in the East and West and South are rallying around the flag and around the ballot-box to-day. City councilmen and saloon-keepers shall not long be synonymous. You Boston Endeavorers are showing yourselves stanch citizens. I understand you are rallying yourselves to the support of the Municipal League in this city in its noble work, and have effected changes in its city charter. To the president of that Municipal League I feel inclined to pay that tribute that was paid to another patriot of this time : that he wastes no time in vague generalities, either of speech or of action, and while others talk of municipal reform, he works to make a better Boston.

I can only speak of a few things that have been done. In Wilkesbarre, Penn., and Newark, N. J., Endeavorers have been doing noble work in securing the enactment of laws, believing, as some one has said, that it is better to have laws made by Lucifer and executed by Gabriel than made by Gabriel and executed by Lucifer. In Philadelphia and in Iron Falls, Me., reading-rooms have been opened to help in educating the public opinion. Pennsylvania and New York Endeavorers have done noble work in executing the laws of the State. In Brooklyn, N. Y., a library has been opened for firemen, and Christian work for the fire department has been begun. In Rochester they have raised the white standard of social purity. In New Hampshire Endeavorers have secured regular hearing in seven of the newspapers, and are going on steadily in their labors. It must be work, not play. We cannot make a heaven on earth in a day-dream. The soil has been watered by blood, — the blood of martyrdom, the blood of the first Christian Endeavor martyr, Robert Ross, of Troy, N. Y., who died defending the ballot-box against repeaters. From that soil shall yet spring a rich harvest of endeavor and achievement. We Christian Endeavorers have done something along these lines this year; we can do more. There is a wonderful amount of energy stored up in youthful hearts and brains. When "I can" becomes "I will," there is no possible reason for pessimism or despair. So shall we be ready for citizenship in that future City where God himself shall reign and we be kings and priests unto him.

Address of Rev. Mungo Fraser.

You have heard from the fair South and the West and the East. I can assure you that the North is all right, and will be right along. But Christian Endeavor is doing for citizenship in that part of the country in which I live a grand work. It is most certainly uniting us together; there is no doubt on that question. All the churches are coming nearer and nearer, it may be imperceptibly, but certainly.

The Christian Endeavor movement, further, is uniting us together for patriotism, the finest and best kind of patriotism. So it is strengthening a body of people for their own various countries. May I be allowed to say that I am sorry on this account that our ranks, the ranks of Christian Endeavor, are even apparently divided up a little by brotherhoods and unions, or other kinds of leagues? I had always hoped that the honored name of Christian Endeavor would be broad and great and good enough for all to rally in the great cause. Christian Endeavor, moreover, is solidifying and consolidating not only patriots but philanthropists.

The Park Sisters then rendered a fine selection, and then Rev. G. L. Morrill, D.D., of Denver, Col., presented the banner to the Syracuse Union for its work in promoting Christian citizenship.

Address of Rev. G. L. Morrill, D.D., Denver, Col.

I have heard of a Presbyterian minister who was very anxious as to what the future of his young son should be. One day he said to his wife, " I will put him in a room by himself, with a Bible, a dollar, and an apple. If he selects the apple, I will make him a farmer; if he selects the dollar, I will make him a merchant; and if he selects the Bible, I will make him a minister." So he put the child in the parlor with the three articles, and then retired. Shortly he returned, and found the boy with the Bible in one hand, the dollar in the other, and the apple in his mouth; whereupon he silently retired and said to his wife, " My wife, the boy is a hog, and I will make a politician out of him." I think Horace Walpole must have had some such idea in mind when he said, " Every man has his price," and Dr. Johnson when he said patriotism was the last refuge of a scoundrel. There are three theories of Church and State. The first is the clerical idea that the State exists by the consent of the Church alone. This idea was illustrated when Henry IV. of Germany stood for three days barefooted and bareheaded in the courtyard before the Palace of Canossa, doing penance to atone for his rebellion against the theory of the Church being supreme over the State. He only received absolution and a return to State power when he promised allegiance, and on condition that he should devote himself to the maintenance of the clerical power. Contrasted with the clerical is the secular idea. The secularist has declared that there is no relation between Church and State as to the function of government, the motive and object to be attained. Therefore, they have said there shall be an eternal divorce. Apart from these two ideas there is the idea of Christian Americanism, which emphasizes the idea which has been forgotten by these other two positions, — the freedom and responsibility of individuals, multiplied by individuals, which gives us a nation whose God is the Lord. It is this idea which shall in the end obtain.

As I understand it this Society believes, " ye shall know the truth," the truth as it is in the Lord Jesus Christ, and this shall make you free. This Society stands this morning here and elsewhere for this idea : that by voice and vote there shall come the time, so help us God, when in Congress there shall be more brain and less of boodle; when in civil service there shall be more of principle and less of partizanship; when in municipal and State affairs there shall be more of conviction and less of corruption; and when Scriptural politics shall be everywhere and saloon politics nowhere. I have heard of three artist liars who wondered who was most proficient in that art. The first one declared that he had painted a piece of wood that looked so much like marble that when placed in a basin of water it sank to the bottom. The second one said, "I painted a picture of the arctic regions which was so natural that when I hung the thermometer by it the thermometer fell twenty-one degrees." And there was one who said, "I will go you one better. I painted a picture of the Count which was so lifelike that the barber had to come and shave it three times a week." But if there is one falsifier greater than all these, it is the man who declares that he is loyal to the Lord Jesus Christ and yet is uninterested in the good government of his own native land. So I declare that the Society is opposed to the brothel, which sends men and women forth from the town with aching heart and head. It is opposed to the gambling-den, whose motto is, "Leave hope behind, all ye who enter here." As such it is further opposed to the saloon, that unchristian institution that diseases the body, and dwarfs the mind, and darkens and damns man's immortal soul. Our forefathers planted "the little red schoolhouse." They did not believe that ignorance was the mother of devotion. They did not believe there was any conflict between science and religion. They felt the danger of the influence of the dark devildom of the Middle Ages; so they had history and they had philosophy and they had geography, and the rich and the poor met together, for God Almighty was the Maker of them all.

I understand Christian citizenship has, in the second place, love of education, which is loyal to the bulwark of our American institutions; which is the same "little red schoolhouse" whose symbol is not a Cross, but "Old Glory" with its red, white, and blue; whose curriculum is not a catechism, but the Constitution of the United States, and for which we pledge ourselves this morning in the presence of "Old Glory" with its red, white, and blue,—that red which was born of suffering upon the battle-field; that blue suggestive of the veins whence came undying hope, and in view of those stars which were as the footsteps of the angels which led our boys to victory.

Christian citizenship stands, in the third place, for liberty. "Liberty" is a new word, but it is an old one. You will remember that down through the centuries there are many whose breasts were stirred by this immortal banner. You will remember how in the sixteenth century the love of education and of religion combined and culminated in the struggle for liberty. William of Nassau had been removed from the throne. Our forefathers came across the wide, weltering waste of the ocean, and He who holds the ocean in the hollow of his hands gave them a safe journey and this paradise regained. They planted a tree whose leaves are free thought, Church, and State, and life for the healing of the nation. Cursed be any lip which utters anathemas against this tree; palsied be any hand which would unpluck it from its base!

And so, in reference to good citizenship, I have the honor of presenting the banner, not to Canada, which we value, not to the West with all its resplendent scenery, not to the fair South with its magical soil, not even to some other places which I might mention, but to the Empire State and to the city of Syracuse and to Rev. H. N. Kinney. May we not feel here this morning, with reference to what we are surrounded by and what others have spoken of, that

> " The Pilgrim spirit is not fled;
>   It walks in noon's broad light;
>   It watches the bed
>   Of the glorious dead,
>   With the holy stars by night.
>   It watches the bed of the glorious dead,
>   And shall guard the ice-bound shore,
>   Till the waves of the bay
>   Where the *Mayflower* lay
>   Shall foam and freeze no more."

Mr. Kinney received the banner on behalf of the union, and made a fitting reply.

After singing, Mr. Patterson introduced Bishop B. W. Arnett, D. D., of Wilberforce, O., who spoke on "The Responsibilities and Possibilities of an American Citizen."

Address of Bishop B. W. Arnett, D. D.

You will accept my hearty congratulations upon our meeting and the prospect that lies before us. It will be our duty to say a word upon the subject of American citizenship, its responsibilities and its possibilities. While discussing this subject you will bear in mind that we have been living under two civilizations: the civilization of Plymouth and Boston, the civilization of Jamestown; the one universal in its applications of the principles of human government, the other circumscribed and limited in its application; the one believing in the Fatherhood of God and the brotherhood of man, the other believing in the Fatherhood of God and the brotherhood of *some* men. It will be my pleasure to try and show you that our institutions were so constructed by our fathers that it has been possible for the strongest and weakest to succeed in accomplishing something for the race, for the age.

At a time when the conflict was fierce and stubborn the Christian Endeavor Association came up as a re-enforcement, with banners flying, and joined in the conflict of the right against the wrong, took its stand in behalf of religious and humane liberty, and called on God's children, of every clime and race, to meet around a common altar to learn the lessons of religion and patriotism. Thus we are here to-day to consider the subject of good citizenship.

In all the conflicts of the past, and in the battle of the present, the hand of God may be seen. It is well to teach our children and instruct them, in reading the history of our country, that they should look for the footprints of the Almighty, and should see the hand of God in our institutions and in our marvellous progress.

The discovery of America happened just at the time when the Church was longing for emancipation, and the State for liberty. The New World presented an enlarged field, where all could have an equal chance in the race of life, where the oppressor and the oppressed could meet on equal footing. Columbus started to find a new way to the Old World; but the result was, he went a new way and found a new world. The world can hardly recognize the good he did for mankind.

August 3, 1492, marks the beginning of one of the most important epochs in the history of man. It looked like a very small thing for Christopher Columbus to sail with three vessels to find a new world, or a new passage to the Old World. But he was confident that a passage could be found. He sailed day after day without seeing land or the prospects of finding land. The sailors on his vessels lost hope, became disobedient and mutinous. Nothing daunted, the bold admiral brought order and peace out of confusion, restored hope to his disheartened sailors, and proceeded on his journey.

The vessels were landed. The Admiral Columbus, accompanied by his officers and crew, stepped on the shore. With tears of joy running down his cheeks, he threw himself upon his knees, kissed the earth, and thanked God. Arising, he drew his sword, planted the Cross, displayed the Castilian banner of Ferdinand and Isabella, and solemnly dedicated the New World to religion and morality. He first gave it to God, and then to Ferdinand and Isabella, recognizing the Divine and humane government in its possession. And in order to show coming generations as to which was superior, humane or Divine government, he called the island " San Salvador," or " Holy Saviour." Thus linking the New and Old World together, Columbus displayed great wisdom, and demonstrated that his mission was providential; and all subsequent events relating to the settlement of the Western Continent have shown the development of the great plan, and of the final triumph of religious and personal liberty.

The landing of the Pilgrim Fathers is another demonstration that God had reserved this continent as a theatre for the final struggle between the powers of intelligence and ignorance, of freedom and oppression, justice and injustice.

The schoolhouse is the hope of the nation; there the coming generations are to be trained in the elements of good citizenship. In the common schools we are to lay the foundation for the building of the character of those who are to form the bone and sinew of the nation.

The schoolmaster occupies the place of an architect, contractor, and builder. He also is to furnish materials for the construction of the edifice of manhood and womanhood. Therefore the schoolmaster is a very important personage in a Republican form of government, where every boy at twenty-one becomes a king and every girl becomes a queen, one ruling in civil life, the other in domestic life; each becoming a centre of moral, social, religious, and political forces which affect directly and indirectly every man, woman, and child in the great Republic. This being true, it is the imperative duty of the citizens to know what their children are taught, to know what lessons are placed before them. Every lover of this country should insist that the school authorities should write over every schoolhouse door, so that every child should learn that obedience to law is the palladium of liberty. They should be taught that the State educates the people for its own good, and not for the good of the citizens as individuals; but that in training the parts, the whole becomes trained, and the parts can do the greatest good for the whole.

Intelligence, loyalty, industry, frugality, are the essential elements of the good citizen. A good citizen will obey all of the laws of the land, and will allow the law to take its course. He will neither precipitate nor encourage the execution of the law by irresponsible persons; he will protect every man, woman, and child in their rights to life, liberty, and the pursuit of happiness, and will use his influence to see that every one accused of a crime has a fair trial before a jury of his peers. The good citizen will respect every right and privilege of his neighbor, and will see that all — rich and poor, intelligent and ignorant, black and white — are protected by the law.

The founders of the American Republic built it on a firm and solid foundation. Its corner-stones are religion, morality, education, and industry. The man, the family, the race, or nation who builds upon these foundations is like unto the man who built his house upon the rock, — "When the rains descended, and the floods came, and the winds blew, the house fell not, because it was upon the rock." Our century-crowned Republic has survived the storms, the rains, the winds. She stands to-day stronger than before her foreign and civil wars. It was said years ago, "Happy are the people whose Lord is God." History, observation, and experience confirm the assertion of the Psalmist.

The people of this country have a strong faith in God. They believe in the Golden Rule, if they do not practise it. Their faith in God is so strong that it has been crystallized and stamped upon every silver dollar throughout the land: "In God we trust." It is true we have two classes of citizens, — one trusting in God, the other trusting in the dollar. Another source of strength to our institutions is the system of common schools, which provides that every child of every race, of every condition of life, shall receive a common-school education. A large majority of the American people are building a high wall of Protection around our institutions, with the Gate of Reciprocity in the East, West, North, and South.

As to citizenship, the good citizen of the great Republic will make a good citizen of Mount Zion. We must teach men to be good citizens of America if they would be good citizens of heaven, for a bad citizen of the Republic will not make a good citizen of the kingdom of grace nor glory. We must teach men to obey the laws of our own government, or they will not obey them there; for if they will not allow, or wait on, human law to have its course, they would not do it in heaven. If a man believe in mob law here as a Christian to take him to heaven, he would do the same there. If a man would murder his brother without trial on earth, if he got into heaven he would do the same there; an unconverted lyncher on earth would be a lyncher in heaven. The citizen who will not obey the law of the land cannot be a good citizen or Christian. Obedience to human and Divine law is essential to good citizenship, for it is written over the pearly gates that no murderer can enter heaven.

To cast a free ballot and have it counted as cast is the right of every citizen. When one makes a choice of a representative in the Congress of the United States he is dealing with the conditions of the commercial, political, educational, and religious questions of sixty-five millions. Then if the voter has been wise in his choice of parties, principles, policies, there will come good to all; but if he has been unwise in his choice of either men or parties, it will be felt by every industry, in every board of trade, and in financial and commercial mart. To be a good citizen one must be intelligent enough to read his own ballot, his Bible, his own newspaper, and the Constitution of his country. The Christian Endeavor is doing much good in requiring every citizen, male and female, to read the Bible once a day.

The advantage of the Christian Endeavor Association is that it gives every man, regardless of race or color, a chance to show what is in him and to achieve whatever place his character and talents merit.

But the possibilities of our government are illustrated in the three decades of the freedom of the negro. Thirty-one years have passed away since Abraham Lincoln issued his Emancipation Proclamation. The questions have often been asked: "Has the emancipation of the negro been a success?" "Is the negro any better off now than he was before the emancipation?" I am old enough to have some knowledge of the negro before the war, of his condition before the war, of his condition during the war, and his progress since the war. I have worked by his side; I have dined at his table; I have slept in his bed; I have attended his prayer meetings and his class meetings, where he related his experiences and his hopes; I have conversed with his moral and religious teachers, and have encouraged them in their work; I have spent the evenings by his fireside; I have listened to the songs of his children and the conversation of his friends; and my observation is that he has made wonderful progress, religiously, intellectually, and socially, as I shall show before I conclude.

The numerical status of the negro at the end of three decades of freedom is as follows: we find that the census says of them, in the Southern States, that in 1840 the number of negroes was 2,688,636; in 1850 the per cent of increase was 21.6, with a total of 3,369,934; in 1860 the per cent of increase was 22.1, and the total, 4,018,389; in 1870 the per cent of increase was 9.9, and the total, 4,242,003; in 1880 the per cent was 34.8, and the total, 5,643,891. In 1890 we find the negro is classed as follows: persons of African descent: Blacks, 6,337,980; Mulattoes (white man and black man), 996,989; Quadroons (mulatto and white), 105,135; Octoroons, 69,936, making a grand total of 7,470,040. The per cent of increase in 1890 was 13.90. This makes an increase from 1860 of 3,451,651.

If we increase as we have in the past, say twenty-five per cent on the present numbers, we will go into the twentieth century with 9,337,560 men, women, and children, all the children of freedom; only a very few of them will have come from the house of bondage. There is great hope for the race to-day, with the advantages of training and culture that belong to all.

Let us examine the decades of religious development. When the negro was emancipated there were only a few distinct negro organizations, and they were confined to the North and not to the South; but as the army pushed on toward the South, the missionaries of the African Methodist Episcopal Church and other followers of the flag followed and organized the moral and religious forces.

The distinctive negro organizations make the following magnificent showing: Regular Baptists, Union A. M. E. Church, American Union Methodist, A. M. E. Zion, Congregational, Methodist, C. M. E. Church, Zion Union Apostolic, Evangelical Missionary, and Cumberland Presbyterian. These have 19,859 organizations, 20,007 church edifices, valued at $22,626,434, with a seating capacity of 5,802,314, a membership of 2,591,129, while adherents and members number 5,650,228.

These organizations are controlled and supported wholly by the negro himself, and are legitimate results of three decades of freedom.

The following denominations are colored organizations in other organizations. They are controlled by white people, but are composed of colored people: Regular Baptist North, Regular Baptist South, Free Will Baptist, Primitive Baptist, Old Two Seed Baptist, Roman Catholic, Christian Connection, Congregational, Disciples of Christ, Methodist Protestant, Methodist Episcopal, Lutheran S. C., Lutheran U. S. South, Independent Methodist, Presbyterians North, Presbyterians South, Reformed Presbyterians, Protestant Episcopal, Reformed Episcopal. Total denominations, 19; organizations, 4,713; church edifices, 4,139; seating capacity, 1,008,651; valuation, $6,236,734; membership, 307,826; total adherents and members, 775,652.

Uniting the two, we have a total in denomination of 29; in organization, 24,572; in church edifices, 21,146; seating capacity, 6,810,965; in valuation, $29,863,168; in members, 2,751,955; in members and adherents, 6,325,880.

These figures will show the result of three decades of the organization of the moral and religious forces of the race. The following will give an idea of what the Methodist denominations have done: —

The Negro Methodist churches have 12,434 pastors, 25,788 local preachers, 1,304,729 members, and 4,316,815 members and adherents. The total number of pastors, ministers, and members is 1,342,951.

The Negro Methodist churches have 13,923 Sunday schools, 110,970 officers and teachers, and 950,047 pupils. Church buildings number 14,850, while church and school property is valued at $29,486,514.

The institutions of learning in the Negro Methodist Church, and used for the education of their children, number 52. They employ 375 teachers, and have 10,556 students. Their school property is valued at $1,817,850.

This is a bird's-eye view of what the Negro Methodism is doing for the moral and religious training of the race. Let us consider the educational development of the negro in three decades. What is he doing toward educating his children during thirty years? Thirty years ago colored schools were scarce. There were not one thousand in all the land. Colored teachers were scarcer, colored professors were a rarity, and of professional men there were only a few; but three decades of freedom give us in all schools of all grades a grand total of 24,038 teachers, 21,674 schools, with an enrolment reaching 1,327,822. After three decades in the schoolroom we furnish at least 20,000 of the teachers to man our own schools; and if we only had the opportunity, we would furnish a teacher for every schoolhouse. All this has been done within the space of thirty years.

The cost of maintaining these schools is borne by the people of the South, both colored and white tax-payers. Within the last three decades the churches and benevolent organizations of the North have contributed at least $20,767,746. Ten Southern States have contributed about $40,377,673, or a total from Church and State and friend, within thirty years, of $61,145,419.

We have found two men during these three decades who have had a million dollars' worth of faith in the possibilities of the negro. But what does the negro pay toward his own education? Is it all a free gift? I find that there are 1,327,822 pupils in the common schools; the books, at $2.00 each, will require an outlay of $2,655,644; to clothe and feed these children, estimating $12.00 each year, or twenty-five cents per week, would cost $15,933,864; or, the total to support the children in the common schools for one year is $18,589,508. Summing up the expense in all schools of all grades, we see that it costs the colored people for board, clothes, books, and transportation, annually, $25,593,457. This is what the negro is laying upon the altar of Christian education every year at the close of three decades.

To illustrate the development of the educational institutions in three decades: the African Methodist Episcopal Church in 1863 had one institution of learning; now there are fifty-two. Then there were three teachers; now, 5,300. Then, value of property was $10,000; now, $576,375. Then the total expense of running the institution was less than $10,000; now the total expense is $604,000. This is only a faint outline of the results of thirty years of freedom as it relates to the negro race.

One of the highest qualities of manhood is that which makes a soldier. It requires obedience, courage, and love of country to constitute a good soldier. He must obey without questioning authority; he must endure fatigue without complaining; he must leave his mother, wife, and children behind without grieving; he must run and not weary; he must walk and not faint.

And during the civil war in America, from 1861 to 1865, there were 178,975 soldiers who enrolled in the United States Volunteer Army. Of this number, 99,337 were enlisted by the authority of the government, 79,638 by the States and Territories, 36,847 soldiers died in the service of the country, and in the 449 engagements in which they participated they proved themselves worthy to be trusted with the nation's flag and honor. And it has become a proverb in military parlance that the colored troops fought nobly.

After the war the Grand Army of the Republic was organized. The negro was admitted as a comrade, and to-day he is received as other comrades in the Grand Army of the Republic, sometimes in separate posts, sometimes together; be it as it may, they have one flag and one country. When the National Guard was organized the negro was received as a soldier, and is treated as all other members of this important branch of public service.

We have companies, regiments, battalions of infantry, cavalry, and of artillery. Colored men to-day bear commissions as captains, majors, colonels, and generals, as well as chaplains.

Among the best military organizations in the country are those of South Carolina, Georgia, and Ohio; and Northern States have encouraged and supported such organizations. In thirty years we have had several young men to attend West Point, and graduated; also to attend the United States Naval Academy at Annapolis, Md. We have a number of regular troops in the regular army. In the last Indian war one of the colored companies distinguished itself for bravery, and saved the army from defeat and destruction. They were commended by the commanding general, thanked by the Secretary of War, and transferred from the field in the West to Washington, D. C., as a mark of distinction for their bravery, and to-day they are guarding the nation's capital. All this in thirty years.

The question now is, "What has the negro done with his thirty years of freedom?" The following are some of his achievements in the field of politics and government: —

Hundreds and thousands have served in ward meetings, city meetings, county and State conventions; hundreds have attended the National Conventions, which nominate the President of the United States; and John R. Lynch and others have presided over the National Convention.

In thirty years the negro has been elected and has served with honor to himself and to his race on the City Council, on Boards of Aldermen, in State Legislatures, in State Senate, in National Congress, and in the United States Senate; and in each of the deliberative bodies has he presided with dignity. What race can show a better record than this? I challenge comparison and wait for a parallel, either from history, tradition, observation, or experience.

Since the negro left the house of bondage he has been elected and has acted as mayor of a town, he has been constable and marshal, county squire and justice of the peace, county sheriff and United States Marshal, the Speaker of the House of Representatives, and Lieutenant-Governor, presiding over the State Senate, acting as Governor of Mississippi, Louisiana, and South Carolina, approving the laws, liberating the convicts, commuting sentences of death to that of life, — the embodiment of law and order for a Commonwealth.

He has presided over the National House of Representatives, and filled the chair of Vice-President of the United States with honor and dignity. The Hon. B. K. Bruce was Register of the United States Treasury, and stamped his name upon the currency of our country, and gave the negro's consent to pay the nation's debt in silver and gold or in greenbacks.

In thirty years the negro has gone from field, shop, and hotel, and has been elected and has served as Secretary of State, Auditor of State, Treasurer of State, Attorney-General of State, Superintendent of Public Schools in County and State; and the negro in the days of reconstruction laid the foundation of the public-school system of the South, and to-day it stands a monument to his love of education and of posterity.

Since 1862 the negro has studied law, been admitted to the bar, been elected city judge, and has presided in the Supreme Court of South Carolina. He has acted as prosecuting attorney and persecuting attorney, too. He has been admitted to practice in the District, Circuit, and Supreme Courts of the United States.

The Hon. Frederick Douglass, the greatest of all American negroes, acted as Marshal of the District of Columbia; he was the representative of law and order of the government, and in a city where less than thirty years ago his kindred were bought and sold. What a wonderful triumph! What marvellous progress has been made in recognizing the rights of the new-made freeman!

Again, inside of thirty years the negro has been appointed by the President of the United States to serve the government as consul in Madagascar, San Domingo, minister resident and consul-general at Hayti, the morning star of negro independence and negro reign; and to Liberia, Africa, the lone star of hope to more than 200,000,000 of men, women, and children, bone of our bone, flesh of our flesh. The negro has assisted in framing the organic laws of many States of the Union since his freedom. He was an important factor in the reconstruction conventions, and has assisted in embodying in the organic law of the land the principles of justice and right.

The trouble in this country is that everybody wants to inform the negro where his place is in society. They do this without consulting him or his friends. It is a common saying both North and South, "I like the negro, but I like him in his place." It means one thing in the North, and it means another in the South. When the old master and the old slave meet it means more than hen two freemen meet.

There must be an understanding with the negro and his friends North and South. The day of reconciliation and organization on the basis of freedom has come. We must now work on other lines than those we fought the battle of liberty on. We must pursue the line of action that will make the largest number of friends and the fewest enemies. It is true and tried friends that we need to-day. We have all the law that is necessary for our happiness, but we want to generate a sentiment in favor of the race, and the only way to do that is by letting each individual make a favorable impression on every one that he comes in contact with, and then the good impressions will be more numerous than the bad ones and we will be respected accordingly.

A great part of this work must be done in the common schools of the North and in the South. The hope of the country is in the instruction of the children, so that they will learn to respect the rights of every one.

Having viewed the past and examined the present condition of the negro, it becomes my duty to give my opinion as to the future, to hang out the danger-signal, and to warn all of the perils that threaten our institutions or imperil the interests of the people. That there are dangers in the future no one can deny. The man with the red flag can be seen by a close observer of the drift of public sentiment. There are two classes of dangers threatening the future of the race. The first are the internal dangers, such as ignorance, poverty, crime, intemperance, and inexperience, with the concomitant evils that follow in the wake of an untrained people having only partially trained leaders. Those of the second class are external and local, coming from intense prejudice and local jealousy among the white people at the progress of the better class of negroes.

As long as the negro is shiftless and worthless he is a good fellow with them; as long as he is unwashed and uncombed, with pants and coats of so many patches that you can hardly distinguish the original material, he is a fine fellow. But as soon as he washes his face, combs his hair, fastens his shoes, dresses himself well, he is a dangerous negro, and must be put out of the community, for " he will spoil all the other negroes." And for the least offence, imagined or otherwise, he is compelled to leave the community, or his low and vicious class circulate a lie, and organize a mob to get rid of this " dangerous negro." The general trouble in the South lies between these two classes, — the mean and extremely low of the negroes and the mean and extremely low of the whites. Their conflicts generally involve to a greater or less degree the better class of whites and the better class of negroes. The work of the future will be for the better class of whites, the better class of negroes, to put down or control the baser elements of both races, and to beget a better feeling between them. Until this is done there lies great danger to the future negro and to the country.

The third danger lies in the coldness and indifference of the North to the cries of the negro in his distress. Northern sentiment has closed its eyes, stopped its ears, locked its mouth, so far as concerns the negro in his sufferings; there is no call nor answer to his danger-signals, and no response to his call of distress.

These are only part of the danger-signals that are hanging by the way of the future of the negro. My advice is as Sherman's advice to his men : " Face the other way, boys, and let us do our duty."

I am here to-day to represent Peter Salem and Crispus Attucks, of the old dispensation; Richard Allen and Christopher Rush, the heroes of the Church; Bishop D. A. Payne, the apostle of an educated ministry; and Frederick Douglass, the highest type of the possibilities of American citizenship, who at the inauguration of Garfield led the procession. Both Garfield and Douglass had travelled a long distance to get their present positions — Garfield, from the tow-path of an Ohio canal; Douglass, from the depths of Lloyd's plantation. Both were representatives of their classes and were honored for their devotion to the sacred cause of liberty.

But, thank God, no child of the Republic will ever have to travel the road travelled by Douglass. The chasm of slavery is filled once for all, and all now start from the plane of a freeman.

As I walk upon the sacred soil of this imperial city, instinctively I raise my hat to the heroes as they pass in memory's gallery. Who will ever forget John Quincy Adams, who at home, in the White House, or in foreign lands, repeated the prayer of his childhood: " Now I lay me down to sleep. If I should die before I wake, I pray the Lord my soul to take "?

He was a pioneer Christian Endeavorer. This Commonwealth has given to Liberty some of her greatest heroes, names that will gild the page of history, the irrepressible conflict for generations, and whose names and examples will be emulated through coming times.

Religion and patriotism are handmaidens, and furnish the cords that bind man to the altar of his country and to his God with a loyalty that is stronger than love of life. He will follow the flag of his country and defend it at the point of the bayonet, or at the cannon's mouth, from the assaults of the enemies of our institutions and the foes of our flag. He will be willing to lay down his life, if need be, to save it from dishonor or disgrace.

There are two flags that every good citizen should love with a holy devotion, — the Stars and Stripes and the Union Jack. The emblems of the three great powers of the earth are the American Eagle, the British Lion, and the Cross of Calvary.

The man or nation that is loyal to each of these is on the road to success; for no man can be loyal to the institutions of America, to the principles of personal liberty of England, and be supremely loyal to the Lord Jesus Christ, without being able to lead the moral and religious forces of Christianity to the conquest of the moral and religious world.

The strength of the Christian Endeavor Association lies in the fact that it teaches the elementary principles of both religion and patriotism, and insists upon good citizenship as the basis of true Christianity.

Wherever the Association has been organized it has supplied the needs of the country and fulfilled every demand made by the various institutions. The true mission of the Christian Endeavor Association is to give to each and every human being bread, truth, love, and faith three times a day: bread for the body, truth for the mind, love for the soul, and faith for mankind,—faith in God, faith in the Bible and the religion of the Bible, faith in the Holy Ghost of the Bible, faith in the cardinal doctrines of Christianity, faith in the moral heroes of the Bible, faith in the Ten Commandments, in the Golden Rule, and in the life and works of the humble Nazarene.

In teaching patriotism to the rising generation, we insist that it shall have an abiding faith in the Declaration of Independence, in the Constitution, with its amendments, in the doctrine of the equality of man, and in an unfaltering faith in the possibilities of every child of the Republic to be an honored and loyal citizen of the Republic of America, and at the same time a citizen of the kingdom of grace and an heir to the kingdom of glory.

Let the sons of God take courage, for right must triumph over might, and justice and truth shall reign from sea to sea. Let the daughters of Zion sing their songs of joy and attune their harps to join in the general jubilee that is sure to come, for virtue, temperance, and education will rout and destroy their last enemy, and will finally reign in every heart, in every home, and in every land.

Roll on, Liberty's ball! roll on until every chain on limb, mind, and heart shall be broken. Roll on till every tyrant shall be crushed beneath thy weight, and until every despot's throne shall be ground to powder. Roll on in the triumphant march until ignorance shall be conquered by intelligence; until crime and sin shall give place to universal righteousness. Roll on until the peerless queen of universal liberty and justice shall sit upon the throne of every heart, shall govern every home, and shall enlighten every mind. Then shall the bell of Liberty that rang out during the World's Fair at Chicago sound the death-knell of religious intolerance, of inequality between man and man, and chime the funeral dirge of color prejudice in Church and State. Let the Christian Endeavor Association do its duty in the future as it has in the past, and the time will come when the nation shall not war with nation, but an arbitration shall settle the difficulties between nation and nation, swords shall be beaten into plowshares, spears into pruning-hooks, and the plow of peace shall turn up the virgin soil, and we shall reap the harvest of security and peace, and every man shall enjoy his right to life and the pursuit of happiness.

Tent Endeavor.

The services at Tent Endeavor called out another great audience, and the occasion proved one of general interest to all in attendance.

The presiding officer of the morning was Trustee Rev. J. M. Lowden, of Boston, and the musical director, Mr. Percy S. Foster.

The usual preliminary singing by the audience without a director was enjoyed, and the Scripture reading following was led by Rev. Walter E. Brooks, D.D., of Washington, D. C., by whom the prayer was also made.

The programme in the tent called for the testimonies of different representatives from the North, East, South, and West, on the important work of Christian citizenship.

The first speaker, the Rev. A. M. Phillips, of Montreal, P. Q., represented Canada.

Address of Rev. A. M. Phillips.

As a principle of action, I will take an extract from the Christian Endeavor active member's pledge: "I promise him (the Lord Jesus Christ) that I will strive to do whatever he would like to have me do." And as an ideal standard, Phil. I. 27, R. V., "Only let your manner of life be worthy of the Gospel of Christ;" literally, "Only live your citizen life in a way worthy of," etc., or as in the margin, "Only behave as citizens worthily of," etc.

I have said "religion in politics," not "religion and politics." They are not twain, but one. It is an unscriptural Christianity and immoral politics that have put asunder "what God hath joined together."

Many, the majority, do not recognize this oneness, and make no connection between religion and politics, between their duty as Christians and as citizens. What is to be done when we recognize that the majority of the people, even of the electorate, are professing Christians? My answers must necessarily be brief: —

1. The citizen must be impressed with the truth that government is a fact "ordained" of God for a definite moral purpose. Forms of government are human, the institution thereof Divine.

2. The citizen must be taught that the same principles of right are binding everywhere alike, on the regenerate professor and the unregenerate non-professor. That there cannot be a double standard of morals applies here. What is right is right for everybody, and what is wrong is right for nobody. There are not two kinds nor two standards of right anywhere in the universe for either God or man.

3. Mankind must be made to feel that it is absolutely wrong to divorce the sacred from the secular — to separate religion from politics. The old cry, "Business is business and religion is religion," is antichristian, as also is the hackneyed objection to mixing religion and politics. Religion is everything and everywhere, or it is nothing and nowhere. It is for time as well as for eternity; for body and mind as well as for soul and spirit; it is as well for politics as for prayer; for the shop as for the Church; for election day as for Sunday; for the office as for the prayer meeting; for the ballot-box as for the communion table; for the masses as for the individual; for the nation as for the home. The true principle is, "Business is religion, politics is religion."

4. The objective point of Christianity as taught must be changed. This, not other worldliness, must become the motive of action. The consummation of Christianity is not in a "happy land, far, far away," but in this real, old, sin-cursed earth; nor is it to be looked for in the distant visionary "good time coming," or the "sweet by and by," but in the "near now and now."

5. The Christian Church must be made to realize fully the spirit and purpose of Christ. Christ came not to establish a church, but a kingdom. The establishment of the kingdom of heaven on earth was the object of his mission.

6. The world must be taught that Christianity is human well-being. Good citizenship in the kingdom of heaven always constitutes good citizenship in the State. Political selfishness has no more a place in life than religious selfishness, and is just as wrong. It is never right for one class of citizens to take an unfair advantage of the necessities of another class.

7. We must secure a correct public sentiment. The sentiment must be created that to enter public life does not mean an abandonment of righteousness. The old maxim, "*Salus populi suprema lex esto*," — "the welfare of the people is the right law," — is the standard "worthy of the Gospel of Christ."

8. The human life of Christ must be taken as the model. "Taking Christ as my example," should become the realized experience of every person and the standard for the State.

9. Denominational pride and bigotry must give way to Christian unity and co-operation. Christianity, as the expression of our Heavenly Father's will, is much more than the denomination as the exponent of any man-made creeds or form of ecclesiastical government. The interests of the kingdom of heaven are much more important than of any church as a human organization.

The next speaker represented the South, Rev. John H. Boyd, D.D., Charlotte, N. C.

Address of Rev. John H. Boyd, D.D.

The voice from the South is going to speak a word as to what Christian citizenship stands for in that section of the country. I want to speak of what it is doing there and call your attention to the conscience vote which is being deposited in the ballot-boxes of the Southern country; and I am glad to represent my section this morning, because I believe there is no part of our common country where public sentiment on moral issues is in so healthy a condition. There is no part of the land where reforms are moving with such rapidity, and are establishing themselves with stability, marked by statute laws and constitutional amendments. Remember that a few years ago in the State of Louisiana there was an institution entrenched behind millions of money; its influence over public sentiment had been established by a mercenary benevolence; the farms of the river valleys were hidden behind levees built by the lottery money; the sick in the metropolis were cared for by the same, and congregations throughout the State were worshipping in sanctuaries that had been built by this money; and yet, notwithstanding all that, the manhood of Louisiana asserted itself, and drove the accursed thing from her borders. Whenever the enactment of a local option law has been mentioned in this Convention, that mention has met with ringing plaudits; but let me tell you that in the South more than eight States already have this law, and under its operation large sections of the country have been won from the power of the saloon. We do not carry on our reform with the din and noise and publicity of the North, but to-day the most prohibition State in the Union is the State of Mississippi. But five counties in that State can license the saloon, and only last week I rode five hundred miles, from one end of the State to the other, and passed but one town where an open saloon exists. Circles of sobriety under the four-mile law of Tennessee have taken one-half that State from the saloon. Georgia is two-thirds under local option. The saloon power as a political element has been destroyed in South Carolina. Therefore, in representing my section this morning, as it stands for practical Christian citizenship and conscience voting, it has a record that I am proud of. Again, you will find that the traditions of our sections are the same. The great Declaration of Independence was signed on Northern soil, but General Cornwallis laid down his sword at Yorktown, thus ending the war. So, then, our traditions are the same, and they are alike precious to North and South. Now, then, look across the Southern country, and you find there to-day a country undeveloped. Your country seems to be finished, your enterprises are established, your fields are cultivated to the fence corners. Interminable forests, arable and yet uncultivated, stretch from one end of the South to the other, and there the wheels of enterprise are destined to run; there the power of wealth is to be established in future. You are the country of the present, and we are the country of the future. And this leads to this point, that millions of American population lie to the South. The colored man in the innermost depths of his being is an American. That flag stands for him: the white of it for the purity of the motives which emancipated him, the red for the blood which was shed for him, and the stars intimate the heavenly hope which has been held before him. The colored man is an American. The blood that flows in the white veins of the South is the blood of the English gentleman, of the Scotch-Irish yeomanry, the blood of the Huguenot artisan. Now this great mixture makes true Americanism. You find no anarchy among us, no infidelity among us, no mobs of strikers among us, no disloyal Romanism among us. But when, with your issues that are pressing upon you to-day, that concern "the little red schoolhouse" and other matters of Church and State — when these issues have been brought to the arbitrament of American controversy, the national ballot-box, understand that from Virginia to Texas you will meet a harmonious American patriotism that will be solid for all that the stars and bars stand for.

The Rev. Dwight M. Pratt, pastor of Williston Church, Portland, Me., was introduced to speak for the East.

Address of Rev. Dwight Mallory Pratt.

I stand here to speak for the East, the far-off, "down-east" portion of this great land. I do so with some degree of confidence, for Maine has endeavored to do her part in the formation of good citizens. She has given this organization to the world, which stands first and last always for the noblest possible type of manhood and womanhood; she has done more in law and practical effort than any other portion of the globe in temperance reform and for the prohibition of the saloon; and last, but not least, it was left to her to furnish a man who had brains and common sense enough to make rules by which a stupid and inefficient Congress could transact business.

One who would fulfil his part as a good citizen must, next to his duty to God, recognize his obligations to his fellowmen. When Abraham Lincoln was President of the United States he summoned President McCulloch, of the Bank of Indiana, to Washington, as Comptroller of the Currency. After two years of incessant, patriotic labor he was again summoned by Mr. Lincoln to the more arduous position of Secretary of the Treasury. It was the darkest hour of the war. The finances of the nation were in a critical condition. Mr. McCulloch felt that he could assume no greater responsibility. Mr. Lincoln called him into his office, looked at him with his sad, weary eyes, and throwing his arms over his shoulder, said, "You *must;* the country needs you." In that spirit of self-surrender and sacrifice, Mr. McCulloch served the country with great unselfishness and devotion. This is good citizenship. This is patriotism.

The determining forces in national life come from private citizens, not from official power. Had there not been consecrated citizens in goodly number who recognized their obligations to humanity, there never would have been a Lincoln to voice those obligations and make them effective in law. The Emancipation Proclamation originated in the writings of a Congregational minister; for Lincoln himself acknowledged that Dr. Leonard Bacon's book on slavery first led him to those clear convictions which issued in the famous proclamation of 1862. Nor is this all. The chief honor here falls to a woman. It is generally conceded that Harriet Beecher Stowe's "Uncle Tom's Cabin" did more than any other one thing to break the fetters of the slave. Look at the formative influences of that remarkable era. John Brown, Garrison, Wendell Phillips, Mrs. Stowe, Dr. Leonard Bacon, made the career of Lincoln possible. A wool dealer, an editor, a lawyer, a minister's daughter, a clergyman, illustrate the forces that go to make up a republic. A devout sense of obligation to humanity on the part of Christians will regenerate society. No man with the spirit of Christ can betray his country in civil office, can surrender to the saloon through fear of disaster to business, can accumulate millions and ignore the wants of suffering humanity, can witness poverty, crime, and growing corruption without being a reformer.

The age calls for men who will place righteousness and the public welfare above personal prosperity. If the evils of the world are ever to be overcome, they will be overcome by the unselfishness and heroism of self-sacrificing love on the part of all who call themselves followers of Jesus Christ. Whether a man be a Phillips Brooks, a Mark Hopkins, an Edison, a Vanderbilt, or a Rockefeller, God calls him in each instance to be alike serviceable to humanity.

The president of the Missouri Christian Endeavor Union, Mr. Thomas Jones, of Kansas City, spoke for the West.

Address of Mr. Thomas Jones.

We of the West are here to-day to get inspiration. We have been trying to march to the music of New England. We were with you in 1776, in 1865, and we want to be with you in 1895. It is said that when Napoleon wanted to inspire his soldiers to noble deeds of heroism and valor he led them to the Pyramids of Egypt, then pointed to the tops and said, "Forty centuries are looking down on you." We have something better than that to inspire our young people, to bring them here to Boston. On Boston Common we point them to the spirit of New England not only in Christian Endeavor, but in good citizenship. You who initiated the cause of good citizenship in Boston and other cities have also inspired us in the West, for our views there are largely like yours. We sprang from the East. You are responsible for our virtue, and in a large measure you are responsible for our vice; so we stand together on common ground. It has become respectable for a Christian man to be more or less in politics. You perhaps remember that when Dr. Parkhurst initiated his work in New York they called it Sunday-school politics. Whenever a Christian man or woman attempted to do anything along that line they called it Sunday-school politics.

I am glad also, whether we are Republicans or Democrats, Populists or Prohibitionists, that our young people write before it these words: "Christian Endeavor" Republican, "Christian Endeavor" Democrat, etc. That means that the vote is to be according to the principle of Christian Endeavor, and we add Republican, Democrat, Populist, or Prohibitionist, as you like to have it. That means that there is a golden thread running through all these parties called Christian Endeavor, and it means that we are bringing conscience into politics. In the West we have been able to do much toward overthrowing the saloon influence. The last two Sundays the door of every saloon in Kansas City, three hundred and forty, has been shut tight as a drum, and some of the saloon-keepers, whether they meant it in sarcasm or not, hung out a placard, "Gone to church." You will find that the law that struck the death-knell of the lottery at the seat of our government was introduced by a Kansas congressman, so that there are some good things yet that can come from the West. We find we are coming together along political, as well as along religious, lines, so that to-day we are all tending toward that golden dream of every Christian man and woman, — one faith and one flag, one God and one country, one duty and one destiny.

Rev. W. G. Clarke, D.D., of Chicago, Ill., conducted the open parliament, the topic being "What Are You Doing for Christian Citizenship?"

Address of Rev. W. G. Clarke, D.D.

I esteem it a high honor to conduct the parliament of patriotism in connection with this Convention, beneath these symbols of patriotism, and above all, in this city of historic memories. For half an hour we shall consider the natural and necessary duties which subsist between the Christian and his community, his city and his country; and as we consider these duties let us all re-vow to consecrate ourselves to loyalty and patriotism. Our life, our thought, our strength, our influence, every relation in us, ought to be permeated with the spirit of Christianity, the commercial and industrial, the social and educational, the civic and political, as truly as the distinctly moral and religious. The Church, the clergy, and the individual Christian have failed of the full measure of usefulness until politics have been moulded by religion, — a religion that demands honesty and competence and fidelity in public office; a religion that demands virtue and intelligence on the part of the citizens. The history of our land is a history of the operation of religion upon our institutions, upon our laws. Where liberty found a fitting shrine Christianity found an ample altar. Bancroft stated that the compact on board the *Mayflower* was the birth of constitutional liberty, but that compact was a religious as truly as a political document. Paternalism was the commingling of patriotism and of piety, and these two streams have marched together in American national life. The first name that this land bore upon an old Roman map was "La Santa Crucis,"—"the Holy Land of the Cross;" and ever since the Cross has extended its arms of blessing in the history of American life. Thomas Jefferson was not forgetful of the sovereignty of God in drafting the Magna Charta of civil liberty, for the Declaration of Independence was still dependent on the protection of Almighty God. And so we find that this has been patent to the foreigners that have examined our conditions, spiritual and religious, and that have commented upon them in glowing terms. Agassiz, whom we love to revere throughout this country and especially in this city, has said, "The foundation of your people is the Bible." Père Hyacinth, looking across the sea from his French pulpit, testified, "The light of this nation is in its faith in Jesus Christ." Gladstone has paid his tribute to New England as the central commanding moral influence of the country; and De Tocqueville, visiting our shores, summed up the situation in these words: "The Americans have combined the notions of liberty and of Christianity so intimately that it is impossible to make them conceive of one without the other."

In every step of our national progress Christianity and civilization have been mixed, from the time that the colonists hurled these words in the teeth of George III.: "We own no Master but Jesus Christ," until the time when the immortal Lincoln testified that the emancipation of the slaves was in pursuance of a solemn vow that he had made to Almighty God: "I have vowed before God that if General Lee be driven out of Pennsylvania I will crown the result with the declaration of freedom to the slaves." The United States Supreme Court has been constrained to declare the United States is a Christian nation. Practical Christianity means among other things the Christian politician and the Christian statesman. Loyalty to God means loyalty to your nation. False to either, and you are false to both. How deeply impressed upon us at the present hour is the need of duty-serving Christians that regard the interests of their land sacred! It is impressed upon us by the abuses which liberty suffers, and the perils that threaten our Commonwealth, which is even yet only an experimental democracy. "Eternal vigilance is the price of liberty." Not yet mayest thou unbrace thy corselet or lay by thy sword; not yet, O Freedom, close thy lids in slumber, for thine enemy never sleeps, and thou must watch and combat till the day of the new era. Allow me to present certain precepts to the good-citizenship committees of our great Christian Endeavor Society, believing that they may achieve a national benefit that is an incalculable good. I will formulate them as a new Decalogue for the sake of brevity.

First commandment: Thou shalt be an intelligent citizen, acquainting thyself by full and fair investigation with the issues of every campaign.

Second commandment: Thou shalt be a virtuous citizen, regarding principle as the best policy, and imparting thy private virtue to the public fund.

Third commandment: Thou shalt be an active citizen, esteeming indifference to public interest and neglect of public duties as forms of treason.

Fourth commandment: Thou shalt employ thy voice and thy pen as truly as thy vote, for however strong the principles are, thou must stand for them or they will fail.

Fifth commandment: Thou shalt cast thy ballot in caucus, primary convention, and at the election, for that white slip is a public trust conveyed to thee, a weapon for good government placed in thy hands, and the ballot-box is the ark of a new covenant.

Sixth commandment: Thou shalt be the inveterate foe of official incompetency and dishonesty and all forms of political corruption.

Seventh commandment: Thou shalt resist all phases of lawlessness, believing that the decay of the authority of law and its violation with impunity is perilous to a republic.

Eighth commandment: Thou shalt not be a slave to thy party, coerced by its tyranny to vote against thy conscience, but shalt maintain that patriotism is superior to partyism, and principle to both.

Ninth commandment: Thou shalt protect our American institutions, the free press, the free schools, and the freedom of religion against all assaults of foreignism or sectarianism, for they are the citadels of our national strength.

Tenth commandment: Thou shalt battle against the tyranny and infamy of the liquor traffic, that is the pregnant source of industrial depression, political corruption, social vice, and indeed, the most universal and colossal evil in our country, and thou shalt not sheathe thy sword until it bears the laurels of a splendid victory.

Young people, by this Decalogue piety, peace, and prosperity will crown the brow of our fair country with a triple crown, whose rays of blessing will shine brighter than the flashing light from Bartholdi's statue of Liberty, to the utmost parts of the world. Remember that if America fails, the world will also fail, but that if America succeeds it will be the success of a new and glorious civilization.

In the open parliament that followed many reports were given of work done along good-citizenship lines.

The presentation of a banner to the Syracuse Union for the best work reported in promoting Christian citizenship was presented by Rev. S. Edward Young, of Newark, N. J. This feature closed the programme for the morning.

Address of Rev. S. Edward Young.

In the cabin of the *Mayflower* the passengers signed the following Christian citizenship pledge: "In the name of God, Amen. We have undertaken for the glory of God and advancement of the Christian faith and honor of our King and country to plant the first colony on the northern part of Virginia." Every charter of every American colony — I have searched the records — plighted troth eternal to the religion of Jesus Christ. The first act of the Continental Congress was the appointment of Rev. Fr. Duché to lead in prayer, followed soon by the act importing 20,000 Bibles, and later by the devising of a coinage such that, if a man should hold a dollar so near his eye as to shut out the whole of heaven, he still would see that little silver creed, "In God We Trust." March 19, 1782, Congress directed citizens to pray "that the religion of our Divine Redeemer, with all its Divine influences, may cover the earth as the waters cover the seas." Seven times, in seven great crises, the nation, in Congress assembled, has re-accented its pristine covenant, the Senate in special resolution, March 2, 1863, expressing the purpose "to seek God through Jesus Christ." After Gettysburg went forth a presidential proclamation, saying, "It has pleased Almighty God to hearken to the prayers and supplications of an afflicted people. Render the homage due to the Divine Majesty. Invoke the influence of his Holy Spirit to lead the whole nation through paths of repentance and submission to the Divine Will back to the perfect enjoyment of union and fraternal peace," — the language of Abraham Lincoln. To America this banner says, "You declared at the outset for God and righteousness, you, the United States, did, and in crucial hours have renewed your vows and covenant. God has kept faith — you must." To citizens of the British Empire this banner says, "The ' *Dei gratia*,' inscribed on coin and signet, is meant in earnest. Verily *by the grace of God* stands firm the throne of England's glorious Queen." To people everywhere this banner says, "The earth is the Lord's and the fulness thereof. Not a nation nor a city, not a man nor a woman in it, not a penny nor an inch of land, not an office nor a ballot-box, rightfully belongs to any one but Jesus Christ." Yes, more; it says an army of young people have enlisted for the absolute subjection of the whole world to Christ. From this moment nearly two and one-half millions of Christian Endeavorers stand for the immediate application of Christianity to all public affairs. The situation can never again be as it has been. Unbound by the fetters, social, political, ecclesiastical, that have withed themselves about the consciences of some farther on in years, these youths are mustering fearlessly for the battle. They will not only scour the gutters for men and women — they will try to keep men and women out of the gutters. They will not be partners to the silent agreement, that *lex non scripta* of other days, that the sole function of Christianity is to balm the wounds that wrong has made. They will go further. They will wage war on the whole wound-making business. What tact and grit and faith and patience it takes to champion well the cause of Christian citizenship! Who shall be efficient for the task? Those only who above the din and strife, louder than the call of party, or friends, or selfish motives, hear and heed the voice of One who must reign till all enemies are put under his foot, who alone is Lord of lords and King of kings. To you, the representative of the Syracuse Union, for splendid work already done and for incitement to nobler achievement in time to come, the United Society of Christian Endeavor present this significant banner.

SATURDAY NOON.

Open-air Meeting on Boston Common.

Just at the hour set for the beginning of the rally on Boston Common the heavens opened, and the delegates, gathered by the thousands around the band-stand, were obliged to flee to their tents, not, however, until ten thousand of them, beneath upraised umbrellas, had joined in three mighty cheers for the venerable author of "America," and had sung, with voices that pierced through the black clouds to heaven itself, one verse of the national anthem, following it with, "God Save the Queen."

It was rather difficult for enthusiasm to find its way up through the black canopy of silk and muslin that covered the crowd, and so the orders were given to disperse to Tent Williston and Tent Endeavor, where the service was continued as two meetings. The enthusiasm was present, however, and not all the waters of the deluge could dampen it.

Tent Endeavor, as being the nearest to the meeting-place on the Common, was thronged to the walls, every seat, every aisle, every niche, and every cranny being occupied by the patriotic Endeavorers. This was the most crowded meeting of all the Convention series. The tents stood the onslaught of celestial artillery in excellent fashion ; and yet through the pole-vents and the joining of the canvas the water found its way in streams, and many delegates had to pay the cost of a thorough drenching for the privilege of participating in the service. Evidently they wanted to receive full value, for certainly the songs were entered into with rare zest, and the addresses were listened to with closest attention.

Dr. Clark's voice would not permit him to fulfil the duties of presiding officer, and he summoned Dr. Nehemiah Boynton to the post. Dr. Boynton, in introducing Rev. S. F. Smith, D.D., to read his original poem, asked that he should be greeted in perfect silence with the Chautauqua salute. It was a wonderful white wave that the venerable patriot beheld, but the love and enthusiasm of the eleven thousand delegates could be satisfied with nothing less than a rousing three cheers. Doubtless the author of "America" never received a nobler ovation.

Then, in complete stillness, he read the following poem, that he had written for the occasion : —

Poem by Rev. S. F. Smith, D.D.

Greetings to all the host,
From mountain, vale, and coast,
   River and seas.
Where'er our bands are found
Send the glad tidings round,
Echo the joyful sound,
   On every breeze.

Greetings to old and young,
Greetings in many a tongue,
   Loudest and best.
Break forth in holy song,
Roll the blest tide along
In accents sweet and strong,
   North, South, East, West.

Onward with purpose brave,
To seek, to lift, to save,
   For God, for man.
Not ours to seek delay,
Nor squander one brief day
Not ours to waste in play
   Life's fleeting span.

All hail, triumphant Lord!
Fulfil Thy gracious word,
   And take Thy throne.
Like watchmen at the gate
Thy youthful servants wait ;
Assume Thy regal state,
   And reign, alone.

When he had departed from the platform, amid a storm of huzzas, the chorus sang, "Arouse Ye, Arouse Ye," the special Convention hymn, of which Dr. Smith is the author. The great band that had been secured for the occasion made the music still more martial and impressive.

Many of the delegates throughout the tent had raised umbrellas, because of the constant dripping of the water. This naturally obstructed the view of those in the rear. Dr. Boynton took a happy and effectual way of remedying the difficulty. Addressing the delegates, he said, " Umbrellas are affiliated members of Christian Endeavor ; but affiliated members would never think of inconveniencing the active members of the association, and I should be very glad if all those affiliated umbrellas could be closed." The umbrellas went down ; and throughout the remainder of the service the delegates had no other shelter than the canvas above them.

Mayor Curtis has been given many cordial greetings ; assemblies of all sorts have been glad to honor him ; but doubtless never before has he been accorded such a reception as the Christian Endeavor delegates gave him when Dr. Boynton led him forward to speak on behalf of the city of Boston. He was scarcely in sight before white handkerchiefs were a-flutter the audience over; and then came roll after roll of thunderous hand-clapping, the whole winding up with a sturdy round of applause.

Address of Mayor Edwin U. Curtis.

Mr. Chairman and Members of the Society of Christian Endeavor,— The watchword of the present day is Municipal Reform. It is the grandest watchword of modern times. Over all our great cities, too long given over to political debauchery, is sweeping a reviving breeze. It brings with it the healing of the people. Upon its wings is borne the cheering news that your Society is making one of its tests of true Christian character a sympathy with this great movement in political life. I congratulate you that this is so, and beg your attention to the discussion of some political considerations which make for good citizenship. "Now, therefore, ye are no more strangers and foreigners, but fellow citizens." As such, let me set before you some of the duties incumbent upon us all.

To make the world better is the chief object of your organization. It is true that its aim is to elevate mankind mainly through Christian work; but at no point do the orbits of the religious and of the secular so nearly coincide as at this point of true citizenship.

Concerning this point I address you, not as an organization, but as individual men and women. Each of you has a part, more or less influential, in the building of society. To enlist such an army of young people in a good cause, it is necessary to appeal to them as individuals. Already in our body politic are far too many cliques, each struggling for recognition upon the basis of some real or fancied right or claim. I should regret the coming of the day when we should hear of the "Christian Endeavor vote."

In municipal affairs, at least, the true reformer also deprecates the existence of too sharp a division upon party lines. The struggle for a well-ordered city government is not properly between those who differ upon economic or fiduciary questions. It is between the upper and the nether world. And by this I do not mean to draw a social, but a moral distinction. As we stand upon the threshold of a new century, the battle for municipal control is between the forces of light and of darkness. The forces of light have heretofore remained far too passive. The organized forces of darkness are unscrupulous and defiant. The forces of light have, far too often, feared to soil their hands by active political work. They have read that to touch pitch is sure defilement. They have imagined that to enter vigorously into the battle for good government is to bring stains upon the skirts of their garments.

It is to such that I would address my appeal to-day. Especially would I beg those to listen who are citizens of our great cities. We have only to turn our eyes to the two great mother cities of the East and of the West — both happily now released from a thraldom of iniquity — to realize the crying need for the upraising of the banners of the forces of light. The vileness of Tammany in New York has long been a reproach to our country. Now, too, the strong searchlight has been turned upon the municipal methods so long in force in Chicago. We find that for years one man has been drawing thirty-one salaries annually from the public treasury; and we realize that none too soon have the forces of righteousness asserted themselves.

The bane of our great cities has been, and still is, indifference. It has been publicly asserted recently that we live in an age of decay of public spirit. But when public spirit decays, the decline is first discovered, not among the worst, but among the best, elements in society. It is lamentable that this is so. The enemies of a pure government never sleep. They never for a moment relax their vigilance. It is those who would fain see truth and honesty prevail who too often slumber in the hour of battle.

Statistics are sometimes uninteresting. Yet it is useful to know that in a single election in this State, out of a total registration of nearly five hundred thousand voters, more than one hundred and fifty thousand failed to visit the polls. There is no reason to believe that Massachusetts is peculiar in this respect. A large number of voters in all our great cities remain at home on election day and refrain, upon frivolous pretexts, from casting their votes. How many of these, think you, belong to the forces of light? How many to the forces of darkness? The political history of our great cities is in itself an answer. The forces of darkness lie not dormant. They are vigilant. They do not miss their opportunities. They gather strength by the supineness of their opponents. Let the true Christian Endeavorer, then, realize that upon him rests, individually, a responsibility for good government. As soon as he reaches man's estate, let him register. His name once upon the voting-list, let him regard it as his Christian duty to cast his vote at every election. The exercise of the suffrage is not merely a right. It is not solely a privilege. It is a solemn duty. See well to it that you neglect it not. Upon this point, one thing more: the true Christian citizen is a Christian citizen in rain as well as in sunshine. Let no inclemency of the weather serve to keep the Christian Endeavorer away from the polls. The forces of darkness dearly love a rainy election day. Do not wait for a carriage to take you to the polls. The rain which falls while on your way to the voting-place is no more damp than that which falls while on your way to your place of business, or to church. Few things are of greater importance than this in the study of good citizenship.

But the responsibility of the Christian citizen does not begin and end here. A conscientious attendance at the polls is not the only duty to be performed. There is a responsibility which begins earlier than this. It begins at the caucus. The good citizen has no right to complain that the ticket offered him is not such as he would have chosen, if he has declined to assist in its formation. Every party has its undesirable elements. Attend the caucus. See to it that the best men possible are chosen as candidates for public office. As a clergyman has said, in discussing this subject, "If the caucus chances on a prayer-meeting night, attend the caucus and leave the women to do the praying." How can the Christian Endeavorer still his conscience when, by his inertness, unworthy candidates have been foisted upon the people? See to it that the sources of political life are pure, that the stream may be pure also.

I have said that the bane of our political life is indifference. Let not this indifference operate to prevent your own candidacy for public office. Too often the man whose service would be the most valuable in municipal affairs pleads his absorption in his own business. He shrinks from possible criticism. He leaves the vacant seat in the councils of the city to be filled by one far less worthy. Public office is not merely a public trust. It is a public duty as well. See to it that you shrink not from it, but perform it as a Christian duty.

The second force which makes for evil in municipal government is an unguided partizanship. As just intimated, a division upon distinctly party lines cannot be conducive to the best results in municipal government. It is not the party "boss" who always finds the warmest place in the affections of his fellow citizens. Especially is this true when the criterion is party fealty rather than honesty and probity. The ideal municipal government is that which makes honesty and capacity indispensable in the selection of candidates for public office. In the selection of a manager of a great business corporation, they would be deemed unwise who should regard party politics as a factor of the greatest importance. How much greater are the interests of a great municipality than those of any corporation within its limits! I am aware that this is not the usual view; but it is rapidly becoming popular. We cannot, however, expect to eliminate all elements of partizanship from our municipal life. As in the nation and in the State, so also in the city must political parties exist. It is well, perhaps, for the health of the body politic that this should be so. And if party lines must exist, then at the municipal caucus let me urge that considerations of purely personal friendship be cast aside. Select your candidates from the field. The aim cannot be too high. Those who read history remember that when John Quincy Adams retired from the presidential chair he returned almost at once to Washington as a member of the lower house of Congress. His constituents aimed high in their choice. He regarded no place in the public service too humble for him to fill. Both constituents and representative displayed the highest wisdom.

No doctrine is more pernicious than that which requires party fealty at the expense of just rule. A man of recognized dishonesty should never be intrusted with the public interests, no matter how earnest a party man he may be. These sentiments are deserving of our most serious thought.

Said President Hayes in his inaugural address: " He serves his party best who serves his country best." It was no new thought. It was a truth that had come down through the ages. The bard of ancient Greece uttered it centuries ago. And yet it is a truth which might well be written in every modern legislative hall.

After a thousand years of darkness the world, in the fourteenth and fifteenth centuries, awoke from its lethargy. New life was infused into mankind. That grand revival of letters, of the arts, of religion, of science, has been most aptly termed the Renaissance. So, too, a political darkness has, of recent years, enshrouded our land, encompassing many of our great municipalities. Our city treasuries have too often been at the mercy of the forces of darkness. Courts of justice have become a mockery. The ballot-box has been dishonored and debased. Our laws have been made, or executed, not in the interest of the orderly, but of the criminal classes.

But the new birth is at hand. We of the United States are approaching our political Renaissance. Already the dawn breaks. The pistol of Bat Shea, at the polling-place in Troy, sought to check its coming. But that shot was one heard all over the land. It stirred to fresh activity the forces of light. It aroused from sleep the languid and the indifferent. It fired the heart of the true lover of righteous government. When, expressing the indignation of the country, a righteous judge pronounced a well-deserved sentence upon John McKane, the glad hour drew nearer. Still nearer it drew when the city of New York was reclaimed from Tammany rule. Higher and higher will rise the wave of reform, if only such as you will give your aid. Broader will grow the band of light which already gilds the horizon, if only such as you will greet the dawn. Welcome the day, speed the hour, when in all our great cities shall rise up men, not singly, but in legions, demanding a righteous rule !

Let us plead, too, for a broad, a true, Americanism. We cannot be too intense in our patriotism. As we lift high the pure banner of reform, let us raise beside it the flag of our country. Let no man in his unworthiness deride it. Let no man fail to respect it. May it be, above and beyond everything, the emblem of all that is noble and true, the token of an exalted patriotism and of a true citizenship.

Every Bostonian was proud of his Mayor when the address had been heard. It was full of the practical wisdom that should be expected from a man engaged in the actual affairs of civic government. The very flags that hung wet and lifeless from the tent-poles seemed almost to flutter with the spirit of the address, and with the enthusiasm it aroused in the audience. With exuberant tone and lively spirit the great meeting closed to the strains of " Marching On."

Tent Williston.

The enthusiasm and earnestness were none the less marked than that in the other tent. Chairman Capen, who presided, was himself one of the attractions of the occasion, and said in the opening of the meeting : —

No one can fail to recognize the significance of this great gathering. It is the fitting outcome of Dr. Clark's memorable address at Montreal two years ago, which for all time and in every land has made good citizenship one of the chief planks in the Christian Endeavor platform. And Boston Common is certainly the ideal spot for the first mass-meeting.

We believe in the sacredness of citizenship and in the new "civic religion," which declare that there can be no piety without patriotism. Patriotism which leaves out God lacks the highest inspiration; and a religion which, in the care of the individual, does not give its best thoughts to purifying the State needs to have a new birth.

Christian Endeavorers, while clinging to the old motto, " For Christ and the Church," believe that one way to hold up the Christ and make the Church universal is to strike down corruption and evil and iniquity wherever it shows itself in public life, helping thereby to make this city and every city more and more a city of God.

Four times during this meeting were three cheers and a tiger given with a will that would have brought down further showers, had the old rain-making theory held good. The first time was when Lieutenant-Governor Wolcott — a prince among orators — stepped forward to speak for the Commonwealth. In the midst of his address the audience began to applaud and cheer once more, apparently without cause. Mr. Wolcott, although but half through an eloquent period, perceived Dr. Smith coming to the platform, and with the quick wit of a true gentleman at once called for another three cheers. When enthusiasm over Dr. Smith had in a measure subsided, the address of Mr. Wolcott was continued, and heard with closest attention to the end.

Address of Lieutenant-Governor Wolcott.

Fellow citizens from all the great sisterhood of forty-four States that make •ur brave and noble country, strangers who have come to us from across the sea and have been adopted into the friendship of common purpose and high endeavor to-day, it is a timely and a happy thought that has determined to devote this noonday of the last week-day of your Convention to the cause of emphasizing the duty and the high privilege of *good citizenship*. The patriot gains by being a Christian, and the Christian loses nothing, thank God, by being a patriot. There has been a long period in the history of our land when our citizens seemed to be too content with the fact that our fathers had established here the most perfect governmental machinery that the world had ever seen, planted on the town meeting, inspired by the education that was given by the public schools, broadly based like a permanent pyramid that should forever stand upon the broad base of universal suffrage. Here was given the most perfect governmental machinery that the hand of man ever devised, but, as I have said, it has seemed that we were too content with the machinery and forgot the thinking citizen that must ever stand behind all machinery, if it is fully to produce the results for which it is adapted. The municipal government of our great cities has not been in all cases such as to command the respect of the world ; it has not been such as to call forth the pride of the great mass of our law-abiding, God-fearing citizens ; it has been in some cases a national disgrace. a great national dishonor, and I thank God that there are signs everywhere of a great revolution in public feeling. In well nigh all our cities we see the formation of civic clubs, of good-citizenship clubs, of municipal leagues, organizations of men and women that are tied together not with the hope of plunder. not with the hope of what they can get out of municipal government, but bound together by the high purpose to carry into municipal government the best thought, the highest consecration, of our people. There is place enough for the active operation of such clubs. Protect our school system and improve it. Protect the home against the curse of intemperance, not only by the wisest legislation that you can conceive, but also by the instruction and the examples of fathers, mothers, and good citizens everywhere. See that the insidious attacks of other forms of vice are not allowed to harm the virtue of our sons and daughters. See to it that your public men are honest and capable and loyal Americans. Keep clear and high this standard of the office holder and office-seeker. Hold the great political parties to the highest virtue of which masses of men and women are capable. See that the vicious, that the unfortunate, are treated with justice and yet with mercy. See that your methods of prison discipline are such as to produce reform wherever on this earth reform is possible. Care tenderly for the poor, for the miserable, for the unhappy.

And so I say rejoice, as do we all, that this idea of good citizenship is taking a high and vital hold upon our people. It may be that the year 1895 shall be known hereafter for giving the first stimulus and impulse to a great reform movement that shall improve our government all over the land, from Maine to San Diego, and from the Great Lakes to the Gulf. Many of you, my friends, have recently, I trust, stood by the bridge at Concord, and looked upon that beautiful statue wrought by the skill of a son of Concord who has attained national fame as a great sculptor. There stands that faithful figure with a look of quick intelligence, of refinement, of educated thought, upon his noble features; his hand rests upon the plow, emblematic of sturdy and useful toil; his ear catches the call of duty and of country as it sounded that night from the galloping horse of Paul Revere through the towns of Middlesex County. In his right hand he grasps a musket, showing that he is willing to do whatever service that call of country may demand of him. I bid you, minute-men of good citizenship, hold yourselves ready, as did that minute-man of '75, ready to obey the call of country. The same type is among us to-day. It went to the front with the same splendid loyalty and devotion in the dark days of the late war. It is living and about us to-day; it is in this tent at this moment — that type of the young American, ready to obey the call of country; not content to live a secluded life, but eager to take his part in the great movement, the great struggle that is going on, and must ever go on, between the forces of good citizenship and of evil citizenship, between the forces of high and enlightened intelligence and the forces of ignorance, easily passing into the forces of vice.

And so, minute-men of this great movement, be you ready to take your part, not with the musket, — thank God that, for the time, may be laid aside, — but with the stern courage, the loyal devotion, that that statue represents. Let your muscles, too, be strung up tense and firm with manly and courageous determination. Go forth into our midst, do the great work that is expected of you. And so the United States of America, in the chapters of her history that will be written by this generation and the generations that are coming, will be the equal in splendor and glory of any chapters that were written by the early settlers of this old Commonwealth of Massachusetts, by the heroes of the Revolutionary War, by the young men who gave their lives, and the young women who poured out their prayers that, under God, this nation founded by our fathers should continue to be the United States of America.

Rev. Donald MacLaurin, D.D., pastor of the First Baptist Church of Detroit, Mich., whose magnificent work for the purity of Detroit entitles him to a place of honor on a Christian Endeavor platform, was the last speaker of the meeting, and his searching thought gave good-citizenship ammunition to Endeavor workers.

Address of Rev. Donald MacLaurin, D.D.

1. Good citizenship is obedient citizenship.

Practically our fathers have not been obedient to the mandate of the supreme authority in spiritual things, as duty related itself to the city and the state and the nation. We must confess that those commonly known as our best people have most neglected all the real duties of citizenship. It is but the bald truth to say that many of them have not done their duty, and do not yet do their duty at all.

Some of them may have occasionally voted, but do any of them work for the right with enthusiasm and regularity at every caucus or primary election of their party?

We fear that they do not, and we fear that they will not until a public sentiment shall be created that shall brand every man in this country who habitually abstains from all participation in civic affairs as a traitor to the Democratic form of government under which he lives.

Citizenship involves privileges and duties. We enjoy the privileges, and we are transgressors of Divine law, and are moral cowards, if not worse, if we neglect our responsibilities and duties.

No less an authority than Justice Henry B. Brown, of the United States Supreme Court, in his address before the Law School of Yale in 1895, points out the directions in which our country is threatened: municipal misgovernment, corporate greed, and the tyranny of labor. To all these questions we must invoke the Divine wisdom to their just and certain solution.

Hear that man of God on America's greatest battle-field — I mean Lincoln: "It is for us to be dedicated to the great task remaining for us; that from the honored dead we are to take increased devotion to the cause for which they gave the last full measure of devotion; that we here highly resolve that these dead shall not have died in vain ; that this nation, under God, shall have a new birth of freedom, and that ' government of the people and by the people and for the people ' shall not perish from the earth."

We cannot be good citizens, then, unless we are obedient to this Divine injunction: that we should act the full part of citizens, worthily of the Gospel of Christ. And this we should do because the State is a Divine institution; the State is a Divine organism. This is God's country, and we must conserve it for him ; this is God's outer vesture, so to speak, and we must, who are his children, preserve it in purity from the hands of the foul and the unclean.

This mighty assembly is a demonstration that the Church is waking up to its duty as the inspirer of good citizenship. Who will doubt the assertion that the Church is on the eve of the mightiest and most beneficent revolution that has marked its wondrous history ! The miracles of progress, we have been informed, came always since Christ's day in the last years of the century. It seems as if the moral forces of the world required a hundred years to prepare them for supreme achievement. Before this century ends the Church will have taken the mightiest strides it has yet taken toward the feet of its Master. Then and only then will she be able to make impossible the hard conditions out of which men and women in a land of such opportunities as ours are forced to exist. Upon the apathy of good men and women, cowardice and folly and the hope of misgovernment and plunder rest.

We hear a great deal now and again about men voting as they pray. "The man who merely prays and votes will never accomplish much for liberty, justice, and good government," some one has said. It is useless to ask God to do what we can do ourselves. Politically, he works through human instrumentalities. That was a wise minister who said in his prayer meeting: "Brethren, a caucus is being held this evening, two blocks away, which will decide whether honest men or thieves and gamblers are going to run this city during the next year. I think we had better leave the sisters to run the prayer meeting, and go ourselves to run the caucus."

2. Good citizenship is an intelligent citizenship.

Just to be an American citizen is the loftiest honor that can come to any one on this globe; and to be an intelligent American citizen is the highest duty of modern civilization. Ignorance of any sort, in these days, is a crime. Ignorance of our civic duties certainly must be high treason.

If we would be good citizens we must know what are the dominant forces in our civic existences. What do we know about the dominant forces in our political life to-day? What are the dominant forces? What is the motor in our legislative action ? What is the power behind the throne? What are the prevailing tendencies in municipal, State, and national legislation and life? Whither are we tending? What will be the result of our present methods, or want of methods? What sort of a vote have I been casting in the years that are gone? Have the elements of an ideal vote entered into it? That ideal vote includes three elements, — intelligence, moral obligation, and patriotism. In my municipal action have I had in mind that a municipal government is business and not politics? Have I thought that the city is a great corporation, in which every citizen is a stockholder, and have I acted with that thought in mind? Have I yet discovered that the trained politician has no idea of reform for the good of the people, but only regards the rebuke of one party's corrupt methods as an invitation to another party to profit by like methods? Has it ever occurred to me that there should be no politics whatever in municipal affairs? Am I broadly intelligent upon these great principles of civic affairs?

We should know all about our municipal life. We should know the duties and functions of our Mayor, or other of our first citizens. We should know the duties and functions of the Board of Aldermen, and their limitations, and the personnel of these aldermen. When a man presents himself as a candidate for this important position, we should know whether he has the capacity to transact so important a business as that of the municipality. What do we know about the functions and duties of the various administrative boards of our municipal life?

Lessons in citizenship should be given at the knee of the mother, and continued throughout the entire educational scheme, which should culminate in the training of men and women to be patriots.

3. Good citizenship is aggressive citizenship.

Something more than good intentions and right motives and intelligence are needed to make a good citizen. Very much of the trouble in the world is caused by people who mean well, who have good intentions, but who do not put their intentions into execution.

Aggressive citizenship will see to it that no man, be he native born, or foreign born, be he high or low, rich or poor, can possess the ballot who does not read in the English tongue the Constitution of the United States, and who is not able to pass a creditable examination therein. No privilege is more exalted than that of citizenship in America, and no one should enjoy that exalted privilege who cannot pass a creditable examination.

Aggressive citizenship will endeavor to arouse the apathy of all the good citizens in every community to do their full duty.

Aggressive citizenship will see to it that the laws we have are strictly and impartially enforced.

Mr. Police Commissioner Theodore Roosevelt has well said, "The greatest source of corruption in any place is unenforced laws."

He is right. Every law upon our statute books ought to be impartially and rigorously and persistently enforced, and if they are unjust or impartial, they ought to be corrected at the very next meeting of the Legislature. But for the sake of our rising men and women, for the sake of all concerned, let aggressive citizenship see to it that every law now upon our statute books against evil of every form is strictly and impartially enforced!

4. Good citizenship is united citizenship.

That is to say, it is not individualistic; but it is otheristic. It does not act alone, without regard to others, but seeks to affiliate with other citizens. Paul says, "Stand in one spirit, with one soul together contending." That means that we should be united in our civic political action for the betterment of civic affairs — that the good should be united as against the bad; it means, indeed, civic organization of the good.

And there is tremendous power in organization. The bad are both cowardly in spirit and inferior in numbers.

In order to effectually accomplish this work, therefore, we need to have in every community, small and great, a union of all the moral forces of that community. That is in the contemplation of Paul for good citizenship. Practical, political community of spirit is really meant. And there is needed a sympathetic unity that finds expression in the word "soul," which he uses. And this unity consists not in uniformity of opinions or beliefs, religious, social, economic, or political, as it relates to national affairs, but in identity of supreme purpose concerning our municipal life. There is only one meeting and mingling place; viz., the high plane of the greatest good of the whole civic community, and there must be one fixed irrevocable purpose—no vacillation, no distraction, no diversion from the purpose to make the municipality a business concern; and that all good citizens, uniting, can have it so must certainly pass without fear of contradiction. Let the union of hearts on the determination for better things be so complete and so welded together that the united purpose shall be immovably fixed.

5. Good citizenship is a fearless citizenship.

[NOTE.—We greatly regret we are unable to give address in full.]

The Junior Rally.

Mechanics' Building. — Saturday Afternoon.

Saturday afternoon was an eventful time for the Junior workers of the country, for then was carried out a programme that must stamp itself upon Junior Christian Endeavor everywhere, and that has fixed the standard for all future Junior rallies. The children had the right of way. Even the pastors were obliged to relinguish their seats upon the platform to the Juniors, and the front of the first floor was reserved for the members of Boston Junior Societies. Five hundred children were on the platform, and two thousand others were elsewhere in the house. Most of the society delegations carried banners, and these added to the impressiveness of the scene. Of course the immense hall was literally packed to the doors long before the service began.

The Junior chorus of about four hundred voices, together with a large orchestra of Juniors, furnished music, under the leadership of Mr. Eustace B. Rice, of Boston. A Boston Junior, Master Walter F. Canavan, spoke the welcome in a voice that could be heard to the remotest corner of the building. Said he : —

> " Friends who come to this Convention,
>   Come so many miles to meet us,
> From the South and East and Northland,
>   From Pacific slopes to greet us;
>
> " Friends who come across the border,
>   Canada's bright sons and daughters ;
> Friends who come from other countries,
>   Come to us across the waters ;
>
> " We, the boys and girls of Boston,
>   Gladly welcome you among us;
> Thank you heartily for coming,
>   Thank you for the songs you 've sung us.
>
> " You have had your larger meetings,
>   Welcomes from the older people ;
> You have seen our goodly Boston,
>   Gazed at every spire and steeple.

> " Now we children give you welcome
> To our part of this Convention,
> While we tell of our Endeavor,
> Ask you for your kind attention.

> " Hear the words of older people,
> Hear the songs we Juniors sing you,
> Hear our tales of other Juniors,
> And the messages we bring you.

> " Quarter of a million children
> Pledged to faithful service ever,
> Send, through us, their greetings to you,
> To the army of Endeavor."

Presiding officer Rev. Henry T. McEwen, D.D., of New York, he of the big voice and bigger heart, made the response.

" Uncle Tom," whom the older folks call Mr. Thomas Wainwright, of Chicago, talked " trap " to the Juniors, using a number of objects to illustrate. There were two mouse-traps to start the talk, then the card trap, the cigarette trap, the drink trap, the bad-company trap, and several others.

The only other speaker, Rev. W. Knight Chaplin, had come all the way from London to attend the Convention, and his address was on flags ; a green flag for faith, a purple flag for gratitude, a red flag for zeal, and a blue flag for consecration were the outline points of his capital .talk.

A pilgrim (Mrs. Geo. W. Coleman, Boston), with cloak, hood, staff, and scallop, advanced to the platform and recited in a clear and feeling voice " The Children's Crusade," as introductory to the exercise of the day. "Christ for the World We Sing," said the music of the choir as the pilgrim retired, and then the roll of the nations was called by Dr. McEwen.

First came the English-speaking nations, represented by thirty children, four of whom wore sailor costumes and spoke as Floating Society Juniors ; and half of the participants carried British flags, and the other half American. As they marched, in beautiful and intricate figures, they sang : —

> " Our eyes behold an army of young soldiers of the Lord,
> A quarter of a million strong, His truth their gleaming sword,
> In His bright armor panoplied, obedient to His word,
> As they go marching on."

Several times during the march the children advanced to the front of the great platform — for nothing less than Mechanics' Hall was large enough for the Junior rally — with the English and American flags crossed. This called forth the most vigorous applause. Next came the responses from heathen lands, and one after another the companies of strangely clad children entered the stage in almost bewildering array.

MESSAGE FROM CHINA:— There are twenty-one Young People's Societies and three bands of Juniors who want to join this crusade and help conquer China for Christ. Forty-five little Chinese boys in Shanghai send you special greeting to-day, and the superintendent of their society writes this letter:—

MIDDLE KINGDOM, SHANGHAI,

SOUTHGATE, OUTSIDE.

Beloved Brethren and Sisters, — How are you? Our respects to you. Now, because of the rich blessing of God, our society is flourishing and greatly differs from former times. Our president very gladly prays for you, beseeching the Heavenly Father the more greatly to give blessedness to you. Though we may not have part with you in your great meeting, yet our hearts share in your fulness of joy. Peace be with you all. We have all been looking through our Bibles for a verse to send as our message, and have chosen this: "Behold, these shall come from far; and lo, these from the north, and from the west, and from the land of Sinim. Lift up thine eyes round about, and behold, all these gather themselves together and come to thee."

MESSAGE FROM INDIA AND CEYLON :— We thank you to-day for the light you have sent to the children of India, so that some of us know of a Father in heaven who loves us, and will always hear us when we pray. The 110 Young People's Societies and six Junior bands are trying to do what they can, but we want your help and your prayers, in leading other children into the light, that they, too, may join our army. The Juniors of India are glad to remember the verse: "The Lord is nigh unto all them that call upon him, to all that call upon him in truth."

MESSAGE FROM SPAIN :— Some of the children in Spain are beginning to know the truth as God has given it in his Book, and in the four Christian Endeavor Societies for the young people and one for the Juniors they are taught to read it every day, and to learn much of it by heart. They ask you to-day to pray for the children of Spain, that they may come to serve God "out of a pure heart, and of good conscience, and of faith unfeigned." The Junior Endeavor Society in San Sebastian sends this verse as their message to the Convention :—

"Si, los ninos y las ninas
Que acuden a Christo,
Son sus joyas escogidas,
Pues las redimio."

(Translation.)

"Yes, the boys and the girls
Who follow Christ
Are his chosen jewels,
For he has redeemed them."

MESSAGE FROM MEXICO :— We thank you that you have begun to come to us already, and that the morning light is breaking over the darkness of Mexico. Pray for us that we may become more energetic Christians, for that was the name first chosen for our societies, and some of them still keep for their motto, "Christian energy." Twenty-three societies of Christian Endeavor are teaching us to love, obey, and serve the Lord truly. Our message to you to-day is this: "Keep on praying all your days."

MESSAGE FROM THE ISLANDS OF THE SEA:—From Madagascar, the West Indies, Bermuda, and Jamaica, from the Sandwich and South Sea Islands, from Samoa and from Micronesia, we bring you the Christian Endeavor greeting to-day. The mission ships have brought us glad tidings, and one hundred and fifty Christian Endeavor Societies are doing what they can to spread the light. Still there are many islands that have never heard of Jesus, and we ask you to remember the words, "The isles shall wait for his law." In the Island of Jamaica there are two Junior Endeavor Societies, with thirty-six active members. The twenty-one members of the Society in Manchioneal send you greeting to-day, and wish to say to the Convention, "We are glad that God so loved the world that he gave his only begotten Son, that whosoever believeth in him might not perish, but have everlasting life."

MESSAGE FROM SOUTH AMERICA : — And a few of us in South America are trying to break the chains that bind, but our numbers are very few. The news of your Endeavor has only just reached our country, and we have not enrolled many in the Endeavor ranks, but believe the day will come when South America, too, will be won for Christ. Our verse is this : " Our help is in the name of the Lord, who made heaven and earth."

MESSAGE FROM JAPAN : — " Japan for Christ." This is the motto of the Endeavorers in our country. Fifty-six older societies and three Junior bands greet you to-day, and give you this verse as our message : " Then shall we know, if we follow on to know the Lord."

MESSAGE FROM AFRICA : — Yet in the Dark Continent there are many bright spots. Twenty-seven Christian Endeavor Societies and three Junior bands have pledged themselves to do whatever Jesus would like to have them do, and follow where he leads. From one of these companies we bring you this message : " Our Junior Endeavor Society in Durban, South Africa, consisting of twenty-two members, do send to the Junior Christian Endeavorers in Boston and other parts of the world Christian greetings. We are but young. Our chief aim, however, is to strive to serve our Lord and Master, and to walk in his footsteps. Pray for us as we do for you. Have we not all one Father? Hath not one God created us? "

MESSAGE FROM TURKEY : — Though we have so much in the Turkish Empire to hinder us and keep away the Gospel light, yet we have a few bands here and there who are trying quietly to work for their Master. Though they may not wear the red cross on their shoulders, nor show their Christian Endeavor badges, yet their hearts are true and loyal. There are thirty-two bands of older Endeavorers in our land, and seven Junior companies. The children of Persia, too, and of Syria, send you greeting, for they also have a few children who are working in Christian Endeavor with you. From all these children we bring you to-day this message : " Fear not, for they that be with us are more than they that be against us."

Eighteen little Armenian girls in the Junior Endeavor Society in Adabazar have met together with their Bibles, and have selected this verse, which their secretary, Huranoosh Bagdasarian, sends to us as their message : " Yete gis gue sirek im badriranneruss bahetzeck." (Translation) " If you love me keep my commandments."

MESSAGE FROM ENGLISH-SPEAKING CHILDREN : — There are about 250,000 children in English-speaking countries who have already joined this crusade, and who are really trying to do what Jesus would like to have them do. In their name we greet you to-day, and ask you to help us in our Endeavor. We want to do whatever children can to help to win the world for Christ. Our verse is this : " All that the Lord hath said we will do, and be obedient."

In every group there was one child bearing on his shoulder the red cross, and he represented the Juniors of that land, and brought to the leader some genuine message of greeting from a real Junior Christian Endeavor Society in the country personated.

The seven nations that have no Junior Society, although they have the Young People's Society of Christian Endeavor, said, through seven children : —

> " For, though we have older Endeavor
> In all our beautiful lands,
> We have not among us — the pity ! —
> One single Junior band."

Six nations that as yet have not received Christian Endeavor in any form — Russia, Sweden, Denmark, Portugal, Italy, and Greenland — pleaded for the light of the Junior Society. The Holy Land told, in the language of Scripture and through six children carrying Turkish flags, how the heathen are come into the inheritance of God, how they have defiled the holy temple and burned up all the synagogues. This was one of the most effective passages of the exercise, and every heart thrilled when the English-speaking children responded with a message full of cheer from the Bible.

The marching throughout had been elaborate and beautiful, but the climax was reached when the hundred participants wound round in a circle about the lands where there is no Christian Endeavor Society, and sang a special hymn, appropriate to the incident. The great audience was by no means sparing in its applause at this and other points during the programme.

To give the whole exercise in a sentence, it was the most graphic and effective demonstration of the extent, power, and possibilities of the Junior movement that has ever been witnessed.

At the close of " The Children's Crusade " there were loud and repeated calls for Mrs. Clark, its composer and compiler. The ovation she received was the most enthusiastic of the day. A brief consecration service, conducted by Dr. McEwen, dismissed the meeting.

Doubtless " The Children's Crusade " will be seen and heard at more than one Christian Endeavor Convention in the months to come. It can be had of the Publishing Department of the United Society of Christian Endeavor for ten cents a copy ; one dollar a dozen.

State Rallies.

One who did not understand the genus of Christian Endeavor would have found cause for wonderment in the delight with which the delegates abandoned the great meetings on Saturday night, and got together by States in their own church headquarters. But it was only an outcropping of the fidelity principle that is the deepest thing in the Society. No meetings were more joyous or jubilant than these State rallies. In most cases, each was a complete convention in itself.

Massachusetts could be accommodated nowhere but in Mechanics' Hall ; Pennsylvania found the great People's Temple all too small for her exuberant host ; Connecticut crowded spacious Berkeley Temple ; and New York was obliged to maintain two meetings, so large was the crowd. Ohio in Shawmut Congregational Church and Illinois in Park Street Church had model meetings, while those bustling " Washington, '96," delegates — we all learned to love them — had a stirring time at Union Congregational Church. Canada, at Phillips Congregational Church, held a meeting that was the inferior of none. Hundreds of the New Hampshire delegates grasped Dr. Clark's hand at his home in Auburndale prior to their church reception, and at no great distance the New Jersey Endeavorers congratulated one another and their hosts — the Allston Congregational Society — on everything in general and the Convention in particular. Vermont, Missouri, Indiana, Rhode Island, Kentucky, Texas, — in short, the entire list of States enjoyed heart-warming meetings. We would not omit to mention the hearty spirit of oneness that made the Floating Society rally memorable.

In most cases, either before or after the speaking, there was a time of genuine Christian Endeavor sociability, when hosts and guests came into closest contact and intelligent fellowship. While many of the addresses were in a lighter vein, there was no small amount of consideration given to the real work of the State unions. The approaching annual conventions were talked of everywhere, and received much stimulus. Nearly all of the best speakers of the Convention addressed these rallies, and most of the utterances were worthy of reproduction through the ever-present note-book.

Sunday's Church Services.

Never again will Christian Endeavor Conventions go back to the former custom of holding regular services on Sunday. The new plan has been a complete and inspiring success. No day of the entire great Convention was more spiritual, more practical, and more helpful than the Sunday spent in the churches and in the services of the sanctuary.

Almost every Protestant church in Boston and vicinity was addressed by visiting pastors and crowded with delegates. At no time in the city's history have the churches been so filled to overflowing. Trinity Church — the pulpit of which Phillips Brooks's presence has made so sacred — was crowded, and many delegates were turned away from the doors disappointed.

But why attempt to enumerate the preachers and the congregations? Dr. Wayland Hoyt, Rev. William Patterson, Rev. W. Knight Chaplin, Rev. W. J. L. Closs, and the whole force of equally stalwart ministers of the Word spoke the pure Gospel to enormous crowds. Music Hall was thronged three times, — in the morning to hear Rev. W. Knight Chaplin, in the afternoon to be inspired by Mr. Woolley, and in the evening to receive Mr. Robert E. Speer's heaven-sent message, "Christ's ownership." Two great meetings were held in the Y. M. C. A. Building; a rousing gospel service was heard by the sailors on board the United States Receiving-Ship *Wabash*, and meetings were conducted in various rescue missions in the slums of the city. Open-air services preached the Gospel on the Common, and various halls and institutions opened their doors for the assembling of the delegates.

With a unity and power that was not of earth, the speeches and sermons set forth the crucified Christ. Every one remarked that even though the temptation to exploit the Christian Endeavor Society and its great Convention was so very strong, the addresses were almost entirely confined to the cardinal principles of Christian life and service. Many of the talks on the reception of the Holy Ghost for service were to the delegates the most precious of any in the entire Convention.

Boston as a whole was affected as it could not possibly have been by meetings in the great auditoriums. The visiting pastors were used as it would have been impossible for them to have been used. From whatever standpoint the matter is viewed, Sunday was a high day in Zion.

MONDAY MORNING.

Mechanics' Building.

At 9 o'clock seats were at a premium in the big hall. At 9.15 standing room was taken. President Clark presided; he said that the subject of the morning was, "The World for Christ," and asked that any foreign missionaries who were in the house would come forward and take the front seats on the platform.

The devotional exercises were conducted by Rev. D. L. Furber, D. D., of Newton, and the venerable Rev. Cyrus Hamlin, D. D., of missionary and college fame in Christian work among the "unspeakable Turks." Dr. Hamlin's name was applauded when it was announced that he would assist in the exercises.

Promptly at the advertised time the missionary roll of honor, which was to be unrolled in the three meeting-places, was brought forward upon a large hose-reel, and Rev. W. C. Bitting, D.D., pastor of Mount Morris Baptist Church of New York City, was introduced. Upon the roll of honor were the names of over 5,000 societies from thirty-five States, seven Territories, seven Provinces, four foreign lands. Each society had given not less than ten dollars to its own denominational home or foreign missionary board for the cause of missions. The total amount as reported on this roll of honor was $149,719.09. In addition to this amount of money which had been given by these 5,551 societies that were enrolled upon the roll of honor, we find that $190,884.45 had been given by these same societies "for Christ and the Church" in other ways, making a total of $340,603.54, the largest amount given by any *one* society being the $1,900 of the Clarendon Street Baptist Church of Boston.

Address of Rev. W. C. Bitting, D.D.

Men have been crying "hard times." This is the answer that we unfurl before them. Here is the official proposition of Christian Endeavor that we economize last of all in our gifts to the kingdom of God.

The spending of the money represented here has more interest for us than its raising. It has accomplished more than magic wands. This roll tells of the transformation of earthly riches into heavenly.

Our financial creed is written here:—

We believe that Christian living and giving are joined in the holy union which none may divorce; that beneficence is an essential evidence of regeneration; that system is the life of the gift; that consecrated gifts have a spiritual power and value; that no one sees the collection-basket as it really is unless he sees in it the scarred palm of Jesus held out for the offering; that the noblest use of wealth is to lay it at the feet of the Master.

We believe not only in sound money honestly made, but in vocalizing our money to sound the Gospel of the King Immanuel.

We believe in monometalism for those who have only one kind of coin, and in bimetalism for those who have two kinds.

We believe in greenbacks for those who are able to give dollars where they now give cents.

We believe in a gold standard for those who have gold, in a silver standard for those who cannot do better, and in a double standard for all.

We believe in a ratio of sixteen to one as the rate of increase in the contributions for the next year over those of the last.

I see the rise of a generation more interested in the cause of Christ than any the world has ever seen, filled with intense desire that the will of God shall be done on the earth as in heaven. I see the pennies grow into dollars, the dollars into eagles, the eagles into hundreds, and the hundreds into thousands and millions. I see in the future fewer wrinkles on the brows of the secretaries of our great societies, heavier bank accounts, with larger balances to the credit of our treasurers, larger checks drawn to our overworked and underpaid missionaries, and the lonely toilers surrounded by the helpers for which they have so long begged.

If we turn the telescope on the local church of the future what do we see? Missionary giving divorced from frantic appeal, the bread and butter of our heroic toilers on the foreign fields no longer placed in jeopardy by the chances of a collection on a rainy Sunday. I see the downfall of the mite-box, as being utterly unworthy of a religion that claims the largest and the best for God, and that the best fruits will be given to him instead of the gleanings.

And now let us look at the interdenominational features of the kingdom through these lenses. I see such a wise economy of force and fund that no worker or society is in the way of any other, that the present wicked waste of men and means is stopped, and that agencies now rivals will be allies. I see our present insularity changed by great spiritual upheavals, the dividing seas of thought and organization pierced by a thousand isthmuses that join our hitherto isolated activities, and the archipelago of denominationalism becoming continental Christianity.

Then the vast audience was informed that the Board of Trustees had prepared a letter for the General Conference of the Methodist Episcopal Church. The " appeal " was read, and was received with applause.

An Appeal for Fellowship.

From the Board of Trustees to the General Conference of the Methodist Episcopal Church.

Dear Fathers and Brethren,— We, the Board of Trustees of the United Society of Christian Endeavor, representing nearly thirty evangelical denominations in a world-wide brotherhood, in view of the fact that your church and the Methodist Episcopal Church, South, are the only churches in the world in which the number of Christian Endeavor Societies is lessening, and in the name of the already wide-spread and rapidly growing fellowship, fraternity, and co-operation, address to you this appeal : —

The Young People's Society of Christian Endeavor is, and is only, a federation of Christian young people within various evangelical churches. Each individual society is under the exclusive control of the denomination to which it belongs. Neither the United Society, nor any State or local union demands or requires any allegiance, levies any taxes, or at all controls the action of any society. The Board of Trustees of the United Society and their officers are but servants of the interests of all the churches; are merely a committee for general suggestion and a bureau of information.

The Christian Endeavor movement is a practical illustration of the gracious fact that Christian spiritual unity is possible without absolute uniformity or centralization of authority. But spiritual union can gain, not by the cold touch of finger-tips through formal fraternal resolutions, but only by heart-to-heart and face-to-face contact.

We regard the Methodist Episcopal Church as one of the foremost in the proclamation of Christian spiritual fraternity, and we greatly desire to welcome the Methodist Episcopal young people, with their glorious fervor, to our delightful interdenominational fellowship.

But Christian Endeavor cannot be simply a mass of miscellaneous societies. Every great movement must necessarily have unity of purpose and some common channels of work along which such purpose can flow. Christian Endeavor took at least general shape, and evinced its equal adaptability to varying ecclesiastical politics, several years before the beginning of similar movements; and since our name has never carried a merely denominational color, and since Christian Endeavor is a distinctly spiritual movement, we have asked that only such societies as are willing to accept our principles and main ways of work, and are under the control of the evangelical bodies to which they belong, take upon themselves our name. Thus, and thus only, can we maintain the peculiar felicity of Christian Endeavor, at once its denominational devotion and its large and beautiful interdenominational fellowship. Can there be any peril to denominational loyalty, for which Christian Endeavor, by its essential principles, has always stood, and must stand, in adding to the distinctive denominational name of a denominational society, as has been done in various Methodist bodies throughout the world, the unifying name of Christian Endeavor?

Cannot the real longing for spiritual interdenominational fellowship, which throbs in the hearts of all young Christians, be thus given a chance of expression in Christian Endeavor, while every denominational conviction and interest shall be at the same time carefully guarded in the name of the one Christ whom we all love? We respectfully ask you to take into consideration this most important matter.

Signed by the following trustees : —

Rev. E. R. Dille, D.D. (Methodist Episcopal).
Rev. N. Boynton, D.D. (Congregational).
Rev. J. F. Cowan, D.D. (Methodist Protestant).
Rev. John Henry Barrows, D.D. (Presbyterian).
Rev. J. T. Beckley, D.D. (Baptist).
Rev. Teunis S. Hamlin, D.D. (Presbyterian).
Bishop Samuel Fallows, D.D. (Reformed Episcopal).
Prof. J. L. Howe (Southern Presbyterian).
Rev. W. W. Andrews (Methodist of Canada).
Rev. J. Z. Tyler, D.D. (Disciples of Christ).
Rev. Canon J. B. Richardson (Protestant Episcopal).
Rev. J. M. Lowden (Free Baptist).
Rev. M. M. Binford (Friends).
Rev. James L. Hill, D.D. (Congregational).
Rev. H. B. Grose (Baptist).
Rev. William Patterson (Canadian Presbyterian).
Rev. Wayland Hoyt, D.D. (Baptist).
Rev. H. C. Farrar, D.D. (Methodist Episcopal).
Rev. W. H. McMillan, D.D. (United Presbyterian).
Rev. W. J. Darby, D.D. (Cumberland Presbyterian).
Rev. M. Rhodes, D.D. (Lutheran).
Rev. Gilby C. Kelly, D.D. (Methodist Episcopal, South).
Rev. Rufus W. Miller (Reformed Church in the United States).
Rev. H. F. Shupe (United Brethren).
President William R. Harper, LL.D. (Baptist).

The next speaker was Miss Ella D. MacLaurin, of Boston, Mass.

Her topic was, "Information Concerning Christian Endeavor and Missions."

Address of Miss Ella D. MacLaurin.

This brief and imperfect sketch will bear the relation to the topic which is borne by a perfectly dry skeleton to a living man. He who looks upon the skeleton must use his own knowledge and clothe it with flesh and blood. Christian Endeavor was born in a mission band. The missionary spirit is its soul and life. Missions are its distinguishing badges among the nations of the earth. The great commission is inwrought into the very warp and woof of our pledge. We are taught by it that missions, world-wide missions, must have the throne in church work. It has taught us that the religion of Christ is aggressive; that while there is a country unevangelized, a soul unsaved, we must preach there "also." We thank God for that word "also." It is the golden link that binds every part of the globe to the heart of Christ and his Church.

Christian Endeavor has revealed to us with a clearness, painful yet gladsome, our relation to whatever in any way was bringing gladness and glory to him. We saw how for his sake we should love all men, know all men, condition ourselves by the conditions of all men, live for all men, labor for all men.

With these revelations before us, the youth of our churches, gathered in young people's societies, have been stirred with the throbbing of this great movement to get an *intelligent missionary education*, to learn all that is knowable of the needs of lost races.

1. *The Missionary Committee.* — Our aim, therefore, is (1) the appointment in every society of a live missionary committee, all at work with this definite purpose.

2. *The Missionary Meeting.* — The monthly missionary meeting, where we introduce Joseph to his brethren, where we are brought face to face with the world's need and our power to meet that need, where we have learned that the evangelization of this lost world comes from Jesus Christ through us, that we are the very channels of communication from the living, saving Son of God to the dead, lost world, and that we must either "go, let go, or help go" into all the world and to every creature.

3. *Missionary Literature.* — There are two powerful foes to missionary endeavor; giants they are, — selfishness and indifference. *The Missionary Library* has proved a successful weapon in slaying these giants. These bright, wide-awake, real live missionary books are mighty in their results. In one society in which the leading member was opposed to foreign missions, by planting some real live missionary books, they began to read, to pray, and to give, one member giving his life to the work.

4. *The Missionary Stereopticon.* — The *missionary stereopticon* has become a mighty factor in our work. With it we have spent the evening in Europe, Africa, Asia, as well as in America, and have looked into the faces of those who have actually known the taste of human flesh, but who have been transformed into "living witnesses known and read of all men." A message that will produce such results ought to be carried at any cost.

5. *Missionary Giving.* — Christian Endeavor has taught us to take a heart and pocket-book interest in the treasury. The first great missionary once said, "Where your treasure is, there will your heart be also." If you would know where men's hearts are to-day, strike for the pocket-book, or better, aim for the heart, and in it you will find the pocket-book. Our giving should be an act of worship. God wants us to give regularly and from principle, ever remembering that it is into the outstretched hand of the world's Saviour we are to place our gifts. Shall our gifts this new year be large enough to cover the scars in those pierced hands?

Results. — This education has resulted in Christian Endeavorers giving their money, their prayers, and their lives, until they have become a mighty power in the great missionary movement of our age. The gifts of the Christian Endeavor Societies to the missionary boards have increased yearly, even when contributions from other sources have decreased.

At the birth of Christian Endeavor our gifts were so small as not to be worthy of mention, while this year the magnificent sum of over $300,000 has passed through the denominational boards, and many societies are supporting their own representatives on the field. A little country society in Illinois, organized in May, 1894, meeting in a schoolhouse, consisting of twenty-two members, support their own missionary in China, eleven members raising the entire salary of $300. They testify to great spiritual blessing received in the work, and are in vital touch with their missionary. Thus we learn that the latent power of our unused money is mighty, and marvellous results will certainly follow its consecration to the Lord's service; but we learn also that the waiting power of the Holy Spirit is almighty, and union with him through the prayer of faith will be nothing less than the linking of our coldness with his warmth, of our ignorance with his wisdom, of our apathy with his energy, and of our weakness with his power.

When the door opened out of the little room of our beloved Dr. Gordon's life into the great Throne and Presence Chamber of the King's Palace, his young people gathered to pray, and with chastened hearts decided to take up the work he had just laid down, and in less than six weeks the Gordon Memorial Fund of $9,373.67 was the result.

The power of prayer is without limitations. It can divide every Red Sea, and cause every Jordan to roll back. It can open the hearts of the heathen in India, and the purses of the Christians at home. If Queen Mary had reason to fear the prayers of John Knox more than an army of 10,000 men, how would the great adversary of Christianity in every form of heathenism be routed, if the great army of Endeavorers will make a chain of prayer that will go over the cable to God's Throne, and lift fallen humanity back to the fellowship and image of God.

Giving Their Lives. — Christian Endeavorers have not only given their money and their prayers, but thousands have looked into the face of the world's Saviour and have asked, " Lord, what wilt thou have me to do? " And this morning from the East and the West, from the North and the South, from away in the heart of Asia, down in Africa, and across in Europe, comes our rallying cry, " For Christ and the Church," and peoples, tribes, and tongues are hearing in their own language the wonderful works of God.

To-day Christian Endeavor with uplifted finger points to the glowing and glorious records on her shining scroll, and solemnly attests the fact that wherever the most consecrated workers are faithfully carrying out the principles of Christian Endeavor there God will set up his standard, display his power, and glorify his Son in the redemption of lost souls.

Dr. Clark then introduced Rev. W. E. Park, D.D., of Gloversville, N. Y., who presented the banner to the local union reporting the best work in promoting systematic and proportionate giving.

Address of Rev. W. E. Park, D.D.

My dear brother, when I present to you this banner I present to you that which means something. It is of no use eliminating the spirituality from man's nature; he is always bound by the ideal. That is valuable only which expresses an idea. What is this beautiful hall? What are these magnificent decorations, this magnificent audience? Resolved to its elements, this hall is of wood, the decorations are bunting, the audience consists of men and women; but we are all magnetized by the grand, colossal idea, " for Christ and the Church," and that binds us all together as one unit, bound and magnetized by the grand idea to which we give ourselves and which harmonizes us.

The banner is valuable as it represents that which stands behind it. Rome stood upon her seven hills, and leaned upon her sword, and she held up the escutcheon — her eagle that meant universal dominion. The fleur-de-lis of France, when it was exchanged for the tricolored ribbon, meant the banner of the people. The cross of St. George has waved victorious over many battles by sea and land; it represents the majesty of England and the world-controlling influence of the British. The Stars and Stripes, dear to our hearts, represent "liberty and union, now and forever, one and inseparable." This banner, detached from the idea connected with it, would mean no more than a roll of silk or a bale of dry goods in the warehouse; but when it is properly inscribed with the idea "for Christ and the Church," that which is dark, that which is opaque, becomes luminous by reason of the majestic idea of which it is the medium.

My brother, the idea is systematic giving; not merely giving, that is an old idea, but giving with system, that is the modern one. That is the idea of the Christian Endeavor, foremost in thought and foremost in usage.

What is the reason of the beggarly support of the Christian Church, for the withering away of the sap of life that should support and build up the kingdom of Christ? Stinginess in the hearts of people; not by any lack of means. I had occasion to investigate the matter a few years ago, and I can tell you that the Church of Christ is a rich body; it is richer than the same number of people outside of the fold. The property of the Church at that time was $10,000,000,000; the annual income, $858,000,000. There is an opportunity to support all our colleges and churches and institutions without asking an outsider for a cent. There was no lack of wealth, but there was a lack in the method of contributing it.

You represent, my brother, beneficence, and a beneficence that is systematic, and I am proud, indeed, to think that this banner goes to the city of Cleveland, — Cleveland, whose munificent hospitality welcomed us last year. And now this emblem of the munificence of your city is returned unto you. If all the churches and Endeavor Societies had your spirit, had your idea of the systematic giving, not much longer would the soul stand at the door and knock, and be thankful for the crumbs that fall from the rich man's table of promise.

You had the banner last year, and it is returned to you. May it ever remain there! As you take it, see that no other city carries it away on a future convention day. Be here annually to receive this banner, and let your constituents put you in a position where you will never fail to get it. I beg of you to make your office eternal, and I give you one text of Scripture that shall sustain you; it is, "Hold fast that which thou hast."

Rev. S. L. Darsie, of Cleveland: — Cleveland gratefully receives again this beautiful standard. Last year, when Christian Endeavor legions were bearing away from Cleveland, '94, the banners won for Christian service, the Society left this banner in our charge. It has been to us a joy and an inspiration. We have brought it back to Boston, '95, and we knew not who would be deemed worthy to carry it until Washington, '96. We shall bear it back to Cleveland, and hang it upon Cleveland's outer wall until Washington, '96.

We prize this banner for what it represents. This banner stands "for Christ and the Church." This banner stands for system in Christian giving, for business in Christianity, for giving as an act of high and solemn devotion, knowing that he prays well who gives well. We prize this banner because it stands for God's portion, because it stands for the tithe, — not only the one-tenth but the nine-tenths also, — the reserve fund on which God draws when he wants to carry on his work.

O brethren, Christ leads the way in giving. He gave loyally; he gave himself. He calls for you and me to suffer in Christian giving. What gift is worthy of our Saviour? The crumbs that fall from your table and mine? Oh no; let Christian Endeavor bring to the feet of our blessed Saviour the alabaster box, and, breaking this box of treasures, let us pour them upon the Church, the body of Christ. The Church needs your giving to-day more than ever. Our work is languishing; glorious projects are before us, if we had the means to carry them on. In the golden age to which we are coming and toward which Christian Endeavor is rapidly leading us, the Church will not beg and implore for funds to carry on her work; she shall have an abundance. In that golden age we shall relegate the church fair and the rented pew to the past. Christian Endeavorers will no longer buy their food and then cook it and then present it to the church, and then eat it and give to Christ in that way by buying it back again. That way is too long, friends, for Christian Endeavorers to follow. In that golden age our gifts will be generous. Alexander the coppersmith will no longer trouble us. The penny, the church-going coin, will be elected to stay at home.

We realize, also, that this banner stands for Christian missions. Well did our Brother Clark say, in his annual address, that the need is not for men but for money. We need money to carry on the work of Christ. The volunteer mission band have received their marching orders; they are ready for the fray, but they are lingering here at home because they have n't the necessary money. We shall see them marching on, aiding them by our systematic giving.

We gladly accept this banner, and we challenge you, Philadelphia and Boston and Chicago and Baltimore — we challenge you in holy emulation; we call you to meet us in Washington in '96, and take this banner if you can.

To which the Ohio delegation responded by singing, "We 're on the Way," and Mr. M. K. Hodges then sang a solo, "The Sword of God."

President Clark then introduced Rev. O. P. Gifford, D.D., of Buffalo, N. Y., who spoke on the subject, "The Light of God the Life of Man." Dr. Gifford received a royal welcome.

Address of Rev. O. P. Gifford, D.D.

"For God, who commanded the light to shine out of darkness, hath shined in our hearts, to give the light of the knowledge of the glory of God in the face of Jesus Christ."

In the Bible, light and life are associated; darkness and death are associated. So long as darkness brooded over the face of chaos, death reigned in the abyss. When light flashed over the face of the waters life leaped into multiform expression.

No man knows what light is. The wise scientist tells us that light is a mode of motion. If we accept his dogmatic statement and are content, we remain in our ignorance. If we ask him, "A mode of motion of what?" he shows his ignorance. Light comes to us with three primary colors,—red, blue, yellow. Red carries with it the power of heat. Blue carries with it the power of chemical action. Yellow carries with it the power of illumination. Without heat, the chemical action, illumination, life is impossible. The dead world lay in the morgue of the universe, at the feet of God, until he lifted up the light of his countenance upon it and it began to live. When the frowns of judgment shall settle upon the Divine Face the earth shall settle back again into the darkness of death. In the world within, as in the world without, darkness is death, and light is life. In Jesus Christ is life, and the life is the light of man, and the light is the life of man when it is comprehended and understood; but when men "choose darkness rather than light because their deeds are evil," they themselves abide in eternal death. Thus, the world within becomes a revelation of the world without, and the world without becomes a revelation of the world above. The universe is natural and supernatural, it is sensuous and supersensuous and all-spiritual, because an expression of a spiritual God.

The invisible things of God are clearly understood, even his eternal power and Godhead being known by the things that he has created. Thus, the visible world runs parallel with the invisible. As the visible steel rails run parallel with the electric wires and the invisible current drives the visible car, so the invisible Spirit of God drives the visible wheels of the machinery of nature.

Life depends upon light in the world of spirit, as in the world of nature. In the world without, and in the world within, knowledge of light depends upon experience. The man who was born blind, who sat by the wayside begging, across the pathway of whose life there fell the benediction of the Son of God, who went to the pool of Siloam and washed, and came away seeing, came ignorant of many things, but this one thing he knew : whereas he was blind, now he sees. The knowledge is direct. The light lay directly upon the nerves of sight. So in the spiritual world the knowledge of God is direct.

As the coin takes the outlined character of the seal that presses it, the soul of man takes the character of the seal of God that presses upon that. The spider delights to weave his silken webs across the beams of the old country barn. The web does not strengthen the beams, but it relieves the spider. The mind of man delights to weave books and lectures. The arguments and the evidences carry no faith, but they work a mighty relief to the man who writes the books and delivers the lectures. The argument and the knowledge of God comes direct; as direct as the knowledge of light to the eye, so direct is the knowledge of God to the soul of man. The blind man knew that it was light, because he trusted his senses and he trusted his soul. If I can trust my senses and trust my soul in my dealings with the world that is outside me, I can trust my soul with the dealings of the unseen God. If I cannot trust myself, then the universe is a living lie; and if I can trust myself, then I can trust God, in whose likeness and image I am. My knowledge, then, of God is direct, and is to be relied upon, because I can trust myself, and through myself, God.

Light reveals its sources in revealing itself. The child creeping upon the nursery floor comes to a spot of sunlight, reaches its hand out to seize it, and finds the sun hidden in the shade and finds its hand bathed in the golden light. At eventide the child cries for the moon that presses its pale, white face against the nursery window. To all intents and purposes sun and moon are peering into the window and are in direct contact with the eye, and thus with the mind, of the child.

Scientific men tell me that every trolley wheel touches the dynamo, so close is the contact between, as the current flashes along the electric wire. To all intents and purposes, every soul of man is in direct personal contact with the living God; and as the thought of Jacob ran up the shining ladder, so the man and soul of man runs up the living revelation of God and finds rest in the light of the uplifted countenance.

God not only reveals himself directly to man, but reveals man to himself. The poet says : —

> " Know, then, thyself; presume not God to scan;
> The proper study of mankind is man."

But you can never study man out of his relation ; and the environment of the soul of man is the living God. You can never study the world at midnight, and you can never study man until you study him in the light of the uplifted face of God.

I once stood in a valley whose tunnel had forced its way as far as eye could see. I was alone in an ocean of mist; not a green hill, not a waiting valley, but pearly, billowy vapors,—a sea of glass mingled with fire. Above the invisible hills there came the eastern sun. The mists shrunk from before it, shrunk down into the waiting valleys, condensed in the river, and disappeared into the distant sea. And then before me there lifted in beauty hill and vale and river, and in the midst clustered a New England home. The sun had revealed the world to me, but the world was made possible before I was, by the shining of the same sun. The light that is in God revealed myself to myself. I did not know myself until I lay in the light of God's love, as a child lies upon its mother's breast, " Where the wicked cease from troubling, and the weary are at rest."

So long as Peter handled the empty net he had nothing to prick the bubble of his self-conceit; but when the net was filled at Jesus' command, Peter fell at his feet, and said, " Depart from me, O Lord, because I am a sinful man." So long as Saul of Tarsus lived under the echoes of Sinai he trusted himself, but when the hand of the risen King smote him from his horse on the sands of Damascus, he shrunk, and cried, " O Christ, what wilt thou have me to do ? "

Man never knows himself until he lies in the light of God's revealing grace, but this light that comes from God is not an end in itself. God gave light that there might be light, and God gave life that there might be spiritual life. The universe is to him like a magnificent organ. We wait, but the angel waits while God presses the foot-boards or the pedals of this earthly realm until the universe shall be filled with the harmony of the thoughts of God.

Life is that man may praise God. "All mountains and little hills, all cedars and fruitful trees, all forms of life on land and sea, praise ye the Lord" until the universe is filled with the antiphonal praises of a redeemed heaven and a redeemed earth. But beyond that, the praise of God, there lies the law of life, "Multiply and subdue the earth." It is always the law of life that it shall reproduce itself and conform the nearest thing that lies to it to the image and likeness of itself. So it comes that the living Church, born into the light of God, manifesting the life of God, loses the light of God if it does not manifest the life of God in the conquest of the world into the light and the life of God. The world lies in darkness. Do not mistake the phosphorescent glow of rotting wood for the living flame of burning logs. Do not mistake the white moonshine of Buddhism that tosses and tumbles the world of paganism for the sun of righteousness that lifts redeemed humanity into clouds of beauty about the Throne of God. Do not mistake the malaria and chills and fever of a worn-out paganism for the inspiration of the indwelling Spirit of the living God. Go you through paganism; go you through the heart of that awful struggle of the world, the flesh, and the devil that lies in the wicked one; then remember that because God has shined in our hearts and made known the knowledge of his glory in the face of Jesus Christ, it were better for us that we were born, bred, and died pagans than that, in being born into the law of life, we resist the law of life.

When Moses was in the heart of the mountain he plead for a revelation of the glory, and God made his goodness to pass before him; but God hath made known the knowledge of his glory in our hearts in the face of Jesus Christ, and the face of Jesus Christ is marred more than the face of any man. He was acquainted with sorrows and grief, and we hid, as it were, our faces from him. The knowledge of the glory of God is in the sacrificial face of the Son of God, and we can only know it as it shines through our sacrificed life to him.

Have you read the last prophecy of the great Christian prophet of Russia, Tolstoi? Have you read the sweet parable that comes to us, voicing the teachings of the peasant of Galilee, "Master and Man"? The man was Nikita, the peasant, one of the million roots of that great Russian tree that saps the vitality of Northern Europe, that casts its threatening shadows over civilization. He was a patient, ox-like man. He would work diligently so long as you fed him and housed him and covered him with coarse clothes. His master's thought was the golden ruble. He prayed by night for the extension of fields, for the accumulation of a bank account.

One severe Russian winter day these two men, master and man, went out to buy a distant forest, and in the blinding whirl of a Russian snow-storm they were tossed into the bosom of a waiting snow-drift, perhaps to die. The man unharnessed the horse and blanketed him. Then in the snow he fastened a banner that should be a prayer for the passing person. He wrapped himself in coarse rugs and lay down to sleep. His master wrapped himself in costly furs and lay down to think, for whether at home, at church, or in field, in storm or in calm, he had but one thought—the getting of gold. The master arose and deserted the servant, mounted the horse, and plunged into the heart of the storm. In a little while the horse threw him off into the snow and turned back to the peasant. The master followed the faithful beast, and, coming over against the peasant, spoke to him, and the peasant, raising himself, swung his hands before his blinding eyes and said, "Look to my wife and child. I feel the touch of death, O Christ." And the merchant, looking at him, felt that instant inspiration of the glory of God, and cried, "Nikita, thou shalt not die," and, throwing open the costly sables, he stretched himself on the body of the man. He nursed him back again to strength, and when, the next noon, the servants, answering the prayer of the uplifted signal, dug them out with shovels, they found that the servant was living, but the master was dead; but in his dying moment he had a vision of the face of God in the life of Jesus Christ, and in losing his life he found it unto life eternal.

Christian Endeavorers of America, stretch yourselves over a dead world. Give the splendid consecration, not alone of money, but of manhood and of womanhood, until the upturned face of an approaching paganism shall be quickened to the lineaments of the face of the Son of God, and you and I shall find our life in losing it, and be lifted into the image of Christ, and be satisfied when we see him as he is.

The chorus and congregation then united in singing, "When the Mists Have Rolled Away."

President Clark then introduced Rev. J. H. W. Stuckenberg, of Cambridge, who spoke on the subject, "The Christian Personality."

Address of Rev. J. H. W. Stuckenberg, D.D.

The prominence attained by the personality is among the most marked signs of the times. From the discussion of nature, of the evolution of life, of the survival of the fittest, emerges the personality to assert its dignity and claim the pre-eminence above the brute in which materialism tried to lose it. The environment was made omnipotent as the former of mind, the creator of character, and the determiner of life; but strong men insisted on determining their own course, and making that environment which could not make them. Whatever natural law might say or the brute demand, the human mind insisted on freedom, pursued ideals, followed reason, and enthroned conscience.

The struggle of the century has been for the rights of the personality, and the victory is assured. Even if matter is the throne, man is the occupant and therefore its lord. "Buckle is wrong," said an eminent scientist, "in subjecting man to nature; only in a low stage of development does it dominate him; in the higher stages the mind is supreme and nature made its minister." That leading physiologist, Du Bois Reymond, advocated the limits of science in the name of science; he recognized certain human factors as beyond its reach. In his "Seven Riddles of the World" he shows that science cannot explain freedom and conscience, the very things which constitute personality. The sceptic Strauss declared that in man nature is constantly striving to transcend nature. We know the reason; there is in him something more than nature. The philosopher Lotze thought it strange that the mind, which alone can understand matter, should ever lose itself in the material universe. As the result of the great conflict we find that the thinkers now, as in all ages, stand in awe in presence of the personality as the object of supreme wonder and profoundest research.

Need I say that this means a new era, the epoch of the personality? We have had an enthusiasm for nature; but now we have a passion for humanity. Things have absorbed the attention; now man is the supreme concern. Political economy has discussed riches, national wealth, value, and such things; but now Roscher, one of the foremost economists, pronounces man himself the beginning and the end of economic science, and Europe and America echo the thought. Coleridge affirmed that property is the grand basis of government; but we are far beyond that, and know that men are the grand basis, while property is but an attachment to the personality. In education the great aim has been to teach men something; now the aim is to make them something. Pestalozzi defines education as human culture, or the culture of the human being; that is, man himself is to be developed; he is not merely to learn what he did not know before, but he is also to become what he was not before. Education is thus an unfolding of the mental powers, an evolution of manhood and womanhood, an enlarging of mind and heart and will. The need of the times is strong character and large souls and grand personalities, and we look to the educators to supply the need.

We need only go deep enough to find how the idea of the personality dominates the age. Formerly it was said that men act as they believe; now we know that men often believe more than they do; but of one thing we are sure: they always do what they are — the life is an outgoing of personality, just as the fruit is the product of the tree. Do faiths and theories and ideas make men? Yes, but there is a deeper truth, — that a man's faith and theory and idea depend on his character. In a man's thoughts and beliefs and prejudices and love and hope and passions the soul mirrows itself and sees itself. As a thinker has said, " As the man is, so is his God, so his faith." It was a philosopher who said that the philosophy of a man depends on his character. And Jesus said, " If any man will do his will, he shall know of the doctrine."

Still another significant fact must be noticed. Not only is the personality enthroned, but the truth itself is turned into personality. Thus the oak turns into oak the richness of the soil, the sunlight, and the rain. Sometimes a man gets religion much as he gets a coat or a dollar ; but it is different when religion gets the man, possesses him, becomes his personality, his inmost self. " The words that I speak unto you, they are spirit, and they are life ; " the Gospel itself becomes the spirit and life of a man, his very personality. Ideas must become personal to be power; they must be flesh and blood, heart and will. It was the Gospel which became Peter, John, James, and Paul, which transformed the world. In this light we must read history; great ideas become powerful when they become personal, as in Augustine, Luther, and Wesley.

What has been said enables us to understand the Christian personality. It means that Christ has been received as the way, the truth, and the life ; that his truth and love have become the personal power of the believer, so that he can truthfully claim to have the mind and spirit of Christ. To be a Christian is simply to be Christlike. The Germans express it by calling every believer a Christ. This embodiment of Christian truth in the personality we express when we say that the believer does not merely receive the truth and grace and light, but he is truthful, he is gracious, he is merciful, he is lovely, he is the light of the world and the salt of the earth. Everywhere we find that little stress is laid on what men profess, but much on what they are. Not doctrine is depreciated, but doctrine as a dead dogma ; doctrine as spirit and life is as much as ever the power of the Church and the world. Never more than now has homage been paid to the Christian truth and light and love which men actually become. The John who becomes love personified is as mighty now in Africa, Japan, in our slums, and in our churches, as was the beloved disciple in Ephesus.

The prominence given to the personality at large is fully shared by the Christian personality. The demand is for Christ embodied in men and women, a living, present reality in his followers, acting, speaking, converting, saving, through them. The great spiritual power in the world is the Bible transformed into Christian personality. A minister sent hundreds of blanks to theologians, preachers, and eminent Christian workers, with the question : " What books aided you most in forming your character and determining your career ? " Many books were named, but the most remarkable fact in the answer was the oft-repeated statement that it was not books at all which had determined the character and the life. The majority attributed their course to personalities as the supreme moulding influence. Some owed everything to a father or mother, in whom they saw Christ personified and faith realized. It was a godly preacher or devout teacher, said many ; not this or that thought, but what he was and what of himself he imparted. Profound thinkers and scholars are named whose systems mark the advance of thought in this century ; but what they themselves were and embodied and lived is emphasized as the supreme power. Sometimes the system taught was rejected, but the personality of the teacher was irresistible. By means of this marvellous, subtle, personal power men reproduce themselves in others, and thus, though dead, they speak.

These truths need be but stated to be accepted. As they are the heart of the Gospel, so they are the vital Christian power of the age. We agree with Luther when he says, " Christ is our Lord because he makes of us such persons as he himself is." So we can echo the thought of Goethe: "Do what one will, the important thing, after all, is the personality." "Take God into your will," exclaims another; and he also says, "Common natures pay an obligation by what they do; grand natures, by what they are." Everywhere the personality is the essence, the heart, out of which are the issues of life. Fathom the meaning of the kingdom of God; what is it? The kingdom of God on earth is a kingdom of persons in whom the Divine Word, the Divine Spirit, the Divine Love, and the Divine Life have become actuality and reality and personality.

But one more thought in order to adapt our theme to the subject for the day. Christ works in believers and through believers; Christ's power on earth is Christ as embodied in Christian personalities. What is the Church? Christian men and women united by the Christ and the spirit in them. Christian organizations are Christian personalities organized as a Christian power for spiritual culture and work. A Christian Endeavorer is Christian Endeavor become personal. Christ in you the hope of glory means also Christ in you the regenerative power in the world. That is, the Christian personality does not make the heart the grave of the truth and love it embodies, but makes it the leaven of the world. The Christian is a social personality, a social power for social transformation, a light on a candlestick, a city set on a hill. We are entering the social epoch when wealth and scholarship and advantage and privilege mean social responsibility and a social mission. How the overwhelming social problem is to be solved I do not know, unless Christian personalities become Christ's social power to the world. What the Christian is to God he is also to be unto men; and what he prays God to do to men God sends him to do unto them. Men who find themselves in Christ want the prodigal world to come to itself and to its Father.

If now we let God interpret his own thought as it lies in the age, this is, I think, the interpretation: let there be a culture of nature, of brutes, of science, of philosophy, but make human culture supreme. Nothing on earth equals God as found in man, his image. Greater than Switzerland and Norway is the humblest inhabitant whom the tourist ignores. From matter to man, that is the trend. We turn from the crushing mass of the world's wealth to its possessor; we refuse to lose the inhabitant in the grandeur of the palace; in the din of the world's machinery and steam power and electricity we search for the human being who gives meaning to all and for whom all work, though he be doomed to be the companion of a lathe; we marvel at a profound thought, but know that the thinker is greater; we listen to a symphony, and express our admiration in the one word Beethoven; we behold the marvellous Transfiguration and wonder at Raphael; the doer is higher than his deed; the singer is more than his song, as the sea is greater than the murmur of its waves; persons mark and make the ages, as Shakespeare, Washington, Lincoln; above the abstraction of the Church we have the Christian, the personality in whom Christ lives and through whom he works to redeem the world. It is not the entire truth to call this the era of human concerns; it is the era of men, of personalities, and of that highest type of humanity, the Christian personality.

President Clark then said : —

Last year, at the Cleveland Convention, New York State received from China a richly embroidered " umbrella of state," for having reported the largest number of societies that had adopted the Fulton plan for giving "two cents a week " per member for missions. The "umbrella of state " is a peculiarly Oriental object, and is usually presented by the Chinese to high officials that have faithfully performed their duty. New York brought the umbrella to Boston, and New York has the pleasure of placing it in the hands of our lively friends from the District of Columbia, it having been decided that this year the umbrella should be awarded to the union having the largest *proportionate* number of societies using the Fulton plan for giving systematically to missions.

Rev. H. T. McEwen, D.D., president of the New York Union, stepped forward.

Remarks of Rev. H. T. McEwen, D.D.

I have been asked this morning, by hosts of friends in the State of New York and in other States, how a man who was going to give away the only banner his State had could look so perfectly seraphic as I do. Well, I am used to it, that is all. I have been at it fourteen years as a pastor in New York. The fight is hot down there, and we are always whipping or getting whipped. So we stand up and take it like men in the churches where the fight between men and Satan is hot, and at the polls where the fight for Christian citizenship is hot. We were accustomed to it when Dr. Howard Crosby was our chivalrous leader; we are accustomed to it with Dr. Charles H. Parkhurst. A good thrashing is the next best thing to a splendid victory.

Next to that I am glad to give the banner away — honestly glad. We received the banner last year, not because we did so much, but because you did so little. I have heard during this Convention, over and over again, a statement which is eloquent but is not true. I hear them say, " The call is now for money; not for men." I tell you No; it is for men. You will get the money when you get the men. The reason why thousands of young men and young women are lingering on our shores when we would hie them to the foreign fields is still that we have not yet captured the men and the women. It is not entire consecration.

I am glad, therefore, that we have received this lesson, and if it will do our State and the other States the good it ought to do in rousing us to our splendid work, then I shall indeed rejoice. There is, however, a little tinge of sadness. Fulton and I walked the streets of New York together; we sat together night after night. We kissed each other good-bye when he set sail for the foreign shore. I love him, and that is the only tinge of sadness about it.

I never believe in carrying a banner that we do not mean. There is also something very pleasant to me that takes something of the sting out of it in presenting it to Washington. It is a state umbrella. Washington is the capital of our nation. What more fitting than that the umbrella of state should be in the capital of the nation! Then, too, those Washington people are a pretty good sort of people. I do not know whether they came it over us with a little guile or not, but we were foolish enough to go home from Cleveland by way of Washington, and innocent enough to set up and show them our umbrella, and they have been wanting it ever since. Then, too, they welcomed me down there last winter, so I forgive them for taking the umbrella, but I warn them that we are coming to Washington in '96 — numerously coming ; doggedly, determinedly coming. All hail to Washington!

MR. MILES M. SHAND, of Washington:— Washington receives this umbrella with very keen appreciation this morning, because it represents some success in a very important department of Christian living. We shall take this token of our successful work back with us with great joy in our hearts that we have been able to enter into the service of our King, the Lord Jesus Christ. It will be to us through all the coming days, we are sure, a source of inspiration and help, and when the next Convention meets,— not only in my city, but in your city, in our city of Washington, the capital of these United States, — we hope that as you gaze upon the Goddess of Liberty on the capitol dome, as she faces the rising sun; as you look upon the finger of the Washington monument as it points to God's heavens; as you walk our beautiful streets, and look into the faces of the heroes of war and of peace; we hope that everywhere, in all the magnificence about you, you may read Immanuel, God with us ; and we trust that you will join with us in this prayer with more reverence and with more feeling than you have ever before uttered it : " Thy kingdom come, thy will be done in earth as it is in heaven."

President Clark then introduced Rev. L. A. Crandall, D.D. of Chicago, who conducted an open parliament on the topic, " The World for Christ."

Remarks of Rev. L. A. Crandall, D.D.

Jesus Christ gave himself to this world that this world might give itself to Jesus Christ. The noblest vision of humanity that the world has ever seen is wrapped up in three words, " Thy kingdom come." These touch only upon the ages of a nobler and more comprehensive vision. There has arisen in these last days somewhat of contention between two factions terming themselves individualists on the one hand and believers in corporate society upon the other. I have sometimes fancied that outside and beyond sociological discussion, even within the lines of religious work and religious discussion, was this disaffection proceeding, until men were coming to classify themselves as believers in individualism in this work.

The "world for Christ " represents corporate society, but that of the whole world as one vast organization. What is your Society doing? for it represents the individual element in the work of winning this world to God, and we cannot do without either. We cannot afford to lose sight of the splendid vision which is afforded us by the words of Jesus Christ when he says that he came " to seek and to save that which was lost." In all the world are we to go in the carrying of his message ; neither can we forget that He who held the whole of the world in his thought, and comprehended all mankind in his love, stooped to touch a sick and needy one by the wayside back into health, or gave his richest and tenderest sentences of love to one sinning and shame-touched woman. Jesus Christ came to save all the world, and yet he gave his earthly work to a little spot of green no larger than our State of New Hampshire. Jesus Christ came to save the world, yet he only touched the world at a few points of contact here and there ; and you and I who seek to save the world can save it only so far as we touch, here and again yonder, some unit of society, and change and transform that unit until it comes unto the Son of God. If we deem our work almost a failure because our voice has not gone afar, and because no one has hung spellbound upon our eloquent speech, and because very few in the great world know that we are at all — if we become discouraged and ill at ease, let us remember that no man in his saying knoweth what he doeth ; no man in his work can predict to what that work shall come.

How many times in the past hours since I came here and looked into the faces of this audience, and realized the tremendous energy and power that is wrapped up in this organization, I have tried to imagine myself in that church in Portland fourteen years ago, and tried to put myself in the place of that man who, in the crucial hour in the history of the Christian Church, gave organization and being to that which we see to-day! Do you dream that our honored brother held in his heart at that moment any faintest dream of that which should be in the years to follow? I believe not. He sowed, and God gave the increase. So must it ever be. The "world for Jesus Christ," and it will be for him in just the measure that you and I are faithful in our personal work. What are you doing, beloved, to this end ? Now, if you are not doing anything, don't say anything; if you are doing something, tell about it. This is an open parliament. It is not often that we fellows, smaller than these great men who have spoken, have a chance to speak.

One society reported supporting a missionary in Siam.

WASHINGTON : Our society has established a mission branch in our church, and supports it. We have also been instrumental in closing twelve saloons.

MASSACHUSETTS : One member of our society has gone to China ; another is a missionary in the West.

CONNECTICUT : Two foreign missionaries supported by our society.

CHICAGO : Our society has two volunteers for the mission field. Besides that we are supporting a native helper in India, a Bible woman in Japan.

ROCHESTER, N. Y.: We raised last year $34.00 for foreign missions in our Christian Endeavor Society. We started the movement in Rochester, N. Y., to close all the saloons on Sunday.

BURMAH : Our society holds gospel meetings in the streets in the Burmese language. It has Sunday schools for heathen children. It entertains strangers who come in from heathen districts requiring the light.

DISTRICT OF COLUMBIA: Two missionaries in India; three young men graduated for the ministry; two home missionaries.

NEW YORK: Supported a native worker in India for four years.

NEW YORK: Have sent three missionaries to South America and three young men into the ministry.

NEW YORK: Fifteen dollars for every one the treasury holds, and we are going to send just as many missionaries into the field as we can.

MICHIGAN: Our society is less than three years old. The first president is studying for the ministry. We have multiplied our offerings by more than ten.

ILLINOIS: In the grand old State of Illinois we are trying to arouse every Christian Endeavorer to intelligent missionary enthusiasm and earnest, prayerful determination to carry the glad tidings of a loving, personal Saviour to those who know him not, or to send those who will go. We believe the time is coming when every Christian Endeavor Society will do the same.

MASSACHUSETTS: One Bible reader in India.

VIRGINIA: Our society has sent six young men into the ministry in the last seven years, and we have three more going.

BALTIMORE JUNIORS: Supporting a Bible reader in India.

NORTH MISSOURI: Endeavorers of the Methodist Protestant Church are supporting a missionary in Japan.

NEW YORK CITY: The Junior Society supports a girl in India.

Then followed singing of the hymn, "I Will Sing the Wondrous Story."

Dr. Clark then took ten minutes to present to the audience the following missionaries; they were received with the Chautauqua salute. Dr. Cyrus Hamlin, of Constantinople; Rev. Mr. Cline, of Japan; Mrs. Newell, of Constantinople; Rev. G. H. Krikorian, of Armenia; Rev. John E. Cummings, of Burmah; Rev. Mr. Rhodes, formerly of Japan; Rev. Mr. Richardson, of Armenia; Rev. and Mrs. Mead, of Turkey; Dr. James H. Ingraham, of Pekin, China.

The meeting then closed by a prayer by Dr. Ingraham and the benediction pronounced by Rev. J. F. Cowen, D.D., of Pittsburgh, Penn.

Tent Williston.

When the services in Tent Williston began this morning songs were sung first, under Mr. Percy S. Foster's direction; then came the devotional exercises. Rev. Wayland Hoyt, D.D., of Minneapolis, presided, in the absence of President William R. Harper, LL.D., of Chicago. President Harper came in and took the chair a little later in the meeting.

Bits of testimony came from all parts of the tent as to what Christ had done for different delegates. This was done at the suggestion of Dr. Hoyt.

Praise from all classes of people, from all parts of the world, followed until the whole enclosure throbbed with the Holy Spirit of God. Then there was a fervent prayer by the chairman and more singing.

Ten minutes for information concerning the religious life in colleges followed. Mr. Franklin D. Elmer, of West Hartford, Conn., himself a college man, was the speaker.

Address of Mr. Franklin D. Elmer.

There occurred recently, and almost simultaneously, in college circles two events; one was reported by newspapers everywhere, with front page position and heavy head-lines; one was mentioned by a few papers directly interested. The one was an athletic contest, while the other was the gathering together of five hundred young men from the schools and universities of the world, to study the Bible, to pray, to fight out great life battles, and to become so filled with the power of God that they might go back and bring their fellow students to the feet of the Master. The people of America know a deal about college athletics, but very little concerning college Christianity. It is a move in the right direction for this body of Christian Endeavor to inquire this morning of those men who are receiving the grandest intellectual opportunities attainable, not, " Men of our universities, what think ye of athletics?" but, " Men of our universities, what think ye of Christ?"

Do we all realize how vastly important it is that our colleges should be Christ's? Statistics show that the intellectual life of America is controlling America, that those men on the walls of whose studies hang college diplomas are being called to undertake the highest offices of State and nation. Is it not important that our rulers and our leaders themselves should be led by Jesus Christ? The hopeful thing about it is that if right means are used students can be reached for Christ perhaps more easily than any other class. Such an idea would have been laughed at a few years ago. Why, there is one estimable old lady, of whom I know, who has lived all her life in a college community and until the other day really believed that there was never such a thing as a prayer meeting held on the campus; she did not think students would tolerate such a thing. This is far from the truth; college men are subjected to awful temptations mental and physical, but they are seeking the truth; day after day they are being trained to seek the truth, and when they find it they know it and gladly receive it. You have only to prove to the college man by the consistent righteousness of your own living that there is a Christ, that he is willing to save, that he is able to save, and no one is more ready to accept that Saviour than he. But students must be reached principally by their fellow students, hand-to-hand living, direct, personal work, fervent, pointed prayer. The probability is that if they are not brought to Christ while undergraduates they never will be.

There are two organized religious influences which make for the kingdom of God among college men. First, the College Branch of the Young Men's Christian Association. I speak of this first because it deals more directly than any other organization with the religious problems of a college community. Breathed upon by the Holy Spirit, this movement was begun eighteen years ago, at Princeton. There were at that time thirty of the higher institutions of learning in this country having Christian associations of some sort; but it seemed, take it all in all, that Christ had a very small hold upon the students of America. The College Young Men's Christian Association took up and has for eighteen years carried on a most gloriously progressive conquest for the honor of Christ and the salvation of souls. The work has wonderfully prospered, stretching out into almost all the seats of learning in the United States and Canada; and now, extending its arms into foreign nations, it is bringing the students of the world into a fellowship broader in extent, scope, and purpose than any other intercollegiate organization, whether social, political, or athletic. It comprehends to-day 60 denominations, 600 associations, and a membership of 35,000, while since its inception it has influenced 3,400 students to enter the gospel ministry, and is sending, through the Volunteer Band, an average of two men per week to the foreign mission fields. The Young Men's Christian Association accomplishes its work in the colleges through Bible classes, prayer and conference meetings, special evangelistic services, personal workers' classes, college secretaries, who go from place to place, supervising the whole, and through summer conferences similar to those held in this country each year at Lake Geneva, Knoxville, and Northfield. In a word, the College Young Men's Christian Association purposes to find out each entering student, and, suiting methods and means to his individual case, help him to build a more Christlike manhood.

The other of these influences is that exerted by the young people's societies of our churches, and I would include them all, as they ought to be included, under the one name, "Christian Endeavor." The college organization in no way undertakes to supplant affection for church homes; into the church home the Christian Endeavor Societies introduce the college man. He is given work to do, offered pleasant and profitable social opportunities, and thus held in the resolves he has formed in the Young Men's Christian Association meeting.

Christian Endeavorer, I want to ask you to-day to co-operate heartily with the Young Men's Christian Association in the bringing of our students to Christ. There are two bits of suggestion I want you to take down in your note-books. First, when a young man from your church congregation leaves home for college or preparatory school, let your corresponding secretary write to the president of the Young Men's Christian Association located at that institution, state that he is going to enter there, that your society is interested in him, and give such facts about his life or experience as you may deem fitting and wise. Second, when the young man comes home for his vacation, if he is a member, or an associate member, of your society, or any other, get him to give to you a careful report of the Christian work in his college.

This address was followed by a special prayer for the young men and women of the colleges and educational institutions throughout the world.

Dr. Hoyt introduced President Gates, of Iowa College, who delivered an address on " The Consecration of an Educated Life."

Address of President Geo. A. Gates, D.D.

The Christian Church has passed through successive phases of activity, ecclesiastical, theological, evangelistic, missionary. These different phases cannot be separated from each other, for all these activities have been present in varying proportion and intensity through the whole history of the Church. But certain periods have with special distinctness emphasized one or another of these lines of work.

It is evident to those who in a fair measure competently read the signs of the times that we are just now entering upon an era which ought to mark a somewhat new and immeasurably greater forward movement than the Church has ever known. There is no one word which so well defines it as the word "social." All civilization seems entering upon a similar movement. It is indeed a world movement. The Church of Christ as a whole has not yet come to realize its importance, but is beginning to perceive it. If the Church can speedily come to realize its opportunities of leadership in this socialization, the whole of Christendom, and hence the world, under the inspiration of such leadership, may in the very early future take a longer step forward than the world has ever seen before, with the single exception of the period at the beginning of our Christian time, when Christ was born in Bethlehem.

The significance of the rise of Christian Endeavor at just such a time as this ought to mean an immeasurable flood of influence in just this direction. The consecrated and inspired lives of the young men and women of the Church universal may fling themselves into the social movements of this period of history with a Divine abandon. They may claim the world and all institutions of human society for Christ in a realer sense and to a completer degree than the ablest Christian prophet has as yet dared to proclaim. There ought to be more hope in the constituency of these young people's societies than anywhere else in the whole Church of God — more than in bishops, or elders, or deacons, conventions, conferences, assemblies, religious or philanthropic congresses. Whether these great and enthusiastic gatherings and movements and impulses of the young people of Christendom can be keen enough of intelligence, pure enough of heart, unselfish enough of life, passionate enough of will, in short, Christlike enough to obey the great law of the Master, the law by which his father, himself, and all moral beings must live, namely the law of service — that remains as yet to be seen. With luminous Oriental imagery Jesus set forth this law in the paradox that he that seeks to save his life will lose it, and only he that loses his life can by any possibility save it. If such a vision can be seen, and such a call can be heard and obeyed, here is immediate hope such as the world has not seen for a thousand years for a new redemption. Not so much reform as re-spirit must be; not reformation, not merely doing a little better, will in any wise meet the present emergency. It must be nothing short of social regeneration. When this reorganization of the affairs of men upon the real Christ basis once sets in, a forward movement will take place compared with which the Protestant Reformation was as child's play. Its beginning we may almost now discover.

Young men and women of the Church, of the schools and colleges of America, are you ready — ready to consecrate your educated lives to such a crusade? Only religious zeal that consumes the life will avail in this new crusade. Your education, if it be anywise right, will guard from all fanaticism this crusade for humanity and a better social order, and hold you steady to Jesus' soldiery, with a Divine self-sacrifice you now little dream of. Verily this generation may not pass till some of these things begin to be. " Be ye also ready."

Singing followed, and the chairman then introduced Rev. Alfred A. Wright, D.D., of Auburndale, Mass., who spoke on " The Bible, the Great Text-book."

Address of Rev. Alfred A. Wright, D.D.

The implications of this theme and the shortness of the time have determined my purpose to make this address an outline and practical.

A text-book implies studies, teachers, plans, methods, and all the aims of a school, set in the environment of an educational system. The formal consideration of the theme would include the following topics: I. The Great Text-book; What It Is. II. The Aim of This Study. III. the Plan of This Study. IV. The Method of This Study. V. The Results of This Study.

I. The Great Text-book; What It Is.—The Great Text-book is the only one that reveals

1. God as one, God as a spirit, God as a person, and God as the creator of the universe.

2. The reality of a life before this universe *had* life.

3. This universe as moral, designed, wrought out, conducted, and preserved to moral utilities.

4. The reality and the imminence of supernatural personality in the current affairs of this universe.

5. Righteousness as the law of happiness in all worlds.

6. The reality of the hereafter and death as God's impartial usher thereto.

7. This present life as a moral probation whose issues come not until the hereafter, and whose issues legally dominate that hereafter endlessly.

8. The moral law of God written in syllables of human language, in commandments, ordinances, institutes, psalms, gospels, parables, epistles, words of Jesus, all harmonious, nay, all singing rather in unison, and all echoing in the conscience of man that one ethical note that man knows God alone can sing.

9. The Great Text-book is .the only book that reveals Providence as a necessity implicated in the very nature of this moral universe.

If this Great Text-book is rightly studied it will be found to claim

1. That I ought to be as anxious for my neighbor to be a Christian as I am anxious for myself to be one.

Just here we put our finger on the second chief nerve-centre of Christian missions; the first is " The love of Christ constraineth us."

2. That I ought to be as anxious for my neighbor to be happy as I am anxious for myself to be happy.

3. That I ought to be as anxious for my Christian brother to become rich as I am anxious for myself to become rich.

4. That in all things I ought to be as anxious about my neighbor's welfare as I am anxious about my own.

5. That in conduct, as in moral purpose, aim, and spirit, I ought to show forth the life of Jesus of Nazareth, who went about doing good, leaving me an example, that I should follow his steps. (1 Pet. II. 21.)

But who is the teacher of the Great Text-book? If it came from God, then he must be the Teacher. Glorious truth! He hath not left himself without witness.

I open the pages of the Great Text-book to learn what it says about the Teacher. "But the Comforter, even the Holy Spirit whom the Father will send in my name, he shall teach you all things, and bring to your remembrance all that I said unto you." (John XIV. 26.)

"But when the Comforter is come, whom I will send unto you from the Father, *even* the Spirit of truth, which proceedeth from the Father, he shall bear witness of me." (John XV. 26.)

"For the Holy Spirit shall teach you in that very hour what ye ought to say." (Luke XII. 12.)

"And I will pray the Father, and he shall give you another Comforter, that he may be with you forever; *even* the Spirit of truth; whom the world cannot receive, for it beholdeth him not, neither knoweth him: ye know him; for he abideth with you, and shall be in you. I will not leave you orphans: I come unto you." (John XIV. 16-18.)

Most wonderful of all is it that in this extraordinary word-play Jesus should identify the Comforter as the Spirit of truth, yet was Jesus himself that Truth; that he should say, "It is expedient for you that I go away: for if I go not away, the Comforter will not come unto you; but if I go, *I* will send him unto you" (John XVI. 7), and also say, "I will pray the Father, and *he* shall give you another Comforter;" that the *Father* would send him in the name of Jesus, and that Jesus would send him from the Father (John XIV. 16); that this Comforter should glorify Jesus; that he should take of the things belonging to Jesus and should declare them to Jesus' own; that all things the Father had were his, and that, therefore, he was justified in saying the Comforter should take of the things of Jesus and declare them, because his Father was he himself, and the Father; that he should promise to give them, yes to send them, another Comforter, and yet he himself was already and even as he spake their Comforter; that this Comforter, *even* the Spirit of truth, the world could not and cannot receive, and, therefore, they are about to crucify him; that while the world knoweth him not, yet they, his own, knew him, for he had made his abode with them, lo, now these three years; that he was even then abiding with them, and that he would be in them; that though he should depart he would not leave them orphans, because *he* would come unto them.

Most wonderful of all is it that the profound mystery of the Trinity should receive this form of statement in the farewell message of the Son of God; that all there is in God should stand thus pledged to man forever to guide him into all the truth.

It is the fashion in certain quarters to belittle the Old Testament of the Great Text-book; but the supernatural Teacher of the supernatural Book gives no warrant for such fatuity. To the scribes and Pharisees, students of the letter of the Scripture who were all the time searching the Scriptures, but finding in them only a creed—to them he said, "Ye search the Scriptures: because ye think that in them ye have eternal life: and these are they which bear witness of me." (John V. 39.) He was eternal life, there, in the midst of them, missed by them, these searchers after God.

II. The Aim of This Study.—The one aim of this study is to discover truth in the widest significations of that word as related to the supreme question of God's spiritual and moral relations to man, and of man's relations to God now and ever.

III.   The Plan of This Study. — To study the Great Text-book, such a book as we know it to be, we must plan widely and wisely and for all worlds. We are not dealing now with the problem of a day, but with the problem of all the days; not with a scheme to develop the intellectual life of man, but with a scheme to develop all there is in man, to develop *God* in man, to bring man's infinite capabilities to their full fruition.   It is true that the chief end of man is to glorify God, and to enjoy him forever.   The Great Text-book makes it clear to one soul at least that the chief end of God, for which he lives to-day in the midst of this mechanism of universal mystery — the chief end of God is to glorify man, and to enjoy him forever.

1. First of all, then, the university of the Bible.   Let it be the one great institution in every Christian nation to which all religious and secular institutions for study of whatever sort shall be co-ordinated.

2. Next in logical order are the theological schools.   The university dominates the college; the secondary schools, the public and private schools of the land.

3. Next come our secular colleges of the liberal arts.   In the scheme here outlined these colleges must be largely reversed in their aim and purpose.   And they ought to be.   The study of physics is of value, but of what value?   This question, " Of *what* value? " is not asked seriously in the colleges of to-day.

4. Next come our secular schools, public and private.   These should be turned with their faces toward the Great Text-book.   To-day they face another way.   But they will yet be saved to Christian education.   Back into " the little red schoolhouse " must that Bible go, and Christian consecration to God and man will soon put it there.

5. Next come our Sabbath schools.   Let these be made more really schools, seriously and systematically at work on the appropriate grade that leads upward through intelligent sentiment and emotion to the truth of God.

Co-ordinate all these and all schools to the Great Text-book study thus, and we shall begin to find out what God is trying to say to us in the Word.

IV.   The Method of This Study. — Philosophically the method of this study must be scientific, as herein defined.   Theologically it must be exegetical, as herein defined.

It has been too generally supposed that only infidels, sceptics, heterodox Christians, come-out-ers, *et id omne genus*, were interested in the application of this method to the examination of the Scriptures.   Moreover, it has been too generally assumed by faithful orthodox believers that the Book is in some special, though indefinite manner, and to a great extent, above the criticism of any minds, however honest and capable.

On the contrary, it is safe to say that men ought to be at least as careful in ascertaining what are the foundations of their belief as in ascertaining what are the foundations of their disbelief, and that inasmuch as that which claims to be God's revelation of his will comes to man in literary form, the tests of validity and of credence applicable in the case of any book are certainly applicable to this Book.   The scientific method ignores no fact, while it rationally accounts for all the facts, immediately involved in the subject of study.   And it is because the scientific method has not been scientifically applied to the Great Text-book that foes have maligned it and friends have mispraised it; foes have attacked friends' opinion of the Book, and friends have scorned to believe that foes could be found friends in disguise.   Friends have assumed the Bible to be true, and have proceeded to believe without questioning their assumption.   Foes have assumed it to be untrue, if not indeed false, and have proceeded to disbelieve without questioning this assumption.   Neither foes nor friends have sufficiently demanded of themselves or of one another the answer to the first of all questions propounded by the scientific method, " What are the Bible facts? "

The scientific method in its application to the Great Text-book, and as a scheme of study supremely valuable, may be exhibited in a general outline as follows: I. Assumptions of fact relating to the Great Text-book. II. The facts within the Great Text-book. III. The facts without the Great Text-book.

The scientific method further exhibits this general outline expanded as follows:—

I. Assumptions of fact relating to the Great Text-book.
1. That God is.
2. That God is what the Great Text-book reveals him to be.
3. That the facts recorded in the Great Text-book are true.
4. That the Great Text-book is God's highest revelation of God's relations to man, and of man's relations to God, now and ever.

II. The facts within the Great Text-book.
1. Identification of these facts as facts.
2. Classification of these facts. (*a*) Here logically belongs the book method of Bible study. (*b*) Here belongs logically the author method of Bible study. (*c*) Here belongs logically the topical method of Bible study. (*d*) Here belongs logically any other method of Bible study. These methods, (*a*) to (*d*), are strictly methods of classification, proceeding largely upon unverified assumptions of fact.

The scientific method identifies fact and verifies truth at every step, and thus lends validity and trustworthiness to every other method. Indeed, the scientific method logically includes all other methods by as much as it accounts either explicitly or implicitly for all the facts.

3. Correlation and comparison of these facts. (*a*) With all similar facts in the Great Text-book; (*b*) with all dissimilar facts in the Great Text-book; (*c*) with all facts without the Great Text-book. See III.

4. Determination of the extent to which these facts thus identified, classified, correlated, and compared strengthen or weaken the assumption of facts at I., relating to the Great Text-book.

III. The facts without the Great Text-book.

Under this head should properly be grouped all topics not philosophically to be included under II., and relating to such departments, for example, as (*a*) inspiration; (*b*) the canon; (*c*) history, (1) monumental, (2) literary, (3) linguistic; (*d*) philosophy of history; (*e*) psychology; (*f*) metaphysics; (*g*) physical sciences; (*h*) mental science; (*i*) moral science; (*j*) biography; (*k*) hermeneutics.

These facts are to be treated precisely as at II. above, the facts within the Great Text-book:—

1. Identification of these facts as facts.
2. Classification of these facts. (*a*) Here belong logically all sciences that are classifications.
3. Correlation and comparison of these facts. (*a*) With all similar facts without the Great Text-book; (*b*) with all dissimilar facts without the Great Text-book; (*c*) with all these facts within the Great Text-book. See II. Under this head logically belong all sciences that are principally correlative and comparative.
4. Determination of the extent to which these facts thus identified, classified, correlated, and compared strengthen or weaken the assumptions of fact I., relating to the Great Text-book.

The scientific method of studying the Great Text-book secures the following advantages:—

1. Increased confidence in the certainty of the conclusions furnishing the basis of faith and hope.
2. Increased independence of thinking.
3. Increased sense of humility because of the vastness of the knowable and the smallness of the known.
4. Increased sharpening and definition of reason's lineaments in the face of the unknown.
5. And the assurance that every hewn stone, whatever its shape or size or color, quarried with these tools of measurement and of work, has (in addition

to its intrinsic worth) a value as ordered and designed in the architectural unity of that Word whose builder and maker is God.

V. The Results of This Study.— The result of all results will be truth. Our questions about God and man will be answered when we come to ask them in all seriousness implicated in the plan and method of this study.

One result will be the suppression of sectarianism. Another result will be, all knowledge, secular as well as religious, will then be co-ordinated rationally as well as logically.

Christian Endeavorers, who knoweth whether ye are not come into your kingdom for such a time, for such a work, as this?

As I look out upon your great organization, as I study its aims and the significance of the movement, I freshly emphasize for myself the glorious confession of my creed concerning the Church of God. Henceforth let me say, " I believe in the holy Church catholic, which is the communion of saints."

Christian Endeavorer, will you personally, individually, and for your own soul's health, and so " for Christ and the Church," study the Great Text-book within the aims and plans and methods herein set forth? You cannot carry out the plan, but you can carry out the method. Within your limitations you can know the truth, and the truth will make you free. Study the greatest truths of the Great Text-book.

At this point President Harper arrived, and Dr. Hoyt resigned his temporary position in his favor. The introduction of Rev. A. C. Peck, of Denver, Col., followed, whose duty it was to unroll the roll of honor.

Address of Rev. A. C. Peck.

I count myself exceedingly happy this morning to be able to wedge in the missionary idea between these educational speeches. It is the central idea of the New Testament, and the New Testament was evolved out of the Old; and Jesus Christ himself first gives expression to it in making himself the first great missionary. I take it to-day that the great movement which we represent, the bringing together of the young blood of this country and of all countries, has a larger signification than any of us this day think.

The work of Christian Endeavorers these days is to be turned to the missionary idea more and more, which, simmered down, is simply this: that this world can be made no better, that society cannot be elevated, that the people who inhabit this earth of ours cannot be raised up to the standard of their Lord and Master, until they have gotten Christ inside; and Christ inside pure hearts means pure politics; it means no saloon; it means no gambling; it means a purified political life all over the world, and this is the missionary idea. And do you say this is hard to do? Suppose it is.

Out in California they had a great tree, a mammoth tree, which they wished to fell; many feet was it in diameter. They got axes with long handles and chopped in as far as they could all round, and still it stood; and then they got saws, and they sawed in all round as far as they could saw, and still the old tree stood; and they got augers and welded long iron handles to them, and they bored as far as they could bore, and still they could not get it down. But one day a western cyclone came along, and the old tree fell. Endeavorers, to-day our business is to go forth and spread this Gospel of the Kingdom, preach it in the country, in the city, give our money to send it to the ends of the earth, until we have this old earth honeycombed with the message of salvation, and then the Holy Ghost will come, and this whole world will be swept into the kingdom of the Lord Jesus Christ.

How are we to do this? It means, in the first place, that every individual society shall do its best; it means that we shall hold missionary meetings and take up missionary collections and circulate missionary literature and not grow weary in well-doing. And then it means, aside from that, that each individual person shall, on his knees, implore the blessing of high heaven to rest upon the efforts thus put forth.

Then followed the presentation of the banner to the Cleveland Local Union, for the best work reported in promoting systematic and proportionate giving.

Address of Rev. A. C. Crews, Toronto, Ont.

In a sermon on " How To Be a Christian in Trade," Dr. Bushnell said that the great problem we have on hand to-day is the Christianizing of the money power of the world. He says what we wait for and what we look for is the consecration of the vast money power to the cause and work of our Lord Jesus Christ. That day, when it comes, will be the morning of a new creation. These words are worthy of our most careful consideration, and it seems to me exceedingly proper that this subject should follow immediately after the presentation of this roll of honor of those who have contributed liberally to the great missionary cause. One of the greatest obstacles in the way is the lack of means to carry on the work of God. Doors are open everywhere, and some of our best young men and women have said, "We are ready to go to any part of the world." What is needed to-day is the consecration of the money power of all our churches in all our denominations. We have had revivals with distinguishing characteristics. Sometimes we have had a revival in which the principal feature has been the spirit of interest aroused in the study of the Bible; sometimes we have had revivals which have been marked by the spirit of prayer. What we need to-day is a revival, the distinguishing characteristics of which shall be liberal giving to the cause of Jesus Christ. And that day, when it comes, will be the prophecy of grander things, for the promise is, " Bring ye all the tithes into the storehouse, that there may be meat in mine house, and prove me now herewith, saith the Lord of hosts, if I will not open you the windows of heaven, and pour you out a blessing, that there shall not be room enough to receive it." Is it the business of the Young People's Society to promote spirituality by the holding of prayer meetings and consecration meetings, while the old folks look after the finances ? I believe that is a great mistake. We ought to promote it not only by these meetings, but by giving to the cause of God. There is a great mine of wealth in our Young People's Societies. We find a great many people who like to testify, but have not yet come up to the level of liberality of giving to the cause of God. You have heard of the parsimonious farmer who went to hear John Wesley preach. There were three divisions of the sermon. The first was, " Get all you can," and the old farmer said, " I like this." The second was, " Save all you can," and he was still more delighted, and said to himself, " I did not suppose I should enjoy this so much." But when the third division came it was, " Give all you can," and the farmer said to himself, " Dear, dear, he has gone and spoiled it all ! " And so we find frequently that a person enjoys the meeting very much, but when we say anything about giving, it spoils his enjoyment. I say the man who prays and speaks ought to give.

It is my pleasure to present this banner for the best work reported in promoting systematic and proportionate giving, and it goes for the second time to the Cleveland Union ; and the fact that it has been won by the Cleveland Union for a second time is an indication that when systematic and proportionate giving is begun it is usually continued.

The audience then sang, and the closing address of the morning was delivered by President Ethelbert D. Warfield, LL.D., of Easton, Penn., upon the subject, " The Attractions of the Ministry to Educated Young Men."

Address of President Ethelbert D. Warfield, LL.D.

I was very much surprised when the invitation came to me to be present this morning and make this address. It seemed to me at first somewhat extraordinary that one who is not a minister of the Gospel himself, but an elder only in the Presbyterian Church, though the president of a Christian college, should be invited to speak to you upon the subject of the attractions of the ministry and yet, upon second thought, it seemed to me rather fitting that one who for a long time has been in the work of preparing men for the pursuit of that calling; one who has been brought up from his earliest days in the midst of a great circle of those who have devoted themselves to the ministry; one who could look back over a long line of ancestry among whom in every generation there were those who had distinguished themselves in the ministry — such a one, coming without any personal feeling as to the dignity of his calling, standing as one somewhat apart, and yet claiming a great share in this glorious work, might very properly be asked to be present upon this occasion and speak to you upon this glorious theme. It is the most glorious theme upon which any man may speak — the attractions of the ministry; the man who bears the message of God to men stands in a position uncommon and wonderful.

The ministry appeals to men because it is the Lord's command to his disciples to go and teach in his name. The Lord's command and the call of the Spirit are the essential conditions of undertaking the work of the ministry. Not overlooking this, we are to consider the attractions of the ministry to educated men. The Church has recognized from the first that men were to be saved by "the foolishness of preaching," but not by foolish preaching; and she has shown in every age that she had a worthy vocation for the highest intellects. The very conception of the minister's office appeals to men of broad and trained minds. The minister is the messenger of God to man. He bears a message of Divine authority, — a message of the deepest import, of the most splendid philosophy, of the most glorious promise. This message comprehends the universe. It anticipates the creation of the world, embraces all philosophy and science, and looks forth beyond the gates of death. All the problems of life are included in the scope of the minister's work, all the domains of thought, all the fields of speculation, but he is not left without a compass and a chart to drift hither and thither at the mercy of every current of human desire, or to be driven by every wind of doctrine. God has given a sure word of revelation, supplementing the revelation which he has made in nature; and in this revelation the minister has, not in a hard and cold code, but in vital, verifying principles, doctrines, lives, the summary of that truth which is above every truth, because it embraces all truth, the plan of God's so great salvation. Within this great system there is room and to spare for the special work of thousands of specialists, while the minister must never forget that his first and great duty is saving souls. The great work of man's redemption is wonderfully rich and varied. It needs great preachers, great teachers, great pastors, great physicians, great scientists, great thinkers and workers in every sphere. Read the twelfth chapter of Romans and learn the lesson of the relation of the members to the body of Christ and the zeal demanded of every faithful member. In the contribution of every generation of ministers to the general fund of human knowledge there is a great and catholic variety, and it is all elevated and dignified by the fact that it has been inspired by a devotion not merely to abstract truth, but by a living love to a personal Lord, who is truth itself.

So varied is the intellectual work of the minister! Mark how rich and varied are the forms in which his intellectual activity finds expression. He is first called on to be a speaker, then a writer, then to influence men by personal contact, interesting, inspiring, teaching, counselling, consoling; in all, a leader among leaders, a thinker among thinkers, a worker among workers. His position sets him at once at the head of an already organized body, who are ready to learn from him, to be led by him, and to look to him for direction. From this nucleus he has unlimited opportunity for influencing the world. If he has a message to his generation the means of proclaiming it are ready to his hand. He need waste no time in organizing a propaganda. The only condition is that he be loyal to the truth as it is in Christ Jesus, that he subordinate all lesser interests to the highest of all, and that he fearlessly preach and faithfully live the Gospel he has undertaken to deliver to men.

Intellectual activity, it must be remembered, does not flourish in an atmosphere of ease, and it must not be thought that the minister's life, because given to the proclamation of universal and glorious truth, is a holiday excursion. It has been represented truly as a conflict. The truth he preaches will be constantly tested by criticism, keen, carping, hostile; his doctrine will be denied, his life sneered at, his counsel refused, his Lord rejected. Every resource of brain and heart and soul will be needed to refute, convince, and win men. Every nerve and muscle will be strained. Intellect itself will become a snare, social advantages an avenue of temptation, only the Lord and his truth will never fail. But the delight of forceful speech, of literary composition, of social leadership, of hard-won triumphs, of high comradeship, of useful service, will grow and brighten till the work shall bring its own reward, a faint but faithful foretaste of the future's, "Well done, good and faithful servant."

Tent Endeavor.

It was peculiarly a young people's service that was held in Tent Endeavor on Monday morning. All of the speakers were comparatively young men, and some were distinctively workers among the youth of the land. The presiding officer of the session, Rev. J. Z. Tyler, D.D., after the devotional service introduced as the first speaker, Rev. A. P. Cobb, D.D., the topic being "Christian Endeavor in Unlikely Places."

Address of Rev. A. P. Cobb, Springfield, Ill.

The first society of Christian Endeavor was for work in unlikely places. It was born amid the whirlwind of human passions.

Over its cradle flashed and flamed the fiery tongue of persecution. Its Founder and all its charter members wear the thorny crown of martyrdom. No more unlikely place could have been found than the one selected for its establishment. In it had been slain so many holy men that a proverb had become current that no prophet could perish out of Jerusalem. Yet there it was that, on the first Pentecost after the glorification of our risen Lord, the first society of Christian Endeavor was organized. It was divinely conceived. It was born of the Holy Spirit. It marked the initial point of a new era. It was the herald of the millennium. God bore witness to its Divine origin in signs and wonders and miracles and gifts of the Holy Spirit. The time was, in one sense at least, auspicious for such a work. The Temple of the Two-Faced Janus was closed for the third time only in all Roman history: once during the Republic, and twice under Augustus. The world was at peace; but, alas! it was the peace of exhaustion. The lion and the lamb lay down together; but only the lamb was visible. Carthage, once mistress of commerce, was obliterated; Greece and Pontus crushed. Hispania, Gallia, Egypt, and the Orient had been subdued. Britain and Germania had felt the iron heel of the autocrat of the Tiber. Over craig and fen, moor and mountain, soared and screamed the fierce eagles of Rome. Brute force reigned everywhere unchecked and defiant. Might made right. To the victor belonged the spoils. Each took what he could, and held it by the title of his sword and strong right arm.

The motto of the age was, "Let him who *can* be king." It was the era of "practical politics."

It was indeed time that a new order of things should be established — time that the reign of righteousness so long before announced by prophets should begin in this sin-cursed world. The fulness of time had come. The new era was to be based on a new idea.

It was to have a new law — the law of love. It was to be embodied in a new institution — the Church of Jesus Christ. Swords were to be beaten into plowshares; spears into scythes. Nations were to learn war no more. The meek were to inherit the earth. The programme of the new movement for the regeneration of the world was published by Isaiah, and reannounced by the Man of Nazareth in the beginning of his public ministry : " The spirit of the Lord is upon me, because he hath anointed me to preach good tidings to the poor; he hath sent me to proclaim release to the captives, and recovery of sight to the blind; to set at liberty them that are bruised; to proclaim the acceptable year of the Lord."

But, alas, such Divine achievements are possible only through the groans and tears and blood of God's elect! The way of the Lord was indeed prepared as was predicted in Holy Writ, his paths were made straight for his feet; but the harbinger sealed his glorious mission with the warm blood of manhood's morning. " Every valley shall be exalted, and every mountain and hill shall be made low: and the crooked shall be made straight, and the rough places plain : and the glory of the Lord shall be revealed, and all flesh shall see it together: for the mouth of the Lord hath spoken it." But if you would know how this is to be accomplished, read the eleventh of Hebrews: " Women received their dead by a resurrection : and others were tortured, not accepting their deliverance; that they obtain a better resurrection : and others had trial of mockings and scourgings, yea, moreover, of bonds and imprisonment: they were stoned, they were sawn asunder, they were tempted, they were slain with the sword: they went about in sheepskins, in goatskins; being destitute, afflicted, evil entreated (of whom the world was not worthy), wandering in deserts and mountains and caves, and the holes of the earth." Shall we not highly prize the sacred gift of spiritual freedom which has been purchased for us at such a price?

It is because of these and such as these, who have not counted their lives dear unto themselves, and have lovingly labored in unlikely places, that you and I meet here this day in this great assembly in this historic city whose very name is a synonym of liberty.

Who would not be an Endeavorer in unlikely places when by so laboring he can have for his companions the noble army of martyrs?

He who thus labors has for his comrades John Huss and Jerome of Prague; Latimer, Ridley, and Savonarola! He is an heir of Holland's heroic struggle for political and spiritual freedom. In his veins flows the blood of Gustavus Adolphus and Oxenstern; of Knox and Wyclif and Luther,— all, all, Christian Endeavorers in unlikely places! Let us thank God unceasingly that we are the spiritual children, and if children, then heirs, of such a race with such a record. Nor has this costly treasure been poured out in vain.

Science teaches that nothing can be destroyed in the material world. We may transform; we cannot destroy. So in the spiritual realm, the blood of the martyrs has been the seed of the Church.

If the trophies of Marathon would not let the Greek patriot sleep, but spurred him on to deeds of lofty valor, ought not the deeds of these heroes and heroines of faith, together with the certainty that the right will finally triumph, inspire us, their spiritual descendants, to the noblest achievements for Christ and his sacred cause? We believe that it was out of this inspiration that the Christian Endeavor Society sprang. And in so far as Endeavorers are true to their mission, they will ever seek the unlikely places, which the lovers of pleasure neglect, and the lovers of fashion despise. They will remember that their Divine Master " pleased not himself," but " though he were a Son, yet learned he obedience by the things which he suffered." They will not forget Paul, the model Endeavorer, who " counted not his life dear unto him." Thus admonished, the true Endeavorer will not despise the lowliest duties nor the humblest place at the Master's feet.

If this be the true principle of Christian Endeavor, that lady could not have been an Endeavorer who said she was so constituted by nature as to be unable to work anywhere but in the lead; for Christian Endeavorers have learned that it is God's purpose so to reconstitute us through grace that we will work anywhere our Lord may place us. The pledge we have all signed is wisely made very comprehensive : " Trusting in the Lord Jesus Christ for strength, I promise him that I will strive to do whatever he would like to have me do."

In that sign we shall conquer not only self, but the world, if we grow not weary in well-doing. No one can long study Christ's life and teaching without discovering that the basis of his approval is not capacity, but faithfulness — not the number of talents committed to us, but the use to which we have put them for the Master's service. In his view, the widow's humble offering outweighed the ostentatious gifts of the opulent. He taught in a thousand divinely gracious ways that in God's sight the wren and the violet have a mission and a sphere as certainly as have the eagle and the rose.

This, it seems to me, is the lesson for Christian Endeavorers to learn. Christ has not many great deeds which he expects of us; but he asks fidelity in the doing of the little deeds which are within our accomplishment. The cup of cold water; the tear that starts when another's heart is burdened; the word in season to him that is weary — these are the ways in which Christ is glad to have us serve him. A little street-sweeper in London pronounced a glowing eulogy, which must have been heard in heaven, when he said, looking after a well-dressed lad who had bidden him a cheery " Good morning " as he passed by: " I likes the looks of you ! It makes me warmer to have you pass by ! " O thou Divine Nazarene, now crowned beside the Father in heaven, make us to know the power and warmth of thine own Divine helpfulness ! Touch with thy wounded hands our cold hearts, and make them glow with love for those for whom thou didst give up all things !

Among the things which I am sure our Saviour would like to have us do are these lowly duties, these little deeds of kindness, each requiring a crucifixion of the natural heart, yet each in the measure of its influence uplifting the world toward heaven and a nobler life.

It may not seem heroic to look up absentees or irregulars for the Sunday school, prayer meeting, or church; to visit the sick, etc.; but the Endeavorer who does these humble and often laborious things will purchase a good degree in the affection of his pastor, and win the approval of the Master who when on earth went about doing good.

He who thus labors has chosen the better part, which neither time nor death shall take from him. And as the Endeavorer, thus trained, passes from circle to circle of enlarging influence, he will ever find unlikely places awaiting his coming, and in which he can labor for the Master. Our good-citizenship leagues are leading the way to some of these unlikely places. Our temperance pioneers point to another. The destitute regions known as the slums are so many invitations " writ large " in human necessity, and appealing to us for a great extension of the Social Settlements, which mark the practical philanthropy of this era. The missionary work needed in this and other countries is still another field in which even the boundless energy of Christian Endeavor can find employment.

In the *Andover Review* for November, 1890, Dr. A. E. Dunning tells us that "there are ninety-five towns and plantations in Maine where no religious services are held, and more villages in Illinois without any Gospel than any other State in the Union." In the *Outlook* for June 15, Dr. E. E. Hale speaks of "the social dangers which come in on our people from the gradual moral decay, if one may so speak, in the extreme outskirts of the smaller towns of the country. We hear the same complaints from the East and from the West."

Judging from the constant desecration of the Lord's Day in picnics, excursions, baseball games, and the like, one might almost be pardoned for saying that this gradual decay is not limited to the " extreme outskirts of the smaller towns of the country."

A friend in England has just sent me a copy of the *Yorkshire Post*, which cites some of these sad facts as to the neglect of many of our smaller towns, and bases upon this neglect an argument against our system of voluntary Church support. It is not the system which is at fault. It is our method of applying that system. We Protestants are cordially seeking to throw upon our pastors nearly the whole duty of religious activity. The crying need of to-day is a return to the activity of the Apostolic Church, whose members, regardless of ordination, went everywhere preaching the Word.

And what agency can so well and so properly lead in this greatly needed reform as can our societies of Christian Endeavor? We dare not expend all this vast enthusiasm of youth and consecration upon ourselves. We cannot go on simply meeting in these grand conventions and rejoicing in our phenomenal growth. To us, as certainly as to other Christians, Christ is saying, "What do ye more than others?" As certainly as other Christian enterprises are judged, so will our tree of Christian Endeavor be judged by the fruits it bears. Without commensurate action our enthusiastic protestations of love and loyalty will petrify into cant, the enemy of God and man. We must then go forward! Great inspirations must be followed by great achievements. Christian Endeavor, like the bicycle, is in stable equilibrium only when advancing. And what mighty incentives are urging us on!

The ancients felt the *gaudia certaminis*, — the joy of conflict. Yet they struggled for a corruptible crown, while before the Christian flames an unfading diadem. Shall we not then gladly go forward? Said Patroclus to Meriones before the walls of renowned Troy: —

> " In deeds, not words, the action of the battle lies;
> Now is not the time to utter swelling phrases, but to fight."

Brief is the period which God gives for achievement here. But three months elapsed between the heroic stand by Captain John Parker at immortal Lexington and his death by ghastly consumption. He seized and utilized that narrow isthmus between two eternities so well that

> " The meanest rill, the mightiest river,
> Rolls murmuring of his fame forever!"

The apostle says, "And what is your life? It is even a vapor that appeareth for a little time, and then vanisheth away." To every man upon this earth, as brave Horatius said, death cometh soon or late. And still is it true, as when he kept the bridge in the brave days of old, that man cannot die better than facing fearful odds for the ashes of his fathers and the temples of his gods. Wendell Phillips advised young men to ally themselves with an unpopular, but righteous cause, that all their strength might be devoted to its growth and triumph. I presume that was also Emerson's meaning when he said, "Hitch your wagon to a star."

Christian Endeavorers should delight in the opportunity of service in unlikely places for Christ's sake. Have we not his promise for companionship? "Lo! I am with you alway." We see his banner daily advancing. We hear the shouts of victory as his hosts forge forward. The kingdoms of this world are becoming the kingdoms of our Lord and of his Christ. Therefore, we gladly join in the conflict which has the world's regeneration for its Divine object, and heaven as its eternal reward.

The banner for systematic and proportionate giving was presented by Rev. Edward M. Noyes, of Newton Centre, Mass.

Address of Rev. Edward M. Noyes.

Christianity is both a science and an art, and the two things are not exactly the same. A science is the theory; an art is the practice. Astronomy teaches the theory and the science of the movements of the heavenly bodies, but many an astronomer who is ignorant of the art of navigation could not find his way across the seas. I know something about harmony; but I can't play an organ. One is theory and the other is art, and art is only learned by practice. Now Christianity is both the theory of science and the art of right living. Its theory is generally conceded. To-day everybody agrees with the man who said, "The man who does not agree with God is a fool." The Christian theory of life, teaching the right relations to God, one's self, and one's fellowmen, is generally conceded; but Christianity is the art of right living also, and the art can only be learned by practice. And the difference between the theory and the art makes me think of the little boy who was asked if his father was a Christian. "Yes," the little fellow replied, "but he is n't working at it nowadays." Our theory of Christian life has to do with the doctrine of Christian stewardship. There is nobody in this audience that would not admit that all that we have is held in trust from God. We hold the truth in trust. A recently converted heathen said it was a violation of the command "Thou shalt not steal," if we did not carry the Gospel to the heathen, because the Gospel does not belong to us; it belongs to God; it belongs to the world; and unless you spread it abroad you are stealing. Well, that is the doctrine of Paul: "I am a debtor to all men." And money is a trust. Every one accepts the doctrine of Christian stewardship; but a large proportion of the Christian Church is not working at it very hard. Out in the West there was an arid plain where for want of water the crops year after year failed. Somebody discovered that underneath was running a vast subterranean river, and they pierced the soil with Artesian wells, and they changed the arid plain into one of the most fertile regions of the whole West. There is a vast region of undeveloped resources in the Christian Church, and the Christian Endeavor Society means by this system of systematic and proportionate giving to reach down and bring up the fountains of benevolence, so, as President Clark said, a debt in a missionary treasury shall be forever an impossibility. There is a difference between systematic and proportionate giving. I knew of an old deacon who said, "When I was a boy at $10.00 a week salary I gave fifty cents a week to the Church, and I have given fifty cents a week ever since." That's systematic giving; but now he is worth a hundred thousand dollars it is not proportionate giving. The banner is to be presented to those who not only believe in systematic but in proportionate giving. You will notice in the report an increasing number of societies and individuals take this pledge: "We covenant with the Lord and with those who enter with us into the fellowship of this consecration that we will devote a proportionate part of our income, not less than one-tenth, to benevolent and religious purposes." The Cleveland, O., Union received last year this banner; and I take great pleasure in again presenting it to the Cleveland Local Union, represented here by our presiding officer, for the best record in systematic and proportionate giving to God.

The congregation and chorus joined in singing "True-Hearted, Whole-Hearted," and then listened to an address by Mr. John R. Mott, of New York, N. Y., on "The Missionary Uprising among the Young."

Address of Mr. John R. Mott.

It is an inspiration to speak to delegates representing an organization which has never apologized for foreign missions. Ignorant indeed must be the man — yes, or thoughtless — who would apologize for this magnificent enterprise! If he apologizes for foreign missions, he would apologize for Christianity, for Christianity is pre-eminently a missionary force; he would apologize at the same time for civilization, for civilization is found solely in the pathway of the missionary host; he would apologize for the Bible at the same time, for missions constitute its central theme; he would apologize for the Apostles' Creed — let him repeat it and see; he would apologize for the prayer of his Lord — he need only pray it in spirit and be convinced; he would apologize for the Fatherhood of God, and at the same time for the brotherhood of man; he would apologize beyond that for his own confession, and in doing these things he would be apologizing for Jesus Christ, who is the propitiation for our sins and those of the whole world. Thoughtless indeed is he, thoughtless or ignorant! But this organization not only does not apologize, but if we may judge from the utterances of its leaders and its conventions, if we may judge from its increasingly fruitful record of the past few years, it emphatically believes in foreign missions. What are the grounds of our belief? Why do you and I believe in foreign missions, and why do we go out of this marvellous Convention with a set determination, formed in the spirit of prayer, that we shall do far more for this world-wide enterprise? Why does the Y. P. S. C. E. as a movement believe in foreign missions? In the first place, because of the relations of our Society to the Church. Dr. John Moore has said that the foreign missions constitute the business of the Church, and not an incident. The Endeavor Society or organization lives in the churches. It must be deeply interested in what constitutes the business of the Church. Those of you in the ranks to-day are to be future leaders of the Church of Christ. To our Cross are coming these young men and women to lead all the enterprises of the Church. Second reason: because we owe it to our members to bring them into active and sympathetic touch with these great movements. There is no subject so broadening, so deepening, so elevating, so inspiring, as the subject of world-wide missions. There is no subject so broadening, it takes in all humanity; no subject so deepening, it takes us right down into the depths of the designs of God; no subject so elevating, nothing which so lifts a man; and therefore there is nothing so inspiring, because it is the spirit that commanded the life, death, and resurrection of Jesus Christ. There is a third reason why we believe deeply in this subject as Endeavorers, and that is that the life and highest inspiration of our societies depend upon their being missionary. As I have travelled throughout all the States of this Union, and through the Provinces of Canada, and in other lands, I have been impressed, in visiting Endeavorers, with this: that the most spiritual, the most aggressive, the most fruitful, societies are those which take the world-wide vision of Jesus Christ. And there is another reason why we believe in this enterprise as members of an organization made up of the youth: because the young have always been the leaders and moving spirit in this enterprise, in full touch with its development, from the time when Jesus said unto the young, " Follow me." From the time when Paul and Apollos and Timothy led their associates into the enterprise to evangelize the then known world; from the days of St. Patrick, and Augustine, and Boniface; from the triumvirate that laid the foundations of Christ's empire in British India; from the time of that other triumvirate that spread it upon the great Dark Continent, — Livingstone, Stanley, and Mackay,— the moving spirits in the missionary enterprise to make Jesus Christ known throughout the world have been the young.

If we want another reason it would be this: that the leaders of the Church to-day, the leaders of the missionary forces, are looking to the young. In this tremendous and unparalleled crisis the missionaries of all foreign fields bring home the same message: that if we are to meet this incoming tide, that if we are to avail ourselves of this strategic point of vantage that comes in the closing days of this century, we must look to the young. We are looking to the young in and out of the colleges to help us turn this crisis in the right direction. Are we looking in vain? Manifestly not. In the whole history of the world there never has been such a missionary awakening as in the last ten years. We believe the two are working on parallel lines,— the Student Volunteer Movement for foreign missionaries interesting the young men and women in the colleges; this mighty Endeavor Society with the purpose of systematic and proportionate giving to make possible the sending of the men. The colleges will furnish the volunteers to go; the Endeavorers will furnish the means to send; and they are doing it. And this great uprising is found not only on this side of the Atlantic. Nothing thrilled me more in the British Isles than, in visiting the universities and churches of the non-conformist bodies as well as the Church of England, to find the same idea had taken possession as never before of the young men and women of the Mother Country. In France, Germany, and Scandinavia the young are throwing themselves into this broad breach, offering themselves and all that they have to carry out this enterprise in their lifetime. Yes, and the word reaches us from South Africa that in the schools there during the last two years over one hundred and fifty young men and women have offered themselves as missionaries to go into the heart of the Dark Continent, and the Young People's Societies are raising money to send them. From India and Japan and other countries the students are associating themselves with the Endeavorers to make possible the completion of this enterprise in this generation. But I would like to go a step further this morning.

Let us not only believe in this enterprise to the extent that we now do, but let us throw ourselves with new energies and determination and enthusiasm into a great forward movement to carry the Gospel of the Son of God to every creature in our lifetime. There is manifest need of it. Might we not take a short trip around the world? Before we leave our own country we might remind ourselves that there is in the United States and Canada, on an average, one Christian worker to every forty-eight people. Let us begin our tour with Mexico and South America. In these two regions there is only one Christian worker to every 32,000 people. On to Japan. Japan is said to be the Sunrise Kingdom; it is in a physical, and, thank God, in a spiritual sense, and yet in Japan to-day there are one hundred thousand more Buddhist temples than individual Christians. On to China. We might have started out several years ago and have taken a horseback ride with Professor Stinson and have cut a swathe a thousand miles by a thousand miles and have touched only one mission station; and since then only a few missionaries have gone into that great expanse. We talk about the needs of our great cities and yet, note, there are in China to-day nine hundred and thirteen walled cities having in them a population of 25,000,000 people without a single missionary. On to Asia Minor. There, in that region where Christ came into the world and founded his religion, there is only one Christian worker to every one hundred thousand people. On to Europe. Take Paris. We can listen to the words of Ney, said shortly before his death: "There are in this city a hundred thousand men who have never had their hands on the Bible, to say less of accepting its saving truths." Before we come back, drop down into Africa. Go to a certain place on the Congo with Mrs. Guinness. A thousand miles in one direction before you come to the first mission station on the great lakes! One thousand, seven hundred miles on the northwest before you come to the Red Sea, and not a single missionary light burning between you and the waters! Two thousand, two hundred miles to the Mediterranean, and not a single missionary there! We are told that it is the great desert. True. It includes the Soudan of 90,000,000 souls; and 2,500 miles to the northwest before you come to the North African station! And 700 miles to the westward before you leave the last station behind you, and a thousand miles to the southwest before you come to the American station at Bihe! Just think of it! An immense circle encompassing 120,000,000 to 180,000,000 people with less than threescore of missionaries!

As we cross the Atlantic let us be reminded that there lie down on this earth every night 200,000,000 people hungry in body, without sufficient food to satisfy the natural craving. But, blacker than that, my friends, remember this: that to-night there will lie down on this round world of ours 1,000,000,000 people hungry in soul, without God, without Christ, without hope; is it proper for us to say without excuse? Yes, is there not need, emphatic need, for this great forward movement and for our throwing ourselves into it with intensity to evangelize the world in this generation? Evangelize! What do we mean? Simply this: to give every person on the face of this earth an opportunity to know Jesus Christ as the Lord and Saviour. That's our responsibility. Are we fulfilling that? That's a stupendous task, but it is our duty, because Jesus Christ commanded it, and he never commanded an impossible thing. It is our opportunity, because to our generation are open all the doors of the nations of the earth. We have the magnificent facilities of nineteenth-century civilization at our disposition. We have the opportunity as no generation that has preceded us. It is a possibility. I notice that the committee of the World's Fair carried the advertising everywhere in two years. And here stands the Church of Christ, purchased with his blood, demanding only 20,000 foreign missionaries. How many would that be? If every two Endeavor Societies would send one missionary, we would have the 20,000. It will require but one out of each one hundred and twenty-five members of Christian Endeavor Societies. If all the other one hundred and twenty-four would give a little more than ten cents apiece each week, that would pay the expense of sending their 20,000 missionaries. It is a possible thing. As my last thought, I wish that I might bring home to you our fivefold personal responsibility. First, lift up your eyes and behold the fields; not simply the field, not this country, this section, but the world-wide mission of Jesus Christ. Second, bring ye all the tithes into the storehouse. Have we done it? Third, are we praying for it? "Pray ye, therefore, the Lord of the harvest that he send forth laborers unto his harvest." Have we faithfully observed it this past week and year? And the fourth, "Go ye into all the world preaching the Gospel to every creature." Does "go" mean Christians to-day or those who gathered round the feet of Jesus Christ? Does "preach the Gospel to every creature" mean to repeat it over and over again to those who have the opportunity of hearing it, or to those who do not have the opportunity? And the last thought applies to those who cannot go; it is this: stay ye, therefore, for foreign missions. We want a generation of young men and women who will stay in this country and back this world-wide enterprise with money, prayers, agitation of an intelligent character. That is one of the great needs. Henry Martyn, as he went out, made this entry in his diary: "Now let me burn out for God." All through our societies we have got young people burning out for pleasure, ambition, burning out for self. Oh that there might be called out a generation that would burn out for God, and we could evangelize this world in this century!

At the close of singing "Speed Away" Rev. Wm. G. Puddefoot, of South Framingham, Mass., addressed the audience.

Address of Rev. W. G. Puddefoot.

One of the hardest things for us to do is the duty that lies nearest to us. So we find people going over to England to stir up the Christian people there over our lynchings in the South. And there were many there whose voices were eloquent over the condition of negroes in America that you cannot stir to help in the needful work that lies all about them. To-day our people, with other nations, are highly indignant with Turkey on account of her treatment of Armenia, and rightly so. Mrs. Julia Ward Howe has lately written to the Boston *Herald*, in which she states that almost 100,000 Armenian Christians have been massacred in 75 years, and we all feel that the unspeakable Turk ought to be made to speak, and to speak plainly; but how many of us are aware that within the last twelve years 50,000 people have been killed by violence in our own land, and that not five per cent of the guilty ones have suffered the extreme penalty of the law, or that the record for homicide has risen from 1,467 in 1882 to 9,800 in 1894? I know that these figures have been disputed by Mr. F. H. Wines, but they are taken from reliable sources, and I believe are approximately correct. Dr. Wayland, in his address at the American Association of Social Science, held in Saratoga in 1894, quotes Mr. Andrew White at the Social Science Association meeting: "Every year 7,000 innocent men are murdered, and not more than 200 murderers are legally executed."

I plead for the 7,000 men innocent of crime who, during the year to come, will be murdered.

Now this is an awful indictment, and what can we do? And why is it so? Some think that these guilty men should be at once executed. Now Mr. F. H. Wines tells us that in 1890 there were 7,386 prisoners in jail charged with homicide. To kill all these guilty ones would be a fearful slaughter, and moreover, from all past experience legal execution never stopped crime. That part of the country where the murderers are the most summarily dealt with is the very part where violence is the most common.

Statistics show that the foreign element furnishes a larger number of criminals per capita than the native; but on the other hand, those States which have the largest percentage of foreign element have the least percentage of homicidal crimes. Our neighbor, Canada, last year reports eleven murders among 5,000,000 people and no town or village without a church. We have thousands of towns, villages, and communities that as yet have no church. These two facts I think explain the real cause of so much crime ; and why have we no churches in these places ? Because every society is in debt. And why are they all in debt ? Simply because the church-members of the entire country give on an average less than two cents per day per member for sustaining the Church, for home and foreign missions, and all benevolent causes. In fact, two cents per day would pay everything, including the $34,000,000 given to colleges last year, and leave millions for new work.

Of course there are other causes of crime. The rapid growth of the city at the expense of the rural district is one, and it is as true in the newer sections as in the old, and it works badly in both places; so that to-day the two points of danger lie on the frontiers and in the great cities.

A great reform has begun in our cities, and you must not let it drop. We are not half civilized as long as we build contagious-disease hospitals instead of cleaning our streets and pulling down the tenements which cause the disease. Mr. F. Harrison says that London could save 30,000 lives a year by better sanitary laws, and London has as clean a bill of health as any large city.

Over seventy-five per cent of the children born in New York die before they are two years old. What was Herod's slaughter of the innocents compared with this ? Over 26,000 children have been abandoned by their mothers in the last twenty years in New York — left with the Sisters of Mercy. We have places in the city to take a young girl in after she has fallen ; but we need places to take her in before she falls. It costs more to make criminals than Christians.

Our jails and courts cost $400,000,000 per year to run them, and the interest money on our jails and penitentiaries comes to more than we raise for home and foreign missions. So there is work ahead for every Christian Endeavorer. The statement is made that we have enough church sittings to let all the people go to church on Sunday, and that is true in one sense, but it is nonsense, all the same; for thousands are too far from any church to reach it by fastest horse-riding all day. Whole counties without a church! Churches whose nearest neighbor is over seventy miles away ! On the other hand, we have hundreds of towns cursed with too many churches — right here in New England, towns of less than 1,400 population building their sixth church. Churches are often built to preach an ism, instead of Christ, and those you must frown down. You must stand up for every good reform, and as Mr. Lang says, " Fear nothing, and make the best of everything," and rejoice that, not withstanding the awful figures given above, we are living in a time that is the best the world ever saw. We are stronger, purer, kinder, richer, and live longer, and are getting to be alive to the fact that we are related to all the human beings on the globe, and that no part can suffer without the other, and that in no possible way can we help that other part so well as by doing the duty nearest to us.

In introducing Rev. Ira Landrith, of Nashville, editor of the *Cumberland Presbyterian*, the chairman said : —

There is to be unrolled now the roll of honor. This has upon it the names of the societies contributing $10.00 or more each for missions through their own denominational boards, and that report the fact to the headquarters of Christian Endeavor.

Address of Rev. Ira Landrith.

I have a little letter to read you just five hundred feet long, containing 5,551 names of Christian Endeavor Societies reported as giving at least $10.00 to their boards of home and foreign missions. It does not contain the whole; there are other thousands that did not report at all. It represents the gifts of thirty-five States, seven Territories, seven Provinces, four foreign lands. It represents a total of gifts of $340,643.54 for Christ's Church. The largest single offering was $1,900, given by the Clarendon Street Baptist Church of blessed Boston. Let it be clearly understood that it represents only those societies that reported,— so many of us did not know that we were to report!— and yet it were worth while to know that one in seven of all the Endeavor Societies of the world has its name upon this noble roll of honor. Did your churches do as well before Christian Endeavor was born? Christian Endeavor needs no apology. We may learn something about the common sense of Christian missions, and one of the things is that there is no difference between Christian missions and common, every-day soul-saving everywhere; that there is no such thing as home and foreign missions; that man, not God, made geography. We may learn, too, that there is a great, wide world to be saved; and we are not asking any longer, Can it be done? but have made up our minds that it must be done, because God said so. And we have made up our minds, also, that there is just one way to do the work of saving this wide world. It is to be done by giving. Let it be heard: giving — first, money; then, men. We have come to the conclusion in Christian Endeavor that C. E. initials do not mean any longer Coppers Exclusively, but Cash—Coin—Everlastingly. We have made up our minds, then, that the money must be given, and that earnestly, cheerfully; but more than that must be done. I think it was R. P. Wilder who said that the demand of foreign missions is the demand of the highway robber: " Your money, or your life." We have concluded that the demand of missions, home and foreign, is, " Your money and your life." So we must win the world by giving not only money, but by giving ourselves. Now somebody tells me, " I am not called." Are n't you? We believe that when God for Christ's sake pardons a human soul, God at that moment calls that soul to be a missionary. And so throughout the length and breadth of Christian Endeavordom they are saying, " Here, here, send me." But I have performed the present service for which I was called to this platform, and I shall perform another service for you by leaving this platform to be taken by one of the noblest weapons of Christian warfare, our own noble, pointed Speer.

Introducing Mr. Speer the chairman said :—

Those who were so fortunate as to attend the great convention in New York City, three years ago, will certainly remember Mr. Robert E. Speer, secretary of the Presbyterian Board of Foreign Missions, and he is the one who will now conduct this service.

Next came the missionary resolution service, topic, " What More Will You Do? What More Will You Give? " conducted by Mr. Robert E. Speer, New York, N. Y.

Address of Mr. Robert E. Speer.

One of the regretable things about our present day way of looking at matters of the Christian life, is the unpopularity into which resolutions have fallen. They stand in very bad odor; so many New Year's resolutions have been made only to be broken, so many total abstinence resolutions have been made only to be forgotten, that the making of resolutions has fallen into pretty bad odor. It was as true in the days of our history as it is to-day, that most resolutions were made to be broken. And yet, because very few people keep the resolutions that they make is no good reason why we should stop making them. It is a good deal better to make resolutions in a good cause and fail to keep them than not to make any resolutions at all in a bad one. If there were two prodigal sons instead of one, and one of them had said, " I will arise and go to my father," and failed to go the first time and the second and the third time he made that resolution, and another had failed to make any resolution, which of the two would have better done the will of his father? I would rather say ten times over, " I intend to do what is right," and succeed in doing it only one of them, than never to say it at all and never get it done. I don't think any of us are afraid of a resolution service just as soon as we know what we are to resolve upon; and this great Convention would end just where it began — yes, back of where it began—unless all of us who are here, having seen more clearly what God's will is in these meetings, had made up our minds to do that will. And when we come, at the close of this morning's service, to the resolution service, and any one says what he will do and what he will give, we have come simply to the test of the success of this whole Convention. All we want to know is, What is it that God wants done? and I believe we are ready here this morning to resolve to do that thing. I would like to know if there is any doubt this morning as to what it is that God wants done. Is there doubt in the mind of any Christian man or woman here? " God so loved the world that he sent his only begotten Son, that the world through him might be saved." That it might be saved! It is not his will that any should perish, but that all should come into life. " God was in Christ reconciling the world unto himself." Jesus Christ came not to condemn, but to save this world; and he died, the propitiation not for our sins, but for the sins of the whole world. It seems to me that it is perfectly clear this morning as to what it is that God wants us to resolve upon. Is there any doubt as to what the Bible wants us to do? From the beginning to the end that Book is a missionary book. It not only contains the music of a missionary psalm, but the more commanding words of Christ. It is a Book that breathes from the beginning to the end with missionary spirit; that proclaims with every one of its tongues that there is a kingdom of Christ to grow out from it, — a kingdom of living men in whom the thought of the world's redemption shall have struck so deep that they will work for that redemption with the same intensity that Christ manifested for it, and will work for it with the same energy that he worked for it. If we read our Bibles and know our God we know perfectly well what things he wants done. Are n't we ready to do them, if only in our hearts we know what it is that he desires? Is not that indication enough for us as to what our resolutions should be ? You are to take as much part in this service as any one else. Let us take it up in a perfectly clear way. What do we propose first of all to do? And let us talk first about our societies rather than about our personal service. What are you going to do as a society in the way of arousing the missionary spirit, in the way of books, pamphlets, and the magazines of your church? I should like to know whether any one has a resolution along that line.

A DELEGATE : A campaign of knowledge.

MR. SPEER: I remember at the convention in New York, when we had this same question, the query was made as to how many had read ten missionary books. Only two people out of 17,000 held up their hands. Only about forty or fifty had read five. Finally, the query was how many had read two, counting the Bible as one, and the vast majority of that great assembly failed to hold up their hands. I don't wonder that you are slow to express any resolutions along the line of missionary knowledge. Have n't you any resolutions ?

VARIOUS DELEGATES : We are going to send for leaflets and distribute them. Pass missionary books around. Keep a bright missionary paper in the Sunday school. Get the literature committee to help.

MR. SPEER: What are you going to do in the matter of missionary meetings during the coming year?

" We propose to have one every month."

" We are going to have two every month."

" We will have one once a month, and have a better one."

" We have one every week; have a missionary extension class with lectures. All of our members do not belong, only a small portion; we have resolved to get them all in."

MR. SPEER: How many believe in monthly missionary meetings? [A great many responded.] What do you propose to do in the matter of prayer when you go back? A missionary reported that they had a twilight band, consisting of almost all the members of the society, that every evening at twilight prayed for the missionary enterprise. What do you propose to do along this line ?

" We propose to spend five minutes in prayer for the missionary work at every Christian Endeavor meeting."

" Our committee are pledged to pray every day at noon when the whistle blows."

MR. SPEER: Now we have told what we propose to do as societies, what do we propose to give as societies? I read over Mr. Baer's report. He said that the societies in the United States gave last year less than $500,000. That is an average of half a cent a week. Now we have been boasting that we gave two cents a week, and we have felt pitifully mean, and yet we have not measured up to that two cents. Half a cent has been the average gift to home and foreign missions. Put together, two cents a week would amount to $2,000,000 during the coming year. What do you propose to give?

A Texas man said, " Our society proposes to give $500."

MR. SPEER: The Boston *Herald* this morning had a list of the amount of wealth of the different States in the United States, and it had Texas at about one-tenth the amount of the State of Massachusetts. Now if that society in Texas can give $500, why can't you keep up the proportion in Massachusetts? In New York the proportion would be greater still.

" Eighty-two members have pledged themselves to raise $300."

" We are going to double last year's gift, — give four or five cents a week."

" We are going to try to make the giving of one-tenth of our income unanimous with our members this year."

MR. SHAW: There are some societies of Christian Endeavor that have an idea that if they give too much for missions they won't have enough for their own needs at home. That's a great mistake. The society that has given the most in the United States for missions is in the Clarendon Street Baptist Church. They gave over $1,900 as a memorial fund for Dr. Gordon. In addition they are supporting two missionaries in the foreign field. In addition to that they are one of the three societies that have given us the most money toward paying the expenses of this Convention; and we find that where the societies are willing to give for missions they have no trouble in carrying on their own home work. There is one young lady here from the State of Rhode Island, a poor girl. And what has she done? She walked from her work to her home every day, in order that the money she would spend for horse-car fares might be used to come here. That girl has walked five hundred miles in order to be able to come to this Convention. How many of us are willing to walk five hundred miles during the year, that we may have something to give for foreign missions? We don't believe in foreign missions or we would give more than half a cent a week for them. When we love missions more and know more about them we won't have to plead for two cents a week for foreign missions.

MR. SPEER: A grocer whose chief stock in trade was crackers did not believe in foreign missions, and the Lord sent him a dream. He thought he stood on the seashore and skipped his crackers out over the sea, and he began to complain, saying, " That's just the way the missionary societies want us to do." And then he dreamed that every cracker came skipping back over the sea a loaf of bread. " There is that scattereth and yet increaseth; and there is that withholdeth more than is meet, but it tendeth to poverty." " The liberal soul shall be made fat, and he that watereth shall be watered also himself." To whom are you going to give your money? Does any Baptist here know where his money is going to?

" The Baptist Missionary Board in Boston, 2A Beacon Street."

MR. SPEER: That's right. Is there a Methodist here? Where are you going to send your money?

" To New York, 150 Fifth Avenue, New York City."

MR. SPEER: The Presbyterians send to 53 Fifth Avenue for foreign missions. Congregationalists send to the Congregational House here in Boston. Thousands of dollars are lost because you have not known where to send them. A friend of mine travelling in Asia encountered a scalawag in Armenia who had been living on money sent by a Young People's Society here because they were n't willing to trust their mission board. What do we propose to do personally? How many of us are willing to talk about missions the coming year? This missionary enterprise is never going to be what we want it unless we are willing to agitate. I should like to know how many of you take the missionary magazine of your church. [Many held up their hands.] How many of you are going to take it? [Many responded.] How many are willing to pray personally for missions the coming year, put it into your prayers every day? This is the place for that suggestion made regarding the noon hour. All who can do it can't do anything better than to resolve here to-day that every day as the clock strikes twelve he will pray that Jesus Christ may see of the travail of his soul and be satisfied. And now, lastly, what do you propose to give personally? It would be a good thing to know how many give a tithe of their income to God. [A great many raised their hands.] Do you suppose that Jesus Christ abrogated the old Jewish law of the tithes? He never withdrew that old law. No, he went further, and he said, " If any man forsake not all that he hath he cannot be my disciple." I do not believe that any Christian is justified in giving less than a tithe of his income to God. And I am very sure that we are missing a part of the spiritual blessing that God means for us in our personal lives if we are not giving the tithe. We have spoken about what we will do as societies and individuals. Have we given ourselves to God? If we will give ourselves in this resolution service here to-day the other things will take care of themselves. This is the time to do it; to give ourselves with all that we have, — energy, strength, talent, time, holding nothing back,

> " Letting all the soul within you,
> For the truth's sake, go abroad;
> Making every nerve and sinew
> Tell on ages, tell for God. "

When the whistles blew, at 12 o'clock, Treasurer Shaw led the congregation in prayer, thus carrying out the suggestion that had been made regarding noontide prayer.

After the "Doxology" the morning session closed with the Mizpah benediction.

MONDAY AFTERNOON.

Patriotic Pilgrimages.

Monday afternoon will long remain to thousands of Endeavorers as a time of wonderful experiences and splendid inspiration. It was a time for the rolling back of the curtains of the years, and the living anew of the thrilling incidents of '75 and '76. Washington, Revere, Franklin, Adams, and the long array of Revolutionary patriots seemed to revive in the presence of this new army of emancipators, and to impart of their spirit to the occasion.

Under the Washington Elm, at Cambridge, the voices that spoke were those of Rev. D. N. Beach, D.D., Cambridge, Rev. S. P. Rose, D.D., Montreal, Rev. W. Knight Chaplin, London, and Mayor William A. Bancroft; but the spirit that permeated the meeting was the spirit of Washington of '76. This pilgrimage was especially popular with the Canadian delegates. Newer Cambridge, with its Lowell, Longfellow, Holmes, Eliot, Higginson, and Harvard, was not neglected; and when the bits of wood from the old elm had been distributed as souvenirs, at the close of the exercises, the delegates scattered to the scores of historic spots about the city.

The Union Jack and the Stars and Stripes were twined as lovingly together at Bunker Hill as if that silent shaft of granite spoke of nothing but peace and good-will. The story of Bunker Hill was told graphically and inspiringly by Hon. Charles Carleton Coffin to the company of two thousand Endeavorers that surrounded the monument. When Rev. Charles R. Brown introduced the next speaker, Prof. W. W. Andrews, of New Brunswick, he called on the audience to sing "God Save the Queen," which it did with heartiest Christian Endeavor spirit. This was a sparkling address, overflowing with the impulses of the occasion, and the audience was wrought to a high pitch of enthusiasm when Professor Andrews closed his address by saying, "Daniel Webster once said that 'all things are possible at Bunker Hill.' It is not impossible to-day that I take the folds of 'Old Mother Glory' [grasping the Union Jack] in one hand and 'Old Glory' in the other, and with the same pin that I used in binding the two flags together at the Convention in St. Louis intertwine the two once more together in the name of Christian Endeavor love and fellowship."

Never has the glorious Old South Church, that saw the patriotic gatherings of Revolutionary days, that heard the burning eloquence of Warren and Adams, seen a fairer sight than greeted it in the Christian Endeavor host that crowded its every portion on Monday afternoon, or heard words better calculated to arouse the noblest sentiments of patriotism than those spoken to these citizens of the future. No man is more thoroughly identified with the Old South Meeting-house than Mr. Edwin D. Mead, editor of *The New England Magazine*. He began his very entertaining and instructive address by reminding the young people that in this church, where our ancestors prayed on the Sabbath, they voted on week-days. "We consider such a union incongruous nowadays, not because the meeting-house is too good, but because the politics are too bad."

In glowing words Mr. Mead ran over the splendid story of the old church, with its memories of Winthrop and Mather, of Andros, of Sewall and Franklin, and of the great town meetings in which our American freedom was born. He especially emphasized the fact that the memories of the Old South contained nothing that all true Englishmen did not rejoice in at the time and rejoice in to-day. Mr. Mead was followed by Rev. H. Montgomery, of Ireland. He spoke in terms of high admiration of what he had seen especially praiseworthy in this country,— our public care for the sick and crippled, our public-school system, and our movement for a better citizenship. The gathering was a most happy one, full of the true spirit of patriotism, and as helpful and inspiring to the subjects of Victoria who were present as to the citizens of our Republic.

"The Cradle of Liberty" was a very comfortable stopping-place for the delegates who took the pilgrimage to Faneuil Hall. The old building, with its many interesting sights, was thoroughly inspected, and then, in three bright addresses, filled with the genius of the hour, the story and teachings of Faneuil Hall and its history were related by Rev. Nehemiah Boynton, D. D., Rev. E. G. Porter, of Boston, and Rev. Anderson Rogers, of Nova Scotia. Dr. Boynton presided as happily as is his wont, and Mr. Porter's address was largely historical. The words of Mr. Rogers were as helpful as fitting.

As many delegates as could possibly crowd into the Old North Church heard with rapt attention the narrative of the events that have given the sacred edifice a shrine in every American heart. The president of the meeting was Rev. Arthur Little, D.D., of Boston, and that prince among Irishmen,— he's a Canadian now, — Rev. William Patterson, was the first speaker. "Families get into trouble and go to the law courts," said he, characteristically, "but by and by the young people fall in love and marry, and then all the past is considered merely a mistake." The point was made that the misunderstanding of '76 has been forgotten in the love of the children.

A pastor whose ripe historical knowledge made him one of the most sought-after men in the Convention, Rev. W. E. Barton, of Boston, closed the exercises with an address descriptive of the history of the old edifice. The delegates lingered long after the meeting to inspect the "vinegar Bible," given by the King to the church in 1773, to gaze upon the bust of Washington that was carried in his funeral procession, and to wonder at the multitude of quaint and curious things that abound in the building. Not a few of the delegates followed Paul Revere's footsteps up into the belfry.

Copp's Hill Burying-ground, Paul Revere's home, the old Hancock house, the dilapidated Thoreau homestead, and the other famous spots in this vicinity were all reverently inspected by the Endeavorers. Every one, especially the young people from the country, dwelt with dismay upon the fact that the heathen have come into the inheritance of these precious places ; and the incongruity of a throng of unwashed Italians peering from windows and doors that are dear to every patriot filled them with surprise. The slums themselves were far from being the least interesting part of the pilgrimage.

THE CLOSING SESSIONS — MONDAY EVENING.

Mechanics' Building.

Such a grand sight as was presented in Mechanics' Building Monday evening, one must be a Christian Endeavorer to imagine.

It was not merely the great crowd that was impressive, but it was the great, strong Christian Endeavor spirit that ran through all the tremendous gathering of delegates to the farewell service of the greatest religious convention ever held.

Open hearts and an entering Christ, entering to bring peace. to impart power, to assume possession — are not these the history of a convention consecration meeting? The last night was the night of the upward look, when eyes were withdrawn from Boston's charms, from the crowds, from the work, from the speakers, and the expectant disciples beheld Jesus only. Pen cannot picture the scene. Words are impotent to describe the mellowed hearts, the vows of consecration, and the eloquent hush and stillness of the last sacred hour.

The mere presence of so great an audience on the closing night of the Convention was indicative of Christian Endeavor principle — there is no flagging of interest in the conventions from beginning to end, and at the last meeting all meet for reconsecration to their principles and endeavors.

The ushers allowed people to fill the hall up to the very limit, which means that there were about 10,000 in Mechanics' Hall.

It was a wonderful meeting, full of power, enthusiasm, pathos, and deep, earnest consecration.

Everything about the service was tinged with this sense of solemnity. The immense company that had gathered at the building and in the sections assigned each State hours before the time of opening was quiet and reverent.

The Committee of Thirteen was presented by President Clark and greeted worthily. Chairman Capen spoke briefly and delightfully. By name the committeemen were introduced, and Chairman Walsh, of the entertainment committee, electrified the audience by the announcement that 56,425 delegates had registered at the Convention.

Chairman Capen read the following resolutions for the Committee of Thirteen: —

The Committee of Thirteen cannot bring its duties to an end without placing upon record its appreciation of the courtesies received from so many in preparing a welcome for the Christian Endeavor host that has honored us by its presence.

We would remember His Excellency Governor Greenhalge, and His Honor Lieutenant-Governor Wolcott, who not only in their eloquent addresses before the Convention but in other ways have shown their helpful interest.

We would especially remember His Honor Mayor Curtis, who in all the preparations for the Convention has most heartily and generously aided the committee in every possible way to make this Convention worthy of the city of Boston. Nothing in his power to grant has at any time been withheld.

We would express to Mr. Doogue, the Superintendent of Public Grounds, our appreciation of the splendid welcome to Boston, '95, which, under the direction of the Mayor, he has prepared for us in the flowers, in Christian Endeavor emblems wrought with such wonderful beauty. We also desire to place in this record our most sincere sympathy with Mr. Doogue in the great sorrow that came to his household just at the opening of the Convention.

We would extend our gratitude to Mr. Wheeler, the Superintendent of Streets, who, at the request of the Mayor, provided for the visit to the city institutions at Long Island and Deer Island, by the trustees of the United Society, the Committee of Thirteen, and our guests from other lands.

To the Honorable Commissioner of Wires, Mr. Murphy, and to the City Messenger, Mr. Peters, we are also grateful for courtesies shown.

This committee and this whole Convention are under very special obligations to the Honorable Board of Police Commissioners, to Superintendent Eldridge, and to the officers and patrolmen who have extended to us such splendid service. Any request made by us day or night has been responded to instantly, and the courtesy of all officers in handling the great throngs under difficult circumstances has been noticed and commended by thousands.

To the press, in this and other cities, we are under the greatest obligations. We believe no religious convention has ever been spread before the world so fully as this. Their editorial columns have recognized in the most kindly way the great purposes we have at heart, and the reporters have in the news columns given careful details at every point.

To the railroad officials at the Union Station, and to those of the New York, New Haven & Hartford and the New York and New England R. R. we desire to express our thanks for their permission to erect booths at their stations, and to all the railroads for enabling us to send our representatives to give upon the incoming trains the first welcome to our guests.

We would gratefully remember the New England Telephone and Telegraph Company, who generously provided us with telephone facilities at the hall and tents; the Estey Organ Company, who prepared the map for our delegates; the many business men who have furnished us with money and with materials of various kinds, and have decorated their stores in crimson and white; the corps of physicians who have been in constant attendance at our meetings, and to all who in care of places of public and historic interest have extended special courtesies to our guests.

Finally we would bear this public tribute of appreciation to the thousands of young women and young men in the choir, and upon the various committees, who have for weeks been giving their time and thought to this Convention. Many of them, though assigned to obscure places, have been showing in the spirit of the Master that greatness in his kingdom consists in service, and that *he loves most who serves best.* The work of this committee would have been of no avail if it had not been for this army of aids of so many kinds who conscientiously and lovingly have responded to every call. He whose Cross they have been trying to "lift a little higher" has noted it all in his book, which will live when this record has forever perished.

Trustee Rev. H. B. Grose then read, for the Board of Trustees, the platform of principles, which was heartily ratified by the audience.

Platform of Principles.

We reaffirm our adherence to the principles which, under God's blessing, have made the Christian Endeavor movement what it is to-day.

First, and foremost, personal devotion to our Divine Lord and Saviour, Jesus Christ.

Second, the covenant obligation embodied in the prayer-meeting pledge, without which there can be no true society of Christian Endeavor.

Third, constant religious training for all kinds of service involved in the various committees, which — so many of them as are needed — are, equally with the prayer meeting, essential to a society of Christian Endeavor.

Fourth, strenuous loyalty to the local church and denomination with which each society is connected. This loyalty is plainly expressed in the pledge; it underlies the whole idea of the movement, and, as statistics prove and pastors testify, is very generally exemplified in the lives of active members. Thus the Society of Christian Endeavor, in theory and in practice, is as loyal a denominational society as any in existence, as well as a broad and fraternal interdenominational society.

Fifth, we re-affirm our increasing confidence in the interdenominational, spiritual fellowship, through which we hope, not for organic unity, but to fulfil our Lord's prayer "that they all may be one." This fellowship already extends to all evangelical denominations, and we should greatly deplore any movement that would interrupt or imperil it.

Sixth, Christian Endeavor stands always and everywhere for Christian citizenship. It is forever opposed to the saloon, the gambling den, the brothel, and every like iniquity. It stands for temperance, for law, for order, for Sabbath-keeping, for a pure political atmosphere — in a word, for *righteousness.* And this it does, not by allying itself with a political party, but by attempting, through the quick conscience of its individual members, to permeate and influence all parties and all communities.

Seventh, that all monies gathered by the various societies of Christian Endeavor for the cause of missions be always sent to the missionary boards of the special denomination to which the particular society belongs.

And, also, Christian Endeavor officers and societies are affectionately reminded that appeals to them for money should come through their pastors and the officers of their churches, and when such appeals are addressed to the societies directly, they should be referred to the pastors and church officers for their approval before being acted on by the societies.

Also, that the causes to which the societies give should be those approved by the denominations to which the societies belong. Thus the societies avoid recognition and support of independent and irresponsible movements.

Eighth, Christian Endeavor has for its ultimate aim a purpose no less wide and lofty than the bringing of the world to Christ. Hence it is an organization intensely evangelistic and missionary in its spirit, and desires to do all it may, under the direction of the churches and the missionary boards, for missionary extension the world around.

These objects it seeks to accomplish while it remembers that it is an influence rather than an institution; that its United Societies and its State, provincial, and local unions have no legislative functions; that they can levy no taxes and control no local society, which is always, and only, under the control of its own church. The duties of these unions are limited to matters of information, inspiration, and fellowship.

We rejoice in the growing friendliness of Christians, and in the fact that more and more as the true spirit of Christian Endeavor is understood in every evangelical Protestant denomination the world around, with but one or two exceptions, our fellowship is constantly growing larger.

We believe that for the sake of Christian fairness and courtesy, in all denominations, and all over the world, the Christian Endeavor principles should go with the name, and the name, either alone or in connection with a distinctive denominational name, should go with the principles.

For the maintenance of these principles of covenant obligation, individual service, denominational loyalty, and interdenominational fellowship, we unitedly and heartily pledge ourselves.

Mr. Grose also read the following petition, drawn up by the trustees to be sent to Queen Victoria and, with appropriate changes, to President Cleveland. This was received with great applause : —

We, the trustees of the Young People's Society of Christian Endeavor, representing a constituency of nearly two millions and a half, assembled in Boston in our Fourteenth Annual International Convention, 50,000 strong, most respectfully address and petition Her Majesty the Queen of England, urging upon her attention the terrible condition of the Christian subjects of Turkey, and praying her, in the name of a common faith and an outraged conscience, to use her great influence and authority to help those who are perishing and to give to that country a safe and just government.

Then followed the singing of an original hymn, written for the Convention by Dr. S. F. Smith, " The Cross and Victory."

Dr. Clark then introduced Rev. H. M. Wharton, D.D., of Baltimore, Md., who delivered the annual sermon.

Sermon of Rev. H. M. Wharton, D.D.

It falls to my lot to-night, dear friends, to give to you a message from God which you will carry to your homes and which I trust may be a blessing to you in the ensuing year. I pray that God may lay it upon your hearts, and that this service may honor his name and bless you and me.

You will find the message in the letter to the Galatians, the sixth chapter, fourteenth verse : " God forbid that I should glory, save in the cross of our Lord Jesus Christ, by whom the world is crucified unto me, and I unto the world." A consecration that grows out of crucifixion, and a glorious enthusiasm crowning all ! He dead to the world, the world dead to him ! He consecrated to Christ and glorying in his Christ ! It is a wonderful thing that that which was the very synonym of sin and shame eighteen hundred years ago and more has now become the pride and glory of many millions on earth.

I was walking once through the Corcoran Art Gallery, in Washington, and I saw a calm, pale face pressed against the grated window of a jail. It was the face of Charlotte Corday. A letter appended to the picture, written to her father, said, " Dear father, do not be distressed about me. It is the crime and not the scaffold that brings disgrace. I have committed no crime; I shall suffer no disgrace." In a higher and more glorious sense it may be said of Jesus that, instead of himself being disgraced by the Cross, he lifted it into glory and glorified it, ever making it the conquering sign of all his followers.

Paul was wonderfully enthusiastic ; and, my friends, I believe in enthusiasm —an enthusiasm that has a backbone to it, an enthusiasm that has life in it, an enthusiasm that has weight and power in it, an enthusiasm that has usefulness in it. Paul was wonderfully enthusiastic, but his enthusiasm was simply the atmosphere in which the wonderful man lived. A physician cannot be very successful unless he is enthusiastic about his profession. A lawyer will never accomplish much unless he has some enthusiasm about his profession ; and I tell you a Christian will never amount to much unless there is enthusiasm in his Christianity. It is just as true of you who sit in the pew as of the preacher who stands in the pulpit. I love to hear a man's heart beat in his sermons when I hear him preach, and I love to see Christians whose hearts are in their religion when they go forth to work for God.

" God forbid that I should glory, save in the cross of our Lord Jesus Christ." Why, the fact of the matter is there is nothing else in which we can glory. Look around you, if you will, in the world, and where will you find anything else in which you can glory ?

Will you young people glory in your health ? You are here now, in the very morning of your life, many of you ; your faces are toward the rising sun ; your hands are stretched forth toward the opening day, and there are many days and years of usefulness for you, let us hope ; and yet, ere the morrow's sun may rise, some of the strongest, some of the best, some of the most useful, may have been called to the other world. We cannot glory in our health ; we cannot glory in our strength, in our young manhood, in our young womanhood.

Can we glory in pleasure ? It is said in these days pleasure is fairly running away with most of our young people ; and I will tell you that most of us who have tried it have come to the conclusion that Burns was right when he wrote : —

> " But pleasures are like poppies spread ;
> You seize the flower, its bloom is shed ;
> Or like the snowflake on the river,
> A moment white, then melts forever."

We cannot glory in the pleasures of this world.

Can you glory in fame ? Why, let those who have accomplished something of fame in the walks of this world answer. Go to the very heights of fame and what will you find ? The man who, to-day, leads in all the affairs of the nation is forgotten to-morrow. Why, it has not been long since a great President in this country, who was no longer a President, was so far forgotten that when he attended the funeral of one of our dead Presidents he was only spoken to by one man in the whole crowd, and that was by a policeman, who requested him to get off the grass.

But perhaps another says, "How about wealth?" The whole world is running mad after wealth; but shall we glory in wealth? It was only a short time ago that the great leaders of wealth in this country were called upon, by one of our most prominent daily papers, to answer whether wealth brought happiness; and every man answered that wealth simply brings care and responsibility, but it does not bring happiness. Well did Mr. Astor say to a man who suggested to him that he must be a very happy man, "Would you attend to my business for your board and your clothes?" "Why," said he, "no, sir." "Well, that is all I get." How much more can any man receive than what he can eat and what he can drink and what he can put on?

We cannot glory in wealth; but perhaps some one may say, "How about the home?" Already your heart is longing for the home and the dear ones, and happiness perhaps is there; but can we glory in it? Shall it endure? I can well remember in my old country home down in Virginia, sitting before the great log fire, father over in that corner, mother over in this, eight children sitting around the fire down to the youngest—and I was the youngest, in my little chair at mother's side. They talked of heaven, and mother, placing her hand upon my head and bending my head back until my face was turned toward hers, said, "Mother wants her boy to be a good boy, serve Jesus, and then go home to heaven." I utterly astonished her by saying, "Mother, I don't want to go to heaven." "What do you mean, my child?" "You are here, father is here, brothers are here, sisters are here; I don't want to go to heaven." It was heaven to my child-heart to have them with me. But where are they now? Mother has crossed over the river, and father, and part of the sisters and brothers have passed to the other side; and if my home had been my heaven, my heaven is broken up.

Why, my friends, we cannot glory in the things of this world. I might mention them one after another, and you might write on every one of them, "This will perish with the using." The German poet Schiller said, as he stood one morning in the door of his father's home and looked far away to the mountain summit that touched the very sky as it seemed to him—he said in his heart, "Some day, when I get to be a big, strong boy, I will go up to the top of yonder mountain, and then I shall be in heaven;" and so one day he started from his home, and across the fields, and up the mountain-side, over ditches and rocks and through the brush. By and by he reached the mountain-top, and when he did, he said heaven was as far away as ever. You may climb any height on earth, and you will find, when you have reached its summit, that heaven is as far away as ever. Therefore, Paul might say, as he took a view of the things in this world, "God forbid that I should glory, save in the cross of our Lord Jesus Christ."

And while it is true that there is nothing on this earth in which we can glory, it is just as true that there is every reason why we can glory in the Cross. You are enthusiastic, wonderfully so. You have a right to be enthusiastic. But, my friends, this enthusiasm is intelligent, and the more we know of the rightfulness of it, the stronger will we be in the glorying of the blessed Cross.

We should glory in the Cross because of its doctrines. What are its doctrines? The blessed old doctrine of sacrifice. There can be no happiness in this world, in its highest sense, unless we sacrifice on our part for somebody else. Sacrifice! Down South a gentleman told me that in Nashville, Tenn., he attended the decoration of the soldiers' graves. I am proud to tell you, as a Southern man, that now, when Decoration Day comes in the South, and our beautiful young women go forth to scatter their roses upon the soldiers' graves, they do not stop to ask whether the man wore the blue or the gray, but on every grave they scatter the flowers, because the men were brave and true, and died for their country's sake, as they honestly believed.

A gentleman said to me that he was standing in the cemetery at Nashville. He saw a cart come through the gate with a marble slab in it. He followed the cart. By and by it came to a grave. A man was standing there, having a place prepared to put this slab. He said he walked up to the man, and said, " Your son, I presume?" "No." "Some near relative?" "No." Well, he did not like to be inquisitive, and did not further insist. The gentleman turned to him and said, " No. I was a member of a company during the war. When the time came for us to go my wife was ill, my children were young. All night long I spent at her bedside, knowing that in the early morning I must leave. Just as the day was breaking I heard a knock at my door, I walked to the door, and there stood one of my young neighbors, a young boy of sixteen, knapsack upon his back, his haversack filled with provisions ; and as he stood there in the early dawn of that morning, the ruddy glow upon his manly cheek, the fire of enthusiasm blazing in his eyes, he said to me, ' I have come to take your place. I am going and answer to your name.' ' Why,' said I, ' my friend, I will give you my farm, I will give you my money, I will give you all I have. It is just what I have desired, that some one might be found to take my place.' ' Oh,' he said, ' I could n't think of taking anything for it. Then I would not be going for you and your wife and children. No, sir; not a cent, not a cent.'" The young man was killed at the battle of Missionary Ridge, near Chattanooga, Tenn., and on that tombstone the gentleman had placed the young man's name, the date of his birth, the date of his death, and under all, " He died for me." And I tell you, every one of us here may place his hand upon his heart and say of Jesus Christ, " He died for me ; " and this blessed doctrine of sacrifice should pass into every act of our every life.

And then the blessed doctrine of substitution ! Jesus Christ taking your place, you taking his place ! He made sin for us that we might be made the righteousness of God in him.

And then the blessed doctrine of the atonement ! That at the Cross of Christ the poor sinner found peace and pardon through reconciliation of the blood of Jesus Christ ! Well might Paul say, who once was a blasphemer, who once, like you and me, was a poor sinner, without God and without hope,— well might he say, since Jesus Christ had sacrificed himself and had taken Paul's place, had atoned for his sins — well might he say, " God forbid that I should glory, save in the cross of our Lord Jesus Christ."

And then another thing : this old Cross has the power to attract. Jesus said, " I, if I be lifted up, will draw all men unto me ; " and is n't it a fact? I say it deliberately, I say it calmly : I do not believe that there is any other power on earth or under the heavens that would have drawn together 56,425 souls in this July of 1895, save and except the Lord Jesus Christ. It is the drawing power, my friends, and it is this that attracts the human heart.

I read some time ago of a mother who went to the police officers in New York City and laid all her money at their feet. She said, " My daughter is gone ? She has been betrayed, and now, with a broken heart and crushed spirit, she has left me." She sought for her child in every direction. She could not find her, and by and by, after the years had passed away, one said to her one day, " Perhaps your daughter may frequent some one of the dance halls and other places of that description in this city. Go there and seek her ; " and one day there appeared in one of these halls this mother. She went up to the superintendent, the man who had charge of the affair, and said to him, " Will you do a poor, broken-hearted mother a favor? " " Why," said he, " what can I do for you ? " She said, " My child ; my child is lost to me. I have spent every cent ; I have done everything ; I have tried everywhere to get my poor child back. There is one more hope ; perhaps she may come to this place." " Well," he said, " suppose she does ; how could I find her ? " She drew from under her shawl a picture, and said, " Will you let that hang on your wall? She might see it, and if she does, perhaps she might come back to me." " Why," he said, " that is not your picture ! " " No," she said, " but it was my picture. She would hardly know me now, but that is the way she did know me." Said he, " Yes, the picture may hang there." A few nights afterwards, after one of the dances was over and the great crowd were promenading round, suddenly he noticed a commotion over in that part of the hall. He walked over there, and he said, " What does this mean here ? " " Why," some one said,

" a girl has fainted here just now. She stood looking at that picture there." He turned and said, " Bring me a carriage to the door there at once ; " and they ordered a carriage. In a few minutes he was in the carriage with her. She came to, and said, " Where are you taking me ? " He said, " I am taking you to your mother. She brought that picture, and hung it there, and she said that perhaps it might bring her wayward child to her ; " and in a few moments she fell into the arms of her loving, devoted, and forgiving mother.

I tell you, brethren, when Jesus Christ died on the Cross God hung up a picture in this world which draws the poor, wayward, wandering ones from earth's remotest bounds up to the Cross, and to the Father's forgiving and loving arms. God forbid that we should glory, save in the Cross that does draw men from every nation and from every clime. Moreover, it has the power to convict. If I wanted to persuade a man here to-day that he is a sinner, I would n't sit down and reason with him about it. I would n't have a long argument about his sinfulness, his depravity. I 'll tell you what I 'd do : I 'd take him to Calvary ; I would lead him up on the hill ; I would let him see the dying Son of God ; I 'd ask him to look at those pierced hands, those feet that wandered homeless through this world, now crushed and bleeding and at rest forever ; I would ask him to look at that pierced side and thorned brow ; I 'd ask him to listen to the groan of that dying One ; and, as he looked upon that picture, I would say, " Your sin did that." Oh, I 'd want no better argument.

Another thing about this glorious Cross, dear friends : it makes us want to give up the world for Christ, " by whom the world is crucified to me, and I to the world." That is the idea which makes us give up everything for God, if truly we are consecrated to his service, and then, oh what a comforting power there is in the Cross ! You know what I am talking about ; I can't tell you. It is in your heart, but there never was language that could explain it.

Young people, I sympathize with you. The world offers many allurements and inducements, but we are dead to the world. Let us not enter in any of its sinful ways. The cards should be utterly repudiated by you. The wine should be forever ostracized. The dance should be in no way indulged in. The theatre should be put back behind you, and these things forever given up. I trust that through your effort a new lesson may be taught to our churches, and that people when they give up card-playing and drinking, and theatre-going and dancing, out in the world, will not come to our churches to find that our church-members are doing the very things they have been called upon to give up. Leave these things, leave them behind. It is the Cross of Jesus Christ that crucifies the world to us, and us to the world. That may be Puritan doctrine, but I stand on Puritan ground, and the blessed old Bible is a Puritan book. Let us give up the world if we would be really consecrated to Christ.

Another word : Search the Scriptures ; turn your enthusiasm to the Bible ; study.

Another word : Be ready everywhere to go to work for the Lord Jesus Christ. If you and I are going to do great work for God, let us do personal work, and let us see to it that every Endeavorer wins a soul for Christ.

And now good-bye until we meet again. Among all the sermons that I have ever heard in all my life, that which made its deepest impression upon me was preached by my precious mother. I remember one night being led, while yet a child, up to her bedside, and they said to me, " Kiss mother and tell her good-bye." I said, " Where 's mother going ? " They said, " She is going away." I never dreamed that mother could leave me. They said, " Mother, here 's your baby boy come to say good-bye ; " and, as I bent over her, I kissed her. It has been nearly forty years since then, and yet it seems to me this evening I can still feel the sweet, soft pressure of those dear lips on mine. They said, " Listen, she is saying something to you," and I put my ear close down to her mouth, and she said, " Meet me in heaven ; " and they closed her eyes and laid her hands across her quiet breast.

At the close of Dr. Wharton's sermon the chorus and congregation joined in singing, and then Dr. Clark opened the consecration service.

Consecration Service.

We have come once more to the supreme hour of the Convention, to the hour to which we have been looking forward for many, many weeks. May it bring the blessing which we every one desire! This stands in the history of Christian Endeavor Conventions as pre-eminently the evangelistic Convention. There have been hundreds and hundreds of evangelistic meetings throughout the city of Boston, and nothing, it seems to me, could better prepare us for this closing hour than these meetings and the atmosphere which has pervaded the city of Boston during this Convention; but it is not what any one can say; it is not a matter of numbers. We will leave the throngs outside of our memory for a moment. We will think little of the eloquence of these three or four days. Let us be alone in the presence of God, if we can, in spirit as we are in our little consecration meetings at home — as we are in our own rooms when there is no one by but God. Let that be the spirit, let that be the atmosphere, of this closing hour, and that alone will make it the greatest crowning hour of the Convention. And now, friends all, will you bow your heads, take the attitude of prayer for a moment, and engage in silent prayer; and then, after we have prayed silently for this coming hour of consecration and God's Spirit, let us all join in singing very softly, without any instrument and with bowed heads, singing as a prayer and as an act of consecration, "Just as I Am, Without One Plea, but that Thy Blood Was Shed for Me." Let us all bow our heads in silent prayer.

Then, after the singing of "Just as I Am, Without One Plea," Dr. Clark continued : —

O God, here we repeat our vows; here and now, utterly and forever, for this night and for all the days and nights to come of all our lives, we are thine,— thine only, thine forever, thine in time, thine in eternity, thine in all that we are and have and hope to be, now and always, through Jesus Christ alone. Amen.

Just one thing I want to say, friends, before the roll is called of the States. Do not think of the numbers as you see them as standing for anything more than individual Christians. It is the same act that it is in your little meeting. It is the same thing as when you stand alone, and, O Endeavorers, be honest in these things that you say and these things that you sing. Do not join in these songs unless you mean them. Do not add your voices to these voices as they are reported. Be honest; be honest before your God; be honest with your own souls in every word that you speak to-night in this consecration meeting. I do not care whether they are old or new; I do not care whether they are original and striking or not; I do not care whether they are repeated over a dozen times to-night. Be honest with yourselves in what you say; mean it all; and then it will be a true consecration.

ALABAMA: We will take Jesus Christ as the passion of our lives.

ARIZONA: I propose, with the inspiration of this great Convention, to go back to my territory and do more for Christ.

ARKANSAS: Being co-workers with God, we are determined whatsoever we do, in word or deed, to do all in the name of our Lord Jesus, and whatsoever our hands find to do, do it with all our might, having for our motto, "Arkansas for Christ."

CALIFORNIA:
> "The land of sunshine bright sends us to you, to-day,
> To bear you a message from far away;
> We want the great Convention on California's slope;
> We'll meet you, '97, for this we pray and hope.
> And in the name of Jesus we'll conquer every foe,
> And Victory will perch upon our banners as we go."

COLORADO: "I will lift up mine eyes unto the hills, from whence cometh my help."

CONNECTICUT: Verse of "Work, for the Night Is Coming!"

DELAWARE: Our motto for evangelistic work is, "Though your sins be as scarlet, they shall be as white as snow; though they be red like crimson, they shall be as wool."

DISTRICT OF COLUMBIA: We consecrate ourselves to the Convention of '96 with this motto: "Not by might, nor by power, but by my spirit, saith the Lord of hosts."

FLORIDA: "Through God we shall do valiantly: for he it is that shall tread down our enemies." Florida for Christ!

GEORGIA: "Not he that crieth, Lord, Lord, shall enter into the kingdom of heaven; but he that doeth the will of my Father which is in heaven."

IDAHO: We will go back to Idaho, from this Mount of Transfiguration, to follow Christ wherever he will have us go.

ILLINOIS: "Trusting in the Lord Jesus Christ for strength," our hope, and pledge, and prayer for Illinois is: A strong and steady advance along our special lines in Christian citizenship, missionary extension, and especially in evangelistic work.

INDIANA: "I can do all things through Christ which strengtheneth me."

PRESIDENT CLARK: I am going to ask Rev. Mr. Closs, who is further away from his home than any one here, Rev. W. J. L. Closs, of Sydney, Australia, to lead us in a brief prayer for the dear friends at home the world around.

Prayer.

Almighty and eternal God, we thank thee for the rich blessing we are receiving at thy hands now, and we pray thee to remember our loved ones, those bound to us in the strong ties of our Christian Endeavor, in Asia, and Africa, and Europe, and America, and Australia, and let a double portion of thy Spirit be borne out upon them; and as they pray for us in this hour, hear thou our prayers for them, and bless them for the riches—the pureness of the riches—that are in Jesus Christ. Amen.

IOWA: "I in them, and thou in me, that they may be made perfect in one; and that the world may know that thou has sent me, and hast loved them, as thou hast loved me." Singing, "Blest Be the Tie that Binds."

KANSAS: "Brethren, I count not myself to have apprehended: but this one thing I do, forgetting those things which are behind, and reaching forth unto those things which are before, I press toward the mark for the prize of the high calling of God in Christ Jesus."

KENTUCKY: "I can do all things through Christ who sent me." "For Christ and the Church." Singing to tune of "Old Kentucky Home."

LOUISIANA: "After this I beheld, and, lo, a great multitude, which no man could number, of all nations, and kindreds, and people, and tongues, stood before the throne, and before the Lamb, clothed with white robes, and palms in their hands; and cried with a loud voice, saying, Salvation to our God which sitteth upon the throne, and unto the Lamb."

MAINE: We expect to do great things for God, and we expect great things from God. Singing, "Tramp, Tramp, Tramp, the Hosts Are Marching."

MARYLAND: "I beseech you therefore, brethren, by the mercies of God, that ye present your bodies a living sacrifice, holy, acceptable unto God, which is your reasonable service." Singing, to tune of "Maryland, My Maryland."

MICHIGAN: Seeking to save and to serve.

MINNESOTA: "And whatsoever ye do in word or deed, do all in the name of the Lord Jesus, giving thanks to God and the Father by him."

MISSISSIPPI: We have taken for our motto "All things are possible with God;" and, with these words inscribed upon our banner, we expect to come up next year, with at least fifty delegates, to Washington.

MISSOURI: "According to my earnest expectation and my hope, that in nothing I shall be ashamed, but that with all boldness, as always, so now also Christ shall be magnified in my body, whether it be by life, or by death." Singing, "Missouri for Christ."

MONTANA: "Thy kingdom come. Thy will be done in all the earth," is the prayer of Montana Endeavorers, and to this end will we work.

NEBRASKA: "Create in me a clean heart, O God; and renew a right spirit within me." Singing, "Wash Me and I Shall Be Whiter than Snow."

NEW HAMPSHIRE: Singing, "The Lord Is My Shepherd."

NEW JERSEY: "If we live in the Spirit, let us also walk in the Spirit."

NEW MEXICO: Scripture passage.

NEW YORK: "Let the word of Christ dwell in you richly in all wisdom; teaching and admonishing one another in psalms and hymns and spiritual songs, singing with grace in your hearts to the Lord." Singing, "Scatter Sunshine."

NORTH CAROLINA: "For I know whom I have believed, and am persuaded that he is able to keep that which I have committed unto him against that day." North Carolina for Christ!

NORTH DAKOTA: We shall carry the blessings that we have received back to our beloved young State, and with God's help we shall press forward "toward the mark for the prize of the high calling of God in Christ Jesus."

OHIO: A stronger faith, a deeper consecration. "Seek ye first the kingdom of God, and his righteousness; and all these things shall be added unto you." Singing, "Nearer, My God, to Thee."

PRESIDENT CLARK: I will ask Rev. W. Knight Chaplin, of London, to lead us in prayer for our associate members, that during the coming year more than 250,000 of this year may be brought to Christ.

Prayer.

O God, our Father, we give thee earnest thanksgiving for the sheaves already garnered. We are thinking now of the sheaves that are yet out on the fields, not gathered in; and the storm-clouds are threatening, and telling of coming judgment and of coming doom. Oh, help us, we pray thee, with the power of God, the Holy Ghost, to reach out to those that are farthest away, and to reach down to those that are lost, and to bring them into saving touch and contact with the Christ who hath died for them. We thank thee for the trophies of grace won in this past year. O our Father, God, with thy power, baptize every Endeavorer and every Endeavor Society so richly and so fully that there shall be, in all our unions, in all our churches, in all our societies, a mighty, a glorious, revival of the work of God. May this result in a multitude of souls, in a multitude of our associates, won for Christ, saved for all eternity. We ask it for thy love's sake. Amen.

OKLAHOMA: Endeavoring in all things, and at all times, for Jesus.

OREGON: We expect to carry back a great blessing from this Convention, and we reconsecrate our lives to Christ again, and go back to our work with more earnest determination that we will work more earnestly, more faithfully, for souls.

PENNSYLVANIA: "Let us lay aside every weight, and run with patience the way that is set before us, looking unto Jesus the author and finisher of our faith." Singing, "Nearer, My God, to Thee."

RHODE ISLAND: "Fear not, little flock; for it is your Father's good pleasure to give you the kingdom."

SOUTH CAROLINA: "I can do all things through Christ which strengtheneth me."

SOUTH DAKOTA: Our State for Christ; and it shall be our aim to bring our lost to him.

TENNESSEE: Tennessee for Christ!

> "We will go where you want us to go, Lord,
> Over mountain, or plain, or sea;
> We will say what you want us to say, Lord;
> We will be what you want us to be."

TEXAS: "Not slothful in business; fervent in spirit; serving the Lord."

> "This is our burden, this is our plea;
> 'Texas for Christ,' our motto shall be."

VERMONT: "Let the words of my mouth, and the meditations of my heart, be acceptable in thy sight, O Lord, my strength, and my redeemer."

VIRGINIA: "As for me and my house, we will serve the Lord."

WASHINGTON: "Search the scriptures, and do good; so shalt thou dwell in the land." "Trusting in the Lord Jesus Christ for strength," we promise a year of better and larger service.

WEST VIRGINIA:

"O Thou who died on Calvary,
To save my soul and make me free,
I consecrate my life to Thee,
My Saviour and my God!

"I'll live for Thee, I'll live for Thee,
And, oh, how glad my soul should be
That Thou didst give Thyself for me,
My Saviour and my God!"

WISCONSIN: "Now thanks be unto God, which always causeth us to triumph in Christ, and maketh manifest the savour of his knowledge by us in every place."

WYOMING: "The Lord is our Master, even Christ; and all we are brethren." The newest star in the Christian Endeavor flag!

ALASKA: We are very grateful for the rich blessings that we have received from this great Convention. Of all the sights that we have seen here and elsewhere, the one that has impressed us the most is the mighty movement of Christianity. The triumphs of this movement are the triumphs of Christ through the instrumentality of his servants.

CANADA: Singing, "Beautiful Zion."

MASSACHUSETTS: Massachusetts Endeavorers saved to serve! Inspired by this Convention, Massachusetts will go forth as never before to seek the perishing ones, to win them to Jesus Christ.

GREAT BRITAIN: The 121,000 Christian Endeavorers of the United Kingdom are determined, by earnest consecration, devoted service, and unswerving loyalty to Christ and the Church, to make the Christian Endeavor Society of this century the Christian Triumph Society of the next.

SCOTLAND: Singing,

"Scotland for Christ, from the court to the palace;
Scotland for Christ; pass the watchword along
Till from her mountains, her glens, and her valleys
Scotland united shall join in our song.
Rally, Endeavorers, swell out the chorus,
Trusting in God and renewing your tryst;
Bright gleams the banner that is marching before us,
Claiming the victory, Scotland for Christ!"

AUSTRALIA: "Fear not: for I am with thee: I will bring thy seed from the east, and gather thee from the west; I will say to the north, Give up; and to the south, Keep not back: bring my sons from far, and my daughters from the ends of the earth." In this great movement our hearts are knit with yours.

JAPAN: By design seek thou the world in his name, for Christ and his Church.

CHINA: China responds for her missionaries in the first two sentences or petitions of the Lord's Prayer.

SPAIN: Our Spanish Endeavorers are trying to carry a pure gospel to every corner of their peninsula.

TURKEY: "Why do the heathen rage," and the Sultan of Turkey "imagine a vain thing? He that sitteth in the heavens shall laugh: the Lord shall have them in derision." Pray for the Christian Endeavorers in Turkey.

BURMAH: Burmah was the first land in Asia to receive the Gospel from America. Burmah had in the past year 35,000 native Christians. The message which I bring you from Burmah to-night is that which Dr. Judson, at the end of the first seven years of his labor, when there was but one convert, sent back to America: "The prospect that the heathen shall be converted is as bright as the promises of God."

MEXICO: I am not ashamed of the Gospel of Christ "for I know whom I have believed, and am persuaded that he is able to keep that which I have committed unto him against that day." Mexico holds out her hands to you for help.

FRANCE: An inspiring message was read from Rev. Theo Monod, D.D., the famous preacher of Paris.

PALESTINE: The response was inaudible.

ARMENIA: I consecrate myself to Christ to-night. I am sure these meetings have impressed me a great deal, and I want especially to urge this, friends: pray for those Christian Endeavorers who are dying in a Turkish dungeon. I want you to carry this Gospel home and pray for us, for our hearts are bleeding.

INDIA: The Cross of our Lord Jesus Christ is exerting the same mighty, attractive power in India that it is exerting here to-day. We are now on our way back to India to proclaim Jesus Christ as God and Saviour, desiring that some day we may see, even in India, a convention like this.

PRESIDENT CLARK: We have most of us had a chance to in some way show our love for our Lord; but perhaps there are some who have been left out in all these different calls, and I want to ask you now, as Christian Endeavorers, to renew your consecration, not only as inhabitants of certain states and provinces and countries, but as workers along different lines. Our pastors have been to the fore in this Convention. Our platforms have been crowded with them. Many have been in the audience—hundreds from whom we have not heard. I want to ask the pastors in this audience if they will rise for a moment before their young people.

Brethren, shall we take for our word this coming year, We will give ourselves continually to prayer and to the ministry of the Word? Will you say that with me? [Repeated by ministers.]

And now, while we stand together, I will ask Prof. James Lewis Howe, of Kentucky, to lead us in prayer for the pastors.

Prayer.

O Thou from whom this Christian Endeavor movement has come, we be seech thee that thou wilt bless these, our leaders. May thy Spirit be poured out upon them. In all their perplexities give them wisdom; in all their weakness give them strength; in all their darkness give them light; in all their ignorance give them knowledge; and may they at all times feel that underneath are the everlasting arms; for Christ's sake. Amen.

The members of the various committees were then called, and took for their mottoes as follows : —

LOOKOUT COMMITTEE: "Look not every man on his own things, but every man also on the things of others."

PRAYER-MEETING COMMITTEE: "Continue in prayer, and watch in the same with thanksgiving."

MISSIONARY COMMITTEE: "Pray ye therefore the Lord of the harvest, that he will send forth laborers into his harvest."

SOCIAL COMMITTEE: "Use hospitality one to another without grudging."

JUNIOR SUPERINTENDENTS: "Whoso shall receive one such little child in my name receiveth me."

All the other committees not then called — the flower, the good-literature, the information, the good-citizenship — were then called, and took for their motto, "Whatsoever ye would that men should do to you, do ye even so to them."

Members of the choir then took for their motto, "I will sing unto the Lord as long as I live."

The presidents and officers of the societies took for their motto, "Speak unto the children of Israel that they go forward."

The active members of Christian Endeavor Societies were then called to stand, and President Clark said : —

"Trusting in the Lord Jesus Christ for strength, I promise him that I will strive to do,"—that is where Endeavor comes in,—"that I will strive to do whatever he would like to have me do,"—and all the rest of our pledge, and all the rest of our Christian Endeavor is embraced in this. Dear friends, will you say this with your hearts; will you say it honestly and solemnly; will you stop and think about it a minute before you do? If you can say this honestly and sincerely, there is nothing you cannot and will not do for Christ this coming year. Will you raise your hands as the old Roman captains raised their hands when the oath of allegiance was read to them? It is an oath we can take; it is something I believe Christ would have us take; it is something we can live up to, for we promise to strive to do it, and I believe God will help us. O soldiers of Jesus Christ, raise your hands and say this with me : "Trusting in the Lord Jesus Christ for strength, I promise him that I will strive to do whatever he would like to have me do." It means faithfulness, service, honesty, loyalty to our own church, an effort to bring others to Christ. All these things are embraced in whatever he would like to have you do.

Dr. Wayland Hoyt then made the following prayer : —

O Lord, behold us, we are before thee; we yield ourselves to thee for service, for better and stronger inner life, for more pioneering attempt and devotion toward others, for all things by which in any wise we may be workers together with thee, for thee and thy Church. Help us through the year to come to keep this pledge more resolutely and accurately than we have ever kept it before. Send upon us, we pray thee, the Holy Spirit. May he dwell in all our hearts; may he manifest himself as he never has before in our hearts, in our societies, in our churches, for Jesus' sake. And now, O Lord, accept our consecration, for thy name's sake, our Saviour, our Redeemer, our Brother, our Friend, our King. Amen.

Then one verse of "God Be with You till We Meet Again," was sung, and Dr. Clark pronounced the Mizpah benediction, "The Lord watch between me and thee, when we are absent one from another. Amen." Dr. Clark then pronounced the Fourteenth International Convention of the Society of Christian Endeavor adjourned.

Tent Williston.

The consecration meeting in Tent Williston was attended by as great a crowd as could possibly get beneath the canvas.

Secretary John Willis Baer presided ; Rev. John Barstow, of Medford, Mass., conducted the devotional exercises ; and Mr. George C. Stebbins, of Brooklyn, N. Y., directed the singing.

After a solo by Mrs. Wm. Patterson, of Toronto, Ont., by rising votes the audience unanimously expressed their hearty agreement with the Platform of Principles and with the petition to Queen Victoria and President Cleveland in behalf of the Armenians ; they gave unmistakable signs of their appreciation of the work of the Committee of Thirteen ; and then the time came for the sermon. At Secretary Baer's suggestion, neither applause nor waving handkerchiefs followed the introduction of Rev. Samuel H. Virgin, D.D., of New York; but everywhere heads were bowed in the hush of silent prayer until the preacher's voice was heard announcing Gal. VI. 1 as the text. From that passage he earnestly and solemnly urged Endeavorers to labor with especial zeal for the restoration of those that have wandered.

Sermon by Rev. S. H. Virgin, D.D.

In the solemn hush of this moment of prayer I announce the Scripture which is to be the basis of our thought as we approach the moments of our consecration. Galatians, sixth chapter, first verse: "Brethren, if a man be overtaken in a fault, ye which are spiritual, restore such an one in the spirit of meekness; considering thyself, lest thou also be tempted."

We are approaching the great climax of our great spiritual feast, when we renew our pledge and consecrate ourselves afresh to larger, nobler, diviner endeavor for Christ and his Church. This, therefore, is no moment for pleasantry, no time for special discussion of controverted questions, but a moment for the consideration of the most momentous and sacred issues of our lives. There are three noble uses which we might make of this sacred privilege. First, we might make it a half-hour of retrospect, going carefully, in thought, over all the field that we have traversed from the opening word of the Convention to this moment. We might, like Ruth, glean again in the fields of Boas and find some sheaves left of purpose; and gathering again into our arms those sheaves that have been piled upon the field, we might recall every sacred inspiration, we might deepen every noble purpose, we might renew every sacred, silent pledge that has been made. Or, in the second place, we might, here in these few moments, just yield ourselves to the absolute luxury of spiritual joy —that joy that has been rising like a mighty tide of the sea, until at this moment it is a joy that is unspeakable and full of glory. We might yield to it and let its waves rise and fall and dash over us, and our experience would be like that of the angels about the Throne at this very moment. Or, in the third place, we might lift our eyes from that which surrounds us and for the moment forget the present, the retrospect, and the joy, and fix our eyes upon the field of service into which in a few hours we shall again be ushered.

The first we shall do anyway. Our minds will traverse and retraverse these hours of sacred privilege; our tongues will rehearse, in the larger circles and in the smaller circles of the country, the words that have been spoken and the inspirations that have been felt; so that we do not need to take time for that here to-night. The second is a fact in experience. Whatever we say, whatever we think, whatever we sing, our souls are filled with joy. There has been rising within us a conscious delight in the Christ we love, in the conquering truth of which he is the centre and the circumference, and we are like the mighty ocean that can rise to its full and bear a million freighted vessels upon its crested waves; so that we need not give ourselves simply to the indulgence of joy.

The third is the wiser and the better use to make of this hour. It is the use that the Master always made. We do not find him returning now and again to the story of Bethlehem, beautiful as it was, and sacred as it must have been to him. We do not find him turning back to the first miracle of Cana again and again, but ever pushing on toward the completion of his sacred work. The eternal ages were to give him the privilege of retrospect. Nor do we find the Master indulging in the ecstacy of joy over what had been accomplished. Multitudes did that. Upon the Mount of Transfiguration it was the lips of the disciples that said, "Let us build three tabernacles, for it is good to be here;" but the Master said, "Let us return to the multitudes that are dying in their sin." Moses looked upon the promised land and not upon the tract of the wilderness. And so to-night, in these few moments before this consecration service, we will look upon the field that is before us and one single line of service to which I want to call the Christian Endeavorers who are here to-night.

The apostle suggests it in the word I have given you from his letter to the Galatians. All over this fair New England there are to-day abandoned farms where once was the sound of joy and revelry from large and happy households. Where once were fields that responded to the scythes of the mower, where once there were orchards that blossomed in the spring and fruited in the autumn, now is there desolation. The old building is in ruins, the out-buildings have fallen into decay, the orchard is waste and ruin, and the fields are tangled with the weeds that have checked the grass. Now and then some son returns, and after a little the old house shows the sign of paint. The window-panes glisten again with the morning and the evening sun. The trees show the pruning-knife, and the blossoms come, and in the autumn the fruit is gathered, and all the village and all the region rejoice in the restored farm.

I have in my possession some pictures that were sent to me from Rome a year or two ago, that present, in the old and beautiful outline, the ruins upon which the eye of the modern traveller rests; and I have taken great delight in thinking of the joy of the world if the old builders could come and rehabilitate those ruins and make the Acropolis of Athens again beautiful in its pristine glory. We have all looked upon pictures from which the faces had faded and darkened and well-nigh gone, until the hand of the modern artist had retouched them into beauty and brought out the old glory of the former artists. There are manuscripts that have come into our possession on which the monks had traced their essays and their sermons, but the modern student has erased the essay and blotted out the sermon and restored the old text of the New Testament Scriptures. Now we rejoice in the restored farm; we are happy in the renewing of the buildings; we are glad over the freshened paintings. But one immortal soul made in the image of God, endowed with all the possibilities of Christly beauty, at the right hand of God, is worth all the farms and buildings and pictures and manuscripts of the world; and the apostle says to us, "Brethren, if a man be overtaken in a fault, ye which are spiritual, restore him." That is not always done. I am thinking of the wanderers. There are 56,000 Christian Endeavorers here. We are glad of it. But I am thinking of those that are not here that once were members of our Society, that once sat at the family altars in Christian homes, whose names are still enrolled upon the Church books, but who have lapsed. Entreaties have been made to them, but slowly and steadily they have lapsed from our thought, and we have said, "Ephraim is joined to his idols; let him alone." And Paul comes to-night into this tent and says, "Restore him." Not simply pray for him, not simply pity him, not condemn him, but restore him.

I chanced a little while ago to be speaking about the recovery of some young man in our great city, and at the close of the service a mother of saintly face and devout spirit came, and with both hands lifted up and the tears streaming down her face said, "Yes, I was glad; but my boy—why was it not my boy?" I am thinking of those that have lapsed to-night, and I bring you this Gospel message.

The attitude of the world is severe, always severe, deadly severe. If the young man has lapsed so that the garments of the prison have come upon him, woe be to him. Heaven pity him, and the world condemns him. He will come out and he will go from store to store, and from office to office, and from man to man, until at length in his sorrow he says, "There is no place for me. I would like to go back to my prison cell again." The world is hard toward the man who has fallen, and the attitude of the Church is unsympathetic. It is not as cold and hard and cruel as that of the world. Oh, I don't like to hear these harsh criticisms of the Church! It is the dearest thing there is in the world; it is the sweetest thing there is in the world; it is the best thing there is in the world, but we must always say the truth; and we may sometimes say with truth that the Church is not as sympathetic as it ought to be. I have in my mind, just at this moment, one who was overtaken in a fault and who fell grievously, and when he had paid the penalty of his failure, and thought of coming back to the Christian Church again, some members of that Church said, "If he comes back into this Church, I go out of it." Sometimes the Church, as well as the world, says, "Yes, I will restore him when he pays me back that money." "Yes, I will restore him, the villain, when I think he is good." No matter how penitent, no matter how loving, he may have become, that is the attitude of the world — and the Church, in many cases — to-day.

And I want to bring to you, as the work of Christian Endeavorers for '95-'96, the blessed work of restoring all these lapsed members. We have in our Church statistics a column of absentees. Who are they? Some of them have moved to other places and have not taken their letters. If there are any such here to-night, ask for your letter as soon as you get home. But a large number is composed of those who have lapsed, who have felt the chill of the world who have been overcome in a fault. And Paul calls us in this solemn moment to restore them. The Church feels that its duty is pretty well done if it prays for them; if it does not absolutely condemn; if it does not ruthlessly strike them off from the list. The Gospel is, "Restore them."

This work of restoration is, in the first place, in thorough harmony with the primal purpose of God in the great work of redemption. I do not know about other worlds; perhaps some of you do. I do not know but there may be worlds that were alien to God from the start, but this world was not. It belonged to our Father. The Garden of Eden was his home, and he came into it and he talked with his children, and they joyed in his presence in the cool of the day.

In that home the man was overtaken in a fault, and the woman. What did the Father do? Destroy them utterly, end their career, destroy all life over the whole planet and start anew? No; he restored them. He would rather have Adam and his posterity back into his heart again than to have a new family started. And when we start into the work of restoration we are in harmony with the primal purpose of God. Don't you wonder at the pathetic patience of God with Israel? Why are they not destroyed? Why are they not cut off from the face of the earth? Because God wants to restore them, and he will do it in time.

This plan of restoration is in thorough harmony, in the second place, with the principle of Jesus Christ. Oh, how I love to think of the Master's love for those men that were his disciples! Do you not remember that there was a time when they all deserted? How strong is that word; they all forsook him and fled! I can think of Peter's denial; but it is hard to think that John fled, it is hard to think that tender-hearted Bartholomew fled. They all forsook him, and when the Master stood before the Sanhedrin he had not a faithful adherent. He recovered Peter partially, as he passed through the crowd, with a tender look. After the Resurrection what did the Master do? Did he gather a new body of apostles and desert the old, and say, "We will have a new company of disciples"? No; the Master was like the Father, and he restored them. He sent the message, "Go, tell my disciples and Peter" — that inclusive remark that went to the heart of the disciple who would say, "I am not a disciple. I am of no use." He gathered them all in. He restored them instead of making a new Church.

This principle of restoration is in thorough harmony with the prayer of godly people of the world. I will show that in a moment as I suggest to you some of the encouragements for this work of restoration. In the first place, it is encouraging because it is along the line of the Divine call. Man goes from God, and God goes after man. He always has. God did not hide from Adam, but Adam hid from God. And in the whole record of the Scripture there is the disclosure of the truth that the heart of the Father has always gone after the children, and the call of the Father is constantly, "Return." There is one passage that has troubled me sometimes not a little: "I hid my face from them for a moment." But we have always taken that in connection with what follows: "But with everlasting kindness will I have mercy upon them." It seems as though the little shadow was given that the long rays of the sunlight might dazzle the eyes of the multitudes forever. It is, then, the call of God that these who have lapsed should return.

In the second place, that kind of work is encouraging because it is in the line of continuous prayer. What is the secret of the success of the Christian Endeavor movement? I venture to say it is because it came in the line of continuous prayer, — prayer for the young people in Christian families, prayer for the young people in Christian homes, prayer for the young people in the Sunday schools, in the congregation. And when by inspiration dear Dr. Clark started his little work in Portland, Me., it spread until it has gathered two millions and a half under its noble banner, because it was working along the line of the petitions of God's people. If you can work while people pray, and as they pray, you have the secret inspiration of God's Holy Spirit with you always. And when we work for those who have gone from the family altar, and from the Christian Endeavor Society, and out of the Church, we work along the line of unlimited petitions.

A third reason for encouragement is that there is an inward longing by those who have been overtaken in a fault for that which they have lost. I hear it often said, " I cannot escape from my training." I urge the families in my church to bring their children to prayer meeting; those children that have come for months and years come steadily, saying, " I cannot get away from my training." And those who have gone from us cannot altogether get away from their training. I heard a young man say in New York the other day, " Pray for me, for sometimes I fear I shall go back. I was never a drunkard, I shall not drink ; I shall not gamble ; I shall not return to lusts ; but my father was an atheist, and I was brought up in a family where the thought of God was absolutely eliminated, and sometimes my training comes back almost to capture me." The contrary is also true. The training of early years, the sweet ecstacy of prayer and praise, the lovely devotion of the house of God, comes back now and then and touches the springs of life and thought in these hearts, and when you work for them you have something to which you can successfully appeal.

And another encouragement is in the added value which they will bring to the service of Christ and his Church. I will not amplify that. You know it well. You have felt the power of the return of the young man who had gone from your meetings, but had been brought back. Your hearts have responded when some old man who long has resisted the prayers of a godly household has at length tremblingly come to the Throne saying, " I return to the God of my youth and to the church of my early manhood."

So, brethren and sisters, beloved in the Lord, I have but one word to leave with you. It is the word of Paul, " Restore the wanderer." As you return to your homes, I pray the Lord of Glory that the sound of the rattling wheels beneath the cars may seem to you to sing, " Restore him ! Restore him !" I pray that when you shall enter your parks and your gardens, in the country or in the city, the travelling feet of the wind along the leafy tree-tops will seem to be saying to you, " Restore him ! Restore him !" I pray that when the stars come up at night over your city or over your village they will make a new constellation that will simply say, in the letters of Divine creation, " Restore him ! Restore him !" I pray that the voice of Jesus, sweeter than all other sounds, may come melting down through the azure that is above us to reach the inner citadel of our being with the sacred command, " Restore him ! Restore him !"

" Sweet Peace, the Gift of God's Love," was sung, another season of silent prayer, and the tender singing of " The Homeland," by Mr. Stebbins, an appeal for consecration by Secretary Baer, and then followed the roll-call.

" God Be with You till We Meet Again," the Mizpah benediction, and the benediction by Dr. Virgin closed the touching service.

Tent Endeavor.

One's thought involuntarily turned back to the great Passover gatherings as he beheld the multitudes who had come up to offer the sacrifice of a willing spirit at the Tent Endeavor consecration service. Rev. Nehemiah Boynton, D.D., guided the meeting, and Bishop B. W. Arnett conducted the devotional service. A stalwart preacher from beyond the border, Rev. John Potts, D.D., of Toronto, delivered a burning message upon the need of Christian Endeavor soul-winning. "Speed Away" fittingly followed, the choir and congregation singing with especial fervor. Resolutions and a Platform of Principles were presented, as in the other meetings.

Sermon by Rev. John Potts, D.D.

And they were all amazed, and they glorified God, and were filled with fear, saying, We have seen strange things to-day.—LUKE V. 26.

The Gospel came to reveal strange things. It has been a history of successive marvels. It has startled humanity with the boldness of its claims, the greatness of its promises, and the grandeur of its results. The Gospel speaks with the voice of Divine authority. It works with the power of the supernatural, in the inner realm of the soul, and in the character and life, and compels the testimony of all classes, "We have seen strange things to-day."

The scene of the text was one of all-absorbing interest, and demonstrative of the divinity of Christ and Christianity. It seems to remind us, who can look upon it as recorded in the Gospel, of the fourteen verse of the first chapter of St. John: "And the Word was made flesh, and dwelt among us (and we beheld his glory, the glory as of the only begotten of the Father), full of grace and truth."

What were the strange things that were seen that day?

The action of the four men who carried the man sick with palsy to Jesus. It meant personal action, and concert of action.

The act of forgiveness pronounced by the Person who attracted the crowd to listen to his words and witness his mighty acts.

The detection, by the great Prophet and Teacher, of the thoughts and feelings of the scribes and Pharisees, who began to reason in their hearts, saying, "Who is this which speaketh blasphemies? Who can forgive sins but God alone?"

The demonstration of Christ's power to forgive sins by the exercise of miracle-working power over disease. "But that ye may know that the Son of man hath power upon earth to forgive sins (he said unto the sick of the palsy), I say unto thee, Arise, and take up thy couch, and go into thine house." Because of all these things it was recorded and testified, "We have seen strange things to-day."

The theme upon which I wish to speak to you, and which I find in this narrative is, "Christian Endeavor in Helping Sinners to Christ."

This is the great need of the Church to-day,—earnestness in soul-saving, earnestness begotten of the Holy Ghost, earnestness inspired by the love of Christ, such as Paul felt when he wrote, "For the love of Christ constraineth us; because we thus judge, that if one died for all, then were all dead: and that he died for all, that they which live should not henceforth live unto themselves, but unto him which died for them, and rose again," earnestness impelled by the peril of the unsaved. The need of to-day is earnestness of Christian testimony, of loving invitation, of all sympathetic effort to help sinners to Christ. God's plan is to save man by man. Earnest Christians alone are successful in soul-saving. Earnestness in politics, in art, in education, in warfare, and in almost everything is applauded and rewarded. Such earnestness would win signal victories for Christ, would overcome the resistance of human hearts, and would greatly increase the population of the heavenly country.

The Record of It as Found in the Narrative. — We may learn how to work for Jesus and for sinners if we carefully study this portion of Divine Truth.

This Christian Endeavor is seen in the act: "And, behold, men brought in a bed a man which was taken with a palsy: and they sought means to bring him in, and to lay him before him." The act was expressive of practical earnestness. See those four men. Their names are not given, their history outside of the act here recorded is not chronicled, but we may safely conclude that their names were in the Book of Life. They have each heard of Christ and, perhaps, were with Jesus as his disciples. They each think of what they might do to extend the fame and glory of the Great Teacher, and also what they might do to help some poor, afflicted fellow-being in their neighborhood. They remember that there is a man sick of the palsy and confined to his bed. He might have been formerly a fellow workman; he was at least an acquaintance of the four men. They consult together and fix upon the afflicted man as the object of their sympathy and effort, and as one whom they believe Jesus could help. They go to his home and find him helpless and hopeless. There is the shadow of despair upon home and hearts. The four men intimate their business. The eye of the invalid beams with hope; wife and children are excited at the bare possibility of such an event as the restoration of husband and father. Visions of the future with husband and father restored fill the eye of their imagination with pictures of joy and gladness. "But," says the sick man, "it may all be true that Jesus has power to heal and that he has a heart of unbounded pity, but he is not likely to come to my house, and I am unable to go to him." "We have come for you; we will carry you to the place where Jesus is; we can do it, and will do it gladly."

See them as they move out of that home carrying upon the bed that helpless man. Were ever those men more nobly employed? Make way for them; they are the observed of heaven. Angels watch their progress and sympathize with their effort, and Christ anticipates their coming. See their practical earnestness in the act thus performed.

Sinners need to-day the help of sympathy, the help of counsel, the help of information, and the help of prayer. What would not such earnestness do now? Alas, how seldom it is seen!

See their earnestness in overcoming obstacles which lay in the way.

There are many hindrances to Christian work reared by sin and Satan. Many obstacles stand in the way between sinners and the Saviour — old habits, sinful companions, former temptations, the fear of the world. How terribly all these stand in the way and seem arrayed in determination to oppose the seeking sinner and the working Church. They can all be overcome and the desired end reached. Let any four Christians unite in the work of helping a sinner to Christ, and it would be strange indeed if they were not successful.

Again, let us fix our eyes upon the four Christian workmen bearing the afflicted to Jesus. Up to a certain point they proceed without interruption. They reach the house where the Prophet of Nazareth and Galilee is teaching. The crowd fills the house, and outside there are many waiting, and anxious to get in. They pause and survey the situation; the sick man cannot be kept long in that position. The multitude are selfish and refuse to make way for the man sick of the palsy. They must not fail; the determination of earnestness is fixed upon their faces. They mean business — the great business of having Christ deal with a poor afflicted sinner. The poor man must not be carried back without at least seeing Jesus. True earnestness has many expedients; it is not easily baffled, and it does things that seem branded with impropriety to such as are strangers to the enthusiasm of earnestness.

We saw their earnestness in going to the man, and now we see it in going to Jesus through all obstacles. A happy thought occurs to one of them. "Let us go up to the roof and make an opening and let down the bed to the place where Jesus is, and we shall succeed." Another concludes that as that is the only possible way, it must be done. Up they take the bed with the man upon it, as expressed in verse nineteen, "And when they could not find by what way they might bring him in because of the multitude, they went upon the housetop, and let him down through the tiling with his couch into the midst before Jesus."

Nothing could hinder such earnestness; devils would tremble before it, and the world would cease its scorning. There is little use in attempting Christian work unless there be the heroism of real earnestness. If there be fear of men or devils, if there be shame, if there be cowardice, if there be hesitancy, if there be solicitude as to what persons may say in praise or blame, you must inevitably fail. But let the Church of God have the deep-toned earnestness of these four men who allowed nothing, neither the multitude nor the roof of the house, to prevent them in their great undertaking, and glorious will be the results. How little dampens our zeal! How little renders us nerveless in Christian effort! How little discourages us in attempting work for Jesus and for souls! How small, how dwarfed, we appear in the sight of these stalwart Christians bearing the sick sinner to the Healer and Saviour of sinners! This earnestness is what is wanted. Not men to act upon committees, not men to organize new enterprises upon paper, not men to give money simply, but workers are wanted, persons to carry sinners to Christ. Earnest workers are the need of the Church and of the world to-day — workers above the power of a sneer and equally above the power of the cold indifference of nominal Christians. These are the great need of the Church. May we soon see such earnestness manifested by all classes of Christians for all classes of sinners.

From the Record We Pass to the Recognition of Christian Endeavor. — By whom? By Jesus, the Master and Saviour and Lord. It may escape the notice of others, but never of Christ. His eye is always fixed upon the toilers in his vineyard and the soldiers of his army. Whether they toil in the full blaze of public recognition and popular glory, or in the quiet private walks of life, they are seen by Him whom they serve, and whom they seek to glorify. Whether they fight splendid battles, and win glorious conquests, like Paul and Luther and Knox and Wesley and other champions of the truth, or are down in the trenches, they are graciously recognized by him who is their King and Captain. Very beautifully does this subject of recognition come before us in this connection. Let us consider it, that it may stimulate us to go and do likewise.

Jesus saw their faith. Jesus saw their efforts overcoming all hindrances, and yet it was the faith that was recognized. Their efforts were but the fruit of their faith. Because they believed in the power and compassion of Jesus they did what they did. Faith is a root principle of Christian life.

Jesus recognized their faith — its active and practical character. They might have felt for the man sick of the palsy — felt even to weeping; they might have prayed for the man sick of the palsy — prayed sincerely, prayed earnestly, prayed as many do now for men sick with sin's dire disease. They might have believed relative to the man sick of the palsy that Christ could cure him, that Christ had power to do it by a word or by a touch, and that Christ would if he were present. They might have talked about the man sick of the palsy — about his need of Jesus, about his pitiable condition, about the benefit it would be to him and to his family, if he were restored, just as many Christian people talk about sinners, their need, and their condition, and the good it would be to them if they were saved. All that might have been done, and Christ might have left the region, and the man sick of the palsy might have lingered for a a few years, and died uncured and unforgiven.

But their faith was an active and practical faith, and as such Jesus recognized it. It is only such faith that is Christ-honoring and soul-saving, — faith that works, that works earnestly, and that works despite all opposition.

Jesus saw their faith. Whose faith? Important question. Our view of it is that their faith means the faith of the five — of the four men and of the sick man. In the act of the four men who let the bed down into the midst where Jesus was, Jesus saw their faith. He saw it when the gracious impulse came into each heart to help that man to him. He saw it when they met together for consultation touching how they might bring their afflicted friend under the healing touch of the Great Physician. He saw it as they approached the sick man, and he saw it in every step of the journey from the home of the sick man to the place where he, Christ, was at that hour. In the countenance of the sick man, whose heart's desire he saw, that pitiful look seemed to say, "Master, I have heard of thy pity and thy power, and of thy willingness to bless afflicted humanity. My friends who carried me here have told me that thou art all-powerful, and what thou hast done for otners thou wilt surely do for me.   Here I am in my helplessness and wretchedness; Master, help me." And thus Jesus saw his faith, perhaps as the outcome of the faith of the four.

I hold this opinion because it accords with the principle upon which God blesses, and it harmonizes with the circumstances as recorded in the narrative. The men had not gone as constables and arrested the sick man, irrespective of his will, and carried him to Jesus. They proposed the matter to him and, doubtless, encouraged him to allow them to bear him to Christ. He went willingly and with faith in the power of Christ. It was this that made their joint faith so influential, so powerful, so successful. When the faith of God's people becomes connected with the faith of sinners seeking salvation nothing can prevent the blessing, hence the importance of securing the co-operation of sinners in the great work of salvation.

The Reward of Christian Endeavor in Helping Sinners to Jesus. — It was twofold; the reward embraced more than was expected. They went for one thing and got two; they went for a secondary favor and got a primary as well. They went for a blessing for the body and got that, but also, and more valuable, a blessing for the soul. Christ never gives less, but always more, than we expect or deserve. It was spiritual — forgiveness. " Man, thy sins are forgiven thee." How those words must have sounded in the ears of the four men on the roof and in the ears and heart of the sinner now pardoned and happy in the favor of God! They looked at each other in glad surprise. It may be that they had thought of it. They had something to do with his salvation.

Forgiveness — what a blessing! It changes a man's relation to God and to Christ and to eternity. It changes a man's immortality from darkness to light, from woe to bliss, from hell to heaven. There is Divine power in the words of Jesus. They were spirit and life to the man sick of the palsy.

The scribes and Pharisees were indignant and said, "Who can forgive sins, but God alone?" Notwithstanding the unbelief of sceptics and infidels, the Son of Man hath power on earth to forgive sins. It is Christ's prerogative still, for he hath been exalted a Prince and a Saviour to give repentance and remission of sins. His voice is a pardoning voice, and it sends a thrill of spiritual joy through the soul of the sinner when he says, " Man, thy sins are forgiven thee."

It was physical as well as spiritual. The palsied, helpless body felt the reviving and transforming Voice as the soul felt the power of " Man, thy sins are forgiven thee." The sick man was instantly well; the feeble man was instantly strong. He who was carried a poor, sinful, diseased sinner to Jesus returned to his house vigorous in body, relieved of sin's guilty burden, but carrying in its stead the blessedness of the forgiven man. How changed the man, how rewarded the men! Did he feel happy? So did they. They shared his joy, and felt that Christ made them partakers with him of Christian blessedness. Know ye this joy? In what light did their earnestness appear to them as they saw the happy man returning to his house and as they felt that Jesus recognized what they had done and blessed their endeavor? Christian service is still rewarded. It carries with it its own recompense. The reward is multiplied in the success achieved, and will be almost infinitely increased when the Master shall say, "It is enough; come up higher," and ultimately when he shall declare to all earnest workers, " Well done, good and faithful servant; enter thou into the joy of thy Lord."

The Result of Christian Endeavor upon the Multitude. — We have had the record, the recognition, the reward, and now we glance at the result. And they were all amazed — amazed at the zeal of the four men. Such intense devotedness always creates astonishment. The manifestation of extraordinary Christian life has the power to startle the ordinary and the careless. It was so on the Day of Pentecost; of the people of Jerusalem it was recorded, " They were all amazed and marvelled." So the people have felt since then when great interest has been manifested by Christian people in the work of God.

They were amazed, also, at the manifested power of Christ in the twofold blessing of forgiveness and healing.

Amazed at the men—there was the man before them who had been carried in a most helpless condition. They saw him unable to rise and walk; they saw him in obedience to the command of Christ, "Rise, take up thy bed, and walk." When they witnessed this done by Jesus they had little difficulty in believing in the power of Christ to forgive sin, and therefore it was no wonder that they stood in amazement. When men become convinced that God is working as well as the Church; when it is seen in changed lives and hearts and homes; when selfish men become unselfish; when worldly men become spiritually minded; when profane men become chaste and pure in conversation; when Sabbath breakers call the Sabbath a delight, the holy of the Lord, and honorable; when careless men begin to pray; when men formerly ashamed of Christ now in simplicity and godly sincerity declare what he has done for them and their willingness to think and speak and work for Christ; when whole families and communities are seeking first the kingdom of God and his righteousness, and making the affairs of the soul supreme in thought and action, and all this is seen, the people are amazed.

They glorified God. The amazement awakened thought, and thought directed to what had occurred led to the people glorifying God. God was glorified in this whole matter. Every work of Christ is God glorifying. The conversion of sinners fills heaven with praise, angelic and redeemed praise, and glorifies the Lord.

They were filled with fear, reverent fear, fear occasioned by the felt presence of the Divine, and they said, "We have seen strange things to-day."

Christ is the same to-day as when he said, "Man, thy sins are forgiven thee," and "Rise, take up thy bed, and walk." The power and compassion and readiness of Christ to bless are as great now as then. Humanity needs forgiveness and spiritual healing, as recorded in Psalm CIII.: "Who forgiveth all thine iniquities and healeth all thy diseases."

It is still the duty of the Church—of all saved ones—to help sinners to the Saviour. Such work needs to be done, and it is still recognized and rewarded by Christ.

To one and all I say, Let nothing keep you from reaching Christ. It is not enough to reach his Book, it is not enough to reach his house, it is not enough to reach his servants; you must reach himself. Let nothing hinder you, it is your safety, your life, your salvation, your heaven. Press through all difficulties, overcome all obstacles, accept of all offered help. If earnest workers will carry you in the arms of sympathy and faith, let them. If they will not, struggle to reach him yourself. If you cannot go, you can cry from where you are, as the blind beggar cried, "Jesus, thou son of David, have mercy on me." Christ will hear and bless and save.

In the light of this subject, in the light of the object for which the Church of Christ was established in the world, and in the light of the dreadful condition of those who are not partakers of the great salvation, what is the need of to-day? Is it not individual and organized earnestness in winning souls for Christ, in helping spiritually diseased and guilty ones to the Healer and Pardoner of sinners? You remember what the band of workers heard on the mountain in Galilee when the risen Christ looked at them, looked at the world in its spiritual destitution, looked forward into the coming centuries of the world's history, and probably looked out into the great eternity, and then said to them as representatives, as witnesses, as stewards, as servants, "All power is given unto me in heaven and in earth. Go ye therefore, and teach all nations, baptizing them in the name of the Father, and of the Son, and of the Holy Ghost: teaching them to observe all things whatsoever I have commanded you: and, lo, I am with you alway, even unto the end of the world."

Dr. Boynton spoke impressively for a few minutes prior to the calling of the roll of States. Message after message, consecration after consecration, each bearing the stamp of unswerving fidelity to the Master and his work, were heard from the States represented. Canada's song was particularly thrilling, and the resolution of the Floating Societies to "Throw Out the Life-Line" was effective to an unusual degree.

It was thought meet that the great assembly should disperse by expressing its adoration, and "All Hail the Power of Jesus' Name" was made the closing hymn. "The Lord watch between me and thee, when we are absent one from another," reverently prayed the delegates, and then, with purpose-filled hearts, they went slowly out into the night.

THE EVANGELISTIC MEETINGS.

"Behold the touch of God that taketh away the sins of the world!" This was the evangel cry that twenty thousand of Boston's work-people heard from the lips of the Convention delegates.

This evangelistic work was the deepest and highest thing about the great assembly. In many ways it was a blessing. As the weeks elapsed after the Convention, it was noticed that the effect of these services upon the delegates themselves became increasingly manifest. But the good seed sown and the harvests gathered among the work-people of Boston cannot be reckoned until we come into the full light of another world.

One of the especially affecting things developed after the departure of the delegates was the fact that Christians in various parts of the land had made these services a subject of special prayer, and that during the noon hour of the Convention days this work and the workers were being borne to God in prayer by faithful souls who themselves were deprived of Convention privileges. Surely, it was in answer to these petitions that such marvellous results were gained.

A word as to the scope of the evangelistic services. They were held in fifty-five different places. The list includes three piano factories, three wood-working establishments, an organ factory, a book bindery, a carriage works, a bank-note company, a clothing house, a rubber store, a screw factory, a coal yard, a printing-house, three laundries, a dry-goods store, a market house, the Chamber of Commerce, the Homœopathic Hospital, the Lend-a-Hand Hospital, a liquor saloon, a fire-engine station, the city jail, the Bromfield Street Methodist Episcopal Church, Faneuil Hall, the steamer *Wabash*, seven rescue missions, fourteen open-air meetings, four wharves, and a service held, at the request of a sick girl, on the pavement before her window.

These meetings were conducted by companies of Endeavorers from the following twenty-two States, District of Columbia, and Canada : Texas, Colorado, Nebraska, Missouri, Mississippi, Florida, Tennessee, Maine, New Hampshire, Vermont, Massachusetts, Rhode Island, Connecticut, New York, New Jersey, Pennsylvania, Delaware, Ohio, Illinois, Iowa, Wisconsin, Minnesota, Washington, D. C., and Montreal, Can. Delegates from other States also entered heartily into the work. The remarkable meetings held at Salem, and in other neighboring towns, are not included in these statistics.

In almost every case arrangements for the services were made in advance by the committee, Rev. James L. Hill, D.D., of Salem ; Rev. Charles Rhodes, of Philadelphia ; and Rev. Charles A. Oliver, of York, Penn. The long weeks of diligent effort spent by these gentlemen in securing the places and arranging with the workers, and the especial labors of Mr. Rhodes and Mr. Oliver, in securing and providing for the shop and factory meetings, call for highest praise.

The conditions were abnormal ; the task was unusually difficult. Three-fourths or more of the people that the Convention aimed to reach were Roman Catholics, most of the places of meeting were a long distance from the Convention hall, and the work was in an experimental stage.

Nevertheless, no fewer than 120 meetings, according to definite reports received, were held by the delegates. At each of these the pure Gospel of a crucified Christ was spoken, and the heart is thrilled by the knowledge that 20,000 persons — an audience equal to twice the number of people that any of the Convention auditoriums could contain at one time — heard these messages of life. The preachers, if we may call those who participated in the service by that name, were 5,850 Christian Endeavor delegates, who themselves were set afire with zeal for the conversion of souls, and who returned to their homes in all parts of the world to continue the work so marvellously begun at Boston.

Of direct results that can be tabulated this much is to be said : several hundred persons — twenty in a single meeting — expressed a desire to become Christians, and scores of actual conversions are recorded.

These things are only surface indications of the interest that was aroused in things spiritual. The eagerness of the people to hear the story of the Cross was affecting to the last degree. Everywhere the earnest invitation was given the Endeavorers to come again. In one case, where the delegation was late in arriving, a workman was sent in a carriage to Mechanics' Hall to ask for a meeting. Bodies of Endeavorers were stopped on the street and asked to enter manufactories and conduct services. In one place the welcome of the visitors took the form of a nicely-prepared lunch, spread by the workmen, that the delegates might not be inconvenienced because of the time spent in this meeting.

In every case except one, where the delegates were thought to be A. P. A.'s, the attention paid was respectful and reverent. In forty-one of the meetings, the statistics of which are before us, a total of 284 work-people took some part, at the invitation of the leaders. In most instances these were Christians. The stimulus that would thus come to these persons to continue the work for their fellows is beyond estimate.

The predominance of Catholic sentiment proved to be no bar to the success of the services. Mr. Oliver relates that when one employer was asked to allow a meeting in his factory he replied that, while he was perfectly willing, yet he felt called upon to state that there were only a dozen or less of Protestants among his more than a hundred employees, and that the meetings would not be attended by any one. The first service in that factory was held in the presence of one hundred and fifty of the workmen, who remained voluntarily. This story was repeated in more than one instance, and the following extract from a letter sent to the committee by a Roman Catholic will show the effect that the work had among the members of the Romish Church.

My Dear Sir,— You cannot imagine what I have gone through since your talk with me. The way the minister prayed, and the equal part every one took, has taken hold of me, and I want to pray to my God myself and for myself. I want to hear speeches or sermons such as I can understand, and in the future I will attend the Protestant Church, after I have seen my priest and talked to him. Will you kindly tell the minister I was afraid to raise my hand to-day, but I want all Christian Endeavorers to pray for me that I may worship God aright? You told me you believed a person must be born again. I don't understand this, but some day I shall, for I have never missed a mass for over two years, or a confession, or a communion, unless I was sick, and I will attend church the same now. It will be strange for me, but I have always believed in God, and I want to be converted, and have some of this faith. Pray for me, and ask others to pray for me. Oh, if you knew the condition of my mind, you would pray out of pity. God will reward you for your words.

(Signed)   Yours,   ——— ———.

Another letter written by a Christian Endeavor worker told how a Roman Catholic had gone to one of the church meetings as a result of a service on the T Wharf, and had confessed Christ, despite the fact that his brother, a priest, and two other Romanists had met him at the door of the church and tried to induce him to remain away. Similar stories, and others equally impressive, could be told in great numbers. In the city jail, the exercises stirred every heart. Seven Bibles were left with especially interested prisoners, by the delegates. Of this same visit it may be said that the Endeavorers held twelve open-air services on the way to the jail.

Particular mention should be made of the success of the noon meetings in Faneuil Hall and the Bromfield Street Church. These were crowded to suffocation, and forcible addresses were made by leading evangelists, such as Dwight L. Moody, Rev. J. Wilbur Chapman, D.D., Rev. Edward S. Smiley, D.D., of Denver, Mr. Charles N. Hunt, of Minneapolis, Rev. Dean Peck, of Denver, and others. Dr. Hill was especially responsible for the success of these meetings.

A word remains to be spoken about the reports from noon services, made at the sunrise prayer meetings. The wonderful words of the workers, literally "words of life," transported the audience straight to the Cross. The power of the early morning exercises was, in most cases, due in a large measure to the spirit imparted by these delegates.

The influence of the evangelistic movement at the Boston Convention, direct, reflex, and incidental, will endure as long as eternity to the glory of God.

NUMBER OF SOCIETIES, JULY 10, 1895

UNITED STATES.

	Young People's.	Junior.	Intermediate.	Mothers'.	Senior.	Total.
Alabama	104	20				124
Alaska Territory	3					3
Arizona Territory	13	3				16
Arkansas	115	26				141
California	742	414			1	1,157
Colorado	207	91	1			299
Connecticut	524	171	3		2	700
Delaware	63	22				85
District of Columbia	86	54				140
Florida	150	40				190
Georgia	143	16				159
Idaho	31	14				45
Illinois	1,676	746	14	17	3	2,446
Indiana	1,291	470	1			1,762
Indian Territory	32	4				36
Iowa	1,204	359				1,563
Kansas	918	315	3	11		1,247
Kentucky	306	63	1			370
Louisiana	48	11				59
Maine	554	141				695
Maryland	340	96		1		437
Massachusetts	930	374	5			1,309
Michigan	814	266	2			1,082
Minnesota	567	284	4			855
Mississippi	37	5				42
Missouri	779	351	2		1	1,133
Montana	33	22				55
Nebraska	503	195	3	1		702
Nevada	6	3				9
New Hampshire	382	84			2	468
New Jersey	718	327				1,045
New Mexico Territory	25	5				30
New York	2,898	920	3		1	3,822
North Carolina	147	23				170
North Dakota	101	20				121
Ohio	2,152	623	8	1	3	2,787
Oklahoma Territory	108	18				126
Oregon	228	104			1	333
Pennsylvania	3,108	1,023	3	2	3	4,139
Rhode Island	140	57				197
South Carolina	62	8	1			71
South Dakota	197	58				255
Tennessee	302	110				412
Texas	251	111	1			363
Utah Territory	44	26			1	71
Vermont	313	110	1			424
Virginia	146	16				162
Washington	227	77	4			308
West Virginia	235	45				280
Wisconsin	562	212	2			776
Wyoming	17	6				23
Total,	24,582	8,559	62	33	18	33,254

CANADA.

	Young People's.	Junior.	Parents'.	Mothers'.	Total.
Alberta	12	2			14
Assiniboia	47	6			53
British Columbia	35	5			40
Manitoba	109	18			127
New Brunswick	140	12			152
Newfoundland	5				5
Nova Scotia	352	36			388
Ontario	1,794	200		1	1,995
Prince Edward Island .	60	2			62
Quebec	204	58	2		264
Saskatchewan	5				5
Total,	2,763	339	2	1	3,105

FOREIGN.

	Young People's.	Junior.	Senior.	Mothers'.	Total
Africa	27	3			30
Asiatic Turkey	1				1
Australia	1,443	62	4		1,509
Austria	2				2
Belgium	1				1
Bermuda	3				3
Brazil	1	1			2
Burmah	14				14
Chili	3				3
Columbia	1				1
China	30	2			32
Egypt	1	1			2
England	2,145	115			2,260
France	64				64
Germany	13				13
Hawaiian Islands	4	3			7
Holland	1				1
India	110	7			117
Ireland	47	6			53
Japan	56	3			59
Laos	9				9
Madagascar	93				93
Mexico	25				25
Norway	2				1
Persia	3	1			4
Samoa	9				9
Sandwich Islands	4				4
Scotland	102	9		1	112
Siam	1				1
South Sea Islands . . .	2				2
Spain	5				5
Switzerland	7				7
Syria	3				3
Turkey	33	6			39
Upper Hebrides	1				1
Wales	158				158
West Indies	60	3			63
Total,	4,484	223	4	1	4,712

RECAPITULATION.

	Young People's.	Junior.	Inter-mediate.	Mothers'	Senior.	Parents'.	Total.
United States	24,582	8,559	62	33	18		33,254
Canada	2,763	339		1		2	3,105
Foreign	4,484	223		1	4		4,712
Floating Societies . . .	157	1					158
Total,							41,229

INDEX.

ILLUSTRATIONS.

www.ingramcontent.com/pod-product-compliance
Lightning Source LLC
Chambersburg PA
CBHW020846090426
42736CB00008B/248